International Relations

Brief Edition

Joshua S. Goldstein

American University, Washington, D.C.

Longman

New York   San Francisco   Boston
London   Toronto   Sydney   Tokyo   Singapore   Madrid
Mexico City   Munich   Paris   Cape Town   Hong Kong   Montreal

To my family

Vice President and Publisher: Priscilla McGeehon
Senior Acquisitions Editor: Eric Stano
Development Director: Lisa Pinto
Development Editor: Barbara A. Conover
Senior Marketing Manager: Megan Galvin-Fak
Print Supplements Editor: Kelly Villella
Media Supplements Editor: Patrick McCarthy
Production Manager: Donna DeBenedictis
Project Coordination, Text Design, and Electronic Page Makeup: Elm Street Publishing
    Services, Inc.
Cover Design Manager: Wendy Ann Fredericks
Cover Designer: Keithley and Associates
Cover Photos: *Top:* Paula Bronstein © Liaison Agency, Inc.; *right:* Franco Silvi © AFP/Corbis;
    bottom: Paulo Whitaker © Archive Photos
Manufacturing Buyer: Roy Pickering
Printer and Binder: Courier/Westford
Cover Printer: Coral Graphic Services

For permission to use copyrighted material, grateful acknowledgment is made to the
copyright holders on p. 465, which is hereby made part of this copyright page.

Library of Congress Cataloging-in-Publication Data
Goldstein, Joshua S., 1952–
    International relations / Joshua S. Goldstein.—Brief ed.
        p. cm.
    Includes bibliographical references and index.
    ISBN 0-321-07063-1
        1. International relations. I. Title.
JZ1242.G65 2002
    327—dc21

2001029549

Please visit our website at http://www.ablongman.com/goldstein or www.IRtext.com

ISBN 0-321-07063-1

2 3 4 5 6 7 8 9 10—CRW—04 03 02

Brief Contents

Website: www.IRtext.com *or* www.ablongman.com/goldstein

Detailed Contents

Note: Each chapter ends with questions on thinking critically and a chapter summary.

CHAPTER 8
Environment and Technology   408

Preface

"The students like it." This is usually the first comment I hear from colleagues who have used a comprehensive edition of *International Relations*. The reason students like it, I believe, is that it makes accessible such an interesting subject. This Brief Edition now offers a concise version that continues to cover all the topics in the comprehensive text in an accessible way and should give instructors more options to integrate other materials in their classrooms. Like the longer edition, it includes a range of interactive learning resources on a multifaceted Website (www.IRtext.com) and a companion Atlas CD-ROM in order to help students with different learning styles to excel and instructors and students to work together in new ways. The Brief Edition puts somewhat more weight on the traditional aspects of the field—especially war and peace—and a bit less emphasis on emerging areas such as international finance, environmental management, and North-South relations.

The rich complexity of international relationships—political, economic, and cultural—provides a fascinating puzzle to try to understand. The puzzle is not just intellectually challenging; it is also emotionally powerful. It contains human-scale stories in which the subject's grand themes—war and peace, tragedy and triumph, intergroup conflict and community—are played out. International relations is also relevant to our daily lives as never before; today's students will graduate into a global economy in which no nation stands alone. This book does not allow the conceptual apparatus of the field to obscure the real people who make up international relations and those whose lives are at stake.

In the 1990s, the rules of world politics were rewritten in large and small ways—a process that is continuing. Students, professors, and policy makers alike are rethinking the subject of international relations. Power still matters, but economic forms of power now rival military ones. Nuclear weapons are still important, but now because of proliferation rather than the superpower arms race. Relations among states remain central to the rules of world politics, but substate and supranational actors and processes are having influence through new avenues as well. Global telecommunications, multinational business networks, and transnational ethnic communities are undermining state sovereignty from within, while the nascent supranational authority of the United Nations and the European Union is doing the same from without. The most important global division is now the North-South gap between the world's rich and poor regions, not the East-West cleavage of the Cold War. At the same time, scholarship in IR has moved in new directions—expanding the scope of the field and often creating uncertain boundaries and a jumble of divergent approaches to the subject.

International Relations, Brief Edition, appears as a new century brings a new focus on the impact of the information revolution on the interstate system. In the coming years, changes in information technologies and advances in human knowledge will profoundly reshape such core IR concepts as power, sovereignty, and national identity. Military forces and the conduct of war are being reshaped by the information revolution, as are global trade and investment. New "Information Revolution" boxes throughout the text explore the impact of the information revolution on IR and pose critical thinking questions. Marginal icons show links onto the World Wide Web and to this book's companion CD-ROM, the Microsoft® Encarta® Interactive World Atlas.

This is also a time to reflect on the past decade, in which the post–Cold War era took form. In some ways, change slowed down after the mid-1990s; for example, few states joined the UN. In other arenas, however, change seems to be accelerating as the post–Cold War era proceeds. For example, economic globalization is shaking up established patterns and creating surprises like the 1997 Asian financial collapse. The decade overall shows some deep trends that are often overlooked in the chaos of day-to-day international events—notably the trend toward a more peaceful world, with lower military spending, fewer and smaller wars, and growing international cooperation in both security and economic relations.

This edition includes up-to-date examples, cases, photos, and theoretical puzzles. I have retained world-order emphases on the Middle East, the former Yugoslavia, and China.

The quantitative data have been updated, usually to 1999. Basic data, presented simply and appropriately at a global level, allow students to form their own judgments and to reason through the implications of different policies and theories. Notable changes in the late 1990s included UN peacekeeping forces (way down), military forces and spending (down), comparative financial positions (North America up; Asia up and down; Russia way down), third world debt (up), foreign aid (down), and AIDS (way up).

Pedagogical Elements

The aim of *International Relations*, Brief Edition, is to present the current state of knowledge in IR in a comprehensive and accessible way—to provide a map of the subject covering its various research communities in a logical order. The subfields of international security and international political economy, although separated physically in this book, are integrated conceptually and overlap in many ways. No longer does one set of principles apply to military affairs and another set to economic relations, as was sometimes argued during the Cold War. Using the concepts of power and bargaining to bridge the two subfields, this book connects both subfields to the real world by using concrete examples to illustrate theories.

Many people in the television generation find information—especially abstract concepts—easier to grasp when linked with pictures. Thus the book uses photographs extensively to illustrate important points. Photo captions reinforce main themes from each section of the text and link them with the scenes pictured.

In a subject like IR, where knowledge is tentative and empirical developments can overtake theories, critical thinking is a key skill for college students to develop. Narratives and boxes present what is known but leave conclusions open-ended in order to encourage critical thinking. The questions at the end of each chapter are designed to engage students in thinking critically about the contents of the chapter. The role of data in encouraging critical thinking by students has been mentioned. In presenting quantitative information, the text uses global-level data (showing the whole picture), rounds off numbers to highlight what is important, and conveys information graphically where appropriate.

Many people come to the study of IR with little background in world geography and history. The first chapter of this book presents background material on these topics. A historical perspective places recent decades in the context of the evolution of the modern international system. The global orientation of the book reflects the diversity of IR experiences for different actors, especially those in the global South.

Three levels of analysis—individual, domestic, and interstate—have often been used to sort out the multiple influences operating in international relations. This book adds a fourth, the global level. Global-level phenomena such as the United Nations, the world environment, and global telecommunications and culture receive special attention.

IR is a large subject that offers many directions for further exploration. Each chapter ends with questions on thinking critically, a chapter summary, and a reminder to try the practice tests on the text's Companion Website.

Structure of the Book

The overall structure of this book follows substantive topics, first in international security (Chapters 1 to 4) and then in international political economy (Chapters 5 to 8). The individual chapters, although convenient for organization, overlap substantively and theoretically, as noted in several places.

Chapter 1 introduces the study of IR and provides some of the geographical and historical context of the subject. Chapters 2 considers various theoretical approaches to the subject, focusing primarily on international security but laying the groundwork for later treatments of international political economy as well. The concepts of power and bargaining, developed in Chapter 2, remain central to later discussions. Chapter 3 introduces the important concepts of interdependence and collective goods and of feminist (and other) critiques of realism. It then examines foreign policy processes and the roles of substate actors in shaping IR. After examining the main sources of international conflict, including ethnic, territorial, and economic conflicts, Chapter 4 considers the conditions and manner in which such conflicts lead to the use of violence.

Chapter 5 introduces theoretical concepts in political economy (showing how theories of international security translate into new issue areas) and discusses the most important topic of international political economy, namely, trade relations. It then describes the politics of international money, banking, and multinational business operations. Chapter 6 shows how international organizations, especially the United Nations and the European Union, and international law have evolved to become major influences in IR. Chapter 7 addresses global North–South relations, paying particular attention to poverty in the third world. It then considers alternatives for third-world economic development in the context of international business, debt, and foreign aid. Concluding the text, Chapter 8 explores the process of international integration through telecommunications and cultural exchange and shows how environmental politics expands international bargaining and interdependence both regionally and globally. A final section of Chapter 8 serves as a vehicle for reflection and critical thinking about the state of international affairs today and its prospects in the future.

Companion Website

Instructors and students are invited to this book's Companion Website at www.IRtext.com or www.ablongman.com/goldstein on the World Wide Web. This online course companion provides a wealth of resources for both students and instructors using *International Relations*, Brief Edition. The site includes a custom search feature and self-loading links to the Microsoft® Encarta® Interactive World Atlas CD-ROM. Students will find chapter summaries, practice tests, interactive exercises tied to the "Information Revolution" boxes in the text, role-playing simulations, web links that are referenced by marginal icons in the book, extensive Selected Readings keyed to page numbers in the text, and more. Instructors will have access to the instructor's manual, downloadable visuals from the text, and teaching links, and they can take advantage of Syllabus Manager, an easy-to-use tool that allows instructors to put their courses online. Find the site at www.IRtext.com or through the publisher's home page at www.ablongman.com/goldstein.

Supplements

Available for Qualified College Adopters

Instructor's Manual/Test Bank

Written by Robert Breckinridge of Mount Aloysius College, this resource includes chapter overviews, learning objectives, lecture outlines, teaching suggestions, ideas for student projects, and key words in addition to numerous multiple-choice, short answer, map and essay questions.

Transparencies

This acetate package based on Goldstein's *International Relations*, Fourth Edition, is composed of 53 tables, figures, and maps drawn from the text.

TestGen EQ Computerized Testing Program

This flexible computerized testing system includes all of the test items in the printed test bank. Instructors can easily edit, print, and expand item banks. Tests can be printed in several formats and include figures such as graphs and tables. The program also includes the Quizmaster EQ program, which allows students to take tests on computers rather than in printed form. It is available in a hybrid platform to accommodate both Macintosh and Windows formats.

Instructor's Guide to the Microsoft® Encarta® Interactive World Atlas CD-ROM

Written by Phil Meeks of Creighton University, this new resource provides numerous tips and strategies on how professors can best use the Microsoft® Encarta® Interactive World Atlas CD-ROM in conjunction with this book.

Available for Students

Microsoft® Encarta® Interactive World Atlas CD-ROM

This multimedia CD maps every corner of the world, providing thousands of interactive maps in 21 different styles, 1.2 million place names, 192 country home pages, 10,000 articles, and thousands of videos and images. This CD, which is available bundled with the book at a steep discount, offers a Map Gallery, Geography Quizzes, a Statistics Center, World Tours, and a Dynamic Multimedia Map. Much of this information is referenced in the text through icons that appear in its margins. (To order the text and discount CD package, give ISBN 0-201-77407-0 to your bookstore.)

Student Workbook for the Microsoft® Encarta® Interactive World Atlas CD-ROM

Written by Bernard-Thompson Ikegwuoha, this new booklet provides exercises that help students utilize the Microsoft® Encarta® Interactive World Atlas CD-ROM in their courses. Engaging activities that can be used with the book help students with geography, statistics, and other areas that will allow them to get the most out of their international relations course.

Longman Atlas of War and Peace

Adapted from the work of Dan Smith, director of the International Peace Institute, introduced by James N. Rosenau of George Washington University, and edited by Joshua S. Goldstein, this series of pedagogical maps and explanations offers a nontraditional approach to cartography: how nations compare to one another in such terms as military spending, ethnic strife, control of natural resources, and internal conflicts. The atlas is available as a stand-alone item or at a discount when packaged with *International Relations.*

New Signet World Atlas

From Penguin-Putnam, this pocket-sized yet detailed reference features 96 pages of full-color maps, plus statistics, key data, and much more. Available for 60 percent off the retail price when ordered packaged!

ContentSelect Research Database for Political Science: www.ablongman.com/contentselect

Give your students free and unlimited access to a customized, searchable collection of thousands of full-text articles from peer-reviewed journals. ContentSelect lets students do research anywhere and anytime they have an Internet connection. Available FREE when ordered packaged with this text.

Quick Guide to the Internet for Political Science

This guide walks students through doing research on the Internet, with an abundance of relevant web addresses and discussions of how to evaluate websites for academic usefulness. FREE when packaged.

Discount Subscription to *Newsweek* Magazine

For more than 80 percent off the regular price, students can receive 12 issues of *Newsweek* magazine delivered to their doors when they order with the discount subscription card packaged with this text.

Writing in Political Science, Second Edition, by Diane E. Schmidt

This book takes students step-by-step through all the aspects of writing for political science courses with an abundance of samples from actual students. 10 percent discount when packaged with the text.

Acknowledgments

Many scholars, colleagues, and friends have contributed ideas that ultimately influenced the various editions of this book. I owe a special debt to Robert North, who suggested many years ago that the concepts of bargaining and leverage could be used to integrate IR theory across four levels of analysis. Recent editions benefited from the assistance of Louis Cooper. For help with military data issues, I thank Randall Forsberg, Ted Postel, David Wright, and William Grimmett. For suggestions, I thank Gerald Bender, Maria Green Cowles, Laura Drake, my colleagues at American University, and the students in my world politics classes. The following reviewers made many useful suggestions:

Philip Baumann, *Moorhead State University*

Robert E. Breckinridge, *Mount Aloysius College*

Gregory A. Cline, *Michigan State University*

Cynthia Combs, *University of North Carolina at Charlotte*

Paul D'Anieri, *University of Kansas*

Patricia Davis, *University of Notre Dame*

Elizabeth DeSombre, *Colby College*

June Teufel Dreyer, *University of Miami*

Larry Elowitz, *George College and State University*

George Emerson, *Miami Dade Community College*

Mark Everingham, *University of Wisconsin—Green Bay*

Jonathan Galloway, *Lake Forest College*

Marc Genest, *University of Rhode Island*

Deborah J. Gerner, *University of Kansas*

Emily O. Goldman, *University of California, Davis*

Vicki Golich, *California State University, San Marcos*

Robert Gregg, *School of International Service, American University*

Wolfgang Hirczy, *University of Houston*

Piper Hodson, *Saint Joseph's College*

Steven W. Hook, *University of Missouri*

Ted Hopf, *University of Michigan*

Zohair Husain, *University of South Alabama*

Akira Ichikawa, *University of Lethbridge*

Matthias Kaelberer, *University of Northern Iowa*

Joyce Kaufman, *University of Maryland at College Park*

John Keeler, *University of Washington*

Michael Kelley, *University of Central Arkansas*

Mark Lagon, *Georgetown University*

William Lamkin, *Glendale Community College*

Wei-Chin Lee, *Wake Forest University*

Renée Marlin-Bennett, *School of International Service, American University*

James Meernick, *University of North Texas*

Karen Mingst, *University of Kentucky*

Richard Moore, *Lewis-Clark State College*

John W. Outland, *University of Richmond*

Salvatore Prisco, *Stevens Institute of Technology*

David Rapkin, *University of Nebraska at Lincoln*

Edward Rhodes, *Rutgers University*

Leonard Riley, *Pikes Peak Community College*

Henry Schockley, *Boston University*

Thomas J. Volgy, *University of Arizona*

David Wilsford, *School of International Service, American University*

The errors, of course, remain my own responsibility.

Joshua S. Goldstein

To the Student

The topics studied by scholars are like a landscape with many varied locations and terrains. This textbook is a map that can orient you to the main topics, debates, and issue areas in international relations. This map divides international relations into two main territories: international security and international political economy. However, these territories overlap and interconnect in many ways. Also, the principles that apply to the interactions of states in security affairs are similar to those that apply to economic relations.

Scholars use specialized language to talk about their subjects. This text is a phrase book that can translate such lingo and explain the terms and concepts that scholars use to talk about international relations. However, IR is filled with many voices speaking many tongues. The text translates some of those voices—of presidents and professors, free-traders and feminists—to help you sort out the contours of the subject and the state of knowledge about its various topics. But ultimately the synthesis presented in this book is the author's own. Both you and your professor may disagree with many points. Thus, this book is only a starting point for conversations and debates.

With map and phrase book in hand, you are ready to explore a fascinating world. The great changes in world politics in the past few years have made the writing of this textbook an exciting project. May you enjoy your own explorations of this realm.

J. S. G.

A Note on Nomenclature

In international relations, names are politically sensitive; different actors may call a territory or an event by different names. This book cannot resolve such conflicts; it has adopted the following naming conventions for the sake of consistency. The United Kingdom of Great Britain (England, Scotland, Wales) and Northern Ireland are called Britain. Burma, renamed Myanmar by its military government, is referred to as Burma. Cambodia, renamed Kampuchea by the Khmer Rouge in the 1970s, is called Cambodia. The 1991 U.S.–led multinational military campaign that retook Kuwait after Iraq's 1990 invasion is called the Gulf War. The war between Iran and Iraq in the 1980s is called the Iran-Iraq War (not the "Gulf War," as some called it at the time). The country of Bosnia and Herzegovina is generally shortened to Bosnia (with apologies to Herzegovinians). The Former Yugoslav Republic of Macedonia is called Macedonia. The People's Republic of China is referred to as China. The former Zaire is now Democratic Congo. Elsewhere, country names follow common usage, dropping formal designations such as "Republic of."

www. IRtext.com

Students are invited to use the learning resources at this book's Companion Website. There, you may take practice tests, follow quick-links onto the web, explore the implications of the information revolution for international relations, find Selected Readings, and take in multimedia explorations from this book's companion CD-ROM, the Microsoft® Encarta® Interactive World Atlas. To use these learning resources, just go to www.IRtext.com or www.ablongman.com/goldstein and enter the page number from this book where an icon appears, to automatically bring up the indicated materials. In the electronic version of the book, all the icons are "hot" and take the user directly to the relevant Web or CD resources.

A Key to Icon Usage

Atlas CD

Atlas CD This icon marks concepts and examples in the text that are illustrated through maps and multimedia presentations on the Microsoft® Encarta® Interactive World Atlas CD-ROM, available for a small charge with new copies of this textbook. After installing the Atlas, follow the Atlas CD icons through this book's Web site to bring up self-loading images from the CD-ROM on your computer. You can quickly download to your computer a folder with all the Atlas CD links, to use the Atlas CD while offline. The first link (p. 3) calls up a map of earth from space. The "+" button (bottom left) zooms in. The "hand" cursor moves the map frame (hold mouse button while moving hand). Click a country for maps, photos, articles, statistics, and Microsoft's web links. Click place names for maps. The "find" box (upper left) toggles the pinpointer on and off.

Web Link

Web Link This icon marks topics for which this book's Companion Website has links to the most important world-wide web sites on a topic or theme. Critical thinking questions accompany each of these links so that students are inspired to think analytically about the information they encounter. Responses to those critical thinking questions can be e-mailed directly to the instructor.

The Information Revolution These boxes in each chapter pose critical-thinking questions about the effects on IR of rapid changes in information technology. To explore these questions, go to this book's Companion Website, follow the indicated links, and then return to the Companion Website to tie together what you have learned.

ONLINE PRACTICE TEST

Take an online practice test at
www.IRtext.com

Online Practice Tests This icon at the end of each chapter reminds you to take a practice test at www.IRtext.com. Get your score and learning tips to improve your weak areas.

Nine Regions of the World

North America

Western Europe

"The North"

"The South"

Russia / Eastern Europe

China

Japan / Pacific

Middle East

Africa

South Asia

Latin America

2000 Kilometers
2000 Miles
0
0

World States and Territories

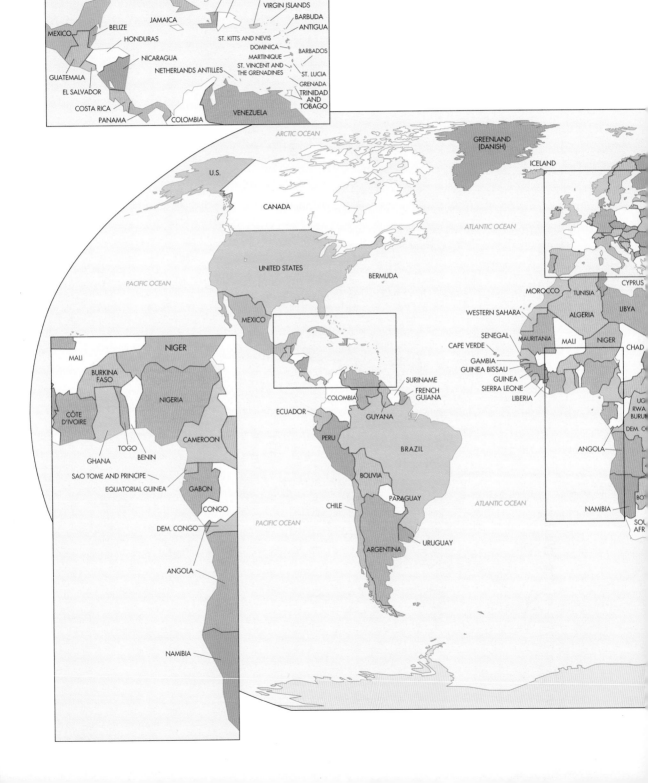

NATO Expansion

Legend:
- NATO members, pre–1999 (France not militarily integrated)
- Joined NATO, 1999
- Leading candidates for next round
- Want to join
- Boundary of former USSR
- Boundary of former Warsaw Pact

0 200 400 Kilometers
0 200 400 Miles

ICELAND

Arctic Circle

ATLANTIC OCEAN

North Sea

NORWAY

SWEDEN

FINLAND

RUSSIA

ESTONIA

LATVIA

LITHUANIA

RUSSIA

BELARUS

DENMARK

IRELAND

UNITED KINGDOM

NETHERLANDS

BELGIUM

GERMANY

LUXEMBOURG

POLAND

UKRAINE

CZECH REP.

SLOVAKIA

MOLDOVA

FRANCE

SWITZ.

AUSTRIA

HUNGARY

SLOVENIA

CROATIA

BOSNIA-HERZEGOVINA

SERBIA-MONTENEGRO

ROMANIA

Black Sea

PORTUGAL

SPAIN

ITALY

BULGARIA

MACEDONIA

ALBANIA

GREECE

TURKEY

Mediterranean Sea

MALTA

Note: All countries on map are members of NATO'S Partnership for Peace program except Switzerland, Croatia, Bosnia-Herzegovina, and Serbia & Montenegro.

China's Neighborhood

North America

Scale 1:38,700,000

Lambert Conformal Conic Projection,
standard parallels 37° N and 65° N

0   500 Kilometers
0   500 Nautical Miles

Boundary representation is
not necessarily authoritative.

RUSSIA

Cherskiy
Pevek
Anadyr
Providéniya
Nome
Barrow
Prudhoe Bay

Arctic Ocean
Chukchi Sea
Bering Strait
Beaufort Sea

UNITED STATES (Alaska)
Bethel
Fairbanks
Anchorage
Valdez
Kodiak
Gulf of Alaska
Juneau
Ketchikan

Inuvik
Dawson
Whitehorse
Prince Rupert
Prince George
Vancouver
Victoria
Seattle
Portland

Great Bear Lake
Echo Bay
Yellowknife
Great Slave Lake
Lake Athabasca
Edmonton
Calgary
Saskatoon
Regina
Winnipeg

CANADA

Banks Island
Victoria Island
Cambridge Bay
Kaujuitoq (Resolune)
Arctic Bay
Queen Elizabeth Islands
Ellesmere Island
Alert
Nord
Thule

Greenland (DENMARK)
Danmark Havn
Itseqqortoormiit
ICELAND
Reykjavík
Denmark Strait
Greenland Sea
Jan Mayen (NORWAY)
Ammassalik
Qeqertarsuaq
Nuuk (Godthåb)
Qaqortoq
Davis Strait
Baffin Bay
Baffin Island
Iqaluit (Frobisher Bay)
Repulse Bay
Churchill
Ivugivik

Hudson Bay
Labrador Sea
Island of Newfoundland
St. John's
St. Pierre and Miquelon (FRANCE)
Schefferville
Happy Valley Goose Bay
Chisasibi (Fort George)
Moosonee

Lake Winnipeg
Thunder Bay
Lake Superior
Lake Huron
Gulf of St. Lawrence
Sydney
Charlottetown
Québec
Fredericton
Bangor
St. John
Halifax
Montréal
Ottawa
Toronto
Lake Ontario
Boston
New York
Detroit
Cleveland
Lake Erie
Chicago
Philadelphia
Washington, D.C.

Great Falls
Boise
Salt Lake City
San Francisco
Las Vegas
Los Angeles
San Diego
Tijuana
Phoenix
Albuquerque
Denver
Minneapolis
Omaha
St. Louis
Louisville
Little Rock
Dallas
El Paso
Ciudad Juárez

UNITED STATES

Atlanta
Charleston
Jacksonville
Norfolk
Bermuda (U.K.)

North Pacific Ocean
North Atlantic Ocean

Houston
New Orleans
Miami
THE BAHAMAS
Nassau

Hermosillo
Chihuahua
Torreón
Monterrey
Matamoros
La Paz
Durango
Mazatlán
Tampico
Gulf of Mexico
Gulf of California
Tropic of Cancer

MEXICO

León
Guadalajara
Mexico
Puebla
Veracruz
Mérida
Oaxaca
Acapulco
Islas Revillagigedo (MEXICO)

Havana CUBA
HAITI
Port-au-Prince
JAMAICA
Kingston
Caribbean Sea

Belmopan
BELIZE
GUATEMALA
Guatemala
San Salvador
EL SALVADOR
HONDURAS
Tegucigalpa
NICARAGUA
Managua

802374 (B01267) 5-95

Central America and the Caribbean

United States
New Orleans
Miami
Gulf of Mexico
Straits of Florida
Tropic of Cancer

North Atlantic Ocean

THE BAHAMAS
Nassau

CUBA
Havana
Isla de la Juventud
Cayman Islands (U.K.)
George Town

Swan Islands (HONDURAS)

GREATER ANTILLES
JAMAICA
Kingston

Guantanamo Bay (U.S. NAVAL BASE)

HAITI
Port-au-Prince

DOMINICAN REPUBLIC
Santo Domingo

Turks and Caicos Islands (U.K.)
Grand Turk

Caribbean Sea

LESSER ANTILLES

British Virgin Islands (U.K.)
Charlotte Amalie
Virgin Islands (U.S.)
San Juan
Puerto Rico (U.S.)

Anguilla (U.K.)
The Valley
Road Town

ANTIGUA AND BARBUDA
St. John's
Basseterre
ST. KITTS AND NEVIS
Plymouth
Montserrat (U.K.)
Guadeloupe (FRANCE)
Basse-Terre
DOMINICA
Roseau
Fort-de-France
Martinique (FRANCE)
ST. LUCIA
Castries
BARBADOS
Bridgetown
ST. VINCENT AND THE GRENADINES
Kingstown
GRENADA
St. George's
Leeward Islands
Windward Islands

Netherlands Antilles (NETHERLANDS)
Bonaire
Curaçao
Willemstad
Aruba (NETH.)
Oranjestad

TRINIDAD AND TOBAGO
Port-of-Spain

VENEZUELA
Caracas
San Cristóbal
Maracaibo
Ciudad Guayana

GUYANA
Georgetown

SURINAME
Paramaribo

French Guiana (FRANCE)
Cayenne

BRAZIL
Boa Vista

COLOMBIA
Bogotá
Barranquilla
Medellín
Cali

ECUADOR

PANAMA
Panama
Colón
Panama Canal
Puerto Limón
COSTA RICA
San José
Isla del Coco (COSTA RICA)

NICARAGUA
Managua
Islas del Maíz (NICARAGUA)
Cayos Miskitos (NICARAGUA)
Isla de Providencia (COLOMBIA)
Isla de San Andrés (COLOMBIA)

HONDURAS
Tegucigalpa
San Pedro Sula

EL SALVADOR
San Salvador

GUATEMALA
Guatemala

BELIZE
Belmopan

MEXICO
Cancún
Isla Cozumel

North Pacific Ocean

Galapagos Islands (ECUADOR)

Tropic of Cancer
Equator

Scale 1:21,500,000
Lambert Conformal Conic Projection, standard parallels 7N and 19N

0   300 Kilometers
0   300 Nautical Miles

Boundary representation is not necessarily authoritative.

802107 (R00769) 8-93

South America

Caribbean Sea

Guadeloupe (FRANCE)
DOMINICA
Martinique (FRANCE)
ST. LUCIA
ST. VINCENT AND THE GRENADINES
BARBADOS
GRENADA

HONDURAS
Puerto Lempira
Tegucigalpa
Puerto Cabezas
NICARAGUA
Managua
Liberia
San José
Colón
Panama
COSTA RICA
David
PANAMA
Isla de San Andrés (COLOMBIA)

North Atlantic Ocean

Barranquilla
Maracaibo
Caracas
Port-of-Spain
TRINIDAD AND TOBAGO
San Cristóbal
VENEZUELA
Ciudad Guayana
Rio Orinoco
Georgetown
Paramaribo
French Guiana (FRANCE)
Medellín
GUYANA
SURINAME
Cayenne
Isla de Malpelo (COLOMBIA)
Bogotá
COLOMBIA
Cali
Boa Vista
Mitú
Macapá
Rio Magdalena

Equator
0
Quito
ECUADOR
Guayaquil
Iquitos
Fonte Boa
Manaus
Santarém
Belém
São Luís
Fortaleza
Rio Negro
Amazon
Amazon
Piura
Trujillo
Rio Branco
Pôrto Velho
BRAZIL
Teresina
Natal
Recife
Huánuco
Rio Marañón
PERU
Lima
Ica
Cusco
Palmas
Aracaju
South Pacific Ocean
Arequipa
Lago Titicaca
Trinidad
BOLIVIA
La Paz
Cochabamba
Santa Cruz
Cuiabá
Goiânia
Brasília
Salvador
Arica
Potosí
Sucre
Rio Xingu
Rio Tocantins
Rio São Francisco
Belo Horizonte
Vitória
Antofagasta
PARAGUAY
Asunción
Rio Paraguai
Rio de Janeiro
São Paulo
20
Tropic of Capricorn
San Miguel de Tucumán
Resistencia
Curitiba
Isla San Félix (CHILE)
Isla San Ambrosio (CHILE)
Florianópolis
Pôrto Alegre
South Atlantic Ocean
CHILE
Córdoba
Salto
URUGUAY
Valparaíso
Mendoza
Rosario
Rio Paraná
Archipiélago Juan Fernández (CHILE)
Santiago
Buenos Aires
Montevideo
ARGENTINA
Concepción
Bahía Blanca
Mar del Plata
San Carlos de Bariloche
Puerto Montt
40
Comodoro Rivadavia

Scale 1:35,000,000

Azimuthal Equal Area Projection

0   250   500 Kilometers
0   250   500 Nautical Miles

Boundary representation is not necessarily authoritative.

Strait of Magellan
Stanley
Falkland Islands (Islas Malvinas) (administered by U.K., claimed by Argentina)
Punta Arenas
Ushuaia

South Georgia and the South Sandwich Islands (administered by U.K., claimed by Argentina)

802376 (545528) 5-95

Africa

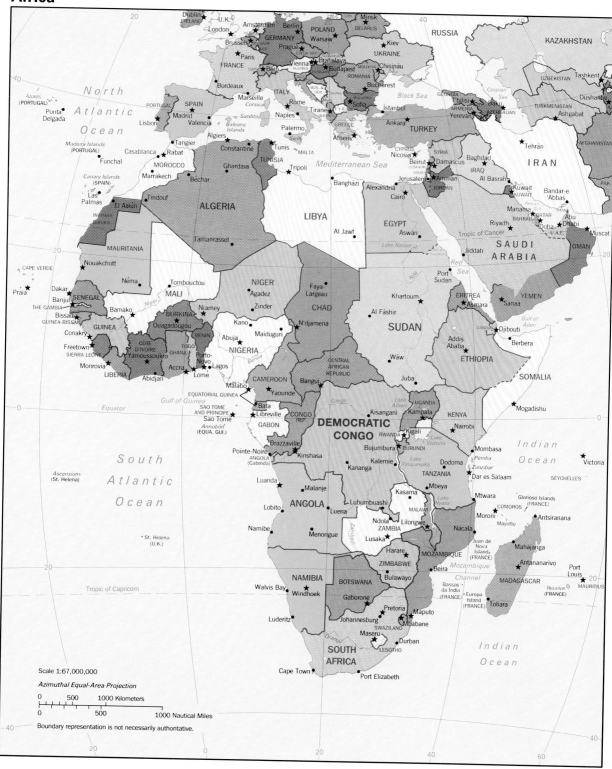

Scale 1:67,000,000

Azimuthal Equal-Area Projection

| 0 | 500 | 1000 Kilometers |

| 0 | 500 | 1000 Nautical Miles |

Boundary representation is not necessarily authoritative.

802380 (R00475) 5-95

Northern Africa and the Middle East

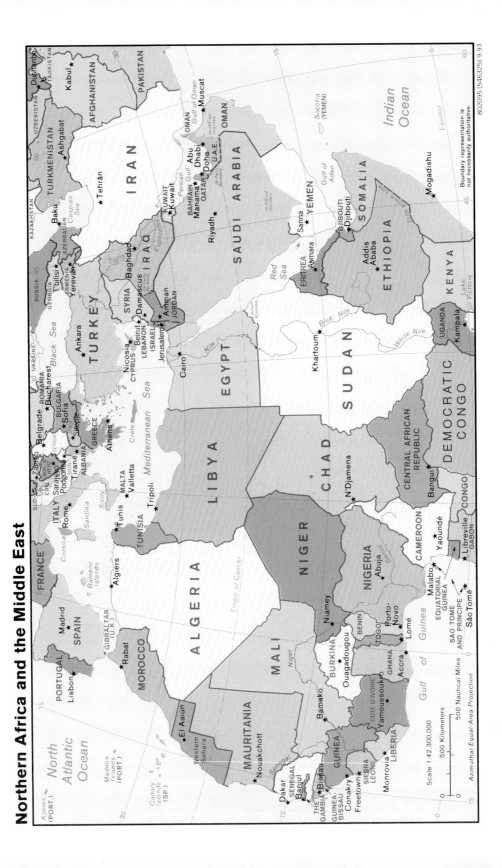

Europe

Serbia and Montenegro have asserted the formation of a joint independent state, but this entity has not been formally recognized as a state by the United States.

Scale 1:19,500,000
Lambert Conformal Conic Projection,
standart parallels 40°N and 56°N

0   300 Kilometers
0   300 Nautical Miles

802377 (R01083) 5-95

Asia

RUSSIA

KAZAKHSTAN

MONGOLIA

CHINA

INDIA

IRAN

AFGHANISTAN

PAKISTAN

NEPAL

BHUTAN

BANGLADESH

BURMA

THAILAND

LAOS

VIETNAM

CAMBODIA

MALAYSIA

INDONESIA

PHILIPPINES

JAPAN

NORTH KOREA

SOUTH KOREA

MONGOLIA

TURKEY

SYRIA

IRAQ

SAUDI ARABIA

YEMEN

OMAN

U.A.E.

QATAR

BAHRAIN

KUWAIT

GEORGIA

ARMENIA

AZERBAIJAN

TURKMENISTAN

UZBEKISTAN

TAJIKISTAN

KYRGYZSTAN

UKRAINE

BELARUS

POLAND

GERMANY

NORWAY

SWEDEN

FINLAND

MOLDOVA

ROM.

HUNG.

SLOV.

CZECH REP.

LITH.

LATVIA

EST.

RUS.

NETH.

DEN.

IRELAND

UNITED KINGDOM

SRI LANKA

MALDIVES

BRUNEI

TAIWAN

Norwegian Sea

Arctic Ocean

Barents Sea

Kara Sea

Laptev Sea

East Siberian Sea

Bering Sea

North Pacific Ocean

Sea of Okhotsk

Sea of Japan

Yellow Sea

East China Sea

Philippine Sea

South China Sea

Bay of Bengal

Arabian Sea

Indian Ocean

Andaman Sea

Laccadive Sea

Black Sea

Caspian Sea

Aral Sea

Lake Balkhash

Lake Baikal

Baltic Sea

North Sea

Persian Gulf

Arctic Circle

Tropic of Cancer

Equator

Franz Josef Land

Severnaya Zemlya

Novaya Zemlya

New Siberian Islands

Wrangel Island

Svalbard (NORWAY)

Sakhalin

Kuril Islands

Okinawa

Spratly Islands

Andaman Islands (INDIA)

Nicobar Islands (INDIA)

Lakshadweep (INDIA)

Hong Kong (China)

Macau (China)

U.S.

Scale 1:50,000,000
Azimuthal Equal-Area Projection

0   500   1000 Kilometers
0   500   1000 Nautical Miles

Occupied by the Soviet Union in 1945, administered by Russia, claimed by Japan.

802382 (R01813) 5-95

Understanding International Relations

CHAPTER OUTLINE

◆ The Study of IR

◆ Actors and Influences

◆ History

The Study of IR

What Is This? The Atlas CD icon means that maps, photos, videos, or articles are available on the *Microsoft Encarta World Atlas* (see p. xvi).

Our world is large and complex. International relations is a fascinating topic because it concerns peoples and cultures throughout the world. The scope and complexity of these groups' interactions make international relations a challenging subject to master.

Strictly defined, the field of **international relations (IR)** concerns the relationships among the world's governments. But these relationships cannot be understood in isolation. They are closely connected with other actors (such as international organizations, multinational corporations, and individuals); with other social structures (including economics, culture, and domestic politics); and with geographical and historical influences. IR is a large subject that overlaps several other fields.

This book's purpose is to introduce the field of IR, to organize what is known and theorized about IR in a logical way, and to convey the key concepts used by political scientists to discuss relations among nations. This first chapter defines IR as a field of study, introduces the actors of interest, and reviews the geographical and historical contexts within which IR occurs.

Atlas CD
Afro-Eurasia from Space; Zoom In *Map*

IR and Daily Life Sometimes international relations is portrayed as a distant and abstract ritual conducted by a small group of people such as presidents, generals, and

1

Reflections of War IR touches our lives in many ways. The Vietnam Veterans Memorial, 1982.

diplomats. This is not accurate. Although leaders do play a major role in international affairs, many other people participate as well. College students and other citizens participate in international relations every time they vote in an election or work on a political campaign, every time they buy a product or service traded on world markets, and every time they watch the news. The choices we make in our daily lives ultimately affect the world we live in. Through those choices, every person makes a unique contribution, however small, to the world of international relations.

In turn, IR profoundly affects the daily lives of college students and other citizens. The prospects for college students' getting jobs after graduation depend on the global economy and international economic competition. Those jobs also are more likely than ever to entail international travel or communication. And the rules of the world trading system affect the goods that students consume, from television sets to gasoline.

Although international economics pervades daily life, war dominates daily life only infrequently. Still, war casts a long shadow. In major wars, students and their friends and family go off to war and their lives change irreversibly. But even in peacetime, war is among the most pervasive international influences in daily life. Children play with war toys; young people go into military service; TV and films reproduce the images of war; and a sizable sector of the world economy is structured around military production.

As technology advances, the world is shrinking year by year. Better communication and transportation capabilities are constantly expanding the ordinary person's contact with people, products, and ideas from other countries.

IR as a Field of Study
As a field of study, IR has uncertain boundaries. As a part of political science, IR is about *international politics*—the decisions of governments concerning their actions toward other governments. To some extent, however, the field is interdisciplinary, relating international politics to economics, history, sociology, and other disciplines. Some universities offer separate degrees or departments for IR. Most, however, teach IR in political science classes. The focus is on the *politics* of economic relationships, or the *politics* of environmental management.

Political relations among nations cover a range of activities—diplomacy, war, trade relations, alliances, cultural exchanges, participation in international organizations, and so forth. Particular activities within one of these spheres make up distinct **issue areas** on which scholars and foreign policy makers focus attention. Examples of issue areas include global trade negotiations, or specific ethnic conflicts such as the Arab-Israeli conflicts. Within each issue area, and across the range of issues in any international relationship, policy makers of one nation can behave in a cooperative manner or a conflictual manner—extending either friendly or hostile behavior toward the other nation. IR scholars often look at international relations in terms of the mix of **conflict and cooperation** among nations.

One kind of politics that has an international character is not generally included in the field of IR: the domestic politics of foreign countries. That is a separate field of political science called *comparative politics*. Comparative politics overlaps with IR to the considerable extent that domestic politics influences foreign policy in many countries. Furthermore, the scholars who know about IR and foreign policies in a certain country or region often are the same people who know the most about domestic politics within that country or region. Despite these overlaps, IR as a field tends to avoid issues that concern domestic politics in the United States or other countries *except* to the extent that they affect international politics.

The scope of the field of IR may also be defined by the *subfields* it encompasses. Traditionally, the study of IR has focused on questions of war and peace—the subfield of **international security** studies. The movements of armies and of diplomats, the crafting of treaties and alliances, and the development and deployment of military capabilities were subjects that dominated the study of IR in the past, especially in the 1950s and 1960s, and they continue to hold a central position in the field. In the 1990s, after the Cold War, the subfield of security studies broadened beyond its traditional focus. Regional conflicts began to receive more attention, and ethnic conflicts became more prominent. Scholars of foreign policy processes increasingly saw themselves as part of this broader security studies community. Meanwhile, interdisciplinary peace studies programs sought to broaden concepts of "security" further—as did feminist scholars. While the study of war, weapons, and military forces continues to be the core concern of international security studies, these trends have expanded the boundaries of the subfield.

In the 1970s and 1980s, as economics became increasingly central to international relations, the subfield of **international political economy (IPE)** became the counterpoint to international security studies as a second main subfield of IR. Scholars of IPE study trade relations and financial relations among nations, and try to understand how nations have cooperated politically to create and maintain institutions that regulate the flow of international economic and financial transactions. These topics mainly relate to relations among the world's richer nations. But, since the 1990s, growing attention has been paid to global North-South relations between rich and poor nations (see pp. 15–19), including such topics as economic dependency, debt, foreign aid, and technology transfer. As the East-West confrontation of the Cold War recedes into history, North-South problems are becoming more salient. So are problems of international environmental management and of global telecommunications. The subfield of IPE is expanding accordingly.

IR scholars now recognize the close connections of IPE with security (after decades of treating them as separate and different). The same principles and theories that help us understand international security (in the first half of this book) also help us to understand IPE (in the second half). Economics is important in security affairs, and vice versa. The organization of this book may seem to create a divide between the two subfields, but in reality they are interwoven.

Theories and Methods

IR scholars want to understand why international events occur in the way they do. Why did a certain war break out? Why did a certain trade agreement benefit one nation more than another? Why are some countries so much richer than others? These "why" questions can be answered in several ways. One kind of answer results from tracing the immediate, short-term sequences of events and decisions that led to a particular outcome. For instance, the outbreak of war might be traced to a critical decision made by a particular leader. This kind of answer is largely *descriptive*—it seeks to describe how particular forces and actors operate to bring about a particular outcome.

Another kind of answer results from seeking general explanations and longer-term, more indirect causes. For example, a war outbreak might be seen as part of a general pattern in which arms races lead to war. This kind of answer is *theoretical* because it places the particular event in the context of a more general pattern applicable across many cases.

Understanding IR requires both descriptive and theoretical knowledge. It would do little good to only describe events without being able to generalize or draw lessons from them. Nor would it do much good to formulate purely abstract theories without being able to apply them to the finely detailed and complex real world in which we live.

Ultimately, IR is a rather practical discipline. There is a close connection between scholars in colleges, universities, or think tanks and the policy-making community in the government—especially in the United States. Some professors serve in the government (for instance, Professor Madeleine Albright became secretary of state in 1997), and sometimes professors publicize their ideas about foreign policy through newspaper columns or TV interviews. Influencing their government's foreign policy enables these scholars to test their ideas in practice. Diplomats, bureaucrats, and politicians can benefit from both the descriptive and the theoretical knowledge produced by IR scholars.

Different IR scholars emphasize different mixes of descriptive and theoretical work. Like other disciplines, IR includes both basic and applied research. Generally, scholars closer to the policy process are more interested in descriptive and short-term explanations that are useful for managing a particular issue area or region. Scholars closer to the academic ivory tower tend to be interested in more abstract, general, and longer-term explanations.

A parallel (though not a perfect one) can be drawn when it comes to the *methods* to use in developing and testing various theories. The methodological approaches can be arrayed roughly along an empirical versus theoretical axis. At one end, many scholars seek knowledge about IR by interviewing people in various places and piecing together their stories—a method well suited to descriptive explanation or to induction (building theories from facts). At the other end, some researchers create abstract mathematical models of relationships that are all theory with no real grounding in the empirical reality of international politics—a method suited to deduction (predicting facts from a theory). Between these approaches are others that mix theory and empirical evidence in various ways. Many IR scholars try to make quantitative measurements of things such as international conflict or trade, and use statistical methods to make inferences about the relationships among those variables. All of these methods of learning about IR can be useful in different ways, though they yield different kinds of knowledge.

IR is an unpredictable realm of turbulent processes and events that catch the experts by surprise, such as the fall of the Berlin Wall in 1989. Most IR scholars are modest about their ability to make accurate predictions—and with good reason. The best theories provide only a rough guide to understanding what actually occurs in IR or predicting what will happen next. Perhaps because of this complexity and unpredictability, IR scholars do not agree on a single set of theories to explain IR or even on a single set of concepts with which to discuss the field. Traditionally, the most widely accepted theories—though never unchallenged by critics—have explained international outcomes in terms of power politics or "realism." But there are many theoretical disagreements—different answers to the "why" questions—both within realism and between realists and their critics. Throughout these discussions, no single theoretical framework has the support of all IR scholars.

Atlas CD
Berlin Wall Fall
Photo

One way to look at the variety of theories is to distinguish three broad theoretical perspectives, which may be called the *conservative*, *liberal*, and *revolutionary world views* (see Figure 1.1, p. 6). In some sense, each is a lens through which the world looks different, and different things seem important. At the same time, the three perspectives can complement each other, and most theories draw on all three, though in different proportions. Each world view encompasses a variety of distinct theoretical approaches.

A *conservative* world view generally values maintenance of the status quo and discounts the element of change in IR. These perspectives focus on the laws of power politics, which are considered timeless and universal. Conservative perspectives find their most fertile ground in the subfield of international security with its logic of military power. They see states as the most important actors (largely because states control the biggest armies). Relative position with regard to other states is more important than the absolute condition of a state, because in the anarchic world with its ever present possibility of war, winning and losing matter above all. Conservative approaches tend to value *order*. Their advocates are prudent and not eager for change, especially rapid change or change that upsets the hierarchy of power in the international system. These perspectives tend to see war as the natural order of things, a sometimes necessary evil for which one should always be prepared. They see international trade as a potential source of national power, a view expressed in IPE as *mercantilism* (the accumulation of national war chests, or the equivalent, through control of trade).

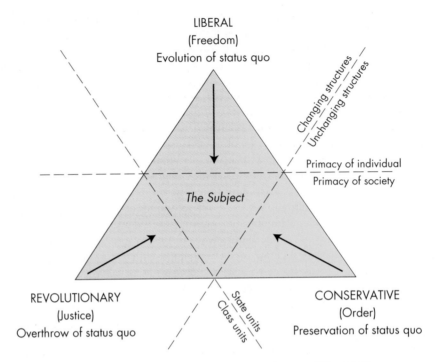

FIGURE 1.1   Conservative, Liberal, and Revolutionary World Views

Source: Adapted from J. S. Goldstein, *Long Cycles: Prosperity and War in the Modern Age.* New Haven: Yale University Press, 1988.

Web Link
Liberalism

What Is This?
The Web Link icon means that links to World Wide Web sites are available at this book's website (see p. xvi).

A *liberal* world view values reform of the status quo through an evolutionary process of incremental change. Theories that build on the liberal tradition often focus on the mutual benefits to be gained in IR through interdependence and reciprocity. Gaining wealth in absolute terms is more important from this perspective than gaining power relative to other countries. Liberal approaches find their most fertile ground in the international-political-economy subfield because of the potentials for mutual gain in trade and exchange, with each nation exploiting its comparative advantage in particular products and services. Liberal approaches tend to value *freedom*, especially free trade and free exchange of ideas. They tend to see war not as a natural tendency but as a tragic mistake, to be prevented or at least minimized by international agreements and organizations.

A *revolutionary* world view values transformation of the status quo by revolutionary and rapid change. These perspectives often focus on the unfair and exploitive aspects of international relationships and on efforts to radically change those relationships. Revolutionary approaches have found resonance in areas of IR scholarship dealing with North-South relations and third world development because of the evident injustice of grinding poverty suffered by a majority of the world's people. Revolutionary approaches tend to value *justice*. They often see war as a product of underlying exploitive economic relationships, and changes in those relationships are key to solving the problem of war.

Real-world politics mixes these three perspectives in various ways. In the United States, for example, most conservative politicians adopt classically liberal positions on free trade and other economic issues. Some European social democrats combine a liberal emphasis on freedom with a revolutionary concern for justice. Similarly, no theory or scholar in IR is purely conservative, liberal, or revolutionary.

In *international security*, a conservative world view strongly influences the contours of "realism" or power politics (taken up in Chapter 2), which holds that a nation rationally uses power to pursue its self-interest. The latest incarnation of realism is "neorealism," which has attempted to make realist principles simpler and more formal. The liberal counterpoint to realism, originally called "idealism" (see Chapter 3), has been less influential in IR scholarship and policy making regarding international security. Its latest version is called *neoliberal institutionalism*; it grants some assumptions of neorealists but claims that the neorealists' pessimistic conclusions about international cooperation do not follow. Several new and more radical critical perspectives have emerged in recent years as serious alternatives to realism as well—feminism, postmodernism, constructivism, and peace studies (also see Chapter 3).

In *international political economy*, the liberal world view dominates scholarship (and often policy). More conservative approaches such as mercantilism have been less influential than those based on liberal "free market" economics. The theoretical contrast of liberalism and mercantilism, and their connection with the collective goods problem, are laid out in Chapter 5. More revolutionary theories of IPE—notably those influenced by Marxism—are taken up in Chapter 7 ("North-South Relations"), where they find greatest resonance.

The theoretical debates in the field of IR are fundamental, but unresolved. They leave IR scholarship in a turbulent condition, racing to try to make sense of a rapidly changing world in which old ideas work poorly. It will be up to the next generation of IR scholars—today's college students—to achieve a better understanding of how world politics works. This book lays out the current state of knowledge without exaggerating the successes of the discipline.

Actors and Influences

Who are the actors in IR? In one sense, the answer is easy. The actors in IR are the world's governments. It is the decisions and acts of those governments, in relation to other such governments, that scholars of IR study.

But in reality, the international stage is crowded with actors large and small who are intimately interwoven with the decisions of governments. These actors are individual leaders and citizens. They are bureaucratic agencies in foreign ministries. They are multinational corporations and terrorist groups. The main contours of the drama are defined by the interactions of large conglomerate characters—nations—while other actors weave in and out of that drama.

State Actors The most important actors in IR are states. A **state** is a territorial entity controlled by a government and inhabited by a population. A state government answers to no higher authority; it exercises *sovereignty* over its territory (to make and enforce laws, to collect taxes, and so forth). This sovereignty is recognized (acknowledged) by other states through diplomatic relations and usually by membership in the

United Nations (UN). (The concepts of state sovereignty and territoriality are elaborated in Chapter 2.) The population inhabiting a state forms a *civil society* to the extent it has developed participatory institutions of social life. All or part of the population that shares a group identity may consider itself a *nation* (see p. 26). The state's government is a *democracy* to the extent that the government is controlled by the members of the population rather than imposed on them. (Note that the word *state* in IR does not mean a state in the United States.)

In political life, and to some extent in IR scholarship, the terms *state*, *nation*, and *country* are used imprecisely, usually to refer to the decisions of state governments. It is common to discuss states as if they were people, as in "France supports the UN resolution" or "Iraq invaded Kuwait." In reality, states take such actions as the result of complex internal processes and the alliances of various domestic groups and interests. Ultimately, only individual human beings are true actors making conscious decisions. But treating states like people makes it easier to describe and explain the relations among them.

Atlas CD
Country
Capitals
Photo Tour

With few exceptions, each state has a capital city—the seat of government from which it administers its territory—and often a single individual who acts in the name of the state. We may refer to this person simply as the "state leader." Often he or she is the *head of government* (such as a prime minister), or the *head of state* (such as a president, or a king or queen). In some countries, the same person is head of state and government. In other countries the prime minister or the president or royalty has become a figurehead symbolic position. In any case the most powerful political figure is the one we mean by "state leader," and these figures are the key individual actors in IR, ever since the days when kings or queens ruled territories by decree. The state actor includes the individual leader as well as bureaucratic organizations (such as foreign ministries) that act in the name of the state.

The **international system** is the set of relationships among the world's states, structured according to certain rules and patterns of interaction. Some such rules are explicit, some implicit. They include who is considered a member of the system, what rights and responsibilities the members have, and what kinds of actions and responses normally occur between states. The international system is discussed in more detail in Chapter 2.

The modern international system has existed for less than 500 years. Before that, people were organized into more mixed and overlapping political units such as city-states, empires, and feudal fiefs. In the last 200 years the idea has spread that nations—groups of people who share a sense of national identity, usually including a language and culture—should have their own states (see pp. 26–29). Most large states today are such **nation-states**. But since World War II, the decolonization process in much of Asia and Africa has added many new states, not all of which can be considered nation-states. A major source of conflict and war at present is the frequent mismatch between perceived nations and actual state borders. When people identify with a nationality that their state government does not represent, they may fight to form their own state and thus to gain sovereignty over their territory and affairs. This substate nationalism is only one of several growing trends that undermine today's system of states. Other such trends include the globalization of economic processes, power of telecommunications, and proliferation of ballistic missiles.

The independence of former colonies and, more recently, the breakup into smaller states of large multinational states (the Soviet Union, Yugoslavia, and Czechoslovakia) have increased the number of states in the world. The exact total depends on the status of a number of quasi-state political entities, and it keeps changing as political units split apart or merge. There were 189 members of the UN in 1999. In addition, one independent state (Switzerland) was a nonmember, and one newly independent area (East Timor) is under UN control and expected to become a member-state. Palestine is widely expected to gain formal, although restricted, statehood in the coming years.

Some other political entities are often referred to as states or countries although they are not formally recognized as states. Taiwan is the most important of these. It operates independently in practice but is claimed by China (a claim recognized formally by outside powers and until recently by Taiwan itself), and is not a UN member. Formal colonies and possessions still exist; their status may change in the future. They include

Atlas CD
Taiwan
Map

Puerto Rico (U.S.), Bermuda (British), Martinique (French), French Guiana, the Netherlands Antilles (Dutch), the Falkland Islands (British), and Guam (U.S.). Hong Kong reverted from British to Chinese rule in 1997, and retains a somewhat separate economic identity under China's "one country, two systems" formula. The smaller former Portuguese colony of Macau also recently reverted to Chinese rule. The status of the Vatican (Holy See) in Rome is ambiguous. Including these various territorial entities with states brings the world total to about 200 state or quasi-state actors. Several would-be states (such as Kurdistan and Western Sahara) also do not fully control the territory they claim and are not universally recognized. Since smaller states may continue to split away from larger ones (for instance, Quebec from Canada), the number of states is likely to grow.

The size of the world's states varies dramatically, from China with more than 1 billion people to microstates with populations of less than 100,000. With the creation of many small states in recent decades, the majority of states now have fewer than 10 million people each, and more than half of the rest have 10 to 50 million each. Only 23 of the world's 200 states have more than 50 million people each. These 23 states contain three-quarters of the world's people. In decreasing order of population, they are China, India, the United States, Indonesia, Brazil, Russia, Pakistan, Japan, Bangladesh, Nigeria, Mexico, Germany, the Philippines, Vietnam, Iran, Egypt, Turkey, Thailand, Britain, France, Italy, Ethiopia, and Ukraine. These are important international actors.

States also differ tremendously in the size of their total annual economic activity—**Gross Domestic Product (GDP)**[1]—from the $8 trillion U.S. economy to the economies of tiny states such as the Pacific island of Vanuatu ($200 million). The world economy is dominated by a few states, just as world population is. The United States

---

[1] GDP is the total of goods and services produced by a nation; it is very close to the Gross National Product (GNP). Such data are difficult to compare across nations with different currencies, economic systems, and levels of development. In particular, comparisons of GDP in capitalist and socialist economies, or in rich and poor countries, should be treated cautiously. GDP data used in this book are mostly from the World Bank. GDP data are adjusted through time and across countries for "purchasing-power parity" (how much a given amount of money can buy). See Summers, Robert, and Alan Heston. The Penn World Table (Mark 5): An Expanded Set of International Comparisons, 1950–1988. *Quarterly Journal of Economics* 106 (2), 1991:327–68. GDP and population data are for 1998 unless otherwise noted.

alone accounts for one-fifth of the world economy; together with six other great powers it accounts for nearly half (see pp. 67–69). The world's 15 largest economies—which together make up three-quarters of the world economy—are the United States, China, Japan, Germany, India, France, Britain, Italy, Brazil, Mexico, Canada, Russia, Indonesia, South Korea, and Spain. All of these are important international actors.

A few of these large states possess especially great military and economic strength and influence, and are called *great powers* (see Chapter 2). The *great-power system* may be defined as the set of relationships among great powers, with their rules and patterns of interaction (a subset of the international system). Great powers have special ways of behaving and of treating each other that do not apply to other states. The most powerful of great powers, those with truly global influence, have been called *superpowers*. This term generally meant the United States and the Soviet Union during the Cold War, but most IR scholars now consider the United States to be the world's only superpower (if indeed it still is one). The great powers and other *major states* (those that have large populations or play important roles in international affairs) are the most important of the state actors. Smaller and weaker states also are important, but taken singly most of them do not affect the outcomes in IR nearly as much as the major states do.

Atlas CD
Tiny States of
Europe
Map Trek

Nonstate Actors National governments may be the most important actors in IR, but they are strongly conditioned, constrained, and influenced by a variety of non-actors. These **nonstate actors** may be grouped in several categories. First, *substate actors*, groups and interests within states, influence the state's foreign policy. For instance, the American automobile and tobacco industries have distinct interests in American foreign economic policy (to sell cars or cigarettes abroad; to reduce imports of competing products made abroad). They are politically mobilized to influence those policies through political action committees, lobbying, and other means. Similarly, farmers in Europe, Japan, and America have organized themselves politically and influenced their governments' positions concerning agricultural trade.

The actions of substate economic actors—companies, consumers, workers, investors—help to create the context of economic activity against which international political events play out, and within which governments must operate. Day in and day out, people extract natural resources, produce and consume goods, buy and sell products and services. These activities of substate actors take place in what is now clearly a world economy—a global exchange of goods and services woven together by a worldwide network of communication and culture.

Increasingly, then, actors operating below the state level also operate across state borders, becoming *transnational actors*. Businesses that buy, sell, or invest in a variety of countries are a good example. The decision of a company to do business with or in another state changes the relationship between the two states, making them more interdependent and creating a new context for the decisions the governments make about each other.

The thousands of multinational corporations (MNCs) are important transnational actors. The interests of a large company doing business globally do not correspond with any one state's interests. Such a company may sometimes even act against its home government's policies, as when the U.S.-based oil company Conoco signed (but then backed out of) a $1 billion deal in 1995 to develop Iranian oil fields while the U.S. gov-

In the Action Nonstate actors participate in IR alongside states, although generally in a less central role. Nongovernmental organizations (NGOs) such as the Catholic Church are becoming increasingly active in IR. Here, Pope John Paul II addresses bishops from North and South America at the Vatican, 1997.

ernment was trying to isolate Iran. MNCs often control greater resources, and operate internationally with greater efficiency, than many small states. MNCs may prop up (or even create) friendly foreign governments. But MNCs also provide poor states with much-needed foreign investment and tax revenues. MNCs in turn depend on states to provide protection, well-regulated markets, and a stable political environment. MNCs as international actors receive special attention in Chapters 5 and 7.

Another type of transnational actor is the **nongovernmental organization (NGO)**. These private organizations, some of considerable size and resources, interact with states, MNCs, and other NGOs. Increasingly NGOs are being recognized, in the UN and other forums, as legitimate actors along with states, though not equal to them. Examples of NGOs include the Catholic Church, Greenpeace, and the International Studies Association. Some of these groups have a political purpose, some a humanitarian one, some an economic or technical one. Sometimes NGOs combine efforts through transnational advocacy networks. There is no single pattern to NGOs.

Finally, states often take actions through, within, or in the context of **intergovernmental organizations (IGOs)**—organizations whose members are national gov-

Web Link
Nongovernmental
Organizations

ernments. The UN and its agencies are IGOs. So are most of the world's economic coordinating institutions such as the World Bank and the International Monetary Fund (IMF). IGOs fulfill a variety of functions, and they vary in size from just a few states to virtually the whole UN membership. For example, the International Atomic Energy Agency seeks to regulate the flow of nuclear technology to developing countries, and the World Trade Organization (WTO) sponsors negotiations on lowering trade barriers worldwide, and enforces the resulting trade rules.

Military alliances such as NATO and political groupings such as the Organization of African Unity (OAU) are also IGOs. The hundreds of IGOs now operating on the world scene (several times more than the number of states) all have been created by their member states to provide some function that those states find useful.

Together, IGOs and NGOs are referred to as international organizations (IOs). In this world of interlaced connections, states are still important. But to some extent they are being slowly pushed aside as companies, groups, and individuals deal more directly with each other across borders, and as the world economy becomes globally integrated. Now more than ever, IR extends beyond the interactions of national governments.

The Information Revolution
Both state and nonstate actors are strongly affected by the present revolution in information technologies. Our information-intensive world promises to reshape international relations profoundly. Technological change dramatically affects actors' relative capabilities and even preferences. Nobody knows where those changes will take us. Already, information capabilities are the central motor of "globalization." Telecommunications and computerization allow economics, politics, and culture alike to operate on a global scale as never before. The ramifications for various facets of IR will be developed in each chapter of this book.

Levels of Analysis
The many actors involved at once in IR contribute to the complexity of competing explanations and theories. One way scholars of IR have sorted out this multiplicity of influences, actors, and processes is to categorize them into different *levels of analysis* (see Table 1.1). A level of analysis is a perspective on IR based on a set of similar actors or processes that suggests possible explanations to "why" questions. IR scholars have proposed various level-of-analysis schemes, most often with three main levels (and sometimes a few sublevels between).

The *individual* level of analysis concerns the perceptions, choices, and actions of individual human beings. Great leaders influence the course of history, as do individual

THE INFORMATION
REVOLUTION

In each chapter, these "information revolution" boxes pose critical-thinking questions about the impacts that rapid changes in information technology have on IR. To explore the questions, go to this book's website at www.IRtext.com, enter the page number in this book, and follow the "information revolution" icon.

TABLE 1.1 Levels of Analysis

Many influences affect the course of international relations. Levels of analysis provide a framework for categorizing these influences and thus for suggesting various explanations of international events. Examples include:

Global Level

North–South gap	Technological change
World regions	Information revolution
European imperialism	Global telecommunications
UN	Worldwide scientific and business
World environment	communities

Interstate Level

Power	IGOs
Balance of power	Diplomacy
Alliance formation and dissolution	Summit meetings
Wars	Bargaining
Treaties	Reciprocity
Trade agreements	

Domestic Level

Nationalism	Political parties and elections
Ethnic conflict	Public opinion
Type of government	Gender
Democracy	Economic sectors and industries
Dictatorship	Military-industrial complex
Domestic coalitions	Foreign policy bureaucracies

Individual Level

Great leaders	Learning
Crazy leaders	Assassinations, accidents of history
Decision making in crises	Citizens' participation (voting, rebelling,
Psychology of perception and decision	going to war, etc.)

citizens, thinkers, soldiers, voters. Without Lenin, it is said, there might well have been no Soviet Union. If a few more people had voted for Nixon rather than Kennedy in the razor-close 1960 election, the Cuban Missile Crisis might have ended differently. The study of foreign policy decision making, which is discussed in Chapter 3, pays special attention to individual-level explanations of IR outcomes because of the importance of psychological factors in the decision-making process.

The *domestic* (or *state* or *societal*) level of analysis concerns the aggregations of individuals within states that influence state actions in the international arena, such as interest groups, political organizations, and government agencies. These groups operate differently (with different international effects) in different kinds of societies and states. Democracies may act differently from dictatorships, and democracies may act differently in an election year from the ways they do at other times. The politics of ethnic conflict and nationalism plays an increasingly important role in the relations among states. Economic sectors within states, including the military-industrial sector, can influence their governments to take actions in the international arena that are good for business. Within governments, foreign policy agencies often fight bureaucratic battles over policy decisions.

The *interstate* (or *international* or *systemic*) level of analysis concerns the influence of the international system upon outcomes. Thus it focuses on the interactions of states themselves, without regard to their internal makeup or their particular leaders. This level pays attention to states' geographic locations and their relative power positions in the international system. It has been traditionally the most important of the levels of analysis.

To these three levels can be added a fourth, the *global* level of analysis. It seeks to explain international outcomes in terms of global trends and forces that transcend the interactions of states. This level deserves particular attention because of the growing importance of global-level processes. The evolution of human technology, of certain worldwide beliefs, and of humans' relationship to the natural environment are all processes at the global level that influence international relations. The global level is also increasingly the focus of IR scholars studying transnational integration through worldwide scientific, technical, and business communities (see Chapter 8). Another pervasive global influence is the lingering effect of historical European imperialism (see pp. 24–26).

Levels of analysis offer different sorts of explanations for international events. For example, there are many possible explanations for the Gulf War in 1991 between Iraq and a U.S.-led coalition of states from around the world. At the individual level, the war might be attributed to the irrational gambles and mistaken judgments of Iraq's leader, Saddam Hussein—or to U.S. President George Bush's efforts to disprove critics who had called him a "wimp." At the domestic level, the war might be attributed to the kind of society and government that Iraq had—a dictatorship in which public opinion could not check a leader's unwise aggression. At the interstate level, the war might be attributed to the end of the U.S.–Soviet bipolar order; the sudden shift in the distribution of power in the international system may have led Iraq to try to exploit a perceived power vacuum. At the global level, the war might be attributed to British imperialism, which had established Kuwait as a state separate from Iraq decades earlier, or to the dependence of the world's rich states on oil imports from the Middle East.

Whereas IR scholars often focus their study mainly on one level of analysis, other levels bear on a problem simultaneously. There is no single correct level for a given "why" question. Rather, levels of analysis help to suggest multiple explanations and approaches in trying to explain a given event. They remind scholars and students to look beyond the immediate and superficial aspects of an event to explore the possible influences of more distant causes. IR is such a complex process that there is rarely any single cause for an outcome. Table 1.1 lists some of the processes operating on each level of analysis. Note that the processes at higher levels tend to operate more slowly than those on the lower levels. Individuals go in and out of office often; the structure of the international system changes rarely.

An analogy can be drawn with scholars who seek to understand a pattern of automobile accidents. In the case of traffic accidents, a serious attempt to understand their causes could consider such factors as the individual drivers (were they drunk?), the kinds of vehicles (mechanically unsound or unsafe?), and the road system (poorly designed?).

Just as different individuals would drive the same car differently, so would different national leaders drive the same state to different international outcomes.

Geography
International relations takes place in the fixed context of geography (as well as history)—an important context to master in order to understand IR. To highlight the insights afforded by a global level of analysis, this book uses a division of the world into nine regions. These *world regions* differ from each other in the number of states they contain and in each region's particular mix of cultures, geographical realities, and languages. But each represents a geographical corner of the world, and together they reflect the overall macro-level divisions of world regions. Later chapters refer back to these regions, especially in discussing the North-South gap (Chapter 7).

The global **North-South gap** between the industrialized, relatively rich countries of the North and the relatively poor countries of the South is the most important geographical element at the global level of analysis. The regions used in this book have been drawn so as to separate (with a few exceptions) the rich countries from the poor ones. The North includes both the West (the rich countries of North America, Western Europe, and Japan) and the old East (the former Soviet Union and its bloc of allies).[2] The South includes Latin America, Africa, the Middle East, and much of Asia. The South is often called the "third world" (third after the West and East)—a term that is still widely used despite the second world's collapse. Countries in the South are also referred to as "developing" countries or "less-developed" countries (LDCs), in contrast to the "developed" countries of the North.

Atlas CD
Europe by Night
Map Trek

In grouping the world's states into nine regions, several criteria were applied in addition to the effort to separate rich from poor states. The regions are geographically contiguous. Countries with similar economic levels, cultures, and languages have been kept together where possible. States with a history of interaction, including historical empires or trading zones, are also placed together in a region. Finally, countries that might possibly unify in the future—notably South Korea with North Korea, and China with Taiwan—are kept in the same region. Of course, no scheme works perfectly, and some states are pulled toward two regions.

The overall world regions are shown on the first map of the map section preceding the text; reference maps for each region follow. (Names of countries are listed on the following map.) The global North is divided into *North America* (the United States and Canada); *Western Europe* (mainly European Union members); *Japan/Pacific* (mainly Japan, the Koreas, Australia, and New Zealand); and *Russia and Eastern Europe* (mainly the former Soviet bloc). The South is divided into *China* (including Hong Kong and Taiwan); the *Middle East* (from North Africa through Turkey and Iran); *Latin America* (Mexico, Central America, the Caribbean, and South America); *South Asia* (Afghanistan through Indonesia and the Philippines); and *Africa* (below the Sahara desert).

With the nine world regions as an organizing framework, Table 1.2 lists the world's states and territories, and an estimate of each state's aggregate GDP. Most of these

---

[2] Note that geographical designations such as the "West" and the "Middle East" are European-centered. From Korea, for example, China and Russia are to the west and Japan and the United States are to the east.

TABLE 1.2 States and Territories with Estimated Total 1998 GDP
(In Billions of 1998 U.S. Dollars)

North America

| United States 7900 | Canada 800 | Bahamas 3 |

Western Europe

Germany 1800	Switzerland[a] 200	Luxembourg 20
France 1300	Austria 200	Iceland 6
Britain 1200	Portugal 100	Malta 5
Italy 1200	Denmark 100	Andorra 1
Spain 600	Norway 100	Monaco 1
Netherlands 300	Greece 100	Liechtenstein 1
Belgium 200	Finland 100	San Marino 1
Sweden 200	Ireland 80	

Japan/Pacific

Japan 2900	Guam/Marianas[b] 2	Nauru 0
South Korea 600	Solomon Islands 1	Marshall Islands 0
Australia 400	Samoa 1	Palau 0
New Zealand 70	Vanuatu 1	Kiribati 0
North Korea 20	Micronesia 0	Tuvalu 0
Papua New Guinea 10	Tonga 0	
Fiji 3	American Samoa[b] 0	

Russia and Eastern Europe

Russia[c] 600	Bulgaria 30	Estonia 10
Poland 300	Croatia 30	Latvia 9
Ukraine[c] 100	Slovenia 20	Turkmenistan[c] 9
Czech Republic 100	Yugoslavia	Tajikistan[c] 7
Romania 90	(Serbia–Montenegro) 20	Albania 7
Hungary 70	Lithuania 20	Macedonia 7
Uzbekistan[c] 70	Azerbaijan[c] 20	Moldova[c] 6
Kazakhstan[c] 60	Armenia[c] 10	Bosnia and Herzegovina 5
Belarus[c] 50	Georgia[c] 10	Mongolia 4
Slovakia 40	Kyrgyzstan[c] 10	

China

| China 3800 | Hong Kong[b] 100 | Macau[b] 10 |
| Taiwan[b] 300 | | |

The Middle East

Turkey 400	Syria 50	Jordan 20
Iran 400	United Arab Emirates 50	Oman 20
Saudi Arabia 200	Iraq 50	Yemen 10
Egypt 200	Tunisia 50	Qatar 10
Algeria 100	Libya 40	Cyprus 10
Israel/Palestine 100	Kuwait 30	Bahrain 10
Morocco/	Lebanon 30	
W. Sahara 90		

Latin America

Brazil 1000	Costa Rica 20	Netherlands Antilles[b] 2
Mexico 800	Paraguay 20	Virgin Islands[b] 2
Argentina 400	Cuba 20	Bermuda[b] 1
Colombia 300	Panama 20	Suriname 1
Venezuela 200	El Salvador 20	French Guiana[b] 1
Chile 200	Honduras 10	St. Lucia 1
Peru 100	Trinidad & Tobago 9	Belize 1
Ecuador 60	Jamaica 9	Antigua & Barbuda 1
Guatemala 50	Nicaragua 9	Grenada 0
Dominican Republic 40	Haiti 9	St. Kitts & Nevis 0
Puerto Rico[b] 30	Martinique[b] 4	St. Vincent &
Uruguay 30	Barbados 3	Grenadines 0
Bolivia 20	Guyana 3	Dominica 0

South Asia

India 1500	Vietnam 100	Cambodia 10
Indonesia 600	Singapore 90	Laos 6
Thailand 400	Sri Lanka 50	Brunei 5
Philippines 300	Burma (Myanmar) 50	Bhutan 1
Pakistan 200	Nepal 20	Maldives 1
Malaysia 200	Afghanistan 10	East Timor 0
Bangladesh 100		

Africa

South Africa 300	Guinea 10	Mauritania 4
Nigeria 100	Botswana 10	Lesotho 4
Kenya 40	Burkina Faso 10	Reunion[b] 3
Sudan 40	Zambia 9	Swaziland 3
Democratic Congo 40	Niger 9	Eritrea 3
Ethiopia 30	Gabon 9	Sierra Leone 2
Côte d'Ivoire (Ivory Coast) 30	Malawi 8	Liberia 2
Ghana 30	Mali 8	Gambia 2
Zimbabwe 30	Namibia 8	Guinea-Bissau 1
Uganda 30	Benin 8	Djibouti 1
Cameroon 30	Chad 7	Comoros Islands 1
Tanzania 20	Togo 6	Cape Verde 1
Angola 20	Rwanda 6	Seychelles 1
Senegal 20	Congo Republic 5	Equatorial Guinea 1
Mozambique 20	Central African Republic 5	São Tomé & Principe 0
Madagascar 10	Burundi 4	
Mauritius 10	Somalia 4	

[a] Nonmember of UN (independent state).

[b] Nonmember of UN (colony or territory).

[c] Commonwealth of Independent States (former USSR).

Note: GDP data are inexact by nature. Estimates for Russia and Eastern Europe, China, and other nonmarket or transitional economies are particularly suspect and should be used cautiously. Numbers below 0.5 are listed as 0.

Sources: Data are author's estimates based on World Bank. Data are at purchasing-power parity. See footnote 1 on p. 9.

TABLE 1.3   Comparison of World Regions

Region	Population (Millions)	GDP (Trillion $)	GDP per Capita (Dollars)
The North			
North America	300	$8.7	$30,000
Western Europe	400	8.0	20,000
Japan/Pacific	200	4.0	17,000
Russia & E. Europe	400	1.7	4,000
The South			
China	1,200	4.2	3,500
Middle East	400	1.9	5,300
Latin America	500	3.5	6,800
South Asia	1,900	3.6	2,000
Africa	600	0.9	1,400
Total North	**1,300 (20%)**	**22.3 (61%)**	**17,000**
Total South	**4,600 (80%)**	**14.2 (39%)**	**3,100**
World Total	**5,900**	**$36.5**	**$6,200**

Note: Data adjusted for purchasing-power parity. 1998 GDP estimates (in 1999 dollars) are from Table 1.2; those for Russia and Eastern Europe, and for China, should be treated especially cautiously.

regions correspond with commonly used geographical names, but a few notes may help. East Asia refers to China, Japan, and Korea. Southeast Asia refers to countries from Burma through Indonesia and the Philippines. Russia is considered a European state, although a large section (Siberia) is in Asia. The Pacific Rim usually means East Asia, Southeast Asia, and Siberia—linked with the west coast of North America and Latin America. South Asia only sometimes includes parts of Southeast Asia. Narrow definitions of the Middle East exclude both North Africa and Turkey. The Balkans are the states of southeastern Europe, bounded by Slovenia, Romania, and Greece.

Table 1.3 shows the approximate population and economic size (GDP) of each region in relation to the world as a whole. As the table shows, income levels per capita are, overall, about five times higher in the North than in the South. *The North contains less than 25 percent of the world's people but 60 percent of its goods and services.* The other three-quarters of the world's people, in the South, have only 40 percent of the goods and services.

Atlas CD
Country List
Articles, Maps,
Photos

Within the global North, Russia and Eastern Europe lag behind in income levels and suffered declines in the 1990s. In the global South, the Middle East, Latin America, and (more recently) China have achieved somewhat higher income levels than have Africa and South Asia, which remain extremely poor. Even in the somewhat higher income regions, income is distributed quite unevenly and many people remain very poor. Note that more than half of the world's population lives in the densely populated (and poor) regions of South Asia and China.

IR scholars have no single explanation of the huge North-South income gap (see Chapter 7). Some see it as part of a natural process of uneven growth in the world economy. Others tie it to the history of imperialism by European states (and by Russia, the United States, and Japan). Some see the gap as a reflection of racism—the North is predominantly white whereas most of the South is nonwhite.

Geography provides one fixed context in which IR takes place; history provides another. The world as we know it developed over many years, step by step. Of special interest in IR are the past 500 years, known as the "modern age," the age of the international system as we know it. The remainder of this chapter reviews the historical development of that system and its context. Special attention is given to the relations between Europe and the rest of the world, in which are found the roots of the present North-South gap.

History

A new millennium finds the world breaking free of the logic of the two world wars and the Cold War that dominated the twentieth century. New possibilities are emerging everywhere, some good and some bad. With so much change, one might wonder whether history is still relevant to understanding the world. It is. Even today, the basic structures and principles of international relations are deeply rooted in historical developments. Our brief discussion of these developments begins with a long-term perspective and gradually focuses on more recent history.

World Civilizations to 2000
The present-day international system is the product of a particular civilization—Western civilization, centered in Europe. The international system as we know it developed among the European states of 300 to 500 years ago, was exported to the rest of the world, and has in the last century subsumed virtually all of the world's territory into sovereign states. It is important to keep in mind, however, that other civilizations existed in other world regions for centuries before Europeans ever arrived. These cultural traditions continue to exert an influence on IR, especially when the styles and expectations of these cultures come into play in international interactions.

North American students should note that much of the world differs from North America in this regard. Before Europeans arrived, native cultures in North America did not have extensive agriculture, cities, irrigation, armies, and other trappings of civilization. Native cultures were exterminated or pushed aside by European settlers. Today's North American population is overwhelmingly descended from immigrants. In other regions, however, the European conquest followed many centuries of advanced civilization in China, India, Japan, the Middle East, and Central America—more advanced than that of Europe. In most of the world (especially in Africa and Asia), European empires incorporated rather than pushed aside indigenous populations. Today's populations are descended primarily from native inhabitants, not immigrants, and are therefore more strongly rooted in their own cultural traditions and history than are most Americans.

WORLD CIVILIZATIONS TO 2000

	Before A.D. 1000	A.D. 1000	1250	1500	1750	2000
Japan	Korean and Chinese influences	samurai	shoguns	Tokugawa isolation	Meiji restoration	WW II → prosperity
China	Dynasties; Great Wall begun; Taoism; Buddhism; paper, gunpowder	Sung dynasty	Mongol dynasty	Ming dynasty	Manchu dynasty	European dominance → People's Republic
S. Asia	Emergence of Hinduism, Buddhism; Ancient India; Arab conquest	Turkish period		Taj Mahal built	European colonialism	independence
Africa	Kingdom of Ghana	Yoruba, Mali, Benin (kingdoms)	Congo	Zimbabwe; slave trade; Buganda	Ashanti	European colonialism → independence
Middle East	Mesopotamia, Egypt, Persia; Jews, Christians; Greeks/Romans; Islam	Crusades; Arab empire		Ottoman Empire		Arab nationalism; European colonialism; Islamic rev.
W. Europe	Ancient Greece; Roman Empire; Vikings; Feudalism	"Dark Ages"	Venice	Renaissance; Protestantism; Empires	French Revolution; German/Italian unifications	WW I/II; loss of empires
Russia & E. Europe	Khazars		Genghis Khan	Ivan the Terrible; czars		Lenin; USSR; WW II; CIS
N. America	(Preagricultural)			Columbus; European colonization	American Revolution; U.S. Civil War; westward expansion	WW II; Cold War
Latin America	Mayans		Aztec & Inca Empires	Portuguese & Spanish conquest	colonialism	European & U.S. interventions; independence; wars, debts, dictators, revolutions

European civilization evolved from roots in the Eastern Mediterranean—Egypt, Mesopotamia (Iraq), and especially Greece. Of special importance for IR is the classical period of Greek city-states around 400 B.C., which exemplified some of the fundamental principles of interstate power politics. By that time states were carrying out sophisticated trade relations and warfare with each other in a broad swath of the world from the Mediterranean through India to East Asia. Much of this area came under Greek influence with the conquests of Alexander the Great around 300 B.C., under the Roman Empire around A.D. 1, and then under the Arab empire around A.D. 600.

China remained an independent civilization during this time. In the "warring states" period, about the same time as the Greek city-states, sophisticated states (organized as territorial political units) first used warfare as an instrument of power politics. By about A.D. 800, when Europe was in its "dark ages" and Arab civilization in its golden age, China under the T'ang dynasty was a highly advanced civilization quite independent of Western influence. Japan, strongly influenced by Chinese civilization, flowered on its own in the centuries leading up to the Shoguns (around A.D. 1200). Japan isolated itself from Western influence under the Tokugawa shogunate for several centuries, ending after 1850 when the Meiji restoration began Japanese industrialization and international trade. Latin America also had flourishing civilizations—the Mayans around A.D. 100 to 900 and the Aztecs and Incas around 1200—independent of Western influence until conquered by Spain around 1500. In Africa, the great kingdoms flowered after about A.D. 1000 (as early as A.D. 600 in Ghana) and were highly developed when the European slave traders arrived on the scene around 1500.

The great Arab empire of about A.D. 600 to 1200 plays a special role in the international relations of the Middle East. Almost the whole of the region was once united in this empire, which arose and spread with the religion of Islam. European invaders—the Crusaders—were driven out. In the sixteenth to nineteenth centuries, the eastern Mediterranean came under the Turkish-based Ottoman Empire, which gave relative autonomy to local cultures if they paid tribute. This history of empires continued to influence the region in the twentieth century. For example, *Pan-Arabism* (or Arab nationalism), especially strong in the 1950s and 1960s, saw the region as potentially one nation again, with a single religion, language, and identity. Iraq's Saddam Hussein in 1991 likened himself to the ruler who drove away Crusaders a thousand years ago. The strength of Islamic fundamentalism throughout the region today, as well as the emotions attached to the Arab-Israeli conflict, reflects the continuing importance of the historic Arab empire.

Atlas CD
Austrian
Fortress, 17th
Century
Photo

Europe itself began its rise to world dominance around 1500, during the Renaissance. The Italian city-states of the period also rediscovered the rules of interstate power politics, as described by Niccolò Machiavelli. Feudal units began to merge into large territorial nation-states under single authoritarian rulers (monarchs). The military revolution of the period created the first modern armies. European monarchs put cannons on sailing ships and began to "discover" the world. The development of the international system, of imperialism, of trade and war, were all greatly accelerated by the *Industrial Revolution* after about 1750. Ultimately the European conquest of the world brought about a single world civilization, albeit with regional variants and subcultures.

In recent decades, the world regions formerly dominated by Europe have gained independence, with their own sovereign states participating in the international system. Independence came earlier in Latin America; most of the nineteenth century was

THE GREAT-POWER SYSTEM, 1500–2000

	1500	1600	1700	1800	1900	2000
Wars		Spain conquers Portugal / Spanish Armada / 30 Years' War	War of the Spanish Succession / 7 Years' War	Napoleonic Wars	Franco-Prussian War	World War I / World War II / Cold War
Major Alliances	Turkey (Muslim) vs. Europe (Christian)	Hapsburgs (Austria-Spain) vs. France, Britain, Netherlands, Sweden	France vs. Britain, Spain	France vs. Britain, Netherlands		Germany (& Japan) vs. Britain, France, Russia, United States, China / Russia vs. U.S., W. Eur., Japan
Rules & Norms	Nation-states (France, Austria)	Dutch independence / Treaty of Westphalia 1648 / Grotius on int'l law	Treaty of Utrecht 1713	Kant on peace / Congress of Vienna 1815 / **Concert of Europe**	League of Nations / Geneva conventions / Communism	UN Security Council 1945– / Human rights
Rising Powers	Britain France	Netherlands	Russia	Prussia	United States Germany Italy / **British hegemony**	China / **U.S. hegemony**
Declining Powers	Venice		Netherlands / Sweden / Spain / Ottoman Empire	**Netherlands hegemony**	Britain France Austria Italy	Russia / U.S.?

absorbed with revolutions, the rise and fall of dictatorships and republics, a chronic foreign debt problem, and recurrent military incursions by European powers and the United States to recover debts.

The Great-Power System, 1500–2000

The modern international system is often dated from the *Treaty of Westphalia* in 1648, which established the principles of independent, sovereign states that continue to shape the international system today. These rules of state relations did not, however, originate at Westphalia; they took form in Europe in the sixteenth century. Key to this system was the ability of one state, or a coalition, to balance the power of another state so that it could not gobble up smaller units and create a universal empire.

This power-balancing system placed special importance on the handful of great powers with strong military capabilities, global interests and outlooks, and intense interactions with each other. (Great powers are defined and discussed in Chapter 2.) A system of great-power relations has existed since around A.D. 1500, and the structure and rules of that system have remained fairly stable through time, although the particular members change. The structure is a balance of power among the six or so most powerful states, which form and break alliances, fight wars, and make peace, letting no single state conquer the others.

The most powerful states in sixteenth-century Europe were Britain (England), France, Austria-Hungary, and Spain. The Ottoman Empire (Turkey) recurrently fought with the European powers, especially with Austria-Hungary. Today, that historical conflict between the (Islamic) Ottoman Empire and (Christian) Austria-Hungary is a source of ethnic conflict in the former Yugoslavia.

Atlas CD
Balkans
Map

Within Europe, Austria-Hungary and Spain were allied under control of the Hapsburg family, which also owned the territory of the Netherlands. The Catholic Hapsburg countries were defeated by mostly Protestant countries in northern Europe—France, Britain, Sweden, and the newly independent Netherlands—in the *Thirty Years' War* of 1618–1648. The 1648 Treaty of Westphalia established the basic rules that have defined the international system ever since—the sovereignty and territorial integrity of states as equal and independent members of an international system. Since then, states defeated in war might be stripped of some territories but were generally allowed to continue as independent states rather than being subsumed by the victor.

In the eighteenth century, the power of Britain increased as it industrialized, and Britain's great rival was France. Sweden, the Netherlands, and the Ottoman Empire declined in power, but Russia and later Prussia (the forerunner of modern-day Germany) emerged as major players. In the *Napoleonic Wars* (1803–1815), France was defeated by a coalition of Britain, the Netherlands, Austria-Hungary, Spain, Russia, and Prussia. The *Congress of Vienna* (1815) ending that war reasserted the principles of state sovereignty in reaction to the challenges of the French Revolution and Napoleon's empire. In the *Concert of Europe* that dominated the following decades, the five most powerful states tried, with some success, to cooperate on major issues to prevent war—a possible precedent for today's UN Security Council. In this period, Britain became a balancer, joining alliances against whatever state emerged as the most powerful in Europe.

By the outset of the twentieth century, three new rising powers had appeared on the scene: the United States (which had become the world's largest economy), Japan,

IMPERIALISM, 1500–2000

	1500	1600	1700	1800	1900	2000
North America	Columbus	British & French colonization		U.S. independence / War of 1812	Canada →	
Latin America	Brazil (Portuguese) / Central & S. America (Spanish)			Independence / European & U.S. interventions →	Mexican Revolution	
East Asia		Russian conquest of Siberia		(China) / Opium Wars ↑	T'ai P'ing Rebellion / Boxer Rebellion / Taiwan & Korea (Japanese) / Japanese empire / Communist China	Korea split / Taiwan autonomous / Hong Kong to China
South Asia	European explorers / Dutch East Indies Company / Indonesia (Dutch) →				India (British) / Philippines (U.S.)	Indian independence / Vietnam War
Africa	Slave trade / Angola, Mozambique (Portuguese)			Scramble for colonies (Brit., Fr., Ger.) ↑		Independence
Middle East	Ottoman Empire ————→				British & French mandates (Palestine) ↑	Algerian independence

and Italy. The great-power system became globalized instead of European. Powerful states were industrializing, extending the scope of their world activities and the might of their militaries. After Prussia defeated Austria and France in wars, a larger Germany emerged to challenge Britain's position. In *World War I* (1914–1918), Germany and Austria-Hungary were defeated by a coalition that included Britain, France, Russia, Italy, and the United States. After a 20-year lull, Germany, Italy, and Japan were defeated in *World War II* (1939–1945) by a coalition of the United States, Britain, France, Russia (the Soviet Union), and China. Those five winners of World War II make up the permanent membership of today's UN Security Council.

After World War II, the United States and the Soviet Union, allies in the war against Germany, became adversaries for 40 years in the Cold War. Europe was split into rival blocs—East and West—with Germany itself split into two states. The rest of the world became contested terrain where each bloc tried to gain allies or influence, often by sponsoring opposing sides in regional and civil wars. The end of the Cold War around 1990, when the Soviet Union collapsed, returned the international system to a more cooperative arrangement of the great powers somewhat similar to the Concert of Europe in the nineteenth century. However, without a common threat from the Soviet Union new strains emerged among the European-American-Japanese "allies."

Imperialism, 1500–2000

European imperialism (see Chapter 7) got its start in the fifteenth century with the development of oceangoing sailing ships in which a small crew could transport a sizable cargo over a long distance. Portugal pioneered the first voyages of exploration beyond Europe. Spain, France, and Britain soon followed. With superior military technology, Europeans gained control of coastal cities and of resupply outposts along major trade routes. Gradually this control extended farther inland, first in Latin America, then in North America, and later throughout Asia and Africa.

In the sixteenth century, Spain and Portugal had extensive empires in Central America and Brazil, respectively. Britain and France had colonies in North America and the Caribbean. The imperialists bought slaves in Africa and shipped them to Mexico and Brazil, where they worked in agriculture and in mining. The wealth produced was exported to Europe, where monarchs used it to buy armies and build states. These empires decimated native populations and cultures, causing immense suffering. Over time, the economies of the colonies developed with the creation of basic transportation and communication infrastructure, factories, and so forth. But they were often molded to the needs of the colonizers, not the local populations.

Decolonization began with the British colonists in the United States who declared independence in 1776. Most of Latin America gained independence a few decades later. The new states in North America and Latin America were, of course, still run by the descendants of Europeans, to the disadvantage of Native Americans and African slaves.

Acquisition of new colonies by Europe through the end of the nineteenth century culminated in a scramble for colonies in Africa in the 1890s. Latecomers such as Germany and Italy were frustrated to find few attractive territories remaining in the world when they tried to build overseas empires in the late nineteenth century. India became Britain's largest and most important colony in the nineteenth century. Only a few non-European areas of the world retained their independence: Japan, most of

Atlas CD
Colonization of
Africa
Map Trek

China, Iran, Turkey, and a few other areas. Japan began building its own empire, as did the United States, at the end of the nineteenth century. China became weaker and its coastal regions fell under the domination, if not the formal control, of European powers.

Atlas CD
Legacies of
Colonialism
Photo Tour

In the wave of decolonization after World War II, it was not local colonists (as in the Americas) but native populations in Asia and Africa who won independence. Decolonization continued through the mid-1970s until almost no European colonies remained. Most of the newly independent states have faced tremendous challenges and difficulties in the postcolonial era. Because long-established economic patterns continue despite political independence, some refer to the postcolonial era as being *neocolonial*. Although the global North no longer imports slave labor from the South, it continues to rely on the South for cheap labor, for energy and minerals, and for the products of tropical agriculture. However, the North in turn makes vital contributions to the South in capital investment, technology transfer, and foreign assistance (see Chapter 7).

The collapse of the Soviet Union and its bloc, which reduced Russia to its size of a century earlier, can be seen as an extension of the post–World War II wave of decolonization and self-determination. There, as in much of the third world, imperialism has left ethnic conflict in its wake, as new political units come to terms with territorial divisions created in distant imperial capitals.

Nationalism, 1500–2000

Many people consider **nationalism**—devotion to the interests of one's nation—to be the most important force in world politics in the last two centuries. A nation is a population that shares an identity, usually including a language and culture. Most of the 60 million inhabitants of France speak French, eat French cuisine, learned French history in school, and are represented by the national government in Paris. But nationality is a difficult concept to define precisely. To some extent, the extension of political control over large territories like France creates the commonality needed for nationhood—states create nations. At the same time, the perceived existence of a nation has often led to the creation of a corresponding state as a people win sovereignty over their own affairs—nations create states.

Around A.D. 1500, countries such as France and Austria began to bring entire nations together into single states. These new nation-states were very large and powerful; they overran smaller neighbors. Over time, many small territorial units were conquered and incorporated into nation-states. Eventually the idea of nationalism itself became a powerful force and contributed to the disintegration of large, multinational states such as Austria-Hungary (in World War I) and the Soviet Union.

The principle of *self-determination* implies that people who identify as a nation should have the right to form a state and exercise sovereignty over their affairs. Self-determination is a widely praised principle in international affairs today (not historically). But it is generally secondary to the principles of sovereignty (noninterference in other states' internal affairs) and territorial integrity, with which it frequently conflicts. Self-determination does not give groups the right to change international borders, even those imposed arbitrarily by colonialism, in order to unify a group with a common national identity. Generally, though not always, self-determination has been achieved by violence. When the borders of (perceived) nations do not match those of states, conflicts almost inevitably arise. Today such conflicts are widespread—in Northern Ireland, Quebec, Israel-Palestine, India-Pakistan, Sri Lanka, Tibet, and many other places.

The Netherlands helped to establish the principle of self-determination when it broke free of Spanish ownership around 1600 and set up a self-governing Dutch republic. The struggle over control of the Netherlands was a leading cause of the Thirty Years' War (1618–1648), in which states mobilized for war in new ways. For instance, Sweden drafted one man out of ten for long-term military service, while the Netherlands used the wealth derived from global trade to finance a standing professional army. This process of popular mobilization intensified greatly in the French Revolution and the subsequent Napoleonic Wars, when France instituted a universal draft and a centrally run "command" economy. Its motivated citizen armies, composed for the first time of Frenchmen rather than mercenaries, marched longer and faster. People participated in part because their nation-state embodied their aspirations, and it brought them together in a common national identity.

The United States meanwhile had followed the example of the Netherlands by declaring independence from Britain in 1776. The U.S. nation held together in the Civil War of the 1860s and developed a surprisingly strong sense of nationalism, considering how large and diverse the country was. Latin American states gained independence early in the nineteenth century, and Germany and Italy unified their nations out of multiple political units (through war) later in that century.

Before World War I, socialist workers from different European countries had banded together as workers to fight for workers' rights. In that war, however, most abandoned such solidarity and instead fought for their own nation. Before World War II, nationalism helped Germany, Italy, and Japan to build political orders based on *fascism*—an extreme authoritarianism undergirded by national chauvinism. And in World War II it was nationalism and patriotism (not communism) that rallied the Soviet people to sacrifice by the millions to turn back Germany's invasion.

Web Link
Understanding
Fascism

In the past 50 years, third world nations by the dozens have gained independence and statehood. Jews worked persistently in the first half of the twentieth century to create the state of Israel, and Palestinians aspired in the second half to create a Palestinian state. While multinational states such as the Soviet Union and Yugoslavia have fragmented in recent years, ethnic and territorial units such as Ukraine and Slovenia have established themselves as independent nation-states. Others, such as Palestine and Kurdistan, are seeking to do so. More than ever, the influence of nationalism is a major factor in international conflict and war.

National identity is psychologically reinforced on a daily basis by symbols such as the national flag, by rituals such as the U.S. Pledge of Allegiance, and by other practices designed to reinforce the identification of a population with its nation and government. In truth, people have multiple identities, belonging to various circles from their immediate family through their town, ethnic or religious group, nation or state, and humanity as a whole (see pp. 158–167). Nationalism has been remarkably successful in establishing national identity as a people's primary affiliation in much of the world. (In many places a sense of local affiliation remains important, however.)

Nationalism harnesses the energies of large populations based on their patriotic feelings toward their nation. The feeling of "we the people" is hard to sustain if the people are excluded from participating in their government. This participation is so important that even authoritarian governments often go through the motions of holding elections (with one candidate or party). Democracy can be a force for peace, constraining the

THE WORLD ECONOMY, 1750–2000

Category	1750–1800	1800–1850	1850–1900	1900–1950	1950–2000
Production	industrialization →			WW I; world depression; Soviet industrialization; WW II	postwar prosperity; Cold War arms race; Japanese & German growth; world recession; Soviet collapse
Energy	steam engine; cotton gin; coal →			oil →	nuclear power → nat. gas →
Leading Sectors		iron & steam →; textiles →	steel →; electricity →	motor vehicles →; electronics; plastics	computers →; biotech →
Transportation	(wooden sailing ships)	iron steamships →; railroads →	Suez Canal	airplanes →; Trans-Siberian Railroad; Panama Canal; automobiles →	jets →; freeways →; high-speed rail →
Trade		British dominance	(free trade)	protectionism; U.S. dominance	GATT →; European integration; WTO; NAFTA
Money			sterling (British) as world currency →	post–WW I inflation; Keynes; U.S. dollar as world currency; Bretton Woods; Marshall Plan; IMF	U.S. drops gold standard; debt crises; Russia joins IMF
Communication			telegraph →; telephone invented; transoceanic cables	radio →	information revolution; communication satellites; Internet; fax, modem, cellular, etc.

power of state leaders to commit their nations to war. But popular influence over governments can also increase conflict with other nations.

Over time, democratic participation has broadened to more countries and more people within those countries. The trend toward democracy seems to be continuing in most regions of the world—in Russia and Eastern Europe, Africa, Latin America, and Asia. Both nationalism and democracy remain great historical forces exerting strong influences in IR.

The World Economy, 1750–2000

In 1750, Britain, the world's most advanced economy, had a GDP of about $1,200 per capita (in today's dollars). That is less than the present level of most of the global South. However, today Britain produces more than ten times that much per person (with a much larger population than in 1750). This accomplishment was due to **industrialization**—the use of energy to drive machinery and the accumulation of such machinery along with the products created by it. The Industrial Revolution started in Britain in the eighteenth century (notably with the inventions of a new steam engine in 1769, a mechanized thread-spinner in 1770, and the cotton gin in America in 1794). It was tied to Britain's emerging leadership role in the world economy. Industrialization—a process at the world level of analysis—spread to the other advanced economies.

Atlas CD
Industry and
Industrialization
Article

By around 1850, the wooden sailing ships of earlier centuries had been replaced by larger and faster coal-powered iron steamships. Coal-fueled steam engines also drove factories producing textiles and other commodities. The great age of railroad building was taking off. These developments not only increased the volume of world production and trade, but also tied distant locations more closely together economically. In this period of mechanization, however, factory conditions were extremely harsh, especially for women and children operating machines.

Britain dominated world trade in the nineteenth century. Because Britain's economy was the most technologically advanced in the world, its products were competitive worldwide. Thus British policy favored **free trade**. Britain also served as the financial capital of the world, managing an increasingly complex world market in goods and services. The British currency, pounds sterling (silver), became the world standard. International monetary relations were still based on the value of precious metals, as they had been in the sixteenth century when Spain bought its armies with Mexican silver and gold.

By the outset of the twentieth century, however, the world's largest and most advanced economy was not Britain but the United States. The industrialization of the U.S. economy was fueled by territorial expansion throughout the nineteenth century, adding vast natural resources. The U.S. economy was attracting huge pools of immigrant labor from the poorer fringes of Europe as well. The United States led the world in converting from coal to oil and from horse-drawn transportation to motor vehicles. New technical innovations, from electricity to airplanes, also helped push the U.S. economy into a dominant world position.

In the 1930s, the U.S. and world economies suffered a severe setback in the Great Depression. Adopting the principles of *Keynesian economics*, the U.S. government used deficit spending to stimulate the economy, paying itself back from new wealth generated by economic recovery. The government role in the economy intensified during World War II.

Following World War II, the capitalist world economy was restructured under U.S. leadership. Today's international economic institutions, such as the World Bank and International Monetary Fund (IMF), date from this period. The United States provided massive assistance to resuscitate the Western European economies (through the Marshall Plan) as well as Japan's economy. World trade greatly expanded, and the world market became more related through air transportation and telecommunications. Electronics emerged as a new leading sector, and technological progress accelerated.

Standing apart from this world capitalist economy in the years after World War II were the economies of the Soviet Union and Eastern Europe, organized on communist principles of central planning and state ownership. The Soviet Union had notable successes in rapidly industrializing the country in the 1930s, surviving the German assault in the 1940s, and developing world-class aerospace and military production capability in the 1950s and 1960s. It launched the world's first satellite (*Sputnik*) in 1957, and in the early 1960s its leaders boasted that communist economies would outperform capitalist ones within decades. Instead, the Soviet bloc economies stagnated under the weight of bureaucracy, ideological rigidity, environmental destruction, corruption, and extremely high military spending. In the 1990s, the former Soviet republics and their Eastern European neighbors tried—with mixed success—to make a transition to some form of capitalist market economy, but found it difficult.

**Atlas CD
Camels and
Satellites**
Photo

Today there is a single integrated world economy that almost no country can resist joining. At the same time, the imperfections and problems of that world economy are evident in the periodic crises and recessions of recent years—in Russia and Eastern Europe, Japan and other Asian economies, and even periodically the mature industrialized countries of North America and Western Europe. Above all, the emergence of a global capitalist economy has sharpened disparities between the richest and poorest world regions. While the United States enjoys unprecedented prosperity, Africa's increasing poverty has created a human catastrophe on a continental scale.

Just as the world economy climbed out of previous depressions in the 1890s and 1930s, it appears that a new wave of technological innovation is pulling the advanced industrialized countries, especially the United States, into a new phase of growth. Much less clear is whether technological change will bypass or empower the global South (see Chapter 7).

The Two World Wars, 1900–1950

World War I (1914–1918) and World War II (1939–1945) occupied only 10 years of the twentieth century, but they shaped its character. Nothing like those wars has happened since, and they remain a key reference point for the world in which we live today. With perhaps just two other cases in history—the Thirty Years' War and the Napoleonic Wars—the two world wars were global or hegemonic wars in which almost all major states participated in an all-out struggle over the future of the international system.

For many people, World War I symbolizes the tragic irrationality of war. It fascinates scholars of IR because it was a catastrophic war that seems unnecessary and perhaps even accidental. After a century of relative peace, the great powers marched off to battle for no good reason. There was even a popular feeling that Europe would be uplifted and reinvigorated by a war—that young men could once again prove their manhood on the battlefield in a glorious adventure. Such ideas were soon crushed by the immense pain and evident pointlessness of the war.

The previous major war had been the Franco-Prussian war of 1870–1871, when Germany executed a swift offensive using railroads to rush forces to the front. That war had ended quickly, decisively, and with a clear winner (Germany). People expected that a new war would follow the same pattern. All the great powers made plans for a quick railroad-borne offensive and rapid victory—what has been called the *cult of the offensive*. Under these doctrines, one country's mobilization for war virtually forced its enemies to mobilize as well. The one to strike first would win, it was believed. Thus, when a Serbian nationalist assassinated Archduke Ferdinand of Austria in 1914 in Sarajevo, a minor crisis escalated and the mobilization plans pushed Europe to all-out war.

The war was neither short nor decisive, however, and certainly not glorious. It bogged down in *trench warfare* along a fixed front—with occasional charges over the top into the enemy machine guns. For example, in 1917 in one battle, the British in three months fired five tons of artillery shells per yard of front line, over an 11-mile-wide front, and then lost 400,000 men in a failed ground attack. The horrific conditions were worsened by chemical weapons and by the attempts of Britain and Germany to starve each other into surrender.

Russia was the first state to crumble. Revolution at home removed Russia from the war in 1917 (and led to the founding of the Soviet Union). But the entry of the United States into the war on the anti-German side that year quickly turned the tide. In the *Treaty of Versailles* of 1919, Germany was forced to give up territory, pay reparations, limit its future armaments, and admit guilt for the war. German resentment against the harsh terms of Versailles would contribute to Adolf Hitler's rise to power in the 1930s. After World War I, U.S. President Woodrow Wilson led the effort to create the **League of Nations**, a forerunner of today's UN. But the U.S. Senate would not approve U.S. participation, and the League did not prove effective. U.S. isolationism between the world wars, along with declining British power and Russia's withdrawal into revolution, left a power vacuum in world politics.

In the 1930s, Germany and Japan stepped into that vacuum, embarking on aggressive expansionism that ultimately led to World War II. Japan had already occupied Taiwan and Korea, after defeating China in 1895 and Russia in 1905. In World War I Japan gained some German colonies in Asia. In 1931, Japan occupied Manchuria (northeast China) and set up a puppet regime there. In 1937, Japan invaded the rest of China and began a brutal occupation that continues to haunt Chinese-Japanese relations.

In Europe, meanwhile, Nazi Germany under Hitler in the 1930s had rearmed, intervened to help fascists win the Spanish Civil War, and grabbed territory from its neighbors under the rationale of reuniting ethnic Germans in those territories with their homeland. In an effort to appease German ambitions, Britain agreed in the **Munich Agreement** of 1938 to let Germany occupy part of Czechoslovakia. Appeasement has

THE TWO WORLD WARS, 1900–1950

	1900	1910	1920	1930	1940	1950
Europe	mobilization plans developed	Balkan crises	*World War I* — Sarajevo; U.S. enters war	Italy invades Ethiopia	Munich Agreement; *World War II* — U.S. enters war; D Day	
Germany	naval arms race with Britain →		Defeat; Weimar Republic; hyperinflation	Hitler wins power; rearmament	invasion of Poland; occupation of Austria, Czech.; occupation of Europe; The Holocaust; strategic bombing; Defeat; occupied by Allied forces	
Russia			Russian Revolution; (civil war); USSR formed	(industrialization)	pact with Hitler; German invasion; Victory	
Asia	U.S. in Philippines	Russo-Japanese War	Japan neutral in WW I	Japan occupies Manchuria (China); Japan invades China	Pearl Harbor; Japan occupies S.E. Asia; island battles; Hiroshima; Occupied by U.S.	
International Norms & Law		Hague Peace Conferences	Versailles treaty; Washington Naval Treaty; League of Nations →	U.S. isolationism; Japan quits League of Nations	Nuremberg Tribunal; United Nations →	
Technology	destroyers		trench warfare; chemical weapons; tanks; submarines	mechanized armor	air war; radar; nuclear weapons	

since had a negative connotation in IR, because the Munich Agreement seemed only to embolden Hitler for further conquest.

In 1939, Germany invaded Poland, and Britain joined the war against Germany in response. Hitler signed a nonaggression pact with his archenemy Joseph Stalin of the Soviet Union and threw his full army against France, occupying most of it quickly. Hitler then double-crossed Stalin and invaded the Soviet Union in 1941. This offensive bogged down and was turned back only after several years. The Soviet Union took the brunt of the German attack and suffered by far the greatest share of the 60 million deaths caused by World War II. This trauma continues to be a powerful memory that shapes views of IR in Russia and Eastern Europe.

The United States joined World War II against Germany in 1942. The U.S. economy produced critically important weapons and supplies for allied armies. The United States played an important role with Britain in the strategic bombing of German cities—including the firebombing of Dresden in February 1945, which caused 100,000 civilian deaths. In 1944, after crossing the English Channel on June 6 (*D Day*), British-American forces pushed into Germany from the west while the Soviets pushed from the east. A ruined Germany surrendered and was occupied by the allied powers.

At its peak, Nazi Germany and its allies occupied virtually all of Europe, except for Britain and part of Russia. Under its fanatical policies of racial purity, Germany rounded up and exterminated 6 million Jews and millions of others, including homosexuals, Gypsies, and communists. The mass murders, now known as the Holocaust, along with the sheer scale of war unleashed by Nazi aggression, are considered among the greatest *crimes against humanity* in history. Responsible German officials faced justice in the *Nuremberg Tribunal* after the war (see pp. 318–325). The pledges of world leaders after that experience "never again" to allow genocide—the systematic extermination of a racial or religious group—have been found wanting as genocide recurred in the post–Cold War era in Bosnia and Rwanda.

While the war in Europe was raging, Japan fought a war over control of Southeast Asia with the United States and its allies. Japan's expansionism in the 1930s had only underscored its dependence on foreign resources: the United States punished Japan by cutting off U.S. oil exports. Japan then destroyed much of the U.S. Navy in a surprise attack at *Pearl Harbor* (Hawaii) in 1941, and seized desired territories including Indonesia, whose oil replaced that of the United States. The United States, however, built vast new military forces and retook a series of Pacific islands in subsequent years. The strategic bombing of Japanese cities by the United States culminated in the only historical use of nuclear weapons in war—the destruction of the cities of *Hiroshima* and *Nagasaki* in August 1945—which triggered Japan's quick surrender.

The lessons of the two world wars seem contradictory. From the failure of the Munich Agreement in 1938 to appease Hitler, many people have concluded that only a hard-line foreign policy with preparedness for war will deter aggression and prevent war. Yet in 1914 it was just such hard-line policies that apparently led Europe into a disastrous war, which might have been avoided by appeasement. Evidently the best policy would be sometimes harsh and at other times conciliatory, but IR scholars have not discovered a simple formula for choosing (see "The Causes of War" in Chapter 4).

THE COLD WAR, 1945–1990

Timeline spanning 1940, 1950, 1960, 1970, 1980, 1990.

Soviet Union — Leaders: Stalin, Khrushchev, Brezhnev, Andropov, Chernenko, Gorbachev
- (WW II alliance)
- A-bomb
- Warsaw Pact →
- Sputnik
- nuclear parity with U.S.
- reforms (perestroika, glasnost)

United States — Leaders: F. D. Roosevelt, Truman, Eisenhower, Kennedy, Johnson, Nixon, Ford, Carter, Reagan, Bush
- NATO →
- containment policy →
- nuclear arms race →
- (nuclear superiority over USSR)
- human rights
- (Iran crisis)
- military buildup
- "Star Wars" (SDI)

China
- civil war (Nationalists-Communists)
- Sino-Soviet alliance
- People's Republic →
- (Taiwan nationalist)
- Taiwan Straits crises (vs. U.S.)
- Sino-Soviet split
- A-bomb
- Cultural Revolution
- Soviet border clashes
- U.S.-China rapprochement
- death of Mao
- joins UN
- neutral to pro-U.S.
- student protests

Confron-tations
- Berlin crisis
- Korean War
- Soviet invasion of Hungary
- Cuban revo-lution
- U-2 incident
- Berlin Wall
- Berlin crisis
- Cuban Missile Crisis
- Vietnam War
- USSR invades Czechoslovakia
- Afghanistan War
- U.S. invasion of Grenada

Proxy Wars
- Greek civil war
- Suez crisis
- Indonesia
- Chile coup
- Arab-Israeli wars
- Somalia vs. Ethiopia
- Cambodia →
- Angola →
- Nicaragua →
- El Salvador →

Co-operation
- Yalta summit
- Geneva summit
- Limited Test Ban Treaty
- Non-Proliferation Treaty
- SALT I
- détente
- SALT II
- START talks
- Paris summit (CFE)
- INF treaty

The Cold War, 1945–1990
The United States and the Soviet Union became the two superpowers of the post–World War II era. Each had its ideological mission (capitalist democracy versus communism), its networks of alliances and third world clients, and its deadly arsenal of nuclear weapons. Europe was divided, with massive military forces of the United States and its *North Atlantic Treaty Organization (NATO)* allies on one side and massive forces of the Soviet Union and its *Warsaw Pact* allies on the other. Germany itself was split, with three-quarters of the country—and three-quarters of the capital city of Berlin—occupied by the United States, Britain, and France. The remainder, surrounding West Berlin, was occupied by the Soviet Union. In 1961, East Germany built the Berlin Wall separating East from West Berlin. It symbolized the division of Europe by what Winston Churchill had called the "iron curtain."

Despite the hostility of East-West relations during the **Cold War**, a relatively stable framework of relations emerged, and conflicts never escalated to all-out war. At a U.S.-Soviet-British meeting at *Yalta* in 1945, when the defeat of Germany was imminent, the Western powers acknowledged the Soviet army's presence in Eastern Europe, allowing that area to remain under Soviet influence. While the Soviet bloc did not join Western economic institutions, all the world's major states joined the UN. The United Nations (unlike the ill-fated League of Nations) managed to maintain almost universal membership and adherence to basic structures and rules throughout the Cold War era.

The central concern of the West during the Cold War was that the Soviet Union might gain control of Western Europe—either through outright invasion or through communists' taking power in war-weary and impoverished countries of Western Europe. This could have put the entire industrial base of the Eurasian landmass (from Europe to Siberia) under one state. The *Marshall Plan*—U.S. financial aid to rebuild European economies—responded to these fears, as did the creation of the NATO alliance. Half of the entire world's military spending was devoted to the European standoff. Much spending was also devoted to a superpower nuclear arms race, in which each superpower produced tens of thousands of nuclear weapons (see pp. 204–206).

Through the policy of **containment**, adopted in the late 1940s, the United States sought to halt the expansion of Soviet influence globally on several levels at once—military, political, ideological, economic. The United States maintained an extensive network of military bases and alliances worldwide. Virtually all of U.S. foreign policy in subsequent decades, from foreign aid and technology transfer to military intervention and diplomacy, came to serve the goal of containment.

The *Chinese communist revolution* in 1949 led to a Sino-Soviet alliance (*Sino* means "Chinese"). But China became fiercely independent in the 1960s following the **Sino-Soviet split**, when China opposed Soviet moves toward *peaceful coexistence* with the United States. In the late 1960s, young radicals, opposed to both superpowers, ran China during the chaotic and destructive *Cultural Revolution*. But feeling threatened by Soviet power, China's leaders developed a growing affiliation with the United States during the 1970s, starting with a dramatic visit to China by U.S. President Richard Nixon in 1972. This visit led to U.S.-Chinese diplomatic relations in 1979, and ended a decades-long argument in the U.S. foreign policy establishment about "who lost China" to communism in 1949. During the Cold War, China generally tried to play a balancer role against whichever superpower seemed most threatening at the time.

In 1950, the *Korean War* broke out when communist North Korea attacked and overran most of U.S.-allied South Korea. The United States and its allies (under UN authority obtained after the Soviets walked out of the Security Council in protest) counterattacked and overran most of North Korea. China sent "volunteers" to help North Korea, and the war bogged down near the original border until a 1953 truce. The Korean War hardened U.S. attitudes toward communism and set a negative tone for future East-West relations, especially U.S.-Chinese relations in the 1950s. U.S. leaders considered using nuclear weapons during the Korean War but decided not to do so.

The Cold War thawed after Stalin died in 1953. The first **summit meeting** between superpower leaders took place in Geneva in 1955. But the Soviet Union sent tanks to crush an uprising in Hungary in 1956 (an action it repeated in 1968 in Czechoslovakia), and the Soviet missile program that orbited *Sputnik* in 1957 alarmed the United States. The shooting down of a U.S. spy plane (the *U-2*) over the Soviet Union in 1960 scuttled a summit meeting between superpower leaders Nikita Khrushchev and Dwight D. Eisenhower. In Cuba, after Fidel Castro's communist revolution in 1959, the United States attempted a counterrevolution in the botched 1961 *Bay of Pigs* invasion.

Web Link
Cuban Missile Crisis

These hostilities culminated in the **Cuban Missile Crisis** of 1962, when the Soviet Union installed medium-range nuclear missiles in Cuba. The Soviet aims were to reduce the Soviet Union's strategic nuclear inferiority, to counter the deployment of U.S. missiles on Soviet borders in Turkey, and to deter another U.S. invasion of Cuba. U.S. leaders considered the missiles threatening and provocative. As historical documents later revealed, nuclear war was quite possible. Some U.S. policy makers favored military strikes before the missiles became operational, when in fact some nuclear weapons in Cuba were already operational and commanders were authorized to use them in the event of a U.S. attack. Instead, President John F. Kennedy imposed a naval blockade to force their removal. The Soviet Union backed down, and the United States promised not to invade Cuba in the future. Leaders on both sides, shaken by the possibility of nuclear war, signed the *Limited Test Ban Treaty* in 1963, prohibiting atmospheric nuclear tests, and began to cooperate in cultural exchanges, space exploration, aviation, and other areas.

The two superpowers often jockeyed for position in the third world, supporting **proxy wars** in which they typically supplied and advised opposing factions in civil wars. The alignments were often arbitrary. For instance, the United States backed the Ethiopian government and the Soviets backed next-door rival Somalia in the 1970s; when an Ethiopian revolution caused the new government to seek Soviet help, the United States switched its support to Somalia.

Web Link
Vietnam War

One flaw of U.S. policy in the Cold War period was to see such regional conflicts through East-West lenses. Its preoccupation with communism led the United States to support unpopular pro-Western governments in a number of poor countries, nowhere more disastrously than in the *Vietnam War* in the 1960s. The war divided U.S. citizens and ultimately failed to prevent a communist takeover. The fall of South Vietnam in 1975 appeared to signal U.S. weakness, especially combined with U.S. setbacks in the Middle East—the 1973 Arab oil embargo and the 1979 overthrow of the U.S.-backed Shah of Iran.

In this period of apparent U.S. weakness, the Soviet Union invaded Afghanistan in 1979. Like the United States in Vietnam, the Soviet Union could not suppress rebel armies supplied by the opposing superpower. The Soviets withdrew after almost a decade of war that considerably weakened the Soviet Union. Meanwhile, President Ronald Reagan built up U.S. military forces to record levels and supported rebel armies in the Soviet-allied states of Nicaragua and Angola (and one faction in Cambodia) as well as Afghanistan. Superpower relations slowly improved after Mikhail Gorbachev, a reformer, took power in the Soviet Union in 1985. But some of the third world battlegrounds (notably Afghanistan and Angola) continued to suffer from brutal civil wars into the new century.

In retrospect, it seems that both superpowers exaggerated Soviet strength. In the early years of the arms race, U.S. military superiority was absolute, especially in nuclear weapons. The Soviets managed to match the United States over time, from A-bombs to H-bombs to multiple-warhead missiles. By the 1970s the Soviets had achieved strategic parity—neither side could prevent its own destruction in a nuclear war. But behind this military parity lay a Soviet Union lagging far behind the West in everything else—sheer wealth, technology, infrastructure, and citizen/worker motivation.

In June 1989, massive pro-democracy demonstrations in China's capital of Beijing (Tiananmen Square) were put down violently by the communist government. Around 1990, as the Soviet Union stood by, one after another Eastern European country replaced its communist government under mass demonstrations. The toppling of the Berlin Wall in late 1989 symbolized the end of the Cold War division of Europe. Germany formally reunified in 1990. The Soviet leader, Gorbachev, allowed these losses of power in hopes of concentrating on Soviet domestic restructuring under his *perestroika* (economic reform) and *glasnost* (openness in political discussion). In 1991, however, the Soviet Union itself broke apart. Russia and many of the other former republics struggled throughout the 1990s against economic and financial collapse, inflation, corruption, war, and military weakness, although they remained political democracies. China remained a communist, authoritarian government but liberalized its economy and avoided military conflicts. In contrast to the Cold War era, China developed close ties with the United States and Russia, and joined the world's liberal trading regime.

Scholars do not agree on the important question of why the Cold War ended. Some believe that U.S. military strength under President Reagan forced the Soviet Union into bankruptcy as it tried to keep up the arms race. Others claim that the Soviet Union suffered from internal stagnation over decades and imploded because of weaknesses in governance that had little to do with external pressure. Indeed, some scholars think the Soviet Union might have fallen apart earlier without the United States as a foreign enemy to bolster the Soviet government's legitimacy with its own people.

The Early Post–Cold War Era, 1990–2000
The post–Cold War era began with a bang, while the Soviet Union was still disintegrating. In 1990, perhaps believing that the end of the Cold War had left a power vacuum in its region, Iraq occupied its neighbor Kuwait in an aggressive grab for control of Middle East oil. Western powers were alarmed—both about the example that such aggression could set in a new era, if unpunished, and about the direct threat to energy supplies for the world economy. The United States mobilized a coalition of the world's major countries (with almost no opposition) to counter Iraq. Working through the UN, the U.S.-led coalition applied escalating sanctions against Iraq—from condemnation, to embargoing Iraq's oil exports,

to threats and ultimatums. President George Bush received from the U.S. Congress authorization to use force against Iraq.

Atlas CD
Persian Gulf
Map

When Iraq did not withdraw from Kuwait by the UN's deadline, the United States and its allies easily smashed Iraq's military and evicted its army from Kuwait in the *Gulf War*. But the coalition did not occupy Iraq or overthrow its government. The costs of the Gulf War were shared among the participants in the coalition, with Britain and France making military commitments while Japan and Germany made substantial financial contributions. This pass-the-hat financing was an innovation, one that worked fairly well.

The final collapse of the Soviet Union followed only months after the Gulf War. The 15 republics of the Union—Russia under President Boris Yeltsin was just one—had begun taking power from a weakened central government, declaring themselves sovereign states. This still-evolving process raised complex problems ranging from issues of national self-determination to the reallocation of property. The Baltic republics (Estonia, Latvia, and Lithuania), incorporated into the Soviet Union only in the 1940s, were leaders in breaking away. The others held long negotiations under Gorbachev's leadership to restructure their confederation, with stronger republics and a weaker center.

The *Union Treaty* outlining this new structure provoked hard-liners in the old central government to try to seize control of the Soviet Union in a military coup in 1991. The failure of the coup—and the role of Russian President Yeltsin in opposing it—accelerated the collapse of the Soviet Union. The Communist party was banned, and soon both capitalism and democracy were adopted as the basis of the economies and political systems of the former Soviet states. The republics became independent states and formed a loose coordinating structure—the **Commonwealth of Independent States (CIS)**—whose future, if any, is still unclear. Of the former Soviet republics, only the three small Baltic states are nonmembers. Russia and Belarus formed a quasi-union in 2000.

Western relations with Russia and the other republics went downhill after 1991. Because of their own economic problems and a sense that Russia needed internal reform more than external aid, Western countries provided only limited aid for the region's harsh economic transition, which had drastically reduced living standards. Russia's brutal suppression of its secessionist province of Chechnya in 1995 and 1999 provoked Western fears of expansionist Russian nationalism, especially after earlier success of ultranationalists in Russian parliamentary elections. Russian leaders feared that NATO expansion into Eastern Europe would place Western military forces on Russia's borders, creating a new division of Europe. Russian President Yeltsin warned of a "Cold Peace." Meanwhile, Japan and Russia could not resolve a lingering, mostly symbolic, territorial dispute.

Despite these problems, the world's great powers increased their cooperation after the Cold War. Russia was accepted as the successor state to the Soviet Union and took its seat on the Security Council. Russia and the United States agreed to major reductions in their nuclear weapons, and carried them out in the 1990s.

U.S. leaders had hoped that the Gulf War would set valuable precedents for the future—punishment of aggression, reaffirmation of sovereignty and territorial integrity (of both Kuwait and Iraq), utility of the UN Security Council, and willingness of the United States to lead the post–Cold War order, which President Bush named the "New World Order." The prime architect of the "New World Order" of the early 1990s was, in many ways, Franklin D. Roosevelt—the U.S. president during most of World War II in the 1940s. His vision was of a great power collaboration through a new United Nations after the defeat of Germany and Japan. Included would be the winners of the war—the United States, the Soviet Union, and Britain, along with France and (for the first time) China. The five would hold permanent seats on the UN Security Council. Germany and Japan would be reconstructed as democracies; the United States would take a strong leadership role in world affairs. Roosevelt's vision was delayed by 40 years while the Soviet Union and United States contested the world order. Then, surprisingly, it came into existence in the early 1990s, close to the original vision.

Hopes for a "New World Order" after the Gulf War quickly collided with less pleasant realities, however. It was in Bosnia-Herzegovina (hereafter called Bosnia for short) that the UN came to have its largest peacekeeping mission and where the gap between the international community's words and deeds was most striking. Just after the Gulf War in 1991, the former Yugoslavia broke apart, with several of its republics declaring independence. Ethnic Serbs, minorities in Croatia and Bosnia, seized about a third of Croatia and two-thirds of Bosnia as territory to form a "Greater Serbia" with the neighboring republic of Serbia. In those territories, with help from Serbia, which controlled the Yugoslav army, the Serb forces massacred hundreds of thousands of non-Serb Bosnians and Croatians and expelled millions more, to create an ethnically pure state. Croatian militias in Bosnia emulated the tactics, though on a smaller scale.

The international community recognized the independence of Croatia and Bosnia, admitting them to the UN and passing dozens of Security Council resolutions to protect their territorial integrity and their civilian populations. But in contrast to the Gulf War, the great powers showed no willingness to bear major costs to protect Bosnia. Instead they tried to contain the conflict by assuming a neutral role as peacekeeper and intermediary, offering a variety of peace plans, economic sanctions and rewards, and other inducements, none of which convinced Serb forces to withdraw. International "neutrality" included an arms embargo imposed on unarmed Bosnia and heavily armed Serbia alike, despite the UN resolutions declaring Serbia the aggressor. The UN sent almost 40,000 peacekeepers to Bosnia and Croatia, at a cost of more than $1 billion per year. NATO threatened military actions repeatedly, only to back down when costs appeared too high.

By 1995, the international community's Bosnia policy was in shambles. The Serbian forces overran two of three UN-designated "safe areas" in eastern Bosnia, expelling the women and slaughtering thousands of the men, but then the tide of battle turned and Serb forces lost ground. Fears of a widening war, along with the pressures of an upcoming U.S. presidential election, finally triggered a more assertive international policy in Bosnia. Two weeks of NATO air strikes (the first serious use of Western military leverage in Bosnia) induced Serb forces to come to terms. U.S. negotiators pushed through the *Dayton Agreement*, which formally held Bosnia together as a single country, but granted Serb forces great autonomy on half of Bosnia's territory (the other half being controlled by a federation of Muslim, Croatian, and multiethnic parties). Sixty thousand heavily armed troops, mostly from NATO (with 20,000 from the United States), went to Bosnia and established a stable cease-fire. With measures of the agreement unimplemented, the international forces extended their mission year after year, fearing that withdrawal would spark renewal of the war. Although Bosnia's people have enjoyed a

Towards Peace or War? Peaceful trends predominated in the 1990s, but hot spots remained. A long war raged on in Afghanistan (the scene is from 1995).

Web Link
Kosovo War

stable cease-fire, the war damaged the United Nations, the Western alliance, and the idea of collective security.

In contrast to their indecision early in the Bosnia crisis, the Western powers acted with dispatch in 1999 when Serbian forces carried out "ethnic cleansing" actions in the Serbian province of Kosovo, where ethnic Albanians made up 90 percent of the population. The guerrilla Kosovo Liberation Army had been conducting a violent campaign for independence, and Serbian forces had responded with massacres and the forced displacement of hundreds of thousands of Albanians. After a Western-sponsored peace initiative collapsed, NATO launched an air war against Serbia. The air campaign escalated incrementally as the Serbian government intensified its cleansing campaign in Kosovo. In response, Serbian strongman Slobodan Milosevic was indicted for war crimes by the UN tribunal for the former Yugoslavia.

NATO came under criticism—notably from Russia and China—for acting without explicit UN authorization and interfering in Serbia's internal affairs. (The international community and the UN considered Kosovo, unlike Bosnia, to be a part of Serbia.) Critics also faulted NATO for relying on air-only tactics in response to atrocities on the ground. Then, Milosevic abruptly conceded. Serbian forces withdrew from Kosovo and were replaced by a UN-authorized, NATO-led international force. Most refugees returned home, although much of the Serbian minority then fled Kosovo in the face of Albanian reprisals. The province's destiny remained unsettled as of 2001. The debate about the limits of air war also remained unsettled, partly because Milosevic's capitulation may have been triggered not by the bombing but by a secret deal with Russia's military to partition Kosovo and retain a Serbian zone. At the end of the war, Russian troops based in Bosnia raced through Serbia and occupied the main airport in Kosovo before NATO troops arrived there. The Russian military's bold actions brought it perilously close to combat with NATO, for the first time since the Cold War. However, the two sides negotiated an agreement to incorporate Russian forces into the international forces in Kosovo. The Kosovo episode nonetheless underscored fears that Russia was sliding toward disaster through a combination of political instability, economic collapse, rampant corruption and crime, an ailing President Yeltsin, and renewed war in secessionist Chechnya province.

Other Western military intervention decisions in the 1990s—outside the strategically important locations of the Persian Gulf and former Yugoslavia—do not easily map onto a "new world order." In Somalia, a U.S.-led coalition sent tens of thousands of troops to suppress factional fighting and deliver relief supplies to a large population that was starving. However, when those forces were drawn into the fighting and sustained casualties, the United States abruptly pulled out, with the UN following by 1995. In Rwanda in 1994, the genocide of more than half a million civilians in a matter of weeks was virtually ignored by the international community. The great powers, burned by failures in Somalia and Bosnia, decided that their vital interests were not at stake. In 1997, the Rwanda conflict spilled into neighboring Zaire (now the Democratic Congo) where rebels overthrew a corrupt dictator. Neighboring countries were drawn into the fighting but the international community steered clear even as conditions worsened. The U.S. military intervened in Haiti to restore the elected president, but the situation there remained bleak for years afterward.

Yeltsin resigned at the end of 1999 and his designated successor, prime minister Vladimir Putin, took office and was elected president a few months later, while Putin's war against Chechen rebels was still popular with Russians. Despite the leadership change, Russian-American relations in 2000 faced the challenges of conflicting interests in multiple areas. Not only has the West provided little aid, in Russia's perspective, but it is pushing NATO's boundaries eastward. It is promoting new pipelines to bypass Russian territory in moving oil from former Soviet republics to Western consumers. It is criticizing the conduct of the war in Chechnya, a province of Russia, yet conducting its own military attacks around the world when it so chooses.

Atlas CD
Russia
Articles, Maps, Photos

The post–Cold War era may seem a conflict-prone period in which savage wars flare up with unexpected intensity around the world, in places such as Bosnia and Rwanda. It is true that the era is complex and unpredictable, leaving some U.S. policy makers susceptible to Cold War nostalgia—longing for a time when world politics followed simpler rules based on a bipolar world order. Despite these new complexities, however, *the post–Cold War era has been a more peaceful one.* World military spending has decreased by about one-third from its peak in the 1980s. Old wars have ended faster than new ones have begun. Latin America and Russia/Eastern Europe have nearly extinguished significant interstate war in their regions, joining a zone of peace already encompassing North America, Western Europe, Japan/Pacific, and China.

Warfare is diminishing worldwide but remains "hot" in an arc of conflict from Africa through the Middle East to South Asia. Even there, almost all wars in the 1990s were internal—even intense ones as in Afghanistan—rather than large-scale interstate wars. Long, bloody wars in South Africa and Mozambique are over. The Israeli-Palestinian conflict has followed a zigzagging course toward peace. Although

Afghanistan's war rages on, Cambodia's has nearly died out. Peace agreements ended long-standing wars in Guatemala and the Philippines. Even the war in Bosnia, which undermined world order in the early 1990s, has been frozen by the international community since late 1995. World order in the 1990s did not spiral out of control.

In international economic relations, the post–Cold War era is one of globalization. Countries worldwide are integrating into a world market, for better or worse. New hubs of economic growth are emerging, notably in parts of Asia with remarkable economic growth in the 1990s (despite a sharp setback in 1997). At the same time, disparities between the rich and poor are growing, globally and within individual countries (including the United States). Globalization has created backlashes among people who are adversely affected or who believe their identities are threatened by foreign influences. The resurgence of nationalism and ethnic-religious conflict—occasionally in brutal form—results partly from that backlash. So does the growing protest movement against world trade, which dominated the failed 1999 Seattle meeting of the World Trade Organization.

Atlas CD
China
Articles, Maps,
Photos

China is becoming more central to world politics as the twenty-first century begins. Its size and rapid growth make China a rising power—a situation that some scholars liken to Germany's rise a century earlier. Historically, such shifts in power relations have caused instability in the international system. China is the only great power that is not a democracy. Its poor record on human rights—symbolized dramatically by the killings in Tiananmen Square (Beijing) in 1989—makes it a frequent target of Western criticism from both governments and NGOs. With the transfer of Hong Kong from Britain in 1997, China acquired a valuable asset and turned to hopes of someday reintegrating Taiwan as well, under the Hong Kong formula of "one country, two systems." The issues of Taiwan and human rights are central to China's relations with the international community, but other issues matter as well: China holds (but seldom uses) veto power in the UN Security Council, and it has a credible nuclear arsenal. China adjoins several regional conflict areas and affects the global proliferation of missiles and nuclear weapons. China is the only great power from the global South. Its population size and rapid industrialization from a low level make China a big factor in the future of global environmental trends such as global warming. All these elements make China an important actor in the coming decades of international relations.

The post–Cold War era has barely begun. The transition has been a turbulent time, full of international changes and new possibilities both good and bad. It is likely, however, that basic rules and principles of IR—those that scholars have long struggled to understand—will continue to apply, though their contexts and outcomes may change. Most central to those rules and principles is the concept of power, to which we now turn.

THINKING CRITICALLY

1. Pick a current area in which interesting international events are taking place. Can you think of possible explanations for those events from each of the four levels of analysis? (See Table 1.1, p. 13.) Do explanations from different levels provide insights into different aspects of the events?

2. For a given nation-state that was once a *colony*, can you think of ways in which the state's current foreign policies might be influenced by this past history?
3. Given the contradictory lessons of World Wars I and II, for which situations in today's world would appeasement (a conciliatory policy) be the best course? For which situations would hard-line containment policies be best? Why?

CHAPTER SUMMARY

◆ IR affects daily life profoundly; we all participate in IR.

◆ IR is a field of political science, concerned mainly with explaining political outcomes in international security affairs and international political economy.

◆ Theories complement descriptive narratives in explaining international events and outcomes, but scholars do not agree on one set of theories or methods to use in studying IR.

◆ States are the most important actors in IR; the international system is based on the sovereignty of (about 200) independent territorial states.

◆ States vary greatly in size of population and economy, from tiny microstates to great powers.

◆ Nonstate actors such as multinational corporations (MNCs), nongovernmental organizations (NGOs), and intergovernmental organizations (IGOs) exert a growing influence on international relations.

◆ The worldwide revolution in information technologies will profoundly reshape the capabilities and preferences of actors in IR, in ways that we do not yet understand.

◆ Four levels of analysis—individual, domestic, interstate, and global—suggest multiple explanations (operating simultaneously) for outcomes observed in IR.

◆ The global level of analysis—a recent addition—draws attention to technological change and the gap in wealth between the industrialized North and the poor South.

◆ A variety of world civilizations were conquered by Europeans over several centuries and forcefully absorbed into a single global international system initially centered in Europe.

◆ The great-power system is made up of about half a dozen states (with membership changing over time as state power rises and falls).

◆ Great powers have restructured world order through recurrent wars, alliances, and the reign of hegemons (states that temporarily gain a preponderance of power in the international system). The most important wars have been the Thirty Years' War, the Napoleonic Wars, World War I, and World War II. Periods of hegemony include Britain in the nineteenth century and the United States after World War II.

◆ European states colonized most of the rest of the world during the past five centuries. Latin American countries gained independence shortly after the United States did (about 200 years ago), while those in Africa, Asia, and the Middle East became independent states only in the decades after World War II.

◆ Nationalism strongly influences IR; conflict often results from the perception of nationhood leading to demands for statehood or for the adjustment of state borders.

- ◆ Democracy is a force of growing importance: more states are becoming democratically governed, and democracies rarely fight each other in wars.
- ◆ The world economy has generated wealth at an accelerating pace in the past two centuries and is increasingly integrated on a global scale, although with huge inequalities.
- ◆ World Wars I and II dominated the twentieth century, yet they seem to offer contradictory lessons about the utility of hard-line or conciliatory foreign policies.
- ◆ For most of the 50 years since World War II, world politics revolved around the East-West rivalry of the Cold War. This bipolar standoff created stability and avoided great-power wars, including nuclear war, but it had harmful consequences for third world states that became proxy battlegrounds.
- ◆ The post-Cold War era that began in the 1990s holds hope of general great-power cooperation despite the appearance of new ethnic and regional conflicts.

ONLINE PRACTICE TEST

Take an online practice test at
www.IRtext.com

2

Power Politics

CHAPTER OUTLINE

- ◆ Realism
- ◆ Power
- ◆ Bargaining
- ◆ The International System
- ◆ Alliances

Realism

No single theory reliably explains the wide range of international interactions, both conflictual and cooperative. But there is a theoretical framework in IR that has traditionally held a central position. This approach, called realism, is favored by some IR scholars and vigorously contested by others, but almost all take it into account. It is a relatively conservative theoretical approach; liberal and revolutionary alternatives will be reviewed in Chapter 3.

Realism (or *political realism*) is a school of thought that explains international relations in terms of power (see "Defining Power," pp. 47–49). The exercise of power by states toward each other is sometimes called *realpolitik*, or just *power politics*. Realism has a long history, and it dominated the study of IR in the United States during the Cold War.

Realism as we know it developed in reaction to a liberal tradition that realists called **idealism** (of course, idealists themselves do not consider their approach unrealistic). Idealism emphasizes international law, morality, and international organization, rather than power alone, as key influences on international events. Idealists think that human nature is basically good; with good habits, education, and appropriate international structures, human nature can become the basis of peaceful and cooperative international relationships. Idealists see the international system as one based on a community of states having the potential to work together to overcome mutual problems (see Chapter 3).

For idealists, the principles of IR must flow from morality. Idealists were particularly active in the period between World Wars I and II, following the painful experience of World War I. U.S. President Woodrow Wilson and other idealists placed their hopes for peace in the League of Nations as a formal structure for the community of nations. Those hopes were dashed when that structure proved helpless to stop German and Japanese aggression in the 1930s. Since World War II, realists have blamed idealists for looking too much at how the world *ought to be* instead of how it *really is*. Sobered by the experiences of World War II, realists set out to understand the principles of power politics without succumbing to wishful thinking. Realism provided a theoretical foundation for the Cold War policies of containment and the determination of U.S. policy makers not to appease the Soviet Union and China.

Web Link

Aggression in the 1930s

Realists ground themselves in a long tradition. The Chinese strategist *Sun Tzu*, who lived 2,000 years ago, advised the rulers of states how to survive in an era when war had become a systematic instrument of power for the first time (the "warring states" period). Sun Tzu argued that moral reasoning was not very useful to the state rulers of the day, faced with armed and dangerous neighbors. Sun Tzu instead showed rulers how to use power to advance their interests and protect their survival.

At roughly the same time, in Greece, *Thucydides* wrote an account of the Peloponnesian War (431–404 B.C.) focusing on relative power among the Greek city-states. He stated that the strong do what they have the power to do and the weak accept what they have to accept. Much later, in Renaissance Italy (around 1500), *Niccolò Machiavelli* urged princes to concentrate on expedient actions to stay in power and to pay attention to war above all else. Today the adjective *Machiavellian* refers to excessively manipulative power maneuvers.

English philosopher *Thomas Hobbes* in the seventeenth century discussed the free-for-all that exists when government is absent and people seek their own self-interest. He called it the "state of nature" or "state of war"—in contrast to the rule of law. Hobbes favored a strong monarchy to prevent the condition, but in international affairs there is no such central authority (see pp. 63–66).

In the nineteenth century, the German military strategist *Karl von Clausewitz* said that "war is a continuation of politics by other means." U.S. admiral *Alfred Mahan* promoted naval power as the key means of achieving national political and economic interests. Realists see in these historical figures evidence that the importance of power politics is timeless and cross-cultural.

After World War II, scholar *Hans Morgenthau* argued that international politics is governed by objective, universal laws based on national interest defined as power (not on psychological motives of decision makers). No nation has "God on its side" (a universal morality) and all nations have to base their actions on prudence and practicality.

Realists tend to treat political power as separate from, and predominant over, morality, ideology, and other social and economic aspects of life. For realists, ideologies do not matter much, nor do religions or other cultural factors with which states may explain their actions. Realists see states with very different religions or ideologies or economic systems as quite similar in their actions with regard to national power.

Today realists share several assumptions about how IR works. They assume that IR can be best (though not exclusively) explained by the choices of states operating as

TABLE 2.1 Assumptions of Realism and Idealism

Issue	Realism	Idealism
Human Nature	Selfish	Altruistic
Most Important Actors	States	States and others including individuals
Causes of State Behavior	Rational pursuit of self-interest	Psychological motives of decision makers
Nature of International System	Anarchy	Community

autonomous actors rationally pursuing their own interests in a system of sovereign states. Sometimes the realist framework is summarized in three propositions: (1) *states* are the most important actors (the state-centric assumption); (2) they act as *rational* individuals in pursuing national interests (the unitary rational-actor assumption); and (3) they act in the context of an international system lacking central government (the *anarchy* assumption). Table 2.1 summarizes some major differences between the assumptions of realism and idealism. We will return to the realism-liberalism debate at the start of Chapter 3.

Power

Power is a central concept in international relations—*the* central one for realists—but one that is surprisingly difficult to define or measure.

Defining Power Power is often defined as the ability to get another actor to do what it would not otherwise have done (or not to do what it would have done). A variation on this idea is that actors are powerful to the extent that they affect others more than others affect them. These definitions treat power as influence. If actors get their way a lot, they must be powerful. One problem with this definition is that we seldom know what a second actor would have done in the absence of the first actor's power. There is a danger of circular logic: power explains influence, and influence measures power. Thus it is hard to use power to explain why international events occur (the aim of realism). A related problem is that common usage treats power as a thing rather than a process: states "have" power.

These problems are resolved by recalling that power is not influence itself, but the ability or potential to influence others. IR scholars believe that such potential is based on specific (tangible and intangible) characteristics or possessions of states—such as their sizes, levels of income, armed forces, and so forth. This is *power as capability*. Capabilities are easier to measure than influence and less circular in logic.

Measuring capabilities to explain how one nation influences another is not simple, however. It requires summing up various kinds of potentials. States possess varying amounts of population, territory, military forces, and so forth. *The best single indicator of a state's power may be its total GDP*, which combines overall size, technological level, and wealth. But even GDP is at best a rough indicator. An alternative method to that fol-

Atlas CD
Mitrovica,
Kosovo
Map

Power as Influence   Power is the ability to influence the behavior of others. Military force and economic sanctions are among the means states use to try to influence each other. A 1999 NATO air war induced Serbia to withdraw from Kosovo province, allowing the ethnic Albanian population there to return home after being expelled. Here, French troops in the powerful international force that now controls Kosovo prevent ethnic Albanians from crossing to the Serbian side of a de facto partition line, Mitrovica, 1999.

Atlas CD
GDP by
Alternative
Method
Statistics

lowed in this book gives GDP estimates that are on average about 50 percent higher for countries in the global North and about 50 percent lower for the global South (see footnote 1 on p. 9). In particular, this alternative method reduces China's GDP substantially from the figures reported in this book. So GDP is a useful estimator of material capabilities but not a precise one.

Furthermore, beyond the tangible capabilities, power depends on intangible elements. Capabilities give a state the potential to influence others only to the extent that political leaders can mobilize and deploy them effectively and strategically. This depends on national will, on diplomatic skill, on popular support for the government (its legitimacy), and so forth. Some scholars emphasize the *power of ideas*—the ability to maximize the influence of capabilities through a psychological process. This process includes the domestic mobilization of capabilities—often through religion, ideology, or (especially) nationalism. International influence is also gained by being the one to form rules of behavior, to change how others see their own national interests. If a state's own values become widely shared among other states, it will easily influence others. For example, the United States has influenced many other states to accept the value of free markets and free trade. This has been called *soft power*.

A state can have power only relative to other states. *Relative po[...]* power two states can bring to bear against each other. It matters little [...] a state's capabilities are rising or declining in absolute terms, only [...] falling behind or overtaking the capabilities of rival states.

Even realists recognize the limits to explanations based on power. [...] provides a general understanding of typical or average outcomes. In actua[...] many other elements at work, including an element of accident or luck. The [...] erful actor does not always prevail. Power provides only a partial explanatio[...]

Estimating Power Any estimate of an actor's overall power must combin[...] elements and will therefore be inexact. But such estimates are nonetheless very us[...]

Consider two examples in which states went to war: Iraq and Iran in 1980, an[...] and the United States in 1991. The logic of power suggests that in wars the more p[...] erful state will generally prevail. Thus, estimates of the relative power of the two ant[...] onists should help explain the outcome of each war. These estimates could take int[...] account the nations' relative military capabilities and the popular support for each one's government, among other factors. But most important is the total size of each nation's economy—the total GDP—which reflects both population size and the level of income per person (per capita). With a healthy enough economy, a state can buy a large army, buy popular support (by providing consumer goods), and even buy allies.

In 1980, Iran and Iraq appeared roughly equal in power. Both were oil-producing countries with middle-range income levels. Both could use oil income to buy arms on world markets, and both had relatively large and advanced military forces (by third world standards). Iran's military had been developed under the Shah in alliance with the United States; Iraq's had been largely supplied by the Soviet Union. Iran's population of 38 million was three times as large as Iraq's but its total GDP was less than double Iraq's.

Counterbalancing Iran's advantage in GDP was its short-term internal disorder. The Shah had been overthrown. Much of the military might offer little support, and perhaps active opposition, to Ayatollah Khomeini and the other leaders who had overthrown the Shah. It seemed that the new government would be unable to mobilize its potential power. By contrast, Saddam Hussein (also known as just Saddam) had recently taken absolute power as leader of Iraq and could count on a loyal military. He invaded Iran, hoping for a quick victory and the installation of a friendly government there.

The key element on which Saddam's plan depended was Iran's low internal cohesion, which would counteract Iran's advantage in size. But Saddam miscalculated this element. The Iranian military pulled together under Khomeini to put up a spirited defense, and its population proved more willing than Iraq's to die for its cause. The tide soon turned against Iraq. Saddam then looked to allies in the Arab world. These, with the tacit support of all the great powers, provided him enough aid to keep from losing (which would expand Iran's power) but not enough to win (which would expand Iraq's power). Thus the two sides were roughly equal in the power they could bring to bear. The war dragged on for ten years, killing a million people, before its end was negotiated with no winner.

The second example could hardly be more different. When Iraq seized its small and rich neighbor Kuwait, it came into a confrontation with the United States (which was determined not to let Iraq control the oil of the Persian Gulf). The power disparity was

Atlas CD
Oil, Source of
Iraqi Power
Photo

GDP, the United States held an advantage of nearly a hundred to one; in
n, more than ten to one. The larger U.S. armed forces were much more capa-
nologically. The United States also enjoyed a power advantage in the moral
macy given it by the UN Security Council. All of this power was augmented by the
tive participation of a broad alliance coalition against Iraq that included the most powerful states regionally and globally. Iraq had few allies of any kind and no strong ones.

Iraq had the advantage in one important element, geography: Kuwait was right next
to Iraq and was occupied by its dug-in troops, whereas the United States was halfway
around the world and had few military forces in the Middle East region at the outset.
Saddam also looked to the internal-cohesion dimension, where (as with Iran) he
expected domestic politics in the United States to sap its will to fight. Again this was a
miscalculation. The U.S. political leadership and citizenry rallied behind the war.

Overall, in this situation, the GDP ratio—nearly one hundred to one—provided a
good estimate of the power imbalance between Iraq and the United States. (In the short
term, of course, other factors ranging from political strategies to military forces to
weather played a role.) When the war began, the U.S.-led coalition established its
dominance within the first few hours and went on to systematically crush Iraq's military
power over six weeks and evict its forces from Kuwait. Thus, despite its lack of precision, GDP is probably the best single indicator of power. It does not always predict who
will win a war, however, as shown by the Vietnam War.

Elements of Power

State power is a mix of many ingredients, such as natural
resources, industrial capacity, moral legitimacy, military preparedness, and popular support
of government. All these elements contribute to an actor's power. The mix varies from
one actor to another, but overall power does relate to the rough quantities of the elements
on which that power is based.

Power resources are elements that an actor can draw on over the *long term*. The power
measure used earlier—total GDP—is in this category. So are population, territory, geography, and natural resources. These attributes change only slowly. Less tangible long-term
power resources include political culture, patriotism, education of the population, and
strength of the scientific and technological base. The credibility of its commitments
(reputation for keeping its word) is also a power resource that a state can nurture over
time. So is the ability of one state's culture and values to consistently shape the thinking
of other states (the power of ideas). Power resources shape an actor's potential power.

The importance of long-term power resources was illustrated after the Japanese surprise attack on the U.S. fleet at Pearl Harbor in 1941, which decimated U.S. naval capabilities in the Pacific. In the short term, Japan had superior military power and was able
to occupy territories in Southeast Asia while driving U.S. forces from the region. In the
longer term, the United States had greater power resources due to its underlying economic potential. Over the next few years it built up military capabilities that gradually
matched and then overwhelmed those of Japan in the Pacific.

Power capabilities allow actors to exercise influence in the *short term*. Military forces are
such a capability—perhaps the most important kind. The size, composition, and preparedness of two states' military forces matter more in a short-term military confrontation
than do their respective economies or natural resources. Another capability is the military-

Atlas CD
Kuwait
Map

Big Economy, Strong Power Military power such as tanks rests on economic strength, roughly measured by GDP. The large U.S. economy produced the military might that defeated Iraq in 1991. Here, a U.S. armored vehicle arrives in a Saudi port shortly after Iraq's invasion of Kuwait, 1990.

industrial capacity to quickly produce tanks, fighter planes, and other weapons. The quality of a state's bureaucracy is another type of capability, allowing the state to gather information, regulate international trade, or participate in international conferences.

As with power resources, some power capabilities are intangible. The support and legitimacy that an actor commands in the short term from constituents and allies are capabilities that the actor can use to gain influence. The loyalty of a nation's army and politicians to its leader (in the short term) is in effect a capability available to the leader. Although capabilities come into play more quickly than power resources, they are narrower in scope. In particular, military capabilities are useful only when military power can be effective in gaining influence. Likewise, economic capabilities are of little use in situations dominated by a military component.

Given the limited resources that any actor commands, there are always trade-offs among possible capabilities. Building up military forces diverts resources that might be put into foreign aid, for instance. Or buying a population's loyalty with consumer goods can reduce the resources available for building up military capabilities. To the extent that one element of power can be converted into another, it is *fungible*. Generally money is the most fungible capability because it can buy other capabilities.

Realists tend to see *military force* as the most important element of national power in the short term, and they see other elements such as economic strength or diplomatic skill or moral legitimacy as being important to the extent that they are fungible into military power. Such fungibility of nonmilitary elements of power into military ones is considerable, at least in the long term. Well-paid soldiers fight better, as do soldiers imbued with moral fervor for their cause, or soldiers using higher-technology weapons. Skilled diplomats can avoid unfavorable military confrontations or provoke favorable ones. Moral foreign policies can help sway public opinion in foreign countries and cement alliances that increase military strength. Realists tend to treat these dimensions of power as important mainly because of their potential military impact. Indeed, realists share this emphasis on military power with revolutionaries such as communist leaders during the Cold War. Chairman Mao Zedong of China said: "All power grows out of the barrel of a gun."

The different types of power capabilities can be contrasted by considering the choice to possess tanks or gold. One standard power capability states want is battle tanks. In land warfare to control territory, the tank is arguably the most powerful instrument, and the leading defense against it is another tank. One can assess power on this dimension by counting the size and quality of a state's tank force (an imprecise but not impossible exercise). A different power capability of time-honored value is the stockpile of *gold* (or its modern-day equivalent in hard currency reserves; see Chapter 5). Gold represents economic power and is a power resource, whereas tanks represent military power and are a power capability.

In the long term, the gold is better because one can always turn gold into tanks (it is fungible), but it might be hard to turn tanks into gold. However, in the short term the tanks might be better because if an enemy tank force invades one's territory, gold will not stop them; in fact, they will soon take the gold for themselves. For example, in 1990 Iraq (which had gone for tanks) invaded its neighbor Kuwait (which had gone for gold). In the short term, Iraq proved much more powerful: it occupied Kuwait and plundered it.

Morality can contribute to power, by increasing the will to use power and by attracting allies. States have long clothed their actions, however aggressive, in rhetoric about their peaceful and defensive intentions. For instance, the U.S. invasion of Panama was named "Operation Just Cause." Military capabilities are most effective in the context of justifications that make state actions seem moral. Of course, if a state overuses moralistic rhetoric to cloak self-interest too often, it loses credibility even with its own population.

Atlas CD
Strategic Suez
Canal
Photo

The use of geography as an element of power is called **geopolitics**. It is often tied to the logistical requirements of military forces (see Chapter 4). Frequently, state leaders use maps in thinking about international power positions and alignments. In geopolitics, the three most important considerations are location, location, location. States increase their power to the extent they can use geography to enhance their military capabilities, such as by securing allies and bases in locations close to a rival power, or by controlling key natural resources. In general, power declines as a function of distance from a home state.

A recurrent geopolitical theme for centrally located, largely land-locked states such as Russia is the threat of being surrounded. In the 1840s, British politician Lord Palmerston warned that "Russia has a basic drive for warm water ports" (free of ice year-round). The 1979 Soviet invasion of Afghanistan was seen by some Western leaders as a step toward Soviet expansion southward to the Indian Ocean, driven by such a motive. Central states such as Germany face a related military problem in the *two-front problem*. Germany had to fight France to the west and Russia to the east simultaneously in

World War I—a problem reduced early in World War II by Hitler's pact with Stalin (until Hitler's disastrous decision to invade the Soviet Union).

For states less centrally located, such as Britain or the United States, different geopolitical problems appear. These states have been called "insular" in that bodies of water protect them against land attacks. Their geopolitical problem in the event of war is to move soldiers and supplies over long distances to reach the scene of battle. This capability was demonstrated in the U.S. participation in the World Wars, the Cold War, and the Gulf War.

Atlas CD
US–Asia
Distance
Map

Bargaining

The exercise of power involves two or more parties, each trying to influence the other more than it is itself influenced. The mutual attempts to influence others constitute a bargaining process. Bargaining is important in various theoretical perspectives (not just realism), though different theories emphasize different motivations, tactics, and outcomes.

Bargaining and Leverage

Bargaining may be defined as tacit or direct communication in an attempt to reach agreement on an exchange of value—that is, of tangible or intangible items that one or both parties value. Bargaining need not be explicit. Sometimes the content is communicated through actions rather than an exchange of words.

A bargaining process has two or more *participants* and sometimes has *mediators* whose participation is nominally neutral. Participants have a direct stake in the outcome; mediators do not. There are one or more *issues* on which each participant hopes to reach agreement on terms favorable to itself, but the participants' *interests* diverge on these issues, creating conflicts. These conflicts define a *bargaining space*—one or more dimensions, each of which represents a distance between the positions of two participants concerning their preferred outcomes. The bargaining process disposes of these conflicts by achieving agreement on the distribution of the various items of value that are at stake. The end result is a position arrived at in the bargaining space.

Such agreements do not necessarily represent a *fair exchange of* value; many agreements are manifestly one-sided and unfair. But in a broad sense, bargains whether fair or unfair contain an element of *mutual gain*. This is possible because the items of value being exchanged have different value to the different parties. To take a clearly unfair example, an armed robber values a victim's wallet more than the victim does, and the victim values his or her own life more than the robber does. The robber "gives" the victim life and the victim "gives" the robber money; thus both gain. As this example illustrates, the mutual gains in bargaining are relative to other possible outcomes, not necessarily to the status quo before the bargain.

Participants bring different means of *leverage* to the bargaining process. Leverage derives from power capabilities that allow one actor to influence the other to reach agreements more favorable to the first actor's interests. Leverage may operate on any of three dimensions of power: the *promise* of positive sanctions (rewards) if the other actor

①

gives one what one wants; the *threat* of negative sanctions (damage to valued items) if not; or an *appeal* to the other's feeling of love, friendship, sympathy, or respect for oneself. For instance, Cuba during the Cold War could obtain Soviet oil by purchasing the oil with hard currency, by threatening to cut its alliance with the Soviet Union unless given the oil at subsidized prices, or by appealing to the Soviet leaders' sense of socialist solidarity.

Bringing a bargaining leverage into play generally opens up a new dimension in the bargaining space, allowing outcomes along this new dimension to be traded off against those on the original dimension (the main issue at stake). Leverage thus helps to get deals done—albeit not always fair ones. One-sided agreements typically result when one side has a preponderance of leverage relative to the other.

The use of violence can be a means of settling conflicts. The application of violent negative leverage can force an agreement that ends a conflict. (Again, the agreement may not be fair.) Because such violence may also create new sources of conflict, agreements reached through violence may not last. Nonetheless, from a realist perspective violence is just another leverage—an extension of politics by other means. Politics itself has been described as the process of deciding "who gets what, when, how."

The same principles of bargaining apply to both international security affairs and international political economy. In both cases power and leverage matter, and structures and institutions have been designed to aid the bargaining process. Economic markets, from the New York Stock Exchange to the local supermarket, serve this purpose. In international security such institutions as diplomatic missions and international organizations facilitate the bargaining process. Realists studying international security focus on political-military bargaining more than economic bargaining because they consider it more important. The economic framework will be elaborated in Chapter 5.

Bargaining that takes place formally—usually at a table with back and forth talking—is called **negotiation**. Because the issues in IR are important and the actors are usually sophisticated players in a game with long-established rules and traditions, most issues of contention reach a negotiating table sooner or later. Often bargaining takes place simultaneously at the negotiating table and in the world (often on the battlefield). The participants talk in the negotiation hall while manipulating instruments of leverage outside it.

Negotiating styles vary from one culture or individual to another. In international negotiations on major political and military issues, problems of cultural difference may become serious obstacles. For example, straight-talking Americans might misunderstand negotiators from Japan, where saying "no" is rude and is therefore replaced by phrases such as "that would be difficult." A good negotiator will take time to understand the other party's culture and bargaining style, as well as its interests and available means of leverage.

Strategies Power strategies are plans actors use to develop and deploy power capabilities to achieve goals. A key aspect of strategy is choosing the kinds of capabilities to develop, given limited resources, in order to maximize international influence. This requires foresight because the capabilities required to manage a situation may need to be developed years before that situation presents itself. Yet the capabilities chosen often will not be fungible in the short term. Central to this dilemma is what size of standing military forces to maintain in peacetime—enough to prevent a quick defeat if war breaks out, but not so much as to overburden one's economy (see pp. 174–179). Strategies also include choices about how capabilities are used in situations—sequences of

Sealing the Deal Bargaining includes both indirect moves and explicit negotiations. Palestinians got a seat at the table in formal Arab-Israeli peace negotiations only in 1991, and the Israeli and PLO leaders first shook hands in 1993. But for decades Israel and the PLO used various power capabilities as leverage in implicit bargaining with each other.

actions designed for maximum effect; the use of deception; the creation of alliances; the use of contingency plans; and so forth. Depending on the situation, most power strategies mix economic instruments (trade, aid, loans, investment, boycotts) with military ones. (In the short term, within a given situation such plans are called *tactics*.)

Strategies include whether (and in what situations) a state is willing to use its power capabilities. For example, in the Vietnam War the United States had overall power capabilities far superior to those of the Vietnamese communists but lost the war because it was unwilling or unable to commit the resources necessary or use them effectively. The *will* of a nation or leader is hard to estimate. Even if leaders make explicit their intention to fight over an issue, they might be bluffing.

The strategic actions of China in recent years exemplify the concept of strategy as rational deployment of power capabilities. China's central foreign policy goal is to prevent the independence of Taiwan, which China considers an integral part of its territory (as does the United Nations and, at least in theory, the United States). Taiwan's government was set up to represent all of China in 1949, when the nationalists took refuge there after losing to the communists in China's civil war. Since 1949, Taiwan has operated more and more independently, and many Taiwanese favor independence. China does not have the military power to invade Taiwan successfully, but it has declared repeatedly that it will go to war if Taiwan declares independence. So far, even though such a war might be irrational on China's part, the threat has deterred Taiwan from formally declaring independence. China might lose such a war, but would certainly inflict immense damage on Taiwan. In 1996, China held war games near Taiwan, firing missiles over the sea. The United States sent two aircraft carriers to signal China that its exercises must not go too far.

Atlas CD
Taiwan, Recent
Decades
Article

Not risking war by declaring independence, Taiwan instead has engaged in diplomacy to gain influence in the world. It lobbies the U.S. Congress, asks for admission to the UN and other world organizations, and grants foreign aid to the 30 or so countries that recognize Taiwan's government. In 1999, Taiwan's president declared that relations with China should be on a "state-to-state" basis, edging closer to declaring independence.

China has used its own diplomacy to counter these moves. It breaks diplomatic relations with countries that recognize Taiwan, and it punishes any moves in the direction of Taiwanese independence. Half the countries that recognize Taiwan are in the Caribbean and Central America, leading to a competition for influence in the region. China has tried to counter Taiwanese ties with those countries by manipulating various positive and negative leverages. For example, in Panama, where China is a major user of the Panama Canal (which reverted to Panama from U.S. ownership in 1999), Taiwan has cultivated close relations, invested in a container port, and suggested hiring guest workers from Panama in Taiwan. But China has implicitly threatened to restrict Panama's access to Hong Kong, or to reregister China's many Panamanian-registered ships in the Bahamas instead. (Bahamas broke with Taiwan in 1997 after a Chinese conglomerate promised to invest in a container port in the Bahamas.)

Two of the five vetoes China has ever used in the UN Security Council were to block peacekeeping forces in countries that extended recognition to Taiwan. With its more recent veto, when the former Yugoslav republic of Macedonia recognized Taiwan in 1999 (in exchange for $1 billion in aid), China terminated a UN peacekeeping mission there at a time of great instability in next-door Kosovo. By contrast, when its Taiwan interests are secure, China cooperates on issues of world order. For example, although China opposed the Gulf War, it did not veto the UN resolution authorizing it.

These Chinese strategies mobilize various capabilities, from missiles to diplomats to industrial conglomerates, in a coherent effort to influence the outcome of China's most important international issue. Strategy thus amplifies China's power. Similarly, during the Cold War China used strategy to amplify power, by playing a balancer role between two superpowers and by playing up the importance of the global South, which it claimed to lead.

Web Link
Camp David

Some individual actors too are better than others at using their capabilities strategically. For instance, U.S. President Jimmy Carter in the 1970s used the great-power capabilities available to him, but his own strategic and interpersonal skills seem to have been the key to success in the Camp David agreements (which achieved the U.S. foreign-policy goal of an Egyptian-Israeli treaty). Good strategies bring together power capabilities for maximum effect, but poor strategies make inefficient use of available capabilities. Of course, even the most skillful leader never has total control of an international situation, but can make best use of the opportunities available while minimizing the effects of bad luck.

In the context of bargaining, actors use various strategies to employ leverage in an effort to move the final agreement point closer to their own positions. One common

Amplifying Power   Coherent strategy can help a state to make the most of its power. China's foreign policy is generally directed toward its most important regional interests, above all preventing Taiwan's formal independence. Despite conflicts with a number of its neighbors, China has had no military engagements for two decades. Here, China uses its veto in the UN Security Council for only the fifth time ever, to end a peacekeeping mission in Macedonia, which had just established ties with Taiwan (1999).

bargaining strategy is to start with extreme demands and then gradually compromise them in an effort to end up close to one's true (but concealed) position. Another strategy is to "drive a hard bargain" by sticking closely to one's original position in the belief that the other participant will eventually accept it. U.S. Secretary of State Henry Kissinger in the 1970s, however, used a policy of preemptive concessions to induce movement on the other side and get to a middle-ground agreement quickly in few steps.

Another common strategy is *fractionation*—splitting up a complex issue into a number of small components so that progress may be sought on solvable pieces. The Arab-Israeli negotiations that began in 1991 had many sets of talks concurrently working on various pieces of the problem. The opposite approach, which some bargainers prefer, is to lump together diverse issues—called *linkage*—so that compromises on one can be traded against another in a grand deal. This was the case in the Yalta negotiations of 1945 among the United States, Britain, and the Soviet Union. On the table simultaneously were such matters as the terms of occupation of Germany, the Soviet presence in Eastern Europe, the strategy for defeating Japan, and the creation of the United Nations.

Reciprocity, Deterrence, and Arms Races

To have the best effect, strategic bargaining over IR outcomes should take into account the other actor's own goals and strategies. Only then can one predict which forms of leverage may induce the other actor to take the actions one desires. But this can be a problem: often states do not know each others' true intentions but can only observe each others' actions and statements (which may be lies). For example, just days before Saddam Hussein's invasion of Kuwait, both U.S. leaders and those in Kuwait interpreted Saddam's actions as intended to threaten an attack but not actually to carry one out.

One very effective strategy for influencing another actor whose plans are not known is **reciprocity**—a response in kind to the other's actions. A strategy of reciprocity uses positive forms of leverage as promises of rewards (if the actor does what one wants); simultaneously it uses negative forms of leverage as threats of punishment (if the actor does not refrain from doing what one does not want). Reciprocity is effective because it is easy to understand. After one has demonstrated one's ability and willingness to reciprocate—gaining a reputation for consistency of response—the other actor can easily calculate the costs of failing to cooperate or the benefits of cooperating.

Reciprocity can be an effective strategy for achieving cooperation in a situation of conflicting interests. If one side expresses willingness to cooperate and promises to reciprocate the other's cooperative and conflictual actions, the other side has great incentive to work out a cooperative bargain. And because reciprocity is relatively easy to interpret, the vow of future reciprocity often need not be stated explicitly. For example, in 1969 China's relations with the United States had been on ice for 20 years. A total U.S. economic embargo against China was holding back the latter's economic development. China's support of North Vietnam was costing many American lives. The two states were not on speaking terms. President Nixon (and adviser Kissinger) decided to try a signal to China in hopes of improving relations (splitting China away from North Vietnam and further away from the Soviet Union). Nixon slightly relaxed the U.S. trade embargo against China. Three days later, with no explicit connection to the U.S. move, China released three U.S. citizens whose boat had earlier drifted into Chinese waters. China reciprocated other U.S. initiatives in the following months, and the two states resumed formal talks within six months. By 1972, Nixon visited China in a spirit of rapprochement. Similarly, in 1992 when President Bush sold fighter jets to Taiwan (to boost the economy in an election year, against China's wishes), China soon sold missiles to Pakistan (against U.S. wishes), though no explicit connection between the two actions was made by either side.

Reciprocity can also help achieve cooperation in the sense of refraining from an undesired action. This is the intent of the strategy of **deterrence**—the threat to punish another actor if it takes a certain negative action (especially attacking one's own state or one's allies). The slogan "peace through strength" reflects this approach. If deterrence works, its effects are almost invisible; its success is measured in attacks that did not occur. Nuclear deterrence is the threat to use nuclear weapons if another state does so.

Generally, advocates of deterrence believe that conflicts are more likely to escalate into war when one party to the conflict is weak. In this view, building up military capabilities usually convinces the stronger party that a resort to military leverage would not succeed, so conflicts are less likely to escalate into violence. A strategy of **compellence**, sometimes used after deterrence fails, refers to the use of force to make another actor take some action (rather than refrain from taking an action). Generally it is harder to get another state to change course (the purpose of compellence) than it is to get it to refrain from changing course (the purpose of deterrence).

One strategy used to try to compel compliance by another state is *escalation*—a series of negative sanctions of increasing severity applied in order to induce another actor to take some action. In theory, the less severe actions establish credibility—showing the first actor's willingness to exert its power on the issue—and the pattern of escalation establishes the high costs of future sanctions if the second actor does not cooperate. These should induce the second actor to comply, assuming that it finds the potential costs of the escalating punishments to be greater than the costs of compliance.

Web Link
Escalation

U.S. actions against Saddam prior to the Gulf War illustrate the strategy of escalation. First came statements of condemnation, then UN resolutions, then formation of an alliance with power clearly superior to Iraq's. Next came the application of economic sanctions, then a military buildup with an implicit threat of force, then explicit threats of force, and finally ultimatums threatening force after a deadline. In this case the strategy did not induce compliance, and only military defeat induced Iraq to accept U.S. terms.

Escalation can be dangerous (especially when with an adversary not as easily defeated as Iraq was). During the Cold War, many IR scholars worried that a conventional war could lead to nuclear war if the superpowers tried to apply escalation strategies. In fact, side by side with the potential for eliciting cooperation, reciprocity in general contains a danger of runaway hostility. When two sides reciprocate but never manage to put relations on a cooperative footing, the result can be a drawn-out, nasty, tit-for-tat exchange of punishments. This characterizes Israeli relations with Islamic guerrillas in southern Lebanon.

An **arms race** is a reciprocal process in which two (or more) states build up military capabilities in response to each other. Since each wants to act prudently against a threat (often a bit overblown in the leaders' perceptions), the attempt to reciprocate leads to a runaway production of weapons by both sides. The mutual escalation of threats erodes confidence, reduces cooperation, and makes it more likely that a crisis (or accident) could cause one side to strike first and start a war rather than wait for the other side to strike. The arms race process was illustrated vividly in the U.S.-Soviet nuclear arms race, which created arsenals of tens of thousands of nuclear weapons on each side.

Rationality

Consistent with the bargaining framework just outlined, most realists (and many nonrealists) assume that those who wield power behave as **rational actors** in their efforts to influence others. First, this rationality implies that the actor exercising power is a single entity that can "think" about its actions coherently and make choices. This is called the *unitary actor* assumption, or sometimes the *strong leader*

Internal Divisions The unitary actor assumption holds that states make important decisions as though they were single individuals able to act in the national interest. For example, Pakistan's decision to build nuclear weapons would reflect decisions of Pakistan's leadership as a unitary entity, rather than conflicting pressure of factions and organizations with differing interests. In truth, Pakistan's Benazir Bhutto (1988) as prime minister struggled frequently with her country's military leadership about national policies.

assumption, and it is used to describe the nature of states as international actors. Although useful, this simplification does not capture the complexity of how states actually arrive at decisions (see Chapter 3).

Second, the assumption of rationality implies that states and other international actors can identify their interests and put priorities on various interests. A state's actions seek to advance its interests. Again, the assumption is a simplification, because the interests of particular politicians, parties, economic sectors, or regions of a country often conflict. Yet realists assume that the exercise of power attempts to advance the **national interest**—the interests of the state itself. President Kennedy, for instance, said that "every nation determines its policies in terms of its own interests."[1]

But what are the interests of a state? Are they the interests of domestic groups (see Chapter 3)? The need to prevail in conflicts with other states (see Chapter 4)? Does the national interest demand cooperation with the international community for mutual benefit (see Chapter 6)? There is no simple answer. Some realists simply define the national interest as maximizing power—a debatable assumption.

Third, rationality implies that actors are able to perform a **cost-benefit analysis**—calculating the costs incurred by a possible action and the benefits it is likely to bring.

---

[1]Address at Mormon Tabernacle, Salt Lake City, UT, September 26, 1963.

Applying power incurs costs and should produce commensurate gains. As in the problem of estimating power, one has to add up different dimensions in such a calculation. For instance, states presumably do not initiate wars that they expect to lose, except in cases where they stand to gain political benefits, domestic or international, that outweigh the costs of losing the war. But it is not easy to tally intangible political benefits against the tangible costs of a war. Even in a winning war, a rational actor can miscalculate costs or benefits, or calculate on the basis of faulty information. And, again, human behavior and fortune (luck) are unpredictable.

These three assumptions about rationality—that states are unitary actors, that they have coherent interests, and that they can make cost-benefit calculations—are simplifications that not all IR scholars accept. But realists consider these simplifications quite useful because they allow scholars to explain in a general way the actions of diverse actors. Power in IR has been compared with money in economics, as a universal measure. In this view, just as firms compete for money in economic markets, states compete for power in the international system.

In order to provide a general explanation of state actions, realism makes a fourth assumption, implicit in the parallel to economics. This is the assumption that all states (or their leaders) have basically the same values and interests—*intersubjective preferences*. (The outcomes valued by an actor are called preferences or *utility*.) Economists assume that everyone prefers more money to less. Realists assume that all states prefer more power to less.

This assumption has been criticized. If a state leader prefers upholding his or her honor by fighting a losing war rather than being dictated to, such an action is rational in terms of the leader's own preferences—even though a U.S. college student or a European prime minister might find it inexplicable in terms of Western cultural norms.

Despite criticism, realists argue that rational-actor models capture not all but the most important aspects of IR. These simplified models provide the foundations for a large body of IR research that represents international bargaining relationships mathematically. By accepting the limitations of the four assumptions of rationality, IR scholars can build very general and abstract models of international relationships.

Game Theory   **Game theory** is a branch of mathematics concerned with predicting bargaining outcomes. A game is a setting in which two or more players choose among alternative moves, either once or repeatedly. Each combination of moves (by all players) results in a set of payoffs (utility) to each player. The payoffs can be tangible items such as money or any intangible items of value. Game theory aims to deduce likely outcomes (what moves players will make), given the players' preferences and the possible moves open to them. Games are sometimes called formal models.

Game theory was first used extensively in IR in the 1950s and 1960s by scholars trying to understand U.S.-Soviet nuclear war contingencies. Moves were decisions to use nuclear weapons in certain ways, and payoffs were outcomes of the war. The use of game theory to study international interactions has become more extensive among IR scholars in recent years, especially among realists, who accept the assumptions about rationality. To analyze a game mathematically, one assumes that each player chooses a move rationally, to maximize its payoff.

Different kinds of situations are represented by different classes of games, as defined by the number of players and the structure of the payoffs. One basic distinction is between **zero-sum games**, in which one player's gain is by definition equal to the other's loss, and *non-zero-sum games*, in which it is possible for both players to gain (or lose). In a zero-sum game there is no point in communication or cooperation between the players because their interests are diametrically opposed. But in a non-zero-sum game, coordination of moves can maximize the total payoff to the players, although each may still maneuver to gain a greater share of that total payoff.

Analysis of a game entails searching for a *solution*—a set of moves by all the players such that no player can increase its payoff by changing its move. It is the outcome at which rational players will arrive. Some simple games have one solution, but many games have multiple solutions or no stable solution.

In the game called *Prisoner's Dilemma (PD)*, the one most commonly studied, rational players choose moves that produce an outcome in which all players are worse off than under a different set of moves. They all could do better, but as individual rational actors they are unable to achieve this outcome. How can this be?

The original story tells of two prisoners questioned separately by a prosecutor. The prosecutor knows they committed a bank robbery but has only enough evidence to convict them of illegal possession of a gun unless one of them confesses. The prosecutor tells each prisoner that if he confesses and his partner doesn't confess, he will go free. If his partner confesses and he doesn't, he will get a long prison term for bank robbery (while the partner goes free). If both confess, they will get a somewhat reduced term. If neither confesses, they will be convicted on the gun charge and serve a short sentence. The story assumes that neither prisoner will have a chance to retaliate later, that only the immediate outcomes matter, and that each prisoner cares only about himself.

This game has a single solution: both prisoners will confess. Each will reason as follows: "If my partner is going to confess, then I should confess too, because I will get a slightly shorter sentence that way. If my partner is not going to confess, then I should still confess because I will go free that way instead of serving a short sentence." The other prisoner follows the same reasoning. The dilemma is that by following their individually rational choices both prisoners will end up serving a fairly long sentence when they could have both served a short one by cooperating (keeping their mouths shut).

In IR, the PD game has been used to gain insight into arms races. Consider the decisions of India and Pakistan about whether to build sizable nuclear weapons arsenals. Both have the ability to do so. In 1998, when India detonated underground nuclear explosions to test weapons designs, Pakistan promptly followed suit. Now, neither side can know whether the other is secretly building up an arsenal, unless they reach an arms control agreement with strict verification provisions. To analyze the game, one must assign values to each possible outcome—often called a *preference ordering*—for each player. This is not simple: if one misjudges the value a player puts on a particular outcome, one may draw wrong conclusions from the game.

The following preferences regarding possible outcomes are plausible: the best outcome would be that one player but not the other had a nuclear arsenal (the expense of building nuclear weapons would be worth it because one could then use them as leverage); second best would be for neither to go nuclear (no leverage, but no expense); third best would be for both to develop nuclear arsenals (a major expense without gaining leverage); worst would be to forgo nuclear weapons oneself while the other developed them (and thus be subject to blackmail).

TABLE 2.2 Payoff Matrix in India-Pakistan PD Game

		Pakistan	
		Cooperate	Defect
India	Cooperate	(3,3)	(1,4)
	Defect	(4,1)	(2,2)

Note: First number in each group is India's payoff, second is Pakistan's. The number 4 is highest payoff, 1 lowest.

The game can be summarized in a *payoff matrix* (see Table 2.2). The first number in each cell is India's payoff, and the second number is Pakistan's. To keep things simple, 4 indicates the highest payoff, and 1 the lowest. As is conventional, a decision to refrain from building nuclear weapons is called "cooperation," and a decision to proceed with nuclear weapons is called "defection." The dilemma here parallels that of the prisoners just discussed. Each state's leader reasons: "If they go nuclear, we must; if they don't, we'd be crazy not to." The model seems to predict an inevitable Indian–Pakistani nuclear arms race, though both states would do better to avoid one.

The model can be made more realistic by allowing the players to play the game repeatedly; as in most IR contexts, the same actors will bargain over this issue repeatedly over a sustained time period. Game theorists have shown that in a *repeated* PD game, the possibility of reciprocity can make it rational to cooperate. Now the state leader reasons: "If we defect now, they will respond by defecting and both of us will lose; if we cooperate they might cooperate too; and if we are suckered once we can defect in the future." The keys to cooperation are the non–zero-sum nature of the PD game and the ability of each player to respond in the future to present moves.

Through analysis of this and other games, IR researchers try to predict what rational actors would do in various situations that may resemble those occurring in world or regional politics. Games can capture and simplify the fundamental dynamics of various bargaining situations. However, a game-theoretic analysis is only as good as the assumptions that go into it. In particular, the results of the analysis depend on the preferences that players are assumed to have about outcomes. And it is difficult to test empirically either the assumptions or the predictions of a formal model against the realities of IR, which are so much more complex in practice.

The International System

States interact within a set of well-defined and long-established "rules of the game" governing what is considered a state and how states treat each other. Together these rules shape the international system as we know it.

Anarchy and Sovereignty
Realists emphasize that the rules of the international system create **anarchy**—a term that implies not complete chaos or absence of

structure and rules, but rather the lack of a central government that can enforce rules. In domestic society within states, governments can enforce contracts, deter participants from breaking rules, and use their monopoly on legally sanctioned violence to enforce a system of law. Both democracies and dictatorships provide central government enforcement of a system of rules. Lack of such a government among states is what realists mean by anarchy. No central authority enforces rules and ensures compliance with norms of conduct. The power of one state is countered only by the power of other states. States must rely on *self-help*, which they supplement with allies and the (sometimes) constraining power of international norms.

Some people think that only a world government can solve this problem. Others think that adequate order can be provided by international organizations and agreements, short of world government (see Chapter 6). But most realists think that IR cannot escape from a state of anarchy and will continue to be dangerous as a result. In this anarchic world, realists emphasize prudence as a great virtue in foreign policy. States should pay attention not to the intentions of other states but rather to their capabilities.

Despite its anarchy, the international system is far from chaotic. The great majority of state interactions closely adhere to **norms (of behavior)**—shared expectations about what behavior is considered proper. Norms change over time, slowly, but the most basic norms of the international system have changed little in recent centuries.

Web Link
Sovereignty

Sovereignty—traditionally the most important norm—means that a government has the right, at least in principle, to do whatever it wants in its own territory. States are separate, are autonomous, and answer to no higher authority (due to anarchy). In principle, all states are equal in status if not in power. Sovereignty also means that states are not supposed to interfere in the internal affairs of other states. Although states do try to influence each other (exert power) on matters of trade, alliances, war, and so on, they are not supposed to meddle in the internal politics and decision processes of other states. For example, it would be inappropriate for Russia or Britain to endorse a candidate for U.S. president. (This rule is often bent in practice.)

In practice, states have a harder and harder time warding off interference in their affairs. Such "internal" matters as human rights or self-determination are, increasingly, concerns for the international community. For example, in the Helsinki agreements that codified East-West détente in the Cold War, the Soviet Union and Eastern Europe promised to respect human rights within their own borders (an internal affair). Also, the integration of global economic markets and telecommunications makes it easier than ever for ideas to penetrate state borders.

Atlas CD
Boundaries
Map Trek

States are based on territory. Respect for the territorial integrity of all states, within recognized borders, is an important principle of IR. Many of today's borders are the result of past wars, or were imposed arbitrarily by third parties such as colonizers. Such borders create many problems—the splitting of nations or ethnic groups into different states, the creation of oddly shaped states that may lack resources or access to ports, and so forth (see pp. 147–150). Despite these imperfections, the international system places the highest value on respect for internationally recognized borders. Almost all of the world's land territory falls under the sovereign control of existing states; very little is considered "up for grabs" (high seas are outside any state's territory; see Chapter 8).

THE INFORMATION REVOLUTION — Cyberspace versus Sovereignty?

The interstate system is based on states' sovereignty within their territories. In the 1990s, the astounding growth of the Internet and World Wide Web created "cyberspace." It is a world of business relationships and communities with shared personal interests, in which geography is irrelevant. How is the growth of cyberspace changing state sovereignty?

To explore this question, go to www.IRtext.com

The territorial nature of the interstate system reflects the origins of that system when agrarian societies relied on agriculture to generate wealth. In today's world, where trade and technology rather than land create wealth, the territorial state may be less important. Information-based economies are linked across borders instantly, and the idea that the state has a hard shell seems archaic. The accelerating revolution in information technologies may dramatically affect the territorial state system in the coming years.

Membership in the international system rests on general recognition (by other states) of a government's sovereignty within its territory. This recognition is extended formally through diplomatic relations and by membership in the UN. It does not imply that a government has popular support but only that it controls the state's territory and agrees to assume its obligations in the international system—to accept internationally recognized borders, to assume the international debts of the previous government, and to refrain from interfering in other states' internal affairs.

States have developed norms of diplomacy to facilitate their interactions. An embassy is considered to be territory of the home state, not the country where it is located (see pp. 316–318). The U.S. embassy in China, for instance, harbored a wanted Chinese dissident for two years after the Tiananmen Square crackdown of 1989, and Chinese troops did not simply come in and take him away. To do so would have been a violation of U.S. territorial integrity.

Realists acknowledge that the rules of IR often create a **security dilemma**—a situation in which states' actions taken to assure their own security (such as deploying more military forces) tend to threaten the security of other states. The responses of those other states (such as deploying more of their own military forces) in turn threaten the first state. The dilemma parallels the Prisoner's Dilemma game discussed earlier; it is a prime cause of arms races in which states waste large sums of money on mutually threatening weapons that do not ultimately provide security. The security dilemma is a negative consequence of anarchy in the international system. Realists tend to see the dilemma as unsolvable, while liberals think it can be solved through the development of norms and institutions (see Chapters 3 and 6).

As we shall see in later chapters, changes in technology and in norms are undermining the traditional principles of territorial integrity and state autonomy in IR. Some

Still Sovereign Territory   Sovereignty and territorial integrity are central norms governing the behavior of states. They give states control within established borders. Embassies are considered the home country's territory. Here, the ruined Russian Embassy grounds in the capital of Afghanistan become a refuge to 15,000 people displaced by war (2000).

IR scholars find states to be practically obsolete as the main actors in world politics, as some integrate into larger entities and others fragment into smaller units. Other scholars find the international system quite enduring in its structure and state units. One of its most enduring features is the balance of power.

Balance of Power

In the anarchy of the international system, the most reliable brake on the power of one state is the power of other states. The term **balance of power** refers to the general concept of one or more states' power being used to balance that of another state or group of states. The term is used in several ways and is imprecisely defined. Balance of power can refer to any ratio of power capabilities between states or alliances; or it can mean only a relatively equal ratio. Alternatively, balance of power can refer to the process by which counterbalancing coalitions have repeatedly formed in history to prevent one state from conquering an entire region. The theory of balance of power argues that such counterbalancing occurs regularly and maintains the stability of the international system. The system is stable in that its rules and principles stay the same: state sovereignty does not collapse into a universal empire. This stability does not, however, imply peace; it is rather a stability maintained by means of recurring wars that adjust power relations.

Web Link
Balance of
Power

Alliances (to be discussed shortly) play a key role in the balance of power. Building up one's own capabilities against a rival is a form of power balancing, but forming an alliance against a threatening state is often quicker, cheaper, and more effective. When such a counterbalancing coalition has a geopolitical element—physically hemming in the threatening state—the power-balancing strategy is called containment. In the Cold War, the United States encircled the Soviet Union with military and political alliances to prevent Soviet territorial expansion.

Sometimes a particular state deliberately becomes a balancer (in its region or the world), shifting its support to oppose whatever state or alliance is strongest at the moment. Britain played this role on the European continent for centuries, and China played it in the Cold War. But states do not always balance against the strongest actor. Sometimes smaller states "jump on the bandwagon" of the most powerful state; this has been called bandwagoning as opposed to balancing. Furthermore, small states create variations on power-balancing themes when they play off rival great powers against each other. For instance, Cuba during the Cold War received massive Soviet subsidies by putting itself in the middle of the U.S.-Soviet rivalry.

In the post–Cold War era of U.S. dominance, balance-of-power theory would predict closer relations among Russia, China, and even France—great powers that are not close U.S. military allies. These predictions appear to be on the mark. Russian-Chinese relations have improved dramatically in such areas as arms trade and demilitarization of the border. In 1997, the two presidents declared jointly that "No country should seek hegemony, practice power politics, or monopolize international affairs."[2] The "country" referred to could only be the United States. On a 1999 visit to China, Russian president Yeltsin pointedly reminded the United States—which had criticized Russia's war in Chechnya, in contrast to China's support for it—that "Russia has a full arsenal of nuclear weapons." France, for its part, contested U.S. positions vigorously in global trade negotiations and discussions of NATO's command structure, and sometimes sided with Russia and China in the UN Security Council.

Great Powers and Middle Powers

Power, of course, varies greatly from one state to another. The *most powerful* states in the system exert most of the influence on international events and therefore get the most attention from IR scholars. By almost any measure of power, a handful of states possess the majority of the world's power resources. At most a few dozen states have any real influence beyond their immediate locality. These are called the great powers and middle powers in the international system.

Although there is no firm dividing line, **great powers** are generally considered the half dozen or so most powerful states. Until the past century the great power club was exclusively European. Sometimes great powers' status is formally recognized in an international structure such as the nineteenth-century Concert of Europe or the UN Security Council. In general, great powers may be distinguished by the criterion that they can be defeated militarily only by another great power. Great powers also tend to share a global outlook based on national interests far from their home territories.

The great powers generally have the world's strongest military forces and the strongest economies to pay for military forces and for other power capabilities. These large economies in turn rest on some combination of large populations, plentiful natural resources, advanced technology, and educated labor forces. Because power is based on these underlying resources, membership in the great-power system changes slowly.

---

[2] *New York Times*, April 24, 1997: A3.

Only rarely does a great power—even one defeated in a massive war—lose its status as a great power, because its size and long-term economic potential change slowly. Thus Germany and Japan, decimated in World War II, are powerful today and Russia, after gaining and then losing the rest of the Soviet Union, is still considered a great power.

What states are great powers today? Seven states appear to meet the criteria: the United States, Russia, China, Japan, Germany, France, and Britain. Certainly the United States qualifies. In total GDP, a measure of potential power, the United States ranks highest by far at almost $8 trillion per year (2000 data). Because of its historical role of world leadership (especially in and after World War II), and its predominant military might, the United States is considered the world's only superpower.

China, with a total GDP of almost $4 trillion, is or soon will be the world's second largest economy. China's GDP is hard to estimate—another method would put it at less than $2 trillion. In any case, China's sheer size (more than 1 billion people) and its rapid economic growth (10 percent annually in the 1990s) make it a powerful state. China has a large but not very modern military, and its orientation is regional rather than global. But, with a credible nuclear arsenal and a seat on the UN Security Council, China qualifies as a great power. It is expected to play a central role in world politics in the twenty-first century. Japan ranks third (perhaps second), with a GDP of $3 trillion. Along with Germany ($1.5 trillion GDP), Japan is an economic great power, but both countries' military roles in international security affairs have been curtailed since World War II. Nonetheless, both Japan and Germany have large and capable military forces, and both have been edging toward using military forces beyond their own territories or regions.

Russia, even after the breakup of the Soviet Union, has a GDP close to $1 trillion—again a hard one to estimate—and very large (though run-down) military forces including a massive nuclear arsenal. France and Britain finish out the list at just more than $1 trillion GDP each. With Russia, they were winners in World War II and have been active military powers since then. Although much reduced in stature from their colonial heydays, they still qualify as great powers by most standards.

The great powers thus include the five permanent members of the UN Security Council—the United States, Russia, France, Britain, and China. The same five states are also the members of the "club" possessing large nuclear weapons arsenals (there are also several recent smaller-scale nuclear states). In world political and economic affairs, Germany and Japan are also great powers (they would like Security Council seats, too; see p. 285). These seven great powers account for about half of the world's total GDP—and hence, presumably, about half of the total power in the world. This concentration of power is especially strong in practice because the remaining half of the world's power is split up among nearly 200 other states (see Figure 2.1).

The slow change in great-power status is evident. Britain and France have been great powers for 500 years, Russia and Germany for more than 250 years, the United States and Japan for about 100 years, and China for 50 years. Only six other states were ever (but no longer are) considered great powers: Italy, Austria (Austria-Hungary), Spain, Turkey (the Ottoman Empire), Sweden, and the Netherlands.

Middle powers rank somewhat below the great powers in terms of their influence on world affairs. Some are large but not highly industrialized; others have specialized capabilities but are small. Some aspire to regional dominance, and many have consider-

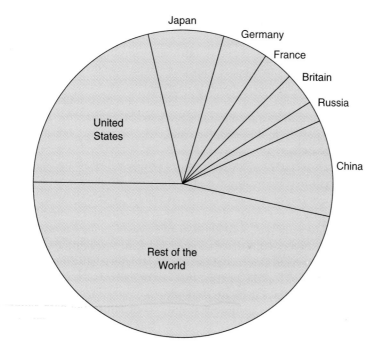

FIGURE 2.1   Great-Power Shares of World GDP, 1998
Note: GDP calculated by purchasing power

able influence in their regions. Even more than with great powers, it is hard to establish a criterion for distinguishing middle powers.

The top rungs of middle powers are easier to identify. Brazil ($1 trillion) and India ($1.5 trillion) are both regional giants that some scholars see as rising powers and possible new great powers in this century. In terms of total GDP, Italy and Canada are just below the range of France and Britain and some would consider them great powers. Both states belong to the Group of Eight (G8) economic powers (along with the United States, Germany, Japan, France, Britain, and Russia, which joined in 1998). Mexico, Indonesia, South Korea, and Spain all have GDPs greater than half a trillion dollars, and are active middle powers. Below this level, GDP estimates become more closely bunched and the order of national economies becomes much harder to sort out.

A list of middle powers (not everyone would agree on it) might include the following states. The first tier would include large states with substantial economic activity, fairly strong military forces, and considerable regional political influence: Canada, Italy, India, Brazil, Mexico, South Korea, Iran, and Turkey. A second tier could include important regional actors with somewhat smaller economies or with strong capabilities on specific dimensions of power: Taiwan, Indonesia, Australia, Spain, Ukraine, Argentina, Israel, Saudi Arabia, Egypt, Pakistan, South Africa, and Kazakhstan. A third tier might include smaller rich states along with middle-sized, middle-income ones and regional "activists" that exercise power beyond their size: the

Atlas CD
Brazil
Map

Netherlands, Belgium, Sweden, Greece, Poland, Nigeria, Venezuela, Vietnam, Syria, Iraq, Serbia, and North Korea.

Middle powers have not received as much attention in IR as have great powers. These states do, however, often come into play in the specific regional conflicts that dominate the day-to-day flow of international news. Smaller, weaker states (not even of middle-power strength) also are often at the center of specific conflicts and crises. But their own actions have only minor influence on world politics; the actions of great powers and middle powers in those conflicts and crises have more impact.

Power Distribution   With each state's power balanced by other states, the most important characteristic of an international system in the view of many realists is the *distribution* of power among states in an international system. Power distribution as a concept can apply to all the states in the world or to just one region, but most often it refers to the great-power system (with most of the world's total power capabilities). Neorealists (so called because they have adopted and refined realism) try to explain patterns of international events in terms of the system structure—the international distribution of power—rather than the internal makeup of individual states. **Neorealism** is thus also called structural realism. Neorealists often use game theory and related models in such analyses. Compared to traditional realism, neorealism is more scientific in the sense of proposing general laws to explain events, but neorealism has lost some of the richness of traditional realism, which took account of many complex elements (geography, willpower, diplomacy, etc.).

Sometimes an international power distribution (world or regional) is described in terms of polarity (a term adopted from physics), which refers to the number of independent power centers in the system. This concept encompasses both the underlying power of various participants and their alliance groupings.

In a **multipolar system** there are typically five or six centers of power, which are not grouped into alliances. Each state participates independently and on relatively equal terms with the others. They may form a coalition of the whole for mutual security through coordination of efforts. Some IR researchers think that multipolarity provides a context for smooth interaction—there are always enough actors present to prevent one from predominating. But to other IR scholars a multipolar system is particularly dangerous, lacking the discipline that predominant states or alliance blocs impose. In a sense, both views are correct: in the classical multipolar balance of power, the great-power system itself was stable but wars were frequently used as power-adjusting mechanisms.

At the other extreme, a unipolar system has a single center of power around which all others revolve. Called hegemony, this will be discussed shortly. The predominance of a single state tends to reduce the incidence of war; the hegemonic state performs some governmental functions, somewhat reducing anarchy in the international system.

A bipolar system has two predominant states or two great rival alliance blocs. Tight bipolar systems, such as the East-West standoff in the 1950s, may be distinguished from looser ones such as developed when China and (to a lesser extent) France split off from their alliance blocs. IR scholars do not agree about whether bipolar systems are relatively peaceful or warlike. The U.S.-Soviet standoff seemed to provide stability and peace to great-power relations (although an icy one). But rival blocs in Europe before World War I did not prove stable or peaceful.

In the fairly rare tripolar system there are three great centers of power (there is a tendency for a two-against-one alliance to form, creating bipolarity). Aspects of tripolarity can be found in the "strategic triangle" of the United States, the Soviet Union, and China in the 1960s and 1970s. Some scholars imagine that in coming decades a tripolar world will emerge, with rival power centers in North America, Europe, and East Asia.

These various polarities can be conceptualized as a pyramid or hierarchy of power in an international system. At the top is the most powerful state, with other great powers and middle powers arrayed below. Such a pyramid is similar to the dominance (or status) hierarchies that many animals use to regulate access to valuable resources such as food—the "pecking order." A multipolar system is one with a relatively flat pyramid—relative equality of status among actors. A unipolar system has a relatively steep pyramid with unequal status. The steepness of the pyramid represents the concentration of power in the international system.

Some IR scholars have argued that peace is best preserved by a relatively equal power distribution (multipolarity) because then no country has an opportunity to win easily. The empirical evidence for this theory, however, is not strong. The opposite proposition has more support: peace is best preserved by hegemony, and next best by bipolarity.

Such is the thrust of power transition theory. This theory holds that the largest wars result from challenges to the top position in the status hierarchy, when a rising power is surpassing (or threatening to surpass) the most powerful state. At such times, power is relatively equally distributed, and these are the most dangerous times for major wars. Status quo powers who are doing well under the old rules will try to maintain them, whereas challengers who feel locked out by the old rules may try to change them. Status disequilibrium refers to a difference between a rising power's status (formal position in the hierarchy) and its actual power. In such a situation, the rising power may suffer from relative deprivation—the feeling that it is not doing as well as others or as well as it deserves, even though its position may be improving in absolute terms. The classic example is Germany's rise in the nineteenth century, which gave it great-power capabilities even though it was left out of colonial territories and other signs of status.

Web Link
Status
Hierarchies
in IR

If the challenger does not start a war to displace the top power, the latter may provoke a "preventative" war to stop the rise of the challenger before it becomes too great a threat. Germany's intensive arms race with Britain (the top power) led to increasing hostility and the outbreak of World War I. After the war there was again a disparity between Germany's actual power (still considerable) and its harsh treatment under the terms of the Versailles Treaty. That disparity may have contributed to World War II.

According to power transition theory, then, peace among great powers results when one state is firmly in the top position, and the positions of others in the hierarchy are clearly defined and correspond with their actual underlying power. Such a situation usually results only from a great war, when one state predominates in power because its rivals and allies alike have been drained. Even then, the different rates of growth among great powers lead to a slow equalization of power and eventually the emergence of challengers: the system becomes more multipolar. For example, the U.S. predominance right after World War II gave way to the bipolar Cold War and perhaps now to a multipolar power structure. But the end of the Cold War also brought a return toward unipolarity—with the United States as the only superpower—so the outcome is complex.

The Enforcer   The United States is the world's most powerful single actor. Its ability and willingness to resume a role as hegemon—as after World War II—are important factors that will shape world order, but its role is still uncertain. This U.S. pilot, operating from an aircraft carrier in the Persian Gulf, helps enforce UN sanctions against Iraq, 1997.

Hegemony   Hegemony is the holding by one state of a preponderance of power in the international system, so that it can single-handedly dominate the rules and arrangements by which international political and economic relations are conducted. Such a state is called a *hegemon*. (Usually hegemony means domination of the world, but sometimes it refers to regional domination.) Sometimes the term is used to refer to the complex of ideas that rulers use to gain consent for their legitimacy and keep subjects in line. By extension, such a meaning in IR refers to the hegemony of ideas such as democracy and capitalism, and to the global predominance of U.S. culture (see pp. 440–441).

Most studies of hegemony point to two examples: Britain in the nineteenth century and the United States after World War II. Britain's predominance followed the defeat of its archrival France in the Napoleonic Wars. Both world trade and naval capabilities were firmly in British hands, as "Britannia ruled the waves." U.S. predominance followed the defeat of Germany and Japan (and the exhaustion of the Soviet Union, France, Britain, and China in the effort). In the late 1940s, the U.S. GDP was more than half the world's total; U.S. vessels carried the majority of the world's shipping; the U.S. military could single-handedly defeat any other state or combination of states; and only the United States had nuclear weapons. U.S. industry led the world in technology and productivity, and U.S. citizens enjoyed the world's highest standard of living.

As the extreme power disparities from major wars slowly diminish (states rebuild over years and decades), hegemonic decline may occur, particularly when hegemons have overextended themselves with costly military commitments. IR scholars do not agree about how far or fast U.S. hegemonic decline has proceeded, if at all, and whether international instability will result from such a decline. And beyond the U.S. and British cases, IR scholars do not agree on historical instances of hegemony. Some see the Netherlands in the early seventeenth century, or Spain in the sixteenth, as cases of hegemony.

The theory of hegemonic stability (see pp. 91–92) holds that hegemony provides some order in the international system, reducing anarchy, and provides some functions similar to a central government—deterring aggression, promoting free trade, and providing a hard currency that can be used as a world standard. Hegemons can help to resolve or at least keep in check conflicts among middle powers or small states.

From the perspective of less powerful states, of course, such hegemony may seem an infringement of state sovereignty, and the order it creates may seem unjust or illegitimate. For instance, China chafed under U.S.-imposed economic sanctions for 20 years after 1949, feeling itself encircled by U.S. military bases and hostile alliances led by the United States. To this day, Chinese leaders use the term *hegemony* as an insult, and the theory of hegemonic stability does not impress them.

Even in the United States itself there is considerable ambivalence about U.S. hegemony. U.S. foreign policy has historically alternated between *internationalist* and *isolationist* moods. It was founded as a breakaway from the European-based international system, and its growth in the nineteenth century was based on industrialization and expansion within North America. In World War I, the country waited three years to weigh in—and refused to join the League of Nations afterward. U.S. isolationism peaked in the 1930s; public opinion polls late in that decade showed 95 percent of the U.S. public opposed to participation in a future great European war, and about 70 percent opposed to joining with other nations to stop aggression.

Internationalists, such as Presidents Theodore Roosevelt and Woodrow Wilson, favored U.S. leadership and activism in world affairs. These views seemed vindicated by the failure of isolationism to prevent World War II (or to allow the United States to stay out of it). U.S. leaders after the war became alarmed by the threat of Soviet (and then Chinese) communism and drummed up U.S. public opinion to favor a strong internationalism during the Cold War. The United States became an activist, global superpower. Despite an inward-looking period after the Vietnam War, the United States has largely continued this internationalist stance ever since—despite a new cost consciousness and the emergence of a new isolationist camp reacting to displacements caused by globalization and free trade.

A second area of U.S. ambivalence is *unilateralism* versus *multilateralism* in U.S. internationalism. Multilateral approaches—working through international institutions—augment U.S. power and reduce costs, but they limit U.S. freedom of action. For example, the United States cannot always get the UN to do what it wants. Polls in the 1990s showed that a majority of U.S. citizens supported working through the UN and other multilateral institutions. However, members of the U.S. Congress, skeptical of the UN and international agencies, often favored a more unilateralist approach, in which the United States dictated terms and expected the world to comply. In the late 1990s Congress passed the *Helms-Burton Act,* which provides for sanctions against countries that do business in Cuba, and the *Iran-Libya Sanctions Act,* which imposes sanctions on countries that invest in Iran or Libya. These unilateralist U.S. policies, naturally, have been resisted by European states and Canada.

A third aspect of ambivalent U.S. hegemony is that of *morality* versus *realism*. Should the United States be a moral guiding light for the world—pursuing goals such as democracy and human rights—or should it concentrate on its own national interests, such as natural resources and geostrategic position? Most U.S. citizens do not want to be "the world's policeman," and some resent paying for the security of allies such as Japan and Europe. After the collapse of the Soviet Union, efforts to win congressional approval of foreign aid for Russia had to be couched in terms of U.S. interests (avoiding a return to costly Russian aggression), not humanitarian assistance or a moral obligation to help a nation achieve freedom and democracy. Yet the U.S. people also think of themselves as a caring nation and a beacon of hope for the world.

Alliances

An *alliance* is a coalition of states that coordinate their actions to accomplish some end. Most alliances are *formalized* in written treaties, concern a *common threat* and related issues of international security, and *endure* across a range of issues and a period of time. If actors' purposes in banding together were shorter term, less formal, or more issue specific, the association might be called a *coalition* rather than an alliance. Informal but enduring strategic *alignments* in a region are discussed shortly. But these terms are somewhat ambiguous. Two countries may have a formal alliance and yet be bitter enemies, such as the Soviet Union and China in the 1960s or NATO members Greece and Turkey today. Or, two countries may create the practical equivalent of an alliance without a formal treaty.

Purposes of Alliances

Alliances generally have the purpose of augmenting their members' power relative to other states. By pooling their power capabilities, two or more states can exert greater leverage in their bargaining with other states. For smaller states, alliances can be their most important power element, and for great powers the structure of alliances shapes the configuration of power in the system. Of all the elements of power, none can change as quickly and decisively as alliances.

Most alliances form in response to a perceived threat. When a state's power grows and threatens to overmatch that of its rivals, the latter often form an alliance to limit that power. Thucydides attributed the outbreak of the Peloponnesian Wars more than 2,000 years ago to the growing power of Athens, and to the fear that this growth caused in Sparta. Sparta turned to its neighbors in the Peloponnesian League, and that alliance defeated Athens.

Alliances are an important component of the balance of power. Except in the rare circumstance of hegemony, every state is weaker than some combination of other states. If states overstep norms of international conduct they may face a powerful alliance of opposing states. This happened to Iraq when it invaded Kuwait in 1990, as it had to Hitler's Germany in the 1940s and to Napoleon's France in the 1800s.

Realists emphasize the fluidity of alliances. Because of the autonomy of states, alliances can be made or broken fairly easily. Alliances are not marriages of love; they are marriages of convenience. Alliances are based on national interests, and can shift as national interests change. This fluidity helps the balance-of-power process to operate effectively.

Marriage of Convenience   Alliances, such as that between Kuwait and the United States, generally result from a convergence of practical interests, not sentimental or ideological reasons. Here, U.S. General Norman Schwarzkopf meets with the emir of Kuwait in 1991, shortly after the Gulf War.

As critics of realism point out, it is not simple or costless to break an alliance: one's reputation may suffer and future alliances may be harder to establish. There is an important norm that says that written treaties should be honored. So states often do adhere to alliance terms even when it is not in their short-term interest to do so.

Nonetheless, because of the nature of international anarchy, there is no mechanism to enforce contracts in IR—the possibility of turning against a friend is always present. Realists would agree with the statement of French president Charles de Gaulle (under whom France withdrew militarily from NATO and developed its own nuclear weapons in the 1960s): "Treaties are like roses and young girls. They last while they last."[3] One hears echoes of Napoleon, 150 years earlier: "Treaties are observed as long as they are in harmony with interests."[4]

Examples are many. Anticommunist Richard Nixon could cooperate with communist Mao Zedong because it was in both nations' interests to do so. Joseph Stalin could sign a nonaggression pact with a fascist, Adolf Hitler, and then cooperate with

---

[3] *Time*, July 12, 1963.
[4] Napoleon. *Maxims, 1804–1815*. See Tripp, Rhoda Thomas. *The International Thesaurus of Quotations*. New York: Thomas Y. Crowell, 1970.

the capitalist West against Hitler. Every time history brings another such reversal in alignments, many people are surprised or even shocked. Realists are not so surprised.

The fluidity of alliances deepens the security dilemma in a world of multiple actors. With only two states, it is possible to match capabilities so that both have adequate defense but cannot attack. But if one adds a third state, free to ally with either side, then each state has to build adequate defenses against the potential alliance of its enemy with the third state. The threat is greater and the security dilemma is harder to escape.

The nightmare of being overpowered looms large when a state faces a potential hostile alliance that could form overnight. For example, in a war Israel could defeat any of its neighbors alone. But to Israel it is only prudent to arm against the worst contingency. Israelis would not feel secure unless they could defeat all their neighbors together. Because the neighbors are not very aligned (and the most important, Egypt and Jordan, are at peace with Israel), Israel's military capabilities appear excessive to those neighbors.

Alliance cohesion is the ease with which the members hold together an alliance. Cohesion tends to be high when national interests converge and when cooperation within the alliance becomes institutionalized and habitual. When states with divergent interests form an alliance against a common enemy, the alliance may come apart if the threat subsides. It did, for instance, with the World War II U.S.-Soviet alliance. Even when alliance cohesion is high, as in NATO during the Cold War, conflicts may arise over **burden sharing** (who bears the costs of the alliance).

The credibility with which an alliance can deter an enemy depends on the alliance's cohesion as well as its total power capabilities. If an alliance is successful at displaying a common front and taking a unified line on issues, a potential enemy is more likely to believe that members will honor their alliance commitments (such as their promise to fight if an ally is attacked). An enemy may try to split the alliance by finding issues on which the interests of the members diverge. For instance, the United States subtly encouraged the Sino-Soviet split, and the Soviet Union subtly tried to wedge European states in NATO away from the United States.

Great powers often form alliances with smaller states, sometimes called client states. In the Cold War, each superpower extended a security umbrella over its allies. The issue of credibility in such an alliance is whether (and under what circumstances) the great power will assist its clients in a war. Extended deterrence refers to a strong state's use of threats to deter attacks on weaker clients—such as the U.S. threat to attack the Soviet Union if it invaded Western Europe.

Great powers face a real danger of being dragged into wars with each other over relatively unimportant regional issues if their respective clients go to war. If the great powers do not come to their clients' protection, they may lose credibility with other clients, but if they do, they may end up fighting a costly war. This happened to Germany when Austria-Hungary helped drag it into World War I.

Web Link
NATO

NATO and the U.S.–Japanese Security Treaty
At present, two important formal alliances dominate the international security scene. By far the more powerful (although with a somewhat uncertain future in the post–Cold War era), is the **North Atlantic Treaty Organization (NATO)**, which encompasses Western Europe and North America. With GDP as a measure of power, the 19 NATO members possess nearly half the world total (roughly twice the power of the United States alone). Members are the United States, Canada, Britain, France, Germany, Italy,

Alliance of the Strong   The NATO alliance has been the world's strongest military force since 1949; its mission in the post–Cold War era is somewhat uncertain. Here, President Kennedy reviews U.S. forces in Germany, 1963.

Belgium, the Netherlands, Luxembourg, Denmark, Norway, Iceland, Spain, Portugal, Greece, Turkey, Poland, the Czech Republic, and Hungary. At NATO headquarters in Brussels, Belgium, military staffs from the member countries coordinate plans and periodically direct exercises in the field. The NATO "allied supreme commander" has always been a U.S. general. In NATO, each state contributes its own military units—with its own national culture, language, and equipment specifications.

NATO was founded in 1949 to oppose and deter Soviet power in Europe. Its counterpart in Eastern Europe during the Cold War, the Soviet-led **Warsaw Pact**, was founded in 1955 and disbanded in 1991. During the Cold War, the United States maintained more than 300,000 troops in Europe, with advanced planes, tanks, and other equipment. After the Cold War ended, these forces were cut to about 100,000. But NATO stayed together because its members believed that NATO provided useful stability even though its mission was unclear.

The first actual use of force by NATO was in Bosnia in 1994, in support of the UN mission there. A "dual key" arrangement gave the UN control of NATO's actions in Bosnia, and the UN feared retaliation against its lightly armed peacekeepers if NATO attacked the Serbian forces to protect Bosnian civilians. As a result, NATO made threats, underlined by symbolic airstrikes, but then backed down after UN qualms; this wavering undermined NATO credibility. More extensive NATO airstrikes in 1995, however, alarmed Russian leaders already concerned by NATO's expansion plans. These problems, along with tensions between the American and European NATO members over Bosnia policy, dogged the first major NATO mission of the post–Cold War era.

In 1999, the European Union decided to form by 2003 its own 60,000-troop rapid deployment force, outside NATO. The decision grew in part from European military weaknesses demonstrated in the 1999 Kosovo war, in which the United States contributed the most power by far. Although the European force will probably work *with* NATO in future operations, it also gives Europe a bit more independence from the United States. Despite other efforts in this direction earlier in the 1990s, currently NATO still dominates European security.

Atlas CD
NATO
Expansion
Map

The biggest question for NATO is eastward expansion, beyond the East-West Cold War dividing line. In 1999, former Soviet-bloc countries Poland, the Czech Republic, and Hungary joined the alliance. Other countries were denied membership but may be admitted in future rounds of expansion. Making the new members' militaries compatible with NATO is a major undertaking, requiring increased military spending by existing and new NATO members at a time of general reductions. Arms industries look forward to new sales as Eastern European countries restructure their military forces. NATO expansion was justified by liberals as solidifying new democracies while keeping Europe peaceful, and by conservatives as protecting against possible future Russian aggression.

Russian leaders oppose NATO's expansion into Eastern Europe as aggressive and anti-Russian. They view NATO expansion as reasserting dividing lines on the map of Europe, but pushed closer to Russia's borders. These fears strengthen nationalist and anti-Western political forces in Russia. To mitigate the problems, NATO created a category of symbolic membership—the Partnership for Peace—which almost all Eastern European and former Soviet states including Russia joined. However, the 1999 NATO bombing of Serbia heightened Russian fears regarding NATO's eastward expansion.

The second most important alliance is the **U.S.-Japanese Security Treaty**, a bilateral alliance. Under this alliance the United States maintains about 50,000 troops in Japan (with weapons, equipment, and logistical support). Japan pays the United States several billion dollars annually to offset about half the cost of maintaining these troops. The alliance was created in 1951 (during the Korean War) against the potential Soviet threat to Japan.

Because of its roots in the U.S. military occupation of Japan after World War II, the alliance is very asymmetrical. The United States is committed to defend Japan if it is attacked, but Japan is not similarly obligated to defend the United States. The United States maintains troops in Japan, but not vice versa. The United States belongs to several other alliances, but Japan's only major alliance is with the United States. The U.S. share of the total military power in this alliance is also far greater than its share in NATO.

Japan's constitution renounces the right to make war and maintain military forces, although interpretation has loosened this prohibition over time. Japan maintains military forces, called the Self-Defense Forces, strong enough for territorial defense but not for aggression. It is a powerful army by world standards but much smaller than Japan's economic strength could support. Japanese public opinion restrains militarism in general and precludes the development of nuclear weapons in particular (after Japanese cities were destroyed by nuclear weapons in World War II). Even the dispatch of unarmed Japanese troops on a UN peacekeeping mission to Cambodia was barely approved in 1992 after a vigorous debate. Japan has little reason to alter its low profile in military affairs because low military spending has contributed to Japan's past economic successes.

Japan is as dependent as ever on natural resources from foreign countries, but Japanese leaders now believe that military capabilities are not useful for obtaining such resources. Instead, economic and diplomatic capabilities assure a smooth flow of resources to Japan and export markets for Japanese goods. The security alliance with the United States—Japan's largest trading partner—provides a stable security framework conducive to business. Japan need not worry that in a dispute over trade barriers the U.S. Navy will arrive to pry Japan's doors open (as it did in 1854). Nonetheless, some Japanese leaders believe that Japan's formal security role should now expand commensurate with its economic power: they call for a Japanese seat on the UN Security Council. The UN in turn is pressing Japan to participate fully in peacekeeping missions.

For its part, the United States has used the alliance with Japan as a base to project U.S. power in Asia, especially during the wars in Korea (1950–1953) and Vietnam (1965–1975) when Japan was a key staging area for U.S. war efforts. The continued U.S. military presence in Japan (as in Europe) symbolizes the U.S. commitment to remain engaged in Asian security affairs. However, these U.S. forces have been drawn down somewhat in the past decade in response to high costs, reduced threats, and some opposition by local residents (especially on Okinawa island).

Parallel with the U.S.-Japan treaty, the United States maintains military alliances with several other states, including South Korea and Australia. Close U.S. collaboration with militaries in other states such as Saudi Arabia make them de facto U.S. allies.

The Former Soviet Republics

Atlas CD
CIS
Article

The 12 members of the *Commonwealth of Independent States (CIS)* comprise the former Soviet republics except the Baltic states (Estonia, Latvia, and Lithuania). Russia is the leading member and Ukraine the second largest. Officially, CIS headquarters is in the city of Minsk, in Belarus, but in practice there is no strong center and meetings rotate around. After its first decade, the CIS remains a loose coordinating institution for states to solve practical problems in economic and (sometimes) military spheres.

When the Soviet Union disintegrated in 1991, a chaotic situation emerged. Power for several years had been shifting from the center in Moscow to the 15 constituent Soviet republics. The Warsaw Pact had collapsed. The Soviet army itself began to break up, and several republics began forming their own military forces using Soviet forces, bases, and equipment located on their territories. At the same time, other former Soviet forces located outside Russia remained in a chain of command centered in Moscow, effectively under Russian control. For years until 1997, Russia and Ukraine debated ownership of the Black Sea fleet, whose port was in Ukraine but whose history was distinctly Russian. (The fleet will be split and Russia's basing rights maintained for 20 years.)

Atlas CD
Russian Influence in CIS States
Photo

One reason for forming the CIS was simply to speed the death of the old Soviet Union and ease the transition to full independence for its republics. After the formation of the CIS at the end of 1991, the Soviet Union quickly dissolved. The extensive property of the Union (including state-owned industry and military forces) went to the individual republics, especially to Russia, which became the USSR's successor state.

The disposition of the Union's property and armed forces was negotiated by CIS members. Although some military coordination takes place through the CIS, plans for a joint military force instead of 12 independent armies did not succeed. Among the largest CIS members, Kazakhstan and Belarus are the most closely aligned with Russia, while Ukraine is the most independent. In 1999, Russia and Belarus formed a confederation that might lead to future economic integration or even an anti-Western military alliance, but currently remains merely symbolic.

It is to the CIS's credit that in the post-Soviet chaos no major war erupted between major CIS member states. Substantial warfare did occur between some of the smaller members (notably Armenia and Azerbaijan), and there was civil violence within several other CIS states (Tajikistan, Moldova, Russia); CIS forces were drawn into a few small clashes. But the large members were not drawn into large wars. The outcome could have been much worse.

The most important relationship within the CIS is between its two largest members, Russia and Ukraine. They distrust each other somewhat but have managed to cooperate fairly effectively since becoming independent. Disputes over issues such as ownership of the Black Sea fleet have been negotiated step by step, often painfully but productively in the end.

One of the first problems facing CIS military forces was what position to take in inter-republic warfare, such as that between Armenia and Azerbaijan, secessionist wars as in Georgia, or civil wars to control republics' governments as in Tajikistan. In some cases, CIS troops from the former Soviet army were stationed close to the fighting, and sometimes they were drawn in or took sides. More often they stood clear or played a peacekeeping role in such conflicts.

Another pressing military problem for the CIS was the disposition of the tens of thousands of nuclear weapons of the former Soviet Union. As the Soviet successor state, Russia assumed control of the weapons and within a year moved all the tactical nuclear weapons out of the other republics and into Russian territory. This was a very touchy operation because of the danger of theft or accident. The United States provided specially designed railroad cars for use in moving the weapons. Still, there were reports that nuclear materials (or perhaps even warheads) had been stolen and sold on the international market by corrupt CIS officers or officials (see the discussion of proliferation in Chapter 4).

The strategic nuclear weapons—those on long-range missiles—presented another kind of problem. These weapons were located in four republics—Russia, Ukraine, Belarus, and Kazakhstan—under control of Russian commanders. They were not easily moved, and the three republic leaders expressed some ambivalence about losing them to Russia. At a minimum they wanted assurances that the nuclear weapons would be destroyed, not retargeted on their own republics. Ukraine toyed with using the missiles as bargaining chips in negotiations with Russia or with the Western powers. But in the end all the former Soviet republics except Russia agreed to become nonnuclear states.

Overall, the CIS is a marriage of convenience. For now the members find it a necessary marriage—especially because of the tight economic integration of the member states—if not always a happy one. A divorce could occur quickly.

Regional Alignments Beyond the three alliances just discussed and the regional IGOs mentioned earlier, most international alignments and coalitions are not formalized in alliances. Among the great powers, a close working relationship (through the UN) developed among the United States, Western European powers, Japan, and Russia after the Cold War. By the mid-1990s new strains had appeared in great-power relations, including economic conflicts among the former Western allies, differences over policy in Bosnia and Kosovo, and Western alarm at Russia's war in the secession-minded Chechnya province. Of the great powers, China continues to be the most independent, but prudently avoids conflict with the others unless China's immediate security interests are at stake.

In the third world, many states joined a **nonaligned movement** during the Cold War, standing apart from the U.S.-Soviet rivalry. This movement, led by India and Yugoslavia, was undermined by the membership of states such as Cuba that were clearly clients of one superpower. In 1992, the nonaligned movement agreed to stay in business, though its future is unclear. One vestige of past centuries is the Commonwealth—a group of countries with historical ties to Britain (including Canada and Australia) working together for mutual economic and cultural benefit. France also maintains ties (including regular summit meetings) with its former colonies in Africa. France had troops stationed in six African countries as of 1997. But France reduced its African ties in the 1990s; it plans to decrease troop levels there, and in 1997 it stood by while friendly governments in Zaire (Democratic Congo) and the Republic of Congo were overthrown.

Web Link
Nonaligned
Movement

In Asia, China has had conflicts with most of its major neighbors. Between 1940 and 1979 it engaged in military hostilities with Japan, South Korea, the United States, India, Russia, and Vietnam. In 1965, China lost its only major regional ally (Indonesia) after a violent change of government there. China has long been loosely aligned with Pakistan in opposition to India (which was aligned with the Soviet Union). The United States tended to favor the Pakistani side as well. But U.S.-Indian relations have improved a bit since the Cold War ended, and U.S.-Pakistani relations have been strained by Pakistan's nuclear weapons program. Vietnam slowly normalized relations with the United States after the wars in Vietnam and Cambodia. The United States has 35,000 troops stationed in South Korea under terms of a formal bilateral alliance dating to the Korean War (North Korea is vaguely aligned with China). Other long-standing U.S. friends in Asia include the Philippines, the Chinese Nationalists on Taiwan (only informally since the 1970s), Singapore, and Thailand. Since 1951 the United States has had a formal military alliance called ANZUS with Australia and New Zealand.

In the Middle East, the Arab-Israeli conflict created a general anti-Israel alignment of the Arab countries for decades, but that alignment broke down as Egypt in 1978 and then the Palestine Liberation Organization (PLO) and Jordan in 1993–1994 made peace with Israel. Syria and Lebanon began down a similar path in early 2000, as Israeli-Palestinian negotiations approached the moment of truth. As the Arab-Israeli peace process inches forward (and at times backward), Arab countries continue to express varying degrees of solidarity with each other and degrees of opposition to Israel. Iraq and Iran are Israel's most intractable enemies as it makes a tenuous peace with all its immediate neighbors. Meanwhile, Israel and Turkey have formed a close military relationship that amplifies Israeli power and links it to the oil-rich Caspian Sea region. Also, despite its small size, Israel has been the largest recipient of U.S. foreign aid since the 1980s (about $3 billion per year).

Atlas CD
Arab-Israeli
Conflict
Map, Article

The United States has similarly close relations with Egypt (since 1978), and cooperates closely with Turkey (a NATO member), Kuwait and Saudi Arabia (cemented by the 1991 Gulf War), and Morocco. But U.S.-Iranian relations remained frosty (despite some recent signs of warming) two decades after the 1979 revolution. The United States has very hostile relations with Iraq as well, with recurrent U.S.-led bombing of Iraqi facilities in the late 1990s and early 2000s. U.S. relations with Libya have also been very hostile.

It is unclear what new international alignments may emerge in the years to come. The fluidity of alliances makes them something of a wild card for scholars to understand, just as they are for policy makers to deal with. For the present, international alignments center on the United States; although several independence-minded states such as China, Russia, France, and Iran keep U.S. hegemony in check, there is little sign that a coherent or formal rival power alignment is emerging to challenge the United States. The leading U.S. role will be central to the course of world politics in the early twenty-first century.

This chapter has focused on the concerns of realists—the interests of states, distribution of power among states, bargaining between states, and alliances of states. Consistent with the realist framework, the chapter has treated states as unitary actors, much as one would analyze the interactions of individual people. The actions of state leaders have been treated as more or less rational in terms of pursuing definable interests through coherent bargaining strategies.

But realism is not the only way to frame the major issues of international security. Chapter 3 reexamines these themes critically, from more liberal and more revolutionary theoretical perspectives, and applies them to the foreign policy decision-making process and its actors.

THINKING CRITICALLY

1. Using Table 1.2 on pp. 16–17 (with GDP as a measure of power) and the maps at the front of the book, pick a state and speculate about what coalition of nearby states might form with sufficient power to oppose the state if it became aggressive.
2. Choose a recent international event and list the power capabilities that participants used as leverage in the episode. Which capabilities were effective, and which were not? Why?
3. The modern international system came into being at a time when agrarian societies relied primarily on farmland to create wealth. Now that most wealth is no longer created through farming, is the territorial nature of states obsolete? How might the diminishing economic value of territory change the ways in which states interact?

CHAPTER SUMMARY

◆ Realism explains international relations in terms of power.
◆ Realists and idealists differ in their assumptions about human nature, international order, and the potential for peace.
◆ Power can be conceptualized as influence or as capabilities that can create influence.
◆ The most important single indicator of a state's power is its GDP.
◆ Short-term power capabilities depend on long-term resources, both tangible and intangible.
◆ Realists consider military force the most important power capability.
◆ International affairs can be seen as a series of bargaining interactions in which states use power capabilities as leverage to influence the outcomes.
◆ Bargaining outcomes depend not only on raw power but also on strategies and luck.

◆ Reciprocity can be an effective strategy for reaching cooperation in ongoing relationships but carries a danger of turning into runaway hostility or arms races.

◆ Rational-actor approaches treat states as though they were individuals acting to maximize their own interests. These simplifications are debatable but allow realists to develop concise and general models and explanations.

◆ Game theory draws insights from simplified models of bargaining situations. In the Prisoner's Dilemma model, selfish participants cannot achieve mutually beneficial cooperation (except over time in some circumstances).

◆ International anarchy—the absence of world government—means that each state is a sovereign and autonomous actor pursuing its own national interests.

◆ The international system traditionally places great emphasis on the sovereignty of states, their right to control affairs in their own territory, and their responsibility to respect internationally recognized borders.

◆ Seven great powers account for half of the world's GDP as well as the great majority of military forces and other power capabilities.

◆ Power transition theory says that wars often result from shifts in relative power distribution in the international system.

◆ Hegemony—the predominance of one state in the international system—can help provide stability and peace in international relations, but with some drawbacks.

◆ States form alliances to increase their power relative to another state or alliance.

◆ Alliances can shift rapidly, with major effects on power relations.

◆ The world's main alliances, including NATO and the U.S.-Japanese alliance, face uncertain roles in a changing world order.

ONLINE PRACTICE TEST

Take an online practice test at
www.IRtext.com

3

Alternatives to Power Politics

CHAPTER OUTLINE

- ◆ Liberalism
- ◆ Foreign Policy and the Decision-Making Process
- ◆ Substate Actors
- ◆ Feminism
- ◆ Other Alternatives to Realism

Liberalism

How well do the assumptions of realism capture what is important about IR? Where are the problems in the realist framework—the places where abstractions diverge too much from the reality of IR, where realism is "unrealistic" in its portrayal?

This chapter revisits the realism-idealism debate and discusses current liberal approaches to international security. It then discusses the roles of decision-making processes and substate actors, which challenge realist assumptions. The chapter concludes by considering several broader and more interdisciplinary alternatives to the realist framework—feminism, postmodernism, and peace studies. Each of these three research communities seeks to radically recast the terms of reference in which we see IR.

Traditional Liberal Critiques Since the time of Sun Tzu in ancient China, idealism has provided a counterpoint to realism. This long tradition of idealism in IR holds that: morality, law, and international organization can form the basis for relations among states; human nature is not evil; peaceful and cooperative relations among states are possible; and states can operate as a community rather than merely as autonomous self-interested agents.

To review the core concepts of realism, states (the central actors in IR) use power to pursue their own interests in the context of an anarchic system lacking central enforcement mechanisms. Power capabilities come into play as leverage in bargaining among states over the outcomes of conflicts. Leverage can be positive (rewards) or negative (punishments); in both cases the purpose is to influence the rational decisions and actions of another state so as to bring about a more favorable outcome for the actor using the leverage. Military force is an important form of leverage—emphasized by realists over all other forms—because of the inherent insecurity of living in an anarchic world.

Traditionally, liberals have offered four major lines of criticism against these assumptions of realism. First, the key assumption of international *anarchy* is no more than a partial truth. Of course, international interactions are structured by power relations, by the distribution of power in the international system—whether a predominant power in the system (hegemony) or a multipolar "concert" of great powers. Realists can accept that anarchy includes international order structured by power. But order also evolves through norms and institutions based on reciprocity and cooperation, even on law. Realists have a harder time reconciling the ever-expanding scope of international interdependence and cooperation with the assumptions of anarchy, of the inevitability of security dilemmas, and of the primacy of military leverage.

Second, liberals criticize the notion of states as *unitary actors*, each with a single set of coherent interests. As the study of foreign policy reveals (see later sections), state actions often do not reflect a single individual set of preferences. Rather, state behavior is shaped by internal bargaining among and within bureaucracies, interest groups, and other actors with divergent goals and interests. Nonstate actors—individuals, NGOs, IGOs, and ethnic groups, among others—further confound the idea that IR can be reduced to interactions of a small number of well-defined state actors pursuing national interests.

Third, the concept of *rationality* is problematical. If states are single actors with coherent interests, they often seem to do a poor job in maximizing those interests. And the evident importance in ethnic conflicts of emotions such as hatred (see Chapter 4) also calls into question the more simplistic realist interpretations of such conflicts as rational bargaining moves by the participating actors.

Finally, *military force* as a form of leverage does not seem nearly as all-important as realism implies. It is a costly way to influence other actors (see Chapter 4), compared with diplomacy, conflict resolution, peacekeeping, and other nonmilitary means. International organizations, laws, and norms create stable contexts for bargaining, making nonmilitary leverage increasingly effective as international organization develops (see Chapter 6). This criticism of realism applies even more to international political economy (Chapters 5, 7, and 8).

Atlas CD
Rebuilding
Beirut
Photo

In addition to these general criticisms of realism, some liberals have argued that changes in the way IR works have made realist assumptions obsolete. Realism may once have been realistic, when European kings and queens played war and traded territories. But states are now interconnected, contradicting the assumptions of autonomy and sovereignty. Borders are becoming fluid, making territorial integrity increasingly untenable. The evolution of norms regarding the use of force has substantially changed the ways in which military force contributes to international power. This line of argument has been prominent in liberal interdependence approaches to IR since the 1970s.

Web Link
Rationality

What Is Rationality?   At the core of the liberal approach is a concept of *rationality* that differs sharply from the realist concept. Realists see rationality as an individual actor's attempt to maximize its own short-term interests. Liberals believe that rational actors are capable of forgoing short-term individual interests in order to further the long-term well-being of a community to which they belong. Such actions are rational because they contribute to the actor's individual well-being, indirectly or over the long term. Thus, 200 years ago, the German philosopher Immanuel Kant argued that states, although autonomous, could join a worldwide federation like today's UN and respect its principles even at the cost of forgoing certain short-term individual gains. To Kant, international cooperation was a more rational option for states than resorting to war. Thus, in realist conceptions of rationality, war and violence appear rational (because they often advance short-term state interests), but liberals tend to see war and violence as irrational deviations that result from defective reasoning and harm the (collective, long-term) well-being of states.

This disagreement is particularly acute when it comes to nuclear weapons. Liberals find it absurd to spend money building weapons that could destroy the world or to claim (as realists do) that there is a rational logic behind their deployment. Furthermore, many realists argue that nuclear deterrence will *prevent* the world from being destroyed—because the state actors owning nuclear weapons are rational; whereas liberals, because they see war as a breakdown in rationality generally, fear that a similar breakdown could cause nuclear weapons to be used, with tragic consequences.

Liberal and realist approaches to *power* reflect the distinction between rationality as seeking narrow self-interest and rationality as seeking to share in long-term collective benefits. Realists define power as the ability to get another actor to do something—or as the capabilities required to so influence an actor (see pp. 47–49). This is *power over others*—a concept that some liberals consider inherently oppressive, rooted in a need to control or dominate other people. This is the power of the bully, to make others do his bidding. But are bullies really the most powerful actors? Do they achieve the best outcomes? And do we really live in an international world populated by bullies?

Another definition of power is based not on power over others but on power to accomplish desirable ends. This power often derives from capitalizing on common interests rather than gaining an edge in bargaining over conflicting interests. Such empowerment often entails the formation of coalitions and partnerships, or the mobilization of the resources of multiple actors for a common purpose. For many liberals, this is a truer, more useful concept of power.

Neoliberalism   In the 1980s, a new liberal critique of realism emerged. The approach stressed the importance of international institutions in reducing the inherent conflict that realists assume in an international system. The reasoning is based on the core liberal idea that seeking long-term mutual gains is often more rational than maximizing individual short-term gains. The approach became known as "neoliberal institutionalism" or **neoliberalism** for short.

The neoliberal approach differs from earlier liberal approaches in that it concedes to realism several important assumptions—among them, that states are unitary actors rationally pursuing their self-interests. Neoliberals say to realists, "Even if we grant your

Happy Family   Liberals emphasize the potential for rivalries to evolve into cooperative relationships as states recognize that achieving mutual benefits is most cost-effective in the long run. The cooperation between U.S. and Soviet/Russian space programs starting in the 1960s is an example. Here, a U.S. shuttle astronaut greets the commander of Russian space station Mir, 1997.

assumptions about the nature of states and their motives, your pessimistic conclusions do not follow." States achieve cooperation fairly often because it is in their interest to do so, and they can learn to use institutions to ease the pursuit of mutual gains and the reduction of possibilities for cheating or taking advantage of another state.

Despite the many sources of conflict in IR, states do attain cooperation most of the time. Neoliberal scholars ask how this is possible in an anarchic world. They try to show that even in a world of unitary rational states the neorealists' pessimism about international cooperation is not valid—states can create mutual rules, expectations, and institutions to promote behavior that enhances (or at least doesn't destroy) the possibilities for mutual gain.

Neoliberals use the *Prisoner's Dilemma (PD)* game (see pp. 62–63) to illustrate their argument that cooperation is possible. Each actor can gain by individually defecting, but both lose when both defect. The narrow, self-serving behavior of each player leads to a bad outcome for both, one they could have improved with cooperation. This is a common situation in IR in which states have a mix of conflicting interests and mutual interests. The dilemma can be resolved if the game is played over and over again—an accurate model of IR, where states deal with each other in repeated interactions.

A strategy of strict reciprocity after an initial cooperative move (nicknamed **tit for tat**) can bring about mutual cooperation in a repeated PD game, because the other player must conclude that any defection will merely provoke a like defection in response. The strategy parallels just war doctrine (see pp. 321–322), which calls for states never to initiate war but to use war in response to war. In international trade, such a strategy calls for opening one's markets but selectively closing them in response to another state's closing its markets (see pp. 229–231).

Reciprocity is an important principle in IR that helps international cooperation emerge despite the absence of central authority. Through reciprocity, not a world government, norms and rules are enforced. In international security, reciprocity underlies the gradual improvement of relations sought by arms control agreements and peace-keeping missions. In international political economy (IPE), where cooperation can create great benefits through trade, the threat to restrict trade in retaliation for unfair practices is a strong incentive to comply with rules and norms.

Although reciprocity is an important norm, it is just one among many norms that mediate states' interactions. For example, diplomatic practices and participation in international organizations (IOs) are both strongly governed by shared expectations about the rules of correct behavior. As dilemmas such as the Prisoner's Dilemma crop up in IR, states rely on a context of rules, norms, habits, and institutions that make it rational for all sides to avoid the self-defeating outcomes that would follow narrow short-term self-interest. Neoliberals study historical and contemporary cases in IR to see how institutions and norms affected the possibilities for overcoming dilemmas and achieving international cooperation. Thus, for neoliberals the emergence of international institutions is key to understanding how states achieve a superior type of rationality that includes long-term self-interest.

Collective Goods The problem of the security dilemma (p. 65), which helps explain costly arms races, is an example of a PD-like dilemma in international security. Such examples are even more common in IPE, where protectionism and other forms of economic nationalism attempt to increase national wealth (relative to other states), at some cost to global wealth (see Chapter 5). The overall efficiency of the world economy is reduced, but the distribution of gains from trade shifts toward one's own state or groups within it. The problem is that if other states take similar actions, global efficiency decreases and the distribution of benefits remains about the same. So all states end up worse off than they could be.

All these situations are examples of the **collective goods problem**. A collective good is a tangible or intangible good, created by members of a group, that is available to all group members, regardless of their individual contributions. As in the security dilemma or Prisoner's Dilemma, participants can gain by lowering their own contribution to the collective good, but if too many participants do so, the good cannot be provided.

For example, it costs less to drive a polluting car than to pay for emission controls, and the air that the car owner breathes is hardly affected by his or her own car. The air quality is a collective good. If too many car owners pollute, all will breathe dirty air. But if just a few pollute, they will breathe fairly clean air; the few who pollute are **free riders**, because they benefit from someone else's provision of the collective good. These important concepts in IPE come up again in later chapters, especially in discussions of international organization and law (Chapter 6) and of the global environment (Chapter 8).

In the Same Boat
Collective goods are provided to all members of a group regardless of their individual contributions, just as these Vietnamese boat people (1984) will sink or float together. Liberal theorists see the community of nations as similarly interdependent. Individual states have conflicting interests over limited resources (as do the boat people) but strong incentives to find ways to maintain collective goods such as peace and stability.

Within domestic society, many collective goods problems are solved by governments, which enforce rules for the common good. Governments can punish free riders who are tempted to avoid contributing. Governments can pass laws against polluting cars or force citizens to pay taxes to support collective goods such as national defense, highways, or schools. In the anarchic international system, the absence of central government sharpens the difficulties created by collective goods. It is difficult to maintain multilateral cooperation when each government is tempted by its own possibility of free riding.

In general, collective goods are easier to provide in small groups than in large ones. In a small group, the defection (free riding) of one member is harder to conceal, has a greater impact on the overall collective good, and is easier to punish. The advantage of small groups helps explain the importance of the great-power system in international security affairs. And it is one reason why the G8 (Group of Eight) industrialized countries have frequent meetings to try to coordinate their economic policies, instead of relying only on groups such as the World Bank or WTO (each of which has more than a hundred member states). Small groups do not solve the problem entirely, however. Whether in small groups or large, the world's states lack a government to enforce contributions to collective goods; states must look elsewhere.

Regimes and Institutions Because of the contradictory interpretations that parties to a conflict usually have, it is difficult to resolve such conflicts without a third party to arbitrate or an overall framework to set common expectations for all parties. These considerations underlie the creation of IOs in the international security field (see Chapter 6). Norms of behavior are at least as important in international economics as in international security because of the great gains to be realized from maintaining a stable framework for smoothly carrying on potentially large economic transactions.

Web Link
International
Regimes

An **international regime** is a set of rules, norms, and procedures around which the expectations of actors converge in a certain issue area (whether arms control, international trade, or Antarctic exploration). The convergence of expectations means that participants in the international system have similar ideas about what rules will govern their mutual participation: each expects everyone to play by the same rules. (This meaning of regime is not the same as that referring to the domestic governments of states, especially governments considered illegitimate or in power for only a short time.)

Regimes can help solve collective goods problems by increasing transparency—everyone knows what everyone is doing, so cheating is more costly. The current revolution in information technologies is strengthening regimes particularly in this aspect. Also, with better international communication, states can identify conflicts and negotiate solutions through regimes more effectively.

Regimes are an important and widespread phenomenon in IR. Several regimes concerning international security will be discussed in Chapter 4. The Ballistic Missile Technology Control Regime (see p. 201) is a set of rules and expectations governing the international trade in missiles. The post–Cold War era of the 1990s has been described as a security regime in which the great powers develop common expectations about the rules for their behavior. In IPE, regimes are even more central. The frameworks within which states carry on trade, monetary relations, communications, and environmental protection policies are key to realizing the benefits of mutual cooperation in these areas.

IR scholars conceive of regimes in several different ways, and the concept has been criticized as too vague. But the most common conception of regimes combines elements of realism and liberalism. States are considered the important actors, and states are seen as autonomous units maximizing their own interests in an anarchic context. Regimes do not play a role in issues where states can realize their interests directly through unilateral applications of leverage. Rather, regimes come into existence to overcome collective goods dilemmas by coordinating the behaviors of individual states. Although states continue to seek their own interests, they create frameworks to coordinate their actions with those of other states if and when such coordination is necessary to realize self-interest (that is, in collective goods dilemmas). Thus, regimes help make cooperation possible even within an international system based on anarchy—exactly the point neoliberals focus on.

Regimes do not substitute for the basic calculations of costs and benefits by states; they just open up new possibilities with more favorable benefit-cost ratios. Regimes do not constrain states, except in a very narrow and short-term sense. Rather they facilitate and empower national governments faced with issues where collective goods problems would otherwise prevent governments from achieving their ends. Regimes can be seen as *intervening variables* between the basic causal forces at work in IR—for realists, the relative power of state actors—and the outcomes such as international cooperation (or lack thereof). Regimes do not negate the effects of power: more often they codify and nor-

THE INFORMATION REVOLUTION Empowering Regimes?

Liberal international regimes codify norms and help solve collective goods problems. "Transparency" reduces cheating or free riding (such as on a treaty, alliance, or cartel), because all states know what the others are doing. As evolving information technologies "illuminate" the world, will international regimes be strengthened and work better, or will information technologies become primarily an instrument of power in states' hands, as realists might argue?

To explore this question, go to www.IRtext.com

malize existing power relations. If the regime works, it will keep less powerful states from gaining leverage they could use against more powerful states.

Hegemonic Stability
Since regimes depend on state power for their enforcement, some IR scholars argue that regimes are most effective when power in the international system is most concentrated—when there is a hegemon to keep order. This theory is known as **hegemonic stability theory**. When one state's power is predominant, it can enforce rules and norms unilaterally, avoiding the collective goods problem. In particular, hegemons can maintain global free trade and promote world economic growth, in this view.

This theory attributes the peace and prosperity of the decades after World War II to U.S. hegemony, which created and maintained a global framework of economic relations supporting relatively stable and free international trade, as well as a security framework that prevented great-power wars. By contrast, the Great Depression of the 1930s and the outbreak of World War II have been attributed to the power vacuum in the international system at that time—Britain was no longer able to act as hegemon, and the United States was unwilling to begin doing so.

Why should a hegemon care about enforcing rules for the international economy that are in the common good? According to hegemonic stability theory, a hegemon basically has the same interests as the common good of all states. Hegemons as the largest international traders have an inherent interest in the promotion of integrated world markets (where the hegemons will tend to dominate). Thus hegemons favor free trade and use their power to achieve free trade. Hegemony, then, provides both the ability and the motivation to maintain regimes that provide a stable political framework for free international trade, according to hegemonic stability theory. This theory is not, however, accepted by all IR scholars.

What happens to regimes when hegemons lose power and decline? Regimes do not always decline with the power of hegemons that created them. Rather, they may take on a life of their own. Although hegemony may be crucial in *establishing* regimes, it is not necessary for *maintaining* them. Once actors' expectations converge around the rules embodied in a regime, the actors realize that the regime serves their own inter-

Hegemony: upset balance of International Power?

ests. Working through the regime becomes a habit, and national leaders may not give serious consideration to breaking out of the established rules.

This persistence of regimes was demonstrated in the 1970s, when U.S. power declined following the decades of U.S. hegemony since 1945. Diminished U.S. power was evident in the loss of the Vietnam War, the rise of OPEC, and the malaise of the U.S. economy. Some IR scholars expected that the entire framework of international trade and monetary relations established after World War II would collapse once the United States was no longer able to enforce the rules of that regime. But that did not happen. The international economic regimes adjusted somewhat and survived.

In part, that survival is attributable to the embedding of regimes in permanent *institutions* such as the UN or NATO. As the rules of the game persist over time, institutions develop around them. These institutions become the tangible manifestation of shared expectations as well as the machinery for coordinating international actions based on those expectations. In international security affairs, the UN and other IOs provide a stable framework for resolving disputes. IPE is even more institutionalized, again because of the heavier volume of activity and the wealth that can be realized from cooperation.

Institutions gain greater stability and weight than do noninstitutionalized regimes. With a staff and headquarters, an international institution can actively intervene to promote adherence to the rules in its area of political or economic life. Important institutions in international security and IPE are discussed in Chapters 4 and 5, respectively.

Collective Security
A major application of liberal conceptions of international security affairs is the concept of **collective security**— the formation of a broad alliance of most major actors in an international system for the purpose of jointly opposing aggression by any actor. The rationale for this approach was laid out by Kant. Since past treaties ending great-power wars had never lasted permanently, Kant proposed a federation (league) of the world's states. Through such a federation, Kant proposed, the majority of states could unite to punish any one state that committed aggression. This would safeguard the collective interests of all the nations together against the narrow self-interest of one nation that might otherwise profit from aggression. The federation would also protect the self-determination of small nations that all too easily became pawns in great-power games.

After the horrors of World War I, a *League of Nations* was actually formed. But it was flawed in two ways. Its membership did not include all the great powers (nor the most powerful one, the United States). And its members proved unwilling to bear the costs of collective action to oppose aggression when it did occur, in the 1930s.

After World War II, the United Nations was created as the League's successor to promote collective security (see Chapter 6). Several regional IGOs also currently perform collective security functions (deterring aggression) as well as economic and cultural ones. In Latin America and the United States, there is the *Organization of American States (OAS)*. In the Middle East (including North Africa), there is the *Arab League*. In Africa (also including North Africa), there is the *Organization of African Unity (OAU)*.

The success of collective security depends on two points. First, the members must keep their alliance commitments to the group. When a powerful state commits aggression against a weaker one, it often is not in the immediate interest of other powerful states to go to war over the issue. It can be very costly to suppress a determined aggressor.

A second requisite for collective security is that enough members must agree on what constitutes aggression. When the United States sent an army half a million strong to try to put down a revolution in South Vietnam in the 1960s, was that aggression? Or was it aggression for North Vietnam to infiltrate its army into the south in support of the rebellion? The UN Security Council is structured so that aggression is defined by what all five permanent members, plus at least four of the other ten members, can agree on (see "The Security Council" on pp. 283–286). This collective security system does not work against aggression by a great power. When the Soviet Union invaded Afghanistan, or the United States mined the harbors of Nicaragua, or France blew up the Greenpeace ship *Rainbow Warrior*, the UN could do nothing—because those states can veto Security Council resolutions.

Both requirements were met in the case of Kuwait in 1990–1991. The aggressor, Iraq, was a member of the UN, as was the victim, Kuwait. It was the first time since the founding of the UN that one member had invaded, occupied, and annexed another member—attempting to erase it as a sovereign state. The invasion was so blatant a violation of Kuwaiti sovereignty and territorial integrity that the Security Council had little trouble labeling it aggression. To the Security Council, the aggression was flagrant, the rules of world order were being redefined as the Cold War ended, and of course the West's oil supply was threatened. In a series of resolutions, the Council condemned Iraq, applied mandatory economic sanctions (requiring all UN members to stop trading with Iraq), and ultimately authorized the use of force by a multinational coalition. Collective security worked in the Iraqi case because the conquest of Kuwait brought all the great powers together and because they were willing to bear the costs of confronting Iraq. (China abstained on the resolution authorizing force and did not contribute to the coalition, but it did not veto the resolution.)

In the case of Bosnia, the aggression was somewhat less clear-cut, since it followed on the disintegration of what had been a single state, Yugoslavia. What would have been an internal matter became an international one when Croatia and Bosnia were recognized as separate states independent of Serbia. Also the conquest of two-thirds of Bosnia was done in the name of Bosnia's minority Serbian population and its political party, though supported and largely directed from Serbia itself. And, traditional ties between Serbia and three Security Council members (Russia, France, and Britain) made these great powers reluctant to punish Serbia.

Atlas CD
Former
Yugoslavia
Map

But the Serb forces' use of genocide and other war crimes demanded a response. And having recognized Bosnia's independence and admitted it to the UN, the Security Council members had some obligation to oppose the conquest and dismemberment of Bosnia. The Security Council was able to agree that Serbia and Bosnian Serb forces were the primary aggressors in Bosnia. Dozens of resolutions were then passed, but their implementation was very problematical.

Ultimately, the sticking point for collective security in Bosnia was not identifying the aggressor; it was cost. Members of the UN (especially the great powers) were not willing to pay a high price to reverse aggression when their own vital national interests

→ Hegemon bears cost, i.e. U.S.

A Lot to Mourn   The UN seemed to work well as an instrument for collective security in the Gulf War, but not in Bosnia, where it took three years to galvanize a credible international response. Partly as a result, the UN lost support and scaled back peacekeeping missions globally. This father in Sarajevo mourns the death of his six-year-old son, 1994.

were not threatened. They patched together an international response that contained the conflict at a modest cost, and contributing states were willing to take on their shares of the overall cost (though not without some cheating). Collective security was thus a collective good in Bosnia, and norms and institutions fell somewhat short in getting members to contribute to provide that good.

The concept of collective security has been broadened in recent years. Toward the end of the Cold War, the liberal premises of international community and mutual state interests provided the foundations for a new idea called *common security* (or "mutual security"), the notion that the security of all states, enemies as well as friends, is interdependent, so the insecurity of one state makes all states less secure. A local dispute in one part of the world can threaten another part; economic and ethnic rivalries can spill over into violent conflicts; the costs of preparing for war can bankrupt great powers even in peacetime. This new reality—if state leaders recognized it—would resolve the security dilemma, because a state's own security interests would be (indirectly) *diminished* if it threatened another state.

The theory and practice of common security were promoted during the late 1980s by Soviet President Gorbachev, who won the Nobel peace prize for his accomplishments (although he was swept from office when the Soviet Union collapsed). Gorbachev and his foreign minister, Eduard Shevardnadze, argued that as states became more closely connected economically and culturally, it was futile and wasteful to arm against each other, especially with nuclear weapons. Of course, domestic economic stagnation was a major factor in Gorbachev's realization that the Soviet Union could no longer afford the Cold War.

Liberals have long sought to reform rather than radically reshape the international system as we know it. They have tried to overhaul the realist model but not to reject its terms of reference entirely (this is one reason that realists and liberals can continue to debate and to understand each other's argument even while disagreeing). Liberal scholars and liberal state leaders alike have argued that international cooperation and the avoidance of violence are ultimately better for states themselves and more rational for state leaders to pursue.

A state is not a single conscious being, however. Its actions are a composite of individual human choices—by its citizenry, its political leaders, its diplomats and bureaucrats—aggregated through the state's internal structures. Next, we shall look at the state from inside out, trying to understand the processes and structures within states that make them take the actions they do toward other states.

Foreign Policy and the Decision-Making Process

Foreign policies are the strategies used by governments to guide their actions in the international arena (various alternative definitions have been proposed). Foreign policies spell out the objectives state leaders have decided to pursue in a given relationship or situation as well as the general means by which they intend to pursue those objectives. Day-to-day decisions are guided by the goal of implementing foreign policies.

Every day, states take actions in international affairs. Diplomats are appointed to posts, given instructions for their negotiations, or recalled home. Trade negotiators agree to reduce their demands by a few percent. Military forces are moved around and occasionally sent into battle. Behind each of these actions are decisions by foreign policy bureaucrats in national capitals. These decisions in turn generally reflect the overall policies states have developed to govern their relationships with other states.

The study of foreign policies includes studying the substance of various states' policies—for instance, what are France's aims with regard to the European Community, or Iran's plans regarding the spread of Islamic revolution in the Middle East? The substantive foreign policies of the United States (as the most powerful actor) have an especially strong influence on IR outcomes. But, in general, IR scholars are less interested in specific policies than in the **foreign policy process**—how policies are arrived at, and implemented, in various states.

States establish various organizational structures and functional relationships to create and carry out foreign policies. Officials and agencies collect information about a situation through various channels; they write memoranda outlining possible options for action; they hold meetings to discuss the matter; they sometimes meet privately to decide how to steer the meetings. Such activities, broadly defined, are what is meant by "the foreign policy process." IR scholars are especially interested in exploring whether certain kinds of policy processes lead to certain kinds of decisions—whether certain processes produce better outcomes (for the state's self-defined interests) than do others.

Foreign policy outcomes result from multiple forces working at once on the various levels of analysis. The outcomes depend on individual decision makers, on the type of society and government they are working within, and on the international and global context of their actions. Since the study of foreign policy concentrates on forces within the state, its main emphasis is on the individual and domestic levels of analysis.

Web Link
Comparative
Foreign Policy

Comparative foreign policy is the study of foreign policy in various states in order to discover whether similar types of societies or governments consistently have similar types of foreign policies (comparing across states or across different time periods for a single state). Such studies have focused on three characteristics: size, wealth, and degree of participation in government (democratic versus authoritarian; see pp. 112–115). An alternative approach categorizes societies according to their relative populations, natural resources, and levels of technology.

A major focus of such studies is whether certain characteristics of a state or society predispose it to be more warlike or aggressive. In particular, during the Cold War scholars debated whether communism or capitalism was inherently more warlike in nature. However, no simple rule has been found to predict a state's warlike tendencies based on attributes such as size, wealth, and type of government. There is great variation among states, and even within a single state over time. Both capitalist and communist states have proven capable of naked aggression or peaceful behavior, depending on circumstances.

Most studies of foreign policy have not focused on the comparison of policies of different states, however; they have instead concentrated on understanding in a more general way the kinds of processes used in various states to reach (and implement) foreign policies. Scholars have tried to probe the effects of these processes on the resulting outcomes. The study of foreign policy processes runs counter to realism's assumption of a unitary state actor; therefore realists tend to reject these approaches.

The foreign policy process is a process of *decision making*. States take actions because people in governments choose those actions. People whose job it is to make decisions about international relations—*decision makers*—have to go through the same kinds of processes, in one way or another, that anyone would go through even in deciding what to eat for dinner.

Web Link
Decision Making

Decision making is a *steering* process in which adjustments are made as a result of feedback from the outside world. Decisions are carried out by actions taken to change the world, and then information from the world is monitored to evaluate the effects of actions. These evaluations—along with information about other, independent changes in the environment—go into the next round of decisions (see Figure 3.1). The steering process, with its external feedback, is based on the *goals* of the decision maker. Along the way to these goals, decision makers set *objectives* as discrete steps to be reached. Objectives fall along a spectrum from core, long-term objectives to very short-term, practical objectives.

Models of Decision Making

A common starting point for studying the decision-making process is the **rational model**. In this model, decision makers calcu-

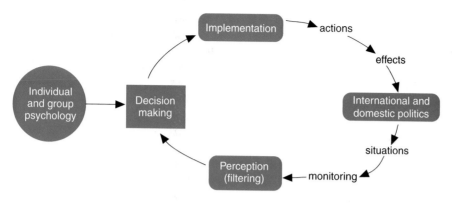

FIGURE 3.1 Decision Making as Steering

late the costs and benefits of each possible course of action and then choose the one with the highest benefits and lowest costs by:

1. *Clarifying goals* in the situation.
2. *Ordering them* by importance (in case different goals conflict).
3. *Listing the alternatives* available to achieve the goals.
4. *Investigating the consequences* (probable and possible outcomes) of those alternatives.
5. *Choosing* the course of action that will produce the best outcome (in terms of reaching one's goals).

The choice may be complicated by *uncertainty* about the costs and benefits of various actions. In such cases, decision makers must attach probabilities to each possible outcome of an action. Some decision makers are relatively *accepting of risk*, whereas others are *averse to risk*. These factors affect the importance that decision makers place on various alternative outcomes that could result from an action. For example, Saddam Hussein's decision to invade Kuwait showed high acceptance of risk. The potential benefits were great (seizing Kuwait's wealth to solve Iraq's economic problems), and Saddam was willing to risk failure on the chance that such a gamble might pay off.

The rational model may imply that decision making is simpler than is actually the case. A decision maker may hold different conflicting goals simultaneously. The goals of different individuals involved in making a decision may diverge, as may the goals of different state agencies. The rational model of decision making thus is somewhat complicated by uncertainty and the multiple goals of decision makers.

An alternative to the rational model of decision making is the **organizational process model**. In this model, foreign policy decision makers generally skip the labor-intensive process of identifying goals and alternative actions, relying instead for most decisions on standardized responses or *standard operating procedures*. For example, the U.S. State Department every day receives more than a thousand cables with reports or inquiries from its embassies around the world and sends out more than a thousand cables to those embassies with instructions or responses. The vast majority of cables are never seen by the top decision makers (the secretary of state or the president); instead, they are handled by low-level decision makers who apply general principles—or who simply try to make the least controversial, most standardized decision. These low-level decisions may not reflect the high-level policies adopted by top leaders, but rather have a life of their own. The organizational process model implies that much of foreign policy results from "management by muddling through."

Web Link
Governmental
Bargaining

Another alternative to the rational model is the **government bargaining** (or *bureaucratic politics*) **model**, in which foreign policy decisions result from the bargaining process among various government agencies with somewhat divergent interests in the outcome. In 1992 the Japanese government had to decide whether to allow rice sushi from California to be imported—a weakening of Japan's traditional ban on importing rice (to maintain self-sufficiency in its staple food). The Japanese Agriculture Ministry, with an interest in the well-being of Japanese farmers, opposed the imports. The Foreign Ministry, with an interest in smooth relations with the United States, wanted to allow the imports. The final decision to allow imported sushi resulted from the tug-of-war between the ministries. Thus, according to the government bargaining model, foreign policy decisions reflect (a mix of) the interests of state agencies.

Although the rational model is the usual starting point for thinking about foreign policy decision making, there are many reasons to question whether decisions can be considered rational, beyond the influences of organizational inertia and government bargaining. These nonrational elements in decision making are best understood from a *psychological* analysis of individual and group decision-making processes.

Individual Decision Makers
Individuals are the only true actors in IR. Every international event is the result, intended or unintended, of decisions made by individuals. IR does not just happen. President Harry Truman, who made the decision to drop U.S. nuclear bombs on two Japanese cities in 1945, understood this. He had a sign on his desk: "The buck stops here." As leader of the world's greatest power, he had nobody to pass the buck to. If he chose to use the bomb (as he did), more than 100,000 civilians would die. If he chose not to, the war might drag on for months with tens of thousands of U.S. casualties. Truman had to choose. Some people applaud his decision; others condemn it. But for better or worse, Truman as an individual human being had to decide, and to take responsibility for the consequences. Similarly, the decisions of individual citizens, although they may not seem important when taken one by one, are what create the great forces of world history.

The study of individual decision making revolves around the question of rationality. To what extent are national leaders (or citizens) able to make rational decisions in the national interest—if indeed such an interest can be defined—and thus to conform to a realist view of IR? Individual rationality is not equivalent to state rationality: states might filter individuals' irrational decisions so as to arrive at rational choices, or states might distort individually rational decisions and end up with irrational state choices. But realists tend to assume that both states and individuals are rational and that the goals or interests of states correlate with those of leaders. Partly this assumption reflects the role of strong individuals such as monarchs and dictators in many states, where the rationality and interests of the leader determine those of the state.

The most simplified rational-actor models go so far as to assume that interests are the same from one actor to another. If this were so, individuals could be substituted for each other in various roles without changing history very much. And states would all behave similarly to each other (or rather, the differences between them would reflect different resources, geography, and similar features, not differences in the nature of national interests). This is at best a great oversimplification.

In truth, individual decisions reflect the *values* and *beliefs* of the decision maker. How can IR scholars characterize an individual's values and beliefs? Sometimes beliefs and values are spelled out in ideological autobiographies such as Hitler's *Mein Kampf*. Other times IR researchers try to infer beliefs through a method called *content analysis*— analyzing speeches or other documents to count the number of times key words or phrases are repeated, and in what contexts. Scholars of IR have also described *operational codes*—routines and methods that mediate between beliefs and practical actions. They have traced out such operational codes, for example, for Soviet communist leaders. Other scholars have created computer-based models of beliefs.

Atlas CD
North Korea
Leadership
Photo

The goals of individuals differ, as do the ways they pursue those goals. Individual decision makers not only have differing values and beliefs, but also have unique personalities—their personal experiences, intellectual capabilities, and personal styles of making decisions. Some IR scholars study individual psychology to understand how personality affects decision making. *Psychoanalytic approaches* hold that personalities reflect the subconscious influences of childhood experiences. For instance, some scholars believe U.S. President Woodrow Wilson's desire for power may have resulted from a feeling of insecurity due to an abusive father and that this insecurity led to his greatest failure, that Congress would not ratify the Versailles Treaty.

Beyond individual *idiosyncrasies* in goals or decision-making processes, there are at least three *systematic* ways in which individual decision making diverges from the rational model. First, decision makers suffer from **misperceptions** and **selective perceptions** (taking in only some kinds of information) when they compile information on the likely consequences of their choices. Decision-making processes must by necessity reduce and filter the incoming information on which a decision is based; the problem is that such filtration often is biased. **Information screens** are subconscious filters through which people put the information coming in about the world around them. Often they simply ignore any information that does not fit their expectations. Information is also screened out as it passes from one person to another in the decision-making process. This kind of selective perception caused Soviet leaders in 1941 and Israeli leaders in 1973 to ignore evidence of pending invasions of their countries.

Misperceptions can affect the implementation of policy by low-level officials as well as its formulation by high-level officials. For example, in 1988, officers on a U.S. warship in the Persian Gulf shot down a civilian Iranian jet that they believed to be a military jet attacking them. The officers were trying to carry out policies established by national leaders, but because of misperceptions their actions instead caused serious embarrassment to their state and damage to its international standing.

Second, the rationality of individual cost-benefit calculations is undermined by emotions that decision makers feel while thinking about the consequences of their actions—an effect referred to as *affective bias*. (Positive and negative affect refer to feelings of liking or disliking someone.) As hard as a decision maker tries to be rational in making a decision, the decision-making process is bound to be influenced by strong feelings held about the person or state toward which a decision is directed.

Big Mistake Foreign policies often deviate from rationality as a result of the misperceptions and biases of decision makers. Nowhere did these processes prove more costly than in the disastrous U.S. war in Vietnam (1967).

Third, *cognitive biases* are systematic distortions of rational calculations based not on emotional feelings but simply on the limitations of the human brain in making choices. The most important seems to be the attempt to produce *cognitive balance*—or to reduce *cognitive dissonance*. These terms refer to the tendency people have to try to maintain mental models of the world that are logically consistent (this seldom succeeds entirely). For instance, after deciding whether to intervene militarily in a conflict, a state leader will very likely adjust his or her mental model to downplay the risks and exaggerate the gains of the chosen course of action.

One implication of cognitive balance is that decision makers place greater value on goals that they have put much effort into achieving—the *justification of effort*. This is especially true in a democracy where politicians must face their citizens' judgment at the polls and so do not want to admit failures. The Vietnam War trapped U.S. decision makers in this way in the 1960s. After sending half a million troops halfway around the world it was difficult for U.S. leaders to admit to themselves that the costs of the war were greater than the benefits.

Decision makers also achieve cognitive balance through *wishful thinking*—an overestimate of the probability of a desired outcome. A variation of wishful thinking is to assume that an event with a *low probability* of occurring will *not* occur. This could be a dangerous way to think about catastrophic events such as accidental nuclear war.

Cognitive balance often leads decision makers to maintain a hardened image of an *enemy* and to interpret all the enemy's actions in a negative light (since the idea of bad people doing good things would create cognitive dissonance). Obviously, this cognitive bias overlaps with the affective bias felt toward such enemies. The enemy-image problem is especially important today in ethnic conflicts (see pp. 160–162).

A *mirror image* refers to two sides in a conflict maintaining very similar enemy images of each other ("we are defensive, they are aggressive," etc.). This happens frequently in ethnic conflicts. A decision maker may experience psychological *projection* of his or her own feelings onto another actor. For instance, if (hypothetically) Indian leaders wanted to gain nuclear superiority over Pakistan but found that goal inconsistent with their image of themselves as peaceful and defensive, the resulting cognitive dissonance might be resolved by believing that Pakistan was trying to gain nuclear superiority (the example works as well with the states reversed).

Another form of cognitive bias, related to cognitive balance, is the use of *historical analogies* to structure one's thinking about a decision. This can be quite useful or quite misleading, depending on whether the analogy is appropriate. As each historical situation is unique in some way, when a decision maker latches onto an analogy and uses it as a shortcut to a decision, the rational calculation of costs and benefits may be cut short as well. For example, U.S. leaders incorrectly used the analogy of Munich in 1938 to convince themselves that appeasement of communism in the Vietnam War would lead to increased communist aggression in Asia. Vietnam then became a potent analogy that helped convince U.S. leaders to avoid involvement in certain overseas conflicts, including Bosnia; this was called the "Vietnam syndrome" in U.S. foreign policy.

All these psychological processes—misperception, affective biases, and cognitive biases—interfere with the rational assessment of costs and benefits in making a decision. Two specific modifications to the rational model of decision making have been proposed to accommodate psychological realities.

First, the model of *bounded rationality* takes into account the costs of seeking and processing information. Nobody thinks about every single possible course of action when making a decision. Instead of **optimizing**, or picking the very best option, people usually work on the problem until they come up with a "good enough" option that meets some minimal criteria; this is called **satisficing**, or finding a satisfactory solution. The time constraints faced by top decision makers in IR—who are constantly besieged with crises—generally preclude their finding the very best response to a situation. These time constraints were described by U.S. Defense Secretary William Cohen, formerly a senator, in 1997: "The unrelenting flow of information, the need to digest it on a minute-by-minute basis, is quite different from anything I've experienced before. . . . There's little time for contemplation; most of it is action."[1]

Second, *prospect theory* provides an alternative explanation (rather than simple rational optimization) of decisions made under risk or uncertainty. According to this theory, decision makers go through two phases. In the editing phase they frame the options available and the probabilities of various outcomes associated with each option. Then in the evaluation phase they assess the options and choose one. Prospect theory holds that evaluations take place by comparison with a *reference point*, which is often the status quo but might be some past or expected situation. The decision maker asks if she or he can do better than that reference point, but the value placed on outcomes depends on how far from the reference point they are. The theory also holds that individuals *fear losses* more than they relish gains. Decision makers are therefore often willing to forgo opportunities rather than risk a setback.

Individual decision making thus follows an imperfect and partial kind of rationality at best. Not only do the goals of different individuals vary, but decision makers face a series of obstacles in receiving accurate information, constructing accurate models of the world, and reaching decisions that further their own goals. The rational model is only

---

[1] *Washington Post*, March 5, 1997: A22.

a simplification at best and must be supplemented by an understanding of individual psychological processes that affect decision making.

Not even an absolute dictator, however, makes decisions all alone. State decisions result from the interactions of groups of people. Leaders surround themselves with advisers to help them think about decisions. Decision-making bodies—from committees and agency task forces to legislatures and political parties—all rely on the interactions of relatively small groups of people reasoning or arguing together. The psychology of group dynamics thus has great influence on the way foreign policy is formulated.

Group Dynamics
What are the implications of group psychology for foreign policy decision making? In one respect, groups promote rationality by balancing out the blind spots and biases of any individual. Advisers or legislative committees may force a state leader to reconsider a rash decision. And the interactions of different individuals in a group may result in the formulation of goals that more closely reflect state interests rather than individual idiosyncrasies. However, group dynamics also introduce new sources of irrationality into the decision-making process. These fall into two general categories: the psychological dynamics that occur within groups, and the ways that the structure of group decision-making processes can bias the outcomes.

The most important psychological problem is the tendency for groups to reach decisions without accurately assessing their consequences, since individual members tend to go along with ideas they think the others support. This is called **groupthink**. The basic phenomenon is illustrated by a simple psychology experiment. A group of six people is asked to compare the lengths of two lines projected onto a screen. When five of the people are secretly instructed to say that line A is longer—even though anyone can see that line B is actually longer—the sixth person is likely to agree with the group rather than believe her or his own eyes.

Unlike individuals, groups tend to be overly optimistic about the chances of success and are thus more willing to take risks. Doubts about dubious undertakings are suppressed by participants because everyone else seems to think an idea will work. Also, the group diffuses responsibility from individuals, so nobody feels accountable for actions.

In a spectacular case of groupthink, President Ronald Reagan's close friend and director of the U.S. Central Intelligence Agency (CIA), William Casey, bypassed his own agency and ran covert operations spanning three continents using the National Security Council (NSC) staff in the White House basement. The NSC sold weapons to Iran in exchange for the freedom of U.S. hostages held in Lebanon, and then used the Iranian payments to illegally fund Nicaraguan Contra rebels. The **Iran-Contra scandal** resulted when these operations, managed by an obscure NSC aide named Oliver North, became public. Because the operation was secret, its few participants seem to have talked themselves into thinking that the operation was a smart idea. They discounted risks such as being discovered and exaggerated the benefits of opening channels to Iranian moderates (who proved elusive). The involvement of a top authority figure surely reassured other participants.

Web Link
Iran-Contra
Scandal

The *structure of a decision-making process*—the rules as to the decision makers, how voting is conducted, and so forth—can affect the outcome, especially when a group has *indeterminate preferences* because no single alternative appeals to a majority of participants. Experienced participants in foreign policy formation are familiar with the techniques for manipulating decision-making processes to favor outcomes they prefer. A common technique is to control a group's formal *decision rules*. These rules include the items of business the group discusses and the order in which proposals are considered (especially important when participants are satisficing). Probably most important is the ability to *control the agenda* and thereby structure the terms of debate. A group's voting procedures also affect the choices it makes. Procedures requiring more votes for adoption tend to favor conservative approaches to policy, whereas those allowing adoption with a mere plurality of votes tend to allow more frequent changes in policy.

The structure of decision making also reflects the composition of a decision group. Who is represented? Often the group is composed of individuals cast in particular *roles* in the group. (Some IR scholars treat role as a distinct level of analysis between the individual and domestic levels.) Roles can be institutional—a participant representing a viewpoint shared by her or his particular group, for example, an intelligence agency. Different sorts of roles within particular groups can be based on factions, mediators, swing voters, and so forth. One adviser might often play the role of introducing new ideas, another the role of defending the status quo, and a third the role of staying neutral so as to gain the leader's ear last.

State leaders often rely on an inner circle of advisers in making foreign policy decisions. The composition and operation of the inner circle vary across governments. For instance, President Lyndon Johnson had "Tuesday lunches" to discuss national security policy with top national security officials. Some groups depend heavily on *informal* consultations in addition to formal meetings. Some leaders create a "kitchen cabinet"—a trusted group of friends who discuss policy issues with the leader even though they have no formal positions in government. For instance, Russian President Boris Yeltsin relied on the advice of his bodyguard, who was a trusted friend.

Informal settings may be used in another way—to shake up formal decision groups and draw participants away from their usual bureaucratic roles. For example, Soviet Premier Leonid Brezhnev in 1972 took President Richard Nixon on a speedboat ride before settling down for discussions at Brezhnev's dacha (villa) in the countryside.

Crisis Management
The difficulties in reaching rational decisions, both for individuals and for groups, are heightened during a crisis. *Crises* are foreign policy situations in which outcomes are very important and time frames are compressed. There is no firm boundary between crises and routine policy making. But if a situation drags on for months or loses the dedicated attention of the top political leaders, it is not considered a crisis anymore. Crisis decision making is harder to understand and predict than is normal foreign policy making.

In a crisis, decision makers operate under tremendous time constraints. The normal checks on unwise decisions may not operate. Communications become shorter and more stereotyped, and information that does not fit a decision maker's expectations is more likely to be discarded simply because there is no time to consider it. In framing options there is a tendency to restrict the choices, again to save time, and a tendency to overlook creative options while focusing on the most obvious ones.

Groupthink occurs easily during crises. During the 1962 Cuban Missile Crisis, President John Kennedy created a small, closed group of advisers who worked together intensively for days on end, cut off from outside contact. Even the president's commu-

Atlas CD
Georgia's
Capital
Photo

Working under Stress Crisis management takes a high toll psychologically and physiologically. President Eduard Shevardnadze of Georgia seems to show this strain in 1992—just the beginning of several years of civil war and perpetual crisis in that country. Shevardnadze, formerly Gorbachev's foreign minister, returned to lead his native Georgia when the Soviet Union dissolved.

nication with Soviet leader Nikita Khrushchev was rerouted through Kennedy's brother Robert and the Soviet ambassador, cutting out the State Department. Recognizing the danger of groupthink, Kennedy would leave the room from time to time—removing the authority figure from the group—to encourage free discussion. Through this and other means, the group managed to identify a third option (a naval blockade) beyond their first two choices (bombing the missile sites or doing nothing).

Participants in crisis decision making are not only rushed, they experience severe psychological *stress*. As most of us have experienced personally, people usually do not make decisions wisely when under stress. Stress amplifies the biases just discussed. Decision makers tend to overestimate the hostility of adversaries and to underestimate their own hostility toward those adversaries. More and more information is screened out in order to come to terms with decisions being made and to restore cognitive balance. Crisis decision making also leads to physical exhaustion. *Sleep deprivation* sets in within days as decision makers use every hour to stay on top of the crisis. Unless decision makers are careful about getting enough sleep, these are the conditions under which vital foreign policy decisions may be made. In addition to sleep deprivation, physiological stress comes from drugs used by top policy makers—often nicotine and caffeine in high doses, and sometimes alcohol.

Because of the importance of sound decision making during crises, voters pay great attention to the psychological stability of their leaders. Before Israeli Prime Minister Yitzhak Rabin won election in 1992, he faced charges that he had suffered a one-day nervous breakdown when he headed the armed forces just before the 1967 war. Not so, he responded; he was just smart enough to realize that the crisis had caused exhaustion and nicotine poisoning; he needed to rest up for a day in order to go on and make good decisions.

Whether in crisis mode or normal routines, individual decision makers do not operate alone. Their decisions are shaped by the government and society in which they work. Foreign policy is constrained and shaped by substate actors ranging from government agencies to political interest groups and industries. Next, we turn our attention to these actors.

Substate Actors

Foreign policy is shaped not only by the internal dynamics of individual and group decision making but also by the states and societies within which decision makers operate.

Bureaucracies   The substate actors closest to the foreign policy process are the state's bureaucratic agencies maintained for developing and carrying out foreign policy. Different states maintain different foreign policy bureaucracies but share some common elements.

Virtually all states maintain a *diplomatic corps*, or *foreign service*, of diplomats working in *embassies* in foreign capitals (and in *consulates* located in noncapital foreign cities), as well as diplomats who remain at home to help coordinate foreign policy. States appoint *ambassadors* as their official representatives to other states and to international organizations. Diplomatic activities are organized through a *foreign ministry* or the equivalent (for example, the U.S. State Department).

Web Link
Diplomats

In many democracies, some diplomats are *political appointees* who come and go with changes in government leaders (often as patronage for past political support). Others are *career diplomats*, who come up through the ranks of the foreign service and tend to outlast changes in administration. Skilled diplomats are assets that increase a state's power.

Diplomats provide much of the information that goes into making foreign policies, but their main role is to carry out rather than create policies. Nonetheless, foreign ministry bureaucrats can often make foreign relations so routine that top leaders and political appointees can come and go without greatly altering the country's relations, for foreign policy is ongoing. The national interest is served, they believe, by the stability of overall national goals and positions in international affairs.

Tension is common between state leaders and foreign policy bureaucrats. Career diplomats try to orient new leaders and their appointees, and to control the flow of information they receive (creating information screens). Politicians struggle to exercise power over the formal bureaucratic agencies because the latter can be too "bureaucratic" (cumbersome, routinized, conservative) to easily control. Also, these agencies are often staffed (at lower levels) mostly by career officials who may not owe loyalty to political leaders.

Size alone does not guarantee power for a bureaucracy. For example, the U.S. Trade Representative (USTR) and the National Security Council (NSC) each have staffs of only about 150 people, compared with 5,000 people with responsibilities for similar matters in the Commerce and State departments. The power of these agencies is their proximity to the U.S. president. It is the NSC chief who traditionally briefs the president every morning on international security issues.

Sometimes, state leaders appoint a close friend or key adviser to manage the foreign policy bureaucracy. Chinese leader Mao Zedong put his loyal ally, Zhou Enlai, in charge of foreign policy, and Soviet President Mikhail Gorbachev had his close ally Eduard Shevardnadze running the foreign ministry. At times, frustration with the bureaucracy leads politicians to bypass normal channels of diplomacy. As President Nixon's national security adviser, Henry Kissinger secretly negotiated with China, the Soviet Union, and North Vietnam outside of the State Department or other formal bureaucratic structures.

INTERAGENCY TENSIONS Tensions between top political leaders and foreign policy bureaucracies are only one form of *interagency* tension in the formulation of foreign policy. Certain agencies traditionally clash, and an endless tug-of-war shapes the foreign policies that emerge. In an extreme example of interagency rivalry, the U.S. State Department and the CIA backed opposite sides in a civil war in Laos in 1960. In the United States and the Soviet Union during the Cold War, the defense ministry was usually more hawkish (favoring military strength) and the foreign ministry or State Department more dovish (favoring diplomacy), with the top leader holding the balance.   In general, bureaucracies promote policies in which their own capabilities would be effective and their power would increase.

Generally, representatives of bureaucratic agencies promote the interests of their own bureaucracy, although sometimes heads of agencies try to appear loyal to the state leader by forgoing the interests of their own agencies. Again, the individuals are somewhat interchangeable. One can often predict just from the job titles of participants how they will argue on a policy issue. The government bargaining model pays special attention to the interagency negotiations that result from conflicts of interest between agencies of the same government. The conflicting and overlapping interests of agencies can be complex, especially in large governments such as those of the great powers, with dozens of agencies that deal with international relations.

Units within agencies have similar tensions. In many countries, the different military services (army, navy, air force) pull in somewhat different directions, even if they ultimately unite to battle the foreign ministry. Bureaucrats working in particular units or projects become attached to them. Officials responsible for a new weapon system will lose bureaucratic turf, and perhaps their jobs, if the weapon's development is canceled.

Of special concern in many poor states is the institutional interest that military officers have in maintaining a strong military. If civilian state leaders allow officers' salaries to fall or the size of the military forces to be cut, they may well face institutional resistance from the military—in the extreme case a military takeover of the government. These issues were factors in attempted military coups in the Philippines, Venezuela, and other states in the 1990s.

Different states develop different institutional capabilities, in terms of both size (of budget and personnel) and specialization. These differences in institutions help explain differences in states' foreign policies.

In general, bureaucratic rivalry as an influence on foreign policy challenges the notion of states as unitary actors in the international system. Such rivalries suggest that a state does not have any single set of goals—a national interest—but that its actions may result from the bargaining of subunits, each with its own set of goals. Furthermore, such a perspective extends far beyond bureaucratic agencies because other substate actors have their own goals, which they seek to advance by influencing foreign policy.

Interest Groups Foreign policy makers operate not in a political vacuum but in the context of the political debates in their society. In all states societal pressures influence foreign policy, although these are aggregated and made effective through different channels in different societies. In pluralistic democracies, interested parties influence foreign policy through interest groups and political parties. In dictatorships similar influences can occur but less visibly. Thus foreign policies adopted by states generally reflect some kind of process of domestic coalition formation. Of course, international factors also have strong effects on domestic politics.

Atlas CD
Solidarity
Labor Union
Photo

Interest groups are coalitions of people who share a common interest in the outcome of some political issue and who organize themselves to try to influence the outcome. For instance, French farmers have a big stake in international negotiations on the European Community (which subsidizes agriculture) and in world trade talks (which set agricultural tariffs). French farmers have turned out in large numbers across the country on several occasions to block roads, stage violent street demonstrations, and threaten to grind the national economy to a halt unless the government adopted their position on tariffs and subsidies. Similarly (but often less dramatically), interest groups form around businesses, labor unions, churches, veterans, senior citizens, members of an occupation, or citizens concerned about an issue such as the environment.

Web Link
Interest Groups

Lobbying is the process of talking with legislators or officials to influence their decisions on some set of issues. Three important elements that go into successful lobbying are the ability to gain a hearing with busy officials, the ability to present cogent arguments for one's case, and the ability to trade favors in return for positive action on an issue. These favors—legal and illegal—range from campaign contributions through dinners at nice restaurants and trips to golf resorts, to securing illicit sexual liaisons and paying bribes. In many states, corruption is a major problem in governmental decision making (see pp. 384–386), and interest groups may induce government officials by illegal means to take certain actions.

Ethnic groups within one state often become interest groups concerned about their ancestral nation outside that state. Many members of ethnic groups feel strong emotional ties to their relatives in other countries; because the rest of the population generally does not care about such issues one way or the other, even a small ethnic group can have considerable influence on policy toward a particular country. Such ethnic ties are emerging as a powerful foreign policy influence in various ethnic conflicts in poor regions. The effect is especially strong in the United States, which is ethnically mixed and has a pluralistic, interest-group form of democracy. For example, Cuban Americans

Atlas CD
Lithuanian
Tensions
Photo

organize to influence U.S. policy toward Cuba, as do Greek Americans on Greece, Jewish Americans on Israel, and African Americans on Africa.

Whether or not a foreign country has a large constituency of ethnic nationals within another country, it can set about lobbying that country's government, as other interest groups do. For example, Israel and Taiwan have strong lobbying presences in the U.S. Congress, and many less visible states have hired U.S. public relations firms to represent their interests in Washington, DC. Meanwhile, oddly, the United States itself openly spends $30 million per year, through the National Endowment for Democracy (NED), to support domestic political actors in foreign countries. For example, the NED's Republican-party wing targeted Mongolia where free elections in 1992 had left former communists in power. U.S. consultants helped opposition politicians organize, and flooded the country with copies of a "Contract with the Mongolian Voter" based on the U.S. Republican party's Contract with America. In the 1997 elections, the opposition won control of the Mongolian government. Clearly, interest groups have goals and interests that may or may not coincide with the national interest as a whole (if indeed such an interest can be identified). As with bureaucratic agencies, the view of the state as a unitary actor can be questioned. The head of General Motors once said that "what's good for General Motors is good for the country, and vice versa." This is not self-evident. Nonetheless, defenders of interest group politics argue that various interest groups tend to push and pull in different directions, with the ultimate decisions generally reflecting the interests of society as a whole.

According to *Marxist* theories of international relations (see Chapter 7), the key domestic influences on foreign policy in capitalist countries are rich owners of big businesses. For instance, European imperialism benefited banks and big business, which made huge profits from exploiting cheap labor and resources in overseas colonies. This is the official view (if not always the operative one) of the Chinese government toward Western industrialized states. During the Cold War, Marxists argued that U.S. foreign policy and that of its Western allies were driven by the profit motive of arms manufacturers.

Web Link
Military-
Industrial
Complex

The Military-Industrial Complex A **military-industrial complex** is a huge interlocking network of governmental agencies, industrial corporations, and research institutes, working together to supply a nation's military forces. Because of the domestic political clout of these actors, the complex was a very powerful influence on foreign policy in *both* the United States and the Soviet Union during the Cold War. Some of that influence remains, though it has diminished. The military-industrial complex was a response to the growing importance of technology (nuclear weapons, electronics, and others) and of logistics in Cold War military planning.

States at war have long harnessed their economic and technological might for the war effort. But during the Cold War military procurement occurred on a massive scale in "peacetime," as the superpowers raced to develop new high-technology weapons. This race created a special role for scientists and engineers in addition to the more traditional role of industries that produce war materials. In response to the Soviet satellite *Sputnik* in 1957, the United States increased spending on research and development and created new science education programs. By 1961, President Dwight Eisenhower warned in his farewell speech that the military-industrial complex (a term he coined) was gaining "unwarranted influence" in U.S. society and that militarization could erode

Flying Pork?   In the post–Cold War era, the military-industrial complex has been hit hard in the United States and harder in the former Soviet Union by cuts in military spending. Here, B-2 long-range stealth bombers (which survived the end of the Cold War despite their enormous cost) are on the assembly line at the Northrop Grumman Corporation in southern California, 1988. Companies like Northrop Grumman have an interest in high military spending—one link in the military-industrial complex.

democracy in the United States. The threat to democracy was that the interest of the military-industrial complex in the arms race conflicted with the interest of ordinary citizens in peace, while the size of the complex gave it more political clout than ordinary citizens could muster.

The complex encompasses a variety of constituencies, each of which has an interest in military spending. *Corporations* that produce goods for the military profit from government contracts. So do military *officers* whose careers advance by building bureaucratic empires around new weapons systems. And so do universities and scientific institutes that receive military research contracts—a major source of funding for scientists in Russia and the United States.

Subcontractors and parts suppliers for big weapons projects are usually spread around many states and congressional districts in the United States, so that local citizens and politicians join the list of constituents benefitting from military spending. Recently, a similar phenomenon has emerged in the European Community, where weapons development programs have been parceled out to several European states. A new fighter jet is less likely to be canceled if one country gets the contract for the wings, another for the engines, and so forth.

Executives in military industries, as the people who best understand their industries, are often appointed as government officials responsible for military procurement decisions and then return to their companies again—a practice called the *revolving door*. In democracies, military industries also try to influence public opinion through *advertising* that ties their products to patriotic themes. Finally, U.S. military industries give generous *campaign contributions* to national politicians who vote on military budgets, and sometimes bribes to Pentagon officials as well. Military industry became an important source of *political action committee (PAC) money*; in the 1996 elections, for example, one company alone, Lockheed Martin, contributed more than $2 million to congressional campaigns.[2]

When the Cold War ended, the military-industrial complex in both superpowers endured cutbacks in military budgets. In Russia, military industries formed the backbone of a political faction seeking to slow down economic reforms and continue government subsidies to state-owned industries. They succeeded in replacing Russia's reformist prime minister with an industrial manager in late 1992. In the United States, meanwhile, the lingering influence of the military-industrial complex may help to explain why Congress kept funding certain Cold War weapons after their purpose seemingly disappeared.

Public Opinion
Military industries and other substate actors seek to influence **public opinion**—the range of views on foreign policy issues held by the citizens of a state. Public opinion has greater influence on foreign policy in democracies than in authoritarian governments. But even dictators must pay attention to what citizens think. No government can rule by force alone: it needs legitimacy to survive. It must convince people to accept (if not to like) its policies, because in the end policies are carried out by ordinary people—soldiers, workers, petty bureaucrats.

Because of the need for public support, even authoritarian governments spend great effort on *propaganda*—the public promotion of their official line—to win support for foreign policies. States use television, newspapers, and other information media in this effort. For instance, when China invited President Nixon to visit in 1972, the Chinese government mounted a major propaganda campaign to explain to its people that the United States was not so bad after all. In many countries the state owns or controls major mass media such as television and newspapers, mediating the flow of information to its citizens; however, new information technologies with multiple channels make this harder to do.

In democracies, where governments must stand for election, public opinion is even more important. An unpopular war can force a leader or party from office, as happened to U.S. President Johnson in 1968 during the Vietnam War. Or a popular war can help secure a government's mandate to continue in power, as happened to Margaret Thatcher in Britain after the 1982 Falkland Islands War. During the war in Bosnia, officials in the U.S. State Department said privately that the main goal of U.S. policy was often just to keep the conflict there off of the front pages of U.S. newspapers (an elusive goal, as it turned out).

---

[2] Washburn, Jennifer. When Money Talks, Congress Listens. *Bulletin of the Atomic Scientists* 53 (4), July/August 1997: 40.

Journalists serve as the gatekeepers of information passing from foreign policy elites to the public. The media and government often conflict, because of the traditional role of the press as a watchdog and critic of government actions and powers. The media try to uncover and publicize that which the government wants to hide, especially in situations such as the Iran-Contra scandal. Foreign policy decision makers also rely on the media for information about foreign affairs. Reportedly, President Kennedy ordered his own subscription to the *New York Times* so that he could anticipate by a day the reports coming to him from the State Department.

Yet the media also depend on government for information; the size and resources of the foreign policy bureaucracies dwarf those of the press. This advantage gives the government great power to *manipulate* journalists by feeding them information, to shape the news and influence public opinion. Government decision makers can create dramatic stories in foreign relations—through summit meetings, crises, and so forth. Bureaucrats can also *leak* secret information to the press to support their view and win bureaucratic battles. Finally, the military and the press have a running battle about journalists' access to military operations; for instance, in the Gulf War, U.S. military censors limited media coverage.

In democracies, where the flow of information and opinions is not tightly restricted by the state, public opinion can be accurately measured through *polling*—analyzing the responses of a sample group to questionnaires, to infer the opinions of a larger population. This is impossible to do in societies where secret police monitor any expressions of opposition to state policies. But in societies where individuals feel free to speak out, polling has developed into an important part of the foreign policy-making process.

Occasionally a foreign policy issue is decided directly by a referendum of the entire citizenry (the United States lacks such a tradition, which is strong in Switzerland and Denmark, for example). In 1992, the Maastricht Treaty on closer European political union (see pp. 304–305) was narrowly defeated in a popular referendum in Denmark, despite the support of the government, all major political parties, labor unions, and other political groups. (A later referendum narrowly approved the treaty.) In France the treaty barely squeaked through. Because of these signs of public opposition to the Maastricht Treaty, European leaders were forced to reconsider the pace of European integration.

Even in the most open democracies, states do not merely *respond* to public opinion. Decision makers enjoy some autonomy to make their own choices, and they are pulled in various directions by bureaucracies and interest groups, whose views often conflict with the direction favored by public opinion at large. Also, public opinion is seldom unified on any policy, and sophisticated polling can show that particular segments of the population (regions of the country, genders, races, etc.) often differ in their perceptions of foreign policy issues. So a politician may respond to the opinion of one constituency rather than the whole population. Public opinion also varies considerably over time. States use propaganda (in dictatorships) or try to manipulate the media (in democracies) to keep public opinion from diverging too much from state policies.

In democracies, public opinion generally has *less effect on foreign policy than on domestic policy*. National leaders traditionally have additional latitude to make decisions in the international realm. This derives from the special need of states to act in a unified way to function effectively in the international system, as well as from the traditions of secrecy and diplomacy that remove IR from the realm of ordinary domestic politics. In the nuclear age, IR was further distanced from everyday political life in the nuclear states by the public's willingness to trust experts and officials to deal with the technical and frightening issues of nuclear strategy. Over time, however, peace movements have sometimes pushed governments toward disarmament.

In the case of Japan, public opinion is a major political force restraining the military spending of the government, its commitment of military forces beyond Japan's borders, and especially the development of nuclear weapons (which is within Japan's technical abilities). The ruling party—under pressure from the United States to share the burden of defense and to shoulder its responsibilities as a great power—has slowly but steadily pushed to increase Japan's military spending and allow Japanese military forces to expand their role modestly (in the 1980s, to patrol Asian sea lanes vital to Japanese trade; in the 1990s, to participate in UN peacekeeping operations). Repeatedly, these efforts have been slowed or rebuffed by strong public opinion against the military. In Japan, people remember the horrible consequences of militarism in the 1930s and World War II, culminating in the nuclear bombings of 1945. They are suspicious of any increase in the size or role of military forces, and dead set against Japan's having nuclear weapons. In this case public opinion strongly constrains the state's conduct of foreign policy.

The *attentive public* in a democracy is that minority of the population that stays informed about international issues. This segment varies somewhat from one issue to another, but there is also a core of people who care in general about foreign affairs and follow them closely. The most active members of the attentive public on foreign affairs constitute a foreign policy *elite*—people with power and influence who affect foreign policy. This elite includes people within governments as well as outsiders such as businesspeople, journalists, lobbyists, and professors of political science. Public opinion polls show that elite opinions sometimes (but not always) differ considerably from those of the general population, and sometimes from those of the government as well.

Governments sometimes adopt foreign policies for the specific purpose of generating public approval and hence gaining domestic legitimacy. This is the case when a government undertakes a war or foreign military intervention at a time of domestic difficulty, to distract attention and gain public support—taking advantage of the **rally 'round the flag syndrome** (the public's increased support for government leaders during wartime, at least in the short term). Citizens who would readily criticize their government's policies on education or health care will often refrain from criticism when the government is at war and the lives of the nation's soldiers are on the line. President Bush enjoyed high popularity ratings in both the 1989 Panama and the 1991 Gulf wars.

However, wars that go on too long, or are not successful, can turn public opinion against the government and even lead to a popular uprising to overthrow the government. In Argentina, the military government in 1982 led the country into war with Britain over the Falkland Islands. At first Argentineans rallied around the flag, but after losing the war they rallied around the cause of getting rid of the military government, and they replaced it with a new civilian government that prosecuted the former leaders.

Atlas CD
Tiananmen
Square
Photo

The Democratic Peace Overall, the differences in the foreign policy process from one state to another are more influenced by a state's type of government than by the particular constellation of bureaucracies, interest groups, or individuals within it. Government types include military dictatorship, communist party rule, one-party (noncommunist) rule, and various forms of multiparty democracy. Relatively democratic

THE INFORMATION REVOLUTION Informed or Brainwashed?

Democratization accelerated in the 1990s worldwide, potentially enlarging the zone of "democratic peace" since democracies rarely fight each other. New information technologies may allow citizens greater access to political processes, including those that cross borders. However, these technologies may also give those with wealth and power new means of influence, as when state-controlled media whip up nationalism or when advertising promotes Western products and values in the global South. Will the information revolution usher in global democracy and peace, or sharpen divisions?

To explore this question, go to www.IRtext.com

states tend to share values and interests, and hence to get along better with each other than with nondemocracies.

Nondemocratic governments are often called **authoritarian**. These governments rule without needing to stand for free elections, to respect civil and political rights, to allow freedom of the press, and so forth. By contrast, a **democracy** is a government of the people, usually through elected representatives, and usually with a respect for individual rights in society (especially rights to hold political ideas differing from those of the government).

In practice, most states lie along a spectrum with some mix of democratic and authoritarian elements. For example, because of campaign contributions, even democracies in North America and Japan give greater influence to rich people than to poor people. In many states, governments control TV and radio stations, putting opposition politicians at a disadvantage in elections. In Angola, relatively fair elections were held in 1992, but the losing side rejected the results and resorted to military attacks. In Algeria in 1992, the military canceled elections midway as Islamic parties were winning.

How do the foreign policies of democracies differ from those of authoritarian governments? We have already referred to a number of differences in the nature of internal decision making, the effects of interest groups, and the importance of public opinion. Although public opinion and interest group activism operate in some form in virtually all states, they are more influential in democracies.

IR scholars have examined empirical data for the idea that democracy is linked to a kind of foreign policy fundamentally different from that of authoritarianism. One theory they considered was that democracies are generally *more peaceful* than authoritarian governments. This turned out to be *not true*. Democracies fight as many wars as do authoritarian states. Indeed, the three most war-prone states of the past two centuries (according to political scientists who count wars) were France, Russia, and Britain. Britain was a democracy throughout, France for part of the period, and Russia not at all.

What *is* true about democracies is that although they fight wars against authoritarian states, *democracies almost never fight each other*. No major historical cases contradict this generalization, which is known as the **democratic peace**. Why this is so is not entirely clear. As there have not been many democracies for very long, the generalization could

Web Link
Democracy

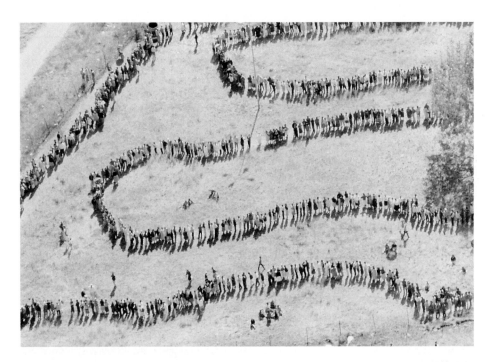

We Want to Vote   Upsurges of democratic movements throughout the world in recent years testify to the power of the idea of democracy. Since democracies rarely fight each other, worldwide democratization might lead to lasting peace. Here, South Africans line up to vote in that country's first all-race elections, which ended apartheid and elected Nelson Mandela as president, 1994.

be just a coincidence, though this seems unlikely. It may be that democracies do not tend to have severe conflicts with each other, as they tend to be capitalist states whose trade relations create strong interdependence (war would be costly since it would disrupt trade). Or, citizens of democratic societies (whose support is necessary for wars to be waged) may simply not see the citizens of other democracies as enemies. By contrast, authoritarian governments of other states can be seen as enemies. Note that the peace among democracies gives empirical support to a long-standing liberal claim that, because it is rooted in the domestic level of analysis, contradicts a fundamental premise of realism—that the most important explanations are to be found at the interstate level.

Over the past two centuries, democracy has become more and more widespread as a form of government, and this is changing the nature of the foreign policy process worldwide. In the past two decades this trend has accelerated in several ways. New democracies emerged in several (though not all) states of the old Soviet bloc. Military governments were replaced with democratically elected civilian ones throughout most of Latin America as well as in several African and Asian countries. South Africa, the last white-ruled African country, adopted majority rule in 1994. In several of these cases (for instance, in the Philippines in 1986), long-standing dictatorships were ended by nonviolent popular movements. Elsewhere (for instance, in Nicaragua) civil wars ended with internationally supervised democratic elections. In several other authoritarian states, such as China, public

Atlas CD
Bulgaria
Democracy
Photo

pressures for greater democratic participation in government became evident. Most recently, long-standing dictatorships or military governments were replaced peacefully by democratic governments in Indonesia and Nigeria, both regional giants. However, movement in the other direction still occurs—military governments took over in Pakistan and in Ivory Coast in 1999, for example—but less often.

We do not know where these trends toward democracy will lead, but because it is now conceivable that someday all or most of the world's states will be democratically governed, wars may become less frequent. As Kant envisaged, an international community based on peaceful relations may emerge. However, although mature democracies almost never fight each other, a period of *transition* to democracy may be more prone to war than either a stable democracy or a stable authoritarian government. Therefore the process of democratization does not necessarily bode well for peace in the short term.

A further caution is in order. By way of analogy, there was a generalization during the Cold War that communist governments never yield power peacefully. That generalization held up beautifully until suddenly a series of communist governments did just that around 1990. As the world has more democracies for a longer time, the generalization about their almost never fighting each other might not hold up.

The attempt to explain foreign policy in a general and *theoretical* way has met only limited success. This is one reason realists continued to find simple unitary actor models of the state useful; the domestic and individual elements of the foreign policy process add much complexity and unpredictability. One area of foreign policy where knowledge stands on a somewhat firmer basis is the *descriptive* effort to understand how particular mechanisms of foreign policy formation operate in various states. This section has largely bypassed such approaches because they belong properly to the field of comparative politics.

To summarize, foreign policy is a complex outcome of a complex process. It results from the struggle of competing themes, competing domestic interests, and competing government agencies. No single individual, agency, or guiding principle determines the outcome. Yet, foreign policy does achieve a certain overall coherence. States do form foreign policy on an issue or toward a region; it is not just an incoherent collection of decisions and actions taken from time to time. Out of the turbulent internal processes of foreign policy formation come relatively coherent interests and policies that states pursue.

Beyond the challenges to realist theories from liberalism and foreign policy analysis, several more sweeping critiques have emerged. These include feminism, postmodernism, and peace studies.

Feminism

Feminist scholarship has cut a broad swath across academic disciplines, from literature to psychology to history. In recent years, it has made inroads in international relations, once considered one of the fields most resistant to feminist arguments. Such resistance perhaps stems from the heavily male composition of the major actors in IR—political decision makers, diplomats, and soldiers. Resistance may also derive from the fact that most IR scholars are themselves male, but not all female scholars are feminists nor do all male scholars reject feminist arguments. Nonetheless, feminist scholarship in IR received increasing interest in the 1990s and produced a rapidly growing literature.

Web Link
Feminism

A Guy Thing   State leaders at a Pacific Rim summit (1997) pose in matching leather bomber jackets. Feminists from various theoretical traditions agree that the gender makeup of such summits is important.

Why Gender Matters
Feminist scholarship encompasses a variety of strands of work, but all have in common the insight that gender matters in understanding how IR works—especially in issues relating to war and international security. Feminist scholarship in various disciplines seeks to uncover hidden assumptions about gender in how we study a subject such as IR. What scholars traditionally claim to be universal often turns out to be true only of males. For instance, feminists criticize medical studies that include only male patients.

Some feminists have argued that the core assumptions of realism—especially of anarchy and sovereignty—reflect the ways in which *males* tend to interact and to see the world. In this view, the realist approach simply assumes male participants when discussing foreign policy decision making, state sovereignty, or the use of military force.

This is a somewhat complex critique. Because in fact the vast majority of heads of state, of diplomats, and of soldiers *are* male, it may be realistic to study them as males. What the feminist critics then ask is that scholars explicitly recognize the gendered nature of their subject (rather than implicitly assuming all actors are male). In this view, our understanding of male actors in IR can be increased by considering how their gender identity affects their views and decision processes. And females also influence IR (more often through nonstate channels than males do)—influences often ignored by realism. Feminist scholars argue that we can better understand IR by including the roles and effects of women than by ignoring them.

Beyond revealing the hidden assumptions about gender in a field of scholarship, feminists often *challenge traditional concepts of gender* as well. In IR, these traditional concepts revolve around the assumptions that males fight wars and run states, whereas females are basically irrelevant to IR. Such gender roles are based in the broader construction of masculinity as suitable to *public* and political spaces, whereas femininity is associated with the sphere of the *private* and domestic. An example of this gendered construction was provided by White House Chief of Staff Donald Regan's comment at a 1985 Reagan-Gorbachev summit meeting that women do not care about throw weights of ICBMs (see p. 193) and would rather watch Nancy Reagan. Later he said that U.S. women would not support sanctions against white-ruled South Africa because they would not want to lose their diamonds (a South African export). Feminists call into question, at a minimum, the stereotypes of women as caring more about fashion and jewelry than arms control and apartheid.

Beyond a basic agreement that gender is important, there is no single feminist approach to IR but several such approaches—*strands* of scholarship and theory. Although they are interwoven (all paying attention to gender and to the status of women) they often run in different directions. On some core issues critiquing realism, the different strands of feminism have conflicting views, creating interesting debates *within* feminism.

One strand, **standpoint feminism**, focuses on valorizing the feminine—that is, valuing the unique contributions of women *as* women. Standpoint feminists do not think women do all things as well as men or vice versa. Because of their greater experience with nurturing and human relations, women are seen as potentially more effective than men (on average) in conflict resolution as well as in group decision making. Standpoint feminists believe there are real differences between the genders that are not just social constructions and cultural indoctrination (although these contribute to gender roles, too). Some standpoint feminists believe there is a core biological essence to being male or female (sometimes called *essentialism*), but the majority think women's standpoint is more culturally than biologically determined. Both perspectives create a *standpoint* from which to observe, analyze, and criticize the traditional perspectives on IR.

Another strand, **liberal feminism**, rejects these claims as being based on stereotyped gender roles. Liberal feminists see the "essential" differences in men's and women's abilities or perspectives as trivial or nonexistent—men and women are equal. They deplore exclusion of women from positions of power in IR but do not believe that including women would basically change the nature of the international system. Liberal feminists seek to include women more often as subjects of study—such as women state leaders, women soldiers, and other women operating outside traditional gender roles in IR.

A third approach combines feminism with postmodernism (discussed later in this chapter). **Postmodern feminism** tends to reject assumptions about gender made by both standpoint and liberal feminists. Where standpoint feminists consider gender differences to be important and fixed, and liberal feminists consider those differences to be trivial, postmodern feminists find them important but arbitrary and flexible.

To some extent the differences among feminist strands—standpoint, liberal, and postmodern—overlap with the general themes of conservative, liberal, and revolutionary world views, respectively. But these parallels are only rough, and overall the feminist approaches to IR can be considered closer to the revolutionary world view than is either realism or liberalism.

The Masculinity of Realism
Standpoint feminism provides a perspective from which to reexamine the core assumptions of realism—especially the assumption of autonomy, from which flow the concepts of sovereignty and anarchy—important con-

cepts for realists. To realists, the international system consists of autonomous actors (states) that control their own territory and have no right to infringe on another's territory. Do these concepts rest on a "masculine" view of the world? If so, what would a "feminine" approach to international security be like? Some standpoint feminists have argued that realism emphasizes autonomy and separation because men find separation easier to deal with than interconnection.

This view rests on psychological research showing that boys and girls grow up from a young age with different views of separateness and connection. In this theory, because a child's primary caretaker is almost always female in the early years, girls form their gender identity around the perception of *similarity* with their caretaker (and by extension the environment in which they live), but boys perceive their *difference* from the caretaker. From this experience, boys develop social relations based on individual *autonomy*, but girls' relations are based on *connection*. As a result, women are held to be more likely than men to fear abandonment, whereas men are more likely to fear intimacy.

In *moral* reasoning, according to this research, boys tend to apply abstract rules and stress individual rights (reflecting their sense of separation from the situation), but girls pay more attention to the concrete contexts of different situations and to the responsibility of group members for each other. In playing *games*, boys resolve disputes through arguments about the rules and then keep playing, but girls are more likely to abandon a game rather than argue over the rules and risk the social cohesion of their group. In *social relations*, boys form and dissolve friendships more readily than girls, who are more likely to stick loyally with friends. All these gender differences in children reflect the basic concept that for girls connection matters more than independence, but for boys the reverse is true. (In addition to its masculine nature, individual autonomy is a *Western* construction that is not as important in many non-Western cultures.)

Realism, of course, rests on the concept of states as separate, autonomous actors that make and break alliances freely while pursuing their own interests (but not interfering in each other's internal affairs). Such a conception of autonomy parallels the masculine psyche just described. Thus, some feminists find in realism a hidden assumption of masculinity. Furthermore, the sharp distinction that realists draw between international politics (anarchic) and domestic politics (ordered) parallels the distinction in gender roles between the public (masculine) and private (feminine) spheres. Thus, realism constructs IR as a man's world, above and beyond the fact that most participants are male.

By contrast, an international system based on *feminine* principles might give greater import to the *interdependence* of states than to their autonomy, stressing the responsibility of people to care for each other with less regard for states and borders. In the struggle between the principles of human rights and of sovereignty (noninterference in internal affairs), human rights would receive priority. In the choice of forms of leverage when conflicts arise between states, violence might be less prevalent. The concept of national security might be based on common security rather than narrow self-interest.

A standpoint feminist reconceptualization of IR also questions the realist preoccupation with the interstate level of analysis, which presumes that the logic of war itself is autonomous and can be separated from other social relationships such as economics, domestic politics, sexism, and racism. A feminist standpoint, however, reveals the *connections* of these phenomena with war. It suggests new avenues for understanding war at the domestic and individual levels of analysis—underlying causes that realists largely ignore.

Her Role and His   Feminist scholars emphasize the importance of gender roles in IR, especially the traditional distinction between males in the political-military roles and females in the domestic-family roles. Here in Sarajevo, a UN soldier provides cover as a Bosnian citizen runs along "sniper's alley" (1994). Realities often diverge from stereotypes, however. In Bosnia, for example, the UN "protection force" mainly protected itself, while ethnic cleansing and siege killed 100,000 women and children.

At the domestic level of analysis, gender relations within a society (both cross-gender and same-gender relationships among both adults and children) may be a cause of war. For example, the psychological theory just discussed suggests that societies in which fathers participate less in child rearing would produce adult males more enamored of autonomy (sovereignty), because more boys would grow up seeing themselves as different from their caregivers. In fact there is some anthropological evidence that war is more frequent in cultures where fathers are distant from their young sons and not affectionate toward them.

Gender in War and Peace   In addition to its emphasis on autonomy and anarchy, realism stresses military force as the key form of leverage in IR. Here, too, many standpoint feminists see in realism a hidden assumption of masculinity. They see war as not only a male occupation, but the quintessentially male occupation. In this view, men are inherently the more warlike sex, and women the more peaceful. Thus, although realism may accurately portray the importance of war and military force in IR as we now know it, this merely reflects the male domination of the international sphere to date—not a necessary, eternal, or inescapable logic of relations among states.

Standpoint feminists find plenty of evidence to support the idea of war as a masculine pursuit. Anthropologists have found that in all hunter-gatherer cultures, males are the primary (and often only) combatants in warfare, despite the enormous diversity of those cultures in so many other ways. Historically, warfare in both agrarian and industrial societies has been an almost exclusively male pursuit. (Of course, so were voting and participation in domestic politics for most of history, yet feminists would hardly call those activities essentially masculine.)

One supposed link between war and masculinity is the male sex hormone testosterone (along with related hormones), which some biologists have connected with aggressive behavior in animals. However, testosterone does not *cause* aggression. Rather, social interactions "feed back" to affect testosterone levels (winners' testosterone rises while losers' levels fall). Thus testosterone is a link in a complex system of relationships between the organism and the social environment. Complex behaviors such as aggression and war cannot be said to be biologically *driven* or predetermined, because humanity's most striking biological capability is flexibility.

Even some feminists who see gender differences as strictly cultural and not biological at all view war as an essentially masculine construction. In one theory, for example, war may fill a void left for men by their inability to give birth; war provides a meaning to life and gives men an opportunity through heroism to transcend their individual isolation and overcome their fear of death—opportunities that women potentially get through childbirth. In addition, heroism on the battlefield, especially before modern mechanized war, promised men a form of immortality, as their deeds would live on in collective memory.

**Atlas CD
Kurdish
Women and
Children**
Photo

By contrast, women are usually portrayed by standpoint feminists as more peaceful creatures than men—whether because of biology, culture, or (most likely) both. These feminists emphasize women's unique abilities and contributions as *peacemakers*. They stress women's roles as *mothers* and potential mothers. Because of such caregiving roles, women are presumed to be more likely than men to oppose war and more likely to find alternatives to violence in resolving conflicts.

Both biologically and anthropologically, there is no firm evidence connecting women's caregiving functions (pregnancy and nursing) with any particular kinds of behavior such as reconciliation or nonviolence. (Of course, researchers have studied females less than males.) The role of women varies considerably from one society to another. Although they rarely take part in combat, women sometimes provide logistical support to male warriors and sometimes help to drive the men into a war frenzy by dancing, shaming nonparticipating males, and other activities supportive of a war effort. Yet in other cultures, women restrain the men from war or play special roles as mediators in bringing wars to an end.

The idea of women as peacemakers has a long history. In ancient Athens, the (male) playwright Aristophanes speculated about how women might end the unpopular Peloponnesian War with Sparta, then in progress. Women have formed their own organizations to work for peace on many occasions. In 1852, *Sisterly Voices* was published as a newsletter for women's peace societies. Bertha von Suttner in 1892 persuaded Alfred Nobel to create the Nobel peace prize (which Suttner won in 1905). During World War I, in 1915, Jane Addams and other feminists founded the Women's Peace Party (now called the Women's International League for Peace and Freedom).

After World War I, the *suffrage* movement won the right for women to vote. Standpoint feminists thought that women would vote for peace and against war, changing the nature of foreign policy, but women generally voted as their husbands did. Similarly, decades later when women participated in liberation struggles against colonialism in the third world, some feminists thought such participation would lead to different kinds of foreign policies in the newly independent countries, but in general such changes did not materialize (partly because women were often pushed aside from political power after the revolution).

Recently, however, U.S. public opinion on foreign policy issues has partially vindicated standpoint feminists. A **gender gap** in polls shows women to be about ten percentage points lower than men on average in their support for military actions (including the Gulf War). This gender gap has been growing over time and has begun to translate into distinctly different average female and male voting patterns (such as women's greater support for President Bill Clinton's reelection in 1996).

Meanwhile, feminists in recent decades have continued to organize women's peace organizations. In the 1980s, Women's Action for Nuclear Disarmament (WAND) opposed the nuclear arms buildup. In 1995, the UN-sponsored Beijing conference on women brought together women activists from around the world, and helped deepen feminists' engagement with global issues such as North-South inequality. In Israel, the "women in black" held vigils to protest their government's military actions against Palestinians.

Through these various actions, standpoint feminists have begun developing a feminist practice of international relations that would provide an alternative to the masculine practice of realism. The motto of the UN Educational, Scientific, and Cultural Organization (UNESCO) is, "Since war begins in the minds of men, it is in the minds of men that the foundations for peace should be sought." For standpoint feminists, war does indeed begin in the minds of men but the foundations for peace would better be sought in the minds of women.

Women in IR

Liberal feminists are skeptical of standpoint critiques of realism. They believe that when women are allowed to participate in IR, they play the game basically the same way men do, with similar results. They think that women can practice realism—based on autonomy, sovereignty, anarchy, territory, military force, and all the rest—just as well as men can. Thus liberal feminists tend to reject the critique of realism as masculine. (In practice many feminists draw on both standpoint and liberal views.)

Liberal feminism focuses on the integration of women into the overwhelmingly male preserves of foreign policy making and the military. In most states, these occupations are typically at least 90 percent male. For instance, in 1995 the world's diplomatic delegations to the UN General Assembly were 80 percent male overall, and the heads of those delegations were 97 percent male. The U.S. military, with one of the highest proportions of women anywhere in the world or in history, is still about 85 percent male.

For liberal feminists, the main effect of this gender imbalance on the nature of IR—that is, apart from its effects on the status of women—is to waste talent. As liberal feminists think that women have the same capabilities as men, the inclusion of women in traditionally male occupations (from state leader to foot soldier) would bring additional capable individuals into those areas. Gender equality would thus increase national capabilities by giving the state a better overall pool of diplomats, generals, soldiers, and politicians.

In support of their argument that, on average, women handle power just as men do, liberal feminists point to the many examples of women who have served in such positions. No distinctly feminine feature of their behavior in office distinguishes these leaders from their male counterparts. Rather, they have been diverse in character and policy. Of course, there is an unavoidable weakness in this line of argument, as women in traditionally male roles may have been selected (or self-selected) on the basis of their suitability to such roles: they may not act the way "average" women would act. Still, they do show that individuals cannot be judged accurately using group characteristics alone.

Female state leaders do not appear to be any more oriented to nonviolent leverage in international conflicts or any less committed to state sovereignty and territorial integrity than are male leaders. It has even been suggested that women in power tend to be more masculine in policy—in particular, more warlike—to compensate for being females in traditionally male roles. However, liberal feminists might dispute this assertion.

Only one female has been the top leader of a great power in the past century—Britain's Margaret Thatcher in the 1980s. She went to war in 1982 to recover the Falkland Islands from Argentina (at issue were sovereignty and territorial integrity). Among middle powers, Indira Gandhi likewise led India in war against Pakistan in 1971, as did Israel's Golda Meir against Egypt and Syria in 1973. But Benazir Bhutto of Pakistan and Corazón Aquino of the Philippines struggled to control their own military forces in the late 1980s. Turkey's Tansu Çiller led a harsh war to suppress Kurdish rebels in the mid-1990s. But the president of Sri Lanka and her mother, the prime minister, tried to make peace with separatist rebels, without much success. Other states, such as Norway and Iceland, have had female leaders when war and peace were not major political issues in those countries. Overall, women state leaders, like men, seem capable of leading in war or in peace as circumstances demand.

Web Link
Women in IR

Within the U.S. foreign policy establishment, the record of women leaders similarly does not show any particular soft or hard tendency relative to their male counterparts. Madeleine Albright, the first female Secretary of State, was considered one of the tougher foreign policy makers in the Clinton administration, as was UN ambassador Jeane Kirkpatrick in the Reagan administration. Nancy Kassebaum (also a Republican) was a voice for compassion in the U.S. Senate, who led efforts to increase humanitarian aid to Africa in 1990s.

In the U.S. Congress, it is hard to compare men's and women's voting records on foreign policy issues because there have been so few women. The U.S. Senate (which approves treaties and foreign policy appointments) was 98 to 99 percent male until 1992, when it dropped to 94 percent male (and later to 93 percent). Women have never chaired the key foreign policy committees (Armed Services and Foreign Relations) in the Senate or House—although Patricia Schroeder was the second-ranking member of the House Armed Services Committee in 1993–1994 and played a major (avowedly feminist) role in Congress on military policy.

In addition to women state leaders and other female foreign policy makers, women in military forces also break from traditional gender roles in IR. Liberal feminists believe that women soldiers, like women politicians, have a range of skills and abilities comparable to men's. Again the main effect of including more women would be to improve the overall quality of military forces. The evidence on women soldiers, like that on women political leaders, seems to support liberal feminists. In the U.S. military in the

Flower Girls   Consistent with liberal feminism's premises, the first female U.S. secretary of state, Madeleine Albright, has been at least as hard-line as her male colleagues. She advocated the use of force in Bosnia and the expansion of NATO in Eastern Europe. Here, however, she told refugee girls from Afghanistan (where the Taliban faction harshly restricts women) that women worldwide "are all the same, and we have the same feelings"—a line more consistent with standpoint feminism (1997).

1990s there were about 200,000 women soldiers (more than 10 percent of the total) and more than 1 million women veterans. Pentagon studies have concluded that women perform comparably to men in a variety of military roles from logistical and medical support to training and command. Women have had similar success in other countries that have allowed them into the military (or, in a few cases, drafted them).

Although women have served with distinction in military forces, they have been excluded from combat roles in almost all those forces. (It is a myth that women in the Israeli army serve in combat infantry roles.) In some countries, military women are limited to traditional female roles such as nurses and typists. Even where women may have nontraditional positions such as mechanics and pilots (as in the United States), most women remain in the traditional roles. And certain jobs still remain off-limits; for instance, women cannot serve on U.S. submarines or in combat infantry. Thus there are only a few cases from which to judge women's abilities in combat.

Power Girls   Women soldiers have performed as well as men in military tasks, as predicted by liberal feminists. But in state armies, women are barred from virtually all infantry combat units worldwide. These Kurdish guerrillas from Turkey (1991)—not part of a state army—are the exception.

Those cases include historical examples of individual women who served in combat (sometimes disguised as men, sometimes not). In the fifteenth century, Joan of Arc rallied French soldiers to defeat England, turning the tide of the Hundred Years' War. (After capturing her, the English burned her at the stake as a witch.) More recent experiences include several in which U.S. women soldiers found themselves in combat (present-day mobile tactics and fluid front lines make it hard to separate combat from support roles). Women helicopter pilots flew in combat zones during the Gulf War of 1991, in which tens of thousands of U.S. women served; 13 were killed, and 2 were captured as POWs. In the late 1990s, women began serving on some U.S. combat ships and airplanes, but not in ground combat units. Women have also repeatedly served in combat in rebel forces fighting guerrilla wars in Vietnam, Nicaragua, and elsewhere, as well as in terrorist or paramilitary units in countries such as Peru, Germany, Italy, and Palestine. All these cases suggest that (at least some) women are able to hold their own in combat.

Sometimes the argument is that women are more vulnerable (that is, to rape) if taken as POWs. Again liberal feminists disagree. All POWs are vulnerable, and both men and women POWs can be sexually abused. In the Gulf War, the 2 U.S. female POWs were sexually abused and the 19 male POWs apparently were not. But the male POWs, and not the females, received severe electric shocks and beatings.

In fact, the main reason that military forces exclude women from combat has little to do with their performance. Rather, it is fear about what effect their presence might have on the male soldiers, whose discipline and loyalty have traditionally been thought to depend on male bonding and single-minded focus. Opponents of women in the military claimed vindication, ironically, from a series of high-profile cases of sex discrimination, harassment, adultery, and rape in the U.S. military in the mid-1990s. The presence of females in the ranks, they said, was breaking down discipline and morale. Liberal feminists reject such arguments and argue that group bonding in military units does not depend on gender segregation. (After all, similar rationales were given for racial segregation and for the exclusion of gay men and lesbians in U.S. military forces.) However, it is clear that all-male traditions in military forces will not adapt painlessly to the presence of women. A 1992 Pentagon survey reported that about one-third of women soldiers experience some form of verbal or physical sexual harassment or abuse. Thus, a heated public debate continues on the question of women in the military.

The effects of war on noncombatant women also received growing attention in the 1990s. Attacks on women in Algeria, Rwanda, Bosnia, and Afghanistan pointed to a possible new trend toward women as military targets. Systematic rape was used as a terror tactic in Bosnia and Rwanda, as it was by Japanese troops in World War II. Rape has long been treated as a normal if regrettable by-product of war, but recently certain instances of rape were declared war crimes by the international war-crimes tribunal for the former Yugoslavia.

In sum, liberal feminists reject the argument that women bring uniquely feminine assets or liabilities to foreign and military affairs. They do not critique realism as essentially masculine in nature but do criticize state practices that exclude women from participation in international politics and war.

Balancing the Feminist Arguments

The arguments of standpoint and liberal feminists may seem totally at odds. Standpoint feminists argue that realism reflects a masculine perception of social relations, whereas liberal feminists think that women can be just as realist as men. Liberal feminists believe that female participation in foreign policy and the military would enhance state capabilities, but standpoint feminists think women's unique abilities can be put to better use in transforming (feminizing) the entire system of international relations rather than in trying to play men's games.

The evidence in favor of both positions can be reconciled to some extent by bearing in mind that the character and ability of an individual are not the same as that of his or her group. Rather, the qualities of individuals follow a bell curve distribution, with many people clustered in the middle and fewer people very high or low on some dimension.

Gender differences posited by standpoint feminists mean that one bell curve is shifted from the other, even though the two may still overlap quite a bit (see Figure 3.2, p. 126). To take a simple example, a few women are physically larger than almost all men, and a few men smaller than almost all women. But on average men are somewhat larger than women. On different dimensions of capability, the women's curve is above the men's on average, but there is still much overlap.

Liberal feminists emphasize the overlap of the two bell curves. They say that individual women—*most* women on most relevant dimensions—are well within the male curve and can perform equally with the men. Indeed, women in nontraditional gender roles may well perform better than their male counterparts, because presumably women who self-select into such roles (such as joining the military) are near the high end of the

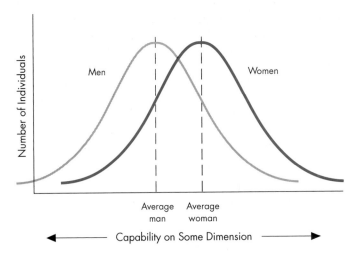

FIGURE 3.2   Overlapping Bell Curves   Bell curves show that individuals differ in capabilities such as physical strength or peace-making ability. Although the genders differ on average, for most individuals (in the area of overlap) such differences do not come into play. Liberal feminists emphasize the area where the curves overlap; essentialist feminists emphasize the overall group differences.

female bell curve, whereas the men are closer to the middle of the male curve (because more of them join). Similarly, women who become state leaders are presumably more adept at foreign policy making than most women (or men), whether or not the foreign policy process as we know it (and as realists describe it) is more compatible with the average man's way of thinking than with the average woman's. Political processes probably tend to select women at the high end of the curve in terms of their affinity for realism.

Standpoint feminists are more interested in the shift in the two bell curves, not their overlap. On average, in this perspective, women tend to see international relations in a somewhat different way from that of men. So, although *individuals* selected to participate in foreign policy and the military may not differ from their male counterparts, women as a group differ. Women voters display different concerns regarding IR than men (the gender gap in opinion polls and voting patterns).

By this logic, then, profound differences in IR—and a shift away from the utility of realism in explaining state behavior—would occur only if many women participated in key foreign policy positions. That is, a *few* women politicians or women soldiers do not change the masculine foundations of IR. Women foreign policy makers today are surrounded by males. But a world in which *most* politicians or soldiers were female might be a different story. Then, instead of women being selected for their ability to fit into men's games, the rules of the game might themselves change to reflect the fact that "average" women would be the main actors in the traditionally important IR roles. Of course, these theories of standpoint feminists have never been tested, because women have never attained predominance in foreign policy making in any country—much less in the international system as a whole.

Overall, then, the standpoint feminist critique of realism is intriguing but hard to demonstrate empirically. It may be, as this critique claims, that realism and neoliberalism alike put too much emphasis on the aspects of IR that fit a typical masculine view of the world—particularly autonomy, sovereignty, and anarchy. If so, realism and neoliberalism miss many important aspects that could help provide fuller and more accurate explanations of why events occur the way they do in IR. But it is hard to test feminist theories against realism and neoliberalism because the empirical reality is that the arena of international power politics is populated overwhelmingly by males.

In addition to the liberal and standpoint strands of feminism, the third strand, postmodern feminism, is connected with the rise of postmodernism.

Other Alternatives to Realism

In addition to feminism, other challenges to realism come from postmodernism, constructivism, and peace studies.

Postmodernism   The theory of **postmodernism**, like feminism, is a broad approach to scholarship that has left its mark on various academic disciplines, especially the study of literature. Because of their literary roots, postmodernists pay special attention to *texts* and to *discourses*—how people talk and write about their subject (IR). Postmodern critiques of realism thus center on analyzing realists' words and arguments.

A central idea of postmodernism is that there is no single, objective reality but a multiplicity of experiences and perspectives that defy easy categorization. For this reason, postmodernism itself is difficult to present in a simple or categorical way. This short discussion will merely convey some important postmodern themes, necessarily oversimplified, and show how postmodernism can help illuminate some problems of realism.

From a postmodern perspective, realism cannot justify its claim that states are the central actors in IR and that states operate as unitary actors with coherent sets of objective interests (which they pursue through international power politics). Postmodern critics of realism see nothing objective about state interests, and certainly nothing universal (in that one set of values or interests applies to all states).

More fundamentally, postmodernism calls into question the whole notion of states as actors. States have no tangible reality; they are "fictions" that we (as scholars and citizens) construct to make sense of the actions of large numbers of individuals. For postmodernists, the stories told about the actions and policies of states are just that—stories. From this perspective, it is an arbitrary distinction that leads bookstores to put spy novels on the fiction shelf whereas biographies and histories go on the nonfiction shelf. None of these is an objective reality, and all are filtered through an interpretive process that distorts the actual experiences of those involved.

Contrary to realism's claim that states are unitary actors, postmodernists see multiple realities and experiences lurking below the surface of the fictional entities that realists construct (states). The Soviet Union, for example, was treated by realists as a single actor with a single set of objective interests. Indeed, it was considered the second most important actor in the world. Realists were amazed when the Soviet Union split into 15 pieces, each containing its own fractious groups and elements. It became clear that the "unitary state" called the Soviet Union had masked (and let realists ignore) the divergent experiences of constituent republics, ethnic groups, and individuals.

Postmodernists seek to "deconstruct" such constructions as states, the international system, and the associated stories and arguments (texts and discourses) with which realists portray the nature of international relations. To *deconstruct* a text—a term borrowed from literary criticism—means to tease apart the words in order to reveal hidden meanings, looking for what might be omitted, or included only implicitly. The hidden meanings not explicitly addressed in the text are often called the **subtext**.

What is the subtext in the stories realists tell about IR? What does realism omit from its accounts of IR? We have just discussed one major omission—gender. Furthermore, in its emphasis on states, realism omits the roles of individuals, domestic politics, economic classes, MNCs, and other nonstate actors. In its focus on the great powers, realism omits the experiences of third world countries. In its attention to military forms of leverage, it omits the roles of various nonmilitary forms of leverage.

Realism focuses so narrowly because its aim is to reduce IR down to a simple, coherent model. The model is claimed to be objective, universal, and accurate. To postmodernists, the realist model is none of these things: it is a biased model that creates a narrow and one-sided story for the purpose of promoting the interests of powerful actors. Postmodernists seek to destroy this model along with any other model that tries to represent IR in simple objective categories. Postmodernists instead want to celebrate the diversity of experiences that make up IR without needing to make sense of them by simplifying and categorizing.

Postmodern Feminism
One line of criticism directed at realism combines feminism and postmodernism. Postmodern feminism seeks to deconstruct realism with the specific aim of uncovering the pervasive hidden influences of gender in IR while showing how arbitrary the construction of gender roles is. Feminist postmodernists agree with standpoint feminists that realism carries hidden meanings about gender roles but deny that there is any fixed inherent meaning in either male or female genders. Rather, feminist postmodernists seek to look at the interplay of gender and power in a more open-ended way. Postmodern feminists criticize liberal feminists for trying merely to integrate women into traditional structures of war and foreign policy. They criticize standpoint feminists for glorifying traditional feminine virtues.

In studying war, postmodern feminists have challenged the archetypes of the (male) "just warrior" and the (female) "beautiful soul." They argue that women are not just passive bystanders or victims in war, but active participants in a system of warfare tied to both identities. Women act not only as nurses and journalists at the "front" but as mothers, wives, and girlfriends on the "home front." They contend World War II is the story of women back home in Colorado as much as of men on the front lines in Europe. They believe that stories of military forces should not omit the roles of prostitutes at military bases, nor should stories of diplomacy omit the roles of diplomats' wives.

Postmodern feminists reject not only realism but also some of the alternative approaches that emphasize the protection of women and other noncombatants. This doctrine is considered too abstract—a set of concepts and rules that does not do justice to the richness of each historical context and the varied roles of individual men and women within it.

Sex in the Subtext   Feminist postmodernists try to reveal hidden subtexts connecting gender with IR, such as the roles of sex and death in the constructions of masculinity by U.S. airmen in England, 1944.

Postmodern feminists have tried to deconstruct the language of realism, especially where it reflects influences of gender and sex. For instance, the first atomic bombs had male gender (they were named "Fat Man" and "Little Boy"). The plane that dropped the atomic bomb on Hiroshima (the *Enola Gay*) had female gender; it was named after the pilot's mother. Similarly, pilots have pasted pinup photos of nude women onto conventional bombs before dropping them. In all these cases, postmodern feminists would note that the feminine gender of vehicles, targets, or decorations amplifies the masculinity of the weapon itself.

These efforts find sex and gender throughout the subtext of realism. For example, the terms *power* and *potency* refer to both state capability and male virility. Military force depends on phallic objects—weapons designed to shoot projectiles, penetrate targets, and explode. In basic training, men chant: "This is my rifle [holding up rifle], this is my gun [pointing to crotch]; one's for killing, the other's for fun." Nuclear weapons are also repeatedly spoken of in sexual terms, perhaps due to their great "potency." Female models are hired to market tanks, helicopter missiles, and other "potent" weapons to male procurement officers at international military trade shows.

Realism and liberalism ignore all the sexual aspects of weaponry, limiting themselves to such issues as a weapon's explosive power, its range, and other technical information about its use as state leverage. But if sexual drives enter (perhaps unconsciously) into decisions about whether and when to use bombs or other military forces, then realism and liberalism cannot adequately explain those decisions. Postmodernism thus reveals another reality—the sexual gratification of male politicians and soldiers—which competes with the realities of realism and neoliberalism, with their focus on maximizing national interests (narrowly or broadly construed). By radically shifting the focus and approach of IR scholarship, postmodernists hope to increase our understanding of IR in general and of the notion of rationality in particular.

Web Link
Constructivism

Constructivism

IR postmodernists have been criticized for spending more time undermining and criticizing realism than developing a positive alternative. A related stream of IR theory, called **constructivism**, tries to fill that gap. While maintaining postmodernists' critical skepticism of the assumptions of realism and liberalism, constructivists seek to develop theory focused on where state interests and identities come from. Realists tend to simply take state interests as given. Thus, like the approach of peace studies discussed shortly, constructivism puts IR in the context of broader social relations.

One constructivist approach focuses on how people use language to make or "construct" the social world and how the social world in turn shapes individuals. Rules are statements telling people how they should behave under certain conditions, and this version of constructivism analyzes rules in terms of the kinds of "speech acts" that compose them. Anarchy, sovereignty, regimes, and other basic IR concepts are then seen in terms of how they relate to rules, in this broad sense.

A different constructivist approach concerns how states' interests are shaped by rule-governed (or norm-governed) interaction. Liberalism also emphasizes rules and norms, but it tends to view them mainly as mediators and coordinators of egoistic states' behavior. For constructivists, however, norms do more than help states to pursue their selfish interests in mutually beneficial ways and to overcome collective goods problems. Rather, norms affect how a state conceives of its interests and, indeed, identity, in the first place. Thus, the state's conception of its interests, its presentation of itself on the international stage, and its behavior all might change as a result of interstate interactions. States, like people, come to see themselves as others see them. Constructivists reject the assumption that states always want more rather than less power and wealth, or the assumption that state interests exist independently of a context of interactions among states.

Constructivists are especially interested in how norms influence state interests and behavior. For example, some cases of humanitarian intervention—military intervention by a state or states to protect citizens or subjects of another—seem difficult to explain in realist or liberal terms. Why, for example, did the United States send troops to Somalia—a country of minimal strategic and economic importance to the United States—as Somalia descended into political chaos and faced the possibility of mass starvation (see p. 41)? A constructivist explanation would point to changing norms about which kinds of people are worthy of protection. The point is not that the international community always responds effectively to humanitarian crises, which it does not, but that it is no longer acceptable to view only Christians or only Europeans as deserving of protection. Thus the evolving construction of norms influences how states act and how they justify their actions.

In sum, through these various methods and concepts, postmodernists and constructivists deliberately undermine the realist foundations of IR. Postmodernists seek to replace an orderly picture with a hall of mirrors in which multiple realities coexist—realities of rationality and power side by side with those of love and interdependence and those of gender and sexuality. They seek to better understand IR by listening to voices silenced by power—the voices of women, of oppressed ethnic minorities, and of others whose interests and actions are not done justice by states or by theories of IR that focus

Atlas CD
Somalia
Map

exclusively on states. Constructivists seek to replace realism's oversimplified assumptions about state interests with much more complex models. All of these approaches are controversial among IR scholars.

Peace Studies

Another approach of growing importance that challenges some fundamental concepts behind both realism and liberalism is peace studies. Many colleges have created interdisciplinary peace studies programs through which scholars and students organize discussions and courses about peace. Typically, such programs include not only political scientists but psychologists who have studied conflict, physicists who have studied nuclear weapons, religious scholars who have studied practical morality, and so forth. With these various disciplinary backgrounds, scholars of peace studies tend to be more eclectic than political scientists and much more broad-ranging in the topics they consider worthy of study in international security affairs. Since peace studies approaches differ more from realism than from liberalism, the focus here will be on critiques of realism.

In particular, peace studies seeks to shift the focus of IR away from the interstate level of analysis and toward a broad conception of social relations. Peace studies connects war and peace with individual responsibility, with economic inequality, with gender relations, with cross-cultural understanding, and with other aspects of social relationships. Peace studies seeks the potentials for peace not in the transactions of state leaders but in the transformation of entire societies (through social revolution) and in transnational communities (bypassing states to connect people and groups globally, ignoring borders).

Another way in which peace studies seeks to broaden the focus of inquiry is to reject the supposed objectivity of traditional (realist and liberal) approaches. Most scholars of peace studies think that a good way to gain knowledge is to participate in action—not just to observe objectively. This approach seeks to integrate theory with practice.

In addition to gaining better knowledge about their theories, peace studies scholars participate in the practice of seeking peace because they want to use their theories and knowledge to influence the world they live in. The main reason for studying war and peace, in this view, is to lessen war and promote the chances for peace. This lack of objectivity is called a **normative bias** because scholars impose their personal norms and values on the subject. Some political scientists (especially realists) dismiss peace studies because it lacks scientific objectivity about outcomes.

Scholars in peace studies are quick to respond, however, that realism itself has normative biases and makes policy prescriptions. Because realism's assumptions—that actors pursue only their own interests, that violence is a normal and acceptable way to achieve ends, that order is more important than justice—are debatable as objective statements of fact, they might better be seen as value statements. Realism, then, becomes more of an ideology than a theory.

Thus scholars in peace studies defend both their broader approach to the subject and their willingness to bring their own values into play when studying that subject. These characteristics of peace studies can be seen in its approach to war—the central topic in international security affairs.

The development and implementation of peaceful strategies for settling conflicts—using alternatives to violent forms of leverage—is known by the general term **conflict resolution**. These methods are at work, competing with violent methods, in virtually all international conflicts. Recently the use of conflict resolution has been increasing, becoming more sophisticated, and succeeding more often.

Peacemaker Conflict resolution offers an alternative avenue for settling conflicts short of violence. Aung San Suu Kyi, a leading practitioner of nonviolent conflict resolution, sought reconciliation with the Burmese military government that had denied her election victory and placed her under house arrest for years (1989 photo). She won the 1991 Nobel peace prize.

Most conflict resolution uses a third party whose role is **mediation** between two conflicting parties. Most of today's international conflicts have one or more mediating parties working regularly to resolve the conflict short of violence. There is no hard-and-fast rule saying what kinds of third parties mediate what kinds of conflicts. Presently the UN is the most important mediator on the world scene. Some regional conflicts are mediated through regional organizations, single states, or even private individuals. For instance, the former president of Costa Rica, Oscar Arias, won the 1987 Nobel peace prize for mediating a multilateral agreement among Central American presidents to end several brutal wars in the region.

The involvement of the mediator can vary. Some mediation is strictly *technical*—a mediator may take an active but strictly neutral role in channeling communication between two states that lack other channels of communication. In facilitating communication, a mediator listens to each side's ideas and presents them in a way the other side can hear. The mediator works to change each side's view of difficult issues. In these roles, the mediator is a translator between the two sides, or a therapist helping them work out psychological problems in their relationship. Sometimes a neutral outside voice can move negotiations forward, as former U.S. Secretary of State James Baker did as a special envoy in Western Sahara in 1997 (where a referendum plan had stalled).

Mediators may also actively *propose solutions* based on an assessment of each side's demands and interests. Such solutions may be compromises, may recognize the greater validity of one side's position (or power), or may be creative ideas that meet the needs of both parties. A fifty-fifty compromise is not always the best or fairest solution—it may simply reward the side with the more extreme starting position.

If both sides agree in advance to abide by a solution devised by a mediator, the process is called *arbitration*. In that case, both sides present their arguments to the arbitrator, who decides on a "fair" solution. For example, the Israelis and Egyptians submitted their border dispute over the hotel at Taba (see p. 147) to arbitration when they could not come to an agreement on their own. When Serbian and Bosnian negotiators could not agree on who should get the city of Brcko, they turned the issue over to arbitration rather than hold up the entire Dayton Agreement. In arbitration it is not uncommon to empower a panel of three people, one chosen by each side unilaterally and a third on whom both sides agree.

Why should a state settle nonviolently a conflict that might be settled by military means? It must see that doing so would be in its interest. To get national leaders to come to this conclusion one must create conditions to bring into play mutual interests that already exist or to create new mutual interests.

In many situations, two conflicting parties could benefit from a solution other than war but lack the trust and communication channels to find such a solution. Neutral mediation with various degrees of involvement can bring about awareness of the two parties' common interests. For example, Egypt and Israel had a common interest in making peace in the late 1970s, but they also had a high level of mistrust. U.S. President Jimmy Carter invited the two heads of state to a private and relaxed setting—his Camp David retreat—where they could go through the issues without the restrictions of formal negotiations.

When heads of state do not see their common interests, ordinary citizens may try to raise awareness of such mutual interests on both sides. Travel and discussion by private individuals and groups toward this end has been called *citizen diplomacy*, and it occurs fairly regularly (though not very visibly) when conflicting states are stuck in a cycle of hostility. Sometimes a private trip takes on historical significance, as when the U.S. wrestling team visited Iran in 1998.

Conflicting parties (and mediators) can also work to *restructure* the terms of bargaining—in effect extending the possible solutions for one or both sides so that their interests overlap. Often a mediator can come up with a win-win solution. This may be as simple as providing means for one or both parties to *save face* when giving up some demand. In other cases, creative solutions may satisfy both parties. For instance, at the Camp David negotiations, Egypt insisted on regaining sovereignty over all its territory in the Sinai desert. Israel insisted on security against the threat of attack from the Sinai. The win-win solution was a return of the territory to Egyptian sovereignty but with most of it demilitarized so that Egypt could not use it to stage an attack.

Another way to create mutual interests is to break a conflict into pieces (fractionation) and start with those pieces in which a common interest and workable solution can be found. These may be largely symbolic *confidence-building* measures at first but can gather momentum as the process proceeds. A gradual increase in trust reduces the risks of nonviolent settlements relative to their costs and creates an expectation that the issues at stake can be resolved nonviolently.

Most scholars in peace studies reject realism's willingness to treat war as normal, or its willingness to be objective about the merits of war or peace. Peace studies resonates

Web Link
Confidence-
Building
Measures

Shadow of War   Militarism in a culture, or the lack thereof, can influence foreign policy. In societies at war, children's psychological trauma contributes to intergroup conflicts decades later. Here, East Timorese children are in the ruins of an Indonesian Army building, 2000. The Army withdrew after backing a terror campaign against East Timorese in 1999.

with Benjamin Franklin's observation that "there never was a good war or a bad peace." In particular, peace studies scholars object to realism's willingness to treat nuclear weapons as just another instrument of state military power. In general, peace studies tries to call into question the nature of war and its role in society.

Peace studies scholars argue that war is not just a natural expression of power, but one closely tied to militarism in (some) cultures. **Militarism** is the glorification of war, military force, and violence through TV, films, books, political speeches, toys, games, sports, and other such avenues. Militarism also refers to the structuring of society around war—for example, the dominant role of a military-industrial complex in a national economy. Militarism is thought to underlie the propensity of political leaders to use military force.

Historically, militarism has had a profound influence on the evolution of societies. War has often been glorified as a "manly" enterprise that ennobles the human spirit (especially before World War I, which changed that perspective). Not only evil acts but also exemplary acts of humanity are brought forth by war—sacrifice, honor, courage, altruism on behalf of loved ones, and bonding with a community larger than oneself.

The culture of modern states—and of realism—celebrates and rewards these qualities of soldiers, just as hunter-gatherer cultures created rituals and rewards to induce participation in warfare. We have holidays in honor of warriors, provide them (or their survivors) with veterans' benefits, and bury them in special cemeteries where their individual identities are symbolically submerged into a larger collective identity. Because militarism seems so pervasive and so strongly associated with the state, many scholars in peace studies question whether the nature of states themselves must change before lasting peace will be possible. In this regard, peace studies differs from both realism and neoliberalism.

Even in the United States—generally sheltered from the world's wars—the militarization of culture is pervasive. In the 1960s and 1970s, the Vietnam War dominated the experiences of young people. In the 1980s, fear of nuclear war returned, and in 1991 came the Gulf War. Scholars in peace studies have made a connection between U.S. uses of military force and the American gun mania, high murder rate, Wild West myths, television violence, and other aspects of American life indicating that violence is socially acceptable.

Peace studies seeks examples of less-militarized cultures to show that realism's emphasis on military force is not universal or necessary. Costa Rica has had no army for 50 years (just lightly armed forces), even during the 1980s when wars occurred in neighboring Nicaragua and Panama. Japan since World War II has developed strong norms against war and violence. Public opinion, more than its constitution, prevents political leaders from considering military force a viable instrument of foreign policy.

Anthropologists have tried to connect the domestic characteristics of hunter-gatherer societies with their external propensity to engage in warfare. There is some evidence that war occurs more frequently in societies with internal (especially gender) inequalities, with harsh childrearing practices, and with fathers who are absent from child rearing. By contrast, relatively peaceful societies are more likely to have open decision-making processes, relative gender equality, and permissive and affectionate childrearing. But all these societal attributes could as well be *effects* of war as causes. And, as virtually all kinds of society seem to have the potential for warfare under some conditions (see Chapter 4), distinctions such as "warlike" are only relative.

Just as war is seen in peace studies as a pervasive aspect of society as a whole, so can peace be reconceptualized in a broader way. According to peace studies scholars, peace should be defined as more than just the absence of war. The mere absence of war does not guarantee that war will not recur. Because realism assumes the normalcy of military conflicts, it recognizes only a negative kind of peace—the temporary absence of war.

By contrast, **positive peace** refers to a peace that resolves the underlying reasons for war—peace that is not just a cease-fire but a transformation of relationships. Under positive peace, not only do state armies stop fighting each other, but they stop arming, stop forming death squads against internal protest, and reverse the economic exploitation and political oppression that scholars in peace studies believe are responsible for social conflicts that lead to war.

Proponents of the positive peace approach see broad social and economic issues—assumed by realists to be relatively unimportant—as inextricably linked with positive peace. Some scholars define poverty, hunger, and oppression as forms of violence—

which they call **structural violence** because it is caused by the structure of social relations rather than by direct actions such as shooting people. Structural violence in this definition kills and harms many more people each year than do war and other forms of direct political violence. Positive peace is usually defined to include the elimination of structural violence because it is considered a source of conflict and war.

Advocates of positive peace also criticize militaristic culture. The "social construction of war"—a complex system of rules and relations that ultimately supports the existence of war—touches our lives in many ways: from children's war toys to patriotic rituals in schools; from teenagers' gender roles to military training for young men; from the taxes we pay to the sports we play. The positive peace approach seeks to change the whole system, not just one piece of it.

Positive peace encompasses a variety of approaches to social change. These include alternative mechanisms for conflict resolution to take the place of war; popular pressure on governments through peace movements and political activism; strengthening of norms against the use of violence; the development of international or global identity transcending national, ethnic, and religious divisions; and egalitarian relations within societies in the economic, social, and political realms. All these topics—not considered legitimate subjects of study by realists—are put on the table for discussion by peace studies.

Atlas CD
Northern
Ireland
Divisions
Photo

Many people think that positive peace would depend on overcoming ethnic conflict, racism, xenophobia, and other sources of tension between groups with different cultures, languages, and religions—tensions that may contribute to war and violence (see "Ethnic Conflict" on pp. 158–162). One approach explores travel, tourism, cultural exchanges (concerts, films), and citizen diplomacy as means of overcoming intergroup conflicts.

Another approach to intergroup conflict is reform in the educational system. For example, Western European countries revised textbooks after World War II to remove nationalistic excesses and promote respect for neighboring countries (see p. 161).

Positive peace is usually defined to include political equality and human rights as well. When a small ruling group or dictator holds political power, fewer checks on government violence operate than when democratic institutions exist. And when avenues of legitimate political participation are open, citizens are less likely to turn to violence.

More controversial within peace studies is the question of whether positive peace requires that states' authority be subordinated to a **world government**. The creation of a world government has long been debated by scholars and pursued by activists; many plans have been drawn up, though none has yet succeeded. Some scholars believe progress is being made (through the UN) toward the eventual emergence of a world government. Others think the idea is impractical or even undesirable (merely adding another layer of centralized control, when peace demands decentralization and freedom).

Peace Movements and Nonviolence
Scholars in peace studies also study how to achieve the conditions for positive peace. Approaches vary, from building a world government to strengthening democratic governance, from redistributing wealth to strengthening spiritual communities. But most peace studies scholars share a skepticism that state leaders left to themselves would ever achieve positive peace. Rather, they believe the practice of IR will change only as a result of pressures from individuals and groups.

Give Peace a Chance   Peace demonstrators play a role in many international conflicts. Here, citizens of the Russian republic of Chechnya form a human chain across the republic to protest the Russian army's invasion in 1994.

The most commonly studied method of exerting such pressure is through **peace movements**—people taking to the streets in protest against war and militarism. Such protests occur in many, though not all, states involved in wars. In peace studies it is believed that people all over the world want peace more than governments do.

In addition to mass demonstrations, common *tactics* of peace movements include getting antiwar messages into the media, participating in civil disobedience (nonviolently breaking laws and inviting arrest to show one's beliefs), and occasionally organizing consumer boycotts. Favorite *targets* of peace movements include the draft, government buildings, taxes, and nuclear test sites. Like other interest groups, peace movements also participate in elections and lobbying. And peace movements try to educate the public by spreading information about a war or arms race that the government may be suppressing or downplaying.

Peace activists often disagree on goals. In the U.S. peace movement since World War I, an *internationalist* wing has seen international organizations (today, the UN) as the best hope for peace and has supported wars against aggression. A *pacifist* wing has opposed all wars, distrusted international organizations whose members are state governments, and favored more radical social change to achieve positive peace.

In other countries, peace movements vary greatly in their goals and character. In Japan, peace movements are extremely broad-based (enjoying wide popular support) and are pacifist in orientation (as a result of reaction against militarism before and during World War II). In the Soviet Union and Eastern Europe during the Cold War, official state-sponsored peace groups linked international peace to the struggle against

Web Link
Peace
Movements

Atlas CD
Nicaragua
Peace Concert
Photo

Western imperialism while unofficial peace groups linked peace to the struggle for human rights and democracy at home.

These divergent tendencies in peace movements come together at peak times in opposition to particular wars or arms races. But beyond this reactive mode of politics, peace movements often have had trouble defining a long-term direction and agenda. Scholars of peace studies are interested in studying the successes and failures of peace movements to understand how popular influence on foreign policy can affect state decisions.

The philosophies of **nonviolence** and **pacifism** are based on a unilateral commitment to refrain from using any violent forms of leverage in bargaining. No state today follows such a strategy; indeed, it is widely believed that in today's world, a state that adopted a nonviolent philosophy would risk exploitation or conquest.

Pacifism nonetheless figures prominently in debates concerning the peaceful solution of conflicts and the achievement of positive peace. Many states contain substantial numbers of citizens, often organized into popular movements, who believe that only pacifism—an ironclad commitment to renounce violence—can change the nature of IR so as to avoid future wars. Japan has a sizable pacifist movement, and pacifists historically have formed the hard core of the peace movement in the United States and Western Europe as well.

Religious faith has often provided a foundation for philosophies of nonviolence and pacifism. Despite the millions killed in the name of religion throughout history, many pacifists draw inspiration from the teachings of religious figures, including Jesus Christ and Buddha. Before the U.S. Civil War, for example, some abolitionists embraced a religiously inspired pacifist philosophy. They relied on moral exhortation, and refused to participate in electoral politics, which they considered a form of collaboration with an unjust and violent system. (Not all abolitionists opposed all resort to violence.)

The term *pacifism* has fallen into disfavor because it has been taken to imply passivity in the face of aggression. The more popular term, nonviolence, reflects especially the philosophy and practice of *Mahatma Gandhi*, who led India's struggle for independence from the British empire before 1948. Gandhi emphasized that nonviolence must be *active* in seeking to prevent violence, to resolve conflicts without violence, and especially to stand up against injustice enforced violently. Gandhi organized Indians to resist the British colonial occupation without resorting to violence, even when British troops shot down unarmed Indian protesters.

As a tool of the *powerless* standing up against injustices by the powerful, nonviolence is often the most cost-effective approach—because the costs of violent resistance would be prohibitive. Thus, nonviolence has traditionally been promulgated by people with the greatest stake in social change but the least access to the instruments of large-scale violence. In the United States, the philosophy of nonviolence spread widely in the 1960s in the civil rights movement, especially through the work of Martin Luther King, Jr. The powerful, unfortunately, have fewer practical incentives to adopt nonviolence because they have greater access to types of leverage that rely on violence.

The dilemma of nonviolence is how to respond to violence. Gandhi believed that there was always a third alternative to passivity or response in kind. Nonviolence does not always succeed when faced with violence, but then neither does violent response. However, political leaders may believe they have done their duty if they respond violently without success, but not if they respond nonviolently without success. Ironically, in order to be effective as a strategy, nonviolence must not appear too strategic—being used only as a practical means to achieve a bargaining advantage. Rather, successful mobilization of the moral leverage implicit in nonviolence depends on its being perceived as steadfast whatever the cost.

Nonviolence overlaps in many ways with the other subjects of interest to the peace studies community, such as peace movements and positive peace. Yet within peace studies there are also substantial differences among scholars who emphasize different aspects of peace and how to achieve it. These differences are deepened by the multidisciplinary nature of peace studies (sociologists, political scientists, psychologists, anthropologists, etc.). Peace studies tends to be inclusive and tolerant, hoping that different scholars (and activists) can find a core of agreement on the meaning of peace. This tolerance can mask incompatibilities within peace studies, however. Those who think that war can be ended through international mediation may find they have little common ground with those who think that individual meditation is the way to end war.

Realist, liberal, and alternative frameworks all seek to understand and manage international relationships, especially international conflicts and the use of military force. Chapter 4 takes up these issues.

THINKING CRITICALLY

1. Inasmuch as democracies almost never fight wars with each other, do existing democracies have a national security interest in seeing democratization spread to China and other authoritarian states? If so, how can that interest be reconciled with the long-standing norm of noninterference in the internal affairs of other sovereign states?
2. Would IR operate differently if most leaders of states were women? What would the differences be? What evidence (beyond gender stereotypes) supports your answer?
3. Peace studies claims that internal characteristics of states (at the domestic level of analysis) strongly affect the propensity for war or potential for lasting peace. For one society, show how internal characteristics—social, economic, and/or cultural—influence that society's external behavior.

CHAPTER SUMMARY

◆ The central claims of realism—regarding anarchy, state actors, rationality, and the utility of military force—have been challenged on a variety of grounds.

◆ Liberals dispute the realist notion that narrow self-interest is more rational than mutually beneficial cooperation.

◆ Neoliberalism argues that even in an anarchic system of autonomous rational states, cooperation can emerge through the building of norms, regimes, and institutions.

◆ Collective goods are benefits received by all members of a group regardless of their individual contribution. Shared norms and rules are important in getting members to pay for collective goods.

◆ International regimes—convergent expectations of state leaders about the rules for issue areas in IR—help provide stability in the absence of a world government.

◆ Hegemonic stability theory suggests that the holding of predominant power by one state lends stability to international relations and helps create regimes.

◆ In a collective security arrangement, a group of states agrees to respond together to aggression by any participating state; the UN and other IGOs perform this function.

◆ Foreign policies are strategies governments use to guide their actions toward other states. The foreign policy process is the set of procedures and structures that states use to arrive at foreign policy decisions and to implement them.

◆ In the rational model of decision making, officials choose the action whose consequences best help to meet the state's established goals. By contrast, in the organizational process model, decisions result from routine administrative procedures, and in the government bargaining (or bureaucratic politics) model, decisions result from negotiations among governmental agencies with different interests in the outcome.

◆ The actions of individual decision makers are influenced by their personalities, values, and beliefs as well as by common psychological factors that diverge from rationality.

◆ Foreign policy decisions are also influenced by the psychology of groups (including "groupthink"), the procedures used to reach decisions, and the roles of participants.

◆ During crises, the potentials for misperception and error are amplified.

◆ Domestic constituencies (interest groups) have distinct interests in foreign policies and often organize politically to promote those interests. Prominent among such constituencies have been military-industrial complexes.

◆ Public opinion influences governments' foreign policy decisions (more so in democracies than in authoritarian states), but governments also manipulate public opinion.

◆ Democracies have historically fought as many wars as authoritarian states, but democracies have almost never fought wars against other democracies. This is called the democratic peace.

◆ Feminist scholars of IR agree that gender is important in understanding IR but diverge into several strands regarding their conception of the role of gender.

◆ Standpoint feminists argue that real (not arbitrary) differences between men and women exist. Men think about social relations more often in terms of autonomy (as do realists), but women think in terms of connection. Standpoint feminists argue that men are more warlike *on average* than women; the participation of large numbers of women would change the character of the international system, making it more peaceful.

◆ Liberal feminists disagree that women have substantially different capabilities or tendencies as participants in IR. They argue that women are equivalent to men in virtually all IR roles. As evidence, liberal feminists point to historical and present-day women leaders and women soldiers.

◆ Postmodern critics reject the entire framework and language of realism, with its unitary state actors. Postmodernists argue that no simple categories can capture the multiple realities experienced by participants in IR.

◆ Postmodern feminists seek to uncover gender-related subtexts implicit in realist discourse, including sexual themes connected with the concept of power.

◆ Constructivists reject realist assumptions about state interests, tracing those interests in part to international rules and norms.

◆ Peace studies programs are interdisciplinary and seek to broaden the study of international security to include social and economic factors ignored by realism.

◆ Peace studies acknowledges a normative bias—that peace is good and war is bad—and a willingness to put theory into practice by participating in politics.

◆ Mediation and other forms of conflict resolution are alternative means of exerting leverage on participants in bargaining. Increasingly these means are succeeding in settling conflicts without (or with no further) use of violence.

◆ Positive peace implies not just the absence of war but addressing conditions that scholars in peace studies connect with violence—especially injustice and poverty.

◆ Nonviolence—the renunciation of force—can be an effective means of leverage, especially for poor or oppressed people with few other means available.

ONLINE PRACTICE TEST

Take an online practice test at
www.IRtext.com

4

Conflict and War

CHAPTER OUTLINE

- ◆ The Causes of War
- ◆ Conflicts of Interest
- ◆ Conflicts of Ideas
- ◆ Means of Leverage
- ◆ The Use of Military Force
- ◆ Control of Military Forces
- ◆ Conventional Forces
- ◆ Weapons of Mass Destruction

The Causes of War

The Roman writer Seneca said nearly 2,000 years ago: "Of war men ask the outcome, not the cause."[1] This is not true of political scientists. They ask two fundamental questions: Why do international actors (states and nonstate actors alike) come into conflict with each other? And why do those conflicts sometimes lead to violence and war? This chapter addresses both questions.

Just as there are many possible outcomes of conflict, many types of war, and varied propensities for violence among states, so too is there great diversity in the ways and means of using force if conflict leads to violence. States develop a wide array of military forces, which vary tremendously in their purposes and capabilities—having in common only that they are instruments used to apply violence in some form. The chapter concludes with a discussion of these forces.

---

[1] Seneca, Hercules Furens. In *Seneca's Tragedies*. Volume 1. Translated by Frank Justus Miller. London: Heinemann, 1917.

Conflict among states is not an unusual condition but an ordinary one. **Conflict** may be defined as a difference in preferred outcomes in a bargaining situation. International conflicts will always exist. In such conflict bargaining, states develop capabilities that give them leverage to obtain more favorable outcomes than they could obtain without such leverage. Whether fair or unfair, the ultimate outcome of the bargaining process is a **settlement** of the particular conflict.

Violence is an effective form of leverage in some bargaining situations (see p. 54). So states develop capabilities for using violence in international conflicts (discussed a bit later). But these capabilities only sometimes come into play in international conflicts. The great majority of international conflicts do not lead to war, but are resolved in other ways. The study of the causes of war, then, is really an effort to understand the *outbreak* of war—the resort to violence as a means of leverage in international conflicts. But understanding the outbreak of war requires studying the underlying conflicts as well.

The question of why war breaks out can be approached in different ways. More descriptive approaches, favored by historians, tend to focus narrowly on specific direct causes of the outbreak of war, which vary from one war to another. For example, one could say that the assassination of Archduke Ferdinand in 1914 "caused" World War I. More general, theoretical approaches, favored by many political scientists, tend to focus on the search for general explanations, applicable to a variety of contexts, about why wars break out. For example, one can see World War I as caused by shifts in the balance of power among European states, with the assassination being only a catalyst.

Theories about War
Broad generalizations about the causes of war have been elusive. Wars do not have a single or simple cause. Some scholars distinguish *necessary* causes (conditions that must exist for a war to occur, but might not trigger one) from *sufficient* causes (conditions that will trigger war but are responsible for only some wars). Many theories about war have been put forward, but few have universal validity. To organize these theories (types of explanations of war) we shall again use levels of analysis. Wars have been viewed as resulting from forces and processes operating on all the levels.

THE INDIVIDUAL LEVEL On the *individual* level of analysis, the question of why conflicts turn violent revolves around the familiar issue of rationality. One theory, consistent with realism, holds that the use of war and other violent means of leverage in international conflicts is normal and reflects *rational* decisions of national leaders: that "wars begin with conscious and reasoned decisions based on the calculation, made by *both* parties, that they can achieve more by going to war than by remaining at peace."[2]

Web Link
Individual Level

An opposite theory holds that conflicts often escalate to war because of *deviations from rationality* in the individual decision-making processes of national leaders (see Chapter 3)—information screens, cognitive biases, groupthink, and so forth. A related theory holds that the education and mentality of whole populations of individuals determine whether conflicts become violent. Here, public nationalism or ethnic hatred—or

---

[2] Howard, Michael. *The Causes of Wars, and Other Essays.* 2nd ed. Cambridge, MA: Harvard University Press, 1984, p. 22. Emphasis in original.

Why War?   Political scientists do not agree on a theory of why great wars like World War II occur, and cannot predict whether it could happen again. The city of Stalingrad (Volgograd) was decimated during Germany's invasion of the Soviet Union, 1943.

even an innate tendency toward violence in human nature—may pressure leaders to solve conflicts violently. Some IR researchers and activists alike believe that the reeducation of populations can result in fewer conflicts turning violent.

Neither theory holds up very well. Some wars clearly reflect rational calculations of national leaders, whereas others clearly were mistakes and cannot be considered rational. Certainly some individual leaders seem prone to turn to military force to try to settle conflicts on favorable terms. But no reliable guide yet predicts who will be a more warlike or more peaceful leader. A man of war can become a man of peace, as did Egypt's Anwar Sadat, for example. Individuals of many cultural backgrounds and religions lead their states into war, as do both male and female leaders.

THE DOMESTIC LEVEL   The *domestic* level of analysis draws attention to the characteristics of states or societies that may make them more or less prone to use violence in resolving conflicts. During the Cold War, Marxists frequently said that the aggressive and greedy *capitalist* states were prone to use violence in international conflicts, while Western leaders claimed that the expansionist, ideological, and totalitarian nature of *communist* states made them especially prone to using violence. In truth, both types of society have used violence regularly in international conflicts.

Likewise, both democracies and authoritarian states fight wars (though democracies almost never fight other democracies) (see Chapter 3). Rich industrialized states and poor agrarian ones both use war at times. In fact, anthropologists have found that a wide range of *preagricultural* hunter-gatherer societies are prone to warfare under certain circumstances. The potential for warfare seems to be universal across cultures, types of society, and time periods—though the importance and frequency of war vary greatly from case to case.

Few useful generalizations can be made about what kinds of domestic society are more prone or less prone to war (given that all are war-prone to some extent). The same society may change greatly over time. For example, Japan was prone to using violence in international conflicts before World War II but averse to such violence since then. The !Kung bush people in Angola and Namibia—a hunter-gatherer society—were observed by anthropologists in the 1960s to be extremely peaceful. Yet anthropologists in the 1920s had observed them engaging in murderous intergroup violence. If there are general principles to explain why some societies at some times are more peaceful than others and why they change, political scientists have not yet identified them.

THE INTERSTATE LEVEL The theories at the *interstate* level explain wars in terms of power relations among major actors in the international system. For example, power transition theory holds that conflicts generate large wars at times when power is relatively equally distributed and a rising power is threatening to overtake a declining hegemon in overall position. At this level, too, there are competing theories that seem incompatible. Deterrence is supposed to stop wars by building up power and threatening its use. But the theory of arms races holds that wars are caused, not prevented, by such actions. No general formula has been discovered to tell us in what circumstances each of these principles holds true.

Scholars use quantitative and statistical methods to test various ideas about international conflict, such as by analyzing data about wars, weapons, and arms races. For example, researchers are analyzing conflicts between democracies to see why they almost never escalate to war (see pp. 112–115). The quality of data, however, is a major problem for statistical studies of infrequent occurrences such as wars.

THE GLOBAL LEVEL At the *global* level of analysis, a number of theories of war have been proposed. Of the several variations on the idea that major warfare in the international system is *cyclical*, one approach links large wars with *long economic waves* (also called *Kondratieff cycles*) in the world economy, of about 50 years' duration. Another approach links the largest wars with a 100-year cycle based on the creation and decay of world orders (see pp. 72–74). These cycle theories at best can explain only general tendencies toward war in the international system over time.

An alternative theory is that war as an outcome of conflict is becoming less likely over time due to the worldwide development of both technology and international norms. Some IR scholars argue that war and military force are becoming *obsolete* as a leverage in international conflicts because these means of influence are not very effective in today's highly complex, interdependent world. A parallel line of argument holds that today's military technology is too powerful to use in most conflicts; this is especially applicable to nuclear weapons.

A possibly complementary theory traces the obsolescence of war to the evolution of international norms against the use of force. War once was seen as a normal way to resolve disputes but now is considered distasteful. An analogy has been drawn to the practices of slavery and dueling—once considered normal but now obsolete. However, all these arguments about the linear evolution of warfare in the international system rest on mixed empirical evidence. In truth, although major wars have become shorter and less frequent, they are more destructive than ever when they occur. And even in the absence of major wars, smaller wars around the world have not yet evolved out of existence. War may be obsolete, but it still occurs with great frequency.

Thus, although the levels of analysis suggest many explanations for why conflicts lead to war, few such generalizations hold up. On all the levels of analysis, competing theories offer very different explanations for why some conflicts become violent and others do not. Political scientists cannot yet predict with confidence which of the world's many international conflicts will lead to war. We can gain insight, however, by studying various types of conflicts to understand better what it is that states are fighting about. We can also examine some of the alternative forms of leverage, violent and non-violent, that states use in conflicts.

Conflicts of Interest

One way of looking at international conflicts is to assume that all states want maximum power relative to other states. Conflict then becomes a universal condition among states, and they fight about power, status, and alliances in the international system. This realist approach offers insights into power rivalries that sometimes become detached from underlying conflicts over territory, religion, or other specific causes. China attacked Vietnam in 1979 to "teach Vietnam a lesson" after Vietnam invaded Cambodia and overthrew the Chinese-aligned Khmer Rouge government there. China did not want Vietnamese territory; it just wanted to administer punishment for an act it disapproved of. In such cases the struggle for power in an abstract sense takes on its own logic.

But why do states want power? Power gives states specific benefits—the ability to gain better outcomes in bargaining over particular issues that matter to their well-being. Most international conflicts, including the dozens going on at present, are disputes about concrete grievances and demands—territorial borders, ethnic hatreds, revolutions, and so forth. To understand the nature of international conflicts, including their potential for becoming violent, one must study the underlying interests and goals of the involved actors.

The following sections discuss six types of international conflict. Three are conflicts over tangible material interests:

1. Territorial border disputes, including secession attempts

2. Conflicts over who controls national governments

3. Economic conflicts over trade, money, natural resources, drug trafficking, and other such economic transactions

The other three types of conflict concern less tangible clashes of ideas:

4. Ethnic conflicts

5. Religious conflicts

6. Ideological conflicts

These six types of conflict are not mutually exclusive, and they overlap considerably in practice. For example, the conflicts between Russia and Ukraine after the 1991 Soviet breakup were complex. The two new states had a *territorial* dispute over the Crimean peninsula, which Soviet leader Nikita Khrushchev had transferred to Ukraine in the 1950s. There and elsewhere, *ethnic* Russians living in Ukraine, and Ukrainians in Russia, experienced ethnic conflict. There are *religious* differences between Ukrainian and Russian forms of Christianity. The two states also had *economic* conflicts over trade and money after the Soviet breakup, which created new borders and currencies. These multiple conflicts did not lead to the use of military force, however. Remember that conflict is not the same as war—most conflicts do not entail the use of violence. Conflicts of interest lie at the heart of all international bargaining, from trade negotiations to arms control. Only sometimes do they turn violent.

Atlas CD
Crimea History
Photo

Territorial Disputes

Among the international conflicts that concern tangible "goods," those about territory have special importance because of the territorial nature of the state (see "Anarchy and Sovereignty" on pp. 63–66). Conflicts over control of territory are really of two varieties: territorial disputes (about where borders are drawn) and conflicts over control of entire states within existing borders (discussed later under "Control of Governments"). Let us first consider differences over where borders between two states should be drawn—that is, about which state should control disputed territory.

Because states value home territory with an almost fanatical devotion, border disputes tend to be among the most intractable in IR. States will seldom yield territory in exchange for money or any other positive reward. Nor do states quickly forget territory that they lose involuntarily. The goal of regaining territory lost to another state is called **irredentism**. This form of nationalism leads directly to serious interstate conflicts.

Because of their association with the integrity of states, territories are valued far beyond any inherent economic or strategic value they hold. For example, after Israel and Egypt made peace in 1978, it took them a decade to settle a border dispute at Taba, a tiny plot of beachfront on which Israeli developers had built a hotel just slightly across the old border. The two states finally submitted the issue for binding arbitration, and Egypt ended up in possession. For Egypt, regaining every inch of territory was a matter of national honor and a symbol of the sovereignty and territorial integrity that defined Egyptian statehood.

Atlas CD
Taba,
Territorial
Settlement
Map

An exception to this attitude toward territories used to exist in regard to colonies and other territorial possessions. Because these were not part of the home territory or associated with the idea of the nation, they were valued only as property to be won, lost, sold, or traded in political deals and wars. France and Russia sold their territories in Louisiana and Alaska, respectively, to the United States. Such territories are valued for their natural resources or their geopolitical location. Britain since 1704 has possessed the tiny Rock of Gibraltar commanding the entrance to the Mediterranean; the United States since 1898 has owned the Pacific island of Guam, used for military bases. But today, with few colonies remaining, most of the world's territory is home territory to some state.

The value states place on home territory seems undiminished despite the apparent reduction in the inherent value of territory over time as technology has developed. Historically, territory was the basis of economic production—agriculture and the extraction of raw materials. Winning and losing wars meant gaining or losing territory, with which came wealth and hence long-term power. Today, however, much more wealth derives from trade and technology than from agriculture. The costs of most territorial disputes appear to outweigh any economic benefits that the territory in question could provide.

MEANS OF CONTROLLING TERRITORY Historically, military means have been the most effective leverage for controlling territory, and wars have often redrawn the borders of states. Military forces can seize control on the ground in a way that is hard to contest by any means except other military forces. When Saddam Hussein redrew the borders of Iraq to include Kuwait, his opponents found no better means to dislodge him (economic sanctions, negotiations, and so on) than to use military force themselves.

Since World War II, however, there has been a strong norm in the international system *against* trying to alter borders by force. Such attempts are considered grave matters by the international community. Thus, when Iraq annexed Kuwait and erased its borders, most states treated the act as not merely distasteful but intolerable. By contrast, it is considered a lesser offense for one state merely to topple another's government and install a puppet regime, even if done violently, because although that state's *sovereignty* has clearly been violated its *territorial integrity* has not. The principle is: governments come and go; borders remain.

The norm of territorial integrity was illustrated in 1992 when a group of Pakistani nationalists tried to march across the border into a part of India populated by fellow Muslims. Pakistani police fired on their own nationalists to keep them from reaching the border. Because the Pakistani action upheld the integrity of the border, Western democracies did not disapprove of Pakistan's use of force against the demonstrators.

SECESSION Efforts by a province or region to secede from an existing state are a special type of conflict over borders—not the borders of two existing states but the efforts by a substate area to draw international borders around itself as a new state. Dozens of secession movements exist around the world, of varying sizes and political effectiveness, but they succeed in seceding only rarely. The existing state almost always tries to hold onto the area in question. For instance, Kurdish nationalists in Turkey, Iraq, and Iran have sought a Kurdish state carved out of those three states; repeatedly in the late 1990s, Turkey sent large military forces into northern Iraq to attack Kurdish guerrilla bases.

Atlas CD
Russia's
Borderlands
Map Trek

As this example suggests, wars of secession can be large and deadly, and they can easily spill over international borders or draw in other countries. This spillover is particularly likely if members of an ethnic or a religious group span two sides of a border, constituting the majority group in one state and a majority in a nearby region of another state, but a minority in the other state as a whole. This pattern occurs in Bosnia-Serbia, Moldova-Russia, Iraq-Iran, and India-Pakistan. In some cases, secessionists want to merge their territories with the neighboring state (as in the effort to carve out a "greater Serbia"), which amounts to redrawing the international border. International norms frown on such an outcome.

The strong international norms of sovereignty and territorial integrity treat secession movements as domestic problems that are of little concern to other states. In the case of Chechnya, the Western governments objected not to Russia's goal of maintaining control of the republic, but only to Russia's methods of waging the war—which included

Territorial Integrity   Efforts by a region to secede from a state are a frequent source of international conflict. But international norms generally treat such conflicts as internal matters unless they spill over borders. Russia's 1995 assault on its mainly Muslim republic of Chechnya, which had declared independence from the Russian Federation, was repelled, but in 1999–2000 Russia regained control over most of the territory in an even fiercer offensive. Despite human rights violations, the international community tacitly accepted Russia's actions. Here the Russian Army takes control of the capital, Grozny, which was totally destroyed in the 2000 attack.

indiscriminate bombing and shelling of civilian areas. These actions violated standards of human rights, which are however a weaker set of norms than those promoting state sovereignty. Even when secession conflicts occasionally spill over international borders, as with Turkey's incursions into Iraq since 1995, the international community tends to treat the matter lightly as long as the cross-border incursion is temporary. The general principle seems to be: "We existing states all have our own domestic problems and disaffected groups or regions, so we must stick together behind sovereignty and territorial integrity."

Messy border problems have been created in some recent cases in which multinational states broke up into pieces. In such cases, borders that had been internal become international; since these borders are new they may be more vulnerable to challenge. Certainly this is the case in the former Yugoslavia, where ethnic groups had intermingled and intermarried, leaving mixed populations in most of the Yugoslav republics. When Yugoslavia broke up in 1991–1992, several republics declared their independence as separate states. Two of these, Croatia and Bosnia, contained minority populations of ethnic Serbs. Serbia seized effective control of significant areas of Croatia and Bosnia that contained Serbian communities or linked such populations geographically. Non-Serbian populations in these areas were driven out or massacred—an **ethnic cleansing**. Then, when Croatia reconquered most of its territory in 1995, Serbian populations in turn fled from Croatia. Ethnic nationalism proved stronger than multiethnic tolerance in both Serbia and Croatia, making borders problematical.

The breakup of a state need not lead to violence, however. Czechoslovakia split into the Czech Republic and Slovakia in a cooperative and civil manner. And the breakup of the Soviet Union did not lead to violent territorial disputes between republics in *most* cases, even where ethnic groups were split across new international borders (such as Ukraine-Russia).

The norm against forceful redrawing of borders does not apply to cases of decolonization. Only the territorial integrity of existing, recognized states is protected by international norms. For example, when Portugal's empire crumbled in 1975, its colony of East Timor was brutally invaded and annexed by neighboring Indonesia. Because East Timor was not a UN member state (most states did not recognize its independence), and because the United States saw Indonesia but not East Timor as strategically important, Indonesia got away with this move (although it has not been officially recognized by most states). As with Chechnya, the problem was treated mainly as one of human rights.

The transfer of Hong Kong from British to Chinese control in 1997 also illustrates how colonial territory is dispensable (Britain's perspective) while home territory is nearly sacred (China's perspective). From neither perspective do the views of the inhabitants of a territory carry much weight. The peaceful transfer of Hong Kong is one of the few recent cases in which territory has changed hands in the international system.

INTERSTATE BORDERS Border disputes between existing states are taken more seriously by the international community but are less common than secessionist conflicts. Because of the norm of territorial integrity, few important border conflicts remain among long-established states. At one time, huge chunks of territory were passed between states at the stroke of a pen (on a peace treaty or marriage contract).

Since the end of World War II, however, only a minuscule amount of territory has changed hands between established states through force. Such efforts have been made, but have failed. For instance, when Iraq attacked Iran in 1980, one objective was to control the Shatt-al-Arab waterway (with access to the Persian Gulf) because of its commercial and strategic value. But ten years and a million deaths later, the Iran-Iraq border was back where it started. Bits of land have changed hands in recent decades through war, but it is remarkable how small those bits have been. (Again, this does not apply to the formation of new states and the fragmenting of old ones.)

Furthermore, when territorial disputes do occur between established states, they *can* sometimes be settled peacefully, especially when the involved territory is small compared with the states disputing it. The Soviet Union simply agreed to China's boundary preferences in 1986 after the two states had disputed ownership of some minor river islands for years. And El Salvador and Honduras got the World Court to adjudicate their border disputes in 1992.

LINGERING DISPUTES Today, only a few of the world's interstate borders are disputed. Nonetheless, those that persist are important sources of international conflict. Among the most difficult are the borders of *Israel*, which have never been firmly defined and recognized by its neighbors. The 1948 cease-fire lines resulting from Israel's war of independence expanded in the 1967 war, then contracted again on the Egyptian border with the Camp David peace treaty of 1978. The remaining pieces of territory occupied in 1967—the *West Bank* near Jordan, the *Gaza Strip* near Egypt, and the *Golan Heights* of Syria—are central to the Arab-Israeli conflict. The Israeli-Palestinian agreements of 1993–1995 tried to move toward Palestinian autonomy in parts of the West Bank and Gaza Strip, but the borders of this Palestinian entity were not resolved as of 2000.

Another major border dispute is in the *Kashmir* area where India, Pakistan, and China intersect. Among the former Soviet republics, the most serious border dispute is over *Nagorno-Karabakh*, an Armenian-populated territory within neighboring Azerbaijan. After a costly war, Armenia gained military control of the region. Russia and Ukraine had a conflict over the Crimean peninsula, formerly Russian but part of Ukraine since the 1950s.

Atlas CD
Nagorno-
Karabakh
Article

Many of the world's other remaining interstate territorial disputes—and often the most serious ones—concern the control of small islands, which often provide strategic advantages, natural resources (such as offshore oil), or fishing rights. China asserts a right to the tiny disputed *Spratly Islands* in the South China Sea. The islands and surrounding waters, which may hold substantial oil reserves, are closer to Vietnam, the Philippines, Malaysia, and Brunei than to China, and are claimed in part or in full by all those countries and by Taiwan (see Figure 4.1). All of those states except Brunei have resorted to military occupation to stake their claims. The Spratly Islands conflict has importance beyond the immediate dispute since it may signal the intentions of a rising great power (China), and show whether a power vacuum has been left by the U.S. military withdrawal from the Philippines.

Another notable island dispute is in the Middle East, where Iran and the United Arab Emirates dispute ownership of small islands near the mouth of the Persian Gulf.

Atlas CD
Iran-UAE
Islands
Map

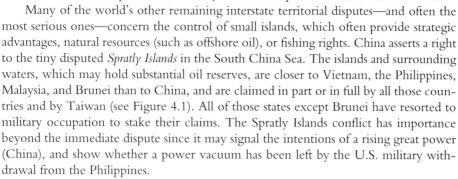

FIGURE 4.1 Disputed Islands   The Spratly Islands exemplify contemporary conflicts over territory and natural resources around islands. All or part of the Spratlys are claimed by China, Vietnam, Malaysia, Brunei, the Philippines, and Taiwan.

In 1995, Iran was reported to have moved military forces, including antiaircraft missiles and possibly chemical weapons, to the disputed islands, from which they could block shipping of Persian Gulf oil to Europe and Japan. However, the Iranian intent may have been defensive (a forward line of air defense for Iran), or economic (claims to off-shore oil deposits). With islands now bringing control of surrounding economic zones, international conflicts over islands will undoubtedly continue in the coming years.

TERRITORIAL WATERS States treat **territorial waters** near their shores as part of their national territory. Definitions of such waters are not universally agreed upon, but norms have developed in recent years, especially after the *UN Convention on the Law of the Sea (UNCLOS)* (see pp. 420–421). Waters within three miles of shore have traditionally been recognized as territorial, but there are disputes about how far out national sovereignty extends and for what purposes. *UNCLOS* generally allows a 12-mile limit for shipping, and a 200-mile *exclusive economic zone (EEZ)* covering fishing and mineral rights (but allowing for free navigation by all). The EEZs together cover a third of the world's oceans.

Atlas CD
Gulf of Sidra
Map

It is because of the EEZs that sovereignty over a single tiny island can now bring with it rights to as much as 100,000 square miles of surrounding ocean. But these zones overlap greatly, and shorelines do not run in straight lines, so numerous questions of interpretation arise about how to delineate territorial and economic waters. For example, Libya claims ownership of the entire Gulf of Sidra, treating it as a bay; the United States treats it as a curvature in the shoreline and insists that most of it is international waters. In 1986, the United States sent warships into the Gulf of Sidra to make its point. U.S. planes shot down two Libyan jets that challenged the U.S. maneuvers. In the Sea of Okhotsk, Russia's EEZ includes all but a small "doughnut hole" of international waters in the middle. Non-Russian boats fish intensively in the "hole," which of course depletes fish stocks in Russia's EEZ.

AIRSPACE **Airspace** above a state is considered the territory of the state. Any airplane that wants to fly over a state's territory must have the state's permission. For example, in a 1986 raid on Libya, U.S. bombers based in Britain had to fly a long detour over the Atlantic Ocean because France (between Britain and Libya) would not grant permission for U.S. planes to use its airspace during the mission.

Outer space, by contrast, is considered international territory like the oceans. International law does not define exactly where airspace ends and outer space begins. However, orbiting satellites fly higher than airplanes, move very fast, and cannot easily change direction to avoid overflying a country. And very few states can shoot down satellites. Since satellites have become useful to all the great powers as intelligence-gathering tools, and since all satellites are extremely vulnerable to attack, a norm of demilitarization of outer space has developed. No state has ever shot down the satellite of another, and doing so would be a severe provocation.

Web Link
Control of
Governments

Control of Governments

Despite the many minor border disputes that continue to plague the world, most of the struggles to control territory do not involve changing borders. Rather, they are conflicts over which governments will control entire states.

In theory, states do not interfere in each other's governance. In practice, states often have strong interests in the governments of other states and use a variety of means of leverage to influence who holds power in those states. When one state wants to alter or replace the government of a second state, a conflict always exists between the two governments. In addition, the first state may come into conflict with other parties that oppose changing the second state's government. These conflicts over governments take many forms, some mild and some severe, some deeply entwined with third parties and some more or less bilateral. Sometimes a state merely exerts subtle influences on another state's elections; at other times, a state supports rebel elements seeking to overthrow the second state's constitutional order altogether.

A severe conflict over government composition arose after the 1991 Gulf War. The U.S. side won the war but the architect of Iraq's aggression—Saddam Hussein—was still in power. Under the official terms of the UN cease-fire, Iraq had to take certain measures before UN economic sanctions would be lifted. In conformity with international norms, the UN conditions did not demand changes in the Iraqi government, only in its behavior. Indeed, the United States stood by when, immediately after the war, Saddam crushed an uprising aimed at toppling his rule. However, the United States used its power on the Security Council to prevent sanctions from being lifted while Saddam was still in power, even several years later when Iraq had largely (but not entirely) complied with the UN conditions. The United States also repeatedly expressed hope that the Iraqi military would overthrow Saddam, and gave money to Iraqi opposition groups in exile.

Occasionally, one state invades another in order to change its government. The Soviet Union did this in Czechoslovakia in 1968; the United States did it in Grenada in 1983 but refrained from doing so in Iraq in 1991. It is sometimes hard for new governments created in this way to gain legitimacy both domestically and internationally. People generally resent having foreigners choose their government for them—even if they didn't like the old government—and the international community frowns on such overt violations of national sovereignty. For instance, the government installed in Afghanistan after the Soviet invasion of 1979 was seen as a Soviet puppet and was finally toppled after a dozen years of rule marked by constant war.

International conflicts over the control of governments—along with territorial disputes—are likely to lead to the use of violence. They involve core issues of the status and integrity of states, the stakes tend to be high, and the interests of involved actors are often diametrically opposed. Other types of conflict are both more widespread and less likely to lead to violence. Chief among these are economic conflicts among states.

Economic Conflict

Economic competition is the most pervasive form of conflict in international relations because economic transactions are pervasive. Every sale made and every deal reached across international borders entail a resolution of conflicting interests. Costa Rica wants the price of coffee, which it exports, to go up; Canada, which imports coffee, wants the price to go down. Angola wants foreign producers of Angolan oil to receive less of the profits from oil sales; those companies' home states want them to take home more profits. In a global capitalist market, all economic exchanges involve some conflict of interest.

Web Link
Economic
Conflict

However, such economic transactions also contain a strong element of mutual economic gain in addition to the element of conflicting interests (see Chapters 2 and 5). These mutual gains provide the most useful leverage in bargaining over economic exchanges: states and companies enter into economic transactions because they profit from doing so. The use of violence would for the most part interrupt and diminish such

Struggle for Control   Conflicts over who controls a national government, especially armed rebellions, can easily become internationalized, especially when economic conflict is also in play. Rebellions in Democratic Congo—where territorial control allows exploitation of valuable natural resources like diamonds—have drawn in military forces from a half dozen neighboring states. The rebels shown here are among three guerrilla groups and two foreign armies headquartered in Kisangani in 1999.

profit by more than could be gained as a result of the use of violence. Thus, economic conflicts do not usually lead to military force and war. Even in the extreme instance where a government nationalizes the property of a U.S.-based corporation, the U.S. Marines do not storm ashore to recover the company's assets, as they might have done some decades ago.

Such restraint has not always been the case. In the sixteenth century, England's Sir Francis Drake intercepted Spanish ships bringing gold and silver from Central America and took the loot in the name of queen and country—a practice known as *privateering*. In the seventeenth century, England fought several naval wars against the Netherlands. An English general, when asked the reason for England's declaration of war in 1652, replied, "What matters this or that reason? What we want is more of the trade the Dutch now have."[3]

Economic conflict seldom leads to violence today because military forms of leverage are no longer very effective in economic conflicts. With the tight integration of the

---

[3] Howard, Michael. *War in European History*. Oxford: Oxford University Press, 1976, p. 47.

world economy and the high cost of military actions, the use of force is seldom justified to solve an economic issue. Thus, most economic conflicts are not issues in international security; they are discussed in Chapters 5 through 8 on international political economy. But economic conflicts do still bear on international security in some ways.

First, many states' foreign policies are influenced by *mercantilism*—a practice of centuries past in which trade and foreign economic policies were manipulated to build up a monetary surplus that could be used to finance war (see pp. 210–212). Because a trade surplus confers an advantage in international security affairs over the long run, trade conflicts have implications for international security relations.

Second, the theory of **lateral pressure** also connects economic competition with security concerns. This theory holds that the economic growth of states leads to geographic expansion as they seek natural resources beyond their borders (by various means, peaceful and violent). As great powers expand their economic activities outward, their competition leads to conflicts and sometimes to war. The theory has been used to help explain both World War I and the expansion of Japan prior to World War II.

Another kind of economic conflict that affects international security concerns *military industry*—the capacity to produce military equipment, especially high-technology weapons such as fighter aircraft or missiles. There is a world trade in such items, but national governments try (not always successfully) to keep control of such production—to try to ensure that national interests take priority over those of manufacturers and that the state is militarily self-sufficient in case of war. Economic competition (over who profits from such sales) is interwoven with security concerns (over who gets access to the weapons). The transfer of knowledge about high-tech weaponry and military technologies to potentially hostile states is a related concern.

Economic competition also becomes a security issue when it concerns trade in *strategic materials* needed for military purposes, such as special minerals or alloys for aircraft production and uranium for atomic weapons. Few countries are self-sufficient in these materials; the United States imports about half the strategic materials it uses. Thus, economic competition as a source of international conflict has important implications for international security. Nonetheless, military force plays a diminishing role in resolving such economic conflicts.

A different kind of economic conflict revolves around the distribution of wealth within and among states. As discussed in Chapter 7, there are tremendous disparities in wealth in our world, disparities that create a variety of international security problems with the potential for violence. Chief among these conflicts is the issue of revolutions in poor countries. Such revolutions are often fueled by disparities of wealth within the country as well as its poverty relative to other countries. These revolutions in turn frequently draw in other states as supporters of one side or the other in a civil war. If successful, revolutions can abruptly change a state's foreign policy, leading to new alliances and power alignments.

Marxist approaches to international relations, discussed in Chapter 7, treat class struggle between rich and poor people as the basis of interstate relations. According to these approaches, capitalist states adopt foreign policies that serve the interests of the rich owners of companies. Conflicts and wars between the global North and South—rich states versus poor states—are seen as reflections of the domination and exploitation of the poor by the rich—imperialism in direct or indirect form. For example, most Marxists saw the Vietnam

War as a U.S. effort to suppress revolution in order to secure continued U.S. access to cheap labor and raw materials in Southeast Asia. Many Marxists portray conflicts among capitalist states as competition over the right to exploit poor areas. For instance, Soviet founder V. I. Lenin saw World War I as a fight over the imperialists' division of the world.

**Atlas CD
Haiti
Map**

Events in *Haiti*, the poorest country in Latin America, illustrate how disparities of wealth can create international security conflicts. For decades, the country was ruled by an absolute dictator, "Papa Doc" Duvalier, backed by a ruthless secret police agency. The dictator and his associates became very rich while the population remained very poor. When the dictator died, his son "Baby Doc" took over. During most of the Cold War, the United States backed the dictatorship because it provided a reliable ally next door to Soviet-allied Cuba. Finally, a popular uprising forced Baby Doc to flee in 1986; a Catholic priest championing the poor, Jean-Bertrand Aristide, was elected president of Haiti. But within a year the military seized power in a coup d'état and began to enrich itself again. This, along with international sanctions against the Haitian economy, led tens of thousands of people to flee on rickety boats heading for the prosperous United States. These boat people were intercepted by the U.S. Navy, and most were sent back to Haiti because they were labeled "economic" refugees (see pp. 363–365)— but the issue caused problems in U.S. domestic politics, forcing a response. The United States sent an invasion force, intimidated the military leaders into leaving, and restored Aristide as president. Then the U.S. military occupation was converted into a UN peacekeeping operation. Thus, the disparities of wealth in Haiti had ramifications for global alliances (in the Cold War), for regional containment (of Cuba), and for international norms concerning military intervention.

DRUG TRAFFICKING As a form of illegal trade across international borders, drug trafficking is smuggling, which deprives states of revenue and violates states' legal control of their borders. But smuggling in general is an economic issue rather than a security one (see p. 229). Unlike other smuggled goods, however, drug trafficking supplies illegal products that are treated as a security threat because of their effect on national (and military) morale and efficiency. Drug trafficking also has become linked with security concerns because military forces participate regularly in operations against the heavily armed drug traffickers. Conflicts over drugs generally concern states on one side and nonstate actors on the other. But other states are drawn in because the activities in question cross national borders and may involve corrupt state officials.

**Atlas CD
Colombia and
Panama
Map**

These international ramifications are evident in the efforts of the U.S. government to prevent *cocaine cartels* based in Colombia from supplying cocaine to U.S. cities. Such cocaine derives mostly from coca plants grown by peasants in mountainous areas of Peru, Bolivia, and Colombia itself. Processed in simple laboratories in the jungle, the cocaine moves from Colombia through other countries such as Panama before arriving in the United States. In each of these states (yes, even the United States), the drug smugglers have bribed some corrupt officials, including military or police officers, to stay clear. But other state officials in each country are working with U.S. law enforcement agencies and the U.S. military to crack down on the cocaine trade.

The truth is that the populations in several of these countries, especially in cocaine-producing regions, benefit substantially from the drug trade. For poor peasants in Bolivia or for residents of the Colombian cocaine cartels' home provinces, the cocaine trade

Drug Wars   Because drug trafficking crosses national borders and involves lots of guns and money, it is a source of interstate conflict. The United States invaded Panama to stop dictator Manuel Noriega's collusion with traffickers shipping illegal drugs to the United States. Here, U.S. forces train in Panama near a billboard advertising the United States's own drug export to Panama (tobacco), 1989.

may be their only access to a decent income. Benefits to corrupt state officials are also substantial. In rural Peru and Colombia, leftist guerrillas have funded their operations by controlling peasants' production of coca.

The cocaine trade thus creates some conflicts between the United States and the states of the region. Most such interstate conflicts are resolved through positive forms of leverage such as U.S. financial or military aid. State officials are also often willing to make common cause with the United States because they are threatened by the drug traffickers, who control great wealth and power, and who, being outlaws, have few incentives against using violence.

Because of the long history of U.S. military intervention in Latin America, state cooperation with U.S. military forces is a sensitive political issue. Governments in the region must respect a delicate balance between the need for U.S. help and the need to uphold national sovereignty. In some countries, governments have faced popular criticism for allowing the "Yankees" to "invade" in the drug war.

Conflicts arising from cocaine trafficking have thus had ramifications for U.S. foreign aid, Latin American sovereignty, the economic well-being of populations in poor countries, guerrilla war in Peru, a military invasion in Panama, and other interstate tensions in the region.

The growing world trade in heroin created some similar conflicts in the late 1990s. Most of the raw material (opium poppies) comes from two poor and conflict-ridden countries with authoritarian governments—Afghanistan and Burma—where Western governments have little leverage. The United States cites six countries for failing to cooperate sufficiently in fighting international drug trafficking, as of 2000—Afghanistan, Burma, Cambodia, Haiti, Nigeria, and Paraguay.

Like the other sources of international conflict discussed so far, conflicts over drug trafficking arise from conflicting interests regarding tangible items such as money, territory, or control of governments. More difficult to understand, in some ways, are international conflicts rooted in clashes of ideas. Of course, the two overlap—especially around the material and intangible aspects of nationalism—but conflicts of ideas also require special attention in their own right.

Conflicts of Ideas

If all international conflicts were strictly material in nature, it might be easier to settle them. Given a large enough positive leverage, any state would agree to another state's terms on a disputed issue. More difficult are the types of conflict in which intangible elements such as ethnic hatred, religious fervor, or ideology come into play.

Atlas CD
Ethnic
Tensions in
Uganda
Photo

Ethnic Conflict Ethnic conflict is quite possibly the most important source of conflict in the numerous wars now occurring throughout the world. **Ethnic groups** are large groups of people who share ancestral, language, cultural, or religious ties and a common *identity* (individuals identify with the group). Although conflicts between ethnic groups often have material aspects—notably over territory and government control—ethnic conflict itself stems from a dislike or hatred that members of one ethnic group systematically feel toward another ethnic group. Ethnic conflict is thus not based on tangible causes (what someone does) but on intangible ones (who someone is).

Ethnic groups often form the basis for *nationalist* sentiments. Not all ethnic groups identify as nations; for instance, within the United States various ethnic groups coexist (albeit uneasily) with a common *national* identity as Americans. But in locations where millions of members of a single ethnic group live as the majority population in their ancestors' land, they usually think of themselves as a nation. In most such cases they aspire to have their own state with its formal international status and territorial boundaries.

Territorial control is closely tied to the aspirations of ethnic groups for statehood. Any state's borders will deviate to some extent (sometimes substantially) from the actual location of ethnic communities. Members of the ethnic group will be left outside its state's borders, and members of other ethnic groups will be located within the state's borders. The resulting situation can be dangerous, with part of an ethnic group controlling a state and another part living as a minority within another state controlled by a rival ethnic group. Frequently the minority group suffers discrimination in the other state and the "home" state tries to rescue or avenge them.

Other ethnic groups lack any home state. Kurds share a culture, and many of them aspire to create a state of Kurdistan. But Kurds reside in four states—Turkey, Iraq, Iran, and Syria—all of which strongly oppose giving up control of part of their own territory to create a Kurdish state (see Figure 4.2). In recent years, rival Kurdish guerrilla armies have fought both Iraqi and Turkish military forces, and each other.

FIGURE 4.2 Kurdish Area Ethnic populations often span international borders. Shaded region shows the approximate area of Kurdish settlements.

Atlas CD
Kurdish Village
Photo

In ethnic conflicts there are often pressures to redraw borders by force. For example, the former Soviet republic of Moldova is inhabited mostly by ethnic Romanians but also by quite a few ethnic Russians, who are concentrated at the eastern end of Moldova (farthest from Romania). A river separates a strip of land at the east end from the rest of Moldova, and ethnic Russians make up the majority in that strip of territory. When Moldova became independent in 1991 and began asserting its Romanian identity—even considering merging into Romania—the Russians living in the eastern strip of land sought to break away and make the river a new international border. Armed conflict ensued, and both Russia and Romania threatened to intervene. Eventually a cease-fire and a peacekeeping arrangement were implemented, with no formal change in borders.

When ethnic populations are minorities in territories controlled by rival ethnic groups, they may even be driven from their land or (in rare cases) systematically exterminated. By driving out the minority ethnic group, a majority group can assemble a more unified, more contiguous, and larger territory for its nation-state, as ethnic Serbs did through "ethnic cleansing" after the breakup of Yugoslavia.

Outside states often worry about the fate of "their people" living as minorities in neighboring states. For instance, Albania is concerned about ethnic Albanians who are the majority population in the Serbian province of Kosovo. But if Kosovo became independent of Serbia (or merged with Albania), then Serbia would worry about the minority of ethnic Serbs living in Kosovo. Similar problems have fueled wars between Armenia and Azerbaijan (in the former Soviet Union) and between India and Pakistan. It appears likely that the dangerous combination of ethnic conflict and territorial disputes will lead to more wars in the future.

In extreme cases, governments use genocide—systematic extermination of ethnic or religious groups in whole or in part—to try to destroy scapegoated groups or political rivals. In Rwanda, where the Hutu group is the majority and the Tutsi group the minority, a Hutu-nationalist government in 1994 slaughtered roughly half a million Tutsis (and Hutus opposed to the government) in a matter of weeks. The weak international response to this atrocity reveals how frail are international norms of human rights compared to norms of noninterference in other states' internal affairs—at least when no strategic interests are at stake. The Hutu ultranationalists quickly lost power when Tutsi rebels defeated the government militarily, but they regrouped across the border in Zaire, with hundreds of thousands of Hutu refugees. In 1997, a Tutsi-led army with support from Rwanda and other neighboring states swept through Zaire, toppled its government, and dispersed or killed many of the refugees. The Hutu-Tutsi conflict thus sparked an intense series of wars that directly affected a half dozen states, brought down several governments, and destroyed or damaged millions of lives.

The Cold War, with its tight system of alliances and authoritarian communist governments, seems to have helped to keep ethnic conflicts in check. In the Soviet Union and Yugoslavia—multinational states—the existence of a single strong state (willing to oppress local communities) kept the lid on ethnic tensions and enforced peace between neighboring communities. The breakup of these states allowed ethnic and regional conflicts to take center stage, sometimes bringing violence and war. These cases may indicate a dilemma in that freedom comes at the expense of order and vice versa. Of course, not all ethnic groups get along so poorly together; after the fall of communism, most of the numerous ethnic rivalries in the former Soviet Union did not lead to warfare, and in Czechoslovakia and elsewhere ethnic rivalries were relatively peaceful.

CAUSES OF ETHNIC HOSTILITY Why do ethnic groups often dislike each other? Frequently there are long-standing historical conflicts over specific territories or natural resources, or over one ethnic group's economic exploitation or political domination of another. Over time, ethnic conflicts may transcend these concrete historical causes and take on lives of their own. They become driven not by tangible grievances (though these may well persist as irritants) but by the kinds of processes described by social psychology that are set in motion when one group of people has a prolonged conflict with another and experiences violence at the hands of the other group.

The ethnic group is a kind of extended *kinship* group—a group of related individuals sharing some ancestors. Even when kinship relations are not very close, a *group identity* makes a person act as though the other members of the ethnic group were family. For instance, African American men who call each other "brother" express group identity as kinship. Likewise Jews around the world treat each other as family even though each community has intermarried over time and may have more ancestors in common with local non-Jews than with distant Jews. Perhaps, as technology allows far-flung groups to congregate in cyberspace, there will be less psychological pressure to collect ethnic groups physically in a territorial nation-state.

Ethnocentrism, or *in-group bias*, is the tendency to see one's own group in favorable terms and an *out-group* in unfavorable terms. Some scholars believe that ethnocentrism

THE INFORMATION

REVOLUTION **Nations and States**

Many current international conflicts result from the mismatch of states' territorial borders with the actual distributions of ethnic or national populations. As technology allows communities to transcend geography, can national identity connect dispersed populations without generating territorial conflicts?

To explore this question, go to www.IRtext.com

has roots in a biological propensity to protect closely related individuals, but this idea is quite controversial. More often in-group bias is understood in terms of social psychology.

No minimum criterion of similarity or kin relationship is needed to evoke the group identity process, including in-group bias. In psychological experiments, even trivial differentiations can evoke these processes. If people are assigned to groups based on a known but unimportant characteristic (such as preferring, say, circles to triangles), before long the people in each group show in-group bias and find they don't much care for the other group's members.

In-group biases are far stronger when the other group looks different, speaks a different language, or worships in a different way (or all three). All too easily, an out-group can be **dehumanized** and stripped of all human rights. This dehumanization includes the common use of animal names—"pigs," "dogs," and so forth—for members of the out-group. U.S. propaganda in World War II depicted Japanese people as apes. Especially in wartime, when people see members of an out-group killing members of their in-group, dehumanization can be extreme. The restraints on war that have evolved in regular interstate warfare are easily discarded in interethnic warfare.

In several countries where long internal wars in the 1990s had led to dehumanization and atrocities—notably in South Africa—new governments used *truth commissions* to help the society heal and move forward. The commission's role was to hear honest testimony from the period, to bring to light what really happened during these wars, and in exchange to offer most of the participants asylum from punishment. Thus, after brutal ethnic conflicts give way to complex political settlements, governments often must balance the need for justice and truth with the need to keep all groups on board.

Experience in Western Europe shows that education over time can overcome ethnic animosities between traditionally hostile nations, such as France and Germany. After World War II, governments rewrote the history textbooks for a new generation. Previously each state's textbooks had glorified its past deeds, played down its misdeeds, and portrayed its traditional enemies in unflattering terms. In a continentwide project, new textbooks that gave a more objective and fair rendition were created. This project helped pave the way for European integration in subsequent decades.

The existence of a threat from an out-group promotes the cohesion of an in-group, thereby creating a somewhat self-reinforcing process of ethnic division. However, ethnocentrism also often causes members of a group to view themselves as disunited (because they see their own divisions up close) and the out-group as monolithic (because they see it only from outside). This usually reflects a group's sense of vulnerability. Furthermore, overstating the threat posed by an enemy is a common way for political leaders to bolster their own position within an in-group. In the Arab-Israeli conflict, Israelis tend to see themselves as fragmented into dozens of political parties and diverse immigrant communities pulling in different directions, while they see Arabs as a monolithic bloc united against them. Meanwhile, Arab Palestinians see themselves as fragmented into factions and weakened by divisions among the Arab states, while Israelis appear monolithic to them.

Over time, rival ethnic groups may develop a pattern of *feuding*. Each side retaliates for actions of the other in a continuing circle of violence. Reflecting in-group bias, each side often believes it is acting defensively and that the other side "started it."

Ethnic conflicts are hard to resolve because they are not about "who gets what" but about "I don't like you." To cast the conflict in terms of a bargaining situation, each side places value on the other's loss of value (see the discussion of game theory on p. 61). A person inflamed with hatred of an enemy is willing to *lose* value in absolute terms—to lose money, the support of allies, or even life—to deprive the enemy of value as well. Almost all the means of leverage used in such conflicts are negative, and bargains are very hard to reach. So ethnic conflicts tend to drag on without resolution for generations.

Ethnic groups are only one point along a spectrum of kinship relations—from nuclear families through extended families, villages, provinces, and nations, up to the entire human race. Loyalties fall at different points along the spectrum. Again there is no minimum criterion for in-group identity. For instance, experts said that of all the African countries, Somalia was surely immune from ethnic conflicts because Somalis were all from the same ethnic group and spoke the same language. Then in 1991–1992 a ruinous civil war erupted between members of different clans (based on extended families), leading to mass starvation and the intervention of foreign military forces (which by 1995 had to withdraw after a humiliating failure to tame the violence).

It is unclear why people identify most strongly at one level of group identity. In Somalia, loyalties are to clans; in Serbia, they are to the ethnic group; in the United States and elsewhere, multiethnic states have managed to gain people's primary loyalty. States reinforce their citizens' identification with the state through flags, anthems, pledges of allegiance, and so forth. Perhaps someday people will shift loyalties further, developing a *global identity* as humans first and members of states and ethnic groups second.

**Atlas CD
World
Religions
Map**

Religious Conflict
One reason ethnic conflicts often transcend material grievances is that they find expression as *religious* conflicts. Since religion is the core of a community's value system in much of the world, people whose religious practices differ are easily disdained and treated as unworthy or even inhuman. When overlaid on ethnic and territorial conflicts, religion often surfaces as the central and most visible division between groups. For instance, most Indians are Hindus and most Pakistanis are Muslims. Most people in Azerbaijan are Muslims; Armenians are Christians. Most Croats are Roman Catholic Christians, whereas most Serbs are Orthodox Christians and most Bosnians and Albanians are Muslims. This is a very common pattern in ethnic conflicts.

Nothing inherent in religion mandates conflicts—in many places members of different religious groups coexist peacefully. But religious differences hold the potential for conflict, and for making existing conflicts more intractable, because religions involve core values that are held as absolute truth. This is increasingly true as *fundamentalist* movements have gained strength in recent decades. (The reasons for fundamentalism are disputed, but it is clearly a global-level phenomenon.) Members of these movements organize their lives and communities around their religious beliefs; many are willing to sacrifice and even die for those beliefs. Fundamentalist movements have become larger and more powerful in recent decades in Christianity, Islam, Judaism, Hinduism, and other religions. Such movements challenge the values and practices of **secular** political organizations—those created apart from religious establishments (the separation of religion and state). For example, an Islamic movement in Turkey and a Christian movement in the United States both seek to change long-standing secular traditions by incorporating religious values into the government.

Among the secular practices threatened by fundamentalist movements are the rules of the international system, whereby states are treated as formally equal and sovereign whether they are "believers" or "infidels." As transnational belief systems, religions often are taken as a higher law than state laws and international treaties. This runs counter to the norms of the international system, and to the assumptions of realism.

Currently, violent conflicts are being prosecuted in the name of all the world's major religions. **Islam**, the religion practiced by **Muslims** (or *Moslems*), has been frequently stereotyped in European and North American political discourse, especially at times of conflict such as the 1973 oil embargo, the 1979 Iranian revolution, and the 1991 Gulf War. Islam is no more conflict-prone than other religions, although Christian-Muslim conflicts are raging in a dozen locations. Islam is in fact broad and diverse. Its divergent populations include Sunni Muslims, Shiite Muslims, and many smaller branches and sects. The areas of the world that are predominantly Islamic stretch from Nigeria to Indonesia, centered in the Middle East (see Figure 4.3). Most countries with mainly Muslim populations belong to the Islamic Conference, an IGO. Many international conflicts around this zone involve Muslims on one side and non-Muslims on the other, as a result of geographical and historical circumstances including colonialism and oil.

Web Link
Islam

In several countries, Islamic fundamentalists reject Western-oriented secular states in favor of governments more explicitly oriented to Islamic values. These movements reflect long-standing *anti-Western* sentiment in these countries—against the old European colonizers who were Christian—and are in some ways *nationalist* movements expressed through religious channels. In some Middle Eastern countries with authoritarian governments, religious institutions (mosques) have been the only available avenue for political opposition. Religion has therefore become a means for expressing opposition to the status quo in both politics and culture. (Similarly political roles have developed for other religions elsewhere, notably the Falun Gong movement in China in the late 1990s.)

Islamic movements have gained strength in recent years. In 1979, an Islamic republic was created in Iran. Pakistan and Sudan adopted Islamic laws without a revolution. An Islamic government was established in Afghanistan in 1992 after a civil war (and following a decade of ill-fated Soviet occupation). Rival Islamic factions then continued the war with even greater intensity for several years. By 1997 a faction called Taliban had taken control of most of Afghanistan and imposed an extreme interpretation of Islamic law—for example, barring women from working and forcing all men to grow beards. The Afghanistan war is perhaps the world's most destructive war in progress (late 1999), and it could fuel conflicts in Russia, China, and other nearby countries where various forms of Muslim nationalism are at odds with state governments. As noted earlier, Afghanistan is also the world's primary source of raw material for illegal narcotics.

Atlas CD
Afghanistan
Map

In Algeria, an especially brutal war evolved in the mid-1990s between the secular military government and an Islamic revolutionary movement. Islamic parties were winning democratic elections for a new Parliament in 1991, when the military intervened to take power and stop the elections. The Islamic movement went underground, and the ensuing war between the military and the rebels killed as many as 100,000 people. In a murky and brutal struggle, both sides eventually turned to seemingly purposeless massacres. In 1999, a reformist politician returned from exile, was elected president, and struck a peace deal with the main rebel faction—raising hopes for a durable peace.

Atlas CD
Islam in
Algeria
Photo

In Jordan, Islamic parties won the largest bloc of seats in Parliament but violence did not ensue. Meanwhile, in the 1990s Islamic parties gained ground in Turkey—a fiercely secular state in which the military has intervened to prevent religious expression in pol-

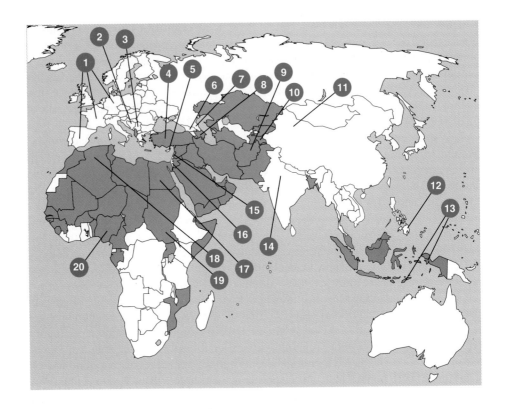

FIGURE 4.3   Members of the Islamic Conference and Areas of Conflict
Shaded countries are members of the conference; numbered regions are areas of conflict between Muslims and non-Muslims or secular authorities.

itics. The leader of the main Islamic party even served briefly as prime minister, in a shaky governing coalition, before the military forced a change.

The more radical Islamic movements not only threaten some existing governments—especially those tied to the West—they also often undermine norms of state sovereignty (for better or worse). They are creating new transnational ties. They reject Western political conceptions of the state (based on individual autonomy) in favor of a more traditional Islamic orientation based on community. Some aspire to create a single political state encompassing most of the Middle East, as existed in A.D. 600–1200.

For better or worse, such a development would create a profound challenge to the present international system—particularly to its current status quo powers—and would therefore be opposed at every turn by the world's most powerful states. From the perspective of some outsiders, the religious conflicts boiling and simmering at the edges of the Islamic world look like an expansionist threat to be contained. The view from within looks more like being surrounded and repressed from several directions—a view reinforced by recent massacres of Muslims in Bosnia, Chechnya, and India.

Overall, Islamic activism (and the opposition to it) is more complex than simply a religious conflict; it concerns power, economic relations, ethnic chauvinism, and historical empires as well. The same forces contribute to religious activism in non-Muslim countries. In India, Hindu fundamentalists have provoked violent clashes and massacres that have reverberated internationally. In 1992, a Hindu mob destroyed a Muslim mosque at Ayodhya, India. The incident provoked days of civil violence in India, mostly directed against Muslims, in which thousands died. In Israel, Jewish fundamentalists have used violence, including the assassination of Israel's own prime minister in 1995, to try to derail Arab-Jewish peace negotiations.

Recently it has been suggested that international conflicts in the coming years may be generated by a clash of civilizations—based on the differences between the world's major cultural groupings, which overlap quite a bit with religious communities. The idea has been criticized for being overly general, and for assuming that cultural differences naturally create conflict.

Ideological Conflict
To a large extent, ideology is like religion: it symbolizes and intensifies conflicts between groups and states more than it causes them. Ideologies have a somewhat weaker hold on core values and absolute truth than religions do, so they pose somewhat fewer problems for the international system.

For realists, ideological differences among states do not matter much, because all members of the international system pursue their national interests in the context of relatively fluid alliances. Over the long run, even countries that experience revolutions based on strong ideologies tend to lose their ideological fervor—be it Iran's Islamic fundamentalism in 1979, China's Maoist communism in 1949, Russia's Leninist communism in 1917, or even U.S. democracy in 1776. In each case, the revolutionaries expected that their assumption of power would dramatically alter their state's foreign policy, because in each case their ideology had profound international implications.

Yet, within a few decades, each of these revolutionary governments turned to the pursuit of national interests above ideological ones. The Soviet Union soon became in many ways just another great power on the European scene—building up its own armed forces, expanding its territory at the expense of Poland, and making alliances with enemies (the Stalin-Hitler pact in 1939 and the alliance with the West during World War II). Likewise, China's Chairman Mao wanted to spread a "prairie fire" of revolution through the third world to liberate it from U.S. imperialism, but within a few decades Mao was welcoming the very embodiment of U.S. imperialism, President Nixon, to pursue mutual national interests.

Sometimes even self-proclaimed ideological struggles are not as ideological as they appear. In Angola in the 1980s, the United States backed a rebel army called UNITA against a Soviet-aligned government—supposedly a struggle of democracy against Marxism. In truth, the ideological differences between the two sides were quite arbi-

Let a Hundred Flowers Bloom   Ideology plays only a limited role in most international conflicts. After revolutions, such as China's in 1949, ideologies such as Maoism may affect foreign policy. But over the next 10 or 20 years such countries typically revert to a foreign policy based more on national interests (for China, territorial integrity and trade-based prosperity) than ideology (communism). Nonetheless, the clashing cultures of U.S.-style democracy and Chinese-style communism still are a source of conflict in U.S.-Chinese relations. Here, students demonstrate for democracy in Tiananmen Square, Beijing, 1989. The violent repression of those demonstrations cast a shadow over U.S.-Chinese relations in the 1990s.

**Atlas CD
Chinese
Communism
*Photo***

trary. The government mouthed Marxist rhetoric to get the Soviet Union to give it aid (a policy that was reversed as soon as Soviet aid dried up). The "democratic" rebels meanwhile adopted democratic rhetoric to get U.S. support but practiced nothing of the sort. In fact, they had earlier received Chinese support and had mouthed Maoist rhetoric. When UN-sponsored elections were won by the government, the "democratic" UNITA refused to accept the results and resumed fighting. This conflict really had nothing to do with ideology.

In the short term, revolutions *do* change international relations—they make wars more likely—but not because of ideology. Rather, the sudden change of governments can alter alliances and change the balance of power. With calculations of power being revised by all parties, it is easy to miscalculate or to exaggerate threats on both sides. Saddam Hussein, for example, miscalculated Iran's power after its revolution (see "Estimating Power" on pp. 49–50). But ideology itself plays little role in this postrevolutionary propensity for wars: revolutions are seldom exported to other states.

We should not assume, however, that ideology and political philosophies play no role at all in international politics. Ideologies can help to *mobilize* national populations to support a state in its international dealings, such as war. Fascism (the Nazi ideology) inflamed German nationalism before World War II, legitimizing German aggression by placing it in an ideological framework. And ideology can sharpen and intensify the conflict between two rivals, as happened to the superpowers during the Cold War. In some third world proxy wars of that era—for instance, Nicaragua in the 1980s—the rebels and governments had real ideological differences that resonated with the Cold War rivalry.

If we consider political democracy to be an ideology, it may be the exception to the rule that ideology does not affect IR much. Democracy has become a global-level force in world politics, transcending the interests of particular states. A commitment to democracy does not yet outweigh a commitment to national interest in states' foreign policies, and perhaps never will, but global democracy is slowly emerging as a norm that states increasingly are pursuing in their dealings with other states (see "Democratic Peace" on pp. 112–115). Democracies and nondemocracies may increasingly find themselves in conflict with each other if this trend continues. Because democracies almost never fight wars with each other (although they still have conflicts), the spread of democratic ideology may have great implications for future prospects for peace.

All six types of conflict just discussed can be pursued through peaceful or violent means. We can better understand conflict by examining the types of leverage, violent and otherwise, that are brought into play in international conflicts.

Means of Leverage

Conflicts are settled when some explicit or implicit bargaining process arrives at an outcome acceptable to both parties (see "Bargaining" on pp. 53–54). Acceptable does not mean that both parties are happy or that the outcome is fair—only that neither party thinks it worth the effort to try to change the outcome. Perhaps both parties are satisfied that they have struck a beneficial or fair deal, or one party has been stripped of its leverage (in the extreme case, destroyed altogether) and has no prospect of improving a bad outcome through further bargaining.

Web Link
Means of
Leverage

War and other violent actions taken in international conflicts are aimed at settling conflicts on favorable terms by inflicting violence as a negative form of leverage. States can also have alternative means of leverage and strategies that often work better than war in resolving conflicts (ending them on mutually acceptable terms).

Types of War
War has been defined in various ways. For present purposes, we may define *war* as sustained intergroup violence (deliberately inflicting death and injury) in which state military forces participate on at least one side—on both sides in the case of *interstate war* and generally on only one side in the case of civil war. Around this definition are gray areas. In a world of standing military forces it is hard to say exactly where peace ends and war begins. A military battle that is not sustained over time may or may not be considered a war. The brief Chinese-Soviet border clashes in March and July 1969, for example, entailed several small battles at a few points along the border, in which some hundreds of people were killed. Similarly ambiguous is a long-term violent struggle involving irregular (substate) forces, such as in Northern Ireland. There, uniformed British military forces waged a sustained violent struggle with a nonstate "army," the Irish Republican Army (IRA), until a cease-fire that has held on and off since 1995.

Gang violence in U.S. inner cities is not considered war by most definitions, unlike the gang-type violence in the former Yugoslavia. One difference is scale—"only" thousands of deaths in the case of U.S. gangs versus hundreds of thousands in Yugoslavia. But the main reason the latter case is generally considered war is the involvement of state military units (and quasi-state military forces created from state armies that disintegrated).

Thus, many different activities are covered by the general term *war*. Consequently, it is not easy to say how many wars are going on in the world at the moment. Political scientists can count the number of militarized disputes or the number of international conflicts that regularly entail violence. But most lists of wars set some minimum criteria—for instance, a minimum of a thousand battle deaths—to distinguish the large-scale violence implied by war from the more common lower-level violence that occurs in many international conflicts. Criteria that are not often used include formal declarations of war (now largely obsolete) or other legal standards. For example, Japan and the Soviet Union never signed a treaty ending World War II but are not considered to be at war.

Table 4.1 summarizes both active wars and those recently suspended by a formal peace process. Of the 26 wars, none is in North America, Western Europe, Japan/Pacific, or China. Almost all are in the global South—mainly in Africa, South Asia, and the Middle East. The largest and most active wars as of January 2000 were in Chechnya (Russia), Afghanistan, Sudan, Democratic Congo, Angola, Turkey (Kurdish area), Sri Lanka, and Colombia. All of these are internal wars (within a state), although some are affected by outside backers. (In early 2000, heavy fighting resumed in the interstate war between Ethiopia and Eritrea.) Wars sputtering on and off are those in Iraq, the Rwanda-Burundi area (including Uganda), Somalia, Burma, Lebanon, and East Timor.

More importantly, a number of intense wars have ended, at least tentatively, in formal peace settlements in recent years. These wars, each of which inflicted grave damage, include those in Liberia, Sierra Leone, the Philippines, Israel-Palestine, Bosnia, Croatia, and Guatemala (along with South Africa and Mozambique earlier in the 1990s). It is an impressive list, indicative of the peaceful trends of the post–Cold War era.

TABLE 4.1   Wars by Region

Region	Most Important Wars, January 2000
Africa	**Ethiopia-Eritrea, Rwanda, Burundi, Uganda, Dem. Congo,** Sierra Leone, Guinea-Bissau, **Sudan**, **Somalia**, **Angola**
South Asia	**Afghanistan,** Sri Lanka, India, Burma, Indonesia, **Philippines**[a]
Middle East	Algeria, Turkey, **Iraq**, **Lebanon,** Israel-Palestine[a]
Russia/E. Europe	Tajikistan/Kyrgyzstan, Russia (Chechnya)
Latin America	Colombia, Peru
N. America, W. Europe, Japan/Pacific, China	None

[a] Apparently settled or in a transitional cease-fire as of January 2000. *Note:* Bold face indicates reported casualties of over 100,000.

Source: Adapted from Center for Defense Information, Washington, DC.

Wars are very diverse. Several types of war tend to arise from different situations and play different sorts of roles in bargaining over conflicts. Starting from the largest wars (which obviously meet the criteria), we may distinguish the following main categories.

Hegemonic war is a war over control of the entire *world order*—the rules of the international system as a whole, including the role of world hegemony (see pp. 72–74). This class of wars (with variations in definition and conception) is also known as *world war*, *global war*, *general war*, or *systemic war*. The last hegemonic war was World War II. This kind of war probably cannot occur any longer without destroying civilization.

Total war is warfare by one state waged to conquer and occupy another. The goal is to reach the capital city and force the surrender of the government, which can then be replaced with one of the victor's choosing. In rare cases, the victor annexes the loser into its own state, as Iraq tried to do with Kuwait. Total war as we know it began with the mass destruction of the Napoleonic Wars, which introduced large-scale conscription and geared the entire French national economy toward the war effort. The practice of total war evolved with industrialization, which further integrated all of society and economy into the practice of war. The last total war among great powers was World War II, which ended with Germany and Japan in ruins and occupied by the Western alliance.

In total war, with the entire society mobilized for the struggle, the entire society of the enemy is considered a legitimate target. In World War II Germany attacked British civilians with V-2 rockets, and British and U.S. bombing killed 600,000 German civilians (and hundreds of thousands more Japanese) in an effort to weaken morale.

Limited war includes military actions carried out to gain some objective short of the surrender and occupation of the enemy. For instance, the U.S.-led war against Iraq in 1991 retook the territory of Kuwait but did not go on to Baghdad to topple Saddam Hussein's government. Many border wars have this character: after occupying the land it wants, a state may stop and defend its gains.

Raids are limited wars that consist of a single action—a bombing run or a quick incursion by land. In 1981 Israeli warplanes bombed an Iraqi nuclear research facility to stop Iraq from making progress toward the development of nuclear weapons. (Without this raid, Iraq might have had nuclear weapons when it invaded Kuwait in 1990.) The action had a narrow objective—destruction of the facility—and was over within hours. Raids fall into the gray area between wars and nonwars because their destruction is limited and they are over quickly. Raiding that is repeated or fuels a cycle of retaliation usually becomes a limited war or what is sometimes called "low-intensity conflict."

Civil war refers to war between factions within a state trying to create, or prevent, a new government for the entire state or some territorial part of it. (The aim may be to change the entire system of government, to merely replace the people in it, or to split a region off as a new state.) The U.S. Civil War of the 1860s is a good example of a secessionist civil war. The war in El Salvador in the 1980s is an example of a civil war for control of the entire state (not secessionist). Civil wars seem to be often among the most brutal wars—sometimes brother fighting brother, often with no clearly defined front lines. One might think that people fighting their own citizens would act less cruelly than those fighting people from another state, but this is not so. The 50,000 or more deaths in the civil war in El Salvador included many at the hands of death squads—killings not based on ethnic differences. (Of course, many of today's civil wars do contain ethnic conflicts as well.)

Atlas CD
Eritrea
Map

Guerrilla war, which includes certain kinds of civil wars, is warfare without front lines. Irregular forces operate in the midst of, and often hidden or protected by, civilian populations. The purpose is not to directly confront an enemy army but rather to harass and punish it so as to gradually limit its operation and effectively liberate territory from its control. U.S. military forces in South Vietnam fought against Viet Cong guerrillas in the 1960s and 1970s, with rising frustration. The United States could easily occupy a location by daylight, but by night the guerrillas would slip back and reclaim control. Efforts to combat a guerrilla army—**counterinsurgency**—often include programs to "win the hearts and minds" of rural populations so that they stop sheltering the guerrillas.

In guerrilla war, without a fixed front line, there is much territory that neither side controls; both sides exert military leverage over the same places at the same time. Thus, guerrilla wars are extremely painful for civilians. The situation is doubly painful because conventional armies fighting against guerrillas often cannot distinguish them from civilians and punish both together. In one famous case in South Vietnam, a U.S. officer, who had ordered an entire village burned to deny its use as a sanctuary by the Viet Cong, commented, "We had to destroy the village to save it."

Warfare increasingly is irregular and guerrilla-style; it is less and less often an open conventional clash of large state armies. But conventional wars such as the Gulf War do still occur. On the whole, state and nonstate actors have a range of political goals that lead them to employ violent forms of leverage, and a range of options for employing force.

Web Link
Terrorism

Terrorism   Terrorism is basically just another step along the spectrum of violent leverage, from total war to guerrilla war. Indeed terrorism and guerrilla war often occur together. Yet terrorism differs from other kinds of wars. *Terrorism* refers to political violence that targets civilians deliberately and indiscriminately. Beyond this basic definition other criteria can be applied, but the definitions become politically motivated: one person's freedom fighter is another's terrorist. More than guerrilla warfare, terrorism is a shadowy world of faceless enemies and irregular tactics marked by extreme brutality.

The purpose of terrorism is to demoralize a civilian population in order to use its discontent as leverage on national governments or other parties to a conflict. Related to this is the aim of creating drama in order to gain media attention for a cause. When the IRA planted bombs in London, it hoped to make life miserable enough for Londoners that they would insist their government settle the Northern Ireland issue; the bombing also sought to keep the issue of Northern Ireland in the news. The government would then be pressured to concede terms more favorable to the IRA than would otherwise be the case. Terrorism is seldom mindless; it is usually a calculated use of violence as leverage. However, motives and means of terrorism vary widely, having in common only that some actor is using violence to send a message to another actor.

The effect of terrorism is psychological. It actually harms very few victims. The number of U.S. citizens killed by terrorists each year is far less than the number killed in fires caused by faulty wiring. Yet terrorism, not faulty wiring, is a national political issue. In part the effectiveness of terrorism in capturing attention is due to the dramatic nature of the incidents, especially as shown on television news. Terrorism also gains attention because of the randomness of its victims. Although only a few dozen people may be injured by a bomb left in a market, millions of people realize "it could have been me," because they, too, shop in markets. In attacks on airplanes this fear is heightened by people's fears of flying. Terrorism thus amplifies a small amount of power by its psychological effect on large populations; this is why it is usually a tool of the powerless.

In the past, most terrorism has occurred in the Middle East, Europe, and South Asia. While U.S. interests and citizens abroad have been repeatedly targeted, little terrorism has taken place in the United States itself. The 1993 bombing of the World Trade Center in New York was an exception. But in an interdependent world, the United States may find increasingly that global problems such as terrorism cannot be kept afar.

Classic cases of terrorism—including those that drew attention to the phenomenon in the 1970s—are those in which a *nonstate* actor uses attacks against *civilians* by secret *nonuniformed* forces, operating *across international borders*, as a leverage against *state* actors. Radical political factions or separatist groups hijack or blow up airplanes, or plant bombs in cafés, clubs, or other crowded places. For example, a Palestinian faction held hostage and then killed Israeli athletes at the 1972 Olympic Games in Munich. Such tactics create spectacular incidents that draw attention to the terrorists' cause. Typically, the message is, "We won't go away; we will make you unhappy until you deal with us."

Often terrorism is used by radical factions of movements that have not been able to get attention or develop other effective means of leverage. It is often a tactic of desperation, and it almost always reflects weakness in the power position of the attacker. For instance, the Palestinian radicals in 1972 had seen Arab states defeated by Israel in war and could not see a way to gain even a hearing for their cause. By capturing media attention worldwide with dramatic incidents of violence—even at the cost of rallying world public opinion against their cause—the radicals hoped to make Palestinian aspirations an issue that Western governments could not ignore. Terrorists are more willing than states are to violate the norms of the international system because, unlike states, they do not have a stake in that system. Conversely, when a political group gains some power or legitimacy, its use of terrorism usually diminishes, as it did with the Palestine Liberation Organization (but not the radical Hamas movement) after the peace process began in 1993.

States themselves carry out acts designed to terrorize their own populations or those of other states, but scholars tend to avoid the label "terrorism" for such acts, preferring to call it repression or war. Russia's indiscriminate attacks on civilian areas of Chechnya province in 1995 are an example. In fact, no violent act taken during a civil or international war—by or toward a warring party—can necessarily fit neatly into the category of terrorism. In the Central American civil wars of the 1980s, both the states and the guerrillas employed tactics that, if taken in peacetime, would easily qualify as terrorism.

The narrowest definition of terrorism would exclude acts either by or against *uniformed military forces* rather than civilians. This definition would exclude the killing of 243 U.S. Marines by a car bomb in Lebanon in 1983 because it was directed at a military target. It would also exclude the bombing of German cities in World War II though the purpose was to terrorize civilians. But in today's world of undeclared war, guerrilla war, civil war, and ethnic violence, there is a large gray zone around clear cases of terrorism.

State-sponsored terrorism refers to the use of terrorist groups by states—usually under control of the state's intelligence agency—to achieve political aims. In 1988 a bomb scattered pieces of Pan Am flight 103 over the Scottish countryside. Combing the fields for debris, investigators found fragments of a tape recorder with a sophisticated plastic-explosive bomb. A tiny strand of wire from the triggering device turned out to be a rare variety, through which the investigators traced the origins of the bomb. The

Crude but Sometimes Effective   Terrorist attacks often reflect the weakness of the perpetrators and their lack of access to other means of leverage. Terror can sometimes amplify a small group's power and affect outcomes. This bombing in Tel Aviv, carried out by the Palestinian faction Hamas, was one of a series credited with provoking a right-wing victory in the 1996 Israeli elections, practically freezing the Israeli-Palestinian peace process (as Hamas wanted). The elections had been called after Israeli Prime Minister Yitzhak Rabin, who was making peace with the PLO, was assassinated (another tool of the weak) by a Jewish right-wing extremist. Opponents of peace on both sides thus used violence to halt the peace process, at least temporarily.

U.S. and British governments identified two Libyan intelligence agents who had smuggled the tape recorder onto flight 103 in Frankfurt. In 1992, backed by the UN Security Council, they demanded that Libya turn over the two agents for trial. When Libya refused, the UN imposed sanctions including a ban on international flights to or from Libya. In 1999, Libya turned over the suspects for trial and the sanctions were lifted.

The United States accuses seven states of supporting international terrorism as of 1998: North Korea, Iran, Iraq, Syria, Libya, Sudan, and Cuba. In 1996, the United States barred U.S. companies from doing business in those states. However, these kinds of sanctions are of limited effect since most industrialized states do not share U.S. views of one or more of these target states. Cuba can do business with Canada, Iran with France, and Libya with Italy. The U.S. position was also undermined when it carved an exception in its rule to allow a U.S. oil company to bid on a lucrative pipeline project in Sudan.

More often, state involvement in terrorism is very difficult to trace. Indeed, had the bomb on flight 103 exploded as scheduled over the Atlantic Ocean, instead of prematurely, the clues would not have been found. When a political faction issues a communiqué claiming credit for a terrorist action, it never includes a statement such as "the participants wish to thank the Iranian government for its generous support, which made today's action possible."

Counterterrorism has become a sophisticated operation as well as a big business. International agencies, notably the *Interpol* police agency (and in Europe, Europol), coordinate the actions of states in tracking and apprehending suspected terrorists (as well as drug traffickers and other criminals). National governments have investigative agencies, such as the FBI and CIA in the United States, to try to break through the wall of secrecy around terrorist operations. Lately, many private companies have expanded the business of providing security services, including antiterrorist equipment and forces, to companies and individuals doing business internationally.

The Use of Military Force

A state leader in a conflict bargaining situation can apply various kinds of leverage to reach a more favorable outcome (see Figure 4.4). One set of levers represent nonviolent means of influencing other states, such as foreign aid, economic sanctions, personal diplomacy, and so forth (less tangible means include use of norms, morality, and other ideas). A second set of levers—the subject of the rest of this chapter—make violent actions occur. They set armies marching or missiles flying.

When state leaders resort to force in an international conflict, they do not push all the violence levers at once. Rather, they choose applications of force that suit their objectives, and their strategies for achieving those objectives. Furthermore, different levers are available to leaders of different states—different military capabilities that they

FIGURE 4.4   Military and Nonmilitary Means of Leverage   Conventional armed force is the most commonly used military form of leverage.

earlier decided to create and maintain. In order to understand the decisions that leaders make about using military force, it is important to know how various military capabilities work, how much they cost, and what effects they have.

Violence as a means of leverage tends to be costly to both the attacker and the attacked. It is therefore not the most effective instrument in most situations: states can generally achieve their objectives in a more cost-effective way using means of leverage such as economic actions (Chapters 5), international organizations (Chapter 6), foreign aid (Chapter 7), and communication (Chapter 8). Military force tends to be a last resort. There is also evidence that the utility of military force relative to nonmilitary means is slowly declining over time. Yet most states still devote vast resources to military capabilities compared to other means of influence. For example, the United States has about 20,000 diplomatic personnel but 2 million soldiers; it spends less than $10 billion a year on foreign aid but more than $250 billion on military forces.

For many states, the reason for this dedication of resources is largely defensive. Military capabilities are maintained in an effort to ensure *security*—the ability to feel safe against the threat of military attack (or other uses of force as leverage by other states). The overall utility of military force in IR may be declining, but for the narrow purpose of repelling a military attack there is often no substitute for military means. Because of the security dilemma, states believe they must devote large resources to military capabilities if even only a few other states are doing so.

Beyond defending their territories, states develop military capabilities for several other purposes. They often hope to *deter* attack by having the means to retaliate. They may also hope to *compel* other states to behave in certain ways, by threatening an attack if the state does not comply.

States are increasingly using military forces for purposes other than fighting (or threatening) wars. These purposes include humanitarian assistance after disasters, surveillance of drug trafficking, and repression of domestic political dissent, among others. Peacekeeping operations (see pp. 287–290) are a growing specialization of certain military forces, and a focus of NATO's Partnership for Peace program (see p. 78).

Military capabilities are generally divided into two types—conventional forces and weapons of mass destruction (nuclear, chemical, and biological weapons). Almost all of the actual uses of military force to date have involved conventional forces. Weapons of mass destruction nonetheless come into play in international bargaining because even the implicit threat of their use is leverage. Though the superpower nuclear arms race has ended, the spread of weapons of mass destruction to new states is an increasing concern.

Military Economics

Given the range of military capabilities available to states (at various costs), how should state leaders choose which to acquire? Choices about military forces depend on the connection between a state's military spending and its economic health. Not long ago, it was widely believed in the United States that "war is good for the economy." If this were true, state leaders would not face difficult choices in setting military budgets. High military spending would give them both more military capabilities for use in international conflicts *and* more economic growth for domestic needs.

Unfortunately for state leaders, the economics of military spending is not so favorable. Over the long run, military spending tends to compete with other economic needs such as investment in civilian industry or government projects. Over time, economic resources for military purposes deprive the rest of the economy and reduce its growth. High-technology military development (using engineers, scientists, etc.) tends to starve civilian sectors of talent and technology. Fewer jobs are created, per dollar of U.S. government funds, in the military than in education, housing, construction, and similar areas. Conversely, reductions in military spending tend to free up economic resources for more productive purposes and strengthen the growth of the economy in the long term.

Thus, over the long term, state leaders face a trade-off between increasing their available military leverage and increasing their overall economic health. This trade-off explains in part why, during the Cold War, the great power with the highest military spending—the Soviet Union, at perhaps 20 percent of GDP—had the worst economic performance, whereas the great power with the lowest military spending (Japan, with around 1 percent of GDP) had the best economic performance.

As the Cold War ended, U.S. leaders cut military spending to reap a peace dividend: more money for cities, education, the environment, and so forth. The savings may not have changed those problems much, but they did help reduce the U.S. budget deficit. U.S. citizens and politicians also began to demand that prosperous U.S. allies in Europe and Japan pay more for maintaining U.S. military forces there—a concept known as *burden sharing*. At the same time, Russia and the other former Soviet republics drastically curtailed military spending, which their tattered economies could not support.

Atlas CD
Russian
Military
Decline
Photo

Unfortunately, the short-term effects of military spending (or reductions in spending) tend to run counter to the long-term effects. The immediate effect of a sharp reduction in military spending (as at the end of a war) is often to throw people out of work and disrupt economic growth. Conversely, the effect of increased military spending in the short term can be to pick up the slack in a national economy operating below capacity. Because of these short-term effects, U.S. military spending cuts after the Cold War deepened a recession in the early 1990s. (Only later in the decade did the United States enjoy unprecedented prosperity.) Russia's cuts in military spending did little to stop its economic free fall. There and throughout the former Soviet Union—and somewhat less desperately in the United States and the West—political leaders scrambled to develop plans for **economic conversion**—use of former military facilities and industries for new civilian production.

Both the long- and short-term effects of military spending are magnified by actual warfare. War not only stimulates high military spending, it destroys capital (people, cities, farms, and factories in battle areas) and causes inflation (reducing the supply of various goods while increasing demand for them). Governments must pay for war goods by borrowing money (increasing government debt), by printing more currency (fueling inflation), or by raising taxes (reducing spending and investment).

Nonetheless, war and high military spending can have certain economic benefits. The short-term stimulation resulting from a boost in military spending has been mentioned. Another potential benefit is the acquisition of territory (containing resources and capital). Serbian ultranationalists made fortunes off the plunder of Bosnians who were "ethnically cleansed." Another potential economic benefit of war is to stir up a population's patriotism so it will work harder for less pay. But overall, the benefits rarely equal the economic costs of war.

State leaders, then, face complex choices in setting overall levels of military spending. Over the long term, lower military spending is economically preferable, but in the short

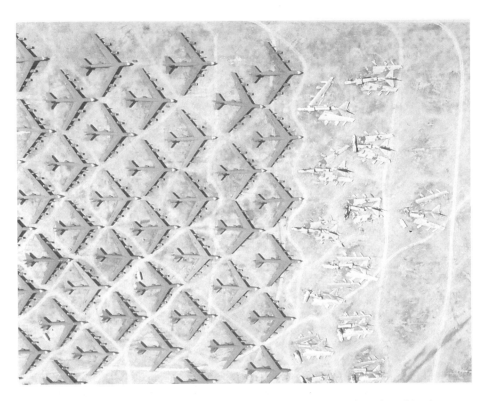

The War Is Over   U.S. and Russian nuclear forces were greatly reduced in the 1990s. Here, U.S. B-52 bombers are being chopped up, under the eye of Russian satellites, to bring force levels down.

term higher military spending can stimulate the economy. Sudden changes in military spending, up or down, are usually disruptive to economic health and stability. But such sudden changes usually reflect the beginnings or ends of wars, which entail even more complex trade-offs of costs and benefits (economic *and* political) for state leaders.

Web Link
Choice of
Capabilities

The Choice of Capabilities   Despite the complexity of these trade-offs, state leaders must adopt military budgets, choose particular military capabilities to obtain, and often structure other economic activities to support those choices (for instance, nurturing the military-industrial complex). Leaders try to assess the threats to their state from other states' military capabilities and then develop affordable strategies to reduce those threats.

The most basic choice facing state leaders is how much to spend on military capabilities. This varies widely, from Costa Rica, with virtually no military spending at all, to states such as North Korea, which devotes 20 percent or more of all economic activity to military purposes. If military budgets are too low, states may be unprepared to meet a security threat; in the worst case, they may even be overrun and conquered militarily. But if leaders set military budgets too high, they will overburden the national economy in the long run. (So far, Costa Rica has not been attacked despite recent wars in neighboring Nicaragua and Panama, whereas North Korea is virtually bankrupt.)

Since the end of the Cold War, U.S. leaders have had to rethink military capabilities. The primary mission of U.S. armed forces during the Cold War—containing the Soviet Union, especially from attacking Western Europe—suddenly became irrelevant. However, the Gulf War suggested a new type of mission based on the ability to deploy a large armed force to a regional conflict area. The U.S. strategy in the post–Cold War era, reaffirmed in 1997, calls for the ability to fight two regional wars at the same time—a scenario that requires ongoing high defense budgets.

Atlas CD
Closing of
Subic Bay
Photo

Outside the United States, other states were making similar assessments—most dramatically in Russia and the other republics of the former Soviet Union. Although they tried to reduce military spending as quickly as possible, there were no jobs for laid-off soldiers and military-industrial workers and no housing for troops brought home from Eastern Europe. For the next few years at least, military forces in Russia and most of the other former Soviet republics appear destined to limp along in a much reduced and weakened condition.

The cutbacks are less dramatic in Western Europe, where NATO members spend several percent of GDP on military forces. In Japan, military spending was already only 1 percent of GDP, so dramatic cutbacks are not in the works. In China, military spending is not critical for economic growth because the army is largely self-supporting (running its own farms, factories, etc.)—which also makes Chinese military spending hard to calculate. Chinese military forces underwent substantial reduction, along with modernization, in the 1980s and 1990s. Because it lags in technology, China's army remains the weakest of the great-power militaries (except perhaps Russia), despite possible circumstances where sheer size or nuclear weapons would be decisive.

Great powers continue to dominate the makeup of world military forces. Table 4.2 (p. 178) summarizes the most important forces of the great powers. Together, they account for two-thirds of world military spending, a third of the world's soldiers, about 50 percent of the weapons, 99 percent of nuclear weapons, and 95 percent of arms exports. The table also indicates the sizable military forces maintained by Germany and Japan despite their nontraditional roles in international security affairs since World War II.

Atlas CD
Military
Spending in
GDP
Statistics

In the global South, military spending varies greatly from one country to another, depending in part on the government in power (military or civilian). Spending also depends heavily on available hard currency, from exports of oil or other products to pay for arms purchases. In the 1980s, well over half of all arms imports by third world countries were in the Middle East, where oil exports created a ready source of funding. The remaining arms purchases were spread fairly evenly across Latin America, South Asia, East Asia, and Africa. More than half these arms came from the United States and the Soviet Union, with two-thirds of the remainder coming from Western Europe. In the 1990s, arms exports to the global South were dominated by the United States.

From a global perspective, the amount of world military spending is decreasing substantially in the post–Cold War era—by about one-third overall in the 1990s. However, it is decreasing from high levels. World military spending is about 2 percent of the total goods and services in the world economy—about $800 billion every year. Most of it is spent by a few big states and about one-third of it by the United States alone. World military spending is a vast flow of money that could, if redirected to other purposes, change the world profoundly and improve major world problems. Of course, "the world" does not spend this money or choose how to direct it; states do.

TABLE 4.2 Estimated Great-Power Military Capabilities, 1996

	Military Expenditures[b] (Billions of U.S. $)	Soldiers[b] (Millions)	WEAPONS[a] Tanks	Carriers/ Warships/ Submarines	Combat Airplanes	Nuclear Warheads[c]	Arms Exported[d] (Billions of U.S. $)
United States	280	1.5	11,000	12/173/ 98	7,000	10,500*	14.1
Russia	40*	1.3	17,000*	2/ 196*/152	4,100	20,000*	3.0
China	35	2.9	10,000	0/ 108/ 62	5,100*	400	0.6
France	50	0.4	1,000	2/ 52/ 19	800	450	3.0
Britain	35	0.2	1,000	3/ 50/ 15	600	185	6.0
Germany	40	0.4	3,000	0/ 19/ 15	700	0	0.5
Japan	50	0.2	1,000	0/ 71/ 18	500	0	0
Approximate % of world total	65%	30%	35%	80/50/70%	50%	99%	95%

Notes: In the 1990s, the military forces of many of these states—Russia above all—were profoundly restructured. Numbers of weapons or soldiers do not indicate quality (levels of technology) or predict how armed forces would actually perform in combat. Russian forces are disorganized and in disrepair, with rampant desertion, nonoperational equipment, and low morale. Chinese forces are lower-tech than the others. Expenditure data are notoriously unreliable for Russia and China.

Data on soldiers exclude reserves. Tanks exclude light armored vehicles. Warships are combat ships over 1,000 tons. Nuclear warheads include both strategic and tactical weapons. Arms exports are deliveries, not orders.

*Problematic data: Russian military expenditure estimates range from $20 billion to $80 billion. A large proportion (probably over half) of Russian tanks and ships are not operational and never will be. Chinese combat aircraft are of Korean War vintage and are of limited military use. U.S. and Russian nuclear warheads include deployed strategic weapons (8,000 U.S., 7,200 Russian) with the remainder being held in reserve or retired (awaiting destruction).

Sources: Author's estimates based on data provided by the Institute for Defense and Disarmament Studies (IDDS), Cambridge, MA. Main sources are: [a] IDDS database; [b] Institute for International and Strategic Studies, *The Military Balance;* [c] Natural Resources Defense Council, in *Bulletin of the Atomic Scientists* March/April 2000: 79; [d] Richard F. Grimmett, *Conventional Arms Transfers to Developing Nations, 1989–1996,* CRS 97-778F (Washington, DC: Congressional Research Service, 1997).

Beyond these considerations about the size of military forces, the configuration of a state's military forces also presents difficult choices. Should the United States emphasize its navy or its air force? Should the army have more soldiers or more tanks? Which bases should be closed in periods of military cutbacks? Should Japan build nuclear weapons? Should Syria buy medium-range missiles?

Different missions require different forces. During the Cold War, about half of all military spending in the U.S. budget—and of world military spending—was directed toward the East-West conflict in Europe. Now other missions—such as intervention in regional and civil conflicts—are more important. Some scholars think such interventions are less necessary now that Soviet influence in third world regions is not a concern; others think that interventions are more important now because North-South threats are replacing East-West ones. And new missions for military forces include humanitarian assistance, drug interdiction, and aid to other nations in building roads and schools.

Decisions about a state's military role give direction to its entire economy. During the Cold War, U.S. scientific research and industrial innovation were concentrated in the military sector. By contrast, Japan's research and development in those years focused on commercial products, contributing to Japan's prosperity.

Whatever configuration of military forces a state maintains, the leaders of the state face ongoing decisions about when and how to use those forces.

Control of Military Forces

The first issue of concern to a state leader in pulling a lever to exert influence is whether the lever is attached to anything. That is, how are the decisions of leaders translated into actual actions in distant locations that carry out the leaders' plans?

Command The use of military force generally requires the coordination of the efforts of thousands, sometimes millions, of individuals performing many different functions in many locations. Such coordination is what is meant by *command*. One cannot take for granted the ability of a state leader to make military forces take desired actions. At best, military forces are large and complex institutions, operating in especially difficult conditions during wartime. At worst, military forces have a mind of their own. Sometimes, as in the Russian Army's attacks in Chechnya province in 1995, the state leader appears to exert only incomplete control over the military.

Web Link
Command

States control military forces through a **chain of command** running from the highest authority through a hierarchy spreading out to the lowest-level soldiers. The highest authority, or commander in chief, is usually the top political leader—the U.S. president, Russian president, and so forth. The military hierarchy consists of levels of officers.

In actual conditions of battle, controlling armed forces is especially difficult, because of complex operations, rapid change, and the fog of war created by the gap between battlefield activity and command-level information. Participants are pumped up with adrenaline, deafened by noise, and confused by a mass of activity that—from the middle of it—may seem to make no sense. They are called on to perform actions that may run

Under Control Through a hierarchical chain of command, states control the actions of millions of individual soldiers, creating effective leverage in the hands of state leaders. Here, Chinese women soldiers march in a military parade, Guangzhou, 1991.

against basic instincts as well as moral norms—killing people and risking death. It is difficult to coordinate forces effectively, to carry out overall plans of action.

These factors reduce the effectiveness of military forces as instruments of state power. But military forces have developed several means for counteracting these problems. First is the principle of military discipline. Orders given from higher levels of the hierarchy must be obeyed by the lower levels—whether or not those at the lower level agree. Failure to do so is insubordination, or a mutiny if a whole group is involved. Leaving one's unit is called deserting. These are serious offenses punishable by prison or death.

But discipline depends not only on punishment but also on patriotism and professionalism on the part of soldiers. Officers play to nationalist sentiments, reminding soldiers that they fight for their nation and family. No military force is better than the soldiers and officers that make it up. Combat, logistics, communication, and command all depend on individual performance; motivation matters.

Whatever the motivation of soldiers, they require training in order to function as instruments of state power. Military training includes both technical training and training in the habit of obeying commands—a central purpose of basic training in every military force. Soldiers are deliberately stripped of their individuality—hair styles, clothes, habits, and mannerisms—to become part of a group. This has both good and bad effects for the individuals, but it works for the purposes of the military. Then in exercises, soldiers practice over and over until certain operations become second nature.

To maintain control of forces in battle, military units also rely on soldiers' sense of group solidarity—soldiers risk their lives because their "buddies" depend on them.

Abstractions such as nationalism, patriotism, or religious fervor are important, but loyalty to the immediate group (along with a survival instinct) is a stronger motivator. Recent debates about participation of women and homosexuals in the U.S. armed forces revolve around whether their presence disrupts group solidarity. (Evidence, though sparse, suggests that it need not.)

Troops operating in the field also rely on logistical support in order to function effectively. For states to use military leverage, they cannot just push armies around on a map like chess pieces. Rather, they must support those armies with large quantities of supplies. Leaders in Prussia (Germany) more than a century ago used well-oiled logistics based on railroads to defeat both Austria and France, which were using rapid offensives.

A further difficulty that states must overcome to use military forces effectively is that top officers and political leaders need accurate information about what is going on in the field—intelligence—to make good decisions. They also need extensive communications networks, including the ability to use codes to ensure secrecy. In the Gulf War, a top U.S. priority was to target Iraqi communications facilities so as to disable Iraq's command and control. Meanwhile, the U.S. side used computers, satellite reconnaissance, and other information technologies to amplify its effectiveness.

Finally, states rely on their military officers to develop and implement effective strategies and tactics. Strategies bring the state's military (and nonmilitary) capabilities to bear in an overall coordinated manner to achieve an end. Tactics do the same but in a more localized setting (a single battle) and in a more standardized way. Strategy and tactics become especially important when a state employs military force in a conflict with another state whose military capabilities are larger or technically superior. For example, Israel defeated the larger Egyptian military forces in 1967 and 1973 partly by employing clever tactics.

Web Link
Homosexuals in the Military

States and Militaries Overcoming chaos and complexity is only part of the task for state leaders seeking to control military forces. Sometimes they must overcome their own military officers as well. Although militaries are considered instruments of state power, in many states the military forces themselves control the government. These **military governments** are most common in third world countries, where the military may be the only large modern institution in the country.

Military leaders are able to exercise political control because the same violent forms of leverage that work internationally also work domestically. In fact, domestically there may be little or no counterleverage to the use of military force. Military officers thus have an inherent power advantage over civilian political leaders. Ironically, the disciplined central command of military forces, which makes them effective as tools of state influence, also lets the state lose control of them to military officers. Soldiers are trained to follow the orders of their commanding officers, not to think about politics.

A **coup d'état** (French for "blow against the state") is the seizure of political power by domestic military forces—a change of political power outside the state's constitutional order. Coups are often mounted by ambitious junior officers against the top generals. Officers who thus break the chain of command can take along with them the sections of the military hierarchy below them. Coup leaders move quickly to seize centers of power—official state buildings, as well as television stations and transmitters—before other units of the military can put down the coup attempt or even create a civil war. Civilian politicians in power and uncooperative military officers are arrested or

Highly Irregular   A coup is a change of government carried out by domestic military forces operating outside the state's constitution. The number of military governments is declining but dozens remain. Soldiers are shown outside the Haitian legislature, which is being forced at gunpoint to name a new president after a coup against elected president Jean-Bertrand Aristide, 1991. (Aristide returned as president in 1995 when the coup leaders surrendered in the face of a U.S. invasion.)

killed. The coup leaders try to create a sense of inevitability around the change in government and hope that fellow officers throughout the military defect to their side.

The outcome of a coup is hard to predict. If most or all of the military go along with the coup, civilian leaders are generally helpless to stop it. But if most of the military officers follow the existing chain of command, the coup is doomed. In the Philippines in the late 1980s, the top general, Fidel Ramos, remained loyal to the civilian president, Corazón Aquino, in seven coup attempts by subordinate officers. In each case, the bulk of the Philippine military forces stayed loyal to Ramos, and the coups failed. In 1992, Ramos himself was elected president with the backing of a grateful Aquino.

Coups may also be put down by an outside military force. A government threatened with a coup may call on foreign friends for military assistance. But because coups are considered largely an internal affair—and because they are over so quickly—direct foreign intervention in them is relatively rare.

Military governments often have difficulty gaining popular legitimacy for their rule because their power is clearly based on force rather than popular mandate, though the public may support the new regime if the old one was really bad. To stay in power, both military and civilian governments require at least passive acceptance by their people.

Even in nonmilitary governments, the interaction of civilian with military leaders—called civil-military relations—is an important factor in how states use force. Military leaders may undermine the authority of civilian leaders in carrying out foreign policies, or they may even threaten a coup if certain actions are taken in international conflicts.

NATO forces operate under strong civilian control. However, military desires continue to run counter to civilian decisions at times. After the Vietnam War, top U.S. military officers became more reluctant to send U.S. forces into combat. The Pentagon now generally supports using military force only when there is a clear goal that can be achieved militarily, when the public supports the action, and when military forces can be used massively for a quick victory. Panama in 1989 and Kuwait in 1991 fit these new conditions. Intervention in the former Yugoslavia generally did not, but Western politicians sent their forces there anyway. Military officers also want autonomy of decision once force is committed, in order to avoid the problems created in the Vietnam War when President Johnson sat in the White House situation room daily picking targets for bombing raids.

Covert operations are the dagger part of the "cloak and dagger" spy business. Several thousand such operations were mounted during the Cold War, when the CIA and its Soviet counterpart, the KGB, waged an ongoing worldwide secret war. CIA covert operations in the 1950s overthrew unfriendly foreign governments—in Iran and Guatemala—by organizing coups against them. The CIA-organized Bay of Pigs invasion in Cuba, in 1961, was its first big failure, followed by other failed efforts against the Castro government (including eight assassination attempts). CIA covert activities were sharply scaled back after congressional hearings in the 1970s revealed scandals. Such covert operations now must be reported to special congressional *oversight* committees. Since the Cold War era, however, intelligence resources are more often targeted at economic capabilities than before, including capabilities of allies. In 1995, France accused four Americans of spying on French trade deals.

The traditions of civil-military relations in a state do not necessarily reflect the extent of democracy there. States in which civilians traditionally have trouble controlling the military include some with long histories of democracy, notably in Latin America. And states with strong traditions of civilian control over military forces include some authoritarian states such as the former Soviet Union (where the Communist party controlled the military). This tradition helps to explain the failure of the attempted coup in August 1991 against the head of the Communist party (Gorbachev). Even with most of the second echelon of party leaders behind them, the coup leaders could not gain the legitimacy needed to take power and to get soldiers to follow their orders.

In a few states, certain military forces operate beyond the reach of the government's chain of command—certainly when rebel guerrilla armies control territories nominally under the jurisdiction of the central government. It is also true in the infrequent but dramatic cases when governmental authority breaks down—in Somalia in 1991–1992, for example. Private armies or militias then answer to local warlords rather than to any national government. But in most of the world, most of the time, military forces follow the commands of state leaders (or are themselves the state leaders).

No matter how firmly state leaders control the military forces at their disposal, those forces are effective only if they are equipped and trained for the purposes the state leaders have in mind. To understand decisions to use military force, one must understand the various types of forces and weapons and the missions they are to perform.

Conventional Forces

The bargaining power of states depends not only on the overall size of their military forces but on the particular capabilities of those forces in various scenarios. State leaders almost always turn to conventional military forces for actual missions, reserving weapons of mass destruction for making or deterring threats.

If a leader decides that an international conflict could be more favorably settled by applying military force, it matters a great deal whether the application involves bombing another state's capital city, imposing a naval blockade, or seizing disputed territory. Armed forces can apply negative leverage at a distance, but various types of forces have evolved over time for different situations and contexts—on water, on land, or in the air. They match up against each other in particular ways. A tank cannot destroy a submarine, and vice versa. A tank can generally prevail against foot soldiers with rifles, though foot soldiers with antitank missiles might prevail.

Whatever their ultimate causes and objectives, most wars involve a struggle to *control territory*. Territory holds a central place in warfare because of its importance in the international system, and vice versa. Borders define where a state's own military forces and rival states' military forces are free to move. Military logistics make territoriality all the more important because of the need to control territories connecting military forces with each other. An army's supplies must flow from home territory along *supply lines* to the field. Thus the most fundamental purpose of conventional forces is to take, hold, or defend territory.

Armies *Armies* are adapted to this purpose. Infantry soldiers armed with automatic rifles can generally control a local piece of territory—using their guns as leverage to "bargain" with people in that zone. When an organized military unit has guns and the other people in the area do not, the latter tend to obey the commands of the former. Military forces with such a presence *occupy* a territory militarily. Although inhabitants may make the soldiers' lives unhappy through violent or nonviolent resistance, generally only another organized, armed military force can displace occupiers.

Foot soldiers are called the **infantry**. They use assault rifles and other light weapons, as well as heavy artillery of various types. Artillery is extremely destructive and not very discriminating: it usually causes the most damage and casualties in wars. Armor refers to tanks and armored vehicles. In open terrain, such as desert, mechanized ground forces typically combine armor, artillery, and infantry. In close terrain, such as jungles and cities, however, foot soldiers are most important.

For this reason, the armies of industrialized states have a greater advantage over poor armies in open conventional warfare, such as in the Kuwaiti desert. In jungle, mountain, or urban warfare, however—such as in Cambodia or Bosnia—such advantages are eroded, and a cheaper and more lightly armed force of motivated foot soldiers or guerrillas may ultimately prevail over an expensive conventional army.

Land mines are used by armies to defend territory by creating zones (mine fields) in which anyone passing through is subject to injury by stepping on (or driving over) a mine. The mine itself is a simple, small, and cheap container of explosives with a trigger activated by contact or sensor. These weapons were a particular focus of public attention in the 1990s because in places like Angola, Afghanistan, Cambodia, and

Web Link
Land Mines

Bosnia, they were used extensively by irregular military forces that never disarmed them. Long after such a war ends, land mines continue to maim and kill civilians who try to reestablish their lives in former war zones. As many as 100 million land mines remain from recent wars; they injure about 25,000 people a year (a third of whom are children); although they are cheap to deploy, they are expensive to find and disarm.

Public opinion and NGOs have pressured governments to restrict the future use of land mines. After the death of Britain's Princess Diana, who had actively supported the campaign, a treaty to ban land mines was signed by more than 100 countries at a 1997 conference organized by Canada. Russia and Japan signed on shortly afterward, but the United States and China refused to sign. The U.S. government argued that land mines were essential for defending South Korea if the massed troops of North Korea tried to invade across the demilitarized zone. A new norm seems to be emerging but its effect on actual military practice is not yet clear.

Atlas CD
Cambodian
Mine-Clearing
Photo

Navies *Navies* are adapted primarily to control passage through the seas and to attack land near coastlines. Unlike armies, navies are not tied to territory because the oceans beyond coastal waters are not owned by any state. Controlling the seas in wartime allows states to move their own goods and military forces by sea while preventing enemies from doing so. In particular, navies protect *sealift* logistical support. Navies can also blockade enemy ports. For most of the 1990s, Western navies enforced a naval blockade against Iraq.

Aircraft carriers—mobile platforms for attack aircraft—are instruments of **power projection** that can exert negative leverage against virtually any state in the world. Merely sending an aircraft carrier sailing to the vicinity of an international conflict implies a threat to use force—a modern version of what was known in the nineteenth century as "gunboat diplomacy." For example, in 1996 the United States dispatched two carriers to the Taiwan area when Chinese war games there threatened to escalate. However, aircraft carriers are extremely expensive and typically require 20 to 25 supporting ships for protection and supply. Few states can afford even one. The United States has 12, France 2, Russia 2, and several other states have a few smaller and less capable carriers (see Table 4.2).

Most warships rely increasingly on guided missiles and are in turn vulnerable to attack by missiles (fired from ships, planes, submarines, or land). Since the ranges of small missiles now reach from dozens to hundreds of miles, naval warfare emphasizes detection at great distances without being detected oneself—a cat-and-mouse game of radar surveillance and electronic countermeasures.

Missile-firing ships are much cheaper and faster than aircraft carriers. They are becoming potent instruments of power projection themselves. Submarines are specialized to attack ships but can also fire missiles at land targets. (Those that fire nuclear missiles are discussed later.) Submarine and antisubmarine warfare places a great premium on detection and evading detection.

Marines (part of the navy in the United States, Britain, and Russia) move to battle in ships but fight on land—amphibious warfare. Marines are also useful for great-power intervention in distant conflicts where they can insert themselves quickly and establish local control. In the 1992–1993 intervention in Somalia, U.S. Marines were already waiting offshore while the UN Security Council was debating whether to authorize the use of force.

Projecting Power Different types of military forces are adapted to different purposes. Aircraft carriers are used for power projection in distant regions. They are so expensive that only a few states have one and only the United States has a dozen. Here, the *USS Independence* enters the Persian Gulf, 1990.

Air Forces *Air forces* serve several distinct purposes—strategic bombing of land or sea targets; "close air support" (battlefield bombing); interception of other aircraft; reconnaissance; and airlift of supplies, weapons, and troops. Missiles—whether fired from air, land, or sea—are increasingly important. Air forces have developed various means to try to fool such missiles, but with mixed results. In the Afghanistan war, the U.S.-made portable missile used by guerrillas took a heavy toll on the Soviet air force.

Traditionally, and still to a large extent, aerial bombing resembles artillery shelling in that it causes great destruction with little discrimination. This has begun to change in a few cases as smart bombs improve accuracy. For instance, laser-guided bombs follow a sensor pointed at the target from the air. Television viewers during the Gulf War watched video images of bombs scoring direct hits (not all were this accurate). But most of the bombing in that war was high-altitude saturation bombing using large numbers of dumb bombs. In other more typical wars, such as Russia's repression of Chechnya in 1995, bombing of cities causes high civilian casualties. In cases of low-intensity conflicts and guerrilla wars, especially where forces intermingle with civilians in closed terrain, bombing is of limited utility.

Even more than ships, aircraft rely heavily on electronics, especially radar. The best-equipped air forces have specialized AWACS (Airborne Warning and Control System) airplanes to survey a large area with radar and coordinate the movements of dozens of aircraft. The increasing sophistication of electronic equipment and high performance requirements of attack aircraft make air forces expensive—totally out of reach for some states. Thus, rich states have huge advantages over poor ones in air warfare. Despite the expense, air superiority is often the key to the success of ground operations in open terrain.

Logistics and Intelligence
All military operations rely heavily on logistical support such as food, fuel, and ordnance (weapons and ammunition). Military logistics are a huge operation, and in most armed forces the majority of soldiers are not combat troops. Before the Gulf War, the United States moved an army of half a million people and a vast quantity of supplies to Saudi Arabia in a six-month effort that was the largest military logistical operation in such a time frame in history.

Global reach capabilities combine long-distance logistical support with various power projection forces. These capabilities allow a great power to project military power to distant corners of the world and to maintain a military presence in most of the world's regions simultaneously. Only the United States today fully possesses such a capability—with worldwide military alliances, air and naval bases, troops stationed overseas, and aircraft carriers plying the world's oceans. Britain and France are in a distant second place, able to mount occasional distant operations of modest size such as the Falkland Islands War. Russia is preoccupied with internal conflicts and its CIS neighbors, and China's military forces are oriented toward regional conflicts and are not global in scope.

Atlas CD
U.S. Base on Guam
Photo

Space forces are military forces designed to attack in or from outer space. Ballistic missiles, which travel through space briefly, are not generally included in this category. Only the United States and Russia have substantial military capabilities in space. (China is poised to join the manned-space club, though with far fewer capabilities.) The development of space weapons has been constrained by the technical challenges and expenses of space operations, and by norms against militarizing space.

Satellites are used extensively for military purposes, but these purposes do not include attack. Satellites perform military surveillance and mapping, communications, weather assessment, and early warning of ballistic missile launches. Satellites also provide navigational information to military forces—army units, ships, planes, and even guided missiles in flight. Analysts pore over masses of satellite reconnaissance data every day in Washington, DC, and other capitals. Poorer states can buy satellite photos on the commercial market—including high-resolution pictures that Russia sells for hard currency. But, in general, outer space is an area in which great powers have great advantages over smaller or poorer states. For instance, U.S. forces in the Gulf War took extensive advantage of satellite reconnaissance, communications, and navigation in defeating Iraqi forces.

Intelligence gathering also relies on various other means such as electronic monitoring of telephone lines and other communications, reports from embassies, and information in the open press. Some kinds of information are obtained by sending agents into foreign countries as spies. They use ingenuity (plus money and technology) to penetrate walls of secrecy that foreign governments have constructed around their plans and capabilities. For example, in 1999 a Russian spy taped conversations from a listening device planted in a high-level conference room at the U.S. State Department.

The U.S. military operates a large intelligence-gathering operation, especially for information relevant to battlefield deployments and other tactical matters. Satellite reconnaissance is now so important and so massive that one agency attends solely to the task. The largest U.S. military intelligence agency is the National Security Agency (NSA), whose mission is encoding U.S. communications and breaking the codes of foreign communications. The NSA is believed to have the most powerful computer facility in the world. Clearly these operations taken together are very large and are growing in importance as the information revolution proceeds.

Web Link
Evolving
Technologies

Evolving Technologies Through the centuries, the lethal power of weapons has increased continuously—from swords to muskets, machine guns to missiles. Technological developments have changed the nature of military force in several ways. First, the resort to force in international conflicts now has more profound costs and consequences than it did at the outset of the international system several centuries ago. Great powers in particular can no longer use force to settle disputes among themselves without risking massive destruction and economic ruin.

A second long-term effect of technological change is that military engagements now occur across greater standoff distances between opposing forces. Missiles of all types are accelerating this trend. Its effect is to undermine the territorial basis of war and of the state itself. The state once had a hard shell of militarily protected borders, but today the protection offered by borders is diminishing. For example, Israel's successful defense of its borders could not stop Iraqi scud missiles from hitting Israeli cities during the Gulf War. This change makes states more interdependent; in the case of Israel, the realization of its vulnerability may have accelerated the search for a peace settlement with its Arab neighbors.

Technology is also changing the loss of power gradient that defines a state's loss of effective power over distance. The gradient still exists; for instance, the United States can more readily apply military force in Haiti or Panama than in Iraq (partly because of the importance of logistics). But technological change is making the gradient less steep. Even smaller states can occasionally extend a long military reach, as Israel did when it once bombed the PLO headquarters in Algeria, 1,800 miles away. Historically, technological developments have often given an inherent advantage to either defense or offense, changing the offense-defense balance over time. Currently, electronics seem to be making small defensive weapons more effective relative to large offensive ones.

The pace of technological change has also made national security more intertwined with economics. Critical technologies with potential military applications are developed by industrialized states and guarded from export. In the 1980s, a major scandal erupted when it was discovered that the Japanese company Toshiba had sold the Soviet Union advanced machinery that would allow the Soviets to produce quieter submarine propellers (an important feature for evading detection).

In recent decades, the technological revolution in electronics has profoundly affected military forces, especially their command and control. **Electronic warfare** (now broadened to *information warfare*) refers to the uses of the electromagnetic spectrum (radio waves, radar, infrared, etc.) in war—employing electromagnetic signals for one's own benefit while denying their use to an enemy. Electromagnetic signals are used for sensing beyond the normal visual range, through radar, infrared, and imaging equipment to see in darkness, through fog, or at great distances. These and other technologies have illuminated the battlefield so that forces cannot be easily hidden.

Electronic countermeasures are technologies designed to counteract enemy electronic systems such as radar and radio communications. **Stealth technology** uses spe-

Smaller Is Better   The information revolution is making smaller weapons more potent. The U.S.-made Stinger antiaircraft missile—portable and shoulder-launched— helped turn the tide against the Soviet Union in the war in Afghanistan in the 1980s, with far-reaching consequences.

cial radar-absorbent materials and unusual shapes in the design of aircraft, missiles, and ships to scatter enemy radar. However, stealth is extremely expensive (each B-2 stealth bomber costs about $2 billion, or about three times its weight in gold) and is prone to technical problems.

Electronics are changing the costs and relative capabilities of weapons across the board. Computer chips in guided missiles have made them a formidable weapon on land, sea, and air. The miniaturization of such weaponry is making smaller and cheaper military forces more powerful than ever. An infantry soldier now can use a shoulder-fired missile costing $10,000 to destroy a main battle tank costing $1 million. Similarly, a small boat firing an antiship missile costing $250,000 can potentially destroy a major warship costing hundreds of millions of dollars.

Technological developments are in some ways increasing the advantages of great powers over less-powerful states, while in other ways undermining those advantages. For example, China's military has been developing lower-cost technological strategies to counter U.S. military power in any future war. Land-based missiles could destroy expensive U.S. aircraft carriers. New Chinese anti-aircraft systems reportedly can detect

THE INFORMATION REVOLUTION   Is Technology an Equalizer?

Information technologies are bringing about revolutionary changes in military tactics and weapons. U.S.-led bombing campaigns against Iraq and Serbia in the 1990s—which used remote sensing and precision-guided munitions extensively—cost far less and caused far fewer civilian casualties than previous air wars had. Yet, "smart" weapons also let guerrillas fire sophisticated anti-aircraft missiles, and new information technologies help China's new radar system detect U.S. "stealth" aircraft. Will the information revolution, despite the advantages it gives Western militaries today, ultimately empower poor states and nonstate actors, equalizing their relationship with the great powers?

To explore this question, go to www.IRtext.com

even "stealth" U.S. aircraft while remaining passive and thus not presenting a target. U.S. forces in turn are developing new battlefield tactics calling for smaller, more mobile weapons and troop units, along with more unmanned systems, linked by intensive communications networks. Strategies for *cyberwar*—disrupting enemy computer networks to degrade command-and-control, or even hacking into bank accounts electronically—were developed by NATO forces during the 1999 Kosovo war, though mostly not implemented, and will probably figure in future wars.

Proposals have been made to restructure great-power military forces to take advantage of changing technologies. One idea, *nonoffensive defense*, is to radically reshape forces for purely defensive missions by taking advantage of electronic technologies that make defense cost-effective. The concept has never been implemented (it was aimed at NATO, which resisted it). But at least one example suggests it could work: in 1991, the breakaway republic of Slovenia used antitank missiles effectively (in mountains) to repel federal Yugoslav armored forces, despite being outnumbered and outspent overall.

Weapons of Mass Destruction

Weapons of mass destruction include three general types—nuclear, chemical, and biological weapons. They are distinguished from conventional weapons by their enormous potential lethality, given their small size and modest costs, and by their relative lack of discrimination in whom they kill. Because of these differences, weapons of mass destruction offer state leaders types of leverage that differ from conventional military forces. When deployed on ballistic missiles, they can be fired from the home territory of one state and wreak great destruction on the home territory of another state.

Until now this has never happened. But the mere threat of such an action undermines the territorial integrity and security of states in the international system. Thus scholars pay special attention to such weapons and the missiles that can deliver them. Of central concern today are the potentials for proliferation—the possession of weapons of mass destruction by more and more states (discussed shortly).

Big Bang   Nuclear weapons were invented during World War II. Here, U.S. soldiers watch a test explosion in 1951, near the start of the nuclear age, before the medical effects of nuclear radiation were fully understood. Since then, tens of thousands of nuclear weapons have been built; eight or nine countries possess at least a few.

Weapons of mass destruction serve different purposes from conventional weapons. With a few exceptions, their purpose is to deter attack (especially by other weapons of mass destruction) by giving state leaders the means to inflict great pain against a would-be conqueror or destroyer. For middle powers, these weapons also provide destructive power more in line with the great powers, serving as symbolic equalizers.

Nuclear Weapons   *Nuclear weapons* are, in sheer explosive power, the most destructive weapons available to states. A single weapon the size of a refrigerator can destroy a city. Defending against nuclear weapons is extremely difficult at best.

To understand the potentials for nuclear proliferation, one has to know something about how nuclear weapons work. There are two types. *Fission* weapons (atomic bombs or A-bombs) are simpler and less expensive than **fusion weapons** (also called thermonuclear bombs, hydrogen bombs, or H-bombs). The term *bomb* refers to a warhead that can be delivered by missile, bomb, artillery shell, or other means.

When a fission weapon explodes, one type of atom (element) is split, or "fissioned," into new types with less total mass. The lost mass is transformed into energy according to Albert Einstein's famous formula, $E=mc^2$, which shows that a little bit of mass is equivalent to a great deal of energy. In fact, the fission bomb that destroyed Nagasaki, Japan, in 1945 converted to energy roughly the amount of mass in a single penny.

Two elements can be split in this way, and each has been used to make fission weapons. These elements—known as **fissionable material**—are uranium-235 (or

U-235) and plutonium. Fission weapons work by taking subcritical masses of the fissionable material—amounts not dense enough to start a chain reaction—and compressing them into a critical mass, which explodes. In the simplest design, one piece of uranium is propelled down a tube (by conventional explosives) into another piece of uranium. A more efficient but technically demanding design arranges high explosives precisely around a hollow sphere of plutonium so as to implode the sphere and create a critical mass. Enhanced designs add an outer sphere of neutron-reflecting material to increase the number of speeding neutrons during the explosion.

Although these designs require sophisticated engineering, they are well within the capabilities of many states and some private groups. The obstacle is obtaining fissionable material. Only ten pounds or less are required for each bomb, but even these small amounts are not easily obtained. U-235, which can be used in the simplest bomb designs, is especially difficult to obtain. Extracting the fissionable U-235, referred to as enriching the uranium up to weapons grade (or high grade), is slow, expensive, and technically complex—a major obstacle to proliferation.

Plutonium is more easily produced, from low-grade uranium in nuclear power reactors—although extracting the plutonium requires a separation plant. But a plutonium bomb is more difficult to build than a uranium one—another obstacle to proliferation. Plutonium is also used in commercial breeder reactors, which Japan in particular has built recently—another source of fissionable material.

Fission weapons were invented 50 years ago by U.S. scientists in a secret World War II science project known as the *Manhattan Project*. In 1945, one uranium bomb and one plutonium bomb were used to destroy Hiroshima and Nagasaki, killing 100,000 civilians in each city and inducing Japan to surrender unconditionally. By today's standards, those bombs were crude, low-yield weapons. But they are the kind of weapon that might be built by a relatively poor state or a nonstate actor.

Fusion weapons are extremely expensive and technically demanding; they are leverage for only the richest, largest, most technologically capable states. In fusion weapons, two small atoms (variants of hydrogen) fuse together into a larger atom, releasing energy. This reaction occurs only at very high temperatures (the sun "burns" hydrogen through fusion). Weapons designers use fission weapons to create these high energies and trigger an explosive fusion reaction. The explosive power of most fission weapons is between 1 and 200 kilotons (each kiloton is the equivalent of 1,000 tons of conventional explosive). The power of fusion weapons is typically 1 to 20 megatons (a megaton is 1,000 kilotons). In the post–Cold War era fusion weapons have become less important.

The effects of nuclear weapons include not only the blast of the explosion, but also heat and radiation. The heat can potentially create a self-sustaining firestorm in a city. The radiation creates radiation sickness, which at high doses kills people in a few days and at low doses creates long-term health problems, especially cancers. Radiation is most intense in the local vicinity of (and downwind from) a nuclear explosion, but some is carried up into the atmosphere and falls in more distant locations as nuclear fallout. Nuclear weapons also create an electromagnetic pulse (EMP) that can disrupt and destroy electronic equipment. Using many nuclear weapons at once (as in a war) would also have substantial effects on global climate, possibly including a nuclear winter in which years of colder and darker conditions would trigger an environmental catastrophe.

Ballistic Missiles and Other Delivery Systems

Nuclear weapons are of little use unless they can be detonated remotely—preferably very remotely! *Delivery systems* for getting nuclear weapons to their targets—much more than the weapons themselves—are the basis of states' nuclear arsenals and strategies (discussed shortly). Inasmuch as nuclear warheads can be made quite small—weighing a few hundred pounds or even less—they are adaptable to a wide variety of delivery systems.

During the Cold War, nuclear delivery systems were divided into two categories. *Strategic* weapons were those that could hit an enemy's homeland, usually at long range (for instance, Moscow from Nebraska). Once carried on long-range bombers, they now are carried mainly on missiles. *Tactical* nuclear weapons were those designed for battlefield use in a theater of military engagement. In the Cold War years, both superpowers integrated tactical nuclear weapons into their conventional air, sea, and land forces using a variety of delivery systems—gravity bombs, artillery shells, short-range missiles, land mines, depth charges, and so forth. As with all conventional forces, missiles assumed a greater role over time, and nuclear warheads were paired with short-range ground-to-ground missiles, ship-to-ship missiles, air-to-ground missiles, ground-to-air missiles, and so forth. Some conventional weapons systems were dual use, carrying either nuclear or conventional warheads.

In part, the integration of nuclear weapons into conventional forces was meant to deter a conventional East-West war (such as a Soviet invasion of Western Europe). In part, military planners simply found nuclear weapons cost-effective. From a strictly military view, if an enemy tank column were advancing, if an enemy airfield had to be neutralized, if an aircraft carrier had to be taken out of the picture, the results would be faster and more reliable using tactical nuclear weapons rather than conventional weapons.

However, the tens of thousands of nuclear warheads integrated into superpower conventional forces posed dangers such as theft or accident. Their actual use would have entailed grave risks of escalation to strategic nuclear war, putting home cities at risk. Thus, both the United States and Russia phased out tactical nuclear weapons almost entirely when the Cold War ended. The tactical weapons deployed in the former Soviet republics were shipped back to Russia for storage and eventual disassembly.

The main strategic delivery vehicles are **ballistic missiles**; unlike airplanes, they are extremely difficult to defend against. Ballistic missiles carry a warhead up along a trajectory and let it drop on the target. A trajectory typically rises out of the atmosphere—at least 50 miles high—before descending. A powerful rocket is needed, and a guidance system adjusts the trajectory so that the warhead drops closer to the target. Various ballistic missiles differ in their range, accuracy, and throw weight (how heavy a warhead it can carry). In addition, some missiles fire from fixed sites, whereas others are mobile (making them hard to target).

The longest-range missiles are **intercontinental ballistic missiles (ICBMs)** with ranges over 5,000 miles (the distance from Chicago to Moscow). Some carry up to ten warheads that can hit different targets. Most ICBMs are owned by the United States and Russia, a few by China. Intermediate- and medium-range missiles have ranges from

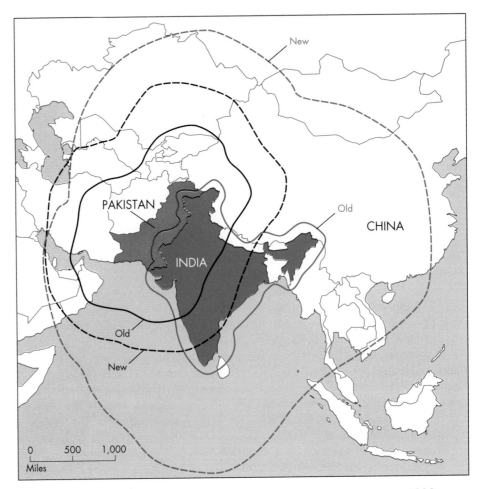

FIGURE 4.5   Expanding Ranges of Indian and Pakistani Missiles, 1999
Source: The Washington Post, May 29, 1999: A32.

somewhat under 1,000 miles to a few thousand miles. They include most submarine-launched ballistic missiles (SLBMs)—which are valued for their protectability under attack—and most of the British, French, and Chinese missiles (and some U.S. and Russian ones). The U.S. and Soviet intermediate nuclear weapons deployed in Europe were eliminated under the 1987 Intermediate Nuclear Forces (INF) Treaty.

Of special interest today are short-range ballistic missiles (SRBMs) with ranges of well under 1,000 miles. The modified scud missiles fired by Iraq at Saudi Arabia and Israel during the Gulf War were (conventionally armed) SRBMs. In regional conflicts, the long range of more powerful missiles may not be necessary. The largest cities of Syria and Israel are only 133 miles from each other; the capital cities of Iraq and Iran are less than 500 miles apart, as are those of India and Pakistan, as shown in Figure 4.5. All these states own ballistic missiles. Short-range and some medium-range ballistic missiles are cheap enough to be obtained and even home-produced by small middle-income states. Table 4.3 lists the capabilities of the 27 states with ballistic missiles.

TABLE 4.3 Ballistic Missile Capabilities, 1997

Country	Range *(Miles)*	Potential Targets
United States[a]	13,000	(World)
Russia[a]	13,000	(World)
China[a]	13,000	(World)
Britain[a]	4,600	(World; submarine-launched)
France[a]	3,700	(World; submarine-launched)
North Korea[b]	800 [3,000?]	South Korea, Russia, China, [Japan]
India[a,c]	150 [1,500]	Pakistan [China, Afghanistan, Iran, Turkey]
Pakistan[a]	175 [400]	India
Iran[b]	300 [1,250]	Iraq, Kuwait, Afghanistan [Israel, Egypt, Turkey, Saudi Arabia, Russia, India]
Saudi Arabia	1,700	Iran, Iraq, Syria, Israel, Turkey, Yemen, Egypt, Libya, Sudan
Israel[a,c]	900	Syria, Iraq, Saudi Arabia, Egypt
Iraq[d]	370	Iran, Kuwait, Saudi Arabia, Syria, Israel
Syria	370	Israel, Jordan, Iraq, Turkey
Egypt	175 [280]	Libya, Sudan, Israel
Yemen	175	Saudi Arabia
United Arab Emirates	175	Saudi Arabia, Iran
Afghanistan	175	Pakistan, Tajikistan, Uzbekistan
South Korea	150	North Korea
Vietnam	175	China, Cambodia
Belarus	300	Russia, Ukraine, Poland
Ukraine	300	Russia, Belarus, Poland, Hungary, Romania
Bulgaria	300	Serbia, Albania, Turkey, Greece, Romania
Slovakia	300	Czech Rep., Hungary, Poland, Ukraine
Czech Republic	175	Slovakia, Poland, Germany
Poland	175	Russia, Belarus, Ukraine, Slovakia, Czech Rep., Germany
Romania	175	Serbia, Ukraine, Moldova, Hungary, Bulgaria
Japan[c]	——	

Number of states with ballistic missiles: 26

[a] States that have nuclear weapons.

[b] States believed to be trying to build nuclear weapons.

[c] States developing space-launch missiles adaptable as long-range ballistic missiles.

[d] Iraq's missile capability was supposedly destroyed after the Gulf War.

Notes: Bracketed range numbers indicate missiles under development. List of potential targets includes both hostile and friendly states, and is suggestive rather than comprehensive. Missile ranges increase with smaller payloads. 175-mile ranges (scud-B) are for a one-ton payload; 300-mile ranges (scud Mod-C) are for a 3/4-ton payload. Saudi range is for a two-ton payload; South Korean range is for a half-ton payload. Iraqi range is for a 1/3-ton payload.

Source: Adapted from *Arms Control Today,* March 1996: 29; and data from David Wright and Ted Postol (MIT), and from Tim McCarthy (Monterey Institute).

Many short-range ballistic missiles, including those used by Iraq during the Gulf War, are highly inaccurate but still very difficult to defend against. With conventional warheads they have more psychological than military utility (demoralizing an enemy population by attacking cities indiscriminately). With nuclear, chemical, or biological warheads, however, these missiles could be deadlier. A number of states now possess short-range ballistic missiles armed with weapons of mass destruction, but none has ever been used.

The accuracy of delivery systems of all ranges improves as one moves to great powers, especially the United States. After traveling thousands of miles, the best U.S. missiles can land within 50 feet of a target half of the time. The trend in the U.S. nuclear arsenal has been toward less-powerful warheads but more accurate missiles, for flexibility.

The newest capable class of delivery system is the **cruise missile**. This is a small winged missile that can navigate across thousands of miles of previously mapped terrain to reach a particular target. Cruise missiles can be launched from ships, submarines, airplanes, or land. As a nuclear-weapon vehicle, it is owned only by the United States and Russia, but several states have developed conventionally armed versions. Argentina scored one of its few successes in the 1982 Falklands War when it hit a British warship with a French-made cruise missile. U.S. leaders have discovered that conventionally armed cruise missiles can attack distant targets without risking U.S. lives—a politically safe strategy used increasingly in recent years. The United States used cruise missiles extensively against Serbian forces in Bosnia in 1995, against Serbia itself in 1999, and for smaller-scale strikes such as at terrorist Osama Bin Laden in Afghanistan.

Conceivably, small states or substate groups that may acquire nuclear weapons in the future could deliver them through innovative means. Because nuclear weapons are small, one could be smuggled into a target state by car, by speedboat, or in diplomatic pouches, and then detonated like any terrorist bomb. One advantage of such methods would be the ease of concealing the identity of the perpetrator.

In all the world's nuclear arsenals, delivery systems include special provisions for command and control. Because the weapons are so dangerous, control is highly centralized. In the United States and Russia, each president is accompanied everywhere by a military officer carrying a briefcase with the secret codes required to order such an attack. So far, at least, control procedures have succeeded in preventing any accidental or unauthorized use of nuclear weapons.

Chemical and Biological Weapons

Several times during the 1991 Gulf War, most of the population of Israel—millions of people—spent nights huddled in special sealed-off rooms in their houses, wearing gas masks and putting infants into little tents. This action was caused by fear of chemical weapons on Iraqi missiles (which turned out to have only conventional warheads).

Web Link
Chemical
Weapons

A *chemical weapon* releases chemicals that disable and kill people. A variety of chemicals can be used, from lethal ones such as nerve gas to merely irritating ones such as tear gas. Different chemicals interfere with the nervous system, blood, breathing, or other body functions. Some can be absorbed through the skin; others must be inhaled. Some persist in the target area long after their use; others disperse quickly.

It is possible to defend against most chemical weapons by dressing troops in protective clothing and gas masks and following elaborate procedures to decontaminate

Vulnerable Civilians are more vulnerable to chemical weapons than soldiers are. A new treaty aims to ban chemical weapons worldwide. Here, Israeli kindergarteners prepare against a chemical warfare threat from Iraq during the Gulf War, 1991.

equipment. But protective suits are hot, and antichemical measures reduce the efficiency of armies. Civilians are much less likely to have protection against chemicals than are military forces (the well-prepared Israeli civilians were an exception). Chemical weapons are by nature indiscriminate about whom they kill. Several times, chemical weapons have been deliberately used against civilians (most recently by the Iraqi government against Iraqi Kurds).

Use of chemical weapons in war has been rare. Mustard gas, which produces skin blisters and lung damage, was widely used in World War I. After the horrors of that war, the use of chemical weapons was banned in the 1925 Geneva protocol, a treaty that is still in effect. In World War II, both sides were armed with chemical weapons but neither used them, for fear of retaliation (the same was true in the Gulf War). Since then (with possibly a few unclear exceptions) only Iraq has violated the treaty—against Iran in the 1980s. Unfortunately, Iraq's actions not only breached a psychological barrier against using chemical weapons, but also showed such weapons to be cheap and effective against human waves of attacking soldiers without protective gear. This stimulated more third world states to begin acquiring chemical weapons. Dozens now have them. During the Gulf War, Iraq deployed but apparently did not use chemical weapons. However, bombing of an Iraqi chemical weapons depot exposed thousands of U.S. troops to chemicals; a link to Gulf War Syndrome (mysterious illnesses affecting veterans of the war) has been suspected but not proven.

Chemical weapons have been called "the poor country's atom bomb"—although nuclear weapons are far more destructive—because chemical weapons are a cheap way for states to gain weapons of mass destruction as potential leverage in international conflicts. Production of chemical weapons can use similar processes and facilities as for pesticides, pharmaceuticals, and other civilian products. It is difficult to locate chemical weapons facilities in suspect countries, or to deny those states access to the needed chemicals and equipment. In 1998, a U.S. cruise missile attack destroyed a suspected weapons facility in Sudan that apparently was only a pharmaceutical factory.

The 1925 treaty did not ban the production or possession of chemical weapons, and several dozen states built stockpiles of them. The United States and the Soviet Union maintained large arsenals of chemical weapons during the Cold War but have reduced them greatly in the past decade. In 1992, a new **Chemical Weapons Convention** to ban the production and possession of chemical weapons was concluded after years of negotiation; it has been signed by 167 states, including all the great powers (but not by Israel, Egypt, Syria, Libya, Iraq, or North Korea). The new treaty includes strict verification provisions and the threat of sanctions against violators including (an important extension) those who are nonparticipants in the treaty. It went into effect in 1997 and the U.S. Senate approved ratification at the last minute. Opponents argued that the treaty would be ineffective, but within months several states (including India, China, South Korea, France, and Britain) admitted to having secret chemical weapons programs, which will now be dismantled under international oversight.

Biological weapons resemble chemical ones, except that instead of chemicals they use microorganisms or biologically derived toxins. Some use viruses or bacteria that cause fatal diseases, such as smallpox, bubonic plague, and anthrax. Others cause nonfatal, but incapacitating, diseases or diseases that kill livestock. Theoretically, a single weapon could spark an epidemic in an entire population, but this is considered too dangerous and use of less-contagious microorganisms is preferred.

Biological weapons have virtually never been used in war (Japan tried some on a few Chinese villages in World War II). Their potential strikes many political leaders as a Pandora's box that could let loose uncontrollable forces if opened. Thus, the development, production, and possession of biological weapons are banned by the 1972 **Biological Weapons Convention**, signed by more than 100 countries including the great powers. The superpowers destroyed their stocks of biological weapons and had to restrict their biological weapons complexes to defensive research rather than the development of weapons. However, because the treaty makes no provision for inspection and because biological weapons programs are, like chemical ones, relatively easy to hide, several states—including Iraq, Libya, and Syria—remain under suspicion of having biological weapons. UN inspections of Iraq in the mid-1990s uncovered an active biological weapons program. In 1997, the U.S. military started to vaccinate all 2.4 million U.S. soldiers against anthrax.

Today the United States and perhaps a dozen other countries maintain biological weapons research (not banned by the treaty). Research programs are trying to ascertain the military implications of advances in biotechnology. Most states doing such research claim that they are doing so only to deter another state from developing biological weapons. There is a security dilemma here (see p. 65) with the potential for a future arms race. But so far such a race has been avoided.

Proliferation

Proliferation is the spread of weapons of mass destruction—nuclear weapons, ballistic missiles, and chemical or biological weapons—into the hands of more actors. Poor states and middle powers want ballistic missiles capable of delivering nuclear weapons—or if that is infeasible, then chemical or biological weapons. This capability provides states with a potentially powerful means of leverage in international conflicts—a threat to cause extreme damage that is impossible to defend against. Because the only practical counterleverage is a threat to retaliate in kind, states also want ballistic missiles with weapons of mass destruction in order to deter their use by others. This causes a security dilemma.

Web Link
Proliferation

The implications of proliferation for international relations are difficult to predict but evidently profound. Ballistic missiles with weapons of mass destruction remove the territorial protection offered by state borders and make each state vulnerable to others. Some realists, who believe in the basic rationality of state actions, are not so upset by this prospect, and some even welcome it. They reason that in a world where the use of military force could lead to mutual annihilation, there would be fewer wars—just as during the superpower arms race of the Cold War. Other IR scholars who put less faith in the rationality of state leaders are much more alarmed by proliferation. They fear that with more and more nuclear (or chemical/biological) actors, miscalculation or accident could lead to the use of weapons of mass destruction on a scale unseen since 1945.

The leaders of great powers tend to side with the second group. They have tried to keep the oligopoly on weapons of mass destruction, in which only great powers had these capabilities and other states generally did not. Slowing down proliferation is a central U.S. foreign policy goal. Proliferation erodes the great powers' advantage relative to middle powers. There is also widespread fear that these weapons may fall into the hands of terrorists or other nonstate actors who would be immune from threats of retaliation (with no territory or cities to defend) and who might be much more willing to use such weapons.

However, states that sell technology with proliferation potential can make money doing so. In the mid-1990s the United States pressured Russia and China to stop selling nuclear technology to Iran (which the United States said was trying to build nuclear weapons). Russia and China would have to give up hundreds of millions of dollars in sales. Industrialized states have competed to sell technology and have simultaneously worked to restrain such sales by other states. This is another international collective-goods problem, in which states pursuing their individual interests end up collectively worse off.

Nuclear proliferation could occur simply by a state or nonstate actor's buying (or stealing) one or more nuclear weapons or the components to build one. The means to prevent this range from covert intelligence to tight security measures to safeguards preventing a stolen weapon from being used. But, for example, the 1998 economic crisis in Russia left hundreds of tons of Russian missile materials—in the control of underpaid civilian workers and military officers at poorly funded facilities with lax security and recurrent corruption—more vulnerable than ever.

A more lasting form of nuclear proliferation is the development by states of nuclear complexes to produce their own nuclear weapons on an ongoing basis. Here larger numbers of weapons are involved and there are strong potentials for arms races in regional conflicts and rivalries. The relevant regional conflicts are those between Israel and the Arab states, Iran and its neighbors, India and Pakistan, the two Koreas, and possibly Taiwan and China. India and Pakistan both have exploded nuclear devices underground, and are moving forward to build arsenals and the missiles to deliver them. In addition, South Africa reported in 1993 that it had built several nuclear weapons but then dismantled them in the 1980s (while still under white minority rule).

Israel has never test-exploded nuclear weapons nor admitted it has them. It claims simply that "Israel will not be the first country to introduce nuclear weapons into the region" (which might imply that weapons hidden away have not been "introduced"). In fact, Israel is widely believed to have a hundred or more nuclear warheads on combat airplanes and medium-range missiles. Israel wants these capabilities to use as a last resort if it were about to be conquered by its neighbors—just as the biblical figure Samson brought down the house upon himself and everyone else. By implicitly threatening such action, Israeli leaders hope to convince Arab leaders that a military conquest of Israel is impossible. But by keeping its weapons secret, Israel tries to minimize the provocation to its neighbors to develop their own nuclear weapons. To prevent Iraq from doing so, Israel carried out a bombing raid on the main facility of the Iraqi nuclear complex in 1981. Without this raid, Iraq probably would have had nuclear weapons by the time of the Gulf War.

Efforts to limit the development of nuclear complexes by these states hinge on stopping the flow of necessary materials and expertise—such as enriched uranium, enrichment equipment, electronic timers, and nuclear engineers. A particular fear in the 1990s was that the nuclear complex of the former Soviet Union could be a source of fissionable material, equipment, or nuclear expertise. From 1992 to 1994, more than 100 attempts to smuggle uranium or plutonium from the former Soviet Union were reported. We do not know whether any such attempts have succeeded.

The **Non-Proliferation Treaty (NPT)** of 1968 created a framework for controlling the spread of nuclear materials and expertise. The International Atomic Energy Agency (IAEA), a UN agency based in Vienna, is charged with inspecting the nuclear power industry in member states to prevent secret military diversions of nuclear materials. However, a number of potential nuclear states (such as Israel) have not signed the NPT, and even those states that have signed may sneak around its provisions by keeping some facilities secret (as Iraq did). Under the terms of the Gulf War cease-fire, Iraq's nuclear program was uncovered and dismantled by the IAEA.

Atlas CD
North Korea
Map

North Korea withdrew from the IAEA in 1993, then bargained with Western leaders to get economic assistance, including safer reactors, in exchange for freezing its nuclear program. North Korea's leader died months later, but the compromise held up. In the late 1990s, North Korea's economic collapse and food crisis combined with the nuclear issue to make the country especially worrisome for Western leaders. Despite fears that its leaders were just playing for time to prop up a failed regime, in 1999 North Korea allowed inspection of a disputed underground complex and agreed to suspend missile tests, in exchange for aid and partial lifting of U.S. trade sanctions.

Nuclear proliferation has been less widespread than was feared decades ago. The five permanent members of the Security Council, who all had nuclear weapons by 1964, have continued to make up the nuclear club of states with large, openly acknowledged arsenals. Several other states have nuclear weapons, but in smaller quantities. India tested one in 1974, and both India and Pakistan tested several in 1998. Pakistan is believed to have more than a dozen nuclear weapons, and India at least several dozen.

A number of middle powers and two great powers (Japan and Germany) have the potential to make nuclear weapons but have chosen not to do so. The reasons for

Hot Stuff The most important hurdle in making nuclear weapons is access to fissionable materials (plutonium and uranium). Here, a plutonium shipment from England is unloaded in Japan, 1999. These imports fuel nuclear reactors, but also give Japan the potential to make hundreds of nuclear weapons if it ever decided to.

deciding against "going nuclear" include norms against using nuclear weapons, fears of retaliation, and practical constraints including cost. Several republics of the former Soviet Union have recently been added to the nonnuclear-by-choice category. Ukraine dragged its feet on commitments to get rid of strategic nuclear missiles—hoping to use them as bargaining chips to obtain Western aid and security guarantees—but ultimately came around.

At present, undeclared nuclear powers include Israel (with perhaps a hundred warheads) and possibly North Korea (with one or two, if any). Newly declared nuclear states are India and Pakistan (with dozens each). Iran has been singled out by the United States recently for trying to develop nuclear weapons (as it had begun to do under the shah in the 1970s), but is not expected to succeed for several more years. Brazil and Argentina seemed to be headed for a nuclear arms race in the 1980s but then called it off as civilians replaced military governments in both countries.

In 1995, the NPT came up for a 25-year review. In that period, the nonnuclear states were supposed to stay nonnuclear; they had largely done so, except for Israel, India, and Pakistan, which had never signed the treaty. The nuclear states were supposed to undertake serious nuclear disarmament; they had largely failed to do so until the 1990s, and still possessed far more potent nuclear arsenals than 25 years earlier. Despite these complaints, the 172 signers of the treaty agreed in 1995 to extend it indefinitely.

The proliferation of ballistic missiles has been more difficult to control. There is a **Missile Technology Control Regime** through which industrialized states try to limit the flow of missile-relevant technology to third world states. One success was the interruption of an Egyptian-Argentinean-Iraqi partnership in the 1980s to develop a medium-range missile. West German companies were induced to stop selling technology secretly to the project. But, in general, the regime has been less successful. At present, short- and medium-range missiles (ranges up to about 2,000 miles) apparently are being developed by Iraq, Iran, Israel, Saudi Arabia, Pakistan, India, North Korea, and possibly Argentina and Brazil. Soviet-made short-range ballistic missiles are owned by a number of third world states. China continues to sell its missiles and technology in the third world (bringing lower prices to buyers and hard currency to China)—a sore point in relations with the West.

Nuclear Strategy Certainly the decision to acquire or forgo nuclear weapons is the most fundamental aspect of a state's *nuclear strategy*. But the term generally is applied to states that have already decided to acquire nuclear weapons; it refers to their decisions about how many nuclear weapons to deploy, what delivery systems to put them on, and what policies to adopt regarding the circumstances in which they would be used.

Web Link
Superpower
Arms Race

The reason for possessing nuclear weapons is almost always to deter another state from a nuclear or conventional attack by threatening ruinous retaliation. This should work if state leaders are rational actors wanting to avoid the huge costs of a nuclear attack. But it will work only if other states believe that a state's threat to use nuclear weapons is credible. The search for a credible deterrent by two or more hostile states tends to lead to an ever-growing arsenal of nuclear weapons.

To follow this logic, let us suppose that Pakistan deployed a single nuclear missile aimed at India (not that Pakistan would really do this or be more likely to than India). Then India would not attack—that is, unless it could prevent Pakistan from using its missile. India could do this by building offensive forces capable of wiping out the Pakistani missile (probably using nuclear weapons, but that is not the key point here). Then the Pakistani missile, rather than deter India, would merely spur India to destroy the missile before any other attack. An attack intended to destroy—largely or entirely—a state's nuclear weapons before they can be used is called a *first strike*.

Pakistan could make its missile survivable (probably by making it mobile). It could also build more nuclear missiles so that even if some were destroyed in an Indian first strike, some would survive with which to retaliate. Weapons that can take a first strike and still strike back give a state *second-strike* capabilities. A state that deploys the fewest nuclear forces needed for an assured second-strike capability (between tens and hundreds) has a minimum deterrent. Possession of second-strike capabilities by both sides is called **mutually assured destruction (MAD)** because neither side can prevent the other from destroying it. The term implies that the strategy, though reflecting "rationality," is actually insane (mad) because deviations from rationality could destroy both sides.

If India could not assuredly destroy Pakistan's missile, it would undoubtedly deploy its own nuclear missile to deter Pakistan from using its missile. India, too, could achieve a second-strike capability. Now the question of credibility becomes important. In theory, India could launch a nonnuclear attack on Pakistan, knowing that rational Pakistani leaders would rather lose such a war than use their nuclear weapons and bring on an Indian nuclear response. The nuclear missiles in effect cancel each other out.

During the Cold War, this was the problem faced by U.S. war planners trying to deter a Soviet conventional attack on Western Europe. They could threaten to use

The Race Is On India and Pakistan are building arsenals of nuclear-tipped missiles that could devastate each other's main cities. Their current arms race follows that of the superpowers during the Cold War. Superpower arms control agreements helped develop norms and expectations about the role of nuclear weapons but did not stop a buildup of tens of thousands of nuclear weapons. Here, India shows off its new intermediate-range ballistic missile, 1999.

nuclear weapons in response, but rational Soviet leaders would know that rational U.S. leaders would never act on such a threat and risk escalation to global nuclear war. Better to lose West Germany, according to this line of thinking, than lose both West Germany and New York. China currently uses a parallel form of this "rational irrationality" in its relations with Taiwan, trying to make credible the threat of war (which would be disastrous for China as well as Taiwan) if Taiwan declares independence (see p. 56).

Nuclear *warfighting*, or *counterforce*, capability specifically targets the other state's forces. Without such a capability, a state's only available lever is to blow up another state's cities—a countervalue capability (targeting something of value to the other side). The trouble with nuclear warfighting forces, however, is that they must be very accurate, powerful, and massive in order to successfully knock out the other side's nuclear weapons. This makes them effective first-strike weapons—very threatening to the other state and likely to provoke a further buildup of the other state's weapons in response. First-strike weapons are considered inherently unstable in a crisis, because they are so threatening that the other side would be tempted to attack them quickly in a first strike of its own. Knowing that this could happen, the first state would itself be tempted to launch its weapons before such an attack—"use 'em or lose 'em."

The problem is accentuated by the use of multiple warheads on a single missile (multiple independently targeted re-entry vehicles, or MIRVs). The more warheads on a missile, the more tempting a target it makes for the other side. (One successful strike can prevent multiple enemy strikes.) Thus, fixed land-based MIRVed missiles are considered destabilizing weapons. In the 1992 START II treaty (unratified as of 1999), the United States and Russia agreed to phase them out.

Defense plays little role in nuclear strategy because no effective defense against missile attack has been devised. However, the United States spent several billion dollars a year for a decade, trying to develop defenses that could shoot down incoming ballistic missiles. The program was called the **Strategic Defense Initiative (SDI)**, or "star wars." It originated in President Ronald Reagan's 1983 call for a comprehensive shield that would make nuclear missiles obsolete. However, the mission soon shifted to a (slightly) more realistic one of defending some U.S. missiles in a massive Soviet attack. After the Cold War the mission shifted again, to one of protecting U.S. territory from a very limited missile attack (at most a few missiles), such as might occur in an unauthorized launch, an accident, or an attack by a small state. Current plans call for deploying (in several years) ground-based, nonnuclear missiles to try to intercept incoming warheads.

In addition to the technical challenges of stopping incoming ballistic missile warheads, a true strategic defense would also have to stop cruise missiles and airplanes, if not more innovative delivery systems. If a rogue state or terrorist group struck the United States with a nuclear weapon, it would probably not use an ICBM to do so. Nobody has an answer to this problem. For now, virtually the only defense against a nuclear weapon is a good offense—the threat to retaliate.

Nuclear Arsenals and Arms Control
During the Cold War, the superpowers' nuclear forces grew and technologies developed. These evolving force structures were codified by a series of arms control agreements. *Arms control* is an effort by two or more states to regulate by formal agreement their acquisition of weapons. Arms control is broader than just nuclear weapons—after World War I the great powers negotiated limits on sizes of navies—but in recent decades nuclear weapons have been the main focus of arms control. Arms control agreements typically require long formal negotiations with many technical discussions, culminating in a treaty. Some arms control treaties are multilateral, but during the Cold War most were bilateral (U.S.-Soviet). Some stay in effect indefinitely; others have a limited term.

At first, the United States had far superior nuclear forces and relied on a strategy of massive retaliation for any Soviet conventional attack. This threat became less credible as the Soviet Union developed a second-strike capability in the 1960s. The superpowers then turned to nuclear arms control to regulate their relations. The superpowers gained confidence from arms control agreements that they could do business with each other and that they would not let the arms race lead them into a nuclear war—fear of which had increased after the Cuban Missile Crisis of 1962. Nuclear arms control talks and agreements did not stop either superpower from developing any weapon it wanted, but they did manage the arms race and bring about a convergence of expectations about its structure.

For example, the first agreements, in the 1960s, banned activities that both sides could easily live without—testing nuclear weapons in the atmosphere and placing nuclear weapons in space. The Non-Proliferation Treaty (1968) built on the superpowers' common fears of China and other potential new nuclear states. Other confidence-building measures were directed at the management of potential crises. The hot line agreement connected the U.S. and Soviet heads of state by telephone. A later agreement on incidents at sea provided for efforts to control escalation after a hostile encounter or accident on the high seas. Eventually, centers and systems for the exchange of information in a crisis were developed.

Several treaties in the 1970s locked in the superpowers' basic parity in nuclear capabilities under MAD, including the 1972 **Antiballistic Missile (ABM) Treaty** and the 1972 and 1979 **Strategic Arms Limitation Treaties (SALT)**. The U.S. arsenal peaked in the 1960s at more than 30,000 warheads; the Soviet arsenal peaked in the 1980s at more than 40,000. More recent arms control agreements substantially reduced nuclear forces after the end of the Cold War. Under the 1987 **Intermediate Nuclear Forces (INF) Treaty**, the 1991 **Strategic Arms Reduction Treaty (START I)**, and the 1992 **START II** treaty, nuclear weapons will be cut by more than half in the next decade. The United States will end up with 3,500 strategic warheads and Russia with 3,000.

A **Comprehensive Test Ban Treaty (CTBT)** to halt all nuclear test-explosions was finally signed in 1996 after decades of stalemate. It aims to impede the development of new types of nuclear weapons. Technological advances—both in the design of weapons (without needing to actually explode one), and in verification that no tests are occurring—overcame the previous reluctance of the great powers to undertake this step. However, the treaty does not take effect until signed and ratified by all 44 states believed capable of building at least a crude nuclear weapon. India did not sign the CTBT, and defied it in 1998 with five nuclear tests. Pakistan followed suit with its own tests. The U.S. Senate voted in 1999 against ratifying the CTBT, whose future thus remains in doubt. Russia ratified it in 2000.

Nuclear arsenals may be further reduced in the coming years. The United States and Russia tentatively agreed in 1997 on a START III treaty allowing about 2,000 warheads on each side. In 1996, 60 retired generals from 17 countries, including a former commander of U.S. nuclear forces, urged deep reductions in nuclear arsenals. Whether nuclear weapons can be eliminated altogether is a more difficult question, because in a nuclear-free world a handful of weapons of mass destruction might become all-powerful.

Overall, the United States has the most potent strategic nuclear arsenal in the world by far, because it has not only the most weapons but the most accurate delivery systems. The reductions in U.S. and Russian arsenals still leave them much larger than those of China, France, and Britain, which each have several hundred weapons. These smaller arsenals are, however, enough for a credible second-strike capability.

Arms control efforts outside the area of nuclear arms have not been very successful. For decades the NATO and Warsaw Pact countries carried on the Mutual and Balanced Force Reduction (MBFR) talks aimed at limiting conventional military forces in Europe. Not until the last years of the Cold War was the **Conventional Forces in Europe (CFE) Treaty** signed, and within two years it was virtually obsolete. Efforts to control conventional arms trade through arms control treaties have had no success. After the Gulf War, the five permanent Security Council members tried to negotiate limits on the supply of weapons to the Middle East. The five participants account for weapons sold in the Middle East. But no participant wanted to give up its own lucrative arms sales in the region, which each naturally saw as justified.

All the weapons of mass destruction are relatively difficult and expensive to build, yet they provide only specialized capabilities that are rarely if ever actually used. As a result, a number of states have decided that such weapons are not worth acquiring, though it would be technically possible to do so. Such cost-benefit thinking also applies more broadly to states' decisions about the acquisition of all kinds of military forces.

States face complex choices regarding the configuration of their military forces in the post–Cold War era. Not only have the immediate contingencies and threats changed drastically, but the nature of threats in the new era is unknown.

Despite the threat of conflict or war and the importance of security concerns, trade, money, and business are playing a more and more powerful role in international relations. In the next chapter we move to a discussion of the politics of international economic activities, the world monetary system, and the role of private companies as nonstate actors in the world economy.

THINKING CRITICALLY

1. How many of the six types of international conflict discussed in this chapter can you connect with the phenomenon of nationalism discussed on pp. 26–29? What are the connections in each case?
2. The rise of fundamentalism among the world's major religions challenges traditional notions of state sovereignty. How might this trend strengthen, or weaken, the United Nations and other attempts to create supranational authority (which also challenge state sovereignty)?
3. Most of the great powers are reconfiguring their military forces in the post–Cold War era. What kinds of capabilities do you think your own country needs in this period? Why?

CHAPTER SUMMARY

◆ War and other forms of international violence are used as leverage to try to improve the terms of settlement of conflicts.

◆ Many theories have been offered as general explanations about when such forms of leverage come into play—the causes of war. Contradictory theories have been proposed at each level of analysis and, with two exceptions, none has strong empirical support. Thus, political scientists cannot reliably predict the outbreak of war.

◆ The two exceptions are (1) that there are virtually no societies in which war and intergroup violence as means of leverage are unknown, and (2) that democratic states almost never fight wars against other democracies.

◆ States come into conflict with each other and with nonstate actors for a variety of reasons. Conflicts will always exist among international actors.

◆ Territorial disputes are among the most serious international conflicts because states place great value on territorial integrity. Conflicts over the control of entire states are also serious and are relatively likely to lead to the use of force.

◆ Economic conflicts lead to violence much less often, because positive gains from economic activities are more important inducements than negative threats of violence.

◆ Drug trafficking creates several kinds of conflict that draw in state and nonstate actors alike.

◆ Ethnic conflicts, especially when linked with territorial disputes, are very difficult to resolve because of psychological biases. It is hard to explain why people's loyalties are sometimes to their ethnic group, sometimes to a multiethnic nation.

◆ Fundamentalist religious movements pose a broad challenge to the rules of the international system in general and state sovereignty in particular.

◆ When violent means are used as leverage in international conflicts, a variety of types of war result. These vary greatly in size and character from guerrilla wars and raids to hegemonic war for leadership of the international system. Thus, the exact definition of war is uncertain.

◆ Like other violent means of leverage, terrorism is used to gain advantage in international bargaining situations. Terrorism is effective if it damages morale in a population and gains media exposure for the cause.

◆ Military forces provide states with means of leverage beyond the various nonmilitary means of influence widely used in international bargaining.

◆ Military spending tends to stimulate economic growth in the short term but reduce growth over the long term. In the 1990s, military forces and expenditures of the great powers—especially Russia—were reduced and restructured.

◆ Military forces include a wide variety of capabilities suited to different purposes. Conventional warfare requires different kinds of forces from those needed to threaten the use of nuclear, chemical, or biological weapons.

◆ Except in time of civil war, state leaders—whether civilian or military—control military forces through a single hierarchical chain of command.

◆ Military forces can threaten the domestic power of state leaders, who are vulnerable to being overthrown by coups d'état.

◆ Control of territory is fundamental to state sovereignty and is accomplished primarily with ground forces.

◆ Small missiles and electronic warfare are increasingly important, especially for naval and air forces. The role of satellites is expanding in communications, navigation, and reconnaissance.

◆ Weapons of mass destruction—nuclear, chemical, and biological—have been used only a handful of times in war.

◆ The production of nuclear weapons is technically within the means of many states and some nonstate actors, but the necessary fissionable material (uranium-235 or plutonium) is very difficult to obtain.

◆ Most industrialized states, and many poor ones, have refrained voluntarily from acquiring nuclear weapons. These states include two great powers, Germany and Japan.

◆ Chemical weapons are cheaper to build than nuclear weapons, they have similar threat value, and their production is harder to detect. More middle powers have chemical weapons than have nuclear ones. A new treaty bans the possession and use of chemical weapons.

- Several states conduct research into biological warfare, but by treaty the possession of such weapons is banned.
- Slowing the proliferation of ballistic missiles and weapons of mass destruction in the third world is a central concern of the great powers.
- The United States and Russia have arsenals of thousands of nuclear weapons; China, Britain, and France have hundreds.
- Arms control agreements formally define the contours of an arms race or mutual disarmament process.

ONLINE PRACTICE TEST

Take an online practice test at
www.IRtext.com

5

Trade and Money

CHAPTER OUTLINE

- From Security to Political Economy
- Markets
- Trade Strategies
- Trade Regimes
- The Currency System
- State Financial Positions
- Multinational Business

From Security to Political Economy

Scholars of *international political economy (IPE)* study the politics of international economic activities. The most frequently studied of these activities are trade, monetary relations, and multinational corporations. Most scholars of IPE focus on the industrialized regions of the world, where most of the world's economic activity occurs. However, the global South has received growing attention, especially because economic relations and conditions there may be a more frequent source of international conflict and war in the post–Cold War era. We shall take up North-South aspects of IPE in Chapter 7.

The conceptual framework used to study international security affairs applies to IPE as well. The core concepts of power and bargaining developed from Chapter 2 on apply to IPE as does the emphasis on states as the most important actors (though not the only important actors) and the idea that states tend to act in their own interests.

However, the major approaches to IPE diverge from realism by downplaying the importance of military leverage in international bargaining. In most conflicts studied in IPE—those over economic transactions—military force would not be a very effective means of influence. The main reason for this ineffectiveness is that using military force would disrupt a range of mutually profitable economic exchanges. Another related divergence from realism is the concept of self-interest; in IPE the realist concept of narrow short-term self-interest competes poorly with the liberal idea that mutually beneficial long-term cooperation can often better achieve a state's self-interest. The collective goods problem is also important throughout IPE. (See Chapter 3.)

Web Link
Mercantilism

Liberalism and Mercantilism On another key assumption of realism—international anarchy—two major approaches within IPE differ. One approach, called **mercantilism**, generally shares with realism the belief that each state must protect its own interests at the expense of others—not relying on international organizations to create a framework for mutual gains. Mercantilists therefore emphasize relative power (as do realists): what matters is not so much a state's absolute amount of well-being but its position relative to rival states.

Liberalism, an alternative approach, generally shares the assumption of anarchy (lack of world government) but does not see this condition as precluding extensive cooperation to realize common gains. It holds that by building international organizations, institutions, and norms, states can mutually benefit from economic exchanges. It matters little to liberals whether one state gains more or less than another—just whether the state's wealth is increasing in *absolute* terms. This concept parallels the idea that IOs allow states to relax their narrow, short-term pursuit of self-interest in order to realize longer-term mutual interests (see Chapter 3 and also Chapter 6, pp. 325–326).

Liberalism and mercantilism are *theories* of economics and also *ideologies* that shape state policies. Liberalism is the dominant approach in Western economics, though more so in *microeconomics* (the study of firms and households) than in *macroeconomics* (the study of national economies). Marxism is often treated as a third theoretical/ideological approach to IPE, along with mercantilism and liberalism. Marxist approaches are attuned to economic exploitation as a force shaping political relations. Chapter 7 explores these theories in depth, as they find their greatest explanatory power in North-South relations.

In IPE, contrary to international security, liberalism is the dominant tradition of scholarship and mercantilism is secondary. Thus, IR has a split personality. In matters of military force and security, scholars focus on anarchy and inherently conflicting interests. In matters of international political economy, however, they focus on international regimes and institutions that allow states to achieve mutual interests.

In truth, most international economic exchanges (as well as security relationships) contain some element of mutual interests—joint gains that can be realized through cooperation—and some element of conflicting interests. Game theorists call this a "mixed interest" game. In international trade, even when two states both benefit from a trade (a shared interest), one or the other will benefit more, depending on the price of the transaction (a conflicting interest).

Liberalism places emphasis on the shared interests in economic exchanges, whereas mercantilism emphasizes the conflicting interests. Liberals see the most important goal of economic policy as the maximum creation of total wealth through achieving optimal *efficiency* (maximizing output, minimizing waste). Mercantilists see the most important goal as the creation of the most favorable possible *distribution* of wealth.

The main reason for the dominance of liberalism in IPE is that in practice great gains have been realized from free trade. In any economic exchange that is not coerced by neg-

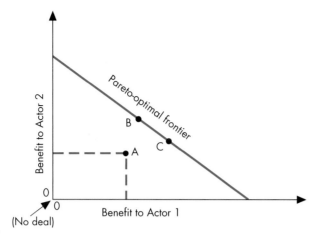

FIGURE 5.1   Joint and Individual Benefits   Any deal struck, such as at point A, yields certain benefits to each actor (dotted lines). Joint benefits are maximized at the Pareto-optimal frontier, but the distribution of those benefits, as between points B and C (both of which are better than A for both actors), is a matter for bargaining. Liberalism is more concerned with joint benefits, mercantilism more with the relative distribution.

ative leverage, both parties gain. Both can gain because they place different values on the items being exchanged. Each party places less value on the item it starts with than the other party does. For instance, when a supermarket sells a head of cabbage, the consumer values the cabbage more than the cash paid for it, and the supermarket values the cash more than the cabbage. This simple principle is the basis for economic exchange.

Atlas CD
Panamania
Free Port
Photo

Even though both parties gain in an exchange, they may not gain equally: the distribution of benefits from trade may not be divided equally among participating states. One party may benefit greatly from an exchange, whereas the other party benefits only slightly. Liberal economists are interested in maximizing the overall (joint) benefits from exchange—a condition called *Pareto-optimal* (after an economist named Pareto). They have little to say about how total benefits are distributed among the parties (see Figure 5.1).

Rather, the distribution of benefits is a matter for implicit or explicit bargaining, and hence a matter for politics and the use of leverage to influence the outcomes. States as participants in the international economy try to realize the greatest overall gains for all states while simultaneously bargaining to maximize their own share of those gains. Power does matter in such bargaining, but the most relevant forms of leverage are positive (the prospect of gains by striking a deal) rather than negative. Because the exchange process creates much wealth, there is much room for bargaining over the distribution of that wealth.

Liberalism sees individual households and firms as the key actors in the economy and views government's most useful role as one of noninterference in economics except to regulate markets in order to help them function efficiently (and to create infrastructure such as roads that also help the economy function efficiently). Politics, in this view, should serve the interests of economic efficiency. With the hand of government removed from markets, the "invisible hand" of supply and demand can work out the most efficient patterns of production, exchange, and consumption (through the mechanism of prices). Because of the benefits of free trade, liberals disdain realists' obsession with international borders, because borders constrain the maximum efficiency of exchange.

For mercantilists, by contrast, economics should serve politics: the creation of wealth underlies state power. Because power is relative, trade is desirable only when the distribution of benefits favors one's own state over rivals. The terms of exchange shape the relative rates at which states accumulate power and thus shape the way power distributions in the international system change over time. As Japan and Germany, for instance, have achieved great prosperity, mercantilists saw them potentially threatening to overtake the United States. Liberals, by contrast, thought Japanese and German wealth boosted the entire world economy and ultimately benefited the United States.

Mercantilism achieved prominence several hundred years ago, and Britain used trade to rise in relative power in the international system around the eighteenth century. At that time mercantilism meant specifically the creation of a trade surplus (see "Balance of Trade" later in this chapter) in order to stockpile money in the form of gold and silver, which could then be used to buy mercenary armies and weapons in time of war. Mercantilism declined in the nineteenth century as Britain decided it had more to gain from free trade than from protectionism. It returned as a major approach in the period between World Wars I and II, when liberal global trading relations broke down. Again in recent years, with the weakening of the liberal international economic order created after World War II, mercantilism has begun to become more prominent.

The distinction between liberalism and mercantilism is in the difference between hegemony and empire. Under hegemony, a dominant state creates an international order that facilitates free trade, but does not try to control economic transactions by itself. An empire, by contrast, controls economic transactions in its area centrally. Historically, empires have a poor record of economic performance; hegemony has been much more successful in achieving economic growth and prosperity. Of course, under hegemony, rival states also share (with the hegemon) in overall growth and prosperity, which can ultimately erode the hegemon's relative power and end its hegemony.

Markets

International exchanges of goods and services now occur in *global markets*. Liberalism supports the use of market processes, relatively unhindered by political elements; mercantilism favors greater political control over markets and exchanges. The stakes in this debate are high because of the growing volume and importance of international trade.

Atlas CD
World Trade
Article

Global Patterns of Trade   International trade amounts to about 15 percent of the total economic activity in the world. Around $5 trillion worth of trade crosses international borders each year.[1] This is a very large number, more than six times larger than the world's military spending, for example. The great volume of international trade reflects the fact that trade is profitable.

---

[1] Data in this chapter are calculated from United Nations. *World Economic and Social Survey 1997: Trends and Policies in the World Economy.* New York: United Nations, 1997.

THE INFORMATION REVOLUTION — Decentralizing Markets

Markets are more efficient when participants have more information about each other. Information systems underlie the rapid growth of international trade. In a world where small producers and consumers meet in cyberspace instead of the village marketplace, how will the character of international trade change?

To explore this question, go to www.IRtext.com

The role of trade in the economy varies somewhat from one region to another, but it is at least as important overall in the third world regions as in the industrialized regions of the world. Nonetheless, in the world economy as a whole, the global South accounts for a relatively small part of all trade, because the third world's economic activity itself is only 40 percent of the world total. This creates an asymmetrical dependence in North-South trade (see Chapter 7).

Overall, most political activity related to trade is concentrated in the industrialized West (North America, Western Europe, and Japan/Pacific), which accounts for about two-thirds of all international trade. Trade between these areas and the global South, although less important in volume, is also a topic of interest to IPE scholars (see Chapter 7). Of special interest currently are trade issues in the former communist transitional economies of Russia and Eastern Europe, which face formidable challenges as they try to join the capitalist world economy.

Web Link
Global Patterns
of Trade

Two contradictory trends are at work in global trading patterns today. One trend is toward the integration of the industrialized regions with each other in a truly global market. The World Trade Organization (discussed below) is especially important to this global integration process. The second trend is the emerging potential division of the industrialized West into three competing trading blocs, each internally integrated but not very open to the other two blocs. Regional free-trade areas in Europe and North America, and perhaps in Asia in the future, raise the possibility of trading zones practicing liberalism inwardly and mercantilism outwardly. However, as information technologies link the world across space, the integrating trend seems to have the upper hand and the more global vision of free trade is shaping the agenda.

Comparative Advantage

The overall success of liberal economics is due to the substantial gains that can be realized through trade. These gains result from the **comparative advantage** that different states enjoy in producing different goods (a concept pioneered by economists Adam Smith and David Ricardo 200 years ago). States differ in their abilities to produce certain goods because of differences in natural resources, labor force characteristics, and other such factors. In order to maximize the overall creation of wealth, each state should specialize in producing the goods for which it has a comparative advantage and then trade for goods that another state is better at producing. Of course, the costs of transportation and of processing the information in the trade

Think Globally   At a Toyota factory in Kentucky, U.S. workers assemble a Japanese car for export to Britain and Japan (car has right-hand drive), 1993. As the world economy becomes more integrated, markets and production are becoming global in scope.

(called *transaction costs*) must be included in the costs of producing an item. But both of these are low (and declining) relative to the differences in the cost of producing items in different locations.

Two commodities of great importance to the world are oil and cars. It is much cheaper to produce oil (or a similar energy source) in Saudi Arabia than in Japan, and much cheaper to produce cars in Japan than in Saudi Arabia. Japan needs oil to run its industry (including its car industry), and Saudi Arabia needs cars to travel its vast territory (including reaching its remote oil wells). Even with accounting for shipping and transaction costs, it saves a huge amount of money to ship Japanese cars to Saudi Arabia and Saudi oil to Japan, compared to the costs if each were self-sufficient.

A state need not have an absolute advantage over others in producing one kind of good to make specialization pay. It need only specialize in producing goods that are lower in cost than other goods relative to world market prices. Imagine that Japan discovered a way to produce synthetic oil using roughly the same mix of labor and capital that it now uses to produce cars, and that this synthetic oil could be produced a bit more cheaply than what it cost Saudi Arabia to produce oil, but that Japan could still produce cars much more cheaply than could Saudi Arabia. From a strictly economic point of view, Japan should keep producing cars (where it had the greatest comparative advantage) and not divert capital and labor to make synthetic oil (where it had only a slight advantage). The extra profits Japan would make from exporting more cars would more than compensate for the slightly higher price it would pay to import oil.

Thus, international trade generally expands the Pareto-optimal frontier by increasing the overall efficiency of production. Free trade allocates global resources to states that have the greatest comparative advantage in producing each kind of commodity. As a result, prices are both lower overall and more consistent worldwide. Increasingly, production is oriented to the world market.

Trade is not without drawbacks, however, when seen from a political rather than purely economic vantage point (see p. 234). One drawback is familiar from the preceding discussions of international security—long-term benefits may incur short-term costs. When a state begins to import goods that it had been producing domestically, there may be disruptions to its economy: workers may need to retrain and find new jobs, and capital (such as factories) may not be easy to convert to new uses. Another problem is that its benefits and costs tend not to be evenly distributed *within* a state. Some industries or communities may benefit at the expense of others. For example, if a U.S. manufacturing company moves its factory to Mexico to take advantage of cheaper labor there, and exports its goods back to the United States, the workers at the old U.S. factory lose their jobs, but U.S. consumers enjoy cheaper goods. The costs of such a move fall heavily on a few workers, but the benefits are spread thinly across many consumers. This kind of unequal distribution of costs and benefits often creates political problems even when the *overall* economic benefits outweigh the costs.

Between states (as well as within each state) the distribution of benefits from trade can also be unequal. The new wealth created by international trade can be divided in any manner between the participants. For instance, it would be worthwhile for Saudi Arabia to import cars even at a price much higher than what it cost Japan to produce them, as long as the price was less than what it would cost Saudi Arabia to produce cars itself (or to buy them elsewhere). Similarly, Saudi Arabia would profit from selling oil even at a price just a bit above what the oil costs to produce (or what it can sell the oil for elsewhere). With so much added value from the exchange process, there is a great deal of room for bargaining over the distribution of benefits.

Atlas CD
Japan Auto
Industry
Photo

If there were only two states in the world, the bargaining over prices (that is, over the distribution of benefits from trade) would essentially be a political process entailing the use of leverage, possibly including military force. But in a world of many states (and even more substate economic actors such as companies and households), this is less true. Prices are set instead by market competition. If Japan's cars are too expensive, Saudi Arabia can buy German cars; if Saudi oil is too expensive, Japan can buy Alaskan oil.

Prices and Markets   The *terms* of an exchange are defined by the price at which goods are traded. Often the *bargaining space*—defined by the difference between the lowest price a seller would accept and the highest price a buyer would pay—is quite large. For example, Saudi Arabia would be willing to sell a barrel of oil (if it had no better option) for as little as, say, $10 a barrel, and industrialized countries are willing to pay as much as $50 a barrel for the oil. (In practice, oil prices have fluctuated in this broad range in recent decades.) How are prices determined within this range? That is, how do the participants decide on the distribution of benefits from the exchange?

When there are multiple buyers and sellers of a good (or equivalent goods that can be substituted for it), prices are determined by market competition. In terms of the above bargaining framework, sellers bargain for a high price, using as leverage the threat to sell to another buyer. Meanwhile buyers bargain for a low price, with the leverage being a threat to buy from another seller. In practice, free markets are supposed to (and sometimes do) produce stable patterns of buying and selling at a fairly uniform price. At this *market price*, sellers know that an effort to raise the price would drive the buyer to seek another seller, and buyers know that an effort to lower the price would drive the seller to seek another buyer. Because of this stability, the process of bargaining is greatly simplified and most economic exchanges take place in a fairly routine manner.

Buyers vary in the value they place on an item (like a barrel of oil); if the price rises, fewer people are willing to buy it, and if the price drops, more people are willing to buy it. This is called the *demand curve* for the item. Sellers also vary in the value they place on the item. If the price rises, more sellers are willing to supply the item to buyers; if the price drops, fewer sellers are willing to supply the item. This is called the *supply curve*.

In a free market, the price at which the supply and demand curves cross is the *equilibrium* price. At this price sellers are willing to supply the same number of units that buyers are willing to purchase. (In practice, prices reflect *expectations* about supply and demand in the near future.) In a trade of Saudi oil for Japanese cars, for example, the prices would be determined by the world demand for, and supply of, oil and cars.

Thus, in liberal economics, *bilateral* relations between states are less important than they are in security affairs. The existence of world markets reduces the leverage that one state can exert over another in economic affairs (the second state can simply find other partners). Imagine Japan trying to exert power by refusing to sell cars to Saudi Arabia. It would only hurt itself; Saudi Arabia would buy cars elsewhere. In IPE, then, power is more diffuse and involves more actors at once than in international security.

The currency in which world prices are expressed is somewhat arbitrary. Prices were once pegged to the value of gold or silver. Now prices are expressed in national currencies, most prominently the U.S. dollar, Japanese yen, and German mark. In practice, the conversion of money among national currencies is complex (see p. 241), but for the sake of simplicity we may proceed as if there were a common currency.

Centrally Planned Economies
One major alternative to a market economy is a **centrally planned** (or *command*) **economy**, in which political authorities set prices and decide on quotas for production and consumption of each commodity according to a long-term plan. This type of economy was for decades the standard in the communist states of the former Soviet Union, Eastern Europe, China, and several smaller countries (it is still in place in Cuba and North Korea). Within the Soviet economic bloc (which included Eastern Europe and Mongolia), international trade also took place at government-controlled prices.

The proponents of central planning claimed it would make economies both more rational and more just. By controlling the economy, governments could guarantee the basic needs of citizens and could mobilize the state fully for war if necessary. Proponents of central planning also hoped that government's long-term view of resources and needs would smooth out the business cycles and avoid the recessions that periodically afflict capitalist economies.

Instead, communist economics has in recent years been discredited as hopelessly inefficient and discarded in whole or in part by virtually all of its former followers. The **transitional economies** of Russia and Eastern Europe stagnated over the Cold War decades while environmental damage and military spending both took an increasing eco-

Atlas CD
Moscow
Market Prices
Photo, Music

Dustbin of History   The unreliable, polluting East German Trabant car reflected the inefficiency of production in the centrally planned economies of the communist countries during the Cold War era. All those countries are now making transitions—by various routes and with various degrees of success—toward market-based economies. This Trabant in East Berlin was discarded as Germany unified, 1990.

nomic toll. Now the former Soviet republics and Eastern Europe are almost all trying to make a *transition* to a market-based economy connected to the world capitalist economy. This transition has proven very difficult. In the first half of the 1990s, the total GDP of the region *shrank* by about *35 percent*—a great depression worse than the one the United States experienced in the early 1930s (see p. 254). Living standards dropped dramatically for most citizens. A program of *shock therapy*— a radical, sudden shift over to market principles—seemed to work in Poland despite short-term dislocation. But a similar program in Russia stalled (or was effectively blocked by old-time communist officials). Through the final years of the Yeltsin administration, Russia's economy remained dysfunctional, owing to depression, corruption, tax delinquency, and the vast differences between the old communist and new capitalist models.

China, whose government continues to follow a Marxist *political* line (central control by the Communist party), has shifted substantially toward a market *economy*. This transition dramatically increased China's economic growth in the 1980s, reaching a sustained annual rate of about 10 percent throughout the 1990s (see pp. 374–377). Perhaps because China is not yet industrialized (and hence is more flexible about how it invests capital profitably), the introduction of market principles in China's economy has been less painful than in the "developed" (but actually mal-developed) economies of Russia and Eastern Europe.

Today, the world's economic activity follows the principles of free markets more than central planning but often falls somewhere between the extremes. Many governments control domestic prices on some goods (for instance, subsidizing certain goods to win political support). Many states *own* (all or part of) industries thought to be vital for the national economy—**state-owned industries** such as oil production companies or national airlines. Some types of goods, such as electricity service, would be inefficient for competing suppliers to provide (each with its own transmission lines running along the street); in such cases governments often regulate prices or supply the service themselves. Also, the government sector of the economy (military spending, road building, Social Security, and so on) makes up a substantial fraction of the industrialized countries' economies. Because they contain both some government control and some private ownership, the economies of the industrialized West are called **mixed economies**.

Politics of Markets A free and efficient market requires a fairly large number of buyers looking for the same item and a large number of sellers supplying it. It also requires that participants have fairly complete information about the other participants and transactions in the market. Also, the willingness of participants to deal with each other should not be distorted by personal (or political) preferences but should be governed only by price and quality considerations. Failures to meet these various conditions are called *market imperfections*: they reduce efficiency (to the dismay of liberal economists). Most political intrusions into economic transactions are market imperfections.

International trade occurs more often at world market prices than does *domestic* economic exchange. No world government owns industries, provides subsidies, or regulates prices. Nonetheless, world markets are often affected by politics. When states are the principal actors in international economic affairs, the number of participants is often small. When there is just one supplier of an item—a *monopoly*—the supplier can set the price quite high. An *oligopoly* is a monopoly shared by just a few large sellers—often allowing for tacit or explicit coordination to force the price up. To the extent that companies band together along national lines, monopolies and oligopolies are more likely.

Governments can use antitrust policies to break up monopolies and keep markets competitive. But home governments often *benefit* from the ability of their companies to distort international markets and gain revenue, whether those companies are state-owned or just taxed by the state. *Foreign* governments have little power to break up such monopolies.

Another common market imperfection in international trade is *corruption*; individuals may receive payoffs to trade at nonmarket prices. The government or company involved may lose some of the benefits being distributed, but the individual government official or company negotiator gets increased benefits (see pp. 377–379).

Politics provides the *legal framework* for markets—assuring that participants keep their commitments, that buyers pay for goods they have purchased, that counterfeit money is not used, and so forth. In the international economy, lacking a central government authority, rules are less easily enforced. As in security affairs, such rules can be codified in international treaties, but enforcement depends on practical reciprocity (see p. 312).

Taxation is another political influence on markets. Taxes are used both to generate revenue for the government and to regulate economic activity by incentives. For instance, a government may keep taxes low on foreign companies in hopes of attracting them to locate and invest in the country. Taxes applied to international trade itself, called tariffs, are a frequent source of international conflict (see "Protectionism," p. 223).

Political interference in free markets is most explicit when governments apply *sanctions* against economic interactions of certain kinds or between certain actors. Political power then prohibits an economic exchange that would otherwise have been mutually beneficial. The United States maintained trade restrictions on 22 states (as of 1998) in response to those states' political actions, such as human rights violations.

Enforcing sanctions is always a difficult task, because there is a financial incentive to break the sanctions through black markets or other means. For instance, despite UN sanctions against trading with Serbia in the early 1990s, many people and companies took risks to smuggle goods across Serbia's borders, because doing so was profitable. Without broad multilateral support for international sanctions, they generally fail. When the United States tried to punish the Soviet Union in the 1970s by applying trade sanctions against a Soviet oil pipeline to Western Europe, it did not stop the pipeline. It just took profitable business away from a U.S. company (Caterpillar) and allowed European companies to profit instead (because European states did not join in the sanctions).

The difficulty of applying sanctions reflects a more general point made earlier—that power in IPE is more diffused among states than it is in security affairs. If one state tries to use economic means of leverage to influence another, other states can profitably take over. Refusing to participate in mutually profitable economic trade often harms oneself more than the target of one's actions, unless nearly all other states follow suit.

Atlas CD
U.S.–Sanctioned Cuban Cigars
Photo

Balance of Trade
Mercantilists favor political control of trade so that trade relations serve a state's political interests—even at the cost of some lost wealth that free markets might have created. Their preferred means of accomplishing this end is to create a favorable balance of trade. The **balance of trade** is the value of a state's imports relative to its exports.

A state that exports more than it imports has a *positive balance of trade*, or *trade surplus*. Japan has run a trade surplus in recent years: it gets more money for cars and other goods it exports than it pays for oil and other imported goods. A state that imports more than it exports has a *negative balance of trade (trade deficit)*. A trade deficit is different from a budget deficit in government spending. In the late 1990s, the U.S. budget deficit became a surplus, but the U.S. trade deficit kept growing. It reached hundreds of billions of dollars per year by 1999, with the majority accounted for by Japan, China, and Taiwan.

The balance of trade must ultimately be reconciled, one way or another. It is tracked financially through the system of national accounts (see pp. 249–250). In the short term, a state can trade for a few years at a deficit and then for a few years at a surplus. The imbalances are carried on the national accounts as a kind of loan. But a trade deficit that persists for years becomes a problem for the state. Japan in recent years has run a trade surplus overall (and in U.S.-Japanese bilateral trade) while the United States has run a deficit. To balance trade, the United States then "exports" currency (dollars) to Japan, which can use the dollars to buy such things as shares of U.S. companies, U.S. treasury bills, or U.S. real estate. In essence (oversimplifying a bit), a state with a chronic trade deficit must export part of its standing wealth (real estate, companies, bank accounts, etc.) by giving ownership of such wealth to foreigners.

This is one reason mercantilists favor national economic policies to create a trade surplus. Then the state can "own" parts of other states, which gives it power over them. Rather than being indebted to others, the state holds IOUs from others. Rather than being unable to find the money it might need to cope with a crisis or fight a war, the state sits on a pile of money representing potential power. Historically, mercantilism literally meant stockpiling gold (gained from running a trade surplus) as a fungible form

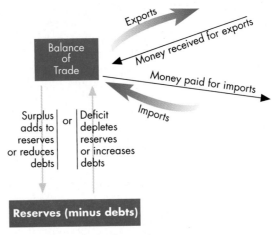

FIGURE 5.2 Balance of Trade

of power (see Figure 5.2). Such a strategy is attuned to realism's emphasis on relative power. For one state to have a trade surplus, another must have a deficit.

There is a price for mercantilist-derived power. Often a trade surplus lowers the short-term standard of living. For instance, if the Japanese people cashed in their trade surplus each year for imported goods, they could enjoy those goods now instead of piling up money for the future. Mercantilists are willing to pay such short-term costs because they are more concerned with power than with standards of living.

Interdependence
When the well-being of a state depends on the cooperation of a second state, the first state is *dependent* on the second. When two or more states are simultaneously dependent on each other, they are *interdependent*. **Interdependence** is a political and not just economic phenomenon. States that trade become mutually dependent on each other's *political* cooperation in order to realize economic gains through trade. In IPE, interdependence refers less often to a *bilateral* mutual dependence than to a *multilateral* dependence in which each state depends on the political cooperation of most or all of the others to keep world markets operating efficiently. Most states depend on the world market, not on specific trading partners (though for large industrialized states each bilateral trade relationship is important as well).

The mutual dependence of two or more states does not mean that their degree of dependence is equal or symmetrical. Often one is more dependent than another. This is especially true because world markets vary in their openness and efficiency from one commodity and region to another. Saudi Arabia, for instance, has more power over the price of oil than Japan has over the price of cars.

The degree of a state's *short-term* dependence on another may differ from its *long-term* dependence. The short-term dislocation that is caused by disrupting exchange with another country is called the *sensitivity* of supply. When oil prices rose sharply in the early 1970s, Japan and other industrialized states did not have policies to cope with the

Unsettling Changes   Growing trade makes states more interdependent. This may make them more peaceful, but can also introduce new insecurities and sources of conflict. Free trade creates both winners and losers. Backlash against free-trade agreements led to a spectacular failure at the WTO summit meeting in Seattle, 1999. As environmentalists and labor unions led protests in the streets, the assembled states could not agree on an agenda for a new round of trade talks.

increases: they were *sensitive* to the disruption, and long lines formed at gas stations. Over the longer term, states may be able to change their policies to take advantage of alternatives that could substitute for disrupted trade. Japan then expanded nuclear power in response to oil price increases—a long-term strategy. A state that *cannot* adjust its policies to cope with disrupted trade, even over the long run, suffers from *vulnerability* of supply.

Over time, as the world economy develops and technology advances, states are becoming *increasingly interdependent*. Some IR scholars point out that this is not entirely new. The great powers were very interdependent before World War I; for instance, international trade was about the same percentage of GDP then as now. But several other dimensions of interdependence show dramatic change. One is the extent to which individual *firms*, which used to be nationally based, now are international in their holdings and interests (becoming MNCs), which makes them dependent on the well-being of other states in addition to their home state and makes them tend to favor free trade.

Another key aspect of interdependence is the tight integration of world markets through the ever-expanding flow of *information* and communication worldwide (see pp.

432–438). This facilitates the free competition of goods and services in global markets as well as the expanding volume of money (capital) that moves around the world every day. Yet another dimension of change is the expansion of *scope* in the global economy, from one based in Europe to a more diffuse network encompassing the world. The rise of China and Southeast Asia, and the integration of Russia and Eastern Europe into the world market economy in the 1990s, are accelerating this trend.

Whether based on a specific bilateral trading relationship, an integrated global (or regional) market, or the international nature of corporate holdings, interdependence arises from comparative advantage—that is, from the greater absolute wealth that two or more states can produce by collaborating. This wealth depends on international political cooperation, which is therefore in the interests of all participants. Furthermore, violence is usually not an effective leverage in bringing about such cooperation. Thus, many IR scholars argue that *interdependence inherently promotes peace*. It alters the cost-benefit calculations of national leaders so as to make military leverage less attractive. (Some IR scholars saw similar trends in international interdependence just before World War I, but war occurred anyway.)

Despite the added wealth that states enjoy as a result of trade and the power that such wealth creates, interdependence does have drawbacks. The more a state gains from trade cooperation, the more its own well-being depends on other states, which therefore have power over it. In situations of asymmetrical interdependence, in particular, the economic benefits of cooperation may come with inherent vulnerabilities. For example, it is cheaper for Japan to import energy than to produce it domestically, but dependence on energy imports has historically put Japan at a disadvantage in terms of international power. Exports as well as imports can create dependence; UN sanctions against Iraq's oil exports deprived it of revenue after its 1990 invasion of Kuwait.

Web Link
Trade and
Conflict

Interdependence thus ties the well-being of a state's population and society to policies and conditions in other states, outside its control. The price of trade-generated wealth (and the power it brings) is a loss of state autonomy and sovereignty. These problems are intensifying as world markets become more closely interwoven, especially in regional integration such as in Europe (see Chapter 6).

As states become more interdependent, power is becoming more, not less, important in IR. The intensification of linkages among states multiplies the number of issues affecting the relations of states and the avenues of influence by which outcomes are shaped. It is true that because power operates on multiple complex dimensions in a highly interdependent world, the importance of one dimension—military power—is gradually diminishing relative to other means of influence (diplomatic, economic, cultural, etc.). But the overall importance of international power on all dimensions combined is increasing as the world becomes more interdependent.

Trade Strategies

To manage the trade-offs of gains and losses in power and wealth, states develop economic strategies—trade strategies in particular—that seek to maximize their own wealth while minimizing their vulnerability and dependence on others. Some strategies can be implemented by single states; most involve participation in some broader framework.

Autarky

One obvious way to avoid becoming dependent on other states, especially for weak states whose trading partners would tend to be more powerful, is to avoid trading and instead try to produce everything one needs by oneself. Such a strategy is called *self-reliance* or **autarky**. As the theory of comparative advantage suggests, such a policy has proven ineffective. A self-reliant state pays a very high cost to produce goods for which it does not have a comparative advantage. As other states cooperate among themselves to maximize their joint creation of wealth, the autarkic state tends to be left further and further behind. Over time, its relative power in the international system falls.

China's experience illustrates the problems with autarky. China's economic isolation in the 1950s and 1960s, resulting from an economic embargo imposed by the United States and its allies, was deepened during its own Cultural Revolution in the late 1960s when it broke ties with the Soviet Union as well. In that period, all things foreign were rejected. For instance, Chinese computer programmers were not allowed to use foreign software such as Assembler language and Fortran—standards in the rest of the world. When China opened up to the world economy in the 1980s, the pattern was reversed. The rapid expansion of trade, along with some market-oriented reforms in its domestic economy, resulted in rapid economic growth, which continued into the late 1990s.

Protectionism

Although few states pursue strategies of autarky, many states try to manipulate international trade so as to strengthen one or more domestic industries and shelter them from world markets. Such policies are broadly known as **protectionism**—protection of domestic industries from international competition. Although this term encompasses a variety of trade policies arising from various motivations, all are contrary to liberalism in that they seek to distort free markets to gain an advantage for the state (or substate actors within it), generally by discouraging imports of competing goods or services.

Government policies discouraging imports can help domestic industries or communities avoid the costs inherent in full participation in world markets. Such costs often fall disproportionately on a small part of the population and lead that group to pressure the government for protection. The benefits of greater global efficiency, by contrast, are spread more broadly across the population and do not create similar domestic pressures.

A state's *motivation* to protect domestic industry can arise from several sources. Often governments simply cater to the political demands of important domestic industries and interests, regardless of the overall national interest. An industry may lobby or give campaign contributions in order to win special tax breaks, subsidies, or restrictions on competing imports (see "Industries and Interest Groups," p. 226).

States often attempt to protect an *infant industry* as it starts up in the state for the first time, until it can compete on world markets. In a number of poor states, the *textile* trade has been a favored infant industry (adding value without heavy capital requirements) that governments have protected. Protection of infant industry is considered a relatively legitimate reason for (temporary) protectionism.

Another motivation for protection is to give a domestic industry breathing room when market conditions shift or new competitors arrive on the scene. Sometimes domestic industry requires time to adapt and can emerge a few years later in a healthy condition. When gas prices jumped in the 1970s, U.S. auto producers were slow to shift to smaller cars, and smaller Japanese cars gained a great advantage in the U.S.

market. The U.S. government used a variety of measures, including import quotas and loan guarantees, to help the U.S. industry through this transition.

Yet another motivation is the protection of industry considered vital to national security. In the 1980s U.S. officials sought to protect the U.S. electronics and computer industries against being driven out of business by Japanese competitors, because those industries were considered crucial to military production. A government-sponsored consortium of U.S. computer-chip companies called Sematech was formed to promote the U.S. capability to produce chips cheaply (ordinarily the government would discourage such a consortium as an antitrust violation). Autarky may not pay in most economic activities, but for military goods states are often willing to sacrifice some economic efficiency for the sake of self-sufficiency. Then, in the event of war the state will be less vulnerable.

Finally, protection may be motivated by a defensive effort to ward off predatory practices by foreign companies or states. *Predatory* generally refers to efforts to unfairly capture a large share of world markets, or even a near-monopoly, so that eventually the predator can raise prices without fearing competition. Most often these efforts entail **dumping** products in foreign markets at prices below the minimum necessary to make a profit. In 1992, Japan was accused of dumping minivans on the U.S. market. How can a company make money selling its products below cost, and why would the importing state complain about such a good deal? It is indeed a good deal for U.S. consumers in the short term, but it weakens the competing U.S. automobile industry in the longer term. The reason a state would want its companies to dump products in foreign markets is that money lost in the short term could lead to dominance of a market, which eventually lets the state's companies raise prices enough to recoup their losses and to profit more.

Within a domestic economy, the government can use antitrust laws to break up an impending monopoly, but in IR no such mechanism exists, so governments try to restrict imports in such situations to protect their state's industries. Such restrictions are recognized as legitimate, but there are great disagreements about whether a given price level is predatory or merely competitive.

Just as there are several motivations for protectionism, so too governments use several methods to restrict imports. The simplest is a **tariff** (or *duty*)—a tax imposed on certain types of imported goods (usually as a percentage of their value) as they enter the country. Tariffs not only restrict imports but also can be an important source of state revenues. If a state is going to engage in protectionism, international norms favor tariffs as the preferred method of protection because they are straightforward and not hidden (see p. 230).

Other means to discourage imports are **non-tariff barriers** to trade. Imports can be limited by a *quota*. Quotas are ceilings on how many goods of a certain kind can be imported; they are imposed to restrict the growth of such imports. The extreme version is a flat prohibition against importing a certain type of good (or goods from a certain country). The U.S. government used quotas to restrict the number of Japanese-made cars that could enter the United States in the 1980s, when the U.S. automobile industry was losing ground rapidly to Japanese imports. Most of those quotas were *voluntary* in that Japan and the United States negotiated a level that both could live with. A disadvantage of this type of quota (based on number, not value) is that Japan could raise the price of its cars (demand remained while supply was restricted) and shift its exports

We Can't Compete

Protectionism uses various means to keep foreign imports from competing with domestic products. Agricultural subsidies, an important non-tariff barrier to trade, are on the WTO agenda and are politically sensitive. Here, Spanish farmers protest European Union imports of Moroccan tomatoes, 2000.

toward more expensive cars. This increased the profits of Japanese automakers relative to their U.S. counterparts. Partly using these profits, Japanese companies then set up their own factories within the United States. These competed effectively with the U.S. automobile companies. U.S. jobs, but not U.S. companies, were protected.

A third way to protect domestic industry is by *subsidies* to a domestic industry, which allow it to lower its prices without losing money. Such subsidies are extensive in, but not limited to, state-owned industries. Subsidies can be funneled to industries in a variety of ways. A state can give *tax breaks* to an industry struggling to get established or facing strong foreign competition. It can make *loans* (or guarantee private loans) on favorable terms to companies in a threatened industry. Sometimes governments buy goods from domestic producers at high *guaranteed prices* and resell them on world markets at lower prices; the European Community does this with agricultural products, to the dismay of U.S. farmers, as does the United States, to the dismay of European farmers.

Fourth, imports can be restricted by *restrictions and regulations* that make it hard to distribute and market a product even when it can be imported. In marketing U.S. products in Japan, U.S. manufacturers often complain of complex bureaucratic regulations and a tight system of corporate alliances funneling the supply of parts from Japanese suppliers to Japanese manufacturers. Imports can also be discouraged by restricting a foreign manufacturer's ability to advertise in local markets. Finally, when a state nationalizes an entire industry, such as oil production or banking, foreign competition is shut out.

Sometimes a country's culture, rather than state action, discourages imports. Citizens may (with or without government encouragement) follow a philosophy of *economic nationalism*—use of economics to influence international power and relative standing in the international system (a form of mercantilism). Many U.S. citizens ignore the advice of liberal economists to buy the best car they can find at the best price, regardless of where it is produced—to participate freely in an international marketplace. Many

Web Link
Subsidies

U.S. citizens prefer to "Buy American" even if it means paying a bit more for an equivalent product. Although such a bias reduces the overall efficiency of world production, it does result in more benefits being distributed to U.S. workers. In Japan, consumers have shown a preference for Japanese-made products even when their government has urged them to buy more imported goods (to reduce Japanese trade frictions with the United States).

Protectionism has both positive and negative effects on an economy, most often helping producers but hurting consumers. For instance, although U.S. automobile manufacturers were aided somewhat by the restrictions imposed on Japanese imports in the 1980s, U.S. automobile consumers paid more for cars as a result (several hundred dollars more per car by some estimates). The costs to consumers may outweigh the benefits to producers (as liberal economists stress), but those costs are spread among millions of households, whereas the benefits are concentrated on a few firms, which are more motivated and politically more powerful. Another problem with protectionism is that domestic industry may use protection to avoid needed improvements and may therefore remain inefficient and uncompetitive—especially if protection continues over many years.

Although it violates liberal principles, temporary protectionism can have a stabilizing effect under certain conditions. When U.S. motorcycle manufacturer Harley-Davidson lost half its U.S. market share in just four years, the U.S. government imposed tariffs on imported Japanese motorcycles. The tariffs started at 45 percent in 1983; they were to decline each year for five years and then be eliminated. With the clock running, Harley scrambled to improve efficiency and raise quality. As a result, Harley regained its market share and the tariffs were lifted a year early. In the late 1980s, a reinvigorated Harley raised its market share even more and began exporting Harleys to Japan. Protectionism worked in this case because it was short-term and straightforward. Most protectionist policies are longer-term, more complex, and more likely to backfire.

Web Link
Interest Groups

Industries and Interest Groups Industries and other domestic political actors often seek to influence a state's foreign economic policies (see "Interest Groups," pp. 107–108). These pressures do not always favor protectionism. Industries that are advanced and competitive in world markets often try to influence their governments to adopt free-trade policies. This strategy promotes a global free-trade system in which such industries can prosper. By contrast, industries that lag behind their global competitors tend to seek government restrictions on imports or other forms of protection.

Means to influence foreign economic policy include lobbying, forming PACs, paying bribes, even encouraging coups. Actors include industry-sponsored groups, companies, labor unions, and individuals. Within an industry, such efforts usually work in a common direction because, despite competition among companies and between management and labor, all share common interests regarding the trade policies. However, a different industry may be pushing in a different direction. For instance, some U.S. industries supported the North American Free Trade Agreement (NAFTA); others opposed it.

A good example of how competing domestic interests can pull in opposite directions on state trade policy is U.S. tobacco exports. U.S. companies have a comparative advantage globally in producing cigarettes. As the U.S. market for cigarettes shrank in the 1980s (due to education about the dangers of smoking), manufacturers more aggressively marketed U.S. cigarettes overseas. They challenged regulations in foreign countries restricting cigarette advertising, claiming that these regulations were protectionist measures aimed at excluding a U.S. product from lucrative markets. In the late 1980s, the U.S. government sided with the U.S. tobacco companies and pressed foreign states to open their markets to U.S. cigarettes, threatening retaliatory trade measures if they refused. Health groups such as the American Cancer Society opposed such U.S. policies, which they saw as unethical. But with the U.S. government's help, the tobacco companies racked up high profits from rapidly growing sales in new foreign markets.

In many countries, government not only responds to industry influence, but works actively with industries to promote their growth and tailor trade policy to their needs. Such **industrial policy** is especially common in states where one or two industries are crucial to the entire economy (and of course where states own industries directly). But it is becoming a major issue in economic relations among great powers as well. In Japan (where industries are mostly not state-owned), the government coordinates industrial policy through the powerful Ministry of International Trade and Industry (MITI), which has had both successes and failures in recent decades. In the Clinton administration, the United States moved toward a more active industrial policy.

Atlas CD
Japan
Electronics
Photo

Interest groups not organized along industry lines also have particular interests in state trade policies. U.S. environmentalists, for example, do not want U.S. companies to use NAFTA to avoid pollution controls by relocating to Mexico (where environmental laws are less strict). U.S. labor unions do not want companies to use NAFTA to avoid paying high wages. However, Mexican-American citizens' groups in the United States tend to support NAFTA because it strengthens ties to relatives in Mexico.

Several industries are particularly important in trade negotiations currently. First is agriculture, which traditionally has been protected from foreign competition on grounds that self-sufficiency in food reduces national vulnerability (especially in time of war). Although such security concerns have now faded somewhat, farmers are well-organized and powerful domestic political actors in Japan, Europe, the United States, and other countries. In France, farmers enjoy wide political support and have a huge stake in the trade policies of the European Community; subsidies to farmers in France (and elsewhere in Europe) protect them against competition from U.S. farmers.

Atlas CD
Agricultural
Trade
Photo Tour

Intellectual property rights are a second contentious area of trade negotiations. Intellectual property rights are the rights of creators of books, films, computer software, and similar products to receive royalties when their products are sold. The United States has a major conflict with some third world states over piracy of computer software, music, films, and other creative works—products in which the United States has a strong comparative advantage globally. It is technically easy and cheap to copy such works and sell them in violation of the copyright, patent, or trademark. Because U.S. laws cannot be enforced in foreign countries, the U.S. government wants foreign governments to prevent and punish such violations. In 1991, the United States threatened China with punitive tariffs unless China enforced a new copyright law. An agreement was reached in 1992, but lack of progress led to the brink of a trade war in 1995. Infringement of intellectual property rights is widespread in many third world countries, on products ranging from videotaped movies to prescription drugs. But the situation is changing: in 1996, for instance, 160 states signed two new treaties covering copyrights for written materials and sound recordings.

Export Product   Intellectual property rights have been an important focus of recent trade negotiations. Here, the U.S. film *Titanic* is being advertised in China, 1998. Under recent agreements, China is to respect copyrights, for example by paying royalties for showing a movie. In many countries, pirated copies of videos, music, and software sell on streets with no royalty payments.

Another key trade issue is the openness of countries to trade in the **service sector** of the economy. This sector includes many services, especially those concerning information, but the key focus in international trade negotiations is on banking, insurance, and related financial services. U.S. companies enjoy a comparative advantage in these areas because of their information-processing technologies and experience in financial management. The North American Free Trade Agreement (NAFTA) allows U.S. banks and insurance companies to operate in Mexico. In general, as telecommunications become cheaper and more pervasive, services offered by companies in one country can be efficiently used by consumers in other countries.

Another especially important industry in international trade is the arms trade, which operates largely outside of the framework of normal commercial transactions because of its national security implications. Governments in industrialized countries want to protect their domestic arms industries rather than rely on imports to meet their weapons needs. And those domestic arms industries become stronger and more economically viable by exporting their products (as well as supplying their own governments). Governments usually participate actively in the military-industrial sector of the economy, even in countries such as the United States that lack industrial policy in other economic sectors (see p. 108). Even when arms-exporting countries agree in principle to try to limit arms exports to a region—as the great powers did for the Middle East in

1991—they have found it extremely difficult to give up the power and profits that such arms exports bring.

Major weapons such as fighter jets are another class of products for which the United States enjoys a global comparative advantage. Indeed, the United States leads the sale of arms internationally, with nearly one-third of the $23 billion in such sales world-wide in 1998. (Germany and France together made up another third, and Russia fell to less than 8 percent of the total.) Generally the world arms market has declined somewhat in the post–Cold War era, despite an arms-buying spree early in the 1990s following the Gulf War. In recent years, the U.S. arms industry, like the tobacco industry, has looked overseas for new customers to offset declining demand at home. The Middle East has been and still is the leading arms-importing region of the global South.

ILLICIT TRADE A different problem is presented by the "industry" of illicit trade, or smuggling. No matter what restrictions governments put on trading certain goods, someone is usually willing to risk punishment to make a profit in such trade. Smuggling exists because it is profitable to sell fake Taiwanese copies of Microsoft Corporation's MS-DOS in Germany, or Colombian cocaine in the United States, even though these products are illegal in those countries. Even with legal goods, profits can be increased by evading tariffs (by moving goods secretly, mislabeling them, or bribing customs officials).

Illegal goods, and legal goods imported illegally, often are sold in black markets—unofficial, sometimes secret markets. Black markets are widespread, and flourish particularly in economies heavily regulated by government, such as centrally planned economies. In many third world countries, black markets are a substantial (though hard to measure) fraction of the total economic activity and deprive the government of significant revenue. Black markets also exist for foreign currency exchange (see p. 241).

The extent of illicit trade varies from one country and industry to another, depending on profitability and enforcement. Drugs and weapons are most profitable, and worldwide illegal trade networks exist for both. A state with enough money can buy—although at premium prices—most kinds of weapons.

Different states have different interests in enforcing political control over illicit trade. In illegal arms exports, the exporting state may gain economically from the trade and the importing state gains access to the weapons; the losers are the other exporters that neither got the export revenue nor kept the weapons out of the hands of the importer. Thus, illicit trade often creates conflicts of interest among states and leads to complex political bargaining among governments, each looking after its own interests.

Cooperation in Trade
Successful trade strategies are those that achieve mutual gains from cooperation with other states. A global system of free trade is a collective good. Given no world government, the benefits of trade depend on international cooperation—to enforce contracts, prevent monopolies, and discourage protectionism. A single state can profitably subsidize its own state-owned industries, create its own monopolies, or erect barriers to competitive imports as long as not too many other states do so. If other states break the rules of free trade as well, the benefits of free exchange slip away from all parties involved.

As with international law generally, economic agreements between states depend strongly on reciprocity for enforcement (see pp. 58–59, 312). If one state protects its industries, or puts tariffs on the goods of other states, or violates the copyright on works produced in other countries, the main resort that other states have is to apply similar measures against the offending state. The use of reciprocity to enforce equal terms of exchange is especially important in international trade, where states often negotiate complex agreements—commodity by commodity, industry by industry—based on reciprocity.

Enforcement of fair trade is complicated by differing interpretations of what is fair. States generally decide what practices of other states they consider unfair (often prodded by affected domestic industries) and then take (or threaten) retaliatory actions to punish those practices. One disadvantage of reciprocity is that it can lead to a downward spiral of noncooperation, popularly called a trade war (the economic equivalent of the arms races discussed on p. 59). To prevent this, states often negotiate agreements regarding what practices they consider unfair. In some cases, third-party arbitration can also be used to resolve trade disputes.

Retaliation for unfair trade practices usually is based on an attempt to match the violation in type and extent. For instance, European barriers to U.S. food exports caused the United States to raise barriers to food imports from Europe. An arbitration panel set up under the GATT (discussed shortly) ruled in early 1992 against the European subsidies, permitting U.S. retaliation if Europe did not lower the barriers. The U.S. government then threatened to impose tariffs of up to 100 percent on $1 billion of imported European "fine foods" such as wine and cheese. The list of European products drawn up by the U.S. trade representative included $2 billion of possible target imports—with a focus on French products because French farmers were considered the main political force behind the European agricultural subsidies. In late 1992, at the last minute, the U.S. and European Community negotiators reached agreement on the phased reduction of European subsidies and a trade war was averted.

In cases of dumping, retaliation is aimed at offsetting the advantage enjoyed by goods imported at prices below the world market. Retaliatory tariffs raise the price back to market levels. For example, U.S. automakers complained to the U.S. government in 1991 that Japanese carmakers were dumping minivans on the U.S. market at below-production cost, in an aggressive effort to take away market share from U.S. producers in one of their few remaining areas of strength. (U.S. producers held 88 percent of the U.S. minivan market, but Japanese producers had gone from 3 to 12 percent in three years.) In 1992, the Commerce Department ruled that Mazda and Toyota had sold minivans in the United States below fair market value. It proposed the use of tariffs to raise prices back to market levels.

Web Link
International
Trade
Commission

Before such tariffs are imposed, another U.S. government agency, the International Trade Commission (ITC), decides whether the low-priced imports have actually hurt the U.S. industry. Meanwhile, importers must put down deposits with the government equal to the difference from market prices. The ITC ruled that U.S. automakers had indeed been hurt, though the minivans were still profitable at prices reduced by Japanese imports. The deposits were kept, and tariffs were imposed on the imported minivans. As a result, U.S. consumers paid substantially more for both domestic and imported minivans.

In this case, there was no third-party ruling as in the European farm subsidy case. The United States unilaterally decided that minivans were being dumped and retaliated in its own way. The Japanese companies disagreed and claimed that their pricing of minivans within Japan was comparable. In fact, the Japanese companies saw the entire incident as election-year pandering by the U.S. government. Was it fair retaliation for unfair trade or an unfair tariff imposed on fair trade? The two sides disagreed.

In practice, states keep close track of the exact terms of trades. Large bureaucracies monitor international economic transactions (prices relative to world market levels, tariffs, etc.) and develop detailed policies to reciprocate another state's deviations from cooperation. In the mid-1990s the United States brought more than two dozen complaints to the WTO (discussed shortly), ranging from European banana tariffs to Japanese liquor taxes to Canadian postal rates. In 1997 the United States issued a report listing 46 states (led by Japan) that erected unfair barriers to U.S. products.

Trade cooperation is easier to achieve under hegemony (see pp. 72–74 and 91–92). The efficient operation of markets depends on a stable political framework such as hegemony can provide. Political power can protect economic exchange from the distorting influences of violent leverage, of unfair or fraudulent trade practices, and of uncertainties of international currency rates. A hegemon can provide a world currency in which value can be universally calculated. It can punish the use of violence and can enforce norms of fair trade. Because its economy is so large and dominating, the hegemon has a potent leverage in the threat to break off trade ties, even without resort to military force. For example, to be denied access to U.S. markets today would be a serious punishment for export industries in many states.

U.S. hegemony helped create the major norms and institutions of international trade in the post–1945 era. Now that U.S. hegemony seems to be giving way to a more multipolar world—especially in economic affairs among the great powers—institutions are even more important for the success of the world trading system. The role and operation of the major trade regimes and institutions are the focus of the next section.

Trade Regimes

Trade regimes are the common expectations governments have about the rules for international trade. A variety of partially overlapping regimes concerned with international trade have developed, mostly since World War II. The most central of these is the World Trade Organization.

The World Trade Organization
The **World Trade Organization (WTO)** is a global, multilateral IGO that promotes, monitors, and adjudicates international trade. Together with the regional and bilateral arrangements described shortly, the WTO is central to the overall expectations and practices of states with regard to international trade. The WTO is the successor organization to the **General Agreement on Tariffs and Trade (GATT)**, which was created in 1947 to facilitate freer trade on a multilateral basis. The GATT was more of a negotiating framework than an administrative institution. It did not actually regulate trade. Before the GATT, proposals for a stronger institutional agency had been rejected because of U.S. fears that overregulation would stifle free trade. In addition to its main role as a negotiating forum, the GATT helped to arbitrate trade disputes (as in the European agricultural subsidy case), clarifying the rules and helping states observe them.

In 1995, the GATT became the WTO. The GATT agreements on manufactured goods were subsumed into the WTO framework and then extended to include trade in services and intellectual property. The WTO has some powers of enforcement and an international bureaucracy (500 people), which monitors trade policies and practices in each member state and adjudicates disputes among members. It is unclear how much power the WTO in practice will eventually be able to wield over states. A growing public backlash against free trade (see below) reflects uneasiness about the potential power of a foreign and secretive organization to force changes in democratically passed national laws. But the WTO is the central international institution governing trade and therefore one that almost all countries want to participate in and develop.

Over time, the membership of the WTO has grown, including some states from the former Soviet bloc. Almost all the world's major trading states were among the WTO's 136 members as of 2000. A breakthrough 1999 U.S.-China trade agreement, after 13 years of negotiations, was expected to lead to China's eventual admission. The most notable remaining nonmember is Russia. It is among several dozen countries seeking admission to the WTO. The United States and other countries demand, as a condition of membership, liberalization of the trading practices of would-be members.

The WTO framework is based on the principles of reciprocity—that one state's lowering of trade barriers to another should be matched in return—and of nondiscrimination. The latter principle is embodied in the **most-favored nation (MFN) concept**, which says that trade restrictions imposed by a WTO member on its most-favored trading partner must be applied equally to all other WTO members. If Australia applies a 20 percent tariff on auto parts imported from France, it is not supposed to apply a 40 percent tariff on auto parts imported from the United States. Thus, the WTO does not get rid of barriers to trade altogether but equalizes them in a global framework to create a level playing field for all member states. States are not prevented from protecting their own industries but cannot play favorites among their trading partners. States may also extend MFN status to others that are not WTO members, as the United States has done with China, for example. President Bill Clinton at first tried to use MFN status, which must be renewed annually, as a form of leverage to induce China to change its human rights practices. When this failed, he unlinked human rights and trade relations with China, granting MFN status unconditionally.

An exception to the MFN system is the **Generalized System of Preferences (GSP)** by which industrialized states give trade concessions to third world states to help the latter's economic development. Preferences amount to a promise by rich states to allow imports from poor ones under lower tariffs than those imposed under MFN.

The WTO continues the GATT's role as a negotiating forum for multilateral trade agreements that lower trade barriers on a fair and reciprocal basis. These detailed and complex agreements specify the commitments of various states and regions to lower certain trade barriers by certain amounts on fixed schedules. Almost every commitment entails domestic political costs, because domestic industries lose protection against foreign competition. Even when other states agree to make similar commitments in other areas, lowering of trade barriers is often hard for national governments.

As a result, negotiations on these multilateral agreements are long and difficult. Typically they last for several years or more in a *round of negotiations*; after it is completed the members begin on a new round. Among the five rounds of GATT negotiations from 1947 to 1995, the Kennedy Round in the 1960s—so called because it started during the Kennedy administration—paid special attention to the growing role of the (increasingly integrated) European Economic Community (EEC), which the United States found somewhat threatening. The Tokyo Round (begun in Tokyo) in the 1970s had to adjust rules to new conditions of world interdependence as, for instance, OPEC raised oil prices and Japan began to dominate the automobile export business.

The **Uruguay Round** started in 1986 (in Uruguay). Although the rough outlines of a new GATT agreement emerged after a few years, efforts to wrap up the Uruguay Round failed at five successive G7 summit meetings in 1990–1994. As the round dragged on year after year, participants renamed the GATT the "general agreement to talk and talk." It was estimated that a successful conclusion to the round would add hundreds of billions of dollars to the world economy over the remainder of the decade. But that money was a collective good, which would be enjoyed both by states that made concessions in the final negotiations to reach agreement and by those that did not. Agreement was finally reached in late 1994. The United States had pressured Europe to reduce agricultural subsidies and third world states to protect intellectual property rights. In the end, the United States got some, but not all, of what it wanted. France held out adamantly and won the right to protect its film industry against U.S. films.

From 1947 the GATT tried to encourage states to use import tariffs rather than other means of protecting industries and to lower these over time. The GATT concentrated on manufactured goods and succeeded in substantially reducing the average tariffs. At present, average tariff rates on manufactured goods in the industrialized West are around 10 to 15 percent of the goods' value. Tariff rates in regions of the global South are around 30 percent (reflecting the greater protection that third world industry is seen as needing).

Agricultural trade is politically more sensitive than trade in manufactured goods and was seriously addressed only in the recent Uruguay Round. Trade in services, such as banking and insurance, is another current major focus of the WTO. Such trade approached one-quarter of the total value of world trade in the 1990s. Trade in telecommunications is a related area of interest. In 1997, 70 states (negotiating through the WTO) agreed on a treaty to allow telecommunications companies to enter each other's markets.

The problems in expanding into these and other sensitive areas became obvious at a 1999 Seattle WTO conference, where trade ministers had hoped to launch a new round of trade negotiations. Most industrialized countries wanted to include provisions, in areas such as environmental protection and child labor, that poorer countries considered an attack on their sovereignty and a way to maintain the North's advantage in trade. (The North's main advantage is technology whereas the South's is cheap labor.) The North-South divide had already developed earlier in the year, when the WTO could not agree on a new leader and split the five-year term between a New Zealander supported mostly by the North and a Thai politician supported mainly by the South (especially Asia). In Seattle, where street protests delayed the conference opening by a day, trade ministers could not agree on a new agenda for trade talks and the meeting broke up in failure. With no Seattle round, free-trade advocates were left to work incrementally, piecing together bilateral and regional agreements within existing frameworks.

In general, states continue to participate in the WTO because the benefits, in terms of global wealth creation, outweigh the costs, in terms of harm to domestic industries or painful adjustments in national economies. States try to change the rules in their favor during the rounds of negotiations (never with complete success), and between rounds they try to evade the rules in minor ways. But the overall benefits are too great to jeopardize by nonparticipation or by allowing frequent trade wars to occur.

Web Link
Resistance
to Trade

Resistance to Trade Globalization of the world economy, which includes growing trade and other aspects (see below and Chapters 6–8), has created a backlash in many parts of the world, including the United States. Global-level integration has fueled a countercurrent of growing nationalism in several world regions where people believe their identities and communities are threatened by the penetration of foreign influences (see Chapter 4). Even more fundamental to the backlash against trade are the material dislocations caused by globalization, which directly affect the self-interests of certain segments of a population.

Workers in industrialized countries, in those industries (from steel and automobiles to electronics and clothing) that face increasing competition from low-wage countries in the global South, are among the most adversely affected by free trade. Inevitably, the competition from low-wage countries holds down wages in those industries in the industrialized countries. It also creates pressures to relax standards of labor regulation, such as those protecting worker safety, and it can lead to job losses if manufacturers close down plants in high-wage countries and move operations to the global South. Not surprisingly, labor unions have been among the strongest political opponents of unfettered trade expansion. (Although the United States stands at the center of these debates, other industrialized countries face similar issues.)

Human rights NGOs have joined labor unions in pushing for trade agreements to include requirements for improving working conditions in low-wage countries; these could include laws regarding a minimum wage, child labor, and worker safety. The U.S. Congress in 1997 banned U.S. imports of goods manufactured by South Asia's 15 million indentured (slave) child laborers. Clothing manufacturers such as Nike and Reebok, meanwhile, stung by criticism of "sweatshop" conditions in their Asian factories, adopted a voluntary program to end the worst abuses; critics claimed it would make little difference, however. About 250 million children under age 14 are working in the global South, according to the UN-affiliated International Labor Organization—about 20 percent of 10- to 14-year-olds in Latin America and Asia and 40 percent in Africa.

Environmental groups also have actively opposed the unrestricted expansion of trade, which they see as undermining environmental laws in industrialized countries and promoting environmentally harmful practices worldwide (see p. 416). For example, U.S. regulations require commercial shrimp boats to use devices that prevent endangered species of sea turtles from drowning in shrimp nets. Indonesia, Malaysia, Thailand, and Pakistan, whose shrimp exports to the United States were blocked because they do not require use of such devices, filed a complaint with the World Trade Organization, arguing that the U.S. regulation unfairly discriminated against them. In 1998, the United States lost the WTO ruling and appeal. Sea turtles became a symbol of environmentalist opposition to the WTO.

In general, unrestricted trade tends to force countries to equalize their regulations in a variety of areas not limited to labor and environmental rules. For example, the WTO ruled in 1997 that Europeans' fears about the use of growth hormones in beef were not

Cheap Labor Labor, environmental, and human rights organizations have all criticized unrestricted free trade. They argue that free-trade agreements encourage MNCs to produce goods under unfair and unhealthy conditions, including the use of child labor. This girl in Honduras makes softballs for export to the United States.

scientifically warranted, and therefore the regulations could not be used to exclude U.S. beef containing hormones. When the European Union persisted, the United States was allowed to impose high tariffs on a list of EU exports such as French cheeses. Meanwhile, U.S. consumers harbored fears about pesticide-laced produce grown in Mexico. In 2000, negotiations on a "Biosafety Protocol," to govern trade in genetically modified food and organisms, pitted U.S. exporters against most other states.

These examples illustrate the variety of sources of backlash against free-trade agreements. Labor, environmental, and consumer groups all portray the WTO as a secretive bureaucracy outside democratic control that serves the interests of big corporations at the expense of ordinary people in both the global North and South. The WTO's critics object to its holding all major deliberations behind closed doors. More fundamentally, these critics distrust the corporate-driven globalization of which the WTO is just one symptom.

Opposition to the WTO came together at the 1999 Seattle WTO meeting. Thousands of demonstrators from labor unions and environmental groups—often on opposite sides in the past—joined in street protests to demand that future trade agreements address their concerns. President Clinton, the host, generally endorsed their goals in his speech. However, many representatives of poor countries argued that they needed trade to raise incomes and could not meet the standards of industrialized countries (who had allowed low wages, harsh working conditions, and environmental destruction when *they* began industrializing). Anarchists "trashed" downtown Seattle and police blanketed the area with tear gas, making tangible the malaise then surrounding the WTO.

The benefits of free trade, as was noted earlier, are much more diffuse than the costs. U.S. consumers enjoy lower prices on goods imported from low-wage countries, such as toys from China. The consumers may spend more money on other products and services, eventually employing more U.S. workers. Cheap imports also help keep inflation low, which benefits citizens and politicians. However, unlike workers, consumers are not politically organized, and the diffuse benefits may receive less attention from politicians than the intense, costly disruptions to people who are negatively affected by free trade.

Bilateral and Regional Agreements
Although the WTO provides an overall framework for multilateral trade in a worldwide market, most international trade is governed by more specific international political agreements. These are of two general types—bilateral trade agreements and regional free-trade areas.

BILATERAL AGREEMENTS Bilateral treaties covering trade are reciprocal arrangements to lower barriers to trade between two states. Usually they are fairly specific. For instance, one country may reduce its prohibition on imports on product X (which the second country exports at competitive prices) while the second country lowers its tariff on product Y (which the first country exports).

Part of the idea behind the GATT/WTO was to strip away the maze of bilateral agreements on trade and simplify the system of tariffs and preferences. This effort has only partially succeeded. Bilateral trade agreements continue to play an important role. They have the advantages of reducing the collective goods problem inherent in multilateral negotiations and facilitating reciprocity as a means to achieve cooperation. As the Uruguay Round of GATT negotiations bogged down, some state leaders began to favor bilateral agreements as more achievable than the global GATT/WTO agreements. Inasmuch as most states have only a few most-important trading partners, a few bilateral agreements can go a long way in structuring a state's trade relations.

FREE-TRADE AREAS Regional free-trade areas are also important in the structure of world trade. In such areas, groups of neighboring states agree to remove the entire structure of trade barriers (or most of it) within their area. With outside countries, trade continues to be governed by bilateral treaties and the WTO framework. (A free-trade area resembles a "common market" or "customs union"; see p. 300.) The creation of a regional free-trade area allows a group of states to cooperate in increasing their wealth without waiting for the rest of the world. In fact, from an economic nationalist perspective a free-trade area can enhance a region's power at the expense of other areas of the world.

The most important free-trade area is in Europe; it is connected with the European Union but with a somewhat larger membership. Europe contains a number of small industrialized states living close together, so the creation of a single integrated market allows these states to gain the economic advantages that come inherently to a large state such as the United States. The European free-trade experiment has been a great success overall, contributing to Europe's accumulation of wealth since World War II (see Chapter 6).

The United States, Canada, and Mexico signed the **North American Free Trade Agreement (NAFTA)** in 1994, following a U.S.-Canadian free-trade agreement in 1988. In the 1990s, Canada and Mexico were the largest and third-largest U.S. trading partners, respectively (Japan was second). In its first year, U.S.-Mexican free trade under NAFTA expanded, but was made more complex and difficult when Mexico's currency dropped drastically relative to the dollar in 1994–1995. The great benefits predicted by NAFTA supporters did not materialize, but neither did the disasters predicted by opponents. The opponents, including various U.S. labor unions and environmental groups, criticized the low wages and poor labor laws in Mexico, which they feared would drag down U.S. labor standards. Environmentalists similarly criticized Mexico's lax environmental laws (relative to the United States) and saw NAFTA as giving U.S. corporations license to pollute by moving south of the border (see p. 416).

Atlas CD
U.S., Canada, Mexico
Map

Many politicians in North and South America spoke in the 1990s of creating a single free-trade area in the Western hemisphere, from Alaska to Argentina—the *Free Trade Area of the Americas*. To empower him to do so, President Clinton asked Congress in 1997 to reinstate fast-track legislation (which commits Congress to vote on trade deals in full without amending them). But Democrats in Congress defeated the measure, demanding that free-trade agreements include requirements for labor and environmental standards for other countries—points on which they found NAFTA's record wanting. This defeat left the future of expanded trade in North America in doubt.

Efforts to create a free-trade area, or even a semi–free-trade area, in Asia began in the late 1980s but moved slowly. Malaysia was the leading country promoting such an arrangement, which it hoped would boost its economic development (though economists expected Japan would benefit most). Unlike the European and North American arrangements, an Asian bloc would include very different kinds of states—rich ones such as Japan, poor ones such as the Philippines; democracies, dictatorships, and communist states. It is unclear how well such a diverse collection could coordinate their common interests, especially because their existing trade patterns are not focused on each other but are spread out among other states including the United States (again in contrast to trade patterns existing before the creation of the European and North American free-trade areas).

During the Cold War, the Soviet bloc maintained its own trading bloc, the Council for Mutual Economic Assistance (CMEA), also known as COMECON. After the Soviet Union collapsed, the members scrambled to join up with the world economy, from which they had been largely cut off. The Commonwealth of Independent States (CIS), formed by 12 former Soviet republics, may become an economic coordinating body and quite possibly a free-trade area. The existing patterns of trade favor a CIS free-trade area because the CIS was previously a free trade zone by virtue of being part of a single state sharing transportation, communication, and other infrastructure links.

Other efforts to create free-trade areas have had mixed results. For example, the Southern Cone Common Market (Mercosur) tripled trade among its members—Brazil, Argentina, Uruguay, and Paraguay—in its first four years, in the early 1990s. By the late 1990s, Chile and Bolivia had joined and Mercosur planned a free-trade agreement with the Andean countries. Nonetheless, Mercosur members trade twice as much with the United States as with each other. A Caribbean common market (CARICOM) was created in

1973, but the area is neither large nor rich enough to make regional free trade a very important accelerator of economic growth.

If regional free-trade areas such as now exist in Europe and in North America gain strength and new ones arise, the WTO may be weakened. The more that states are able to meet the political requirements of economic growth through bilateral and regional agreements, the less they may depend on the worldwide agreements developed through the WTO.

Web Link
Organization of Petroleum Exporting Countries

Cartels A **cartel** is an association of producers or consumers, or both, of a certain product—formed to manipulate its price on the world market. It is an unusual but interesting form of trade regime. Most often it is producers and not consumers that form cartels, because there are usually fewer producers than consumers and it seems possible for them to coordinate their actions so as to keep prices high. Cartels can use a variety of means to affect prices; the most effective is to coordinate limits on production by each member so as to lower the supply, relative to demand, of the good.

The most prominent cartel in the international economy is the **Organization of Petroleum Exporting Countries (OPEC)**. Its member states together control well more than $100 billion in oil exports annually—about half the world total and enough to significantly affect the price. (A cartel need not hold a monopoly on production of a good to be effective.) Two decades ago—at OPEC's peak of strength—the proportion was even higher. OPEC maintains a headquarters in Vienna, Austria (not a member), and holds negotiations several times a year to set quotas for each country's production of oil to keep world oil prices in a target range. Members and their export levels (before and after the Gulf War) are shown in Table 5.1. After 1991, Saudi Arabia increased its exports to compensate for the loss of Iraqi and Kuwaiti production, keeping prices relatively stable on world markets before and after the Gulf War.

Atlas CD
Petroleum Production Statistics

OPEC illustrates the potential that a cartel creates for serious collective goods problems. Individual members of OPEC can (and do) cheat a bit by exceeding their pro-

TABLE 5.1   OPEC Members and Oil Production, 1998

Member State	Thousands of Barrels/Day	Member State	Thousands of Barrels/Day
Saudi Arabia	8,400	Indonesia	1,500
Iran	3,600	Libya	1,400
Venezuela	3,200	Algeria	1,200
United Arab Emirates	2,300	Qatar	700
Nigeria	2,200		
Iraq	2,200	Total OPEC	28,800
Kuwait	2,100	Percent of World	43%

Note: Major oil exporters not in OPEC include Russia and Kazakhstan (the Soviet Union was the world's largest exporter in the late 1980s, although exports have since dropped sharply), Mexico, China, Britain, and Norway. Ecuador and Gabon, minor exporters, left OPEC in 1992 and 1995, respectively. The United States, until several decades ago a major oil exporter, is now a major importer.

Source: Data adapted from United States Dept. of Energy, International Petroleum Statistics Report.

duction quotas while still enjoying the collective good of high oil prices. The collective good breaks down when too many members exceed their quotas, as has happened repeatedly to OPEC. Then world oil prices drop. (Iraq's accusations that fellow OPEC member Kuwait was exceeding production quotas and driving oil prices down was one factor in Iraq's invasion of Kuwait in 1990.)

OPEC may work as well as it does only because one member, Saudi Arabia, has enough oil to unilaterally manipulate supply enough to drive prices up or down—a form of hegemonic stability within the cartel. Saudi Arabia can take up the slack from some cheating in OPEC (cutting back its own production) and keep prices up. Or if too many OPEC members are cheating on their quotas, it can punish them by flooding the market with oil and driving prices down until the other OPEC members collectively come to their senses. Even with Saudi predominance, high oil prices in the 1970s led non-OPEC states to increase production and importing states to improve energy conservation, so that by the 1980s even OPEC could not prevent a severe decline in world oil prices.

Consumers usually do not form cartels. However, in response to OPEC the major oil-importing states formed their own organization, the *International Energy Agency (IEA)*, which has some of the functions of a cartel. The IEA coordinates the energy policies of major industrialized states—such as the maintenance of oil stockpiles in case of a shortage on world markets—in order to keep world oil prices low and stable. The largest importers of oil are the large industrialized states.

For a few commodities that are subject to large price fluctuations on world markets—detrimental to both producers and consumers—joint producer-consumer cartels have been formed. In order to keep prices stable, producing and consuming states use the cartel to coordinate the overall supply and demand globally. Such cartels exist for coffee, several minerals, and some other products. In the coffee cartel, Colombia argued in the late 1980s for a higher target price for coffee, so that Colombian peasants would have an incentive to switch from growing coca (for cocaine production) to coffee. But the United States, as the major coffee-consuming state, would not agree to the proposal for higher prices.[2]

In general, the idea of cartels runs counter to liberal economics because cartels are deliberate efforts to distort free markets. However, in occasional cases where free markets create large fluctuations in price, the creation of a cartel can bring some order to chaos and result in greater efficiency. Cartels usually are not as powerful as market forces in determining overall world price levels: too many producers and suppliers exist, and too many substitute goods can replace ones that become too expensive, for a cartel to corner the market. The exceptions, such as OPEC in the 1970s, are rare.

States have found it worthwhile to expand trade steadily, using a variety of regimes and institutions to do so—the WTO, free-trade areas, bilateral agreements, and cartels. Overall, despite a loss of state sovereignty as a result of growing interdependence, these efforts have benefited participating states. Stable political rules governing trade allow states to realize the great economic gains that can result from international exchange. Such political stability is equally important in international monetary and business relations, which will be discussed next.

---

[2] Bates, Robert H. *Open-Economy Politics: The Political Economy of the World Coffee Trade*. Princeton: Princeton University Press, 1997.

The Currency System

Imagine a world *without* money. In order to conduct an economic exchange, the goods being exchanged would have to be brought together in one place and traded in quantities reflecting the relative values the parties placed on them. This kind of trade, involving no money, is called *barter*. It still occurs sometimes when monetary systems do not operate well. For example, during the Chinese-Soviet hostility of the 1960s and 1970s, Soviet money was worthless in China, and Chinese money was worthless in the Soviet Union. So traders brought goods to the border, agreed on their value (expressed nominally in Swiss francs), and traded the appropriate quantities.

With money, goods can move directly from sellers to buyers without having to meet in a central place. In a world economy, goods can flow freely among many states—the exchange of money keeps track of who owes whom for what. Money provides a single medium against which all goods can be valued. Different buyers and sellers place different values on goods, but all buyers and sellers place about the same value on money, so it serves as a standard against which other values can be measured.

Money itself has little or no inherent value. What gives it value is the widespread belief that it has value—that it can be exchanged for goods. Because it depends on the willingness of people to honor and use it, money's value rests on trust. Governments have the job of creating money and of maintaining public confidence in its value. For money to have stable value, the political environment must be stable. Political instability erodes public confidence that money today will be exchangeable for needed goods tomorrow. The result is inflation (discussed later in this chapter).

The international economy is based on national currencies, not a world currency, because of the nature of state sovereignty. One of the main powers of a national government is to create its own currency as the sole legal currency in the territory it controls. The national currencies are of no inherent value in another country, but can be exchanged one for another. How can the value of goods or currencies be judged in a world lacking a central government and a world unit of money?

Traditionally, for centuries, the European state system used *precious metals* as a global currency, valued in all countries. *Gold* was most important, and *silver* second. These metals had inherent value because they looked pretty and were easily molded into jewelry or similar objects. They were relatively rare, and the mining of new gold and silver was relatively slow. These metals lasted a long time, and they were difficult to water down or counterfeit.

Over time, gold and silver became valuable *because* they were a world currency—because other people around the world trusted that the metals could be exchanged for future goods—and this overshadowed any inherent functional value of gold or silver. Bars of gold and silver were held by states as a kind of bank account denominated in an international currency. Gold has long been a key power resource with which states could buy armies or other means of leverage.

In recent years the world has not used such a **gold standard** but has developed an international monetary system divorced from any tangible medium such as precious metal. Until recently, and still to some extent, private investors have bought stocks of gold or silver at times of political instability, as a haven that would reliably have future value. But gold and silver have now become basically like other commodities, with

It's Just Money Money has value only because people trust its worth. Inflation erodes a currency's value if governments print too much money or if political instability erodes public confidence in the government. Brazil initially survived the loss of confidence in emerging markets that resulted from the 1997 Asian financial crisis. The next year, however, Brazil had to devalue its currency. This trader reacts to a stock market crash in 1998, after domestic politics threatened a $41 billion IMF agreement and shook investors' confidence in Brazil's economy.

unpredictable fluctuations in price, and their role even as private havens is diminishing. The change in the world economy away from unwieldy bars of gold to purely abstract money makes international economics more efficient; the only drawback is that without tangible backing in gold, currencies may seem less worthy of people's confidence.

Today, national currencies are valued against each other, not against gold or silver. Each state's currency can be exchanged for a different state's currency according to an **exchange rate**—defining, for instance, how many Canadian dollars are equivalent to one U.S. dollar. These exchange rates are important because they affect almost every international economic transaction. Consider first the mechanics by which exchange rates are set and adjusted, then the factors influencing the longer-term movements of exchange rates, and finally the banking institutions that manage these issues.

Web Link
Exchange Rates

International Currency Exchange
Most exchange rates are expressed in terms of the world's most important currencies—the U.S. dollar, Japanese yen, and German mark. Thus, the rate for exchanging Danish kroner for Brazilian reals depends on the value of each relative to these leading currencies. Exchange rates that most affect the world economy are those *within* the G7 states—dollars, marks, yen, British pounds, French francs, Canadian dollars, and Italian lire.

The relative values of currencies at a given point in time are arbitrary; only the *changes* in values over time are meaningful. For instance, the German mark happens to be fairly close to the U.S. dollar in value, whereas the Japanese yen is denominated in units closer to the U.S. penny. In itself this says nothing about the desirability of these currencies or the financial positions of their states. However, when the value of yen rises (or falls) *relative* to dollars, because yen are considered more (or less) valuable than before, the yen is said to be strong (or weak).

Some states do not have **convertible currencies**. The holder of such money has no guarantee of being able to trade it for another currency. Such is the case in states cut off from the world capitalist economy, such as the former Soviet Union. Few such states remain, but a lingering challenge is to make the Russian ruble a fully convertible currency (see p. 254). In practice, even nonconvertible currency can often be sold, in black markets or by dealing directly with the government issuing the currency, but the price may be extremely low.

Some currencies are practically nonconvertible because they are inflating so rapidly that holding them for even a short period means losing money (this was the biggest problem with the ruble in the 1990s). The 10-billion-dinar notes printed by Serbia in 1993 were worth only pennies after hyperinflation reached 100 trillion percent per year. (In early 1994, a new currency tied directly to the German mark was issued, cutting inflation to nearly zero for a year before inflation began accelerating again.) Nobody wants to hold currency that is rapidly inflating—losing value relative to goods and services. So inflation reduces a currency's value relative to more stable (more slowly inflating) currencies.

The industrialized West has kept inflation relatively low—mostly below 5 percent annually—since 1980 (see Table 5.2). (The 1970s saw inflation of more than 10 percent per year in many industrialized economies, including the United States.) The global South has had less success with inflation, although in the mid-1990s Latin America brought inflation from 750 percent to under 20 percent, while China and South Asia got inflation rates below 10 percent. Most dramatically, in Russia and other former Soviet republics inflation rates of more than 1,000 percent came down to less than 50 percent. Extremely high, uncontrolled inflation—more than 50 percent per month, or 13,000 percent per year—is called **hyperinflation**. Even at less extreme levels, currencies can lose 95 percent of their value in a year. In such conditions, money loses 5 percent of its value every week, and it becomes hard to conduct business domestically, let alone internationally.

TABLE 5.2   Inflation Rates by Region, 1993–1999

Region	INFLATION RATE (percent per year)		
	1993	1996	1999*
Industrialized West	3	2	1
Russia and Eastern Europe	1,400	48	67
China	15	8	2
Middle East	27	34	35
Latin America	750	19	12
South Asia	6	6	6
Africa	112	37	9

Note: Regions are not identical to those used elsewhere in this book. * Data are estimates based on partial data for 1999.
Source: Adapted from United Nations, *World Economic and Social Survey 1999* (New York: United Nations, 1999), p. 270.

By contrast with nonconvertible currency, **hard currency** is money that can be readily converted to leading world currencies (which now have relatively low inflation). For example, a Russian oil producer can export oil and receive payment in German marks or another hard currency, which can then be used to pay for imported goods from outside Russia. But a Russian sausage producer selling products within Russia would be paid in rubles, which could not be used outside the country.

States maintain **reserves** of hard currency. This is the equivalent of the stockpiles of gold in centuries past. National currencies are now backed by hard-currency reserves, not gold. Some states continue to maintain gold reserves as well. The industrialized countries have financial reserves roughly in proportion to the size of their economies.

One form of currency exchange uses **fixed exchange rates**. Here governments decide, individually or jointly, to establish official rates of exchange for their currencies. The Canadian and U.S. dollars were for many years equal in value; a fixed rate of 1-to-1 was maintained (this is no longer true). States have various means for trying to maintain, or modify, fixed rates in the face of changing economic conditions (see p. 244).

Floating exchange rates are now more common and are used for the world's major currencies. Rates are determined by global currency markets in which private investors and governments alike buy and sell currencies. There is a supply and demand for each state's currency, with prices constantly adjusting in response to market conditions. Just as investors might buy shares of General Motors stock if they expected its value to rise, so they would buy a pile of Japanese yen if they expected that currency's value to rise in the future. Through short-term speculative trading in international currencies, exchange rates adjust to changes in the longer-term supply and demand for currencies.

There are major international currency markets in a handful of cities—the most important being New York, London, Zurich (Switzerland), Tokyo, and Hong Kong—linked by instantaneous computerized communications. These markets are driven in the short term by one question: What will a state's currency be worth in the future relative to what it is worth today? These international currency markets involve huge amounts of money—a trillion dollars every day—moving around the world (actually only the computerized information moves). They are private markets, not as strongly regulated by governments as are stock markets.

National governments periodically *intervene* in financial markets, buying and selling currencies in order to manipulate their value. (These interventions may also involve changing interest rates paid by the government; see pp. 246–247.) Such government intervention to manage the otherwise free-floating currency rates is called a **managed float** system. The leading industrialized states often, but not always, work together in such interventions. If the price of the U.S. dollar, for instance, goes down too much relative to other important currencies (a political judgment), governments will step into the currency markets, side by side with private investors, and buy dollars. With this higher demand for dollars, the price may then stabilize and perhaps rise again. (If the price got too high, governments would step in to sell dollars, increasing supply and driving the price down.) Such interventions usually happen quickly, in one day, but may be repeated several times within a few weeks in order to have the desired effect. In their interventions in international currency markets, however, governments are at a disadvantage because even acting together they control only a small fraction of the money moving on such markets; most of it is privately owned.

A successful intervention can make money for the governments at the expense of private speculators. If, for example, the G8 governments step in to raise the price of dollars by buying them around the world (selling other hard currencies), and if they succeed, the governments can then sell again and pocket a profit. However, if the intervention fails and the price of dollars keeps falling, the governments will *lose* money and may have to keep buying and buying in order to stop the slide. In fact, the governments might run out of money before then and have to absorb a huge loss. So governments have to be realistic about the limited effects they can have on currency prices.

These limits were well illustrated in the *European currency crisis* of September 1992. The European Union (EU) tried to maintain the equivalent of a fixed exchange rate among the various European currencies while letting the European currencies as a whole float freely relative to the rest of the world (see p. 303). For 1992, the British pound was pegged at 2.95 German marks, and if it slipped from that rate, European governments were supposed to take various actions to bring it back into line. This was called the **Exchange Rate Mechanism (ERM)**, and it was a step toward a single currency for Europe (see p. 305).

In September 1992, certain long-term forces were pushing apart the values of the German mark and British pound. Germans feared inflation due to the costs of reunifying their country and wanted to restrict money supply to prevent this. Britons were worried about recession and unemployment, which a tight money supply would only worsen. As a result, currency speculators began to gamble that Britain would not be able to maintain the value of the British pound relative to the German mark.

As the pound began to fall, the British government intervened to buy pounds and drive the price back up. But speculators, who controlled far more money than the European governments, kept selling pounds. The speculators were convinced that the British government would be unable to prop up the pound's value, and they proved correct. With no way to stop the decline, Britain pulled out of the ERM and allowed the pound to float freely; it quickly fell in value. All the pounds that the British government had bought during its intervention were then worth less—a loss of billions of dollars. The government's loss was the private speculators' gain.

Atlas CD
Inflation in
Russia
Photo, Music

Why Currencies Rise or Fall

In the short term, exchange rates depend on speculation about the future value of currencies. But over the long term, the value of a state's currency tends to rise or fall relative to others because of changes in the long-term supply and demand for the currency. *Supply* is determined by the amount of money a government prints. Printing money is a quick way to generate revenue for the government, but the more money printed, the lower its price on international currency markets. Domestically, printing too much money creates inflation because the amount of goods in the economy is unchanged but more money is circulating to buy them with. *Demand* for a currency depends on the state's economic health and political stability. People do not want to own the currency of an unstable country because political instability leads to the breakdown of economic efficiency and of trust in the currency issued by that government.

A *strong* currency is one that increases its value relative to other currencies—not just in day-to-day fluctuations on currency markets, but in a longer-term perspective. A weak currency is the opposite. The strength of a state's currency tends to reflect that

Prices Subject to Change   Changes in the dollar-yen exchange rate—reflecting underlying trends in the two national economies as well as the two governments' monetary policies—directly affect the prices of imported goods like these U.S.–made Apple computers for sale in Japan, 1992.

state's monetary policy and economic growth rate. Investors seek currency that will not be watered down by inflation and that can be profitably invested in a growing economy.

To some extent, states have *common* interests—opposed to those of private investors—in maintaining stable currency exchange rates. Despite these shared interests, states also experience *conflicts* over currency exchange, as we have seen in the example of Britain and Germany in the 1992 European currency crisis. States often prefer a *low* value for their own currency relative to others, because a low value promotes exports and helps turn trade deficits into surpluses—as mercantilists especially favor (see p. 219).

For example, the rise in the value of the yen in 1995 made Japanese exports to the United States more expensive. If Japanese politicians were economic liberals (which they were up to a point), they might have wanted to enjoy cheaper goods imported from the United States. But if they were economic nationalists, they would have wanted to maintain a trade surplus and would have agreed to bring the yen back down only at the point at which the stability of the world economic system was endangered (the collective good of stable exchange rates might not be provided). Decisions about the target rates of currency exchange—those the great powers will cooperate to enforce through market interventions—are thus a major arena of international political bargaining. To keep currency speculators from profiting at the expense of all governments, most such bargaining occurs in secret.

To some extent, exchange rates and trade surpluses or deficits tend to adjust automatically toward equilibrium (the preferred outcome for liberals). An *overvalued* currency is one whose exchange rate is too high, resulting in a chronic trade deficit. The deficit can be covered by printing more money, which in turn waters down the currency's value and brings down the exchange rate (assuming it is allowed to float freely).

Because they see adjustments as harmless, liberals are not bothered by exchange rate changes such as the fall of the dollar relative to the yen, and of the Mexican peso relative to the dollar, in 1995. These are viewed as mechanisms for allowing the world economy to work out inefficiencies and maximize overall growth.

A unilateral move to reduce the value of one's own currency by changing a fixed or official exchange rate is called a **devaluation**. Generally, devaluation is a quick fix for financial problems in the short term, but it can create new problems. It causes losses to foreigners who hold one's currency (which is suddenly worthless). This reduces the trust people place in the currency. As a result, demand for the currency drops, even at the new lower rate. Investors become wary of future devaluations, and indeed such devaluations often follow one after another in unstable economies. A currency may be devalued by allowing it to float freely, often bringing a single sharp drop in values. This is what Britain did in the European currency crisis just discussed.

The weakening of a currency, while encouraging exports, carries dangers. When the currency used by 14 African countries (based on the French franc) was devalued by half in early 1994, financial experts praised the long-term benefits the move would bring to those economies. But in the short term, the urban poor had to tighten their belts as prices jumped. Thus, depending on what goods an economy imports and exports, a weaker currency that raises the price of imported goods may disrupt economic growth. In general, any sharp or artificial change in exchange rates tends to disrupt smooth international trade and hence interfere with the creation of wealth.

Web Link
Central Banks

Central Banks Governments control the printing of money. In some states, the politicians or generals who control the government directly control the amounts of money printed. It is not surprising that inflation tends to be high in those states, because political problems can often be solved by printing more money to use for various purposes. But in most industrialized countries, politicians know they cannot trust themselves with day-to-day decisions about printing money. To enforce self-discipline and enhance public trust in the value of money, these decisions are turned over to a **central bank**.

The economists and technical experts who run the central bank seek to maintain the value of the state's currency by limiting the amount of money printed and not allowing high inflation. Politicians appoint the people who run the bank, but generally for long terms that do not coincide with those of the politicians. Thus, central bank managers try to run the bank in the national interest, a step removed from partisan politics. If a state leader orders a military intervention the generals obey, but if the leader orders an intervention in currency markets the central bank does not have to comply.

In the United States, the central bank is the *Federal Reserve*, or the Fed. The "reserve" is the government's stockpile of hard currency. The Fed can affect the economy by releasing or hoarding its money. Internationally, it does this by intervening in currency markets as described earlier. Multilateral interventions are usually coordinated by the heads of central banks and treasury (finance) ministries in the leading countries. The long-term, relatively nonpartisan perspective of central bankers makes it easier for states to achieve the collective good of a stable world monetary system.

Domestically, the Fed exercises its power mainly by setting the **discount rate**—the interest rate the government charges when it loans money to private banks. (Central banks have only private banks, not individuals and corporations, as their customers.) In effect, this rate controls how fast money is injected into the economy. If the Fed sets too low a discount rate, too much money will come into circulation and inflation will result. If the rate is set too high, too little money will circulate and consumers and businesses will find it hard to borrow as much or as cheaply from private banks; economic growth will be depressed. Again, a state leader cannot order the central bank to lower the discount rate and inject more money into the economy but can only ask for such action.

Central bank decisions about the discount rate have important international consequences. If interest rates are higher in one state than another, foreign capital tends to be attracted to the state with the higher rate. And if economic growth is high in a foreign country, more goods can be exported to it. So states care about other states' monetary policies. This often creates international conflicts that can be resolved only politically (such as at G8 summit meetings), not technically—because each central bank, although removed from domestic politics, still looks out for its own state's interests.

Although central banks control sizable reserves of currency, they are constrained by the limited share of world money that they own. Most wealth is controlled by private banks and corporations. As economic actors, states do not drive the direction of the world economy; in many ways they follow it, at least over the long run. However, states still have key advantages as actors in the international economy. Most important, states control the monopoly on the legal use of force—violent leverage—against which even a large amount of wealth usually cannot stand. Ultimately, political power is the state's trump card as an economic actor.

The World Bank and the IMF   Because of the importance of international cooperation for a stable world monetary system and because of the need to overcome collective goods problems, international regimes and institutions have developed around norms of behavior in monetary relations. Just as the UN institutionally supports regimes based on norms of behavior in international security affairs (see Chapter 6), the same is true in the world monetary regime.

As in security affairs, the main international economic institutions were created near the end of World War II. The **Bretton Woods system** was adopted at a conference of the winning states in 1944 (at Bretton Woods, New Hampshire). It established the *International Bank for Reconstruction and Development (IBRD),* more commonly called the **World Bank**, as a source of loans to reconstruct the European economies after the war and to help states through future financial difficulties. (Later, the main borrowers were third world countries and, in the 1990s, Eastern European ones.) Closely linked with the World Bank was the **International Monetary Fund (IMF)**. The IMF coordinates international currency exchange, the balance of international payments, and national accounts (discussed shortly). The World Bank and the IMF continue to be the pillars of the international financial system. (The roles of the World Bank and the IMF in third world development are taken up in Chapter 7.)

Web Link
World Bank

Bretton Woods set a regime of stable monetary exchange, based on the U.S. dollar and backed by gold, that lasted from 1944 to 1971. During this period, the dollar was given a fixed value equal to 1/35 of an ounce of gold, and the U.S. government guaranteed to buy dollars for gold at this rate (from a Fort Knox, Kentucky, stockpile). Other states' currencies were exchanged at fixed rates relative to the dollar. These fixed exchange rates were set by the IMF based on the long-term equilibrium level that could be sustained for each currency (rather than short-term political considerations). The international currency markets operated within a very narrow range around the fixed rate. If a country's currency fell more than 1 percent from the fixed rate, the country had to use its hard-currency reserves to buy its own currency back and thus shore up the price. (Or, if the price rose more than 1 percent, it had to sell its currency to drive the price down.)

The gold standard was abandoned in 1971—an event sometimes called the "collapse of Bretton Woods." The term is not quite appropriate: the institutions survived, and even the monetary regime underwent more of an adjustment than a collapse. The U.S. economy no longer held the overwhelming dominance it had in 1944—mostly because of European and Japanese recovery from World War II, but also because of U.S. overspending on the Vietnam War and other programs. Throughout the 1950s and 1960s, the U.S. had spent dollars abroad to stimulate world economic growth and fight the Cold War, but these had begun to far exceed the diminishing stocks of gold held by the Federal Reserve. So successful were the efforts to reinvigorate the economies of Japan and Europe that the United States suffered a relative decline in its trade position.

As a result, the dollar became seriously overvalued. By 1971, the dollar was no longer worth 1/35 of an ounce of gold, and the United States had to abandon its fixed exchange rate—much as Britain did in its 1992 crisis. President Nixon unilaterally dumped the dollar-gold system, and the dollar was allowed to float freely; soon it had fallen to a fraction of its former value (gold was worth several hundred dollars an ounce, not $35).

The abandonment of Bretton Woods was good for the United States and bad for Japan and Europe, where leaders expressed shock at the unilateral U.S. actions. The interdependence of the world capitalist economy, which had produced record economic growth for all the Western countries after World War II, had also created the conditions for new international conflicts.

To replace gold as a world standard, the IMF created a new world currency, the **Special Drawing Right (SDR)**. The SDR has been called "paper gold" because it is created in limited amounts by the IMF, is held as a hard-currency reserve by states' central banks, and can be exchanged for various international currencies. The SDR is today the closest thing to a world currency that exists, but it cannot buy goods—only currencies. And it is owned only by states (central banks), not by individuals or companies.

The value of the U.S. dollar was pegged to the SDR rather than to gold, at a fixed exchange rate (but one that the IMF periodically adjusted to reflect the dollar's strength or weakness). SDRs are linked in value to a basket of several key international currencies. So when one currency rises a bit and another falls, the SDR does not change value much; but if all currencies rise (worldwide inflation), the SDR rises with them.

Since the early 1970s, the major national currencies have been governed by the managed float system. Transition from the dollar-gold regime to the managed float regime was difficult. The United States was no longer dominant enough to single-handedly provide stability to the world monetary system. States had to bargain politically over the targets for currency exchange rates in the meetings now known as G7 summits.

The technical mechanisms of the IMF are based on each member state's depositing financial reserves with the IMF. Upon joining the IMF, a state is assigned a *quota* for such deposits, partly of hard currency and partly of the state's own currency (this quota is not related to the concept of trade quotas, which are import restrictions). The quota is based on the size and strength of a state's economy. A state can then borrow against its quota (even exceeding it somewhat) to stabilize its economy in difficult times, and repay the IMF in subsequent years. Unlike the UN General Assembly or the Security Council, the IMF and the World Bank use a *weighted voting* system—each state has a vote equal to its quota. Thus the G7 states control the IMF, although nearly all the world's states are members. The United States has the single largest vote, and its capital city is headquarters for both the IMF and the World Bank.

Since 1944, the IMF and the World Bank have tried to accomplish three major missions. First they sought to provide stability and access to capital for states ravaged by World War II, especially Japan and the states of Western Europe. This mission was a great success, leading to growth and prosperity in those states. Then, especially in the 1970s and 1980s, the Bank and the IMF tried to promote economic development in newly independent third world countries. That mission was far less successful—as seen in the lingering (and even deepening) poverty in much of the global South (see Chapter 7). The third mission, in the 1990s, was the integration of Eastern Europe and Russia into the world capitalist economy. The outcome of this ambitious effort is far from certain.

State Financial Positions

As currency rates change and state economies grow, the overall positions of states relative to each other shift.

National Accounts

The IMF maintains a system of *national accounts* statistics to keep track of the overall monetary position of each state. A state's **balance of payments** is like the financial statement of a company: it summarizes all the flows of money in and out of the country. The system itself is technical and not political in nature. Essentially, three types of international transactions go into the balance of payments: the current account, flows of capital, and changes in reserves (see Table 5.3).

The *current account* is basically the balance of trade discussed earlier. Money flows out of a state to pay for imports and flows into the state to pay for exports. The goods imported or exported include both merchandise and services. For instance, money spent by a British tourist in Florida is equivalent to money spent by a British consumer buying Florida oranges in a London market; both are money flowing into the U.S. current account. The current account includes two other items. *Government transactions* are military and foreign aid grants, as well as salaries and pensions paid to government employees abroad. *Remittances* are funds sent home by companies or individuals outside a country. For example, a Ford Motor Company subsidiary in Britain may send profits back to Ford in Detroit. Conversely, a British citizen working in New York may send money to her parents in London.

The second category in the accounts is *capital flows*, which are foreign investments in, and by, a country. Capital flows are measured in *net* terms—the total investments and loans foreigners make *in* a country minus the investments and loans that country's companies, citizens, and government invest in *other* countries. Most of such investment is pri-

TABLE 5.3 Balance of Payments Accounts, 1995

In Billions of 1997 U.S. Dollars

	United States	Germany	Japan
Current Account			
Exports (goods and services)	1,018	742	721
− Imports (goods and services)	-1,136	-721	-597
= Trade balance	-119	21	125
+ Government transactions and remittances	-37	-43	-8
= Current account balance	-156	-22	117
Capital Flows (net money received)			
+ Foreign investment received	61	1	-62
+ Loans and other capital inflow, and discrepancies	-6	29	9
Changes in Reserves			
= Changes in reserves	-101	+8	+64

Source: Data adapted from World Bank, *World Development Indicators on CD-ROM*, Feb. 1997.

vate, although some is by (or in) government agencies and state-owned industries. Capital flows are divided into **foreign direct investment** (or *direct foreign investment*)—such as building a factory, company, or real estate in a foreign country—and indirect *portfolio investment*, such as buying stocks and bonds or making loans to a foreign company. These various kinds of capital flows have somewhat different political consequences (see below and p. 263), but they are basically equivalent in the overall national accounts picture.

The third category, *changes in foreign exchange reserves*, makes the payments balance in the national accounts. Any difference between the inflows and outflows of money (in the current account and capital flows combined) is made up by an equal but opposite change in reserves. These changes in reserves consist of the state's purchases and sales of SDRs, gold, and hard currencies other than its own, and changes in its deposits with the IMF. If a state has more money flowing out than in, it gets that money from its reserves. If it has more money flowing in than out, it puts the money in its reserves.

Thus, national accounts always balance in the end. At least, they almost balance; there is a residual category—errors and omissions—because even the most efficient and honest government (many governments are neither) cannot keep track of every bit of money crossing its borders. But basically the payments balance.

International Debt In one sense, an economy is constantly in motion, as money moves through the processes of production, trade, and consumption. But economies also contain *standing wealth*. The hard-currency reserves owned by governments are one form of standing wealth, but not the most important. Most standing wealth is in the form of homes and cars, farms and factories, ports and railroads. In particular, *capital* goods (such as factories) are products that can be used as inputs for further production. Nothing lasts forever, but standing wealth lasts for enough years to be treated differently than goods that are quickly consumed. The main difference is that capital can be used to create more wealth: factories produce goods, railroads support commerce, and so forth. Standing wealth creates new wealth, so the economy tends to grow over time. As it grows, more standing wealth is created. In a capitalist economy, money makes more money.

Interest rates reflect this inherent growth dynamic. *Real* interest rates are the rates for borrowing money above and beyond the rate of inflation (for instance, if money is loaned at an annual interest rate of 8 percent but inflation is 3 percent, the real interest rate is 5 percent). Businesses and households borrow money because they think they can use it to create new wealth faster than the rate of interest on the loan.

Borrowing and lending are like any other economic exchange; both parties must see them as beneficial. The borrower values the money now more than the promise of more money in the future, whereas the lender values the promise of more money in the future more than the money now. The distribution of benefits from the exchange is, as usual, subject to bargaining. Imagine that a profitable business can use a loan to generate 10 percent annual profit (above the inflation rate). At one extreme, the business could pay 1 percent real interest and keep 9 percent for itself; at the other, it could pay 9 percent interest and keep 1 percent.

The actual split, reflected in prevailing interest rates, is determined by the market for money. Lenders seek out businesses profitable enough to pay high interest; businesses seek out lenders with enough idle cash to lend it at low interest rates. In an imperfect but workable way, the supply and demand for money determine interest rates.

Imagine now that the business borrowing the money is an entire state—the government, companies, and households. If the state's economy is healthy, it can borrow money from foreign governments, banks, or companies and create enough new wealth to repay the debts a few years later. But states, like businesses, sometimes operate at a loss; then their debts mount up. In a vicious circle, more and more of the income they generate goes to paying interest, and more money must be borrowed to keep the state in operation. If its fortunes reverse, a state or business can create wealth again and over time pay back the principal on its debts to climb out of the hole. If not, it will have to begin selling off part of its standing wealth (buildings, airplanes, factories, and the like). The *net worth* of the state or business (all its assets minus all its liabilities) will decrease.

When a state's debts accumulate, the standing wealth of the state is diminished as assets are sold off to pay the debts. In some third world countries, debts accumulated in the 1970s and 1980s to the point of virtual national bankruptcy, or zero net worth. The debts became unpayable, and the lenders (banks and governments) had to write them off the books or settle them at a fraction of their official value.

The industrialized states, by contrast, have enough standing wealth that even in their most indebted times they still have substantial net worth. Still, rising debts are encumbrances against the future creation of wealth, and foreign lenders come to own a greater share of the state's total standing wealth. Naturally, such a situation horrifies mercantilists. National debt to them represents a loss of power. It is the opposite of the pile of reserves that mercantilists would like to be sitting on.

Why do states go into debt? One major reason is a trade deficit. In the balance of payments, a trade deficit must be made up somehow. It is common to borrow money to pay for a trade deficit. A second reason is the income and consumption pattern among households and businesses. If people and firms spend more than they take in, they must borrow to pay their bills. The credit card they use may be from a local bank, but that bank may be getting the money it lends to them from foreign lenders.

A third reason for national debt is government spending relative to taxation. Under the principles of **Keynesian economics** (named for economist John Maynard Keynes), governments sometimes spend more than they take in—*deficit spending*—to stimulate economic growth. If the strategy works, increased economic growth eventually generates higher tax revenues to make up the deficit. The government lends money to the nation and recovers it later from a healthier economy. Where does the government get this money? It could print more money, but this would be inflationary and central banks try to prevent it. So the government often borrows the money, from both domestic and foreign sources.

Government decisions about spending and taxation are called **fiscal policy**; decisions about printing and circulating money are called **monetary policy**. These are the two main tools available for government to manage an economy. There is no free lunch: high taxation chokes off economic growth, printing excess money causes inflation, and borrowing to cover a deficit places a mortgage on the state's standing wealth. This is why, for all the complexities of governmental economic policies and international economic transactions, a state's wealth and power ultimately depend more than anything on the underlying health of its economy—the education and training of its labor force, the amount and modernity of its capital goods, the morale of its population, and the skill of its managers. In the long run, international debt reflects these underlying realities.

The U.S. Position

The United States is an extraordinarily wealthy and powerful state. Its most *unique* strengths may be in the area of international security—as the world's only superpower—but its economic strengths are also striking. It is not only the world's largest economy but the most technologically advanced one in such growth sectors as computers, telecommunications, aviation and aerospace, and biotechnology. The U.S. position in scientific research and higher education is unparalleled in the world.

The U.S. position in the international economy, however, has shifted over the decades. U.S. hegemony peaked after World War II, then gradually eroded as competitors gained relative ground (especially in Western Europe and Asia). In the early 1950s, the U.S. economy (GDP) was about twice the size of the next six advanced industrial states *combined*. By the 1980s, its relative share of world GDP had dropped almost by half. In 1950, the United States held half of the world's financial reserves; by 1980 it held less than 10 percent. This long-term decline after the extraordinary post–1945 U.S. hegemony was a natural and probably unavoidable one.

In the 1980s, however, the U.S. financial position worsened much more rapidly, causing great alarm. The U.S. national debt increased dramatically as the government financed a military buildup while reducing taxes—without stimulating faster growth. In the private sector, the United States started the 1980s with well more than $100 billion more invested in foreign countries than foreigners had invested in the United States. By 1988, foreigners had more than $500 billion more invested in the United States than U.S. investors had in foreign countries.

The country slipped into *recession* (a shrinking GDP) in the early 1990s. The U.S. government continued to slide further into debt by hundreds of billions of dollars each year.

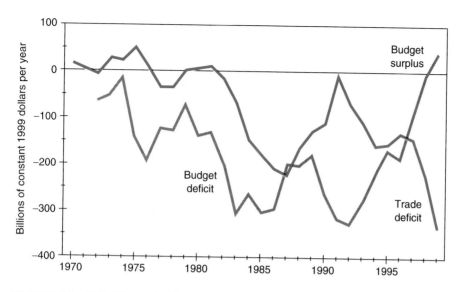

FIGURE 5.3   U.S. Financial Position, 1970–1999   In the 1980s and 1990s the United States imported more than it exported (the current account balance or trade deficit), and its government spent more than its income (the budget deficit). The budget deficit has finally been closed but leaves behind a large national debt, and the trade deficit remains especially large after the 1997 Asian financial crisis.

Note: Trade deficit refers to current balance account.

Source: Based on data from World Bank and IMF.

The United States was losing net worth and having to sell off its standing wealth to pay the bills. Where the United States had once sat on a pile of gold, it now sat under a pile of debt.

The shifting U.S. financial position in the 1980s and 1990s is illustrated in Figure 5.3. The budget deficit grew to $300 billion per year in the early 1980s while the trade deficit (exports minus imports) grew from near zero to $200 billion in just a few years. The trade deficit recovered to nearly zero again, but then returned to nearly $300 billion a year by 1998. The U.S. trade deficit is reflected in the U.S. national accounts for 1995, shown in Table 5.3 (p. 250). The circled "–119" shows a trade deficit of $119 billion, whereas Germany and Japan had $21 billion and $125 billion surpluses, respectively. The circled "61" shows $61 billion more of investments coming into the country than Americans were investing outside the country. And the circled "–101" indicates that in 1995 the United States depleted its reserves by $101 billion to make ends meet. All these numbers reflect the fall in U.S. economic standing in the 1980s and early 1990s.

The U.S. economy showed remarkable resiliency in the mid- to late-1990s, as those of other industrialized countries (notably Japan) stumbled. The United States ended the 1990s with all-time low unemployment, low inflation, robust growth, and stock market gains. The budget deficit shrank dramatically in the 1990s and turned to a modest surplus, owing to this economic performance and the downsizing of some parts of government (including military forces).

Web Link
Trade Deficit

Although the U.S. budget deficit has been at least temporarily curbed, the accumulated debt from 20 years of deficit spending remains. The U.S. government's **national debt** grew from about $1 trillion at the beginning of the 1980s to $3 trillion by the end of that decade, and nearly the equivalent of one year's GDP by the mid-1990s. The interest payments were equivalent to what would otherwise be a healthy rate of economic growth. Not long ago, the United States was the world's leading lender state; now it is the world's leading debtor state.

These U.S. financial trends have profound implications for the entire world political economy. They seemed to first undermine (in the 1980s) and then reconstruct (in the 1990s) the leading U.S. role in stabilizing international trade and monetary relations, in assuring the provision of collective goods, and in providing capital for the economic development of other world regions. In a more decentralized, more privatized world economy with an uncertain U.S. role, collective goods problems may be harder to solve and free trade may be harder to achieve. Some troubling signs of economic instability appeared in the early 1990s, in the turbulent, recession-plagued years that followed the end of the Cold War, and again in the financial collapses in Asia in 1997 and Russia in 1998.

The Position of Russia and Eastern Europe
Russia and Eastern Europe are immediate victims of U.S. financial weakness, in the sense that the United States cannot provide the capital (investments, loans, and grants) to help get this region on its feet again after the Cold War. Were the United States stronger economically, it might repeat in Russia and Eastern Europe the successful aid program that stimulated new growth in Western Europe and Japan after World War II.

Atlas CD
Uzbekistan
Scenes
Video

Instead, states in this region face daunting challenges as they try to convert from centrally planned to capitalist economies and to join the world capitalist economy. These challenges include integration into the world trading system (membership in the WTO, bilateral trade agreements, and so forth) and attracting foreign investment. Among the most difficult tasks are the attempts of states in this region to join the international monetary system. This matters greatly because having a stable and convertible currency is a key element in attracting foreign business and expanding international trade.

Web Link
The IMF in
Russia

Most of the states of the former Soviet bloc became members of the IMF and were assigned quotas. But the IMF and the World Bank would not make loans available freely to these states until their governments took strong action to curb inflation, balance government budgets, and assure economic stability. Such stability would have been easier to achieve with the foreign loans, however, creating a chicken-and-egg problem.

All the economies of the region experienced a deep depression (shrinking GDP) in 1989–1991. By 1992, only Poland had resumed economic growth—a 1 to 4 percent annual growth of GDP following a 20 percent shrinkage in 1990–1991. The rest of Eastern Europe (except Bulgaria and Slovakia) stopped shrinking by 1994. But the states of the former Soviet Union continued downward, until by 1996 the total economic activity of those states had been cut by half over seven years (see Table 5.4).

Atlas CD
Eastern Europe
Map

In general, the Eastern European countries appeared to have better prospects of stabilizing their economies than did the states of the former Soviet Union. Among the latter, Russia was better off than some others; it had inherited much of the Soviet Union's economic infrastructure and natural resources and was large enough to gain the attention of the West. But internal power struggles created political instability in Russia, discouraging foreign investment. Russia was not a WTO member as of 2000. Inflation

TABLE 5.4   Economic Collapse in Russia
and Eastern Europe

Country	Cumulative (10-Year) Change in GDP, 1990–1999
Former Soviet Republics[a]	-50%
Former Yugoslavia	-35%
Estonia, Latvia, and Lithuania	-29%
Bulgaria	-29%
Romania	-28%
Albania	-12%
Czech Republic	-11%
Slovakia	-1%
Hungary	-1%
Poland	+21%

[a] Russia, Ukraine, and 10 other CIS members.

Source: Author's estimates based on United Nations, *World Economic and Social Survey 1999* (New York: United Nations, 1999), p. 263.

reached 1,500 percent in 1992 and nearly 1,000 percent in 1993, but was brought down to less than 50 percent by 1996. The costs of the disastrous 1995 war in Chechnya made matters worse, however, and with Russia again at war in Chechnya in 2000, Russia's future remains uncertain—perhaps the most important uncertainty in IR today.

Ukraine had even more severe economic woes (as did some other former Soviet republics). By 1992, Ukraine had inflation of 2,700 percent, with the government printing ever-larger quantities of coupons (denominated in Russian rubles) that served as money. The coupons themselves had become devalued by more than half their value in less than a year. As a result, almost two-thirds of all economic transactions in Ukraine were on a barter basis. Meanwhile, the government had enacted almost no market-oriented economic reforms (former communists were in power) and continued to funnel huge subsidies to state-owned industries (in the form of freshly printed coupons). Inflation was near 9,000 percent in 1993, according to one estimate.

By 1994, with Ukraine's GDP at half its 1990 level and inflation at around 5,000 percent, Ukrainian voters elected a reformer as president. He pushed through "shock therapy" economic reforms but faced a backlash from antireform political forces. In next-door Belarus, democratic reforms evaporated and the transition from a centrally planned economy was sluggish. The prospects for Ukraine and Belarus, as for Russia and the other former Soviet republics, are still uncertain.

Thus, the various states of the region had varying experiences, ranging from Poland's relative speed in making the transition away from communism to Ukraine's relative slowness. Russia was somewhere in between—itself a mix of successes and failures. During the transition, the gold reserves of the former Soviet Union—previously among the world's largest—were sold off to make ends meet.

The region's financial problems were similar to those facing third world countries trying to stabilize their economies (see Chapter 7), but they were compounded by special problems resulting from the breakup of the Soviet Union. First, some states printed

Bitter Fruits   Inflation and unemployment in Russia and other former Soviet republics in the 1990s have cut the GDP about in half and created political turmoil. These women in Moscow try to make ends meet by selling pickled vegetables grown in their yards, 1999.

Atlas CD
Hungary's
Private Farms
Photo, Music

their own currency while others kept using the Russian ruble (through the framework of the CIS). In the case of Ukraine, which planned to print its own currency, the rubles already in circulation there threatened to flood back into Russia in trade for Russian goods—expanding the ruble supply and fueling inflation in Russia. In other former Soviet republics—Azerbaijan, Armenia, Georgia, and Tajikistan—devastating wars wrecked economies and further fueled inflation.

The soaring inflation and general economic collapse throughout the region made it much harder to resolve all these problems and arrive at a stable political and economic environment in which IMF and World Bank assistance would be useful and not just wasted. Nonetheless, the former Soviet republics joined the IMF after negotiating reform plans. In 1996, creditor states renegotiated (to a longer-term basis) $40 billion in previous Russian debts; this reduced interest payments but did not address the underlying causes of the debts.

Several billion dollars were collected from the major economic powers in the early 1990s to create a "ruble-convertibility fund" that could be used to intervene in currency markets to shore up the value of the Russian ruble if necessary. This fund, combined with other forms of economic assistance (mostly loans rather than grants), made about $20 billion available for the task of helping the region through its transition. Such a sum, however, was inadequate for such a massive, historic, and unprecedented transition of an entire economic system. By way of comparison, international bail-outs of much smaller countries with less severe financial problems, such as Mexico and South Korea in the 1990s, each required tens of billions of dollars.

To get access to these assistance funds, Russia had to take steps to control inflation and government spending, sell off state-owned industry, and institute a market system throughout its economy. The attempt to implement such measures turned out to be even more painful than expected. The chaos of transition also provided fertile ground for corruption among government officials.

In Lithuania, which had led the way among republics breaking away from the Soviet Union, severe economic problems led voters in late 1992, in that state's first free elections after independence, to return the former communists to power. Then a number of other states in the region followed suit, electing former Communist parties. Some of these in turn switched again to reformers.

The economic and financial problems of the region were compounded by security problems—ethnic and national conflicts along the southern rim of the former union—which disrupted trade and monetary relations. For example, rail traffic from Russia was disrupted by separatists in Georgia, and Azerbaijan cut off energy supplies to Armenia. The main oil pipeline from Azerbaijan went right through the bombed-out capital of Chechnya, and was shut down for years.

It appears that for the next few years at least, Russia and Eastern Europe will struggle to find the economic and political stability that will allow them to integrate into the world capitalist economy. Until then, most of these states remain largely cut off from the potential benefits that could result from stable convertible currencies, expanded trade, and increased foreign investment.

The Position of Asia

Financial positions in the leading economies of Asia in some ways were reversed from the U.S. path in the 1980s and 1990s. Whereas the U.S. position deteriorated in the 1980s and early 1990s but strengthened in the late 1990s, the main Asian economies enjoyed a tremendous boom of economic growth in the 1980s and early 1990s but serious financial deterioration in the late 1990s. (China appeared immune from the deterioration.)

Atlas CD
Asia-Pacific
Map

Japan led these Asian trends. Following decades of robust growth since the devastation of World War II, Japan by the 1980s seemed to be emerging as a possible rival to the United States as the world's leading industrial power. Japanese auto manufacturers gained ground on U.S. rivals when smaller cars became popular after the oil-price shocks of the 1970s. In electronics and other fields, Japanese products began to dominate world markets, and Japanese capital became a major economic force in nearby developing economies (such as China and Thailand) and even in the United States where Japanese creditors financed much of the growing U.S. national debt.

These successes masked serious problems. The go-go economic growth of the 1980s drove prices of stocks and real estate to unrealistic levels based on speculation rather than inherent value. When these collapsed at the end of the 1980s, many banks were left with outstanding loans that had been secured by stocks and real estate, which could no longer be collected. These bad loans were covered up, however, partly because the Japanese government did not stringently regulate the banking system (and partly because bankers were political supporters of the government). Corruption and fraud added to the basic problems of the financial system. All of these problems were supposed to be solved in the

Atlas CD
Tokyo Scenes
Video

Is My Money Safe? The Asian financial crisis of 1997 led to currency devaluations, bank failures, and stock market crashes in a number of fast-growing Asian economies. Ordinary people faced hardships as a result, and financial analysts worried that the effects could seriously impact U.S. financial markets. Here, depositors gather outside a Hong Kong bank after a rumor of a run on the bank during the 1997 crisis.

early 1990s, but in fact persisted for years afterward. By 1997, Japan's financial position had weakened and large brokerages and banks began to go out of business.

Despite the example of Japan's financial system, these mistakes were repeated almost exactly in the 1990s by the newly industrializing countries of East and Southeast Asia. Real estate and stocks became overvalued as rapid economic growth led to speculation and ever-rising expectations. Banks made massive bad loans based on these overvalued assets and got away with it because of political corruption and cronyism. In 1997, these economies suffered a serious financial crisis, which jumped across international borders and sent shock waves around the globe that reverberated for two years.

The 1997 Asian crisis began when currency speculators began selling off the currencies of Southeast Asian countries. Thailand, the Philippines, Malaysia, and Indonesia were forced to let their currencies be devalued. Such pressure on currencies creates pressure on prospects for economic growth—because governments will have to cut back money supplies (raise interest rates) in response. The reduced prospects for economic growth in turn put pressure on stock prices, since companies will be less profitable. Also, currency devaluation reduces foreign investment (because investors lose confidence) and makes foreign loans harder to repay (since more local currency is needed to repay each unit of foreign currency). Thus, the currency problems of Asian countries led to stock market crashes in several of them. Other so-called *emerging mar-*

kets around the world—for example, Brazil—also suffered as investors generalized the developments in Asia.

The Philippines addressed the problem in the manner that international agencies and foreign investors preferred. After losing $1 billion unsuccessfully defending its currency's value, the Philippines let its currency float and then asked the IMF for a $1 billion stabilization loan, which the IMF approved in a week. In return for the IMF loan, the Philippines' government agreed to keep interest rates high and budget deficits low (to reduce inflation), to pass a tax reform law, and to tighten control of banks that had made bad real estate loans. These kinds of tough measures create political problems, especially when banks are politically connected or when governments are corrupt. The Philippines, by addressing such problems, won international approval.

Thailand at first refused to seek an IMF loan, but reversed itself by late July 1997. To gain a $16 billion IMF bail-out, Thailand agreed to close dozens of indebted banks, raise taxes, cut government deficits, and lower economic growth rates by more than half. The government of Thailand, a shaky coalition based on political patronage, soon collapsed as street protests vented anger at the economic downturn. A reform-minded prime minister was appointed and the situation stabilized.

Other Asian countries did not act decisively. In Malaysia, the prime minister annoyed foreign investors by accusing currency speculators of political motives in undermining Asian economies, because of racism and differences regarding human rights; he said that currency speculation should be illegal. (There is no evidence that speculators acted from any motivation other than making money, however.) The currency speculators, meanwhile, moved on to attack Indonesia, which had to let its currency fall, raise interest rates, and let its stock market drop. Within a few months, Indonesia too had to seek tens of billions of dollars in IMF loans, with the usual conditions attached. Indonesia resisted implementing the promised reforms, however, and its economy continued to slide (as did its political stability) in 1998. Riots and student protests eventually forced Indonesia's President Suharto to resign after 30 years of dictatorship. Overall, in Thailand, Malaysia, and Indonesia, stock markets lost about half their value and currencies about a quarter of their value in the first nine months of 1997. Observers declared the "Asian economic miracle" to be at an end.

China was exempt from these pressures for several reasons. Its economic growth had been less speculative (although rapid), its currency was not freely convertible, it held massive reserves of hard currency, and its government had shown the discipline necessary to bring inflation under control. Bringing down the economic growth rate from 14 to 10 percent annually, the government reduced inflation from 20 percent to less than 4 percent in 1995–1997. China then rode out the Asian crisis without devaluing its currency, by further drawing down the growth rate to 7 percent by 1999, still a very healthy pace.

In the fall of 1997, just months after being taken over by China, Hong Kong became the central target of currency speculators. To maintain the Hong Kong dollar, which for years had been pegged at a fixed rate per U.S. dollar, the Hong Kong government had to raise interest rates drastically and watch the stock market lose a third of its value in a few weeks. The Hong Kong stock crash triggered a huge global sell-off, but the Hong Kong government remained firm in maintaining its currency's value—which it saw as critical to foreign investors' long-term confidence—despite the costs of financial collapse and economic slowdown. In the first test of China's "one country, two systems" formula,

Atlas CD
Hong Kong
Stock
Exchange
Photo

the Chinese government did not intervene—allowing the Hong Kong administration to manage the crisis. After failing to bring down the Hong Kong dollar, currency speculators tried the Brazilian currency but ran into an equally firm policy there.

At the end of 1997, when South Korea caught the "Asian flu," the stakes increased. South Korea is the largest of the NICs, an economic power in the region ranking behind only Japan and China. With South Korea's currency down 20 percent, its stock markets collapsing, and its banks saddled with $50 billion in bad loans based on cronyism, the IMF stepped in with a $60 billion international bail-out—the largest ever—and the Korean government adopted stringent austerity measures. South Koreans first responded with a wave of nationalism, calling the day of the IMF agreement a Day of National Humiliation, and turning in foreign currency at public gatherings to help the national currency. Then they elected a new reformist president, Kim Dae Jong, a former political prisoner. After he convinced South Koreans that foreign investment was positive, they accepted the IMF; in fact, they began using the IMF as a face-saving way to reduce the costs of extravagant status-oriented weddings and funerals. Thus in South Korea, as in Thailand and Indonesia, the financial crisis brought about democratization and reform as well as pain.

The Asian crisis suddenly dried up huge sums of capital that had poured into Southeast Asia, doubling every two years and reaching nearly $100 billion annually. In 1997 and 1998, about $10 billion annually moved *out* of Southeast Asia. The capital flight also hit other so-called emerging markets. Russia's economy took a sharp downturn in 1998, and South America staggered along. Brazil in particular was the target of currency speculators recurrently, because Brazil found it hard to pass legislation to stem a huge government deficit. Every time the Brazilian political system seemed to stumble in making reforms promised as part of an IMF agreement, Brazil's stock market would fall and its currency would come under attack.

In theory, the free flow of capital instantly around the world—a result of global communications technologies—should stabilize economies. Investors can shift money quickly, and thus incrementally, as conditions indicate shifting strength and weakness of different currencies and economies. Instead of waiting for governments to devalue or revalue currencies when problems are far along, markets can gradually adjust values day by day. In practice, however, the global liquidity of capital has also shown a destabiliz-

THE INFORMATION

REVOLUTION   Liquid Capital

Technology has allowed electronic transfer of money around the world. As a result, more than $1 trillion crosses borders daily in international currency exchanges, and international investment capital can quickly bail out of emerging markets in crises, as happened in 1997. Currency speculators can drive foreign governments and economies into ruin, but in so doing may stimulate needed reforms. Will the liquidity of international capital ultimately prove destabilizing to the global economy?

To explore this question, go to www.IRtext.com

ing tendency, as small events can be amplified and reverberate in distant locations. Thus the problems of Thailand became an Asian crisis and then an emerging-markets crisis, as liquid capital fled for cover at the speed of light.

Total outstanding bank loans from the industrialized West to emerging-market countries, despite the sudden pull-out of some capital, still came to $1 trillion (mid-1998), with two-thirds from European banks, one-fifth from Japan, and one-eighth from U.S. banks. This relatively low U.S. exposure may help explain why the United States was not harmed by shock waves from the Asian crisis. Some aspects even benefited the United States—low oil prices that resulted from lower demand in 1998–1999, and cheaper imports from Asian countries that had devalued.

The Southeast Asian economies continued to shrink in 1998, but began growing again in 1999. The crisis had delayed, but not derailed, the fast-growing Asian economies. China, surprisingly, emerged as the rock of stability in the Asian turbulence. Japan was reduced in stature from a decade before. The Japanese government tried to stimulate more spending—in a population accustomed to saving—first by lowering interest rates to zero, then by tax cuts, and finally by giving out coupons in 1999 that could only be spent, not saved.

The Asian financial crisis of 1997 illustrates the importance of currency exchange rates in overall economic stability and growth. Governments face a dilemma in that politically desirable policies—from stimulating growth and keeping taxes low to supporting banks and businesses owned by friends and relatives—tend to undermine currency stability. If allowed to continue, such policies may lead to an economic collapse and the loss of foreign investment, but tough policies to maintain currency stability may cause a government to lose power.

In all the regions just discussed—North America, Asia, and especially Russia and Eastern Europe—the role of private businesses is expanding relative to that of the state. Throughout the world, private business now plays a role in the economy that exceeds that of the state. The remainder of this chapter considers the international political issues related to the operation of private businesses across state borders.

Multinational Business

Although states are the main rule makers for currency exchange and other international economic transactions, those transactions are carried out mainly by private firms and individuals, not governments. Most important among these private actors are MNCs.

Multinational Corporations
Multinational corporations (MNCs) are companies based in one state with affiliated branches or subsidiaries operating in other states. There is no exact definition, but the clearest case of an MNC is a large corporation that operates on a worldwide basis in many countries simultaneously, with fixed facilities and employees in each. With no exact definition, there is also no exact count of the total number of MNCs, but a reasonable estimate is around 10,000 worldwide.

Most important are *industrial corporations*, which make goods in factories in various countries and sell them to businesses and consumers in various countries. For example, the Ford Motor Company has more than 300,000 employees in 30 countries and in 1994

Web Link
Multinational
Corporations

**Atlas CD
German Car
Factory
*Photo***

merged its European and North American operations into one administrative unit, producing a "world car." Many of the largest industrial MNCs are based in the United States, though the relative U.S. share has declined in recent decades while the shares of Japan and Germany have increased. The automobile, oil, and electronics industries have the largest MNCs. Almost all of the largest MNCs are based in G7 states.

Financial corporations (the most important being banks) also operate multinationally—though often with more restrictions than industrial MNCs. Among the largest commercial banks worldwide, the United States does not hold a leading position—reflecting the traditional U.S. antitrust policy that limits banks' geographic expansion and restricts them from certain financial services (such as stock brokerage and insurance). Most of the world's largest banks are Japanese or European. The growing international integration of financial markets was spectacularly illustrated in 1995, when a single 28-year-old trader in Singapore lost $1 billion speculating on Japanese stock and bond markets and bankrupted his employer, a 200-year-old British investment bank. The 1997 stock market crash in Hong Kong also created a wave of sell-offs across international time zones as markets opened in Europe and then North America. Money moves across borders at the rate of $1.5 trillion per day. In this context, financial corporations are becoming more internationalized.

Some MNCs sell *services*. McDonald's fast-food chain and American Telephone and Telegraph (AT&T) are good examples. So are the international airlines, which sell tickets in dozens of states (and currencies) for travel all over the world. More down-to-earth service businesses such as retail grocery stores can also become MNCs. During the Gulf War, U.S. personnel could shop at Safeway supermarkets in Saudi Arabia. The United States predominates in service MNCs as it does in industrial ones (though service companies are generally somewhat smaller and less internationalized).

The role of MNCs in international political relations is complex and in some dispute. Some scholars see MNCs as virtually being agents of their home national governments. This view resonates with mercantilism, in which economic activity ultimately serves political authorities; thus MNCs have clear national identities and act as members of their national society under state authority. A variant of this theme (from a more revolutionary world view) sees national governments as virtually being agents of their MNCs; state interventions (economic and military) serve private, monied interests.

An opposite, liberal view of MNCs sees them as virtual citizens of the world beholden to no government. The head of Dow Chemical once said he dreamed of buying an island beyond any state's territory and putting Dow's world headquarters there. In such a view, MNCs act globally in the interests of their (international) stockholders and owe loyalty to no state. In any case, MNCs are motivated by the need to maximize profits, and managers who fail to do so are likely to be fired. Only in the case of state-owned MNCs—an important exception but a small minority of the total companies worldwide—do MNC actions reflect state interests. Even then, managers of state-owned MNCs have won greater autonomy to pursue profit in recent years (as part of the economic reforms instituted in many countries), and in many cases state-owned enterprises are being sold off (privatized).

As independent actors in the international arena, MNCs are increasingly powerful. Dozens of industrial MNCs have annual sales of tens of billions of dollars each (more than $100 billion each for GM, Ford, and Exxon). Only 36 states have more economic activity per year (GDP) than does the largest MNC, General Motors. A more apt comparison might be between MNCs and IOs as nonstate actors operating in the international arena. MNCs more than match most such organizations in size and financial resources. The largest IGO (the UN) has about $2 billion a year in revenue, compared to more than $150 billion for the largest MNC (GM). However, the largest *government* (the United States) has revenues of more than $1 trillion—about ten times larger than GM. Thus the power of MNCs does not rival that of the largest states but exceeds that of many poorer states and many IOs; this affects MNC operations in the global South (see p. 387).

Giant MNCs contribute to global interdependence. They are so deeply entwined in so many states that they have a profound interest in the stable operation of the international system—in security affairs as well as in trade and monetary relations. MNCs prosper in a stable international atmosphere that permits freedom of trade, of movement, and of capital flows (investments)—all governed by market forces with minimal government interference. Thus MNCs are, overall, a strong force for liberalism in the world economy, despite the fact that particular MNCs in particular industries do push for certain mercantilist policies to protect their own interests.

Most MNCs have a world management system based on *subsidiaries* in each state in which they operate. The operations within a given state are subject to the legal authority of that state's government. But the foreign subsidiaries are owned (in whole or in substantial part) by the parent MNC in the home country. The parent MNC hires and fires the top managers of its foreign subsidiaries.

Corporations that do business internationally and the states that host them have created a global *infrastructure* of facilities, services, communication links, and the like, that facilitate the conduct of business. The business infrastructure is a key aspect of *transnational relations*—linkages among people and groups across national borders. In addition to the direct connections among members of a single MNC, the operations of MNCs support a global business infrastructure connecting a transnational community of businesspeople. A U.S. manager arriving in South Korea, for instance, does not find a bewildering scene of unfamiliar languages, locations, and customs. Rather, she or he moves through a familiar sequence of airport lounges, telephone calls and faxes, international hotels, business conference rooms, and CNN broadcasts—most likely hearing English spoken in all.

Foreign Direct Investment

MNCs do not just operate in foreign countries, they also own capital (standing wealth) there—buildings, factories, cars, and so forth. For instance, U.S. and German MNCs own some of the capital located in Japan, and Japanese MNCs own capital located in the United States and Germany. *Investment* means exchanging money for ownership of capital (for the purpose of producing a stream of income that will, over time, more than compensate for the money invested). Investments in foreign countries are among the most important, and politically sensitive, activities of MNCs.

Web Link
Foreign Direct
Investment

Portfolio investment refers to paper securities such as stocks, bonds, and T-bills, whereas *foreign direct investment* involves tangible goods such as factories and office buildings (including ownership of a sizable fraction of a company's total stock, as opposed to a portfolio with little bits of many companies). Paper can be traded on a global market relatively freely, but direct investments cannot be freely moved from one state to another when conditions change. Direct investment is long term, and it is more visible than portfolio investment. Investments in the manufacturing sector usually entail the greatest investment in fixed facilities, which are difficult to move, and in training workers and managers. Investments in the extraction of minerals or fuels are less expensive, but even less movable. Investments in the service sector tend to be less expensive and easier to walk away from if conditions change.

Mercantilists tend to view foreign investments in their own country suspiciously. In third world countries, foreign direct investment often evokes concerns about a loss of sovereignty, because governments may be less powerful than the MNCs that invest in their country. These fears also reflect the historical fact that most foreign investment in the third world used to come from colonizers.

But many poor and transitional states also desperately need capital from any source to stimulate economic growth, so foreign direct investment is generally welcomed and encouraged despite these fears of economic nationalists (North-South investment is discussed further in Chapter 7.) Most foreign direct investment is not in the third world, however, but in industrialized countries.

Economic nationalists in industrialized countries also worry about losing power and sovereignty due to foreign investment. In Canada, for instance, mercantilists are alarmed that U.S. firms own more than half of Canada's manufacturing industry and more than two-thirds of Canada's oil and gas industry. Canada is much smaller than the United States, yet it depends heavily on U.S. trade. In this asymmetrical situation, some Canadians worry that they are being turned into an annex of the United States—economically, culturally, and ultimately politically—losing their own national culture and control of their economy.

Meanwhile, U.S. economic nationalists have similar concerns over foreign direct investment in the United States. Partly this reflects alarm over the accumulation of U.S. debts. Mercantilists see a loss of power when foreign investors buy up companies and real estate in a debtor country. Such concerns seem to be stronger when a foreign MNC buys an existing company or building than when it builds a new factory or other facility. For example, when Japanese investors bought Columbia movie studios in Los Angeles and (temporarily) Rockefeller Center in New York, many Americans saw these properties as somehow representative of the American spirit, and their sale was seen as a U.S. loss. But when Honda built a new car factory in Ohio, adding jobs and facilities to the U.S. economy, no such loss was perceived.

Liberalism does not condone such arguments. Liberal economists emphasize that global efficiency and the increased generation of wealth result from the ability of MNCs to invest freely across international borders. Investment decisions should be made solely on economic grounds, not nationalistic ones. Liberals also point out a glaring inconsistency in the U.S. public's preoccupation with Japanese investment in the United States in the late 1980s: more than half of all foreign investment in the United States was from Western Europe, and only a third as much was from Japan. Yet there was little outcry about a loss of U.S. sovereignty to Europe. Presumably this reflects either racism or a lingering shadow of World War II in the U.S. public's perceptions. The tables were turned in the late 1990s when financial crises in Japan made Americans worry that Japanese investors would pull out of the United States, not that more would come in.

In the view of liberal economists, foreign investments in the United States help, rather than hurt, the U.S. economy. Many of the benefits of a profitable Japanese factory in the United States accrue to U.S. workers at the plant and U.S. consumers of its

It's a Job   Foreign direct investment is often sought by host governments because it stimulates employment and economic growth, though at wages that home countries would not tolerate. Here, Muslim women in Indonesia assemble Barbies at a Mattel factory. Note that along with investment, a host country imports certain cultural trappings of the MNC's activity—such as Mattel's rendition of femininity in its doll. (This is a literal case of what postmodern feminists call the social construction of gender roles.)

products, even if some profits go back to Japan (and even those profits may be reinvested in the United States). Also, U.S. MNCs have more than $1 trillion of foreign direct investment outside the United States, so the picture is by no means one-sided.

Host and Home Government Relations   A state in which a foreign
MNC operates is called the **host country**; the state where the MNC has its headquarters is called its **home country**. MNC operations create a variety of problems and opportunities for both the host and home countries' governments. Conflicts between the host government and the MNC may spill over to become an interstate conflict between the host government and home government. For example, if a host government takes an MNC's property without compensation or arrests its executives, the home government may step in to help the MNC.

Because host governments can regulate activities on their own territories, in general an MNC cannot operate in a state against the wishes of its government. Conversely, because MNCs have many states to choose from, a host government cannot generally force an MNC to do business in the country against the MNC's wishes. At least in theory, MNCs operate in host countries only when it is in the interests of both the MNC and the host government. Common interests result from the creation of wealth in the host country by the MNC. Both the MNC and the host government benefit—the MNC from profits, the government directly by taxation and indirectly through economic growth (generating future taxes and political support).

However, there are also conflicts in the relationship. One obvious conflict concerns the distribution of new wealth between the MNC and host government. This distribution depends on the rate at which MNC activities or profits are taxed, as well as on the ground rules for MNC operations. Before an MNC invests or opens a subsidiary in a host country, it sits down with the government to negotiate these issues. Threats of violent leverage are largely irrelevant. Rather, the government's main leverage is to promise a favorable climate for doing business and making money; the MNC's main leverage is to threaten to take its capital elsewhere.

Governments can offer a variety of incentives to MNCs to invest. Special terms of taxation and of regulation are common. National and local governments may offer to provide business infrastructure—such as roads, airports, or phone lines—at the government's expense. (An MNC could also offer to build such infrastructure if allowed to operate on favorable terms in the country.) Over time, certain locations may develop a strong business infrastructure and gain a comparative advantage in luring MNCs to locate there.

These issues all concern the distribution of the new wealth that will be created by MNC operations. MNCs seek host governments that will let the MNC keep more of that wealth; governments seek MNCs that will let the government keep more. With many MNCs and quite a few governments involved in such negotiations, there is a sort of market process at work in the worldwide investment decisions of MNCs.

In addition to these relatively straightforward questions of distribution, MNC relations with host governments contain several other sources of potential conflict. One is the potential for governments to break their agreements with MNCs and change the terms of taxes, regulations, or other conditions. The extreme case is nationalization, in which a host government takes ownership of MNC facilities and assets in the host country (with or without compensation). However, governments hesitate to break their word with MNCs because then other MNCs may not invest in the future. Nationalization of foreign assets is rare now.

Another source of conflict is the trade policies of the host government. Government restrictions on trade seldom help foreign MNCs; more often they help the host country's own industries—which often directly compete with foreign MNCs. Ironically, although they favor global free trade, MNCs may funnel direct investment to states that restrict imports, because MNCs can avoid the import restrictions by producing goods in the host country (rather than exporting from the home country). Trade restrictions are thus another form of leverage that states have in luring foreign direct investment.

Trade regulations often seek to create as many jobs and as much taxable income as possible within the host country. If Toyota assembles cars at a factory in the United States (perhaps to avoid U.S. import restrictions), the U.S. government tends to pressure Toyota to use more U.S. parts in building the cars (such "domestic content" rules were part of the 1992 North American Free Trade Agreement). With parts and supplies now routinely converging from many countries to go into a product completed in one country, it is difficult to say exactly where the product was made. The question is a complex one that entails long negotiations between MNCs and host governments.

Monetary policy also leads to conflicts between MNCs and host governments. When a state's currency is devalued, imports suddenly become more expensive. A foreign

MNC selling an imported product (or a product assembled from imported parts) in the host country can be devastated by such a change. For example, if the dollar falls relative to the yen, Toyota-U.S.A. may have to charge more U.S. dollars for its cars in order to pay for the parts it brings in from Japan. Therefore, an MNC making a long-term investment in a host country wants the country's currency to be reasonably stable.

Finally, MNCs may conflict with host governments on issues of international security as well as domestic political stability. When an MNC invests in a country, it counts on its facilities there operating profitably over a number of years. If a war or revolution takes away the MNC's facility, the company loses not just income but capital—the standing wealth embodied in that facility.

In negotiating over these various sources of conflict, MNCs use a variety of means to influence host governments. These generally follow the same patterns as those used by domestic corporations (see pp. 107 and 226). MNCs hire lobbyists, use advertisements to influence public opinion, and offer incentives to host-country politicians (such as locating new facilities in their districts). Such activities are politically sensitive because host-country citizens and politicians may resent foreigners' trying to influence them. If Toyota-U.S.A. ran television ads supporting a U.S. presidential candidate who supported free trade, U.S. voters might react negatively to this foreign intrusion into U.S. politics.

Corruption is another means of influence over host governments that cannot be overlooked. Nobody knows the full extent to which MNCs use payoffs, kickbacks, gifts, and similar methods to win the approval of individual government officials for policies favorable to the MNC. Certainly this happens quite a bit with host governments in the third world (where government officials may be more desperate for income), but corruption also occurs regularly in rich industrialized countries. For example, in the early 1990s the Bank of Commerce and Credit International (BCCI) was found to have operated a vast illegal worldwide network of money laundering, fraud, and corruption.

MNCs have a range of conflicts with their home governments (where their headquarters are located), just as they do with their host states. Because MNCs are not foreigners but citizens in their home states, they have somewhat more freedom of action in influencing their home governments than they do in influencing host governments. For instance, U.S. MNCs routinely contribute to U.S. politicians' campaigns in hopes that those politicians will support policies favorable to the MNCs' global operations.

Some MNC conflicts with home governments are the same as with host governments. Taxation is an important one, as is trade policies. One recurrent complaint of MNCs against home governments is that policies adopted to punish political adversaries—economic sanctions and less extreme restrictions—end up harming the home-country MNCs more than the intended target. Usually, a competing MNC from another country is able to step into the gap when a government restricts its own MNCs. Unless ordered to do so, MNCs tend to go on doing business wherever it is profitable, with little regard for the political preferences of their governments. For example, the U.S.-based oil company Unocal described as "positive" the 1996 capture of Afghanistan's capital by the fundamentalist Taliban faction, whose treatment of women Secretary of State Albright called "despicable." The oil company hoped that if any faction, of whatever political or religious beliefs, could capture all of Afghanistan and end a civil war, then a multibillion dollar natural gas pipeline crossing Afghanistan could be built.

Sometimes governments do prevail, since MNCs often need the support of their home governments. For example, the U.S.-based Conoco oil company agreed to a bil-

Hard Place to Do Business   International business prospers in stable political environments. Foreign investors tend to be wary of putting money into a business environment like Russia's, where inflation constantly erodes the value of currency, and rampant crime and corruption take a huge economic toll. Here, a woman in Moscow trades rubles for dollars in 1994, bailing out after a one-day drop of more than 25 percent in the ruble's value.

lion-dollar oil development project in Iran, just when the U.S. government was trying to isolate Iran as a rogue state. Under pressure from the U.S. government, Conoco quickly decided to back out of the deal. This saved Conoco a fight with its home government, but cost Conoco a lucrative contract that went instead to a European company.

The location of an MNC's headquarters determines its home nationality. The shareholders and top executives of an MNC are mostly from its home country. But as the world economy becomes more integrated, this is becoming less true. Just as MNCs are increasingly doing business all over the world and assembling products from parts made in many countries, so are shareholders and managers becoming more international in composition.

Business Environments   All business activity takes place within an environment shaped by politics. In some places, states allow private businesses to compete freely with little interference from government; elsewhere, states own and operate their own businesses and forbid competition altogether. In some places, goods flow freely from producers to consumers; elsewhere, the same goods may be taxed or even stolen on their way to the consumer. In some places, markets are dominated by oligopolies; elsewhere, large companies are forcibly broken up into smaller ones.

The international business environment most conducive to the creation of wealth by MNCs is one of stable international security. It is difficult and risky to make money in a situation of international conflict, especially one that threatens to degenerate into violence and war. War destroys wealth, reduces the supply of labor, and distorts markets in many ways. Certainly some businesses profit from international instability and the threat of war—such as arms merchants and smugglers—but these are the exceptions.

In part, the MNCs' great interest in stability derives from the nature of investment, which pays back a stream of income over time. Money invested today may not be recovered for many years into the future. Any disruption of the economic framework in which MNCs expect to do business may mean the loss of investments. Large corporations, and especially banks, put much effort into political **risk assessment** before making international investments. They want to determine the probability that political conditions in future years (during which the investments will be paid back) will change so radically that the flow of income is disrupted. These future political conditions include not only wars but also international exchange rates, taxation policies, and trade policies. However, international security risks are among the most threatening to business.

In favoring stable international security, MNCs illustrate the fundamental connection between peace and prosperity in the liberal view of IPE. The world in which realists and mercantilists think we are doomed to live is, from a liberal perspective, an impoverished world. According to liberalism, the growing interdependence and growing prosperity of our world go hand in hand and create the conditions for stable peace. MNCs are merely the leading edge of a strong trend in IR: actors would rather make money than make war, and making war is not an effective way to make money.

Beyond these international security concerns, MNCs favor political stability in the broader rules of the game governing international business. When an MNC decides to do business in a new country, it hopes to know at the outset what to expect in terms of trade regulations, monetary policies, tax rates, and even public sentiments toward foreign companies. In a way, the actual policies of states regarding tax rates, exchange rates, tariffs, and so forth matter less than the stability of those policies. Businesses can easily adapt to a variety of conditions, but they adapt to rapid changes in those conditions less easily.

In monetary policy, international business benefits from the stability of rates that the managed float system tries to achieve. In trade policy, business benefits from the stability of tariff levels in the slowly shifting GATT framework. In norms of international law, business benefits from the traditions holding governments responsible for their predecessors' debts and requiring compensation for foreign assets nationalized.

MNCs also depend on national governments to provide security domestically for business operations. If Toyota builds a factory in Italy, it wants the Italian government to apprehend criminals who kidnap Toyota executives or steal Toyota payrolls, not to mention terrorists who might plant bombs to protest Toyota's presence. Many corporations have their own security personnel, and independent companies provide security services to businesses. But such capabilities do not compare with those of the armed forces maintained by states, so MNCs ultimately rely on host and home governments to provide a secure environment for business.

In the postcolonial era, military interventions by industrialized countries in the third world continue to occur, and some IR scholars see those interventions as efforts to impose on smaller states the political arrangements for profitable MNC operations. This is an area of controversy, however. IR scholars continue to study the relationships between the international economic activities of MNCs and the international security activities of their home governments.

MNCs themselves influence the evolving international security environment. Just as states form alliances to augment their capabilities, so do companies ally with other companies to enhance their pursuit of wealth. Corporate alliances involving MNCs often have international implications. When business alliances in an industry that has international markets occur within a single state, the alliances may in effect promote economic nationalism. Increasingly, however, corporate alliances are forming across national borders. Such alliances tend to promote liberalism rather than economic nationalism.

These international business alliances undermine both economic nationalism and the concept of a world splitting into rival trading blocs based in Europe, North America, and East Asia. In fact, international business alliances create interdependence among their home states. National interests become more intertwined and interstate conflicts tend to be reduced. By operating in multiple countries at once, all MNCs have these effects to some degree. But because they are based in one home country, MNCs are foreigners in other countries. International alliances of MNCs, however, are at home in several countries at once.

We do not yet live in a world without national borders—by a long shot—but the international activities of MNCs are moving us in that direction. The next chapter considers first the United Nations and its limited supranational role; then the European Union, the most highly developed intergovernmental organization; and finally the structure and norms governing international law and how they are changing the nature of world order.

THINKING CRITICALLY

1. Suppose your state had a chance to reach a major trade agreement by making substantial concessions. The agreement would produce $5 billion in new wealth for your state, as well as $10 billion for each of the other states involved (which are political allies but economic rivals). What advice would a mercantilist give your state's leader about making such a deal? What arguments would support the advice? How would liberal advice and arguments differ?

2. China seems to be making a successful transition to market economics and is growing rapidly. It is emerging as the world's second-largest economy. Do you think this is a good thing or a bad thing for your state? Does your reasoning reflect mercantilist or liberal assumptions?

3. If you were representing an MNC such as Toyota in negotiations over building an automobile factory in a foreign country, what kinds of concessions would you ask the host government for? What would you offer as incentives? If instead you were representing the host state in the negotiations and reporting to top state leaders, what would be your negotiating goals and the focus of your report?

CHAPTER SUMMARY

◆ Mercantilism emphasizes the use of economic policy to increase state power relative to other states. It is related to realism.

◆ Liberalism emphasizes international cooperation—especially through worldwide free trade—to increase the total creation of wealth (regardless of its distribution among states). Liberalism is conceptually related to idealism.

◆ Most international exchanges entail some conflicting interests and some mutual interests on the part of the states involved. Deals can be made because both sides benefit, but conflict over specific outcomes necessitates bargaining.

◆ The volume of world trade is very large—about 15 percent of global economic activity—and is concentrated heavily in the states of the industrialized West (Western Europe, North America, and Japan/Pacific).

◆ Trade creates wealth by allowing states to specialize in producing goods and services for which they have a comparative advantage (and importing other needed goods).

◆ The distribution of benefits from an exchange is determined by the price of the goods exchanged. With many buyers and sellers, prices are generally determined by market equilibrium (supply and demand).

◆ Communist states during the Cold War operated centrally planned economies in which national governments set prices and allocated resources. Almost all these states are now in transition toward market-based economies, which seem to be more efficient in generating wealth. The transition has been very painful in Russia and Eastern Europe, less so in China.

◆ Politics intrudes into international markets in many ways, including the use of economic sanctions as political leverage on a target state. However, sanctions are difficult to enforce unless all major economic actors agree to abide by them.

◆ Mercantilists favor trade policies that produce a trade surplus for their own state. Such a positive trade balance generates money that can be used to enhance state power.

◆ States are becoming more and more interdependent, in that the well-being of states depends on each other's cooperation. States that have reduced their dependence on others, by pursuing self-sufficient autarky, have failed to generate new wealth to increase their well-being. Self-reliance, like central planning, has been largely discredited as a viable economic strategy.

◆ Through protectionist policies, many states try to protect certain domestic industries from international competition. Such policies tend to slow down the global creation of wealth but do help the particular industry in question. Protectionism can be pursued through various means, including import tariffs (the favored method), quotas, subsidies, and other non-tariff barriers.

◆ Certain products—especially food, intellectual property, services, and military goods—tend to deviate more than others from market principles. Political conflicts among states concerning trade in these products are frequent.

◆ A world market based on free trade is a collective good (available to all members regardless of their individual contribution) inasmuch as states benefit from access to foreign markets whether or not they have opened their own markets to foreign products.

◆ Because there is no world government to enforce rules of trade, such enforcement depends on reciprocity and state power. In particular, states reciprocate each other's cooperation in opening markets (or punish each other's refusal to let in foreign products). Although it leads to trade wars on occasion, reciprocity has achieved substantial cooperation in trade.

◆ The World Trade Organization, formerly the GATT, is the most important multilateral global trade agreement. In successive rounds of GATT negotiations over nearly 50 years, states have lowered overall tariff rates (especially on manufactured goods).

◆ The GATT was institutionalized in 1995 with the creation of the World Trade Organization (WTO), which expands the focus on manufactured goods to include agriculture and services.

◆ Although the WTO provides a global framework, states continue to operate under thousands of bilateral trade agreements specifying the rules for trade in specific products between specific countries.

◆ Regional free-trade areas (with few if any tariffs or non-tariff barriers) have been created in Europe, North America, and several other less important instances. The North American area includes Canada, Mexico, and the United States.

◆ International cartels are occasionally used by leading producers (sometimes in conjunction with leading consumers) to control and stabilize prices for a commodity on world markets. The most visible example in recent decades has been the oil producers' cartel, OPEC.

◆ Free-trade agreements have led to a backlash from politically active interest groups adversely affected by globalization; these include labor unions, environmental and human rights NGOs, and certain consumers.

◆ Each state uses its own currency. These currencies have no inherent value but depend on people's belief that they can be traded for future goods and services.

◆ Gold and silver were once used as world currencies that had value in different countries. Today's system is more abstract: national currencies are valued against each other through exchange rates.

◆ The most important currencies—against which most other states' currencies are compared—are the U.S. dollar, German mark, and Japanese yen.

◆ Inflation, most often resulting from the printing of currency faster than the creation of new goods and services, causes the value of a currency to fall relative to other currencies. Inflation rates vary widely but are generally much higher in the third world and former Soviet bloc than in the industrialized West.

◆ States maintain reserves of hard currency and gold. These reserves back a national currency and cover short-term imbalances in international financial flows.

◆ Fixed exchange rates can be used to set the relative value of currencies, but more often states use floating exchange rates driven by supply and demand on world currency markets. Governments cooperate to manage the fluctuations of (floating) exchange rates but are limited in this effort by the fact that most money traded on world markets is privately owned.

◆ Over the long term, the relative values of national currencies are determined by the underlying health of the national economies and by the monetary policies of governments (how much money they print).

◆ To ensure discipline in printing money—and to avoid inflation—industrialized states turn monetary policy over to semiautonomous central banks such as the U.S. Federal Reserve.

◆ The World Bank and the International Monetary Fund (IMF) work with states' central banks to maintain stable international monetary relations. Since 1971 the system has used Special Drawing Rights (SDRs)—a kind of world currency controlled by the IMF—rather than gold.

◆ The IMF operates a system of national accounts to keep track of the flow of money into and out of states. The balance of trade (exports minus imports) must be balanced by capital flows (investments and loans) and changes in reserves.

◆ International debt results from a protracted imbalance in capital flows—a state borrowing more than it lends—in order to cover a chronic trade deficit or government budget deficit.

◆ The U.S. financial position declined naturally from an extraordinary predominance immediately after World War II. The fall of the dollar-gold standard in 1971 reflected this decline. In the 1980s, the U.S. position worsened dramatically. A chronic budget deficit and trade deficit expanded the country's debt burden. Economic growth in the mid-1990s helped bring the budget deficit back down.

◆ The positions of Russia and the other states of the former Soviet bloc have declined drastically as they have tried to make the difficult transition from communism to capitalism. Though rampant inflation in the early 1990s subsided in the late 1990s, the economies of the former Soviet republics are about half their former size. Western states have not extended massive economic assistance to Russia and Eastern Europe.

◆ Multinational corporations (MNCs) do business in more than one state simultaneously. The largest are based in the leading industrialized states, and most are privately owned. MNCs are increasingly powerful in international economic affairs.

◆ MNCs contribute to international interdependence in various ways. States depend on MNCs to create new wealth, and MNCs depend on states to maintain international stability conducive to doing business globally.

◆ MNCs try to negotiate favorable terms and look for states with stable currencies and political environments in which to make direct investments. Governments seek such foreign investments on their territories so as to benefit from the future stream of income.

◆ MNCs try to influence the international political policies of both their headquarters state and the other states in which they operate. Generally MNCs promote policies favorable to business—low taxes, light regulation, stable currencies, and free trade. They also support stable international security relations, because war generally disrupts business.

◆ Increasingly, MNCs headquartered in different states are forming international alliances with each other. These inter-MNC alliances, even more than other MNC operations across national borders, are creating international interdependence and promoting liberal international cooperation.

◆ MNCs sometimes promote economic nationalism over liberalism, however, especially in the case of state-owned MNCs or alliances of MNCs based in a single country.

ONLINE PRACTICE TEST

Take an online practice test at
www.IRtext.com

6

International Organization and Law

CHAPTER OUTLINE

- ◆ Supranationalism
- ◆ The United Nations
- ◆ The European Union
- ◆ International Law

Supranationalism

This chapter continues to develop a theme from the discussion of MNCs—that of non-state actors in interaction with state actors. Although MNCs are *substate* actors in the formation of state foreign policy (see pp. 105–115), they are also *transnational* actors bridging national borders and creating new avenues of interdependence among states. This chapter discusses transnational and international nonstate actors whose roles and influences are **supranational**—they subsume a number of states within a larger whole.

The UN has some supranational aspects, but they are limited by the UN Charter, which is based on state sovereignty. The European Union (EU) is a somewhat more supranational entity than the United Nations (UN); other regional organizations have tried to follow Europe's path as well, with mixed success. These cases all contain a struggle between the contradictory forces of *nationalism* and *supranationalism*—between state sovereignty and the higher authority (in level but not yet in power or legitimacy) of supranational structures.

Overall, the density of connections across national borders is increasing year by year. Formal IGOs such as the UN and the EU are not the only way that supranationalism is developing. In a less tangible way, people are also becoming connected across international borders through the meshing of ideas, including norms, rules, and international laws. The final section of this chapter discusses these influences.

Roles of International Organizations International organizations

(IOs) include *intergovernmental organizations (IGOs)* such as the UN, and *nongovernmental organizations (NGOs)* such as the International Committee of the Red Cross. The number of IOs has grown more than fivefold since 1945, reaching about five hundred IGOs and tens of thousands of NGOs (depending somewhat on definitions). New NGOs are created around the world daily. This weaving together of people across national boundaries through specialized groups reflects world interdependence (see "Interdependence" on pp. 220–222).

Some IGOs are global in scope, others are regional or just bilateral (having only two states as members). Some are general in their purposes, others have specific functional purposes. Overall, the success of these IGOs has been mixed; the regional ones have had more success than the global ones, and those with specific functional or technical purposes have worked better than those with broad purposes. IGOs hold together because they promote the national interests (or enhance the leverage) of their member states—not because of vague ideals.

Among *regional* IGOs, the European Union encompasses some of the most important, but it is not the only example. Others include the Association of South East Asian Nations (ASEAN), the Latin American Integration Association, and locust control organizations in Africa (on regional security alliances, see pp. 76–79). The functional roles of IOs are important to their overall effect on international relations. Here we will rely on the more general theoretical discussion of international institutions begun in Chapter 3.

Global IGOs (aside from the UN) usually have functional purposes involving coordinating actions of some set of states around the world. The IGO called Intelsat, for example, is a consortium of governments and private businesses that operates communications satellites. Members of the Organization of Petroleum Exporting Countries (OPEC) are major oil producers, who meet periodically in Vienna to set production quotas for members in an effort to keep world oil prices high and stable.

NGOs tend to be more specialized in function than IGOs. Many NGOs have economic or business-related functions. The International Air Transport Association coordinates the work of airline companies. Other NGOs have global political purposes—for instance, Amnesty International (for human rights), or Planned Parenthood (for reproductive rights and family planning). Still other NGOs have cultural purposes—for example, the International Olympic Committee.

Religious groups are among the largest NGOs, whose memberships often span many countries. Both in today's world and historically, sects of Christianity, Islam, Buddhism, Judaism, Hinduism, and other world religions have organized themselves across state borders, often in the face of hostility from one or more national governments. Missionaries have deliberately built and nurtured these transnational links. The Catholic Church historically held a special position in the European international system, especially before the seventeenth century. NGOs with broad purposes and geographical scope often maintain observer status in the UN so that they can participate in UN meetings about issues of concern.

A web of international organizations of various sizes and types now connects people in all countries. The rapid growth of this network, and the increasingly intense communications and interactions that occur within it, are indicative of rising international interdependence. These organizations in turn provide the institutional mesh to hold together some kind of world order even when leaders and contexts come and go, and even when norms are undermined by sudden changes in power relations. At the center of that web of connection stands the most important international organization today, the UN.

The United Nations

The UN and other international organizations have both strengths and weaknesses in the anarchic international system. State sovereignty creates a real need for such organizations on a practical level, because no central world government performs the function of coordinating the actions of states for mutual benefit. However, state sovereignty also severely limits the power of the UN and other IOs, because governments reserve power to themselves and are stingy in delegating it to the UN or anyone else. The UN has had a mixed record with these strengths and weaknesses—in some ways providing remarkable global-level management and in other ways appearing helpless against the sovereignty of even modest-sized states (not to mention great powers).

The UN System The UN is a relatively new institution, about 50 years old. Even newer is the more prominent role that the UN has played in international security affairs since the Cold War ended. Despite this new prominence, the main purposes of the UN are the same now as when it was founded right after World War II.

PURPOSES OF THE UN The UN is the closest thing to a world government that has ever existed, but it is not a world government. Its members are sovereign states that have not empowered the UN to enforce its will within states' territories except with the consent of those states' governments. Thus, although the UN strengthens world order, its design acknowledges the realities of international anarchy and the unwillingness of states to surrender their sovereignty. Within these limits, the basic purpose of the UN is to provide a global institutional structure through which states can sometimes settle conflicts with less reliance on the use of force.

The **UN Charter** is based on the principles that states are *equal* under international law; that states have full *sovereignty* over their own affairs; that states should have full *independence* and *territorial integrity*; and that states should carry out their international *obligations*—such as respecting diplomatic privileges, refraining from committing aggression, and observing the terms of treaties they sign. The Charter also lays out the structure of the UN and the methods by which it operates.

The UN does not exist because it has power to force its will on the world's states; it exists because states have created it to serve their needs. A state's membership in the UN is essentially a form of indirect leverage. States gain leverage by using the UN to seek more beneficial outcomes in conflicts. The cost of this leverage is modest—UN dues and the expenses of diplomatic representatives, plus the agreement to behave in accordance with the Charter (most of the time).

States get several benefits from the UN, foremost among which is the international stability (especially in security affairs) that the UN tries to safeguard; this allows states to realize gains from trade and other forms of exchange. The UN is a *symbol* of international order and even of global identity. It is also a *forum* where states promote their views and bring their disputes. And it is a *mechanism for conflict resolution* in international security affairs. The UN also promotes and coordinates development assistance (see Chapter 7) and other programs of *economic and social development* in third world countries. This reflects the belief that economic and social problems—above all, poverty—are an important source of international conflict and war. Finally, the UN is a coordinating system for *information* and planning by hundreds of internal and external agencies and programs, and for the publication of international data.

Despite its heavy tasks, the UN is still a small and fragile institution—a 55-year-old infant. Compare, for instance, what states spend on two types of leverage for settling conflicts—military forces and the UN. Every year, the world spends $800 billion on the military and about $2 billion on the UN. That proportion is about the same in the United States: each U.S. citizen pays (on average) about $1,000 a year for U.S. military forces and about $2 a year for UN dues and assessments (yet the United States is more than $1 billion behind in paying its dues). The UN costs about as much as the military budget of a single mid-sized country such as Malaysia or Egypt, or less than what a country such as Thailand or Switzerland spends on military forces.

≈ **STRUCTURE OF THE UN** The UN's structure (see Figure 6.1) centers around the **UN General Assembly**, where representatives of all states sit together in a huge room, listen to speeches, and pass resolutions. The General Assembly coordinates a variety of third world development programs and other autonomous agencies through the *Economic and Social Council (ECOSOC)*. Parallel to the General Assembly is the **UN Security Council**, in which five great powers and ten rotating member states make decisions about international peace and security. The Security Council has responsibility for the dispatch of peacekeeping forces to trouble spots. The administration of the UN takes place through the **UN Secretariat** (executive branch), led by the secretary-general of the UN. The *World Court* (International Court of Justice, discussed below) is a judicial arm of the UN.

National delegations to the UN, headed by ambassadors from each member state, work and meet together at UN headquarters in New York City. They have diplomatic status in the United States, which as host country also assumes certain other obligations to facilitate the UN's functioning. For example, the U.S. government has permitted people such as Fidel Castro—normally barred from entry to the United States—to visit New York long enough to address the UN.

A major strength of the UN structure is the *universality of its membership*. There were 189 members in 2000. Virtually every territory in the world is either a UN member or formally a province or colony of a UN member. Switzerland, which maintains a strict autonomy from the international system, is not a UN member but its "observer" mission participates in meetings. Formal agreement on the Charter (even if sometimes breached) commits all states to a set of basic rules governing their relations. (A major flaw in the old League of Nations was the absence of several important actors.)

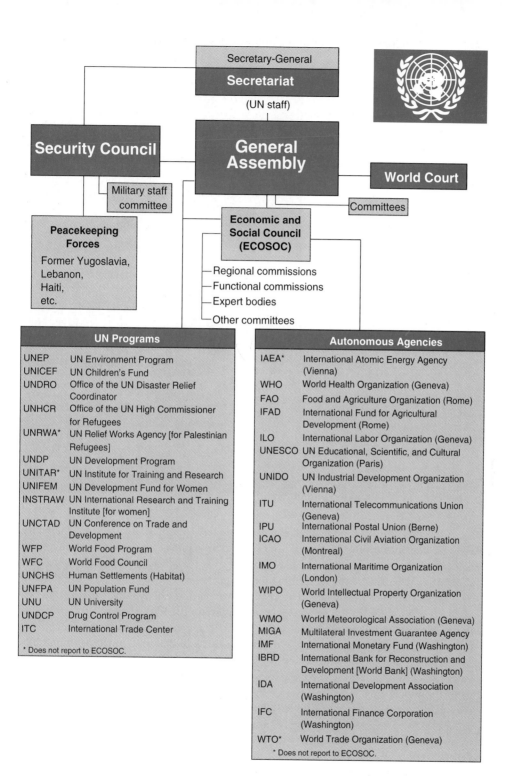

Secretary-General

Secretariat

(UN staff)

Security Council

General Assembly

World Court

Military staff committee

Committees

Peacekeeping Forces

Former Yugoslavia,
Lebanon,
Haiti,
etc.

Economic and Social Council (ECOSOC)

— Regional commissions
— Functional commissions
— Expert bodies
— Other committees

UN Programs	
UNEP	UN Environment Program
UNICEF	UN Children's Fund
UNDRO	Office of the UN Disaster Relief Coordinator
UNHCR	Office of the UN High Commissioner for Refugees
UNRWA*	UN Relief Works Agency [for Palestinian Refugees]
UNDP	UN Development Program
UNITAR*	UN Institute for Training and Research
UNIFEM	UN Development Fund for Women
INSTRAW	UN International Research and Training Institute [for women]
UNCTAD	UN Conference on Trade and Development
WFP	World Food Program
WFC	World Food Council
UNCHS	Human Settlements (Habitat)
UNFPA	UN Population Fund
UNU	UN University
UNDCP	Drug Control Program
ITC	International Trade Center

* Does not report to ECOSOC.

Autonomous Agencies	
IAEA*	International Atomic Energy Agency (Vienna)
WHO	World Health Organization (Geneva)
FAO	Food and Agriculture Organization (Rome)
IFAD	International Fund for Agricultural Development (Rome)
ILO	International Labor Organization (Geneva)
UNESCO	UN Educational, Scientific, and Cultural Organization (Paris)
UNIDO	UN Industrial Development Organization (Vienna)
ITU	International Telecommunications Union (Geneva)
IPU	International Postal Union (Berne)
ICAO	International Civil Aviation Organization (Montreal)
IMO	International Maritime Organization (London)
WIPO	World Intellectual Property Organization (Geneva)
WMO	World Meteorological Association (Geneva)
MIGA	Multilateral Investment Guarantee Agency
IMF	International Monetary Fund (Washington)
IBRD	International Bank for Reconstruction and Development [World Bank] (Washington)
IDA	International Development Association (Washington)
IFC	International Finance Corporation (Washington)
WTO*	World Trade Organization (Geneva)

* Does not report to ECOSOC.

FIGURE 6.1   The United Nations

Assembly of Equals The universal membership of the United Nations is one of its strengths. All member states have a voice and a vote in the General Assembly. Here, it votes on a comprehensive nuclear test ban treaty, 1996. It passed 158–3, with India—which set off five nuclear tests two years later—voting "no."

One way the UN induced all the great powers to join was to reassure them that their participation in the UN would not harm their national interests. Recognizing the role of power in world order, the UN Charter gave five great powers each a veto over substantive decisions of the Security Council.

The UN Charter establishes a mechanism for *collective security*—the banding together of the world's states to stop an aggressor. Chapter 7 of the Charter explicitly authorizes the Security Council to use military force against aggression if the nonviolent means called for in Chapter 6 have failed. However, because of the great-power veto, the UN cannot effectively stop aggression by (or supported by) a great power. Thus Chapter 7 was used only once during the Cold War—in the Korean War when the Soviet delegation unwisely boycotted the proceedings (and when China's seat was held by the nationalists on Taiwan). It was under Chapter 7 of the Charter that the UN authorized the use of force to reverse Iraqi aggression against Kuwait in 1990.

HISTORY OF THE UN The UN was founded in 1945 in San Francisco by 51 states. It was the successor to the League of Nations, which had failed to effectively counter aggression in the 1930s—Japan simply quit when the League condemned Japanese aggression against China. Like the League, the UN was founded to increase international order and the rule of law to prevent another world war.

There has long been a certain tension between the UN and the United States as the world's most powerful state. (The United States had not joined the League, and it was partly to assure U.S. interest that the UN headquarters was placed in New York.) The UN in some ways constrains the United States by creating the one coalition that can rival U.S. power—that of all the states. A certain isolationist streak in U.S. foreign policy runs counter to the UN concept. However, the UN *amplifies* U.S. power because the United States leads the global UN coalition. Also, the United States is not rich or strong enough to keep order in the world by itself. And, as a great trading nation, the United States benefits from the stability and order that the UN helps to create.

In the 1950s and 1960s, the UN's membership more than doubled as colonies in Asia and Africa won independence. This changed the character of the General Assembly, where each state has one vote regardless of size. The new members had different concerns from the Western industrialized countries and in many cases resented having been colonized by Westerners. Many third world states, even more so then than today, believed that the United States enjoyed too much power in the UN. They noticed that the UN is usually effective in international security affairs only when the United States leads the effort (because U.S. interests are at stake in the matter).

The growth in membership thus affected voting patterns in the UN. During the UN's first two decades, the Assembly had regularly sided with the United States, and the Soviet Union was the main power to use its veto in the Security Council to counterbalance that tendency. But as newly independent third world states began to predominate, the United States found itself in the minority on many issues, and by the 1970s and 1980s it had become the main user of the veto.

Another change took place in 1971. China's seat on the Security Council (and in the General Assembly) had been occupied by the nationalist government on Taiwan island, which had lost power in mainland China in 1949. The exclusion of communist China was an exception to the UN principle of universal membership, and in 1971 the Chinese seat was taken from the nationalists and given to the communist government. Today, the government of Taiwan—which functions autonomously in many international matters despite its status as a Chinese province—is not a member of the UN.

Throughout the Cold War, the UN had few successes in international security because the U.S.-Soviet conflict prevented consensus. The UN appeared somewhat irrelevant in a world order structured by two opposing alliance blocs. There were a few notable exceptions, such as agreements to station peacekeeping forces in the Middle East, but the UN did not play a central role in solving international conflicts. The General Assembly, with its predominantly third world membership, concentrated on the economic and social problems of poor countries, and this became the main work of the UN.

Third world states also used the UN as a forum to criticize rich countries in general and the United States in particular. By the 1980s, the U.S. government showed its displeasure with this trend by withholding U.S. dues to the UN (eventually more than $1 billion) and by withdrawing from membership in one UN agency, UNESCO.

After the Cold War, the bipolar world order gave way to one in which multilateral action was more important. The great powers could finally agree on measures regarding international security. Also, third world states could not hope to play off the super-powers against each other, so they cautiously avoided alienating the United States. In this context the UN moved to center stage in international security affairs.

The UN had several major successes in the late 1980s in bringing to an end violent regional conflicts (in Central America and the Iran-Iraq War). Cease-fires were negotiated under UN auspices, and peacekeeping forces were dispatched to monitor the situation. By the 1990s, the UN had emerged as the world's most important tool for settling international conflicts. Between 1987 and 1993, Security Council resolutions increased from 15 to 78, peacekeeping missions from 5 to 17, peacekeepers from 12,000 to 78,000, and countries sending troops from 26 to 76.

**Atlas CD
United Nations
in Somalia
*Photo***

The new missions ran into serious problems, however. Inadequate funding undermined peacekeeping efforts to some extent. In Angola, the UN sent only a few peacekeepers, and when the government won internationally observed elections in 1992, the rebels took to arms and the civil war resumed. In Cambodia, the Khmer Rouge faction refused to disarm according to the UN-brokered peace plan it had signed; later a coup interrupted Cambodia's transition to democracy.

Such problems were most dramatic in the former Yugoslavia, where the UN in 1993–1995 undertook its largest peacekeeping mission with nearly 40,000 foreign troops, costing more than $1 billion annually. The mission was deeply flawed by a mismatch between the types of forces sent (lightly armed, equipped for humanitarian operations) and the situation itself (territorial aggression by heavily armed forces). This unhappy combination was known as "peacekeeping where there is no peace to keep."

In response to these problems (and to the unpaid U.S. dues), the UN scaled back peacekeeping operations in 1995–1997 (from 78,000 to 19,000 troops) and carried out reductions and reforms in the UN Secretariat and UN programs. The changes grew out of a financial crisis in the mid-1990s that saw Secretary-General Boutros Boutros-Ghali declare at the UN's fiftieth anniversary that "practically, the United Nations is bankrupt." Overseeing reforms and reductions has occupied his successor, Kofi Annan, who took over in 1997. In Annan's first year, CNN founder Ted Turner gave him a boost with a $1 billion private contribution (pledged over ten years), the equivalent of almost a year's (nonpeacekeeping) UN operating budget.

The United States still failed to pay its bills, though a new Secretary General shrank budgets and jobs as the United States had demanded. Congress first refused to allocate funds, then attached abortion-related riders that triggered presidential vetoes. Congress also delayed confirming the new U.S. ambassador to the UN, Richard Holbrooke, leaving the position vacant for a year. In 1997, the U.S. owed the UN $1.6 billion; Japan, Russia, and Ukraine each owed more than $200 million. Only 30 states paid their 1997 assessments on time. The United States was also hundreds of millions of dollars behind in payments to other international organizations including the World Bank and the Food and Agriculture Organization. This U.S. free-riding shows that support of intergovernmental organizations presents a difficult collective goods problem (see pp. 88–89).

A vigorous 1999 lobbying campaign by American UN supporters including the former secretaries of state from both parties (with Turner-funded media spots) pointed out that "Great nations pay their bills." The highest-ranking American in the UN staff called the U.S. failure to pay up "tragic shortsightedness" based on "ignorance." Close U.S. allies became outspoken in criticizing the U.S. failure to honor its international commitments. Finally, U.S. legislation was enacted in 1999 to pay the back dues, but only at a lesser rate than originally committed, and only on condition of various further UN reforms. It was unclear, in 2000, whether the other UN member-states would accept the offer, which many openly criticized as arrogant.

The UN is in some ways just beginning to work as it was originally intended to, through a concert of great powers and universal recognition of the Charter. However, as states turned increasingly to the UN after the Cold War, its modest size and resources became seriously overburdened, leading to contraction of missions and funding. The UN today is more important than ever, yet more in danger of failing. In the coming few years the UN must continue to grapple with the challenges of its new role and the limitations of its new budget.

The Security Council

The Security Council is responsible for maintaining international peace and security, and for restoring peace when it breaks down. Its decisions are *binding* on all UN member states. The Security Council has tremendous power to *define* the existence and nature of a security threat, to *structure* the response to such a threat, and to *enforce* its decisions through mandatory directives to UN members (such as to halt trade with an aggressor).

Web Link
UN Security
Council

In 55 years, the Council has passed about 1,250 resolutions, with new ones now added by the week. These resolutions represent the great powers' blueprints for resolving the world's various security disputes, especially in regional conflicts. The resolutions reflect what the great powers can all agree upon.

The five *permanent members* of the Council—the United States, Britain, France, Russia, and China—are the most important. The Council also has ten *nonpermanent members* who rotate onto the Council for two-year terms. Nonpermanent members are elected (five each year) by the General Assembly from a list prepared by informal regional caucuses. Usually there is a mix of regions and country sizes, though not by any strict formula. The Council's *chairperson* rotates among the Council members monthly. Sometimes this matters: in 1990 the United States pushed for action against Iraq before the chair passed from the United States to Yemen, which opposed the U.S. position.

Substantive Security Council resolutions require *nine* votes from among the 15 members. But a "no" vote by any permanent member defeats the resolution—the *veto* power. Many resolutions have been vetoed by the permanent members, and many more have never been proposed because they would have faced certain veto.

Members can *abstain* on resolutions, an option that some permanent members use to register misgivings about a resolution without vetoing. China abstains with regularity, because it generally reserves its veto for matters directly affecting Chinese security. Its 1997 veto of a resolution on Guatemala (a country with strong ties to Taiwan) was its first veto in nearly 25 years. As a power with more regional than global interests, China avoids alienating other great powers by blocking their actions in distant parts of the world. (If the Security Council tried to condemn China, no such restraint would apply.) The United States has abstained several times to register a middle position on resolutions critical of Israel. (Nonpermanent members may also abstain.)

The Security Council *meets irregularly* (in the New York UN headquarters) upon request of a UN member—often a state with a grievance regarding another state's actions. When Kuwait was invaded, when Bosnia was being overrun, the victim called on the Security Council—a kind of 911 phone number for the world (but one without a standing police force). Because international security continues to be troublesome in many

Council of Power   Collective security rests with the UN Security Council, here voting in November 1990 to authorize the use of force if Iraq did not withdraw from Kuwait by January 15. Foreign ministers attended personally on this occasion, and the presidency, which rotates monthly, was held by U.S. Secretary of State James Baker *(top right)*. Soviet Foreign Minister Shevardnadze *(top center)* voted "yes." China *(at right)* abstained but did not use its veto, and the resolution passed 12–2 with only Cuba and Yemen opposed. UN staff sit in center, with UN Secretary-General Perez de Cuellar next to Baker.

regions and because these troubles often drag on for months or years, meetings of the Council are frequent.

The Security Council's *power is limited* in two major ways; both reflect the strength of state sovereignty in the international system. First, the Council's decisions depend entirely on the interests of its member states. The UN ambassadors who represent those states cannot change a Council resolution without authorization from their governments. Second, although Security Council resolutions in theory bind all UN members, member states in practice often try to evade or soften their effect. For instance, trade sanctions are difficult to enforce because it is tempting and relatively easy to cheat by trading with a sanctioned state. A Security Council resolution can be enforced in practice only if enough powerful states care about it.

The Security Council has a formal mechanism for coordinating multilateral military action in response to aggression, called the *Military Staff Committee*. It is composed of military officers from the permanent Council members. But the United States opposes placing its forces under non-U.S. commanders, and the committee has never been used. Instead, military forces responding to aggression under the auspices of Security Council resolutions have remained under national command. For example, U.S. forces in the Gulf War had the mission of enforcing UN resolutions but did not display UN insignia or flags, nor did the 20,000 U.S. soldiers sent to Somalia in late 1992 to restore humanitarian relief efforts disrupted by civil war. In most *peacekeeping* operations, however, UN forces operate under UN command, wear UN insignia (including blue helmets or berets), travel in UN-marked vehicles, and so forth.

Even when the Security Council cannot agree on means of enforcement, its resolutions shape the way disputes are seen and ultimately how they are resolved. Security Council Resolution 242 after the Arab-Israeli war of 1967 laid out the principles for a just peace in that conflict—primarily the right of all states in the region to live within secure and well-defined borders and the return by Israel of territories captured in the 1967 war. (The parties are still arguing about whether territories to be returned by Israel means "all" territories.) Reaffirmed in Resolution 338 after the 1973 war, these resolutions helped shape the 1978 Camp David agreement; later they formed the basis for peace negotiations between Israel and its Arab neighbors that began in 1991.

After the end of the Cold War, the prestige of the Security Council rose and it became more active than before. The first *summit meeting* of Council members in 1992 brought together for the first time the leaders of the "big five." The summit reaffirmed the universal commitments of states to the security principles embodied in the UN Charter and to the Security Council as a structure for implementing those principles. However, in the second half of the 1990s, the Council lost influence or was marginalized in such hot-spots as Iraq, Angola, Macedonia, and the large Ethiopia-Eritrea war. Most importantly, the 1999 NATO bombing campaign against Serbia proceeded without authorization from the Security Council, in contrast to most great-power military interventions in the 1990s. After the fact, the Security Council authorized an international force for Kosovo since Serbia had agreed to it.

Proposed Changes The structure of the Security Council is not without its problems. Japan and Germany are great powers that contribute substantial UN dues (based on economic size) and make large contributions to UN programs and peacekeeping operations. Yet they have exactly the same formal representation in the UN as tiny states with less than one-hundredth of their populations: one vote in the General Assembly and the chance to rotate onto the Security Council (in practice they rotate on more often than the tiny states). As global trading powers, Japan and Germany have huge stakes in the ground rules for international *security* affairs, because a stable security climate is good for international business. The security rules are written in the Security Council. Naturally, Japan and Germany would like seats at the table.

But including Japan and Germany as permanent Council members would not be simple. If Germany joined, three of the seven permanent members would be European, giving that region unfair weight (especially from the viewpoint of former European colonies in the third world). The three European seats could be combined into one (a rotating seat or one representing the European Union), but this would water down the power of Britain and France, which can veto any such change in the Charter. Also, if Japan or Germany were given a seat, then what about India, with 20 percent of the world's population? It, too, has only a lone vote in the General Assembly and so is badly underrepresented in the present scheme. But China (with a veto) would not welcome rival India onto the Council. Shouldn't an expanded Security Council include at least one predominantly Islamic country? But which state could represent such a diverse set of countries? Finally, what about Latin America and Africa? One plan to overhaul the Security Council, proposed by Brazil in 1992, would give permanent seats, but without veto power, to Japan, Germany, India, Brazil, Nigeria, Egypt, and perhaps others—expanding the Council to around 25 members. But neither this plan nor others made headway in the 1990s.

Any overhaul of the Security Council would require a change in the UN Charter, possibly opening other issues of Charter reform on which member states disagree. Any change in membership would reduce the power of the current five permanent members, any one of which could veto the change. Thus, changes in the structure of the Security Council are difficult to achieve, barring a compelling reason to act.

Table 6.1 shows the recent rotations of members onto the Security Council. The system of nomination by regional caucuses has worked to keep the regional balance on the Council fairly constant as individual states come and go. Major regional actors, including those mentioned as candidates for possible new permanent seats (shown at right in the table), tend to rotate onto the Council more often than do less important states.

TABLE 6.1   Regional Representation on the UN Security Council

Region	Permanent Members[a]	Nonpermanent Members[b]			Possible Contenders for New Permanent Seats[c]
		2000	1999	1998	
North America W. Europe	United States Britain France	Canada Netherlands	Canada Netherlands	Sweden Portugal	Germany
Japan/Pacific				Japan	Japan
Russia & E. Europe	Russia	Ukraine	Slovenia	Slovenia	
China	China				
Middle East		Tunisia	Bahrain	Bahrain	Egypt?
Latin America		Jamaica Argentina	Brazil Argentina	Brazil Costa Rica	Brazil, Mexico?
South Asia		Malaysia Bangladesh	Malaysia		India, Indonesia?
Africa		Namibia Mali	Namibia Gambia Gabon	Kenya Gambia Gabon	Nigeria?

[a] The five permanent members hold veto power.

[b] Nonpermanent members are elected for two-year terms by the General Assembly, based on nominations by regional caucuses.

[c] Possible new permanent seats might have fewer if any veto powers.

Peacekeeping Forces

Peacekeeping forces are not mentioned in the UN Charter. The Charter requires member states to place military forces at the disposal of the UN, but such forces were envisioned as being used in response to aggression (under collective security). In practice, when the UN has authorized force to reverse aggression—as in the Gulf War in 1990—the forces involved have been *national* forces not under UN command.

Web Link
Peacekeeping
Forces

The UN's *own* forces—borrowed from armies of member states but under the flag and command of the UN—have been *peacekeeping* forces to calm regional conflicts, playing a neutral role between warring forces. These forces won the Nobel peace prize in 1988 in recognition of their growing importance and success. However, such neutral forces acting as neutrals do not succeed well in a situation where the Security Council has identified one side as the aggressor.

PEACEKEEPING MISSIONS The secretary-general assembles a peacekeeping force for each mission, usually from a few states totally uninvolved in the conflict, and puts it under a single commander. Peacekeeping forces serve at the invitation of a host government and must leave if that government orders them out (as Egypt did in 1967 and Croatia briefly threatened to do in 1995).

Authority for peacekeeping forces is granted by the Security Council, usually for a period of three to six months that may be renewed—in some cases for decades. In one early case, the Suez crisis in 1956, the General Assembly authorized the forces under the "Uniting for Peace" resolution, allowing the Assembly to take up security matters when the Security Council was deadlocked. But today the Security Council controls peacekeeping operations.

Funds must be voted by the General Assembly, and lack of funds is today the single greatest constraint on the use of peacekeeping forces. Special assessments against member states pay for peacekeeping operations. With the expansion of peacekeeping in 1988–1994, the expenses of these forces came to exceed the rest of the UN budget by more than 2 to 1, but the sharp reduction in peacekeeping forces in 1994–1997 reduced costs to about the same level as the regular UN budget (each about $1 billion annually). Member states owed about $1.5 billion in unpaid peacekeeping assessments in 1997 (in addition to substantial back UN dues). The United States alone owed more than $1 billion in assessments by the mid-1990s when it unilaterally reduced its share of peacekeeping contributions from 31 to 25 percent (a reduction not accepted by the UN).

RECENT MISSIONS In late 1999, the UN maintained 32,000 troops from dozens of countries in 17 separate peacekeeping or observing missions, spanning five world regions (see Table 6.2, p. 288). (Missions change from year to year.) The size and cost of peacekeeping rose modestly in 1997–1999, but remained well below half the mid-1990s peak levels.

Atlas CD
East Timor
Map

The largest peacekeeping mission at the end of 1999 was in East Timor. In 1999, the UN oversaw elections in which residents of East Timor—a former Portuguese colony occupied by neighboring Indonesia for two decades—voted for independence. In response, the Indonesian army presided over a campaign of killing and burning by pro-Indonesian militias, evidently aimed at deterring provinces of Indonesia itself

TABLE 6.2   UN Peacekeeping Missions as of Late 1999

Location	Region	Size	Annual Cost (million $)	Role	Since
Sierra Leone	Africa	11,100	$209	Observe peace agreement	1999
Central African Republic	Africa	1,200	33	Peacekeeping	1998
Democratic Republic of the Congo	Africa	500	unknown	Observe cease-fire	1999
Western Sahara	Africa	15	60	Organize referendum in Moroccan-held territory	1991
East Timor	South Asia	10,800	unknown	Peacekeeping; humanitarian relief	1999
India/Pakistan	South Asia	45	7	Observe cease-fire between India and Pakistan	1949
Kosovo	Russia/E. Europe	3,000	67	Administer executive, legislative, judicial gov't; humanitarian relief	1999
Bosnia/Herzegovina	Russia/E. Europe	2,000	166	Observe peace agreement	1995
Croatia	Russia/E. Europe	30	190	Monitor demilitarization	1996
Georgia	Russia/E. Europe	100	20	Observe cease-fire in civil war	1993
Tajikistan	Russia/E. Europe	35	19	Observe cease-fire in civil war	1994
Cyprus	Middle East	1,300	45	Monitor cease-fire between Greek and Turkish sides	1964
Lebanon	Middle East	4,500	149	Monitor cease-fire near border with Israel	1978
Syria (Golan Heights)	Middle East	1,000	35	Monitor cease-fire between Israel and Syria	1974
Israel	Middle East	143	24	Observe Arab-Israeli truce	1948
Iraq/Kuwait	Middle East	1,100	51	Observe cease-fire along border	1991
Haiti	Latin America	300	30	Professionalization of national police	1997
Total		32,000	$1,100		

Note: Size indicates total personnel (mostly troops but some civilian administrators).

from pursuing separatism. Indonesia then agreed to withdraw, and an Australian-commanded international force under a UN mandate took control. The UN itself then began running a transitional administration which is expected to lead to statehood for East Timor over several years.

The UN's other largest peacekeeping operations in late 1999 were in Sierra Leone, Lebanon, and former republics of Yugoslavia, which had the largest concentration of UN peacekeepers in the mid-1990s. Although 5,000 peacekeepers still serve in Bosnia-Herzegovina, Croatia, and the Kosovo province of Serbia, these operations were reduced greatly after the 1995 Dayton Agreement under which NATO-led forces

Birth of a Nation   After a sharp reduction in peacekeeping operations, the United Nations has tried combining a UN–authorized but nationally commanded military force with a UN–run civil government, in East Timor and Kosovo. Braving intimidation from pro-Indonesian militias, the population of East Timor voted overwhelmingly for independence in a 1999 UN–sponsored referendum.

largely replaced UN peacekeepers in Bosnia (and, later, took military control of Kosovo). UN operations in these countries focus on civilian governmental functions, leaving security matters largely to UN-authorized but independently commanded international forces. Since the same approach is being used in East Timor, we may see it again elsewhere in the future.

At its peak in the early 1990s, the UN ran several other large peacekeeping operations in addition to those in the former Yugoslavia and in Lebanon. One of the most important was in *Cambodia*. There, 15,000 peacekeepers were coupled with a large force of UN administrators who took over substantial control of the Cambodian government under a fragile pact that ended (for the most part) a long and devastating civil war. Despite difficulty in obtaining the cooperation of the Khmer Rouge faction (which refused to disarm as it had agreed), the UN pressed forward to hold elections in 1993 that chose a Cambodian government (which, however, proved unstable).

The lessons learned in Cambodia helped the UN accomplish a similar mission more easily in *Mozambique*. A peace agreement ended a long and devastating civil war there, setting up mechanisms for disarmament, the integration of military forces, and the holding of internationally supervised elections for a new government. Overall, Mozambique was perhaps the most successful of the UN's large missions of the early 1990s; those in the former Yugoslavia, Somalia, Rwanda, and Lebanon all experienced major problems.

Atlas CD
Southern
Africa
Map

OBSERVING AND PEACEKEEPING "Peacekeepers" actually perform two different functions—observing and peacekeeping. *Observers* are unarmed military officers sent to a conflict area in small numbers simply to watch what happens and report back to the UN. With the UN watching, the parties to a conflict are often less likely to break a cease-fire. Observers can *monitor* various aspects of a country's situation—cease-fires, elections, respect for human rights, and other areas. (Often this monitoring is organized by IGOs and NGOs outside the UN as well.) This kind of monitoring was useful, for example, in the transitions from war to democracy in Nicaragua and El Salvador in the 1990s.

The function of *peacekeeping* is carried out by lightly armed soldiers (in armored vehicles with automatic rifles but without artillery, tanks, and other heavy weapons). Such forces play several roles. They can *interpose* themselves physically between warring parties to keep them apart (more accurately, to make them attack the UN forces in order to get to their enemy). UN peacekeepers often try to *negotiate* with military officers on both sides. This channel of communication can bring about tactical actions and understandings that support a cease-fire. But the UN forces in a war zone cannot easily get from one side's positions to those of the other to conduct negotiations.

Peacekeeping is much more difficult if one side sees the UN forces as being *biased* toward the other side. Israel feels this way about UN forces in southern Lebanon—on occasion Israeli forces have broken through UN lines to attack enemies, and they allegedly have targeted UN outposts on occasion. In Cambodia and the former Yugoslavia in the early 1990s, one party deliberately attacked UN forces many times, causing a number of deaths. In general, when cease-fires break down, UN troops get caught in the middle. More than 1,500 have been killed over the years—most of them in the Congo (Zaire) in 1960–1964, in Cyprus since 1964, in southern Lebanon since 1978, and in the former Yugoslavia in the 1990s. In some conflicts, peacekeepers organized outside the UN framework have been used instead of UN-commanded forces; for example, U.S. forces have acted as peacekeepers in Egypt's Sinai desert since the 1970s.

Atlas CD
Cyprus
Map

PEACEMAKING In the past, peacekeeping forces have generally been unable to make peace, only to keep it. To go into a shooting war and suppress hostilities requires military forces far beyond those of past UN peacekeeping missions. Thus, peacekeepers are usually not sent until a cease-fire has been arranged, has taken effect, and has held up for some time. Often dozens of cease-fires are broken before one sticks—wars may simmer along for years, taking a terrible toll, before the UN gets its chance.

To address this problem, the secretary-general in 1992 proposed to create UN *peacemaking* (or *peace enforcement*) units that would not only monitor a cease-fire but enforce it if it broke down. These forces would be more heavily armed than peacekeeping forces because they would weigh into the battle. Also, they would be able to respond within a few days, rather than within several months as with past peacekeeping forces. The secretary-general called for member states to make available 1,000 soldiers each—specially trained volunteers—to create a standby UN army that could respond quickly to crises. Chapter 7 of the UN Charter allows the UN to draw on resources of member states in this way, but these provisions have not yet been used. Control over the deployment and operation of these forces would be held by the Security Council.

Not only did the member states refuse the request for soldiers, they shot down the idea of peacemaking and did not provide peace enforcement forces for Bosnia where the need was most pressing. (In 1995, a more combat-ready "reaction force" was tried out in Bosnia, but it was soon replaced when NATO-led forces took over from the UN there.)

Within a few years, the great powers halted the expansion of peacekeeping operations generally, and oversaw a drastic scaling back of peacekeeping. In some cases, the great powers turned down the secretary-general when he urgently requested a peacekeeping mission to head off an impending disaster—for example, in Burundi in 1995, when the same Hutu-Tutsi conflict as in Rwanda threatened to become another genocide.

One current experiment moves in the direction of improving peacekeeping forces rather than just reducing them. Seven countries—Denmark, Norway, Sweden, Poland, the Netherlands, Austria, and Canada—agreed in 1996 to form a 4,000-troop UN Standby High Readiness Brigade, headquartered in Denmark and available to deploy to conflict areas in two to four weeks. The brigade is controlled by the Security Council.

The Secretariat
The secretary-general of the UN is the closest thing to a "president of the world" that exists. But the secretary-general represents member states—especially the five permanent Security Council members—and not the world's six billion people. The past secretary-general, Boutros Boutros-Ghali, was fond of calling himself just the "humble servant" of the member states. Judging from his inability to get the Security Council to follow his lead on peacekeeping, his humility would seem well justified.

The secretary-general is *nominated* by the Security Council—requiring the consent of all five permanent members—and must be *approved* by the General Assembly. The term of office is five years and may be renewed. Boutros-Ghali in 1996 fought for a second term, with the support of almost every UN member, but the United States opposed him and prevailed. Kofi Annan, the current secretary-general, finally emerged as a consensus choice.

The Secretariat of the UN is its executive branch, headed by the secretary-general. It is a bureaucracy for administering UN policy and programs, just as the State Department is a bureaucracy for U.S. foreign policy. In security matters, the secretary-general personally works with the Security Council; third world development programs are coordinated by a second-in-command—the Director-General for Development and International Economic Co-operation. The Secretariat is divided into functional areas, with undersecretaries-general and assistant secretaries-general.

The *UN staff* in these areas includes administrative personnel as well as technical experts and economic advisers working on various programs and projects in the member countries. The staff numbers about 9,000 people (down from 12,000), and the total number of employees in the UN system is just more than 50,000—about the same as in Disneyland and Disneyworld. There is a concentration of UN-related agency offices in Geneva, Switzerland (even though Switzerland itself is not a UN member). Geneva is a frequent site of international negotiations and is seen by some as more neutral than New York. A few third world development programs are headquartered in third world cities.

One purpose of the UN Secretariat is to develop an *international civil service* of diplomats and bureaucrats whose loyalties are at the global level, not to their states of origin. The UN Charter sets the secretary-general and staff apart from the authority of national governments and calls on member states to respect the staff's "exclusively international character." The UN has been fairly successful in this regard; the secretary-gen-

Whole World in His Hands   The UN secretary-general has a lofty mission but limited power and resources. Kofi Annan (1997) was the first to rise through the UN bureaucracy to the top position. He was selected after the United States blocked a second term for his predecessor.

eral is most often seen as an independent diplomat thinking about the whole world's interests, not a pawn of any state. But in the early 1990s the UN bureaucracy came under increasing criticism for both inefficiency and corruption. These criticisms, coming especially from the United States, which saw itself as bearing an unfair share of the costs, led to a reform program. By the late 1990s, UN staff was reduced by one-quarter compared to a decade earlier, and budgets were being scaled back year by year.

The secretary-general is more than a bureaucratic manager. He (it has not yet been a she) is a visible public figure whose personal attention to a regional conflict can move it toward resolution. The Charter allows the secretary-general to use the UN's "good offices" to serve as a neutral mediator in international conflicts—to bring hostile parties together in negotiations. For example, Boutros-Ghali was personally involved in trying to mediate conflicts in Somalia and the former Yugoslavia, and Annan personally tried to talk Iraq into compliance with UN inspections in 1997.

The secretary-general also works to bring together the great-power consensus on which Security Council action depends—a much harder job than mere bureaucratic management. The secretary-general has the power under the Charter to bring to the Security Council any matter that might threaten international peace and security, and so to play a major role in setting the UN's agenda in international security affairs.

Boutros Boutros-Ghali was the secretary-general from 1992 through 1996. He was a "diplomat's diplomat" from Egypt, with decades of experience in foreign service and the UN. Boutros-Ghali tried to expand UN peacekeeping and peacemaking in local conflicts before they escalated and spread. But his assertiveness in the Security Council caused frictions with permanent members of the Council. He scolded them for giving him big mandates without adequate resources to carry them out.

By contrast, the current secretary-general, Kofi Annan (1997–2001), an American-educated manager who knows the UN bureaucracy well, is focusing on reforming the UN Secretariat's finances and operations and improving relations between the UN and the United States. Annan is the first secretary-general from sub-Saharan Africa (Ghana), and the first to rise through the UN civil service. He was previously undersecretary-general for peacekeeping operations, who gained a reputation for making the best of ill-conceived peacekeeping missions in Somalia and Bosnia in the early 1990s.

Just as the U.S. president has tensions with Congress over foreign policy, the secretary-general sometimes has tensions with the Security Council. But the secretary-general is chosen by the Security Council and has less autonomy than the U.S. president. When the secretary-general asks for authority for a peacekeeping mission for six months, the Security Council is likely to say "three months." If the secretary-general asks for $10 million he might get $5 million. Thus the secretary-general remains, like the entire UN system, constrained by state sovereignty.

Past secretaries-general have come from various regions of the world but never from a great power. They are Trygve Lie (from Norway, 1946–1952), Dag Hammarskjöld (Sweden, 1953–1961), U Thant (Burma, 1961–1971), Kurt Waldheim (Austria, 1972–1982), Javier Perez de Cuellar (Peru, 1982–1992), and Boutros Boutros-Ghali (Egypt, 1992–1996).

The General Assembly

The General Assembly is made up of all 189 member states of the UN, each with one vote. It usually meets every year, from late September through January, in *plenary session*. State leaders or foreign ministers, including the U.S. president, generally come through one by one to address this assemblage. The Assembly sessions, like most UN deliberations, are simultaneously translated into dozens of languages so that delegates from around the world can carry on a single conversation. This global town hall is a unique institution and provides a powerful medium for states to put forward their ideas and arguments. Presiding over it is a president elected by the Assembly—a post without much power.

Web Link
The General Assembly

The Assembly convenes for *special sessions* every few years on general topics such as economic cooperation. The UN special session on disarmament in June 1982 provided the occasion for the largest political rally in U.S. history—a peace demonstration of a million people in New York. The Assembly has met in *emergency session* in the past to deal with an immediate threat to international peace and security, but this has happened only nine times and has now become uncommon.

The General Assembly has the power to accredit national delegations as members of the UN (through its Credentials Committee). For instance, in 1971 the delegation of the People's Republic of China was given China's seat in the UN (including on the Security Council) in place of the nationalists in Taiwan. For decades, neither North nor South Korea became members of the UN (because both claimed the whole of Korea), but they finally took seats as separate delegations in 1991. Some political entities that fall short of state status send *permanent observer missions* to the UN, which participate without a vote in the General Assembly; these include the Vatican (Holy See), the Palestine Liberation Organization (PLO), and the Koreas before becoming members.

The General Assembly's main power lies in its *control of finances* for UN programs and operations, including peacekeeping. It also can *pass resolutions* on various matters, but these are purely advisory and at times have served largely to vent frustrations of the third world majority. The Assembly also *elects members* of certain UN agencies and programs. Finally, the Assembly coordinates UN programs and agencies through its own system of committees, commissions, councils, and so forth.

The Assembly coordinates UN programs and agencies through the Economic and Social Council (ECOSOC), which has 54 member states elected by the General Assembly for three-year terms. ECOSOC manages the overlapping work of a large number of programs and agencies. Its *regional commissions* look at how UN programs work together in a particular region; its *functional commissions* deal with global topics such as population growth, narcotics trafficking, human rights, and the status of women; its *expert bodies* work on technical subjects that cut across various UN programs in areas such as crime prevention and public finances. Outside ECOSOC, the General Assembly operates many *other specialized committees*. Standing committees ease the work of the Assembly in issue areas such as decolonization, legal matters, or disarmament.

Many of the activities associated with the UN do not take place under tight control of either the General Assembly or the Security Council. They occur in functional agencies and programs having various amounts of autonomy from UN control.

UN Programs Through the Economic and Social Council, the General Assembly oversees more than a dozen major programs to advance economic development and social stability in poor states of the third world. Through its programs, the UN helps to manage global North-South relations: it organizes a flow of resources and skills from the richer parts of the world to support development in the poorer parts.

The programs are *funded* partly by General Assembly allocations and partly by contributions that the programs raise directly from member states, businesses, or private charitable contributors. The degree of General Assembly funding, and of operational autonomy from the Assembly, varies from one program to another. Each UN program has a staff, a headquarters, and various operations in the field, where it works with host governments in member states.

The *UN Environment Program (UNEP)* grew in importance in the 1990s as the economic development of the third world and the growing economies of the industrialized world took a toll on the world environment (see Chapter 8). UNEP grapples with global environmental strategies, guided by principles adopted at the Earth Summit (the UN Conference on Environment and Development) in Brazil in 1992. UNEP provides technical assistance to member states, monitors environmental conditions globally, develops standards, and recommends alternative energy sources.

UNICEF is the UN Children's Fund, which gives technical and financial assistance to third world countries for programs benefiting children. Unfortunately, the needs of children in many countries are still urgent, and UNICEF is kept busy. Financed by voluntary contributions, UNICEF has for decades organized U.S. children in an annual Halloween fund drive on behalf of their counterparts in poorer countries.

Helping Out An array of UN programs, operating under the General Assembly, aim to help countries in the global South to overcome social and economic problems. Here are vehicles of the UN High Commissioner for Refugees (UNHCR) at a camp in Somalia, 1992.

The *Office of the UN High Commissioner for Refugees (UNHCR)* has also been kept busy in recent years. UNHCR coordinates efforts to protect, assist, and eventually repatriate the many refugees who flee across international borders each year to escape from war and political violence. (The longer-standing problem of Palestinian refugees is handled by a different program, the *UN Relief Works Agency*, or *UNRWA*.)

The *UN Development Program (UNDP)*, funded by voluntary contributions, coordinates all UN efforts related to third world development. With about 5,000 projects operating simultaneously around the world, UNDP is the world's largest international agency for technical development assistance. The UN also runs several development-related agencies for training and for promoting women's role in development.

Many third world countries depend on export revenues to finance economic development, making those countries vulnerable to fluctuations in commodity prices and other problems involved in international trade. The **UN Conference on Trade and Development (UNCTAD)** seeks to negotiate international trade agreements to stabilize commodity prices and promote third world development. Because third world countries do not have much power in the international economy, however, UNCTAD has little leverage with which to promote third world interests in trade (see p. 394).

Other UN programs manage problems such as disaster relief, food aid, housing, and population issues. Throughout the poorer countries, the UN maintains an active presence in economic and social affairs.

Autonomous Agencies In addition to its own programs, the UN General Assembly maintains formal ties with about 20 autonomous international agencies not under its control. Most are specialized technical organizations through which states pool their efforts to address problems such as health care and labor conditions. The only such agency in international security affairs is the *International Atomic Energy Agency (IAEA)*, headquartered in Vienna, Austria. It was established under the UN but is formally autonomous. Although the IAEA has an economic role in helping to develop civilian nuclear power plants, it mainly works to prevent nuclear proliferation (see p. 200). With nuclear proliferation threats causing great international concern in recent years, the IAEA is a busy agency.

In the area of health care, the **World Health Organization (WHO)** based in Geneva provides assistance to improve conditions in the third world and conducts major immunization campaigns in poor countries. In the 1960s and 1970s, WHO led one of the great public health victories of all time—worldwide eradication of smallpox. Today WHO is a leading player in the worldwide fight to control AIDS (see pp. 354–356).

In agriculture, the *Food and Agriculture Organization (FAO)* is the lead agency. In labor standards, it is the *International Labor Organization (ILO)*. UNESCO—the *UN Educational, Scientific, and Cultural Organization*—facilitates international communication and scientific collaboration. The *UN Industrial Development Organization (UNIDO)* promotes industrialization in the third world.

The longest-established IOs, with some of the most successful records, are those specialized agencies dealing with technical aspects of international coordination. For instance, the *International Telecommunications Union (ITU)* allocates radio frequencies. The *Universal Postal Union (UPU)* sets standards for international mail. The *International Civil Aviation Organization (ICAO)* sets binding standards for international air traffic. The *International Maritime Organization (IMO)* facilitates international cooperation on shipping at sea. The *World Intellectual Property Organization (WIPO)* seeks world compliance with copyrights and patents, and promotes third world development and technology transfer within a legal framework that protects such intellectual property. Finally, the *World Meteorological Association (WMO)* promotes the exchange of weather information.

The major coordinating agencies of the world economy (discussed in Chapters 5 and 7) are also UN-affiliated agencies. The World Bank and the International Monetary Fund (IMF) give loans, grants, and technical assistance for economic development (and the IMF manages international balance-of-payments accounting). The World Trade Organization (WTO) sets rules for international trade.

Overall, the density of connections across national borders, both in the UN system and through other IOs, is increasing year by year. These interconnections are furthest developed in the European Union.

The European Union

Like the UN, the **European Union (EU)** was created after World War II and has developed since. But whereas the UN structure has changed little since the Charter was adopted, the EU has gone through several waves of expansion in its scope, membership, and mission over the past 45 years.

Integration Theory

The theory of international integration can help to explain these developments, which challenge once again the foundations of realism (state sovereignty and territorial integrity). **International integration** refers to the process by which supranational institutions replace national ones—the gradual shifting upward of sovereignty from state to regional or global structures. The ultimate expression of integration would be the merger of several (or many) states into a single state—or ultimately into a single world government. Such a shift in sovereignty to the supranational level would probably entail some version of federalism, in which states or other political units recognize the sovereignty of a central government while keeping certain powers for themselves. This is the form of government adopted (after some debate) in the U.S. Constitution.

Today one hears occasional calls for a "United States of Europe"—or even of the world—but in practice the process of integration has never gone beyond a partial and uneasy sharing of power between state and supranational levels. States have been unwilling to give up their exclusive claim to sovereignty and have severely limited the power and authority of supranational institutions. The UN, certainly, falls far short of a federal model. It represents only a step in the direction of international integration. Other modest examples of the integration process have been discussed in Chapter 5—for example, NAFTA and the WTO. But these arrangements hardly challenge states' territorial integrity, much less their political sovereignty. Nor do states give up much sovereignty in either monetary regimes or dealings with MNCs, although all these aspects of IPE do have supranational elements.

Web Link
United States
of Europe

The most successful example of the process of integration by far—though even that success is only partial—is the European Union. Although we can observe aspects of international integration at work elsewhere in the world, these processes have gone much further in Europe than anywhere else. The regional coordination now occurring in Western Europe is a new historical phenomenon achieved only since World War II.

Until 50 years ago the European continent was the embodiment of national sovereignty, state rivalry, and war. The international system was invented in Europe. For 500 years until 1945, the states of Europe were locked in chronic intermittent warfare; in the twentieth century alone two world wars left the continent in ruins. The European states have historical and present-day religious, ethnic, and cultural differences. The 15 members of today's EU speak 13 different official languages. If ever there were a candidate for the failure of integration, Europe would appear to be it. Even more surprising, European integration began with the cooperation of Europe's two bitterest enemies over the previous 100 years, enemies in three major wars since 1870—France and Germany (references to "Germany" refer to West Germany from 1944 to 1990, and unified Germany since).

Atlas CD
Europe
Language Map

That Western European states began forming supranational institutions and creating an economic community to promote free trade and coordinate economic policies caught the attention of IR scholars, who used the term *integration* to describe what they observed. Seemingly, integration challenged the assumption of realism that states were strictly autonomous and would never yield power or sovereignty. These scholars proposed that European moves toward integration could be explained by *functionalism*—growth of specialized technical organizations that cross national borders. According to functionalists, technological and economic development lead to more and more supranational structures as states seek practical means to fulfill necessary *functions* such as delivering mail

Tear Down the Walls

Integration processes in Europe and elsewhere are making state borders more permeable to people, goods, and ideas—increasing interdependence. The European Union is deepening economic integration while contemplating eastward expansion. Here, the opening of the Berlin Wall makes integration very tangible, 1989.

Atlas CD
Reunited
Berlin
Photo, Music

Atlas CD
Channel
Tunnel
Photo

from one country to another or coordinating the use of rivers that cross borders. Some IR scholars tried to measure the extent of functional connections in Europe, for instance, by counting flows of mail and other communications among countries. As these connections became denser and the flows faster, functionalism predicted that states would be drawn together into stronger international economic structures.

The European experience, however, went beyond the creation of specialized agencies to include the development of more general, more political supranational bodies, such as the European Parliament. **Neofunctionalism** is a modification of functional theory by IR scholars to explain these developments. Neofunctionalists argue that economic integration (functionalism) generates a *political* dynamic that drives integration further. Closer economic ties require more political coordination in order to operate effectively and eventually lead to political integration as well—a process called *spillover*.

Some scholars focused on the less-tangible *sense of community* ("we" feeling) that began to develop among Europeans, running contrary to nationalist feelings that still existed as well. The low expectation of violence among the states of Western Europe created a **security community** in which such feelings could grow. The emergence of a European identity was also assisted by such efforts as the textbook revision project (see p. 161).

Elsewhere in the world, economies were becoming more interdependent at both the regional and global levels. The Andean Common Market, begun in 1969, promoted a limited degree of regional integration in the member states of Venezuela, Colombia, Ecuador, Peru, and Bolivia. In Asia, the Association of South East Asian Nations (ASEAN) chalked up some successes in promoting regional economic coordination over several decades.

Interest in integration theory among IR scholars has waxed and waned with the uneven pace of European integration. In the 1960s and 1970s, European integration seemed to slow down; regional efforts elsewhere in the world also failed to develop as hoped. For most of the Cold War decades, integration took a secondary position among IR scholars (and policy makers) to the concerns of East-West conflict, nuclear weapons, and related security issues. Then, in the 1980s, Europe accelerated its progress toward integration again, the Cold War ended, and the North American Free Trade Agreement took form; the scholarly interest in integration expanded again.

COSTS OF INTEGRATION Ironically, the new wave of integration in Europe and elsewhere is encountering limits and setbacks just as scholars are reinvigorating the theory of integration. Integration reduces states' ability to shield themselves and their citizens from the world's many problems and conflicts. For example, China found that its new openness to foreign trade also exposed it to the AIDS epidemic. Germany found that accepting foreign refugees meant living with more domestic ethnic conflict.

Integration can mean greater centralization at a time when individuals, local groups, and national populations demand more say over their own affairs. The centralization of political authority, information, and culture as a result of integration can threaten both individual and group freedom. Ethnic groups want to safeguard their own cultures, languages, and institutions against the bland homogeneity that a global or regional melting pot would create. As a result, many states and citizens, in Europe and elsewhere, responded to the new wave of integration with resurgent nationalism in the 1990s.

Indeed these forces have set in motion a wave of *disintegration* of states running counter to (though simultaneous with) the integrating tendencies in today's world. The wave of disintegration in some ways began with the decolonization of former European empires after World War II. Currently disintegration is most evident in Russia and Eastern Europe—especially in the former Soviet Union and former Yugoslavia. States in other regions—Somalia, Iraq, and Afghanistan—appear in danger of breaking into pieces, in practice if not formally. The result of the Soviet breakup *might* end up resembling that of Western Europe under the most optimistic scenario for the future of the CIS. But the result of that experiment is not yet known, and few scholars are optimistic. A challenge to integration theorists in the future will be to account for these new trends running counter to integration.

Throughout the successful and unsuccessful efforts at integration runs a common thread—the tension between nationalism and supranational loyalties (regionalism or globalism). In the less-successful integration attempts, nationalism stands virtually unchallenged, and even in the most successful cases nationalism remains a potent force locked in continual struggle with supranationalism. This struggle is a central theme even in the most successful case of integration—the European Union.

The Vision of a United Europe

Europe in 1945 was decimated by war. Most of the next decade was spent recovering with help from the United States through the Marshall Plan. But already two French leaders, Jean Monnet and Robert Schuman, were developing a plan to implement the idea of functionalism in Europe—that Europe

Web Link
Jean Monnet

could be saved from future wars by creating economic linkages that would eventually bind states together politically.

In 1950, Schuman as French foreign minister proposed a first modest step—the merger of the French and German steel (iron) and coal industries into a single framework that could most efficiently use the two states' coal resources and steel mills. Coal and steel were key to European recovery and growth. The Schuman plan gave birth in 1952 to the *European Coal and Steel Community (ECSC)*, in which France and Germany were joined by Italy (the third large industrial country of continental Europe) and by three smaller countries—Belgium, Netherlands, and Luxembourg (together called the Benelux countries). These six states worked through the ECSC to reduce trade barriers in coal and steel and to coordinate their coal and steel policies. The ECSC also established a High Authority that to some extent could bypass governments and deal directly with companies, labor unions, and individuals. Britain did not join, however.

Atlas CD
Europe,
Political
Map

If coal and steel sound like fairly boring topics, that was exactly the idea of functionalists. The issues involved were matters for engineers and technical experts, and did not threaten politicians. Since 1952, technical experts have served as the leaders of the integration process in other aspects of European life and outside Europe.

International scientific communities deserve special mention in this regard. If German and French steel experts had more in common than German and French politicians, this is even more true of scientists. Today the European scientific community is one of the most internationally integrated areas of society. For example, the EU operates the European Space Agency and the European Molecular Biology Laboratory. This illustrates the importance of technical communities in functionalist integration.

Although technical cooperation succeeded in 1952, political and military cooperation proved much more difficult. In line with the vision of a united Europe, the six ECSC states signed a second treaty in 1952 to create a European Defense Community to work toward integrating Europe's military forces under one budget and command. But the French Parliament failed to ratify the treaty, and Britain refused to join such a force. The ECSC states also discussed formation of a European Political Community in 1953, but could not agree on its terms. Thus, in economic cooperation the supranational institutions succeeded but in political and military affairs state sovereignty prevailed.

The Treaty of Rome

In the **Treaty of Rome** in 1957, the same six states (France, Germany, Italy, Belgium, Netherlands, Luxembourg) created two new organizations. One extended the coal-and-steel idea into a new realm, atomic energy. **Euratom**, the European Atomic Energy Community, was formed to coordinate nuclear power development by pooling research, investment, and management. It continues in operation today with an expanded membership. The second organization was the *European Economic Community (EEC)*, later renamed the *European Community (EC)*. After its founding in 1957, the EEC was often called simply the *Common Market*. Actually a common market was not immediately created but was established as a goal, which has since been largely realized.

In Chapter 5, the terms *free-trade area*, *customs union*, and *common market* were not distinguished; we now define them more precisely. Creating a **free-trade area** meant lifting tariffs and restrictions on the movement of goods across (EEC) borders, as was done shortly after 1957. Today the *European Free Trade Association (EFTA)* is an extended free-trade area associated with the EU; its members are Norway, Iceland, Liechtenstein, and Switzerland. (All but Switzerland became, with the EU, the European Economic Area, participating in the "Europe 1992" single market described below.)

A **customs union** means that participating states adopt a unified set of tariffs regarding goods coming in from outside the free-trade area. Without this, each type of good could be imported into the state with the lowest tariff and then reexported (tariff-free) to the other states in the free-trade area; this would be inefficient. The Treaty of Rome committed the six states to creating a customs union by 1969. A customs union creates free and open trade within its member states, bringing great economic benefits. Thus the customs union remains the heart of the EU and the one aspect widely copied elsewhere in the world.

A **common market** means that in addition to the customs union, member states allow labor and capital (as well as goods) to flow freely across borders. For instance, a Belgian financier can invest in Germany on the same terms as a German investor. Although the Treaty of Rome adopted the goal of a common market, even today it has been only partially achieved.

One key aspect of a common market was achieved, at least in theory, in the 1960s when the EU (then the EC) adopted a **Common Agricultural Policy (CAP)**. In practice, the CAP has led to recurrent conflicts among member states and tensions between nationalism and regionalism (see pp. 226–229). To promote national self-sufficiency in food, many governments give subsidies to farmers. The CAP was based on the principle that a subsidy extended to farmers in any EC country should be extended to farmers in all EC countries. That way, no EC government was forced to alienate politically powerful farmers by removing subsidies, yet the overall policy would be equalized throughout the community in line with the common market principle. As a result, subsidies to farmers today absorb about two-thirds of the total EU budget and are the single greatest source of trade friction between Europe and the United States (see pp. 229–231).

The fourth step in the plan for European integration (after a free-trade area, customs union, and common market) was an *economic and monetary union (EMU)* in which the overall economic policies of the member states would be coordinated for greatest efficiency and stability. In this step, a single currency would replace the separate national currencies now in use (see below). A future fifth step in economic integration would be the supranational coordination of economic policies such as budgets and taxes.

To reduce state leaders' fears of losing sovereignty, the Treaty of Rome provides that changes in its provisions must be approved by all member states. For example, France vetoed Britain's application for membership in the EEC in 1963 and 1967. However, in 1973 Britain did finally join, along with Ireland and Denmark. This expanded the EC's membership to nine, including the largest and richest countries in the region.

In 1981, Greece was admitted, and in 1986 Portugal and Spain joined. Inclusion of these poorer countries with less industry and lower standards of living created difficulties in effectively integrating Europe's economies which persist today, as the richer European states give substantial aid to the poorer ones in hopes of strengthening the weak links. Greece, Portugal, Spain, and Ireland are called the "*poor four*" within the EU.

Structure of the European Union
The structure of the EU reflects its roots in technical and economic cooperation. The coal and steel experts have been

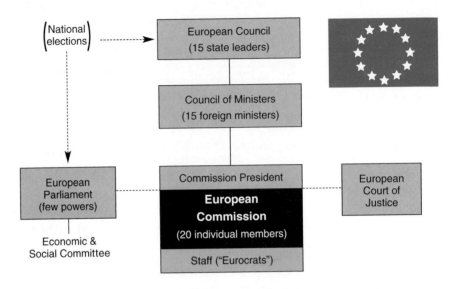

FIGURE 6.2 Structure of the European Union (EU)

joined by experts on trade, agriculture, and finance at the heart of the community. The EU headquarters and staff have the reputation of colorless bureaucrats—sometimes called "*Eurocrats*"—who care more about technical problem solving than about politics. These supranational bureaucrats are balanced in the EU structure by provisions that uphold the power of states and state leaders.

Although the rule of Eurocrats follows the functionalist plan, it has created problems as the EU has progressed. Politicians in member states have qualms about losing power to the Eurocrats. Citizens in those states have become more uncomfortable in recent years with the growing power of faceless Eurocrats over their lives. Citizens can throw their own political leaders out of office in national elections, but the Eurocrats seem less accountable.

The EU's structure is illustrated in Figure 6.2. The Eurocrats consist of a staff of about 5,000, organized under the **European Commission** at EU headquarters in Brussels, Belgium. The Commission has 20 individual members—one or two from each member state—who are chosen for four-year renewable terms. Their role is to identify problems and propose solutions to the Council of Ministers. They select one of their members as the commission president. These individuals are supposed to represent the interests of Europe as a whole (supranational interests) and not their own states, but this goal has been only imperfectly met. For instance, in the 1992 agricultural trade dispute with the United States, critics of Commission President Jacques Delors said he had impeded a settlement in order to appease French farmers because he planned a future political career in his native France. (He opted not to run for president of France after his EU term.)

The European Commission lacks formal autonomous power except for day-to-day EU operations. Formally the Commission reports to, and implements the policies of, the **Council of Ministers**. The Council is a meeting of the relevant ministers (foreign, economic, agriculture, finance, etc.) of each member state—politicians who control the bureaucrats (or who try to). This formal structure reflects states' resistance to yielding sovereignty. It also means that the individuals making up the Council of Ministers vary from one meeting to the next, and that technical issues receive priority over political ones. The arrangement thus gives some advantage back to the Commission staff. Recall similar tension between politicians and career bureaucrats in national foreign policy making (see pp. 105–107).

The Council of Ministers in theory has a weighted voting system based on each state's population, but in practice it operates by consensus on major policy issues (all 15 members must agree). On other issues, decisions can be made by qualified majorities, overriding national sovereignty. The Council has a rotating presidency (with limited power). The Council of Ministers must approve the policies of the European Commission and give it general directions.

In the 1970s, state leaders (prime ministers or presidents) created a special place for themselves in the EC, to oversee the direction of the community; this structure again shows the resistance of state leaders to being governed by any supranational body. This *European Council* of 15 state leaders meets with the Commission president on a twice-a-year basis. They are the ones with the power to get things done in their respective national governments (which still control most of the money and power in Europe).

There is a **European Parliament**, which might someday operate as a true legislature passing laws for all of Europe. At present it operates more as a watchdog over the Commission, with little power to legislate. The Parliament must approve the Commission's budget but cannot control it item by item. The Parliament serves mainly as a debating forum and a symbol of European unity. However, in 1999 an independent commission created by the Parliament found waste and fraud in the Commission, leading all 20 commissioners to resign. Since 1979, voters throughout Europe have directly elected their representatives to the European Parliament, according to population. Political parties are organized across national lines, with all Christian Democrats from all 15 countries, for instance, sitting together. But many of the most heated debates are between national delegations *within* a party—reflecting the continuing influence of nationalism.

Web Link
European
Parliament

An *Economic and Social Committee* discusses continentwide issues that affect particular industries or constituencies. This committee is purely advisory; it lobbies the Commission on matters it deems important. It is designed as a forum in which companies, labor unions, and interest groups can bargain transnationally.

A **European Court of Justice** in Luxembourg adjudicates disputes on matters covered by the Treaty of Rome—which covers many issues. Unlike the World Court (see pp. 313–314), the European Court has actively established its jurisdiction and not merely served as a mechanism of international mediation. The Court can overrule national law when it is in conflict with EU law—giving it unique powers among international courts. It hears cases brought by individuals, not just governments. In hundreds of cases, the Court has ruled on matters ranging from discrimination in the workplace to the pensions of Commission staff members.

The Single European Act

European integration has proceeded in a step-by-step process that produces tangible successes, reduces politicians' fears of losing sovereignty, and creates pressures to continue the process. Often major steps forward are followed by periods of stagnation or even reversals in integration. The first major revision of the

Treaty of Rome—the 1985 **Single European Act**—began a new phase of accelerated integration. The EU set a target date of the end of 1992 for the creation of a true common market in Europe. This comprehensive set of changes was nicknamed *Europe 1992*.

The 1992 process centered on about 300 directives from the European Commission, aimed at eliminating nontariff barriers to free trade in goods, services, labor, and capital within the EC. The issues tended to be complex and technical. For instance, professionals licensed in one state should be free to practice in another; but Spain's licensing requirements for, say, physical therapists, may have differed from those of Britain. The Commission bureaucrats worked to smooth out such inconsistencies and create a uniform set of standards. Each national government had to pass laws to implement these measures.

For example, a dispute raged for decades over the definition of chocolate. Belgium—famous for its chocolates—requires the exclusive use of cocoa butter for a product to be called chocolate; Britain and other countries use a cheaper process that partially substitutes other vegetable oils. With deepening integration and seamless trade, Belgium worried that it would lose its competitive advantage in the $30 billion worldwide chocolate market (half of which came from Europe). Britain and six other EU countries won an exemption from the all-cocoa rule that applies to the other eight EU members. Under the pressure of integration, however, the EU is moving to unify standards such as food regulations. The chocolate wars well illustrate that the seemingly simple concept of economic integration sets in motion huge forces of change that reach into every corner of society and affect the daily lives of millions of people.

The Single European Act also gave a new push to the creation of a European Central Bank, and a single currency and monetary system—longstanding goals that have now been accomplished. As long as the economies of the EU members were tied to separate states (with separate central banks), efforts to maintain fixed exchange rates were difficult. For example, British politicians in 1992 were reluctant to deepen a recession in Great Britain in order to save German politicians from inflation.

The 1992 process moved economic integration into more political and controversial areas, eroding sovereignty more visibly than before. It also deepened a trend toward the EU's dealing directly with provinces rather than the states they belong to—thus beginning to "hollow out" the state from below (stronger provincial governments) as well as from above (stronger Europewide government). However, Europe 1992 continued to put aside for the future the difficult problems of political and military integration.

Web Link
Maastricht
Treaty

The Maastricht Treaty
The **Maastricht Treaty**, signed in the Dutch city of Maastricht in 1991, renamed the EC as the EU and committed it to further progress in three main areas. The first is monetary union (discussed shortly), in which the existing national currencies were to be abolished and replaced by a single European currency. A second set of changes, regarding Justice and Home Affairs, created a European police agency and responded to the new reality that borders were opening to immigrants, criminals, and contraband alike. It also expanded the idea of citizenship, so that, for example, a French citizen living in Germany can vote in local elections there. A third goal of Maastricht is even more controversial—political and military integration. The treaty commits European states to work toward a common foreign policy with a goal of eventually establishing a joint military force. All three of these areas of change infringe on state sovereignty.

The Maastricht Treaty encountered problems soon after its signing. One problem was the fractious response of EU members to the war in the former Yugoslavia—next door on the European continent. Efforts by the EU to mediate the conflict failed repeatedly as the war spread and a humanitarian and refugee crisis deepened. In 1992, French President Mitterrand secretly flew straight from an EU summit meeting to the embattled Bosnian capital, Sarajevo; this unilateral initiative reflected the EU's inability to act in unison. Over time, the EU's response became more unified, but the policy still was ineffective until the United States began leading the effort in 1995 (see p. 39).

Closer to home, some citizens of Europe began to react strongly against the loss of national identity and sovereignty implicit in Maastricht. Through the years of European integration, public opinion has been largely supportive. In recent years, polls have shown a strong majority of European citizens in favor of greater political and military integration, and of expanding the powers of the European Parliament—although support for political union is weak in Denmark and Britain. Perhaps the Eurocrats took public support too much for granted, for a substantial and growing minority was having second thoughts—parallel to the backlash against free trade discussed in Chapter 5.

As an amendment to the Treaty of Rome, Maastricht had to be ratified by all (then 12) members. The ratification process stirred up strong public feelings against closer European union in several countries. British politicians had already gotten assurances that allowed Britain to stay outside a monetary union and a unified European social policy, if it so chose. In other EU states, however, political leaders and citizens had not fully anticipated the public reactions to Maastricht before signing it. Suddenly, citizens and leaders in several countries seemed to realize that faceless Eurocrats in Brussels were stripping away their national sovereignty!

In a 1992 referendum, Danish voters narrowly rejected the treaty despite the support of the major political parties, industries, and labor unions (in a second 1993 vote Danes approved the treaty, with provisions like Britain's). A referendum in Ireland passed easily, but one in France just barely passed. As a result, EU leaders had to admit that public opinion in several countries reflected deep reservations about a closer European union. Although the EU implemented the Maastricht treaty, it did so more slowly and with fewer participating countries than originally hoped. Economic and technical integration, including a monetary union among 11 of the 15 members, is proceeding.

The future of political and military integration is much more uncertain. The EU decided in 1999 to develop a 60,000-troop military force (see p. 77), but NATO will continue to be more important and may even subsume the new force in practice. The struggle between nationalism and supranationalism seems precariously balanced between the two; the transition to supranationalism has not yet been accomplished as to sovereignty and foreign and military policy. Even after 40 years of preparation, spillover is elusive.

Monetary Union
Under the Maastricht process, EU members are creating a European currency, called the **euro**. Today it is an abstract unit like the IMF's SDR (see p. 248), used by national governments and for international exchange. But by 2002 the euro is to replace 11 of Europe's national currencies, which will cease to exist. A European Central Bank is taking over the functions of states' central banks.

Monetary union is difficult for both economic and political reasons. In participating states, fundamental economic and financial conditions must be equalized. One state

Integration Marches On

The Maastricht Treaty called for a monetary union with a common currency. Despite unexpected public resistance in several European countries, the Euro currency is coming into effect in eleven countries. This Italian shop posts a "Euro welcome" sign, 1998.

cannot be allowed to stimulate its economy with low interest rates while another cools inflation with high interest rates. (Divergent inflation rates would make a single currency unworkable; see pp. 241–244.) As the 1992 currency crisis (see pp. 244–246) indicates, the necessary uniform conditions across Europe do not yet exist. This is a problem because the EU will not be able to handle differences across countries well, such as a recession in one country while another is booming. In an integrated economy that is also politically integrated, the central government can reallocate resources, as the United States might do if Texas were booming and Massachusetts were in recession. But the EU does not have centralized powers of taxation or control of national budgets.

One solution is to work toward equalizing Europe's economies. For example, to reduce the disparity between rich and poor EU states, the Maastricht Treaty increased the EU budget by $25 billion annually to provide economic assistance to the poorer members. But the richer EU members pay the cost for this aid—in effect carrying the poor countries as free riders on the collective good of EU integration. Partly for this reason, $25 billion annually is far too small to truly equalize the rich and poor countries.

The main solution adopted at Maastricht was to restrict membership in the monetary union, at least in the first round, to only those countries with enough financial stability not to jeopardize the union. To join the unified currency, a state had to achieve certain benchmarks: a budget deficit less than 3 percent of GDP, a national debt less than 60 percent of GDP, an inflation rate no more than 1.5 percentage points above the average of the three lowest-inflation EU members, and stable interest rates and national currency values.

Atlas CD
Luxembourg's
Finance Niche
Photo

These targets proved difficult to meet for many EU members. Soon after Maastricht, only France and Luxembourg could have qualified; then it appeared that France might not make the cut. Clearly a euro with only Luxembourg participating would not work! Germany's participation is central because the mark is the strongest European currency. In a sense, the euro will replace the mark and the other countries will tag along. Proponents of monetary union hope that Germany's sacrifice of its own respected currency, the mark, will help reassure Europe that German reunification (see p. 37) does not threaten other European countries.

Within several years the entire push for monetary union appeared endangered. In response, EU members decided to redouble their efforts and forge ahead. There was talk of loosening the standards for admission, but EU leaders believed this to be a dangerous course that could undermine the ultimate stability of the euro. Instead, the leaders of states wishing to participate agreed to buckle down and try to meet the standards. This meant hard choices by governments in France, Spain, Italy, and other countries, to cut budgets and benefits and to take other politically unpopular moves. French workers responded with massive strikes on several occasions. Governments fell to opposition parties in several countries, but the new leaders generally kept to the same course. As a result of the newfound fiscal discipline, Germany and France qualified to join the euro in the first round, as did the Benelux countries, Austria, Finland, and Ireland.

Somewhat to their own surprise, Italy, Spain, and Portugal—all of which had been presumed too unstable financially to qualify for the euro—took firm measures to control their finances in 1997, and won inclusion in the monetary union as well. Italian leaders in particular were able to harness national pride to gain public acceptance of required fiscal measures. The successes of Italy, Spain, and Portugal left only Greece excluded for not meeting the criteria for joining the euro.

Three other members, however—Britain, Denmark, and Sweden—decided to stay outside the monetary union at least for a few years. This decision reflected broad concerns about loss of sovereignty as well as practical economic worries. These countries may join a monetary union later if it proves successful.

Money is more political than steel tariffs or chocolate ingredients. A monetary union infringes on a core prerogative of states—the right to print currency. Because citizens use money every day, a European currency along these lines could deepen citizens' sense of identification with Europe—a victory for supranationalism over nationalism. However, precisely for this reason some state leaders and citizens resist the idea of giving up the symbolic value of their national currencies. These problems were reflected in the task of designing euro banknotes and coins. How could any country's leaders or monuments become Europewide symbols? The solution was to put generic architectural elements (not identifiable by country) on the front of the banknotes and a map of Europe on the back. Coins will come in various member-state designs.

So far the EU has met its timetable to get the euro off the ground. Production of euro banknotes and coins began in 1998. Currency exchange rates were frozen in 1999 (for the 11 national currencies against the euro), and a transition to European Central Bank control begun. International currency markets began trading the euro instead of the 11 currencies. Cash registers across Europe were reprogrammed, and prices displayed in both euros and national currencies for the transition years. The circulation of euros as legal tender, and the cancellation of national currencies, is set for 2002.

Beyond launching the euro on schedule, the EU faces uncharted waters in actually making a monetary union work without political unification. In its first 16 months, the value of the euro slumped (from $1.17 to $0.93) as investor confidence in the experiment proved shaky. The creation of a European currency is arguably the largest financial over-haul ever attempted in history, so nobody knows how it will really work in practice.

Web Link
Expanding the
European Union

Expanding the European Union Despite the resistance encountered in the Maastricht process, the EU has been successful enough to attract neighboring states that want to join. In fact, the larger and more integrated the EU becomes, the less attractive is the prospect of remaining outside of it for any state in the vicinity of Europe. The EU is beginning to come to terms with the possibility of going from 15 members to 20 or 30, with potentially far-reaching changes in how the community operates.

Spain and Portugal, admitted in 1986 as the eleventh and twelfth members, filled out the western side of Europe. In 1995, Austria, Sweden, and Finland joined the EU. They are located on the immediate fringe of the present EU area, and as relatively rich countries they will not disrupt the EU economy. Norway applied to join and was accepted, but its citizens voted down the idea in a referendum in 1994, leaving the EU with 15 members since 1995—all but two of the main states of Western Europe. (Switzerland's plans to join were, like Norway's, halted by a popular referendum in the early 1990s; citizens preferred to maintain their traditional strict neutrality even at a possible cost to the Swiss economy.)

To the south, three others had applied to join but faced less hopeful prospects for acceptance—Turkey, Cyprus, and Malta. They were poorer states, on the fringe of Europe, that could add to the problems the EU already had in absorbing poor states such as Greece. Turkey also had drawn criticism for its human rights record, especially regarding Kurdish rebels and journalists, and as a predominantly Muslim (though secular) country it faced European biases. Thus, in 1997 the EU opened talks on future membership only with Cyprus and the more prosperous of the Eastern European states.

The 1999 Kosovo war apparently convinced EU leaders that future expansion should be more inclusive. The prospect of EU membership could promote stability and democratization of nonmember countries to the east and southeast, building a "firewall" between the war-ravaged Balkans and troubled CIS states of the former Soviet Union. By 1999 Turkey had made progress on human rights and the Kurdish conflict. Thus, the EU in 1999 extended invitations to apply for membership to Turkey (conditionally), Malta, Bulgaria, Romania, Slovakia, Lithuania, and Latvia, in addition to the states invited in 1997 (Cyprus, Slovenia, Hungary, the Czech Republic, Poland, and Estonia).

If all of these candidate states joined the EU in the coming years, the EU membership would grow to 28 from the current 15. By Western European standards, the new members would be relatively poor. Existing EU members are wary of being dragged down by these economies, most of which are still embroiled in the painful transition from socialism to capitalism and sometimes lack stable currencies. Their prospects for joining a European monetary union appear some years in the future at best.

The implications of ongoing EU expansion are considerable. The expansion from 12 to 15 members in 1995 changed the dynamics of the EU in several ways. The Commission, previously a cumbersome committee with 17 members, became more cumbersome with 20 members. If the states now beginning talks on membership join the EU, the Commission would have 33 members. The Parliament would grow to more than 1,000 members. The ability of the EU to reach decisions by consensus could become more elusive. The working time required to make decisions in the Council of

Ministers would expand with potential conflicts and alliances on a particular issue among 28 rather than 12 or 15 members. In addition to being cumbersome, and worsening collective goods problems, an expanded community could make the achievement of unified policies more difficult. The more states that are represented in the EU, each with national interests, the harder it may be to identify any coherent supranational interest of the group as a whole (one that also serves the interests of the individual members). The tensions between nationalism and supranationalism would presumably intensify, with more states pulling in more directions at once.

Beyond these problems, the addition of new members in the south and east could add to problems of disparity in wealth already existing with the "poor four." If $25 billion annually is needed to stabilize currencies of the "poor four" and bring them into a monetary union, much more will be needed to bring in new Eastern European states.

Thus the future expansion of the EU remains uncertain despite the extension of invitations to begin talks. Some observers see a choice for the EU—deepening the community through a monetary union and other measures envisioned by Maastricht, or broadening it by adding members. States that favor deepening the EU—France especially—argue that an enlarged membership would prove unwieldy and would endanger the gains the EU has made. Those that favor broadening (such as Britain) argue that the ideal of a united Europe requires the EU to take in those who want to join, even though progress toward economic integration would be slowed down. Britain is less eager to deepen the European Union and favors expansion partly because it will slow down such deepening.

Perhaps as a result of these pressures, the EU in the late 1990s showed signs of dividing into "inner" and "outer" layers—those states such as France and Germany joining a currency union and deepening their integration, and those such as Britain and perhaps the new members operating at the edges of the EU with more autonomy. This division of the EU was illustrated in 1995 when seven countries from Portugal to Germany abolished border controls and the need for passports but in turn tightened border controls between themselves and the eight other EU members that did not join the free-movement zone.

Beyond the EU itself, Europe is a patchwork of overlapping structures with varying memberships (see Figure 6.3, p. 310). Despite the Single European Act, there are still many Europes. Within the EU are the "inner six," the "poor four," and the possible new joiners, each with its own concerns. Around the edges are the EFTA states participating in the European Economic Area. NATO membership overlaps partly with the EU. Russia and even the United States are European actors in some respects.

One truly universal intergovernmental organization exists in Europe—the *Organization for Security and Cooperation in Europe (OSCE)*. Operating by consensus, with a large and expanding universal membership, the OSCE has little actual power except to act as a forum for multilateral discussions of security issues. (The name was upgraded in 1994 from "Conference" to "Organization"—CSCE to OSCE.) In the late 1990s, the OSCE shifted into new tasks such as running elections in Bosnia under the Dayton Agreement.

Thus, international integration is not a matter of a single group or organization but more a mosaic of structures tying states together. These various structures of the European political system, centered on the EU, are IGOs composed of states as members. IOs impinge on state sovereignty by creating new structures (both supranational and transnational) for regulating relations across borders. International law and international norms

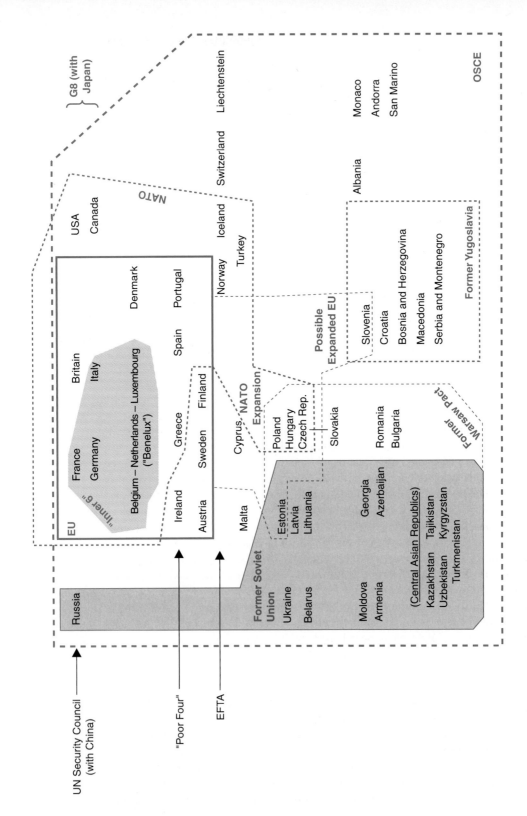

FIGURE 6.3 Overlapping Memberships of European States

limit state sovereignty in another way. They create principles for governing international relations that compete with the core realist principles of sovereignty and anarchy.

International Law

International law, unlike national laws, derives not from actions of a legislative branch or other central authority, but from tradition and agreements signed by states. It also differs in the difficulty of enforcement, which depends not on the power and authority of central government but on reciprocity, collective action, and international norms.

Sources of International Law
Laws within states come from central authorities—legislatures or dictators. Because states are sovereign and recognize no central authority, international law rests on a different basis. The declarations of the UN General Assembly are not laws, and most do not bind the members. The Security Council can compel certain actions by states, but these are commands rather than laws: they are specific to a situation. No body of international law has been passed by a legislative body. Where, then, does international law come from? Four sources of international law are recognized: treaties, custom, general principles of law (such as equity), and legal scholarship (including past judicial decisions).

Web Link
Sources of
International
Law

Treaties and other written conventions signed by states are the most important source. International treaties now fill more than a thousand thick volumes, with tens of thousands of individual agreements. There is a principle in international law that treaties once signed and ratified must be observed. States violate the terms of treaties they have signed only if the matter is very important or the penalties for such a violation seem very small. In the United States, treaties duly ratified by the Senate are considered to be the highest law of the land, equal with acts passed by Congress.

Treaties and other international obligations such as debts are *binding on successor governments* whether the new government takes power through an election, a coup, or a revolution. After the revolutions in Eastern Europe around 1990, newly democratic governments were held responsible for debts incurred by their communist predecessors. Even when the Soviet Union broke up, Russia as the successor state had to guarantee that Soviet debts would be paid and Soviet treaties honored. Although revolution does not free a state from its obligations, some treaties have built-in escape clauses that let states legally withdraw from them, after giving due notice, without violating international law.

Because of the universal commitment for all states to respect certain basic principles of international law, the UN Charter is one of the world's most important treaties. Its implications are broad and far-reaching, in contrast to more specific treaties such as a fishery management treaty. The specialized agreements are usually easier to interpret and more enforceable than broad treaties such as the Charter.

Custom is the second major source of international law. If states behave toward each other in a certain way for long enough, their behavior may become generally accepted practice with the status of law. Western international law (though not Islamic law) tends to be *positivist* in this regard—it draws on actual customs, the practical realities of self-interest, and the need for consent rather than on an abstract concept of divine or natural law.

General principles of law also serve as a source of international law. Actions such as theft and assault, recognized in most national legal systems as crimes, tend to have the same meaning in an international context. Iraq's invasion of Kuwait was illegal under treaties signed by Iraq (including the UN Charter and that of the Arab League) and under the custom Iraq and Kuwait had established of living in peace as sovereign states. Beyond treaty or custom, the invasion violated international law because of the general principle that one state may not overrun its neighbor's territory and annex it by force. (Of course, a state may still think it can get away with such a violation of international law.)

The fourth source of international law, recognized by the World Court as subsidiary to the others, is *legal scholarship*—the written arguments of judges and lawyers around the world on the issues in question. Only the writings of the most highly qualified and respected legal figures can be taken into account, and then only to resolve points not resolved by the first three sources of international law.

Often international law lags behind changes in norms; law is quite tradition-bound. Certain activities such as espionage are technically illegal but are so widely condoned that they cannot be said to violate international norms. Other activities are still legal but have come to be frowned upon and seen as abnormal. For example, China's shooting of student demonstrators in 1989 violated international norms but not international law.

Enforcement of International Law
Although these sources of international law distinguish it from national law, an even greater difference exists as to the *enforcement* of the two types of law. International law is much more difficult to enforce. There is no world police force, no prison in the UN building to hold aggressors. Enforcement of international law depends on the power of states themselves, individually or collectively, to punish transgressors or force compliance.

Enforcement of international law depends heavily on practical reciprocity (see pp. 58–59). States follow international law most of the time because they want other states to do so. The reason neither side in World War II used chemical weapons was not that anyone could *enforce* the treaty banning use of such weapons. It was that the other side would probably respond by using chemical weapons, too, and the costs would be high to both sides. International law recognizes in certain circumstances the legitimacy of *reprisals*: actions that would have been illegal under international law may sometimes be legal if taken in response to the illegal actions of another state.

States also follow international law because of the general or long-term costs that could come from disregarding international law (rather than just immediate retaliation). If a state fails to pay its debts, it will not be able to borrow money on world markets. If it cheats on the terms of treaties it signs, other states will not sign future treaties with it. The resulting isolation could be very destructive to the state's security interests.

A state that breaks international law may also face a collective response by a group of states, such as the imposition of *sanctions*—agreements among other states to stop trading with the violator, or to stop some particular commodity trade (most often military goods) as punishment for its violation. Over time, a sanctioned state can become a *pariah* in the community of nations, cut off from normal relations with others. This is very costly in today's world, when economic well-being everywhere depends on trade and economic exchange in world markets. Iraq and Serbia have been pariahs for the last decade.

International law enforcement through reciprocity and collective response has one great weakness—it depends entirely on national power. Reciprocity works only if the aggrieved state has the power to inflict costs on the violator. Collective response works only if the collectivity cares enough about an issue to respond. This makes it relatively easy to cheat on small issues (or to get away with major violations if one has enough power). The international community repeatedly condemned Serbia's violations of international law in 1992 but was reluctant to bear the costs of punishing and reversing them.

If international law extends only as far as power reaches, what good is it? The answer lies in the uncertainties of power (see Chapter 2). Without common expectations regarding the rules of the game and adherence to those rules most of the time by most actors, power alone would create great instability in the anarchic international system. International law, even without perfect enforcement, creates expectations about what constitutes legal behavior by states. Thus violations or divergences from those expectations stand out, making it easier to identify and punish states that deviate from accepted rules. When states agree to the rules by signing treaties (such as the UN Charter), violations become more visible and clearly illegitimate. Thus, in most cases, although power continues to reside in states, international law establishes workable rules for those states to follow. The resulting stability is so beneficial that usually the costs of breaking the rules outweigh the short-term benefits that could be gained from such violations.

The World Court

As international law has developed, a general world legal framework in which states can pursue grievances against each other has begun to take shape. The rudiments of such a system now exist in the **World Court** (formally called the **International Court of Justice**), although its jurisdiction is limited and its caseload light. The World Court is a branch of the UN. Only states, not individuals or businesses, can sue or be sued in the World Court. When a state has a grievance against another, it can take the case to the World Court for an impartial hearing. The Security Council or General Assembly may also request advisory Court opinions on matters of international law.

Web Link
The World Court

The Court is a panel of 15 judges elected for nine-year terms (five judges every three years) by a majority of both the Security Council and General Assembly. The Court meets in The Hague, Netherlands. It is customary for permanent members of the Security Council to have one of their nationals as a judge at all times. Ad hoc judges may be added to the 15 if a party to a case does not already have one of its nationals as a judge.

The great *weakness* of the World Court is that states have not agreed in a comprehensive way to subject themselves to its jurisdiction or obey its decisions. Almost all states have signed the treaty creating the Court, but only about a third have signed the *optional clause* in the treaty agreeing to give the Court jurisdiction in certain cases—and even many of those signatories have added their own stipulations reserving their rights and limiting the degree to which the Court can infringe on national sovereignty. For example, Iran refused to acknowledge the jurisdiction of the Court when sued by the United States in 1979 over its seizure of the U.S. embassy in Iran. In such cases, the Court may hear the case without one side participating and usually rules in favor of the participating side—but has no means to enforce the ruling.

In one of its most notable successes, the World Court in 1992 settled a complex border dispute between El Salvador and Honduras. By mutual agreement, the two states had asked the Court in 1986 to settle territorial disputes about six stretches of border, three islands, and territorial waters. The disputes dated from 1861 and had led to a war in 1969. This was the most complex case ever handled by the Court, entailing 50 court sessions and years of deliberation over documents and precedents. In its ruling, the

Atlas CD
Honduras–
El Salvador
Border
Map

World Court drew borders that gave about two-thirds of the total land to Honduras and split the territorial waters among both countries and Nicaragua. Despite some misgivings among residents of certain disputed territories, the national governments pledged to abide by the decision.

A main use of the World Court now is to arbitrate issues of secondary importance between countries with friendly relations overall. The United States has settled commercial disputes with Canada and with Italy through the Court. Because security interests are not at stake, and because the overall friendly relations are more important than the particular issue, states have been willing to submit to the Court's jurisdiction.

There are other international forums for the arbitration of grievances (by mutual consent) as well. Some regional courts, notably in Europe, resemble the World Court in function. Various bodies are capable of conducting arbitration—as when Israel and Egypt submitted their dispute about the tiny territory of Taba to binding arbitration after failing to reach a settlement. Arbitration can remove domestic political pressures from state leaders by taking the decision out of their hands. But for major disputes involving issues of great importance to states, there is still little effective international legal apparatus.

Because of the difficulty of winning enforceable agreements on major conflicts through the World Court, states have used the Court infrequently over the years—a dozen or fewer cases per year (only 61 judgments and 23 advisory opinions since 1946). The number has been increasing, however.

International Cases in National Courts   Most legal cases concerning international matters—whether brought by governments or by private individuals or companies—remain entirely within the legal systems of one or more states. National courts hear cases brought under national laws and can enforce judgments by collecting damages (in civil suits) or imposing punishments (in criminal ones).

A party with a dispute that crosses national boundaries gains several advantages by pursuing the matter through the national courts of one or more of the relevant states, rather than through international channels. First, judgments are enforceable. The party that wins a lawsuit in a national court can collect from the other party's assets within the state. Second, individuals and companies can pursue legal complaints through national courts (as can subnational governmental bodies), whereas in most areas of international law states must themselves bring suits on behalf of their citizens. (In truth, even national governments pursue most of their legal actions against each other through national courts.)

Third, there is often a choice of more than one state within which a case could legally be heard; one can pick the legal system most favorable to one's case. It is up to each state's court system to decide whether it has *jurisdiction* in a case (the right to hear it), and courts tend to extend their own authority with a broad interpretation. Traditionally, a national court may hear cases concerning any activity on its national territory, any actions of its own citizens anywhere in the world, and actions taken toward its citizens elsewhere in the world. Noncitizens can use the national courts to enforce damages against citizens, because the national court has authority to impose fines and if necessary seize bank accounts and property.

The United States is a favorite jurisdiction within which to bring cases for two reasons. First, U.S. juries have the reputation of awarding bigger settlements in lawsuits than juries elsewhere in the world (if only because the United States is a rich country).

Second, because many people and governments do business in the United States, it is often possible to collect damages awarded by a U.S. court.

There are important limits to the use of national courts to resolve international disputes, however. Most important is that the authority of national courts stops at the state's borders, where sovereignty ends. A court in Zambia cannot compel a resident of Thailand to come and testify; it cannot authorize the seizure of a British bank account to pay damages; it cannot arrest a criminal suspect (Zambian or foreigner) except on Zambian soil.

To bring a person outside the state's territory to trial, the state's government must ask a second government to arrest the person on the second state's territory and hand him or her over for trial. This is called *extradition*, which is a matter of international law because it is a legal treaty arrangement *between* states. If there is no such treaty, the individual generally remains immune from a state's courts by staying off its territory.

There are gray areas in the jurisdiction of national courts over foreigners. If a government can lure a suspect onto the high seas, it can nab the person without violating another country's territoriality. More troublesome are cases in which a government obtains a foreign citizen from a foreign country for trial without going through extradition procedures. In a famous case in the 1980s, a Mexican doctor was wanted by U.S. authorities for allegedly participating in the torture and murder of a U.S. drug agent in Mexico. The U.S. government paid a group of bounty hunters to kidnap the doctor in Mexico, carry him forcibly across the border, and deliver him to the custody of U.S. courts. The U.S. Supreme Court gave the U.S. courts jurisdiction in the case—showing the tendency to extend state sovereignty wherever possible—although international lawyers and Mexican officials sharply disagreed. The U.S. government had to reassure the Mexican government that it would not kidnap Mexican citizens for trial in the United States in the future. (Ironically, the doctor returned home after the case was thrown out for lack of evidence.)

The principle of territoriality also governs **immigration law**. When people cross a border into a new country, the decision about whether they can remain there, and under what conditions, is up to the new state. The state of origin cannot compel their return. National laws establish conditions for foreigners to travel and visit on a state's territory, to work there, and sometimes even to become citizens *(naturalization)*. Many other legal issues are raised by people traveling or living outside their own country—passports and visas, babies born in foreign countries, marriages to foreign nationals, bank accounts, businesses, taxes, and so forth. Practices vary from country to country, but the general principle is that *national laws prevail on the territory of a state.*

The former Chilean military dictator Augusto Pinochet was arrested in England in 1999 on a Spanish warrant, based on crimes committed against Spanish citizens in Chile during Pinochet's rule. His supporters claimed that he should have immunity for acts taken as head of state, but since he was not an accredited diplomat in England (where he had gone for medical treatment), and no longer head of state, the British courts held him on Spain's request to extradite him for trial there. Once on British soil without current diplomatic immunity, Pinochet was subject to British law, including its extradition treaties. However, the British government eventually let him return to Chile, citing his medical condition.

Despite the continued importance of national court systems in international legal affairs and the lack of enforcement powers of the World Court, it would be wrong to conclude that state sovereignty is supreme and international law impotent. Rather, there is a balance of sovereignty and law in international interactions. The remainder of this chapter discusses particular areas of international law, from the most firmly rooted and widely respected, to newer and less-established areas. In each area, the influence of law and norms runs counter to the unimpeded exercise of state sovereignty. This struggle becomes more intense as one moves from long-standing traditions of diplomatic law to recent norms governing human rights.

Laws of Diplomacy

The bedrock of international law is respect for the rights of diplomats. The standards of behavior in this area are spelled out in detail, applied universally, and taken very seriously. The ability to conduct diplomacy is necessary for all other kinds of relations among states, except perhaps all-out war. Since the rise of the international system five centuries ago, it has been considered unjustifiable to harm an emissary sent from another state as a means of influencing the other state. Such a norm has not *always* existed; it is natural in some ways to kill the messenger who brings an unpleasant message, or to use another state's official as a hostage or bargaining chip. But today this kind of behavior is universally condemned, though it still happens from time to time.

The status of embassies and of an ambassador as an official state representative is explicitly defined in the process of **diplomatic recognition**. Diplomats are *accredited* to each other's governments (they present "credentials"), and thereafter the individuals so defined enjoy certain rights and protections as foreign diplomats in the host country.

Diplomats have the right to occupy an *embassy* in the host country as though it were their own state's territory. On the grounds of the U.S. embassy in Kuwait, for instance, the laws of the United States, and not those of Kuwait, apply. The U.S. armed forces (Marines) occupy the territory, and those of Kuwait may not enter without permission. This principle of international law explains why, when Iraq invaded Kuwait, it did not set foot inside the U.S. embassy compound even though it could have overrun the facility easily. Instead Iraq placed the compound under siege, eventually forcing the staff and ambassador to leave.

A flagrant violation of the sanctity of embassies occurred in Iran after Islamic revolutionaries took power in 1979. Iranian students seized and occupied the U.S. embassy compound, holding the U.S. diplomats hostage for more than a year. The Iranian government did not directly commit this act but did condone it and did refuse to force the students out of the embassy. (Host countries are expected, if necessary, to use force against their own citizens to protect a foreign embassy.)

Diplomats enjoy **diplomatic immunity** even when they leave the embassy grounds. The right to travel varies from one country to another; diplomats may be restricted to one city or free to roam about the countryside. Alone among all foreign nationals, diplomats are beyond the jurisdiction of the host country's national courts. If they commit any crimes, they may not be arrested and tried. All the host country can do is to take away a diplomat's accreditation and *expel* the person from the host country. However, strong countries can sometimes pressure weaker ones to lift immunity so that a diplomat may face trial for a crime. This happened twice in 1997, when the United States and France were allowed to prosecute diplomats from Georgia and Zaire, respectively, for reckless driving that killed children.

U.S. commitments as host country to the UN include extending diplomatic immunity to the diplomats accredited to the UN. The UN delegates thus cannot be prose-

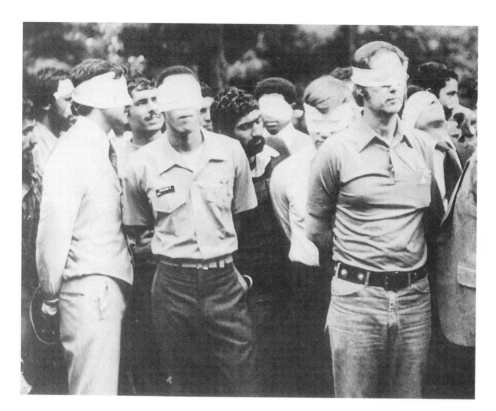

Against the Law   International law prohibits attacks on diplomats. This fundamental principle, like others in international law, can ultimately be enforced only by applying the power of other states (through such leverage as imposing economic sanctions, freezing relations, or threatening military force). Here are U.S. diplomats on their first day as hostages in the U.S. embassy, Tehran, Iran, 1979.

cuted under U.S. law. Given this immunity, delegates each year, for example, simply tear up thousands of parking tickets. Occasionally, UN representatives are accused of more serious crimes (murder, in one case in the 1980s), but they cannot be brought to trial in the United States for those crimes—much less for their parking offenses.

Because of diplomatic immunity, it is common to conduct espionage activities through the diplomatic corps, out of an embassy. Spies are often posted to low-level positions in embassies, such as cultural attaché, press liaison, or military attaché. If the host country catches them spying, it cannot prosecute them, so it merely expels them. Diplomatic norms (though not law) call for politeness when expelling spies; the standard reason given is "for activities not consistent with his/her diplomatic status." If a spy operates under cover of being a business person or tourist, then no immunity applies: the person can be arrested and prosecuted under the host country's laws.

A *diplomatic pouch* is a package sent between an embassy and its home country. As the name implies, it started out historically as a small and occasional shipment, but today there is a large and steady volume of such shipments all over the world. Diplomatic pouches, too, enjoy the status of home country territoriality: they cannot be opened, searched, or confiscated by a host country. Although we do not know how much mischief goes on in diplomatic pouches (because they are secret), it is safe to assume that illicit goods such as guns and drugs regularly find their way across borders in diplomatic pouches.

To *break diplomatic relations* means to withdraw one's diplomats from a state and expel its diplomats from one's own state. This tactic is used to show displeasure with another government; it is a refusal to do business as usual. When a revolutionary government comes into power, some countries may withdraw recognition. The U.S. has not had diplomatic relations with Cuba since the 1959 revolution, for example.

When two countries lack diplomatic relations, they often do business through a third country willing to represent a country's interests formally through its own embassy. This is called an *interests section* in the third country's embassy. Thus the practical needs of diplomacy can overcome a formal lack of relations between states. For instance, U.S. interests are represented by the Swiss embassy in Cuba, and Cuban interests are represented by the Swiss embassy in the United States. In practice, these interests sections are located in the former U.S. and Cuban embassies and staffed with U.S. and Cuban diplomats.

States register lower levels of displeasure by *recalling their ambassadors* home for some period of time; diplomatic norms call for a trip home "for consultations" even when everyone knows the purpose is to signal annoyance. Milder still is the expression of displeasure by a *formal complaint*. Usually the complaining government does so in its own capital city, to the other's ambassador.

The law of diplomacy is repeatedly violated in one context— terrorism. Because states care so much about the sanctity of diplomats, the diplomats make a tempting target for terrorists, and because terrorist groups do not enjoy the benefits of diplomatic law (as states do), they are willing to break diplomatic norms and laws. An attack on diplomats or embassies is an attack on the territory of the state itself—yet can be carried out far from the state's home territory. Being a diplomat has become a dangerous occupation, and many have been killed in recent decades. Because terrorist actions are seldom traceable to governments, international law (enforced through reciprocity or collective response) is of limited use in stopping terrorist attacks on diplomats.

War Crimes

War Crimes After the law of diplomacy, international law regarding war is one of the most developed areas of international law. Laws concerning war are divided into two areas—laws in war *(jus in bello)* and laws of war *(jus ad bellum)*. Consider these in turn, beginning with laws in wartime, violations of which are considered **war crimes**.

In wartime, international law is especially difficult to enforce, but there are extensive norms of legal conduct in war that are widely followed. After a war, losers can be punished for violations of the laws of war (war crimes). In the 1990s, for the first time since World War II, the UN Security Council authorized an international war crimes tribunal, directed against war crimes in the former Yugoslavia. A similar tribunal was later established for genocide in Rwanda. Both tribunals are headquartered in The Hague, Netherlands. The tribunal on the former Yugoslavia issued indictments against the top Bosnian Serb leaders and other Serbian and Croatian officers, and in 1999 against Serbian strongman Slobodan Milosevic during the expulsion of Albanians from Kosovo. The tribunal was severely hampered by lack of funding and by its lack of power to arrest suspects who enjoyed the sanctity of Serbia and Croatia. A new Croatian government that won elections in 1999 pledged much greater cooperation with the tribunal,

Prime Suspects   War crimes include mistreatment of prisoners of war (POWs) and unnecessary targeting of civilians. An international war crimes tribunal is hearing cases from the former Yugoslavia. The top leaders of the Bosnian Serb forces, Radovan Karadzic and Ratko Mladic, were indicted in 1996 for genocide and war crimes including the execution of 7,000 Muslim prisoners of war in 1995. As of 2000 they had not been arrested, however (photo, 1992).

leaving Serbia as the holdout. Of 76 suspects indicted, 31 were still at large as of March 2000. (An unknown number of additional indictments had been sealed to avoid tipping off the suspect.) Sporadically since 1997, NATO forces have arrested 17 suspects and killed one, but have not yet tried to arrest the top leaders of Serb forces.

Unlike at Nuremberg, the aggressor had not been conquered and its leaders arrested. So, as with most international law, the enforcement of laws of war occurs mostly through practical reciprocity and group response, reinforced by habit and legitimacy. A state that violates laws of war can find itself isolated without allies and subject to reprisals.

The most important principle in the laws of war is the effort to limit warfare to the combatants and to protect civilians when possible. It is illegal to target civilians in a war unless there is a compelling military utility in doing so. Even then the amount of force used must be *proportional* to the military gain, and only the *necessary* amount of force can be used.

To help separate combatants from civilians, soldiers must wear uniforms and insignia; for example, U.S. armed forces typically have a shoulder patch with a U.S. flag. This provision is frequently violated in guerrilla warfare, making that form of warfare particularly brutal and destructive of civilian life. If one cannot tell the difference between a bystander and a combatant, one is likely to kill both when in doubt. By con-

Web Link
Nuremberg

trast, in a large-scale conventional war such as the Gulf War, it is much easier to distinguish civilians from soldiers, although the effort is never completely successful.

Soldiers have the right under the laws of war to surrender, which is to abandon their status as combatants and become **prisoners of war (POWs)**. They give up their weapons and their right to fight, and earn instead the right (like civilians) not to be targeted. POWs may not be killed, mistreated, or forced to disclose information beyond their name, rank, and serial number. During the Gulf War, the United States took many thousands of Iraqi prisoners and respected their right to drop out of the fight. Iraq's treatment of a handful of U.S. POWs—including physical mistreatment—was among Iraq's many violations of international law in that war. The law of POWs is enforced through practical reciprocity. Once, late in World War II, German forces executed 80 POWs from the French partisan forces. The partisans responded by executing 80 German POWs.

The laws of war reserve a special role for the **International Committee of the Red Cross (ICRC)**. The ICRC provides practical support—such as medical care, food, and letters from home—to civilians caught in wars and to POWs. Exchanges of POWs are usually negotiated through the ICRC. Armed forces must respect the neutrality of the Red Cross, and most of the time they do so (again, guerrilla war is more problematical).

The laws of warfare impose moral responsibility on individuals in wartime, as well as on states. The Nuremberg Tribunal after World War II established that participants can be held accountable for war crimes they commit. German officers defended their actions as "just following orders," but this was rejected; the officers were punished, and some executed, for their war crimes.

Not all Nuremberg defendants were found guilty, however. For example, laws of war limit the use of force against civilians to that which is necessary and proportional to military objectives. That can be a high limit in a total war. In World War II, the German army besieged the Russian city of Leningrad (St. Petersburg) for two years, and civilians in the city were starving. Sieges of this kind are permitted under international law if an army cannot easily capture a city.

CHANGING CONTEXT The laws of warfare have been undermined by the changing nature of war. Conventional wars by defined armed forces on defined battlegrounds are giving way to irregular and "low-intensity" wars fought by guerrillas and death squads in cities or jungles. The lines between civilians and soldiers blur in these situations, and war crimes become more commonplace. In the Vietnam War, one of the largest problems faced by the United States was an enemy that seemed to be everywhere and nowhere. This led frustrated U.S. forces into attacking civilian villages seen as supporting the guerrillas. In one infamous case, a U.S. officer was court-martialed for ordering his soldiers to massacre hundreds of unarmed civilians in the village of My Lai in 1968 (he was convicted but given a light sentence). In today's irregular warfare, frequently inflamed by ethnic conflicts, the laws of war are increasingly difficult to uphold.

Another factor undermining laws of war is that states now rarely issue a *declaration of war* setting out whom they are warring against and the cause of their action. This practice, common until about 50 years ago, helped distinguish belligerents from bystanders, protecting neutral countries and invoking the rights and responsibilities of the warring states. Today, such declarations are seldom used because they bring little benefit to the state declaring war and incur obligations under international law. States just fight wars without declaring them. In many cases, such as revolutionary and counterrevolutionary civil wars in the third world, a declaration would not even be appropriate, because wars are declared only against states, not internal groups. In undeclared wars the distinctions between participants and nonparticipants are undermined (along with the protection of the latter).

Just War Doctrine
In addition to the laws about how wars are fought (war crimes), international law distinguishes **just wars** (which are legal) from wars of aggression (which are illegal). This area of law grows out of centuries-old religious writings about just wars (which once could be enforced by threats to excommunicate individuals from the church). Today, the legality of war is defined by the UN Charter, which outlaws aggression. Above and beyond the legal standing of just war doctrine, it has become a strong international norm, not one that all states follow but an important part of the modern intellectual tradition governing matters of war and peace that evolved in Europe.

The idea of aggression, around which the doctrine of just war evolved, is based on a violation of the sovereignty and territorial integrity of states. It assumes recognized borders that are legally inviolable. Aggression refers to a state's use of force, or an imminent threat to do so, against another state's territory or sovereignty—unless the use of force is in response to aggression. Tanks swarming across the border constitute aggression, but so do tanks massing at the border if their state has threatened to invade. The lines are somewhat fuzzy—for a threat to constitute aggression (and justify the use of force in response) it must be a clear threat of using force, not just a hostile policy or general rivalry.

In Iraq's invasion of Kuwait, Iraq's complaint that Kuwait had unfairly taken joint oil resources could not justify Iraq's invasion. Instead, Iraq justified its invasion on the grounds that Kuwait's territorial integrity had never existed, because it was historically a province of Iraq. The argument's flaw was that Iraq and Kuwait had both signed the UN Charter binding them to respect each other's territorial integrity! The international community had little trouble determining that Iraq's invasion was aggression.

States have the right to respond to aggression in the only manner thought to be reliable—military force. Just war doctrine is not based on nonviolence. Responses can include both the *repelling* of the attack itself and the *punishment* of the aggressor. Responses can be taken by the victim of aggression or by other states not directly affected—as a way of maintaining the norm of nonaggression in the international system. The collective actions of UN members against Iraq after its invasion of Kuwait are a classic case of such response.

Response to aggression is the only allowable use of military force according to just war doctrine. The just war approach thus explicitly rules out war as an instrument to change another state's government or policies, or in ethnic and religious conflicts. In fact, the UN Charter makes no provision for "war" but rather for "international police actions" against aggressors. The analogy is with law and order in a national society, enforced by police when necessary. Because only aggression justifies military force, if all states obeyed the law against aggression there would be no international war.

Just war doctrine has been undermined, even more seriously than laws of war crimes, by the changing nature of warfare. In civil wars and low-intensity conflicts, the belligerents range from poorly organized militias to national armies, and the battleground is often a patchwork of enclaves and positions with no clear front lines (much less borders). It is harder to identify an aggressor in such situations, and harder to balance the relative merits of peace and justice.

Another change in the nature of warfare is the development of nuclear weapons. It is generally recognized that nuclear war could not be an adequate response to aggression. Thus, the use of nuclear weapons could never be just in the view of most scholars of the subject. More difficult to answer is whether it can be just to possess such weapons.

For a war to be *morally* just, it must be more than a response to aggression; it must be waged for the *purpose* of responding to aggression. The *intent* must be just. A state may not take advantage of another's aggression to wage a war that is essentially aggressive. Although the U.S.-led war effort to oust Iraq from Kuwait was certainly a response to aggression, critics found the justness of the war to be compromised by the U.S. interest in obtaining cheap oil from the Middle East—not an allowable reason for waging war.

Human Rights   One of the newest and least developed areas of international law concerns **human rights**—the universal rights of human beings against certain abuses of their *own* governments. The very idea of human rights flies in the face of the sovereignty and territorial integrity of states. Efforts to promote human rights are routinely criticized by governments with poor human rights records (such as China or Russia) as "interference in our internal affairs." This charge puts human rights law on shaky ground.

Atlas CD
Grozny in 1995
Photo

Yet norms and even laws concerning human rights continue to develop, if only because what happens within one state can so easily spill over national borders. A prime example occurred when Iraq cracked down brutally on a Kurdish uprising in northern Iraq. The norm of noninterference in Iraq's internal affairs would dictate that the slaughter was Iraq's business alone. But when the Kurds fled in huge numbers to the Turkish border, they threatened to overwhelm the resources of Turkey and perhaps inflame a Kurdish uprising in Turkey. The anti-Iraqi alliance therefore declared the matter an international concern and imposed their own armed forces within northern Iraq to provide security and coax the Kurds back home. Eventually the Kurdish groups gained virtual autonomy under foreign military cover, compromising Iraq's sovereignty. Because of Iraq's lack of military reach into the area, Turkey was able to invade several times in 1995–1998 to try to cut off the roots of the Kurdish guerrillas operating in Turkey.

Even in cases that do not so directly spill over national borders, the world is more interconnected and interdependent than ever. A government's abuses of its citizens can inflame ethnic conflicts, undermine moral norms of decency, and in other ways threaten the peace and stability of the international community. At least this is the rationale for treating human rights as a question of international law and norms. Human rights are also considered by some state leaders as a legitimate international concern because the presence or absence of democracy (including respect for rights) is thought to strongly influence states' foreign policies and propensities for violence (see pp. 112–115).

Laws concerning human rights date back to the Nuremberg trials. Beyond the war crimes committed by German officers were their acts of *genocide* (attempts to exterminate a whole people) in which about ten million civilians had been killed in death camps. Clearly this ranked among the most wicked crimes ever committed, yet it did not violate either international law or German law. The solution was to create a new category of legal offenses—**crimes against humanity**—under which those responsible were punished. The category was not applied again until 1994–1995, when the tribunal for the former Yugoslavia handed down indictments for genocide.

Soon after the experience of World War II, in 1948, the UN General Assembly adopted the *Universal Declaration of Human Rights*. It does not have the force of international law, but it sets forth (hoped-for) international norms regarding behavior by governments toward their own citizens and foreigners alike. The declaration roots itself in the principle that violations of human rights upset international order and in the fact that the UN Charter commits states to respect fundamental freedoms. The declaration proclaims that "all human beings are born free and equal" without regard to race, sex, language, religion, political affiliation, or the status of the territory on which they were born. It goes on to promote norms in a wide variety of areas, from banning torture to guaranteeing religious and political freedom to the right of economic well-being.

Web Link
Universal
Declaration on
Human Rights

Clearly this is a broad conception of human rights, and one far from today's realities. No state has a perfect record on human rights, and states differ as to areas they respect or violate. When the United States criticizes China for prohibiting free speech, China notes that the United States has 40 million poor people, the highest ratio of prison inmates in the world, and a history of racism and violence. Overall, despite the poor record of the world's states on some points, progress has been made on others. For example, slavery has been abandoned worldwide in the past 150 years.

The *Helsinki Agreements* in the 1970s, reached during a period of détente in U.S.-Soviet relations, made human rights a legitimate subject in an East-West treaty for the first time in the Cold War. The Soviet Union and Eastern European states agreed to guarantee certain basic rights of political dissent in their countries. These agreements were often breached but still provided important norms by which governments' behavior was judged (including, later, by their own people, who overthrew those governments).

Today, human rights efforts center on winning basic political rights in authoritarian countries—beginning with a halt to the torture, execution, and imprisonment of those expressing political or religious beliefs. The leading organization pressing this struggle is **Amnesty International**, an NGO that operates globally to monitor and try to rectify glaring abuses of human rights. Amnesty International has a reputation for impartiality and has criticized abuses in many countries, including the United States. Other groups, such as Human Rights Watch, work in a similar way but often with a more regional or national focus. The UN also operates a Commission on Human Rights with a global focus. In 1993, the General Assembly after 40 years of debate created the position of high commissioner for human rights (whose powers do not, of course, include making states do anything, but do include publicizing their abuses).

Enforcement of norms of human rights is difficult, because it involves interference in a state's internal affairs. Cutting off trade or contact with a government that violates human rights tends to hurt the citizens whose rights are being violated by further isolating them. The most effective method yet discovered is a combination of *publicity* and *pressure*. Publicity entails digging up information about human rights abuses, as Amnesty International does. The pressure of other governments, as well as private individuals and businesses, consists of threats to punish the offender in some way through nonviolent means. For instance, one faction in the U.S. Congress repeatedly sought in the early 1990s to link the terms of U.S.-Chinese trade to China's human rights record. But inasmuch as

Execution Leader

International norms concerning human rights conflict with state sovereignty, causing friction in relationships like China's with the United States. China executes thousands of people each year, more than any other country. Here, a city official convicted of taking $1 million in bribes is led to his execution, 1995. China considers human rights an internal affair.

most governments seek to maintain normal relations with each other most of the time, this kind of intrusive punishment by one government of another's human rights violations is rare—and not reliably successful. In 1994, the U.S. government unlinked China's trade status from its human rights record. However, in 1997 the United States imposed sanctions on Burma (a far less important trade partner) over human rights abuses.

The U.S. State Department has actively pursued human rights since the late 1970s. An annual U.S. government report assesses human rights in states around the world. In cases where abuses are severe or becoming worse, U.S. foreign aid has been withheld from these states or their armed forces. (But in other cases, CIA funding supported the abusers.)

Currently, human rights are one of the two main areas of conflict (along with Taiwan) in China's relationship with the United States. Several practices draw criticism; these include imprisoning political opponents of the government, the use of prison labor, and a criminal justice system prone to abuses. In the 1990s, according to Amnesty International, China executed more people than the rest of the world combined—nearly 5,000 in 1996 alone—sometimes within days of the crime and sometimes for relatively petty crimes.

A variety of covenants and conventions on human rights have been drawn up as legally binding (though not easily enforceable) treaties. These include a major covenant on civil and political rights (ratified by the United States) and on economic, social, and cultural rights (not U.S.-ratified). More specific conventions cover genocide, racial discrimination, women's rights, torture, and the rights of the child. The treaties have been ratified by various groups of the world's states. Some states (including both the United States and China) have general concerns about the loss of sovereignty implicit in such treaties. In 1998 China promised to sign the Covenant on Civil and Political Rights, which the United States ratified in 1992. China and all but four

UN members (one of which is the United States) have ratified the 1990 Convention on the Rights of the Child.

Despite many limitations, concern about human rights is a force to be reckoned with in international relations. There are now widely held norms about how governments *should* behave, and someday governments may actually adhere to those norms. With the downfall of authoritarian and military governments in the former Soviet Union, Eastern Europe, Latin America, and Africa, a growing emphasis on human rights seems likely.

The Evolution of World Order

The growing importance of IOs and international law reflects the fact that most international conflicts are not settled by military force. Despite the anarchic nature of the international system based on state sovereignty, the security dilemma does not usually lead to a breakdown in basic cooperation among states. States generally refrain from taking maximum short-term advantage of each other (such as by invading and conquering). States work *with* other states for mutual gain and take advantage of each other only "at the margin." Unfortunately the day-to-day cooperative activities of states often are less newsworthy than states' uses of force.

States work together by following rules they develop to govern their interactions. States usually *do* follow the rules. Over time, the rules become more firmly established and institutions grow up around them. States then develop the habit of working through those institutions and within the rules. They do so because of self-interest; great gains can be realized by regulating international interactions through institutions and rules, thereby avoiding the costly outcomes associated with a breakdown of cooperation.

International anarchy thus does not mean a lack of order, structure, and rules. In many ways, actors in international society now work together as cooperatively as actors in domestic society—more so than some domestic societies. Today, most wars are civil, not interstate, wars; this reflects the general success of international norms, organizations, and laws—and the balance of power—in maintaining peace among states.

International anarchy, then, means simply that states surrender sovereignty to no one. Domestic society has government with powers of enforcement; international society does not. When the rules are broken in IR, actors can rely only on the power of individual states (separately or in concert) to restore order.

Over the centuries, international institutions and rules have grown stronger, more complex, and more important. International order started out based largely on raw power, but it has evolved to be based more on legitimacy and habit (and power). *Domestic law*, too, was once enforced only by the most powerful for the most powerful. The first states and civilizations were largely military dictatorships. Law was what the top ruler decreed. International law and organization likewise began as terms imposed by powerful winners on losers after wars.

The international institutions and rules that operate today took shape especially during periods of hegemony (see pp. 72–74), when one state predominated in international power after a hegemonic war among the great powers. The organizations that today form the institutional framework for international interactions—such as the UN, the Organization of American States, and the World Bank—were created under U.S. leadership.

Rules of international behavior have become established over time as norms and are often codified as international law. This is a more incremental process than the creation of institutions; it goes on between and during periods of war and of hegemony. But still the most powerful states, especially hegemons, have great influence on the rules and values that have become embedded over time in a body of international law.

For example, the principle of free passage on the open seas is now formally established in international law. But at one time warships from one state did not hesitate to seize the ships of other states and make off with their cargoes. This was profitable to the state that pulled off such raids, but of course their own shipping could be raided in return. Such behavior made long-distance trade itself more dangerous, less predictable, and less profitable. The trading states could benefit more by getting rid of the practice. So over time a norm developed around the concept of freedom of navigation on the high seas. It became one of the first areas of international law—developed by the Dutch in the mid 1600s, a time when they dominated world trade and could benefit most from free navigation.

Dutch power, then, provided the backbone for the international legal concept of freedom of the seas. Later, when Britain was dominant, the principle of free seas was enforced through the cannons of British warships. As the world's main trading state, Britain benefited from a worldwide norm of free shipping and trade. With the world's most powerful navy, it was in a position to define and enforce the rules for the world's oceans.

Likewise, twentieth-century world order depended heavily on the power of the United States (and, for a few decades, on the division of power between the United States and the Soviet Union). The United States at times came close to adopting the explicit role of "world police force." But in truth the world is too large for any single state—even a hegemon—to police effectively. Rather, the world's states usually go along with the rules established by the most powerful state without constant policing. Meanwhile they try to influence the rules by working through international institutions (to which the hegemon cedes some of its power). In this way, although states do not yield their sovereignty, they vest some power and authority in international institutions and laws and generally work within that framework.

The rules that govern most interactions in IR are rooted in moral norms. **International norms** are the expectations held by state leaders about normal international relations. The invasion of Kuwait by Iraq was not only illegal, it was widely viewed as immoral—beyond the acceptable range of behavior of states (that is, beyond the normal amount of cheating that states get away with). Political leaders in the United States and around the world drew on moral norms to generate support for a collective response to Iraq. Thus morality is an element of power (see pp. 50–53).

These norms are widely held; they shape expectations about state behavior and set standards that make deviations stand out. International morality differs somewhat from morality within states, which is strongly influenced by the particular culture and traditions of the particular state. By contrast, international morality is a more universal set of moral standards and rules applicable to the interactions of states themselves.

The attempt to define universal norms follows a centuries-long philosophical tradition. Philosophers such as Kant argued that it was natural for autonomous individuals (or states) to cooperate for mutual benefit because they could see that pursuing their narrow individual interests would end up hurting all. Thus, sovereign states could work together through structures and organizations that would respect each member's autonomy and not create a world government over them. In the nineteenth century, such ideas were embodied in practical organizations in which states participated to manage specific issues such as control of traffic on European rivers.

THE INFORMATION REVOLUTION — Consolidating Norms

The post–Cold War era has created uncertainty about international norms—the shared expectations about how states should behave. The new rules are still being written and tested. One unsettled aspect of international norms is the changing view of when outsiders can interfere in states' internal affairs. Will technological change tear down walls and force states to accept international norms in such areas as human rights, nonproliferation, and environmental protection?

To explore this question, go to www.IRtext.com

Agreed norms of behavior, institutionalized through such organizations, become *habitual* over time and gain *legitimacy*. State leaders become used to behaving in a normal way and stop calculating whether violating norms would pay off. For instance, the U.S. president does not spend time calculating whether the costs of invading Canada would outweigh the benefits. The willingness to maintain normal behavior has psychological roots in "satisficing" and in aversion to risk (see pp. 98–102). Legitimacy and habit explain why international norms can be effective even when they are not codified and enforced.

International norms and standards of morality do not help, however, when different states or world regions hold different expectations of what is normal. To the United States, it was a moral imperative to punish Iraqi aggression against Kuwait. But from the perspective of leaders in Jordan and Yemen, the U.S. response represented immoral imperialistic aggression. In cases of diverging norms, morality can be a factor for misunderstanding and conflict rather than a force of stability.

The **"New World Order"** envisioned by U.S. President George Bush during the Iraq-Kuwait crisis included four principles: peaceful settlement of disputes, solidarity against aggression, reduced and controlled arsenals, and just treatment of all peoples. Note that some of the principles are based more on practical considerations (reduced arsenals) and others on more explicitly moral standards (just treatment of all peoples). These principles represent the interest that the United States and other great powers have in a stable world order.

This new order found little solid ground to stand on in the post–Cold War era, however. One problem with rapid change is that nobody knows what to expect; norms break down because leaders do not have common expectations. Through a long process of coping with a sequence of cases, international leaders build up new understandings of the rules of the game. In the 1990s, the rules clearly changed. For example, President Bush's last secretary of state, who helped keep the United States aloof from the Bosnia crisis in 1992, said later that if the Cold War had still been going on he would have advised U.S. leaders to "jump in with both feet." Thus, the end of the Cold War put basic expectations, such as when U.S. military intervention is warranted, up for grabs.

These new norms remained unsettled in 2000. New expectations were emerging in such areas as human rights, UN peacekeeping, Russia's and China's roles as great powers, and the role of the U.S. as a superpower. Three factors have combined to shake up inter-

Atlas CD
Sarajevo's
Place in
History
Photo, Music

Crossing Borders   International norms are evolving in such areas as humanitarian assistance and refugee flows. These norms help define the relevance of morality in IR and the roles of international organizations (IOs). Here, Rwandan refugees cross the border from Tanzania, 1996.

national norms—the end of the Cold War, the shifts in economic position of various regions and states, and the effects of technological change in creating a "small world." Domestic and local politics now play out on a global stage. In the coming years, international norms may settle down in a new configuration—perhaps with a lessened emphasis on national sovereignty. These changes will play out in a world increasingly marked by the gap between rich and poor countries—the subject of Chapter 7.

THINKING CRITICALLY

1. Suppose you were asked to recommend changes in the structure of the UN Security Council (especially in permanent membership and the veto). What changes would you recommend, if any? Based on what logic?

2. Functional economic ties among European states have contributed to the emergence of a supranational political structure, the EU, which has consider-

able though not unlimited power. Do you think the same thing could happen in North America? Could the U.S.-Canadian-Mexican NAFTA develop into a future North American Union like the EU? What problems would it be likely to face, given the experience of the EU?

3. Although international norms concerning human rights are becoming stronger, China and many other states continue to consider human rights an internal affair over which the state has sovereignty within its territory. Do you think human rights are a legitimate subject for one state to raise with another? If so, how do you reconcile the tensions between state autonomy and universal rights? What practical steps could be taken to get sovereign states to acknowledge universal human rights?

CHAPTER SUMMARY

◆ Supranational processes bring states together in larger structures and identities. These processes generally lead to an ongoing struggle between nationalism and supranationalism.

◆ International rules operate through institutions (IOs), with the UN at the center of the institutional network.

◆ The UN embodies a tension between state sovereignty and supranational authority. In its Charter and history, the UN has made sovereignty the more important principle. This has limited the UN's power.

◆ The UN particularly defers to the sovereignty of great powers, five of whom as permanent Security Council members can each block any security-related resolution binding on UN member states.

◆ In part because of its deference to state sovereignty, the UN has attracted virtually universal membership of the world's states, including all the great powers.

◆ Each of the 189 UN member states has one vote in the General Assembly, which serves mainly as a world forum and an umbrella organization for third world social and economic development efforts.

◆ The Security Council has ten rotating member states and five permanent members: the United States, Russia, China, Britain, and France.

◆ The UN is administered by international civil servants in the Secretariat, headed by the secretary-general.

◆ The regular UN budget plus all peacekeeping missions together amounts to far less than 1 percent of what the world spends on military forces.

◆ Voting patterns and coalitions in the UN have changed over the years with the expanding membership and changing conditions. Currently the U.S. role is strong but controversial, because the United States has demanded UN reforms but is more than $1 billion behind in its payments to the UN.

◆ UN peacekeeping forces are deployed in regional conflicts in five world regions. Their main role is to monitor compliance with agreements such as cease-fires, disarmament plans, and fair election rules. They were scaled back dramatically in 1995–1997.

◆ UN peacekeepers operate under UN command and flag. Sometimes national troops operate under their own flag and command to carry out UN resolutions.

◆ IOs include UN programs (mostly on economic and social issues), autonomous UN agencies, and organizations with no formal tie to the UN. This institutional network helps to strengthen and stabilize the rules of IR.

◆ International integration—the partial shifting of sovereignty from the state toward supranational institutions—is considered an outgrowth of international cooperation in functional (technical and economic) issue areas.

◆ Integration theorists thought that functional cooperation would spill over into political integration in foreign policy and military issue areas. Instead, powerful forces of disintegration are tearing apart previously existing states in some regions (especially in the former Soviet Union and Yugoslavia).

◆ The European Union (EU) is the most advanced case of integration. Its 15 member states have given considerable power to the EU in economic decision making. However, national power still outweighs supranational power even in the EU.

◆ The most important and most successful element in the EU is its customs union (and the associated free-trade area). Goods can cross borders of member states freely, and the members adopt unified tariffs with regard to goods entering from outside the EU.

◆ Under the EU's Common Agricultural Policy (CAP), subsidies to farmers are made uniform within the community. Carrying out the CAP consumes two-thirds of the EU's budget. EU agricultural subsidies are a major source of trade conflict with the United States.

◆ The EU has long worked toward a monetary union with a single European currency (the euro). Such a union will require roughly comparable inflation rates and financial stability in participating states. EU leaders plan to complete the monetary union among 11 states by 2002.

◆ In structure, the EU revolves around the permanent staff of "Eurocrats" under the European Commission. The Commission's president, individual members, and staff all serve Europe as a whole. However, the Council of Ministers representing member states (in national roles) has power over the Commission.

◆ The European Parliament has members directly elected by citizens in EU states, but it has few powers and cannot legislate the rules for the community. The European Court of Justice also has limited powers, but has extended its jurisdiction more successfully than any other international court.

◆ The Single European Act, or "Europe 1992," created a common market throughout the EU, with uniform standards, open borders, and freedom of goods, services, labor, and capital within the EU.

◆ With its Exchange Rate Mechanism (ERM), the European Monetary System maintains relatively fixed rates of exchange within the EU while allowing EU currencies together to fluctuate in value relative to other world currencies. However, Britain, Italy, and Spain dropped out in 1992 when they could not maintain the required value of their own currencies because of underlying economic pressures.

◆ The 1991 Maastricht Treaty on closer European integration (monetary union and political-military coordination) provoked a public backlash in several countries. Some citizens began to resent the power of EU bureaucrats over national culture and daily life. The treaty was ratified despite these difficulties, however.

- The EU faces challenges in deciding how far to expand its membership (especially in Eastern Europe). To some extent the broadening of membership conflicts with the deepening of ties among the existing members.

- In addition to the EU and the associated European Free Trade Association (EFTA), there are a variety of overlapping groupings, formal and informal, that reflect the process of integration in Europe.

- International law, the formal body of rules for state relations, derives from treaties (most importantly), custom, general principles, and legal scholarship—not from legislation passed by any government.

- International law is difficult to enforce and is enforced in practice by national power, international coalitions, and the practice of reciprocity.

- The World Court hears grievances of one state against another but cannot infringe on state sovereignty in most cases. It is an increasingly useful avenue for arbitrating relatively minor conflicts.

- Most cases involving international relations are tried in national courts, where a state can enforce judgments within its own territory.

- In international law, the rights of diplomats have long had special status. Embassies are considered to be the territory of their home country.

- Laws of war are also long-standing and well-established. They distinguish combatants from civilians, giving each certain rights and responsibilities. Guerrilla wars and ethnic conflicts have blurred these distinctions.

- Wars of aggression violate norms of just war—one waged only to repel or punish aggression. It is sometimes (but not always) difficult to identify the aggressor in a violent international conflict.

- International norms concerning human rights are becoming stronger and more widely accepted. However, human rights law is problematical because it entails interference by one state in another's internal affairs.

- International anarchy is balanced by world order—rules and institutions through which states cooperate for mutual benefit.

- World order has always been grounded in power, but order mediates raw power by establishing norms and habits that govern interactions among states.

- States follow the rules—both moral norms and formal international laws—much more often than not.

- The "New World Order" is a set of norms, proposed by former President George Bush, for international behavior in the post–Cold War era.

ONLINE PRACTICE TEST

Take an online practice test at
www.IRtext.com

North-South Relations

Poverty

This chapter concerns the world's poor regions—the global South—where most people live. States in these regions are called by various names, used interchangeably—third world countries, **less–developed countries** (LDCs), *underdeveloped countries* (UDCs), or **developing countries**. The chapter first discusses the gap in wealth between the industrialized regions (the North) and the third world (the South) and then considers international aspects of economic development in the South.

Third world poverty may be viewed from several theoretical perspectives. IR scholars do not all agree on the causes or implications of such poverty, or on solutions (if any) to the problem. Thus, they also disagree about the nature of relations between rich and poor states (North-South relations). Everyone agrees, however, that much of the global South is extremely poor.

Such poverty is difficult for North Americans to grasp. It is abject poverty—far worse than the poverty of U.S. ghettos. The extreme on the scale is starvation. As conveyed in pictures from places such as Somalia and Sudan, starvation is dramatic and horrible. But it is not the most important aspect of poverty, because it affects few of the world's poor people. Starvation is generally caused by war or extreme drought or both. In most places, people who die from poverty do not starve but succumb to diseases after being weakened by malnutrition. A lack of adequate quality of nutrition kills many more people than outright starvation does—but less dramatically because people die in many locations day in and day out rather than all at once in one place. Hunger and malnutrition are sometimes caused by war but more often by other factors that displace people from farmable land to cities where many are unable to find other income (see pp. 360–361).

People who die from malnutrition do not die because of a lack of food in the world, or usually even a lack of food in their own state, but because they cannot *afford* to buy food. Likewise, people lack water, shelter, health care, and other necessities because they cannot afford them. The widespread, grinding poverty of people who cannot afford necessities is more important than the dramatic examples of starvation triggered by war

Dirt Poor   Nearly a billion people in the global South live in abject poverty; the majority lack such basic needs as safe water, housing, food, and the ability to read. China still contains large areas of impoverished countryside, despite rapid economic development in the coastal cities. Here, a peasant moves dirt in a Chinese village where the average income is below $100 per year, 1997.

or drought, because chronic poverty affects many more people. Of all the world's people, about half are without adequate supplies of safe drinking water. About half live in substandard housing or are homeless altogether. About a third are malnourished, and one in seven is chronically undernourished (unable to maintain body weight). Nearly half are illiterate, and 99 percent do not have a college education. Multiplied by six billion people, these percentages add up to a staggering number of extremely poor people.

Globalization in the 1990s increased the gap between the world's richest and poorest countries. The number of people living on less than $1 per day grew worldwide from 1.2 billion in 1987 to 1.5 billion in 1999. The 1997 Asian economic crisis—and harsh cutbacks implemented in response—contributed to this rise. However, the greatest setbacks have been in Africa, where 29 of the 34 lowest-ranked countries are located, and where the AIDS epidemic is worsening a bad situation (see pp. 353–356). For example, Democratic Congo, one of the worst, saw annual GNP per person fall from $225 to $97 between 1985 and 1997. Some 60 countries are worse off than 20 years ago, even while other countries in the South rise gradually out of poverty. Environmental disasters linked to deforestation, climate change, and urbanization have also contributed to the dire situation of the poorest countries in recent years, driving 25 million people from their homes in 1998, for example. The El Niño weather shift triggered drought in Indonesia, ultimately leading to both massive forest fires and food riots.

Atlas CD
Democratic
Congo and
Neighbors
Map

Globalization has sharpened inequality within both the North and the South, as well as between the North and the South. As North America and Western Europe enjoy unprecedented prosperity, incomes in Russia and Eastern Europe have shrunk by nearly half. As China and parts of Southeast Asia, along with much of Latin America, climb gradually out of poverty, much of Africa slips further into it. In the global South as a whole, some trends such as environmental degradation are alarming, while others such as reduced warfare and slow reductions in hunger are encouraging. Clearly, globalization creates both winners and losers, with the world's poorest billion people mostly among the losers.

Web Link
Children in
Poverty

In all, about a billion people live in utter, abject poverty, without access to basic nutrition or health care. They are concentrated in the densely populated states of South Asia and in Africa. The average income per person in South Asia—home to nearly two billion people—is only $2,500 per year, and in Africa less than $1,500 (even after adjusting for the lower costs of living in these regions compared to richer ones). In fact, half of all people globally have incomes of less than $2 a day ($730 a year).

If these statistics are difficult to digest, consider the bottom line. Every three seconds, somewhere in the world, a child dies as a result of malnutrition. That is more than 1,000 every hour, 30,000 every day, 10 million every year. The world produces enough food to nourish these children and enough income to afford to nourish them, but their own families or states do not have enough income. They die, ultimately, from poverty. Consider that in the same three seconds in which another child dies this way, the world spends $75,000 on military forces. A thousandth of that amount would save the child's life. This reality shadows the moral and political debates about North-South relations.

Atlas CD
Infant
Mortality
Statistical Map

Theories of Accumulation

How do we explain the enormous gap between income levels in the world's industrialized regions and those in the third world? What are the implications of that gap for international politics? There are several very different approaches to these questions; we will concentrate on two contrasting theories of wealth accumulation, based on more liberal and more revolutionary world views.

Economic Accumulation
A view of the problem from the perspective of capitalism is based on liberal economics—stressing overall efficiency in maximizing *economic growth*. This view sees the third world as merely lagging behind the industrialized North. More wealth creation in the North is a good thing, as is wealth creation in the South, and the two are not in conflict.

A more revolutionary view of things, from the perspective of socialism, is concerned with the distribution of wealth as much as the absolute creation of wealth. It sees the North-South divide as more of a zero-sum game in which the creation of wealth in the North most often comes at the expense of the South. It also gives politics (the state) more of a role in redistributing wealth and managing the economy than does capitalism. Socialism thus parallels mercantilism in some ways. But socialists see economic classes rather than states as the main actors in the political bargaining over the distribution of the world's wealth. And mercantilism promotes the idea of concentrating wealth (as a power element), whereas socialism promotes the broader distribution of wealth.

For socialists, international exchange is shaped by capitalists' exploitation of cheap labor and cheap resources—using states to help create the political conditions for this exploitation. Thus, whereas mercantilists see political interests (of the state) as driving economic policies, socialists see economic interests (of capitalists and of workers) as driving political policies.

Capitalist and socialist approaches are rather incompatible in their language and assumptions about the problem of third world poverty and its international implications. The next several sections somewhat favor socialist approaches, focusing on the past history of imperialism as a central cause and on revolutionary strategies and massive redistribution of wealth as solutions to it, whereas those concluding the chapter lean toward capitalist approaches.

Economic development is based on **capital accumulation**—the creation of standing wealth (capital) such as buildings, roads, factories, and so forth. For human populations and their capital to grow, they must produce an **economic surplus** by using capital to produce more capital. This is done by investing money in productive capital rather than using it for consumption. The more surplus an economy produces, the more resources are available for investment above the minimum level of consumption needed to sustain human life.

Early human societies had a very simple stock of capital—mostly clothes and hand tools—and produced little surplus. Then came the discovery of agriculture about 10,000 years ago. A group of people could produce a surplus—more grain than they could eat—decade after decade. The extra grain could feed specialists who made tools from metals, built houses, and constructed irrigation works. Ever since, the human species has been on an uninterrupted growth cycle based on economic surplus. More and more wealth has accumulated, and the human population has grown larger and larger.

The Industrial Revolution of several centuries ago greatly accelerated this process of world accumulation, drawing on large amounts of energy from fossil fuels. But, industrialization has occurred very unevenly across the world regions. The North has accumulated vast capital. The South produces spurts of wealth and has pockets of accumulation, but in most areas it remains a basically preindustrial economy. This is why the North consumes nearly ten times as much commercial energy per person as the South does.

Information technology now is making a fuel-burning infrastructure relatively less important, in the advanced economies. The countries of the global South may need to pass through a phase of heavy industrialization, as countries in the North did, or perhaps they can develop economically along different paths, using new technology from the start. The problem is that, just as industrial infrastructure is located mostly in the North, so is the world's information infrastructure (see pp. 432–434). While students in industrialized countries go online, poorer countries still struggle to extend literacy to rural populations.

Nonetheless, neither the absolute size of GDP nor its size relative to other countries indicates whether a national economy is growing or shrinking. Accumulation, or profit, in a national economy corresponds with the *economic growth rate*. States that operate profitably grow from year to year; those that operate at a loss shrink. (GDP and related concepts refer here to real values after adjusting for inflation.)

A state's economic growth rate does not indicate how much wealth it has accumulated in the past. On a global scale, the South will continue to lag behind the North in GDP (income), even if its economic growth rate continues to be higher than the North's, as it has been in the last few years. The concentration of surplus in the world economy (in the North) tends to be self-reinforcing for two reasons. First, concentrating wealth allows it to be invested more efficiently, which generates more wealth. Second, the more wealth is concentrated, the more power its owners gain. With 60 percent of the world's wealth, the North dominates world politics. Because socialists see a conflict of interest between the rich and poor, they see the North's political power as oppressive to the South.

Ultimately, the distribution of the benefits of world accumulation is an issue for international bargaining, just as the distribution of benefits from trade is (see pp. 210–212). In the bargaining between rich and poor regions over the process of world accumulation, the two sides have very unequal power.

Capitalism Earlier chapters referred to capital in a general way as standing wealth. More precisely, *capital* is the set of goods that are used in producing other goods. Thus,

THE INFORMATION REVOLUTION **Sharpening Disparities?**

The concentration of surplus tends to be self-reinforcing: the rich get richer. The information revolution is no exception, in that richer countries and individuals tend to have much greater access to information technologies than do poorer ones. Will the information revolution give the industrialized West more power than ever, and increase the North-South gap in wealth?

To explore this question, go to www.IRtext.com

a warehouse full of refined tin is capital, as is a tin can or a canning factory—all these goods go into producing further goods. But a stamp collection, a set of Lego toys, and a pleasure boat are not capital in this sense, even though they have value; they are **consumption goods**. Their consumption does not contribute directly to the production of other goods and services.

A cycle of accumulation depends on capital goods more than consumption goods. Mines, factories, oil refineries, railroads, and similar goods contribute directly to the cycle of surplus production by which more factories and oil refineries are produced.

Investment competes with consumption. Foregoing consumption for investment is another case where short-term costs produce long-term benefits (as do aspects of trade and population policies where collective goods problems are successfully overcome).

Capitalism is a system of *private ownership of capital* that relies on market forces to govern distribution of goods. Under capitalism, the cycle of accumulation is largely controlled by private individuals and companies. When a surplus is produced, it is profit for the owners of the capital that produced the surplus (after taxes). Private ownership encourages reinvestment of surplus because private individuals and companies seek to maximize their wealth. The concentration of capital ownership in few hands also allows investment to be shifted easily from less productive sectors and technologies to more productive ones. Capitalism concentrates wealth, promoting efficient and rapid accumulation; it does not seek an equitable distribution of benefits.

In reality, no state is purely capitalistic. Almost all have some form of mixed economy that includes both private and state ownership. Also, in most capitalist countries the government balances the inhuman side of capitalism by redistributing some wealth downward (and regulating capitalists). A "welfare state" provides education, certain health benefits, welfare for the poor, and so forth. Over the past century, capitalism became more responsive to the need to balance efficiency with equity.

The principles of capitalism underlie the global economy with its great disparities of wealth. The concentration of capital in the global North furthers the development of global trade, of technology, and of reinvestment for maximum profit (overall growth). The private ownership of companies and of currency makes international markets operate more efficiently. Capital can be moved around from less productive to more productive countries and economic sectors. If wealth were distributed equally across world regions, these efficiencies might be lost and world economic growth might be slower.

Socialism
Socialism—the idea that workers should have political power—favors the *redistribution of wealth* toward the workers who produce that wealth. Because such redistribution does not happen naturally under capitalism, socialism generally endorses the use of the state for this purpose. It favors *governmental planning* to manage a national economy rather than leaving such management entirely to market forces. Often, socialists advocate *state ownership* of capital, rather than private ownership, so that the accumulation of wealth is controlled by the state, which can distribute it equitably.

Socialism includes many political movements, parties, and ideologies, historical and present-day. No socialist party has been influential in U.S. politics since the 1930s, but elsewhere in the global North socialist or social-democratic parties held important roles in the late 1990s as governing parties (Britain, France), parts of governing coalitions (Germany, Japan), or main opposition parties (Russia). In the third world, where great

Atlas CD
Libyan Oil
Photo

Web Link
Socialism

poverty and disparities of wealth make the idea of redistributing wealth popular, most revolutionaries and many reformers consider themselves socialists of some sort.

Communist governments, including those in China and the former Soviet Union, base their political philosophy on socialism as well. In practice, however, they tend to extract wealth toward the center and have thus been called a form of state capitalism. For example, in the Soviet Union under Stalin in the 1930s there was a tremendous concentration of capital, which allowed rapid industrialization but starved millions of people. This took place under dictatorial political control rather than workers' control.

Marxism is a branch of socialism that includes both communism and other approaches. (Not all socialists are Marxist.) Marxism is most influential in third world countries where capital is still scarce and labor conditions are wretched.

Like capitalism, socialism does not exist anywhere in a pure form. There is an element of socialism in mixed economies. China now calls its economic system "market socialism"—a combination of continuing state ownership of many large industries, capitalism at the local level, and openness to international investment and trade.

Some socialist theories argue that state ownership of industry increases efficiency by avoiding problems that arise from the fragmentation of decision making under capitalism. But after decades of experimentation, it is clear that whatever its benefits in equity, state ownership is not very efficient. State planners who set quotas for production at each factory cannot adjust to economic conditions as efficiently as market-based prices can. State ownership is still promoted in many countries in order to redistribute wealth, to coordinate development of key industries, or to maintain self-sufficiency in military production—but not because it is more efficient in general.

Atlas CD
Laos Economic
Reforms
Photo

Russia and Eastern European states are now trying to make a transition to market economies because of the failure of centrally planned economies. Many third world countries are also moving to sell off large state-owned industries—*privatization*—in hopes of increasing growth. Phone companies, oil companies, railroads—all are going on the auction block.

Privatization is proceeding quickly in several Eastern European and former Soviet republics, where the state owned virtually the whole economy during decades of communism. Before Czechoslovakia split in two, citizens received coupons representing a small bit of stock in state-owned companies. They could sell the coupons for cash or invest them in any of several new mutual funds established by entrepreneurs. The mutual fund managers pooled the coupons and bought up state-owned companies they thought would be profitable. Lured by promises of large profits, most Czechoslovak citizens invested as new capitalists in this way. But when a similar scheme was tried in Russia, citizens weary from economic depression did not put much value in the coupons. Many Russians invested in a leading mutual fund that promised high profits but then went bankrupt.

Thus, in the region of Russia and Eastern Europe, communism had collapsed under the weight of inefficiency, but the beginning stages of capitalism were even more inefficient, leading to a reduction of economic activity by roughly half over several years. Some countries, including Russia, slowed the pace of reforms in response, while reformists argued that what was needed was a speedup to get through the transition. Some countries democratically threw out the reformers and brought back the old communist leaders. In coming years, it is likely that the various experiments being tried by the different countries of Eastern Europe and the former Soviet Union will sort themselves out, making clearer the best routes of transition.

Imperialism

Marx's theories of class struggle were oriented toward *domestic* society in the industrializing countries of his time, not toward poor countries or international relations. Traditional Marxists looked to the advanced industrialized countries for revolution and socialism, which would grow out of capitalism. In their view, the third world would have to develop through its own stages of accumulation from feudalism to capitalism before taking the revolutionary step to socialism. What actually happened was the opposite. Proletarian factory workers in industrialized countries enjoyed rising standards of living and did not make revolutions. Meanwhile, in the backward third world countries, oppressed workers and peasants have staged a series of revolutions, successful and failed, over the past 70 years.

Web Link
Proletariat

The Globalization of Class
Why did this happen? The answer largely shapes how one sees North-South relations today. Marxists have mostly (but not exclusively) followed a line of argument developed by *V. I. Lenin*, founder of the Soviet Union, before the Russian Revolution of 1917. Russia was then a relatively backward state, as the third world is today, and most Marxists considered a revolution there unlikely (looking instead to Germany).

Lenin's theory of **imperialism** argued that European capitalists were investing in colonies where they could earn big profits and then using part of these to *buy off* the working class at home. The only limit Lenin saw was that after the scramble for colonies

Rich and Poor   Disparity of wealth is a microcosm of global North-South relations. Marxists see international relations and domestic politics alike as being shaped by a class struggle between the rich and the poor. Here, squatter huts are seen next to comfortable homes in Manila, Philippines, 1986.

in the 1890s, few areas of the world were left to be colonized. Imperialist expansion could occur only at the expense of other imperialist states, leading to interimperialist competition and wars such as World War I. Seizing on Russia's weakness during that war, Lenin led the first successful communist revolution there in 1917.

Lenin's general idea still shapes a major approach to North-South relations—the idea that industrialized states exploit poor countries and buy off their own working classes with the profits. Through this *globalization of class relations*, world accumulation concentrates surplus toward the rich parts of the world and away from the poor ones. Revolutions, then, would be expected in poor regions.

Many third world revolutionaries have sought to break loose from exploitation by the European colonizers. After European colonization ended, the United States as the world's richest country (with large investments in the third world and a global military presence) became the target of revolutionaries agitating against exploitation in poor countries. In a number of countries, imperialists were thrown out (often violently, sometimes not) and revolutionary nationalists took power.

One of the most important such revolutions was in China, where Mao Zedong's communists took power in 1949 on a Leninist platform adapted to the largely peasant-based movement they led. Mao declared that "China has stood up"—on its own feet, throwing off foreign domination and foreign exploitation. In India at the same time, the movement led by Gandhi used a different means (nonviolence) to achieve similar ends—national independence from colonialism. This pattern was repeated, with variations, in dozens of countries.

According to the revolutionaries in these countries, exploitation of third world countries by rich countries takes away the economic surplus of the third world and concentrates the accumulation of wealth toward the rich parts of the world. By breaking free of such exploitation, third world states can then retain their own surplus and begin to accumulate their own wealth. Eventually they can generate their own self-sustaining cycles of accumulation and lift themselves out of poverty. In reality such an approach has not worked well. A policy of autarky does not foster growth. And within a single poor country, trade-offs arise between concentrating or distributing wealth. For former colonies, the realities of economic development after independence have been complex.

Not all Marxist approaches favor a policy of self-reliance after revolution. *Leon Trotsky*, a Russian revolutionary, felt that after the 1917 revolution Russia would never be able to build socialism alone and should make its top priority the spreading of revolution to other countries to build a worldwide alliance. Trotsky's archrival Stalin wanted to build "*socialism in one country*," and he prevailed (and had Trotsky killed). Indeed, most third world revolutions since then have had a strongly nationalist flavor.

The World-System

The global system of regional class divisions has been seen by some IR scholars as a **world-system** or a *capitalist world economy*. This view is Marxist in orientation (focusing on economic classes) and relies on a global level of analysis. In the world-system, class divisions are regionalized. Third world regions mostly extract raw materials (including agriculture)—work that uses much labor and little capital, and pays low wages. Industrialized regions mostly manufacture goods—work that uses more capital, requires more skilled labor, and pays workers higher wages. The manufacturing regions are called the **core** (or *center*) of the world-system; the extraction regions are called the **periphery**.

The most important class struggle today, in this view, is between the core and periphery of the world-system. The core uses its power (derived from its wealth) to concentrate surplus from the periphery, as it has been doing for about 500 years. Conflicts among great powers, including the two world wars and the Cold War, basically result from competition among core states over the right to exploit the periphery.

The core and periphery are not sharply delineated. Within the periphery, there are also centers and peripheries (for instance, the city of Rio de Janeiro compared to the Amazon rain forest) as there are within the core (such as New York City compared to the Mississippi Delta). The whole global structure is one of overlapping hierarchies. The concentration of capital and the scale of wages each form a continuum rather than a sharp division into two categories.

In world-system theory, the **semiperiphery** is an area in which some manufacturing occurs and some capital concentrates, but not to the extent of the most advanced areas in the core. Eastern Europe and Russia are commonly considered to be semiperipheral, as are some of the newly industrializing countries (see pp. 372–374) such as Taiwan and Singapore. The semiperiphery acts as a kind of political buffer between the core and periphery because poor states can aspire to join the semiperiphery instead of aspiring to rebel against domination by the core.

Over time, membership in the core, the semiperiphery, and the periphery change somewhat, but the overall global system of class relations remains. Areas that once were beyond the reach of Europeans, such as the interior of Latin America, become incorporated as periphery. Areas of the periphery can become semiperiphery and even join the core, as North America did. And core states can slip into the semiperiphery if they fall behind in accumulation, as Spain did in the late sixteenth to early seventeenth centuries. Because world-system theory provides only general concepts but not firm definitions of what constitutes the core, semiperiphery, and periphery, it is hard to say exactly which states belong to each category.

The actual patterns of world trade support world-system theory to some extent. Table 7.1 (p. 342) shows the net exports (exports minus imports) of each world region for several types of goods. As the circled numbers indicate, different regions specialize in exporting different kinds of goods. The core (industrialized West) exports $310 billion more than it imports in machinery, chemicals, and similar heavy manufactured goods. All the other regions import more than they export in such goods.

Asia—here including Taiwan, Hong Kong, and South Korea (but not Japan)—has a niche in light manufacturing including textile production; it exports $62 billion more of these goods than it imports. Such a pattern fits the semiperiphery category. China's $28 billion in net exports of light manufactures (double the number just four years earlier) suggests that China is rising into the global semiperiphery.

The Middle East and Africa (here including North Africa) specialize in exporting oil (net exports of energy are $111 billion and $49 billion, respectively). This is an extraction role typical of the periphery. Latin America has net exports of $52 billion in food, agricultural products, and minerals—also typical of the periphery. These regions' patterns of specialization must be kept in perspective, however: all regions both import and

Atlas CD
Tin Mining in Nigeria
Photo

TABLE 7.1 Commodity Structure of World Trade by Region

Net Exports (Exports Minus Imports) for 1997, in Billions of 1999 Dollars

Region[a]	Manufactured Goods		Raw Materials	
	Machinery/ Chemicals[b]	Textiles and Other Light	Agriculture and Minerals	Energy
North America/Western Europe/Japan	(310)	-99	-18	-171
Russia and Eastern Europe	-48	1	16	23
China[c]	-31	(28)	1	-2
Middle East[d]	-67	1	-18	(111)
Latin America	-84	4	(52)	22
Asia[c]	-38	(62)	-39	-32
Africa[d]	-42	3	6	(49)

[a] Regions do not exactly match those used elsewhere in this book. World total imports exceed exports owing to discrepancies in data from national government. [b] Machinery, metal manufactures, and chemicals. [c] Taiwan, Hong Kong, and South Korea are here included in Asia. [d] North African oil-exporting states here are included in Africa, not in the Middle East as elsewhere in this book.

Source: Calculated from data in United Nations, *World Economic and Social Survey 1999* (New York: United Nations, 1999), pp. 279–82.

export all these types of goods, and the net exports listed in the table amount to only a small part of the world's $5 trillion in trade.

Web Link
Colonialism

European Colonialism

For most third world states, the history of having been colonized by Europeans is central to their national identity, foreign policy, and place in the world. For these states—and especially for those within them who favor socialist perspectives—international relations revolves around their asymmetrical power relationships with industrialized states. Capitalists tend to pay less attention to history and to focus on present-day problems in the South such as unbalanced economies, unskilled work forces, and corrupt governments.

Today's global disparities did not exist until a few centuries ago. Eight hundred years ago there were a variety of relatively autonomous, independent civilizations in the world, none of which held power over each other—the Sung dynasty in China, the Arab empire in the Middle East, the Aztecs and Incas in Central America, the African kingdoms near present-day Nigeria, the shoguns in Japan, Genghis Khan's society in Siberia, and the feudal society of Europe (see pp. 19–23).

Europe between the twelfth and fifteenth centuries saw the rise of capitalism, a merchant class, science, and stronger states. Technological improvements in agriculture, industry, and the military gave Europe an edge over other world civilizations for the first time. European states conquered and colonized different world regions at different times (see pp. 23–26). Decolonization in some regions (such as the United States in 1776) overlapped with new colonizing in other regions. But most of the world's territory was colonized by Europe at one time or another.

Decolonization occurred only 20 to 50 years ago in most of Asia, Africa, and the Middle East. In Asia, the most important British colony was India (which included today's Pakistan and Bangladesh). Hong Kong was until 1997 a British colony serving as the gateway to China. British possessions also included Malaysia, Singapore, New Guinea, Australia, New Zealand, and others. Almost all the Asian colonies became independent around the time of World War II and the two decades afterward.

In Africa, European colonizers included Portugal, the Netherlands, Britain, France, Belgium, Germany, and Italy. In the late nineteenth century, European states rushed to grab colonies there (France and Britain gaining the most territory). Thus, Africa became a patchwork collection of colonies without coherent ethnic or geographic foundations.

The Middle East came under European influence as the Ottoman Empire disintegrated in the late nineteenth and early twentieth centuries—and as oil became a key fuel. Britain and France were most prominent there as well. Present-day Israel and Jordan were British-run until 1948. Syria and Lebanon were French. Iraq's claims on Kuwait stem from Britain's creation of Kuwait as an independent territory. The Arab-Israeli conflict also is strongly influenced by the history of British rule.

European conquerors treated their colonies as possessions that could be traded, seized as booty in wars, or given as mandates to new rulers. For instance, the island of Guam in the Pacific was once Spanish territory, then German, then Japanese, and then American.

Being colonized has a devastating effect on a people and culture. Foreigners overrun a territory with force and take it over. They install their own government, staffed by their own nationals. The inhabitants are forced to speak the language of the colonizers, to adopt

My Doll, My Self? European colonialism worldwide promoted values and norms implying that the colonizer's culture was superior to the indigenous culture. Lingering effects remain in postcolonial societies. Here, mixed-race girls play with a European-featured doll, Lima, Peru, 1992.

their cultural practices, and to be educated at schools run under their guidance. The inhabitants are told that they are inherently, racially inferior to the foreigners.

White Europeans in third world colonies in Africa and Asia were greatly outnumbered by native inhabitants but maintained power by a combination of force and (more important) psychological conditioning. After generations under colonialism, most native inhabitants either saw white domination as normal or believed that nothing could be done about it. The whites often lived in a bubble world separated from the lives of the local inhabitants.

Colonialism also had certain negative *economic* implications. The most easily accessible minerals were dug up and shipped away. The best farmland was planted in export crops rather than subsistence crops. The infrastructure that was built served the purposes of imperialism rather than the local population—for instance, railroads going straight from mining areas to ports. The education and skills needed to run the economy were largely limited to whites. As a result, when colonies attained independence and many of the whites departed, what remained was an undereducated population with a distorted economic structure and many of the valuable natural resources gone.

Atlas CD
Angola's
Capital City
Photo

The economic effects were not all negative, however. Colonialism often fostered local economic accumulation (although controlled by whites). Cities grew up. Mines were dug and farms established. It was in the colonial administration's interest to foster local cycles of capital accumulation. Much of the infrastructure that exists today in many third world countries was created by colonizers. In some cases, colonization combined disparate communities into a cohesive political unit with a common religion, language, and culture, thus creating more opportunities for economic accumulation. In some cases, the local political cultures replaced by colonialism were themselves oppressive to the majority of the people.

Anti-Imperialism
Wherever there were colonizers, there were anticolonial movements. Independence movements throughout Africa and Asia gained momentum during and after World War II, when the European powers were weakened. Through the 1960s, a wave of successful independence movements swept from one country to the next, as people stopped accepting imperialism as normal or inevitable (see Figure 7.1 on African decolonization).

Although many third world countries gained independence around the same time, the methods by which they did so varied. In India, the most important colony of the largest empire (Britain), Gandhi led a movement based on nonviolent resistance to British rule (see pp. 138–139). However, nonviolence broke down in the subsequent Hindu-Muslim civil war, which split India into two states—India mostly with Hindus, and Pakistan (including what is now Bangladesh) mostly with Muslims.

Web Link
Colonialism and
Vietnam

Some colonies (for example, Algeria and Vietnam) won independence through warfare to oust their European masters; others won it peacefully by negotiating a transfer of power with weary Europeans. The Soviet Union supported such movements, and the United States opposed them. But in most cases the appeal of liberation movements was the general theme of anticolonialism rather than any ideology.

Across the various methods and ideologies of liberation movements in the third world, one common feature was reliance on nationalism for strong popular support. Nationalism was only one idea that these movements took from Europe and used to

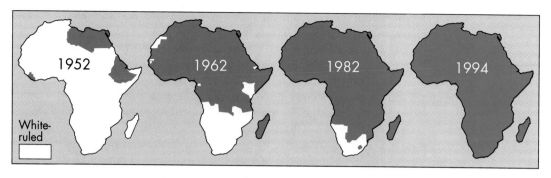

FIGURE 7.1 Areas of White Minority Rule in Africa, 1952–1994 Colonialism as a factor in international relations has been swept away over the past 40 years. However, postcolonial dependency lingers on in many former colonies.

Source: Adapted from Andrew Boyd, *An Atlas of World Affairs*, 9th ed. New York: Routledge, 1992, p. 91.

undermine European control; others included democracy, freedom, progress, and Marxism. Leaders of liberation movements often had gone to European universities. Furthermore, under European control many states developed infrastructures, educational and religious institutions, health care, and military forces on the European model. Europe's conquest of the third world thus gave tools to undo that conquest.

Postcolonial Dependency
If imperialism concentrated the accumulation of wealth in the core and drained economic surplus from the periphery, one might expect that accumulation in the third world would take off once colonialism was overthrown. Generally this has not been the case. A few states, such as Singapore, have accumulated capital successfully since becoming independent. But others, including many African states, seem to be going backward—with little new capital accumulating to replace the old colonial infrastructure. Most former colonies are making only slow progress in accumulation. Political independence has not been a cure-all for poor countries.

One reason for these difficulties is that under colonialism the training and experience needed to manage the economy were often limited to white Europeans. A few native inhabitants went to Europe for university training, but most factory managers, bankers, and so forth were whites. Often the white Europeans fled the country at the time of independence, leaving a huge gap in technical and administrative skills.

Another problem faced by newly independent states was that, as colonies, their economies had been narrowly developed to serve the needs of the European home country. Many of these economies rested on the export of one or two products. For Zambia, it was copper ore; for El Salvador, coffee; for Botswana, diamonds; and so forth.

Such a narrow export economy would seem well suited to use the state's comparative advantage to specialize in one niche of the world economy. But it leaves the state vulnerable to price fluctuations on world markets. Given the North-South disparity in power, the raw materials exported by third world countries do not tend to receive high prices (oil, from the mid-1970s to the mid-1980s, was an exception). The liberal free-trade regime based around the WTO corrected only partially for the North's superior bargaining position in North-South trade. And GATT allowed agriculture (exported by the periphery) to remain protected in core states (see p. 233).

It is not easy to restructure an economy away from the export of a few commodities. Nor do state leaders generally want to do so, because the leaders benefit from the imports that can be bought with hard currency (including weapons). In any case, coffee plantations and copper mines take time and capital to create, and they represent capital accumulation—they cannot just be abandoned. In addition, local inhabitants' skills and training are likely to be concentrated in the existing industries. Furthermore, infrastructure such as railroads most likely was set up to serve the export economy. For instance, in Angola and Namibia the major railroads lead from mining or plantation districts to ports. Political borders also may follow lines dictated by colonial economies. For example, an Angolan enclave (surrounded by Democratic Congo) contains the area's most profitable oil wells. A South African enclave, surrounded by Namibia, controls the best port in the area.

The newly independent states inherited borders that were drawn in European capitals by foreign officers looking at maps. As a result, especially in Africa, the internal rivalries of ethnic groups and regions made it very difficult for the new states to implement coherent economic plans. In a number of cases, ethnic conflicts within third world states contributed to civil wars, which halted or reversed capital accumulation.

In quite a few cases, the newly independent countries of Africa were little more than puppet governments serving their former colonizers. According to a recent memoir by a French official, France in the 1960s punished and even helped assassinate African leaders who opposed French policies. Those supporting France gave France open-ended permission for military intervention. French officials auditioned a potential president of Gabon before allowing him to take office, and the self-declared emperor of the Central African Republic (later accused of cannibalism) called President de Gaulle of France "Papa."

Finally, governments of many postcolonial states did not function very effectively, creating another obstacle to accumulation. In some cases, corruption became much worse after independence (see pp. 384–386). In other cases, governments tried to impose central control and planning on their national economy, based on nationalism, mercantilism, or socialism.

In sum, liberation from colonial control did not change underlying economic realities. The main trading partners of newly independent countries were usually their former colonial masters. The main products were usually those developed under colonialism. The administrative units and territorial borders were those created by Europeans. The state continued to occupy the same peripheral position in the world-system after independence as it had before. And in some cases it continued to rely on its former colonizer for security.

For these reasons, the period after independence is sometimes called **neocolonialism**—the continuation of colonial exploitation without formal political control. This concept also covers the relationship of the third world with the United States, which (with a few exceptions) was not a formal colonizer. And it covers the North-South international relations of Latin American states, independent for almost two centuries.

DEPENDENCY   Marxist IR scholars have developed **dependency theory** to explain the lack of accumulation in the third world. They noticed that after World War II, Latin American states seemed on the verge of self-sustaining growth, in which a country's own capital would produce goods for its own markets. But this did not happen. These scholars define dependency as a situation where accumulation of capital cannot sustain itself internally. A dependent country must borrow capital to produce goods; the debt payments then reduce the accumulation of surplus. (Dependency is a form of international interdependence—rich regions need to loan out their money just as poor ones need to borrow it—but it is an interdependence with an extreme power imbalance.)

Dependency theorists focus not on the overall structure of the world-system (center and periphery) but on how a peripheral state's own internal class relationships play out. The development (or lack of development) of a third world state depends on its local conditions and history, though it is affected by the same global conditions as other countries located in the periphery. Recall that within the third world there are local centers and local peripheries. There are capitalists and a national government within the state in addition to the external forces. These various forces can take on different configurations.

One historically important configuration of dependency is the **enclave economy**, in which foreign capital is invested in a third world country to extract a particular raw material in a particular place—usually a mine, oil well, or plantation. Here the cycle of capital accumulation is primed by foreign capital, is fueled by local resources, and completes itself with the sale of products on foreign markets. Such an arrangement leaves the country's economy largely untouched except to give employment to a few local workers in the enclave and to provide taxes to the state (or line the pockets of some state officials). Over time, it leaves the state's natural resources depleted.

Angola's Cabinda province, located up the coast from the rest of Angola, is a classic enclave economy. Chevron pumps oil from a large field of offshore wells, with the money going to Angolan government officials who spend some on weapons for the civil war there and pocket large sums in flagrant acts of corruption. The people of Cabinda, aside from a tiny number who work for Chevron, live in poverty with crumbling infrastructure, few government services, few jobs, and recurrent banditry by unpaid soldiers. Inside the Chevron compound, however, U.S. workers drive on paved roads, eat American food, and enjoy an 18-hole golf course. The Americans rarely leave the fenced compound, which Chevron is believed to have surrounded with land mines.

Atlas CD
Angola's
Cabinda
Enclave
Map

A different historical pattern is that of nationally controlled production, in which a local capitalist class controls a cycle of accumulation based on producing export products. The cycle still depends on foreign markets, but the profits accrue to the local capitalists, building up a powerful class of rich owners within the country. This class—the local bourgeoisie—tends to behave in a manner consistent with the interests of rich industrialized countries (on whose markets the class depends). The local capitalists, in alliance with political authorities, enforce a system of domination that ultimately serves the foreign capitalists. This is another form of dependency.

After World War II a third form of dependency became more common—the penetration of national economies by MNCs. Here the capital is provided externally (as with the enclaves), but production is for local markets. For instance, a GM factory in Brazil would produce cars mostly for sale within Brazil. To create local markets for such manufactured goods, income must be concentrated enough to create a middle class that can afford such goods. This sharpens disparities of income within the country (most people remain poor). The cycle of accumulation depends on local labor and local markets, but because MNCs provide the foreign capital they take out much of the surplus as profit.

Web Link
MNCs in the
Third World

According to dependency theory, the particular constellation of forces within a country determines which coalitions form among the state, the military, big landowners, local capitalists, foreign capitalists (MNCs), foreign governments, and middle classes. On the other side, peasants, workers, and sometimes students and the church, form alliances to work for more equal distribution of income, human and political rights, and local control of the economy. These class alliances and the resulting social relationships are not determined by any general rule but by concrete conditions and historical developments in each country. Like other Marxist theories, dependency theory pays special attention to class struggle as a source of social change.

Some people think that under conditions of dependency, economic development is almost impossible. Others think that development is possible under dependency, despite certain difficulties. We will return to these possibilities later in the chapter.

Population

North-South disparities are sharpened by population growth in the South. World population is growing by nearly 100 million each year—more than a quarter of a million more people every day—and passed 6 billion in 1999.

Atlas CD
Youthful
Djibouti
Photo

Forecasting future population is easy in some respects. Barring a nuclear war or an environmental catastrophe, today's children will grow up and have children of their own. For the coming 20 to 30 years, world population growth will be driven, rather mechanistically, by the large number of children in today's third world populations. The projected world population in 25 years will be around 8 billion people, and there is little anyone can do to change that projection. Of the increase in population in that period, 97 percent will be in the global South, with one-third in Africa alone.

Forecasting beyond 25 years is more difficult. When today's children grow up, the number of children they bear will be affected by their incomes (due to the "demographic transition" discussed shortly). To the extent that third world countries accumulate wealth (see pp. 334–339), their populations will grow more slowly. A second factor affecting the rate of population growth will be government policies regarding women's rights and birth control.

Web Link
Population

Because of these two uncertainties, projections beyond a few decades have a range of uncertainty (see Figure 7.2). By 2050, world population will probably be around 9 billion, with a final leveling out around 10 billion in the next 200 years. A decade ago, population projections were revised upward because in the 1980s the decline in birthrates stalled in a number of countries and economic growth in the third world fell below expectations. However, successes in third-world regions outside Africa—in raising incomes and lowering birthrates in the 1990s—brought a downward revision in 1999. The actions of states and IOs *now* will determine the earth's population in 200 years.

Two hundred years ago, British writer *Thomas Malthus* warned that population tends to increase faster than food supply and predicted that population growth would limit itself through famine and disease. Today, experts and officials who warn against world overpopulation are sometimes called *Malthusian*. Critics point out that technology has kept pace with population in the past, allowing more food and other resources to be extracted from the environment even as population keeps growing. However, leaders of

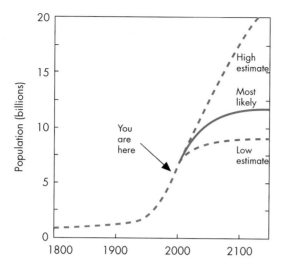

FIGURE 7.2 World Population Trends and Projections

Source: Based on data from the UN Population Office.

most third world states now recognize that unrestrained population growth drags down per capita income. But actions taken to slow population growth tend to have short-term costs and long-term benefits. Doing nothing is the cheapest and often most politically acceptable course in the short run—and the most expensive in the long run.

The Demographic Transition Population growth results from a difference between rates of birth (per 1,000 people) and rates of death. In agrarian (preindustrial) societies, both birthrates and death rates are high. Population growth is thus slow—even negative at times when death rates exceed birthrates (during a famine for instance).

The process of economic development—of industrialization and the accumulation of wealth on a per capita basis—brings about a change in birth and death rates that follows a fairly universal pattern called the **demographic transition** (see Figure 7.3, p. 350). First, death rates fall as food supplies increase and access to health care expands. Later, birthrates fall as people become educated, more secure, and more urbanized, and as the status of women rises. At the end of the transition, as at the beginning, birthrates and death rates are fairly close to each other, and population growth is limited. But during the transition, when death rates have fallen more than birthrates, population grows rapidly.

One reason poor people tend to have many children is that under harsh poverty a child's survival is not assured. Disease, malnutrition, or violence may claim the lives of many children, potentially leaving parents with no one to look after them in their old age. Having many children helps ensure that some survive. (The collective goods problem appears again, because each family wants more children but when all pursue this strategy the economic development of the community or state is held back.)

As a state makes the demographic transition, the structure of its population changes dramatically. At the beginning and middle of the process, most of the population is young. Families have many children, and adults do not have a long life expectancy.

Atlas CD
Kenya
Demographic
Transition
Photo

Atlas CD
Family Size
Photo, Tour

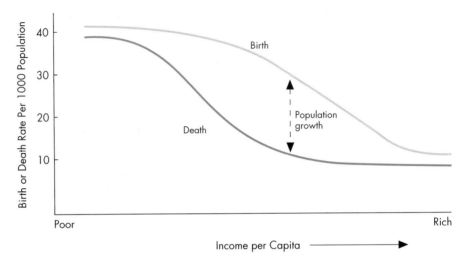

FIGURE 7.3 The Demographic Transition As income rises, first death rates and then birthrates fall. The gap between the two is the population growth rate. Early in the transition, the population contains a large proportion of children; later it contains a large proportion of elderly people.

Because children are not very productive economically, the large number of children in poor countries tends to slow down the accumulation of wealth. But by the end of the demographic transition, adults live longer and families have fewer children, so the average age of the population is much older. Eventually a substantial section of the population is elderly—a different nonproductive population that the economy must support.

The industrialized countries have been through the demographic transition and now have slow population growth—even negative growth in a few states. Most third world countries are in the middle of the transition and have rapid population growth.

The dilemma of the demographic transition is this: rapid population growth and a child-heavy population are powerful forces lowering per capita income. Yet the best way to slow population growth is to raise per capita income.

Population growth thus contributes to a vicious cycle in many poor states. Where population rises at the same rate as overall wealth, the average person is no better off over time. Even when the economy grows faster than population, so that the *average* income rises, the total *number* of poor people may increase. From 1970 to 1985, according to the UN Population Fund (UNFPA), the *proportion* of people living in poverty in the third world dropped from 52 to 44 percent. But the actual *number* of people living in poverty increased from about 950 million to 1.1 billion.

The demographic transition tends to widen international disparities of wealth. States that manage to raise incomes a bit enter an upward spiral—population growth slows, so income levels per capita rise more, which further slows population growth, and so forth. Meanwhile, states that do not raise incomes have unabated population growth; per capita incomes stay low, which fuels more population growth—a downward spiral.

Globally, this disparity contributes to the gap in wealth between the North and South. Within the South disparities are also sharpened, as a few countries manage to slow population growth and raise incomes while others fail to do so. Even within a single country, the demographic transition sharpens disparities. Cities, richer classes, richer ethnic groups, and richer provinces tend to have low birthrates compared to the countryside and the poorer classes, ethnic groups, and provinces. In countries such as France, Israel, and the United States, wealthier ethnic groups (often white) have much slower population growth than poorer ethnic groups (often nonwhite).

Recent trends suggest that the third world is splitting into two groups of states. Around 1970, nearly 50 states including China and India entered the phase of the demographic transition marked by falling birthrates. But in nearly 70 other poor states, death rates were still falling faster than birthrates, leading to accelerating population growth. In the 1980s, few new states moved from the second category to the first. These population trends contributed to disparities within the global South that emerged in the 1990s, notably between Africa and Asia.

Although the demographic transition is universal in its outlines, particular changes vary depending on local conditions and government policies.

Population Policies The policies that governments adopt—not just economic and demographic conditions—influence the birthrate. Among the most important policies are those regarding birth control (contraception). State policies vary widely.

Atlas CD
Single-Child
Families in
China
Photo

At one extreme, China uses its strong government control to try to enforce a limit of one child per couple. Penalties for having a second child include being charged for services that were free for the first child and being stigmatized at work. Beyond two children, the penalties escalate. Contraceptives and abortions are free, and citizens are educated about them. China's policy has lowered growth rates considerably in the cities but less so in the countryside, where 80 percent of the people live. Still, in a single decade (the 1970s) China's fertility rate fell from 6 children per woman to about 2.5, a dramatic change.

But the Chinese policy has drawbacks. It limits individual freedom in favor of government control. Forced or coerced abortions have been reported. In traditional Chinese society, sons are valued more than daughters. Couples who have a daughter may keep trying until they have a son. In some cases, Chinese peasants have reportedly had abortions if they knew the baby was going to be female, or have even killed newborn daughters so they could try for a son. (Simply bribing or paying fines became a more common route in the 1990s.)

India's policies are less extreme but have been slower to reduce the birthrate, which fell from just under 6 per woman to about 4.7 in the 1970s. India's government, strongly committed to birth control, has tried to make information and means widely available, but as a democracy it does not have China's extreme control over society. India's birthrate leveled out from 1977 to 1984 but resumed a gradual decline by the 1990s.

Countries with somewhat higher incomes than India or China can succeed more easily. Mexico cut birth rates in half over 15 years (to 2.7 per woman) with a strong but noncoercive family-planning program adopted in 1974.

At the other extreme from China are governments that encourage or force childbearing, and outlaw or limit access to contraception. Such a policy is called **pronatalist** (pro-birth). Traditionally, many governments have adopted such policies because population was seen as an element of national power. More babies today meant more soldiers

One Is Enough Few governments still promote high birthrates (pronatalism), but states vary widely in their family planning policies. The two most populous countries, China and India, have different approaches to birth control, each with strengths and weaknesses. Both are bringing down birthrates (China faster), with important long-term implications for world population growth. This poster promotes China's one-child policy, advising "practice birth control to benefit the next generation," 1983.

later. Recall (from p. 49) that the major difference in potential power between Iraq and Iran was population—Iran's being three times larger. On the battlefield, this power played out as "human wave" assaults of Iranian men and boys (who were slaughtered by the tens of thousands), which ultimately wore the Iraqis down.

Communist countries, including the Soviet Union, often adopted pronatalist policies. They gave awards for mothers who produced large numbers of children for the fatherland—an extension of the factory quota system of centrally planned production.

Today, only a few third world governments have strongly pronatalist policies, but many do not make birth control or sex education available to poor women. In some such states, population is not considered a problem (and may even be seen as an asset); in other states, the government simply cannot afford effective measures to lower birthrates. (Again, birth control has short-term costs and long-term benefits.) According to the UNFPA, 300 million women today do not have access to effective contraception.

Industrialized states have provided financial assistance for family planning programs in poor countries. One reason the drop in birthrates slowed in the 1980s is that international financial assistance slowed. After growing by 460 percent from the 1960s to the 1970s, such assistance grew by only 16 percent from the 1970s to the 1980s. The U.S. government, providing more than a quarter of the voluntary contributions that financed the UNFPA's annual budget of $225 million, terminated these contributions in 1976 after U.S. antiabortion activists protested that some UNFPA funds were financing abortions.

WOMEN'S STATUS Perhaps most important, birthrates are influenced by the status of women in society. In cultures that traditionally see women as valuable only in producing babies, great pressures exist against women who stop doing so. Many women do not use birth control because their husbands will not allow them to. These husbands may think that having many children is proof of their manliness. As women's status improves and they can work in various occupations, own property, and vote, women gain the power as well as the education and money necessary to limit the size of their families.

According to the UNFPA, improving the status of women is one of the most important means of controlling world population growth. Government policies about women's status vary from one state to another. International programs and agencies, such as the UN commission on the status of women, are working to address the issue on a global scale. International economic aid programs have been criticized for paying insufficient attention to the status of women (see pp. 362–363).

Mortality and AIDS
Population growth is determined by the death rate as well as the birthrate. In a way, the death rate is more complicated than the birthrate: births have only one source (sex involving women of childbearing age), whereas people die from many different causes at different ages. In poor countries, people tend to die younger, often from infectious diseases; in richer countries, people live longer and die more often from cancer and heart disease. The proportion of babies who die within their first year is the **infant mortality rate**. It reflects a population's access to nutrition, water, shelter, and health care. In rich countries, infant mortality is 1 percent or less. In the poorest countries, it is as high as 20 percent, and it is even higher in local pockets of extreme poverty.

Although death rates vary greatly from one state or region to another, the overall trends are stable from decade to decade. Wars, droughts, epidemics, and disasters have an effect locally but hardly matter globally. In the poorest countries, which are just beginning the demographic transition, the death rate has declined from nearly 30 deaths per thousand population in 1950 to less than 15 in 1990. In the *industrialized countries*, the death rate bottomed out around 10 per thousand by 1960. In the *midtransition* countries (including China and India), the death rate fell from 25 in 1950 to 10 in 1980 and has been slightly lower than in the rich countries since then. In this middle group of developing countries, infant mortality is generally much lower than in the poorest countries.

These stable trends in mortality mean that the death rate is not a means by which governments or international agencies can affect population growth—worsening poverty may cause famine and a rising death rate, but this is not a realistic way to control population growth. It would mean moving backward through the demographic transition, which would wreck any chance of lowering birthrates. Nor can wars kill enough people to reduce population growth (short of global nuclear war). Even a major famine or war, one killing a million people, hardly alters world population trends because every year about 75 million people die—200,000 every day. In short, most of the world is already at or near the end of the transition in *death* rates; the key question is how long birthrates take to complete the transition.

Two mortality factors, however—smoking and AIDS—deserve special attention because they have begun to exact very high costs even if they do not alter overall population trends. In both cases, actions taken in the short term have long-term consequences, and once again there are short-term costs and long-term benefits. In the case of smoking, states that fail to curb the spread of nicotine addiction face high future costs in health care—costs that are just beginning to come due in many third world countries.

Web Link
AIDS in the
Developing
World

AIDS By contrast, AIDS is a worldwide epidemic in which the failure of one state to control the spread of HIV (human immunodeficiency virus) makes it more likely that people in other states will eventually become infected as well. There is a delay of five to ten years after infection by the virus before symptoms appear, and during this period an infected individual can infect others (through sex or blood). AIDS spreads internationally, through travel, reflecting the interdependence of states.

By 1999, an estimated 34 million people had been infected with HIV worldwide. Of these, about 23 million were in Africa, 6 million in South Asia, 2 million in Latin America, 1 million in North America, half a million each in Europe and East Asia, and about 200,000 each in the Middle East and Russia/Eastern Europe. Of these 34 million, only a small fraction had yet developed AIDS (most did not even know they were infected), so most of the costs—human, economic, and political—are yet to come as infected individuals become ill. Each year, 6 million new people are infected with HIV, and more than 2 million die from AIDS, including nearly half a million children. About 85 percent of people with AIDS are in the global South. Because of systematic underreporting none of the totals are firm, and other estimates revise them upward.

In Africa, already the world's poorest and most war-torn region, AIDS has emerged as one of several powerful forces driving the region backward into deeper poverty. About 8 percent of adults are infected with HIV, more than half of them women. In the most affected African countries in southern Africa, AIDS has lowered life expectancy by 20 years, while infection rates in some cities have reached 30 percent of adults. In many central African armies more than half the soldiers are already infected—with direct implications for international security in a war-plagued zone.

In North America and other industrialized regions, new drug therapies dramatically lowered the death rate from AIDS in the late 1990s. But these treatments are far too expensive to do any good in Africa and other poor regions. Of worldwide spending on AIDS, less than 10 percent has been in third world countries where more than 80 percent of infected people live. Thus, the global North-South division is deepening as a result of the AIDS epidemic.

States can adopt policies to slow the spread of AIDS. It is primarily a sexually transmitted disease; its transmission can be prevented by using condoms. Drug users and medical personnel can use only new or disinfected needles; hospitals can screen blood. Although there is a massive scientific effort to develop a vaccine, for now the most effective measures boil down to public education and the distribution of condoms and clean needles—none of which can make individuals act responsibly. The World Bank has provided about $1 billion in AIDS-related development funds in the global South.

States have only two means to protect themselves from infection from the outside —a particular concern in countries with current low infection rates, such as China. First is to seal themselves off from contact with foreigners or to monitor foreigners on their territory. Considering the benefits of economic exchange (and the realities of interdependence), this is not a very practical approach. The second and more practical approach is to cooperate with other states worldwide to try to bring the epidemic under

Be Careful Out There
AIDS is spreading rapidly in Southeast Asia and Africa. The worldwide effort to slow AIDS, coordinated by the World Health Organization (WHO), illustrates how global-level problems like AIDS are making IOs like WHO more important. Here is an AIDS poster in Hanoi, Vietnam, 1992.

control. These international efforts are coordinated primarily by WHO and funded mainly by the industrialized countries. But WHO depends on national governments to provide information and carry out policies, and governments have been slow to respond. Governments falsify statistics to underreport the number of cases, and many governments are reluctant to condone or sponsor sex education and distribution of condoms because of religious or cultural taboos.

In the late 1990s, HIV spread rapidly in three new regions—South Asia, China, and Russia/Eastern Europe—where prostitution and drug use are growing. Thailand was especially vulnerable because of its huge prostitution industry and acceptance of male promiscuity. Thailand's AIDS epidemic has special international significance because of Thailand's large tourism industry. Tourism and prostitution overlap in "sex tours" that attract thousands of foreign men each year to visit Thai brothels. (This phenomenon has spread beyond Thailand to other Southeast Asian countries.)

Thailand is one of the few developing countries ever to develop an effective anti-AIDS program, which focuses on public education. Thanks to these education efforts, condom use among prostitutes went from 20 percent to 90 percent in four years (1988–1992), and cases of sexually transmitted diseases among men (an indicator of HIV spread) dropped by 80 percent. Thailand still faces serious problems with AIDS but it dramatically lowered the infection rate in the 1990s.

The international response to the AIDS epidemic is crucial to its ultimate course. AIDS illustrates the transnational linkages that make international borders less meaningful than in the past. Effective international cooperation could save millions of lives and significantly enhance the prospects for economic development in the poorest countries in the coming decades. However, there is once again a collective goods problem regarding the allocation of costs and benefits from such efforts. A dollar spent by WHO has the same effect regardless of which country contributed it.

Population and International Conflict

Population issues are sometimes portrayed as simply too many people using up too little food and natural resources. This is too simplified a picture. In particular, the idea that overpopulation is the cause of hunger in today's world is not really accurate. Poverty and politics more than population are the causes of malnutrition and hunger today (see pp. 360–361). There is enough food in the world to feed all the world's people. There is also enough water, enough petroleum, enough land, and so forth—but these are unequally distributed.

Nonetheless, growing populations put more strain on resources, regionally and globally. Though resources do not usually run out, it costs more to extract them as the quantity needed increases. New agricultural land is less productive than existing plots; new oil or water supplies must come from greater depths; and so on. For example, food production grew more slowly than population in two-thirds of the developing countries in the 1980s. In the 1960s and 1970s, the "green revolution" increased yields enough to stay ahead of population growth (see pp. 388–389). But local environmental damage—such as soil erosion and water table depletion—has begun to reduce agricultural productivity in some areas. The faster populations grow, the more pressing will be world food problems.

Growing populations exacerbate all the international conflicts over natural resources discussed earlier. Conflicts over water, which are very serious in several regions, become worse as populations grow. So do a range of issues such as overfishing, deforestation, and the loss of agricultural land to urban sprawl. There is not a simple linear relationship between the number of people in a state and its need for resources. Rather, as an economy develops, population growth slows but the demand for resources continues to rise. The resources are then needed for raising incomes (industrialization) rather than just feeding more mouths. The type of resources needed also changes—less food and more petroleum—as the state's technological style evolves. But overall, while more states moving through the demographic transition more quickly will slow population growth, it will not decrease the quantity of resources they use or the environmental damage they cause. More likely the opposite is true.

If population growth can be limited at lower income levels—shifting the demographic curve by using government policies to encourage lower birthrates—strains on the environment will be less. A country would then not only increase its per capita income sooner and faster but would do so at lower total population levels. This would reduce the load on the environment and resources as compared with industrializing at a higher level of population. Presumably, international conflicts would be reduced.

Some IR scholars have argued that population growth leads states to expand outward in search of resources. During the rise of Germany from the mid-nineteenth century through World War II a consistent theme of German expansionists was the need for "living space" for the growing German population. This need was as much psychological as physical, but it was used to justify German territorial expansion, imperialism, and aggression.

Another source of international conflict connected with demographics is migration from poor states with high population growth to rich states with low population growth. For example, illegal immigration from Mexico to the United States is an irritant in U.S.-Mexican relations. Refugees are a recurrent source of interstate conflict as well (see pp. 363-365). Palestinians living in refugee camps for several generations have become a chronic focal point of Arab-Israeli conflict.

Demographics can exacerbate ethnic conflicts (which in turn often fuel international conflicts due to ethnic ties with foreign states). Often one ethnic group is richer than another, and usually the poorer group has a higher rate of population growth (because of the demographic transition). In Lebanon, Muslims have a higher birthrate than Christians. At the time of Lebanese independence in 1944, a power-sharing arrangement was devised between Christian and Muslim political groups. By the 1970s, the size of the two populations had changed but the political structure had remained frozen in place. This was a factor in the Lebanese civil war of the late 1970s and 1980s. That civil war, in turn, pulled in outside states including Syria, Israel, and the United States. The seizure of (Christian) U.S. hostages by (Muslim) militants in Lebanon set the stage for the arms-for-hostages scandal during Ronald Reagan's presidency.

Thus, population pressures are not a simple explanation for the world's problems but contribute in various ways to international conflicts. Demographic and environmental factors are playing a larger role and receiving more attention from IR scholars.

The State of the South

In the postcolonial era, some third world states have made progress toward accumulation; some have not. Some (though not all) are caught in a cycle of abject poverty. Until incomes rise, the population will not move through the demographic transition; population growth will remain high and incomes low.

Basic Human Needs   In order to put accumulation on a firm foundation, and to move through the demographic transition, the **basic human needs** of most of the population must be met. People need food, shelter, and other necessities of daily life in order to feel secure. Furthermore, as long as people in the third world blame imperialism for a lack of basic needs, extreme poverty fuels revolution, terrorism, and anti-Western sentiments.

Children are central to meeting a population's basic needs. In particular, education can allow a new generation to meet other basic needs and move through the demographic transition. Literacy—which UNESCO defines as the ability to read and write a simple sentence—is the key component of education. A person who can read and write can obtain a wealth of information about farming, health care, birth control, and so forth. In industrialized states, more than 95 percent of the population is literate. In most middle-income third world countries, the majority of the population is literate—more than 90 percent in a few states. But in poorer countries the rate varies from more than 50 percent to just 10 percent of the population.

There is also great variation in schooling. Primary school attendance is fairly high in most poor states, which bodes well for future literacy. Secondary education—middle and high school—is another matter. In the North, about 90 percent are enrolled, but in most of the third world, less than half are enrolled. The rest are already working full-time and are unable to continue their schooling. College is available to only a small fraction of the

Atlas CD
Education
Policy
Photo Tour

Hanging On Children are a main focus of efforts to provide basic human needs in the global South. In Sudan (1993), famine and war forced this starving girl to set out for a feeding center, stalked by a vulture at one point. She survived the incident, but the photographer committed suicide the next year, haunted by the photo (which had won a Pulitzer prize).

population. Relative to population size, the United States has more than 30 times more college students than Africa.

Effective health care in poor countries is not expensive—just $4 per person per year for primary care. For instance, UNICEF has promoted four inexpensive methods that together are credited with saving the lives of millions of children each year. One method is growth monitoring—it is estimated that regular weighing and advice could prevent half of all cases of malnutrition. A second method is oral rehydration therapy (ORT), which stops diarrhea in children before they die from dehydration. A facility that produced 300 packets of the simple sugar-salt remedy daily at a cost of 1.5 cents each was built in Guatemala for just $550. Child deaths from diarrhea were cut in half in one year. The third method is immunization against six common deadly diseases: measles, polio, tuberculosis, tetanus, whooping cough, and diphtheria. In the past two decades, the number of children immunized in third world countries has risen from 5 percent to more than 50 percent.

The fourth method is the promotion of breast feeding as opposed to the use of infant formula. Many poor mothers consider baby formula more modern and better for a baby—a view promoted at times by unethical MNCs eager to market formula to large third world countries. In the worst cases, salespeople dressed like nurses gave out free samples to new mothers. But once mothers started using formula, their own milk dried up and they had to continue with the costly formula, which is inferior to breast milk and can be dangerous when water supplies are unsafe and means of sterilization and refrigeration are lacking. After a consumer boycott of a well-known MNC (Nestlé), formula producers agreed in the 1980s to abide by WHO guidelines for selling formula in poor countries.

Globally, the disparities in access to health care are striking. The 75 percent of the world's people living in the South have about 30 percent of the world's doctors and nurses. In medical research, less than 5 percent of world expenditures are directed at problems in developing countries, according to WHO. The biggest killers are acute respiratory infections (7 million deaths per year), diarrhea (4 million), tuberculosis (3 million), and malaria and hepatitis (1 to 2 million each). About 600 million people are infected with tropical diseases—almost 300 million with malaria alone. Yet, because the people with such diseases are poor, there is often not a large enough market for drug companies (MNCs) in the industrialized world to invest in medicines for them.

Atlas CD
Rwanda
Health Care
Photo

In one case, the U.S. Army created a lotion that can protect against infection by snail-borne worms that carry schistosomiasis, which WHO considers the second-worst public health problem in the world. Soldiers who serve in tropical areas can now be protected, but the drug company that produces the lotion has no plans to make it available to ordinary people because the market cannot afford the product.

Safe water is another essential element of meeting basic human needs. In many rural locations, people must walk miles every day to fetch water. Access to water is not running water in every house, but a clean well or faucet for a village. Unfortunately, many third world people lack such access—half or more of the population in India, Bangladesh, and Pakistan; two-thirds in Nigeria and Indonesia; one-quarter even in relatively well-off Brazil and Mexico. Even among those with access to safe drinking water, many lack sanitation facilities such as sewers and sanitary latrines. Half the world's population does not have access to sanitation and as a result suffers from recurrent epidemics and widespread diarrhea, which kill millions of children each year.

For shelter, like water, the needs are minimal—safe structures that keep weather out and do not collapse on the inhabitants. It is taken for granted that large families live in a single room. Even so, in shantytowns shelter is inadequate and unsafe—especially in potential areas of earthquakes or monsoons (hurricanes). Refugees from war also lack shelter unless they are lucky enough to reach a well-equipped refugee camp.

Atlas CD
Human
Habitation
Video

In theory, providing for basic needs should give poor people hope of progress and should ensure political stability. However, it does not always work out. In Sri Lanka, a progressive-minded government implemented one of the world's most successful basic needs strategies. The policy showed that even a very poor country could meet basic needs at low levels of per capita income. Then an ethnic civil war broke out. The war became more and more brutal—with death squads and indiscriminate reprisals on civilians—until it consumed the progress Sri Lanka had made. Today Sri Lanka is one of the world's most dangerous places, with basic needs in great jeopardy.

War in the third world—both international and civil war—is a leading obstacle to the provision of basic needs and political stability. War causes much greater damage to society than merely the direct deaths and injuries it inflicts. In war zones, economic infrastructure such as transportation is disrupted, as are government services such as health care and education. Civil wars kill more children than soldiers, according to a

1994 UNICEF report. Wars also drastically reduce the confidence in economic and political stability on which investment and trade depend.

It is noteworthy that almost all the wars of the past 40 years have taken place in the third world. The shadow of war stretches from Central America through much of Africa, the Middle East, and South Asia. These wars may be the single greatest obstacle to economic development in the third world. War is often part of a vicious circle for states unable to rise out of poverty.

There is a trade-off for third world governments between spending funds on the military or on poor people. Many third world governments import expensive weapons—whether because of real security conflicts with their neighbors, to put down internal challenges, or just as status symbols. These military forces are so expensive that even if they are never used they may deplete a state's ability to pursue basic needs and economic development. The nearly $1 trillion spent annually on military forces (mostly in the North) could easily provide for the basic needs of all the world's poor people. Instead, industrialized states compete to sell their advanced weapons to third world governments as a source of export earnings. Disarmament alone would not solve all the problems of poor states, but continual militarization certainly makes those problems worse.

Web Link
World Hunger

World Hunger Of all the basic needs of people in the third world, the most central is *food*. About 10 million children die each year from causes related to **malnutrition** (malnourishment)—the lack of needed foods including protein and vitamins. The term *hunger* refers broadly to **malnourishment** or outright **undernourishment**—a lack of calories. Hunger does not usually kill people through outright starvation, but it weakens them and leaves them susceptible to infectious diseases that would not ordinarily be fatal.

Nearly 800 million people—about one in eight worldwide—are chronically undernourished (see Table 7.2). Their potential contribution to economic accumulation is wasted because they cannot do even light work. They cannot forgo short-term consumption for long-term investment. And they are a potential source of political instability—including international instability—as long as they stay hungry. At a World Food Summit

TABLE 7.2 Who's Hungry?
Chronically Undernourished People by Region, c. 1996

Region	Number (millions)	Percentage of Population	16 Years Earlier
South Asia and China	526	17%	32%
Africa	180	33%	37%
Latin America	53	11%	13%
Middle East	33	9%	9%
Total "South"	792	18%	29%

Notes: Data are from 1995–1996 and 1971–1981. Regions do not exactly match those used elsewhere in this book. Chronic undernourishment means failing to consume enough food on average over a year to maintain body weight and support light activity.

Source: Based on FAO, *The State of Food Insecurity in the World 1999* (Rome: FAO, 1999), p. 29.

in 1996, world leaders adopted a goal to cut hunger in half by 2015. By 1999, with the number of undernourished people falling but only by 8 million a year and only in selected countries, the FAO stated that "there is no hope of meeting that goal."

The world has the potential to produce enough food to feed all the world's people. The problem is not so much that there is an absolute shortage of food (though that condition does exist in some places) but that poor people do not have money to buy food.

Traditionally, rural communities have grown their own food—**subsistence farming**. Colonialism disrupted this pattern, and the disruption has continued in postcolonial times. Third world states have shifted from subsistence to commercial agriculture. Small plots have been merged into big plantations, often under the control of wealthy landlords. By concentrating capital and orienting the economy toward a niche in world trade, this process is consistent with liberal economics. But it displaces subsistence farmers from the land. Wars displace farmers even more quickly, with similar results.

Commercial agriculture relies on machinery, commercial fuels, and artificial fertilizers and pesticides, which must be bought with cash and often must be imported. To pay for these supplies, big farms grow **cash crops**—agricultural goods produced for export to world markets. Such crops typically provide little nutrition to local peasants; examples include coffee, tea, and sugar cane. Subsistence farmers end up working on plantations at very low wages or migrating to cities in search of jobs. Often they end up hungry.

Atlas CD
Coffee in
Uganda
Photo

Many third world governments support commercial agriculture with loans, subsidies, irrigation projects, or technical help. This government support reflects both the political power of the big landowners and the government's ability to obtain hard-currency revenues from export crops, but not from subsistence crops.

International food aid itself can sometimes contribute to these problems. Agricultural assistance may favor mechanized commercial agriculture. And if an international agency floods an area with food, prices on local markets drop, which may force even more local farmers out of business and increase dependence on handouts from the government or international community. Also, people in a drought or famine often have to travel to feeding centers to receive the food, halting their work on their own land.

Rural and Urban Populations

The displacement of peasants from subsistence farming contributes to a massive population shift that typically accompanies the demographic transition. More and more people move to the cities from the countryside—**urbanization**. This is hard to measure exactly; there is no standard definition of when a town is considered a city. But industrialized states report that about 70 to 90 percent of their populations live in cities. By contrast, China is only 20 percent urbanized—a level typical of Asia and Africa. Most Middle Eastern states are a bit more urban (40 to 50 percent), and South American ones are 70 to 85 percent urban.

Urbanization is not caused by higher population growth in cities than in the countryside. In fact, the opposite is true. In cities, the people are generally better educated, with higher incomes. They are further along in the demographic transition, and have lower growth rates than people in the countryside. Rather, the growth of urban population is caused by people moving to the cities from the countryside. They do so because of the higher income levels in the cities—economic opportunity—and the hope of more chances for an exciting life. They also move because population growth in the countryside stretches available food, water, arable land, and other resources—or

Atlas CD
Country
and City
Map Trek

because they have been displaced from subsistence farming as land is turned to commercial cultivation (or have been displaced by war).

Capital accumulation is concentrated in cities. To some extent this makes urban dwellers more politically supportive of the status quo, especially if the city has a sizable middle class. Governments extend their influence more readily to cities than to the countryside—Chinese government policies adopted in Beijing often have little bearing on actual village life. But urban dwellers can also turn against a government: they are better educated and have rising expectations for their futures. Often rebellions arise from frustrated expectations rather than from poverty. By contrast, the conservatism of peasants can make them a base of governmental support, as in China after the 1989 protests in Beijing.

In many cities, the influx of people cannot be accommodated with jobs, housing, and services. In third world slums, basic human needs often go unmet. Many states have considered policies to break up large land holdings and redistribute land to poor peasants for use in subsistence farming—**land reform**. Socialists almost always favor land reform, and many capitalists favor it in moderation. The main opponents of land reform are large landowners, who often wield great political power because of their wealth and their international connections to markets, MNCs, and other sources of hard currency. Landowners have great leverage in bargaining with peasants—from using the legal system to maintaining virtual private armies.

Web Link
Women and
Development

Women in Development Economic accumulation in poor countries is closely tied to the status of women in those societies. This is a recent revelation; most attention in the past has focused on men as supposedly the main generators of capital. Governments and international reports concentrated on work performed by male wage earners; women's work, by contrast, often is not paid for in money and does not show up in financial statistics. But women in much of the world work harder than men and contribute more to the economic well-being of their families and communities. Women are key to efforts to improve the lot of children and reduce birthrates. In nutrition, education, health care, and shelter, women are central to providing the basic needs of people in poor countries.

Yet women hold inferior social status to men in the countries of the South (at least as much as in the North). For instance, when food is in short supply, men and boys often eat first, with women and girls getting what is left. Because of this, of the world's malnourished children, 80 percent are female, according to Oxfam America.

Discrimination against girls is widespread in education and literacy. In Pakistan, 50 percent of boys but less than 30 percent of girls receive primary education. Throughout Asia, Africa, and the Middle East (though not in Latin America), more boys receive education, especially at the secondary level. At university level, only 30 percent of students are women in China and the Middle East, a bit more than 20 percent in South Asia and Africa (but 45 percent in Latin America). In China, 80 percent of men, but only 50 percent of women, are literate. In India, the rates are 55 percent for men and 25 percent for women. Only in Latin America do women's literacy rates approach those of men.

Atlas CD
Women's Roles
Photo Tour

States and international agencies have begun to pay attention to ending discrimination in schooling, assuring women's access to health care and birth control, educating mothers about prenatal and child health, and generally raising women's status in

Bride Available   The status of women in countries of the global South affects their prospects for economic development. Women are central to rural economies, to population strategies, and to the provision of basic human needs including education. This Asian 12-year-old, a prostitute's daughter, wears a wedding dress to invite a marriage proposal.

society (allowing them a greater voice in decisions). These issues occupied the 1995 UN women's conference in Beijing, China, attended by tens of thousands of state and NGO representatives.

For example, UNICEF has helped women get bank loans on favorable terms to start up small businesses in Egypt and Pakistan, and cooperative farms in Indonesia. Women have organized cooperatives throughout the third world, often in rural areas, to produce income through weaving and other textile and clothing production, retail stores, agriculture, and so forth. In the slums of Addis Ababa, Ethiopia, for example, women heads of household with no land for subsistence farming had been forced into begging and prostitution. Women there established the Integrated Holistic Approach Urban Development Project, which organized income-producing businesses from food processing to cloth weaving and garment production. These profitable businesses earned income for the women and helped subsidize health and sanitation services in the slums.

Migration and Refugees   The processes just outlined—basic-needs deprivation, displacement from land, urbanization—culminate in one of the biggest political issues affecting North-South relations—**migration** from poorer to richer states. Millions of people from the global South have crossed international borders, often illegally, to reach the North.

Atlas CD
Human
Migration
Video

Someone who moves to a new country in search of better economic opportunities, a better professional environment, or better access to their family, culture, or religion is engaging in migration (emigration from the old state and immigration to the new state). Such migration is considered voluntary. The home state is not under any obligation to let such people leave, and, more important, no state is obligated to receive migrants. As with any trade issue, migration creates complex patterns of winners and losers. Immigrants often provide cheap labor, benefiting the host economy overall, but also compete for jobs with (poor) citizens of the host country.

Most industrialized states try to limit immigration from the third world. Despite border guards and fences, many people migrate anyway, illegally. In the United States, such immigrants come from all over the world, but mostly from nearby Mexico, Central America, and the Caribbean. In Western Europe, they come largely from North Africa, Turkey, and (increasingly) Eastern Europe. Some Western European leaders worry that the loosening of border controls under the process of integration (see pp. 304–305) will make it harder to keep out illegal immigrants. Indeed, fear of immigration is one reason why Swiss voters rejected membership in the EU.

Web Link
Refugees

International law and custom distinguish migrants from **refugees**, people fleeing to find refuge from war, natural disaster, or political persecution. (Fleeing from chronic discrimination may or may not be grounds for refugee status.) International norms obligate countries to accept refugees who arrive at their borders. Refugees from wars or natural disasters are generally housed in refugee camps temporarily until they can return home (this can drag on for years). Refugees from political persecution may be granted asylum to stay in the new state. Acceptance of refugees—and the question of which states must bear the costs—is a collective goods problem. The number of international refugees in the world grew from 3 million in 1976 to 22 million by 1998. In addition, more than 20 million more people are displaced within their own countries. The majority of refugees and internally displaced people have been displaced by wars (see Table 7.3).

TABLE 7.3 Refugee Populations, 1998

Region	Millions	Main Concentrations (millions)
Middle East and South Asia	6.2	Iran, Afghanistan, Pakistan (3.7), Sri Lanka and India (0.9)
Africa	5.6	Rwanda/Uganda/Congo area (2.3), Sierra Leone/Liberia/Guinea area (2.0)
China	0.3	
Latin America	0.1	
Western and Eastern Europe	8.0	Former Yugoslavia (2.3), Russia/CIS (2.9), W. Europe, various regions of origin (2.5)
North America	1.3	Various regions of origin
Japan/Pacific	0.1	
World Total	21.5	

Note: Includes refugees, asylum-seekers, returned refugees, and internally displaced people.
Source: UNHCR.

The political impact of refugees has been demonstrated repeatedly in recent years. After the Gulf War, Iraq's persecution of rebellious Iraqi Kurds sent large numbers of Kurdish refugees streaming to the Turkish border, where they threatened to become an economic burden to Turkey. Turkey closed its borders, and the Iraqi Kurds were left stranded in the mountains. The United States and its allies then sent in military forces to protect the Kurds and return them to their homes in Iraq (violating Iraq's territorial integrity but upholding the Kurds' human rights). When the Kurdish-controlled area of Iraq became a base for Kurdish guerrillas in Turkey, the Turkish Army in 1995 invaded the area (another violation of Iraqi sovereignty). The close connection of economics and international security is seen in this episode—a security-related incident (the war) caused an economic condition (starving Kurds) that in turn led to other security ramifications (U.S. military protection of Kurdish areas of Iraq; Turkish invasion of the area).

The connection of economics and security appears in other refugee questions as well. Palestinian refugees displaced in the 1948 and 1967 Arab-Israeli wars (and their children and grandchildren) live in "camps" that have become long-term neighborhoods, mainly in Jordan and Lebanon. Economic development is impeded in these camps because the host states and Palestinians insist that the arrangement is temporary. The poverty of the refugees in turn fuels radical political movements among the camp inhabitants.

It is not always easy to distinguish a refugee fleeing war or political persecution from a migrant seeking economic opportunity. Illegal immigrants may claim to be refugees in order to be allowed to stay, when really they are seeking better economic opportunities. In recent decades this has become a major political issue throughout the North.

In Germany, France, Austria, and elsewhere, resentment of foreign immigrants has fueled upsurges of right-wing nationalism in domestic politics. Germany, with lax regulations for asylum seekers, became a favored destination for growing numbers of immigrants—most of whom were not political refugees. At a time of economic difficulty following German reunification, around 1992, neo-Nazi youths staged violent attacks on foreigners and forced the government to tighten restrictions on immigration. (Hundreds of thousands of Germans then demonstrated against the neo-Nazis.) In 1999, Austria alarmed its EU partners by including a far-right party in a coalition government.

Atlas CD
Refugees in
Germany
Photo

After a 1991 coup in Haiti deposed the elected (socialist) president, tens of thousands of poor people set off for U.S. shores in small boats. Were they fleeing from persecution or just looking for better economic opportunities (especially plausible given U.S.-led economic sanctions that had damaged Haiti's economy)? The U.S. government screened the Haitians, granted asylum to a few, and shipped most back to Haiti. As the numbers grew, the United States began intercepting boats on the high seas and returning them directly to Haiti—a practical response that nonetheless violated international law. President Clinton promised to change the U.S. policy if elected, but he reversed himself when thousands of Haitians prepared to set sail on his inauguration day. Evidently the only solution to the Haitian problem was to seek a political solution within Haiti itself (and then drop the U.S. sanctions). Thus, the United States ultimately intervened militarily to restore Haiti's president to power.

In general, South-North migration creates problems for the industrialized states that, it seems, can only be solved by addressing the problems of the South itself. To the extent that the North does not help address those problems, people in the South seem likely to turn to their own solutions, which often include revolutionary strategies.

Revolution

Poverty and lack of access to basic human needs are prime causes of revolutions, especially when poor people see others living much better. Most revolutionary movements espouse egalitarian ideals—a more equal distribution of wealth and power. Political revolutions seek to change the form of government; social revolutions also seek changes in the structure of society, such as class relations. Most third world countries have had active revolutionary movements at some time since their independence.

Revolutionary Movements During the Cold War years, the classic third world revolutionary movement was a communist insurgency based in the countryside. Such a revolution typically was organized by disenchanted students, professionals, and educated workers—usually committed to some variant of Marxist ideology—who won support from laborers and peasants. Its targets were the state, the military forces backing up the state, and the upper classes whose interests the state served. Usually "U.S. imperialism" or another such foreign presence was viewed as a friend of the state and an enemy of the revolution.

Sometimes the U.S. government gave direct military aid to governments facing such revolutionary movements; in a number of countries, U.S. military advisers and even combat troops were sent to help put down the revolutions and keep communists from taking power. The United States often tried (but rarely with success) to find a third force, between repressive dictators and communist revolutionaries, that would be democratic, capitalist, and committed to peaceful reform. For its part, the Soviet Union often armed and helped train the revolutionaries. If a revolution won power, then it was the Soviet Union that armed the new government and sent military advisers, and the United States that supported antigovernment rebels.

Thus the domestic politics of third world countries became intertwined with great-power politics in the context of the North-South gap. In reality, many of these governments and revolutions had little to do with global communism, capitalism, or imperialism. They were local power struggles into which great powers were drawn.

Some third world revolutions succeeded in taking power: they gained strength, captured some cities, and (often following the defection of part of the government army) marched on the capital city and took control. New foreign policies quickly followed (see pp. 368–370).

Elsewhere, and more frequently, revolutions failed: ever-smaller numbers of guerrillas were forced ever farther into the countryside with dwindling popular support. A third outcome has become more common in recent years—a stalemated revolution in which after ten or twenty years of guerrilla warfare neither the revolutionaries nor the government defeats the other. In these cases, the international community may step in to negotiate a cease-fire and the reincorporation of the revolutionaries, under some set of reforms in government practices, into peaceful political participation. This happened successfully in El Salvador and elsewhere in the late 1980s with varying degrees of success.

The Chinese revolution of the 1930s and 1940s was the model of a successful communist revolution for decades thereafter. In Southeast Asia, communist guerrillas ultimately took power in South Vietnam, Cambodia, and Laos, but lost in Thailand,

Burma, and Malaysia. In Latin America, Fidel Castro's forces took power in Cuba in 1959 after years of guerrilla war. But when Castro's comrade-in-arms, Che Guevara, tried to replicate the feat in Bolivia, Guevara failed and was killed.

By the early 1990s, these communist third world revolutions seemed to have played themselves out—winning in some places, losing in others, and coming to a stalemate in a few countries. The end of the Cold War removed superpower support from both sides, and the collapse of the Soviet Union and the adoption of capitalist-oriented economic reforms in China undercut the ideological appeal of communist revolutions.

Islamic Revolutions   Although third world revolutions almost always advocate for the poor versus the rich and for nationalism versus imperialism, the particular character of these movements varies across regions and time periods. In Africa, where colonialism left state boundaries at odds with ethnic divisions, many revolutionary movements have a strong tribal and provincial base; this may fuel secessionism by a province (such as Eritrea from Ethiopia). Asian revolutionary movements tapped into general anticolonial sentiments, as when Vietnamese communists fought to oust the French colonizers and then saw the war against the United States as a continuation of the same struggle. In Latin America, where national independence was won long ago, revolutions tended to be couched in terms of class struggle against rich elites and their foreign allies.

In the post–Cold War era, some of the most potent revolutionary movements are Islamic, not communist. Islam is now a key focal point of global North-South conflict. Islamic political activists in Middle Eastern countries, like revolutionaries elsewhere, derive their main base of strength from championing the cause of the poor masses against rich elites. Like other revolutionaries throughout the third world, Islamic movements in countries such as Turkey and Egypt draw their base of support from poor slums, where the revolutionaries sometimes provide basic services unmet by the government.

Islamic revolutionary movements often criticize the Westernized ways of the ruling elite. For example, in Iran the shah had been armed by the United States as a bulwark against Soviet expansion into the Middle East. The Islamic revolutionaries who overthrew him in 1979 (led by Ayatollah Khomeini) declared the United States, as the leading political and cultural force in the industrialized West, to be the world's "great Satan." (Later, reformers in Iran offered other, less confrontational, interpretations of Islam.)

Atlas CD
Western
Influences
on Turkey
Photo

Some Islamic perspectives reject the European-based cultural framework on which the modern international system rests. This rejection was dramatically illustrated when, after its revolution, Iran refused to protect the safety of U.S. diplomats and the territorial integrity of the U.S. embassy in Iran (see pp. 316–318). Western values regarding human rights and women's roles have been similarly rejected, notably in the extreme policies of the Taliban movement controlling Afghanistan. Of course, Islam encompasses a broad spectrum of political practices and forms of government, mostly not revolutionary.

Whereas Iran's revolution was directed against a U.S.-backed leader, an Islamic guerrilla war in Afghanistan showed that similar ideas could prevail against a Soviet-backed leader. Here it was communism and Soviet domination, rather than capitalism and Western domination, that Islamic revolutionaries overthrew. After a decade of destructive civil war (in which U.S. aid helped the revolutionaries), the Islamic forces took power in 1992. However, the Islamic factions then began fighting among themselves—based

Islamic Democracy In some Muslim-populated countries, Islam is a political rallying point with anti-Western connotations. However, in the leading such case, Iran, relatively pro-Western reformers gained in power when a vibrant democratization movement emerged twenty years after the 1979 Islamic revolution. Here are street posters for municipal elections, 2000.

partly on ethnic and regional splits and partly on the different foreign allies of different factions. The fundamentalist Taliban faction seized control of the capital and most of Afghanistan in 1996, but the war continued.

In the Middle East, Islamic movements are particularly active in Algeria, Tunisia, Jordan, and Tajikistan. In Jordan, Islamic parties for years controlled the largest bloc of seats in the parliament. In the former Soviet republic of Tajikistan they are a major faction in civil strife (since the Soviet Union's demise). Middle Eastern Islamic revolutionaries also took a keen interest in the fate of Muslims targeted for genocide in Bosnia from 1992 on. They saw this conflict as part of a broad regional (or even global) struggle of Western, Christian imperialism against Islam—a struggle dating back to the Crusades almost a thousand years ago. In the mid-1990s Muslim civilians were targeted by Christians in wars in Bosnia, Azerbaijan, and Chechnya.

Postrevolutionary Governments
When revolutionaries succeed in taking power, their state's domestic and international politics alike are affected. This occurred in China in 1949; Cuba in 1959; Algeria in 1962; South Vietnam, Cambodia, Angola, and Mozambique in 1975; Nicaragua and Iran in 1979; and Afghanistan in 1992.

Even though revolutionaries advocate the broad distribution of wealth, they tend to find after taking power that centralizing accumulation is more practical: it gives the state more control of wealth and power (with which to meet the needs of the masses, or line the pockets of the new leaders, as the case may be). Over time, the new elite may come to resemble the old one, although individuals change places. Similarly, revolutionaries often advocate improving women's status, but after taking power male revolutionaries have tended to push aside their female comrades, and traditional sex roles have reappeared.

More relevant to international relations are the problems that beset successful revolutionaries due to violence—usually backed directly or indirectly by foreign states. After many revolutions, the meeting of basic human needs has been severely impeded by continuing political violence and even civil war. For example, the socialist government that took power in Angola in 1975 wanted to improve the lot of poor people, but instead civil war ravaged the country for more than 15 years and the poor ended up much hungrier than ever. In Vietnam, the war that brought the communists to power was so fierce that it left the country devastated.

Such problems reached an extreme under the communist Khmer Rouge faction that took power in Cambodia in 1975. They sought to radically alter the society by destroying economic classes, destroying concentrations of capital, destroying ideas that ran contrary to the revolution, abolishing money, and rebuilding the entire nation in the image of their own ideology. The Khmer Rouge first executed almost everyone associated with government, business, or universities, or who had independent ideas. They then evacuated the populations of cities into the countryside, where hundreds of thousands starved to death. After losing power in 1979 to Vietnam, the Khmer Rouge continued for more than a decade to wage guerrilla war. A UN-administered peace plan was implemented in the early 1990s (though against Khmer Rouge resistance), but the country had been decimated. The Khmer Rouge disaster showed that merely destroying concentrations of capital does not help meet poor people's basic needs.

Violence and war—both international and civil war—are tremendous obstacles to economic accumulation and the provision of basic human needs. It is a great contradiction of violent revolutions that they rely on the methods of war to gain power, supposedly to redistribute wealth and meet people's basic needs. Yet rich and poor alike are often caught in a downward spiral of indiscriminate violence and destruction. And after taking power, violent revolutionaries often face continuing civil or international war in the struggle to keep power. Successful revolutions often induce neighboring states either to contain the revolution or to take advantage of the new government's instability. For example, within a year of the 1979 revolution in Iran, Iraq had attacked in hopes of conquering Iran while it was weak.

In foreign policy, revolutionary governments often start out planning radically different relationships with neighbors and great powers. The pattern of international alliances often shifts after revolutions, as when a Cold War client of one superpower shifted to the other after a change of government.

But the new government usually discovers that, now that it holds power, it has the same interest as other states in promoting national sovereignty and territorial integrity. The rules of the international system are working for the revolutionaries instead of against them. Their state also has the same geographical location as before, the same historical conflicts with its neighbors, and the same ethnic ties. So it is not unusual over time to find similar foreign policies emanating from a revolutionary government as from its predecessor.

After revolutionaries have been in power for a decade or two, they tend to become less revolutionary. Power tends to corrupt or co-opt even the best-intentioned socialists, and officials find some of the same opportunities for corruption as those in the previous government did. Even for the most honest leaders, the need to develop the economy often creates pressures to build up new concentrations of capital. Perhaps these are now owned by the state, rather than by private banks or landowners. But hierarchies tend to reappear. Furthermore, violent revolutions most often lead to authoritarian rule (for fear that counterrevolutionaries will retake power), not to multiparty democracy. Thus the revolutionary party has a monopoly on power, year after year, which leads to a certain conservatism. For example, in China the revolutionaries who took power in 1949 were able to make common cause with the U.S. imperialists by 1971, and by 1989 they were the conservative rulers shooting down student protesters in the streets of Beijing.

Thus, although revolutions create short-term shifts in foreign policy, over the longer term the rules of international relations have tended to triumph over revolutionary challenges. Likewise, though revolutions promise great economic change, the overall state of economic conditions and relations—especially between North and South—has been resistant to change.

Overall, North-South relations show how difficult it has become to separate political economy from international security. The original political relations contained in European imperialism led to economic conditions in the South—from high population growth to urbanization and concentrations of wealth—that in turn led to political movements for independence, and later to revolutions. The various aspects of the North-South gap considered in the first half of this chapter—from hunger and refugees to the structure of commodity exports—all contain both economic and political-military aspects.

Marxists emphasize that the economic realities of accumulation, or the lack of accumulation, lie beneath all the political struggles related to global North-South relations. But Marxists' strategies—from armed revolutions to self-reliance to state ownership—have not been very successful at changing those realities. The remainder of the chapter therefore turns to the question of how economies in the South can develop the accumulation process and what role the North can play in that process.

Development Experiences

Economic development refers to the combined processes of capital accumulation, rising per capita incomes (with consequent falling birthrates), increasing skills in the population, adoption of new technological styles, and other related social and economic changes. The most central aspect is the accumulation of capital (with its ongoing wealth-generating potential). The concept of development has a subjective side that cannot be measured statistically—the judgment of whether a certain pattern of wealth creation and distribution is good for a state and its people. But one simple measure of economic development is the per capita GDP—the amount of economic activity per person.

By this measure, most of the third world made progress on economic development in the 1970s, with real per capita GDP growth of almost 3 percent annually. This rate was a bit higher than in the global North (despite the higher population growth in the South, which pulls down per capita GDP). However, in the 1980s this economic development came to a halt except in Asia. In the 1990s, real economic growth returned across much of the South—about 5 to 6 percent annual growth for the South as a whole, compared to 2 to 3 percent in the global North. By the late 1990s,

China stood out among the regions of the South as making rapid progress toward economic development. All the other regions of the global South showed much slower progress, if any, and faced serious problems. (China slowed down in 1998–1999 after the Asian crisis, but only modestly.)

Growth varies greatly across regions and countries, as well as within countries. The gap between rich and poor—both within countries and globally—is widening, according to a 1996 UN report. In countries with the greatest internal disparities in income, such as Brazil and Guatemala, the poorest fifth of the population lives on incomes one-tenth of the national average. Also, although the global South as a whole grew in the 1990s, this growth bypassed many countries. In 89 countries economic conditions are worse now than a decade ago, and in 70 countries incomes are lower than in the 1960s and 1970s. Nineteen of those countries have lower incomes than in 1960, almost 40 years earlier. These conditions lead some observers to wonder if the global South is dividing into two parts, one moving forward and one stalled.

Regarding how income is distributed and spent, the perspectives and prescriptions of capitalism and socialism again diverge (see pp. 336–339). Capitalists tend to favor the concentration of capital as a way to spur investment rather than consumption. In line with liberalism, capitalists favor development paths that tie third world states closely to the world economy and international trade. They argue that although they defer equity, such development strategies maximize efficiency. Once a third world state has a self-sustaining cycle of accumulation under way, it can better redress poverty in the broad population. To do so too early would choke off economic growth, in this view.

The same concept applies broadly to the world's development as a whole. From a capitalist perspective, the North-South gap is a stage of world development in which capital accumulation is concentrated in the North. This unequal concentration creates faster economic growth, which ultimately will bring more wealth to the South as well. There is no practical way, in this view, to shift wealth from the North to the South without undermining the free-market economics responsible for global economic growth.

Socialists argue that meaningful third world development should improve the position of the whole population and of the poor—sooner rather than later. Thus, socialists tend to advocate a more equitable distribution of wealth; they dispute the idea that greater equity will impede efficiency or slow down economic growth. Rather, by raising incomes among the poorer people, a strategy based on equity will speed up the demographic transition and thus lead more quickly to sustained accumulation. Such a strategy seeks to develop a state's economy from the bottom up instead of the top down.

On a global level, socialists do not see the North-South disparities as justified by global growth benefits. They favor political actions to shift income from North to South in order to foster economic growth in the South. Such a redistribution, in this view, would create faster, not slower, global economic growth—as well as more balanced and stable growth.

In reality, most states in the South use a mix of the two strategies in their economic policies, as do the industrialized states in shaping their roles in third world development. Welfare capitalism, such as most industrialized states practice, distributes enough wealth to meet the basic needs of almost everyone while letting most wealth move freely in capitalist markets. Such a mix is harder to achieve in a third world state where the smaller total amount of wealth may force a choice between welfare and capitalism. Fortunately, the amount of income a state needs to satisfy its population's basic needs is not large—around $6,000 per capita per year, even if that income is distributed unequally as it typically is. Unfortunately, many states are still below this level of per capita income.

The capitalist theory that unequal income distributions are related to higher economic growth is only weakly supported by empirical evidence. Many states with fairly equitable income distributions have high growth rates (including South Korea, Taiwan, Singapore, and Hong Kong); many with unequal distributions have grown slowly if at all (Zambia, Argentina, and Ghana). But there are also cases of relatively equitable countries that grow slowly (India) and inequitable ones that grow rapidly (Malaysia).

The Newly Industrializing Countries Although much of the third world went backward in the 1980s, some Asian states continued to develop and China began to raise its GDP per capita rapidly, though from a low starting level (see Figure 7.4). This indicates that a single, simplified model of the South does not apply to all third world countries. One must consider the various experiences of different countries as they try different approaches to development.

Given the extent of poverty in the third world, is it even possible for a third world country to lift itself out of poverty? The answer is "yes," at least for some countries. A handful of poor states—called **newly industrializing countries (NICs)**—have achieved self-sustaining capital accumulation, with impressive economic growth. These semiperiphery states, which export light manufactured goods (see pp. 257–261), posted strong economic growth in the 1980s and early 1990s. They ran into serious problems in the late 1990s (see pp. 340–342) because growth had been pushed too fast, with overly idealistic loans, speculative investments, and corrupt deals. Notwithstanding these set-

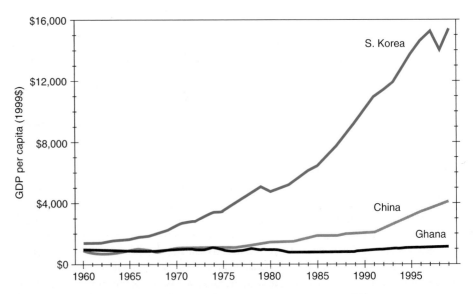

FIGURE 7.4 Per Capita GDP of South Korea, China, and Ghana
Source: Based on Penn World Tables and World Bank and IMF data.

backs, the NICs began growing again in 1998–1999 and have still developed much further and faster than most of the global South.

The most successful NICs are the **"four tigers"** or **"four dragons"** of East Asia—South Korea, Taiwan, Hong Kong, and Singapore. Each has succeeded in developing particular sectors and industries that are competitive on world markets. These sectors and industries can create enough capital accumulation within the country to raise income levels not just among the small elite but across the population more broadly.

Many third world countries are trying to apply the model of the NICs, but so far few have succeeded. Most poor states remained mired in poverty, with as many failures as successes. Scholars do not know whether the NICs are just the lucky few that have moved from the periphery to the semiperiphery of the world-system, or whether their success can eventually be replicated throughout the world.

South Korea, with iron and coal resources, developed competitive steel and automobile industries that export globally, creating a trade surplus (see pp. 219–220). Hyundai cars and trucks, sold in the United States and elsewhere, are produced by the giant South Korean MNC, Hyundai. The state has been strongly involved in industrial policy, trying to promote and protect such industries. By the mid-1990s, South Korea had an income level per capita equivalent to that of Spain; Korean companies began to move manufacturing operations to Britain where production costs were lower.

Web Link
South Korean
Development

Taiwan too has a strong state industrial policy. It specializes in the electronics and computer industries, where Taiwanese products are very successful worldwide, and in other light manufacturing.

Hong Kong—controlled by China since 1997—also has world-competitive electronics and other light industries, but its greatest strengths are in banking and trade—especially trade between southern China and the rest of the world. Hong Kong is a small territory with some of the world's highest real estate prices, and great internal disparities of wealth. Its rich neighborhoods are jammed with high-rise office buildings and expensive apartments, and Hong Kong is a financial center for much of Asia.

Atlas CD
Hong Kong
Port
Photo

Singapore is a trading city located at the tip of the Malaysian peninsula—convenient to the South China Sea, the Indian Ocean, and Australia. Singapore has developed niches in light manufacturing, and has tried to attract MNCs to locate headquarters there.

For different reasons, each of these states holds a somewhat unusual political status in the international system. South Korea and Taiwan—both former colonies of Japan—are hotspots of international conflict. South Korea and North Korea are separate states in practice, but have not recognized each other since fighting the Korean War in 1950–1953. Taiwan is formally part of China, but in practice operates independently. Both South Korea and Taiwan came under the U.S. security umbrella during the Cold War. Both then were militarized, authoritarian states intolerant of dissent, although they later became democratic. U.S. spending in East Asia during the Cold War benefited South Korea and Taiwan. In these cases military conflict did not impede development because the conflicts served to transfer some wealth from the United States to these states.

Hong Kong and Singapore have a different political profile. They are both former British colonies. They are more city-states than nation-states, and their cities are trading ports and financial centers. Although not as repressive nor as militarized as South Korea and Taiwan during the Cold War era, Hong Kong and Singapore were not democracies either. Hong Kong was ruled by a British governor (and since 1997 by the government in Beijing), Singapore by a dominant individual (who once banned sales of the *Asian Wall Street Journal*, hardly a radical newspaper, after it criticized him).

Thailand has been suggested as a potential "fifth tiger." It received enormous foreign investment in the 1980s (mostly from Japan) and created a sizable middle class. But its growth masked serious problems that put Thailand at the center of the 1997 financial crisis in Asia. It is not yet clear whether Thailand will recover and resume its path toward becoming another NIC. *Malaysia* is also trying to follow closely in the footsteps of the tigers. *Indonesia* set itself a goal in 1969 to become an NIC by 1994. It fell short of that goal but has made some progress in attracting foreign investment. With 200 million people, Indonesia's major assets are cheap labor (an average wage of about 25 cents per hour) and exportable natural resources, including oil. All of these Asian countries were caught in the 1997 financial downturn; at best, their growth will be slowed for several years.

A few other states have had some success in industrializing but are not considered to be models as widely applicable as the "four tigers." *Israel* has developed economically in an unusual manner. It received sustained infusions of outside capital from several sources—German reparations, U.S. foreign aid, and contributions from Zionists in foreign countries. This outside assistance was particular to the history of German genocide against Jews during World War II and the efforts of Jews worldwide to help build a Jewish state afterward. Few if any third world countries could hope to receive such outside assistance (relative to Israel's small size). In common with the other NICs, however, Israel has a strong state involvement in key industries, and it has carved out a few niches for itself in world markets (notably in cut diamonds and military technology).

Thus, it is unclear whether there are general lessons to be learned from the success of the "four tigers." Two NICs (Hong Kong and Singapore) are small trading cities located at the intersection of industrialized and third world regions (Japan/Pacific, South Asia, and China). There are no equivalents elsewhere in the third world. The other two came of age while enmeshed in security relationships with the United States that no longer apply to most third world countries, if they ever did.

The Chinese Experience
Very few of the third world's people live in NICs. The largest, South Korea, has fewer than 50 million. China is more than 20 times its size. This alone makes China's efforts to generate self-sustaining accumulation worthy of study. But China has also had one of the fastest-growing third world economies in recent years. Between the communist victory of 1949 and the Cultural Revolution of the late 1960s, Chinese economic policy emphasized national self-sufficiency and communist ideology. The state controlled all economic activity through central planning and state ownership. An "iron rice bowl" policy guaranteed basic food needs to all Chinese citizens (at least in theory).

Web Link
Mao Zedong

After Mao died in 1976, China under Deng Xiaoping instituted waves of economic reforms and transformed its southern coastal provinces into **free economic zones** open to foreign investment and run on capitalist principles. Peasants work their own fields, instead of collective farms, and "get rich" (by Chinese standards) if they do well. Entrepreneurs start companies, hire workers, and generate profits. Foreign investment has flooded into southern China, taking advantage of its location, cheap labor, and relative political stability. Other areas of China have gradually opened up to capitalist principles as well. The state now requires more industries to turn a profit and gives more initiative to managers to run their own companies and spend the profits as they see fit.

China Boots Up   China's rapid economic growth has raised incomes dramatically, especially for a growing middle class. These successes followed China's opening to the world economy and adoption of market-oriented reforms. China's leaders hope to use information technology to further these economic trends without undermining their political rule. An agreement for China to join the WTO will allow foreign investment in Internet businesses in China. Here, a Beijing computer store brings in customers by offering free Internet use for twenty minutes, 1999.

Economic growth has been rapid since these policies were instituted. Standards of living are rising substantially. However, China is also recreating some of the features of capitalism that Mao's revolutionaries had overturned. New class disparities are emerging, with rich entrepreneurs driving fancy imported cars while poor workers find themselves unemployed (earlier, socialism guaranteed everyone employment despite reduced efficiency). Unprofitable state-owned industries laid off 10 million workers in the 1990s, with more coming each year. In the countryside, areas bypassed by development still contain 200 million desperately poor Chinese peasants. Social problems such as prostitution have returned, as have economic problems such as inflation. Most frustrating for ordinary Chinese is the widespread official corruption accompanying the get-rich atmosphere.

Popular resentment over such problems as inflation and corruption led industrial workers and even government officials to join students in antigovernment protests at Beijing's Tiananmen Square in 1989. Authorities used the military to violently suppress the protests, killing hundreds of people and signaling its determination to maintain tight political control while economic reform proceeded. This policy was reaffirmed at the Party Congress in 1992 and again in 1997.

China's leaders felt vindicated by subsequent economic performance. Foreign investors returned quickly after the political disruption of 1989, and economic growth roared ahead at 12 percent per year in 1992–1994. Inflation returned, however, reaching 22 percent in 1994 as a result of what the government called "mistakes." The government then devalued the Chinese currency and successfully tamed inflation by trimming growth back to 10 percent annually—a difficult task requiring both economic skill and political will. By 1997, with inflation in check and growth proceeding rapidly, Shanghai's mayor estimated that his city alone was using 18 percent of the world's construction cranes.

After the death of Deng Xiaoping in 1997, Chinese President Jiang Zemin consolidated power and reaffirmed Deng's principles, while the government's chief inflation-fighter was named prime minister. Hong Kong joined China in 1997 under the "one country, two systems" formula. China and the United States resumed summit meetings, which had been frozen since 1989.

At that moment of Chinese strength, the Asian financial crisis introduced new doubts about China's prospects. China was guilty of many of the excesses of the Asian growth economies—debt, bad bank loans, money-losing state industries, real estate overbuilding, speculative investment, and corruption. Since China's currency was not freely traded on world markets, however, China was immune in the short term from the "Asian flu" that led to currency and market crashes in neighboring countries targeted by international currency speculators.

Nonetheless, the 1997 financial crisis affected China in several ways. First, Hong Kong's dollar was freely traded, and maintaining its value (which China especially wanted to do after gaining control in Hong Kong) required measures that led to stock market and real estate crashes there. Second, the devaluation of neighboring states' currencies made the exports of those countries more competitive with China's, so that Chinese prospects for exporting to the United States and elsewhere diminished. But if China in turn devalued its currency, a new round of devaluations by the neighboring states might follow, leading to a downward spiral of competitive devaluations such as happened in the Great Depression of the 1930s. Third, much foreign investment into China had been coming from those countries (including Japan), and their financial woes were expected to reduce the flow of capital into China. Therefore, it appeared that China's growth would, at best, slow down somewhat from its 8 to 10 percent annual rate. Given China's environmental problems (see p. 411) and the social and political dislocations just mentioned, a somewhat slower growth path might not be a bad thing for China. By 1999, with growth down to about 7 percent and a new trade deal reached with the United States, China appeared to have weathered the Asian flu in good health.

The new trade agreement and China's expected membership in the WTO raise new questions about how the ongoing Chinese opening of its economy to the world can coexist with continued political authoritarianism under communist rule. In the first four years of the new century, 25 million Chinese are expected to become Internet users for the first time. They will be able to communicate with overseas partners, monitor shipments, and follow economic trends globally. They will also be able to bypass government-controlled sources of political information. Some observers expect economic integration in an information era to inexorably open up China's political system and lead to democratization, whereas other experts think that as long as Chinese leaders deliver economic growth, the population will have little appetite for political change.

THE INFORMATION REVOLUTION   China and the Net

China is emerging as a more globally oriented great power, one that can put astronauts in space, stabilize Asian financial crises, and join the World Trade Organization. China's leaders need the Internet as a connecting point with the world economy, yet fear its political impacts. Can China open to the world as a great trading power without letting information in and out freely? Will new information channels affect China's form of government?

To explore this question, go to www.IRtext.com

It is unclear what lessons China's economic success over the past decade holds for the rest of the third world. The shift away from central planning and toward private ownership was clearly a key factor in its success, yet the state continued to play a central role in overseeing the economy (even more than in the NICs). Perhaps the earlier socialist policies had met basic needs adequately enough to allow capitalism into the mix without impoverishing most of the population. Then again, China's socialist policies may merely have delayed its accumulation of wealth. Perhaps authoritarian political control facilitated the difficult transition to a more capitalist, growth-oriented economy, as China's leaders seem to think. Then again, such control may only have closed off economic opportunities. These topics are being debated vigorously as China navigates the post–Deng era and as other poor states look to China's experience for lessons.

Other Experiments Other sizable third world states have pursued various development strategies, with mixed successes and failures. *India*, like China, deserves attention because of its size. Its economy was until recently based loosely on socialism and state control of large industries but on private capitalism in agriculture and consumer goods. The state subsidizes basic goods and gives special treatment to farmers. Unlike China, India has a relatively democratic government—and a fractious one, with various autonomy movements and ethnic conflicts. India's government is corrupt from top to bottom; this has held back accumulation.

Indian state-owned industries, like those elsewhere, are largely unprofitable. To take an extreme example, 12 years after a fertilizer plant was built, it employed 3,000 workers but had not produced any fertilizer. India's socialist philosophy and widespread poverty also limit the growth of a middle class to support capital accumulation and state revenue: less than 1 percent of the population pays any income tax. Furthermore, bureaucracy in India has discouraged foreign investment. In the 1990s, China received many times the foreign investment that India did.

The 1991 collapse of the Soviet Union—India's main trading partner—threw India into a severe economic crisis that nearly caused it to default on its international debts. India sought help from the IMF and the World Bank, and committed itself to far-reaching economic reforms such as reducing bureaucracy and selling money-losing state-owned industries (see pp. 392–393). It was unclear several years later how far these reforms would go and what effect they would have on India's economic growth.

Among other sizable Asian countries, *Indonesia* and *Thailand* are trying, with some limited success, to follow a Pacific Rim NIC strategy like that of South Korea and Taiwan. Thailand's military government followed China's example in 1992 by shooting student demonstrators, but this did not work. Afterward, some military commanders were forced off lucrative positions on the boards of directors of state-owned enterprises.

Other large Asian states—*Bangladesh, Pakistan, Vietnam,* and the *Philippines*—are more deeply mired in poverty and have dimmer prospects for capital accumulation in the coming years. All have problems with state bureaucracies and corruption. Vietnam is a communist state trying to follow a reform model parallel to China's. The Philippines is trying to overcome a rebellion in the countryside and a history of political instability that discourages foreign investment. It has not fully recovered from the looting of its economy and treasury under the Marcos dictatorship in the 1970s and early 1980s. Pakistan also faces political instability and a chronic danger of war with India. Bangladesh is just extremely poor, with no apparent foothold to get accumulation started.

**Atlas CD
Vietnam
Economic
Reforms
*Photo***

Brazil and *Mexico* are the largest third world states in the Western hemisphere. Brazil built up a sizable internal market by concentrating income in a growing middle and upper class, especially after a military coup in 1964. However, its cities are still ringed with huge slums filled with desperately poor people. In the 1980s, Brazil returned to democratic civilian rule and began economic reforms such as selling off unprofitable state-owned enterprises, promoting free markets, and encouraging foreign investment.

Nonetheless, by the early 1990s, Brazil remained well more than $100 billion in debt—the largest foreign debt in the third world. It had annual inflation of 200 percent and more, causing the currency's value to fall drastically. The president was impeached in a corruption scandal. The positive side of this embarrassing episode for Brazil was a constitutional, civilian transfer of power. With faster economic growth and foreign investment, a bigger grain harvest, and a substantial trade surplus, Brazil's main problem by 1993 was inflation. The anti-inflation plan of finance minister Fernando Cardoso was so successful that he was elected president in 1995, and other countries tried to copy his methods. In the 1997 currency crisis, Cardoso was able to scare off currency speculators, though at the cost of a dramatic slowdown in Brazil's economy.

**Web Link
Mexico's
Economy**

In Mexico, similar economic reforms were undertaken in the 1980s. Like Brazil, Mexico had pockets of deep poverty and a sizable foreign debt. Unlike Brazil, Mexico had oil to export (a good source of hard currency, despite low world prices). Mexico has also enjoyed relative political stability, though corruption is a problem. Leaders hoped that the NAFTA free-trade agreement of 1994 would accelerate foreign investment, creating jobs and export opportunities. Mexico also sold off more than $20 billion of state-owned companies (sparing the strategic oil industry) to help lower its debt and bring down inflation. But assassinations and other political upheaval, including an armed rebellion in the South that broke out in response to the NAFTA accord, complicated Mexico's development problems. In 1994–1995 Mexico's currency collapsed and standards of living for many consumers took a sharp drop. With help from the United States, Mexico undertook new economic reforms and began to rebuild the economy and restore international and domestic confidence.

In Africa, *Nigeria* is the largest country and, with oil to export, one of the less impoverished. In 1980, when oil prices were high, Nigeria began building a huge,

Soviet-style steel plant, which leaders hoped would serve as the cornerstone of Nigerian economic development. Twelve years and $5 billion later, the plant was ready to start producing steel. It is the biggest industrial project in sub-Saharan Africa. But its products will not be competitive in the world steel industry, so government subsidies may be required indefinitely. Meanwhile, as world oil prices fell drastically in the 1980s, the country went in debt by $35 billion. Corruption consumed a sizable sum of money in the course of building the steel plant. This pattern of centralized industrialization under Nigeria's military government faces uncertain prospects at best, although oil exports provide continuing income. Nigeria canceled a planned experiment in democracy in the early 1990s, and a military dictatorship continued in power by mid-decade. African Americans began an unusual campaign to press for democracy in Nigeria, in order to move Africa's largest country forward in both human rights and overall development. But Nigeria's government seemed resistant to all such pressures. In 1995 it ignored international pleas and executed a popular leader of an oil-rich but impoverished region. Finally, the dictator died and his successor held elections in which a civilian president took power in 1999. Nigeria's economic state remains tenuous, however.

Atlas CD
Nigeria
Traffic Jam
Photo

In the Middle East, the small countries with large oil exports—such as *Saudi Arabia*, *Kuwait*, and *Bahrain*—have done well economically. But they are in a special class; their experience is not one that third world states without oil can follow. *Iran* and *Iraq* are somewhat larger countries that have also benefited from oil exports. After the Iran-Iraq War ended in 1988, Iran began to grow robustly and to attract foreign investment. However, its Islamic radicalism creates frictions with Western powers and makes some investors wary. Meanwhile, Iraq squandered oil revenues on military adventures in Iran and Kuwait; its economic development was set back enormously during the Gulf War.

Turkey has been fairly successful in developing its economy without oil, a rare case. Like South Korea and Taiwan, Turkey was an authoritarian state for many years but has recently allowed political liberalization; it has developed under a U.S. security umbrella (NATO) and has received considerable U.S. foreign aid. Turkey is trying to join its richer neighbors—the EU. Turkey also hopes to develop strong ties with the five former Soviet Asian republics. Unlike Iran, Turkey espouses a secular politics, with Islam relegated to the religious and cultural sphere. (In the 1990s, a small but growing Islamic movement began challenging the secular basis of Turkish society.)

Egypt is mired in poverty despite substantial U.S. aid since the late 1970s. The state owns 70 percent of industry, operates the economy centrally, imposes high import tariffs, and provides patronage jobs and subsidized prices in order to maintain political power. A major portion of Egypt's foreign debt was forgiven after it helped the anti-Iraq coalition in the Gulf War, but Egypt remains about $30 billion in debt. It runs a trade deficit of billions of dollars each year, and 20 percent of the work force is unemployed. Corruption is widespread at all levels of the bureaucracy. Islamic militants have gained increasing strength as Egypt's economy weakens, despite state repression against them.

These examples from all third world regions illustrate the many approaches to economic development that third world states have tried and the mixed success they have met. Clearly, the largest third world states are following somewhat different strategies with somewhat different results. But several common themes recur. These themes concern trade, the concentration of capital, authoritarianism, and corruption.

Import Substitution and Export-Led Growth Throughout the third world, states are trying to use international trade as the basis of accumulation. For the reasons discussed in Chapter 5, a policy of self-reliance or autarky is at best an extremely slow way to build up wealth. But through the creation of a trade surplus, a state can accumulate hard currency and build industry and infrastructure.

One way to try to create a trade surplus—used frequently a few decades ago—is through **import substitution**—the development of local industries to produce items that a country had been importing. These industries may receive state subsidies or tariff protection. This might seem to be a good policy for reducing dependency—especially on the former colonial master—while shrinking a trade deficit or building a trade surplus. But it is against the principle of comparative advantage and has not proven effective in most cases. Some scholars think that import substitution is a policy useful only at a very early phase of economic development, after which it is counterproductive. Others think it is never useful.

Recently, more and more states have shifted to a strategy of **export-led growth**, a strategy used by the NICs. This strategy seeks to develop industries that can compete in specific niches in the world economy. The industries may receive special treatment such as subsidies and protected access to local markets. Exports from these industries generate hard currency and create a favorable trade balance. The state can then spend part of its money on imports of commodities produced more cheaply elsewhere.

Atlas CD
Zambia
Copper Mine
Photo

Such a strategy has risks, especially when a state specializes in the export of a few raw materials (see pp. 345–348). Such a specialty leaves poor countries vulnerable to sudden price fluctuations for their export products. For example, when world copper prices fell from $3,000 to $1,300 per ton in 1974, income fell accordingly in Zambia, which got 94 percent of export earnings from copper. It had to cut back imports of needed goods drastically and suffered a 15 percent decline in its (already low) GDP.

The overall relationship between the prices of exported and imported goods—called the **terms of trade**—affects an export strategy based on raw materials. There is some evidence that in the 1950s and 1960s, and again in the 1980s, the terms of trade eroded the value of raw materials. A third world state trying to create trade benefits by exporting such goods would have to export more and more over time in order to import the same manufactured goods—a major obstacle to accumulation.

Because of both terms of trade and price fluctuations, states have looked to exporting manufactured goods, rather than raw materials, as the key to export-led growth. However, in seeking a niche for manufactured goods, a third world state must compete against industrialized countries with better technology, more educated work forces, and much more capital. For example, Nigeria's steel exports are unlikely to provide the desired trade surplus (although South Korean steel did so). Thus, third world countries need to be selective in developing export-oriented industrial strategies. It is not enough to subsidize and protect an industry until it grows in size; someday it has to be able to stand its own ground in a competitive world or it will not bring in a trade surplus.

Concentrating Capital for Manufacturing Manufacturing emerges as a key factor in both export-led growth and self-sustaining industrialization (home production for home markets). It is not surprising that third world states want to increase their own manufacturing base and change the global division of labor based on manu-

Capital Intensive
Successful economic development in South Korea meant investing in moderately capital-intensive factories to manufacture such goods as TVs and cars competitively. Foreign investment, international debt, and domestic inequality all can help concentrate the necessary capital for manufacturing. Here, TVs are being manufactured by assembly line workers in a factory in South Korea.

facturing in the core and resource extraction in the periphery. One great difficulty in getting manufacturing started is that capital is required to build factories. Competitive factories in technologically advanced industries can require large amounts of capital—such as the $5 billion for Nigeria's steel plant. Nigeria got much of the money from oil exports, but most third world states lack such a source of funds.

To invest in manufacturing, these countries must *concentrate* what surplus their economies produce. They face the familiar trade-off between short-term consumption and long-term investment. Money spent building factories cannot be spent subsidizing food prices or building better schools. Thus the concentration of capital for manufacturing can sharpen disparities in income. A political price must often be paid in the short term for reducing public consumption, even in industrialized states. In third world states there is little margin for reducing consumption without causing extreme hardship. The result may be crowds rioting in the streets or guerrillas taking over the countryside.

The problem is compounded by the need to create domestic markets for manufactured goods. Because it is unlikely that a manufacturing industry in a poor country will be immediately competitive on world markets, one common strategy is to build up the industry with sales to the home market (protected by tariffs and subsidies) before pursuing world markets. But home markets for manufactured goods do not come from poor peasants in the countryside or the unemployed youth in city slums. Rather, wealth must be concentrated in a *middle class* that has income to buy the manufactured goods.

The growing disparity of income in such a situation often triggers intense frustration on the part of poorer people, even those whose income is rising. (Political rebellion is fueled by relative deprivation as much as by absolute poverty.) A common way states respond to such problems is to crack down hard with force to stamp out the protests of the poor and of other political opponents (see the next section).

Such problems might be minimized by reducing the amount of capital that needs to be squeezed from a third world state's domestic economy. Capital for manufacturing can come from foreign investment or foreign loans, for instance. This strategy reduces short-term pain, but it also reduces the amount of surplus (profit) available to the state in the long term. Another way to minimize the capital needs of manufacturing is to start out in low-capital industries. These industries can begin generating capital, which can in turn be used to move into somewhat more technologically demanding and capital-intensive kinds of manufacturing. A favorite starter industry is *textiles*. The industry is fairly labor-intensive, giving an advantage to countries with cheap labor, and does not require huge investments of capital to get started. Many third world states have built their own textile industries as a step toward industrialization. For this reason, many states impose high tariffs on textiles, which are among the least freely traded commodities.

Atlas CD
Textile
Industry in
Hong Kong
Photo

There are some problems with concentrating capital for manufacturing. One is that it creates conditions ripe for corruption (discussed shortly). The problem is especially severe when authoritarian political control is used to enforce compliance with hardships that may accompany the concentration of wealth. In many cases—Brazil, Nigeria, India, China, and others—too much of the money ends up in the hands of corrupt bureaucrats.

An approach that received international attention in the 1980s is based on a Peruvian entrepreneur's analysis of the **informal sector** in Lima's economy—black markets, street vendors, and other private arrangements. These modes of business are often beyond state control and may not even show up in state-compiled economic statistics. Markets operate rather freely, and some scholars have begun to see such markets, rather than large manufacturing industries, as the core of a new development strategy.

Web Link
Microlending

A related approach to capitalization in very poor countries, growing in popularity in recent years, is **microcredit** (or *microlending*). Based on a successful model in Bangladesh (the Grameen Bank), microcredit uses small loans to poor people, especially women, to support economic self-sufficiency. The borrowers are organized into small groups, and take responsibility for each other's success, including repaying the loans. Repayment rates have been high, and the idea is spreading rapidly in several regions. In one high-tech twist, village women have begun using small loans to start businesses offering cellular phone booths (or huts) where people pay to make domestic or international calls. Microcredit is the opposite of a trickle-down approach, instead injecting capital at the bottom of the economic hierarchy. A loan to buy a goat or cell phone may do more good, dollar for dollar, than a loan to build a dam. However, the idea has not been tried on a large enough scale to test its overall potential for international development.

Authoritarianism and Democracy Several decades ago, many scholars expected that third world states would follow the European and North American states in economic and political development. The gradual accumulation of capital would be accompanied by the gradual extension of literacy and education, the reduction of class and gender disparities, and the strengthening of democracy and political participation. The United States could be a model for third world development in this view. It had gone from poor colony to industrializing state to rich superpower. Political rights (including the vote) had been steadily extended to more segments of the population.

In reality, democracy has not accompanied economic development in a systematic or general way. In fact, the fastest-growing states have generally been authoritarian states, not democracies. This has led to the theory that economic development is incompatible with democracy. Accordingly, political repression and the concentration of political control are necessary to maintain order during the process of concentrating capital and starting accumulation. Demands by poor people for greater short-term consumption must be refused. Class disparities must be sharpened. Labor discipline must be enforced at extremely low wage levels. Foreign investors must be assured of political stability—above all, that radicals will not take power and that foreign assets will not be nationalized in a revolution. A democracy may be inherently incapable of accomplishing these difficult and painful tasks, according to this theory.

The NICs did not achieve their success through free and open democratic politics, but through firm state rule permitting little dissent. Chinese leaders, for example, contrast their recent economic successes, achieved under tight political control, with the failed Soviet efforts under Gorbachev to promote economic reform by first loosening political control.

It has been suggested that a strong state facilitates capital accumulation. Only a strong state in this view has the power to enforce and coordinate the allocations of wealth required to start accumulation going. But scholars do not agree on the definition of a strong state; some refer to the size of the state bureaucracy or its ability to extract taxes, others to its legitimacy or its ability to enforce its will on the population.

In reality, the theory that authoritarianism leads to economic development does not hold up, just as the theory that democracy automatically accompanies economic development does not hold up. Many authoritarian states have achieved neither political stability nor economic development. Others have realized political stability but have failed at economic accumulation. The many military dictatorships in Africa are among the least successful models in the third world. In Latin America, the poorest country, Haiti, had the most authoritarian government for decades. By contrast, in both Brazil and Argentina, democratization in the 1980s was eventually followed by financial progress in increased growth in the mid-1990s.

Furthermore, authoritarian states can lead to greater political instability, not less. The harder the state cracks down, the more resentment the population feels. Instead of peaceful protests, violent insurgencies often grow out of such resentments. In Guatemala, a military government harshly repressed rural revolutionaries and their peasant sympathizers for decades until a peace agreement was reached in 1996. Since the 1960s, in this country of 9 million, repression and war killed 100,000 people, and another 45,000 "disappeared." Guatemala's government at times received substantial U.S. aid (based on "anticommunism") and at other times was banned from receiving such aid (based on violations of human rights). But its decades of authoritarian rule did not stop dissent, bring political stability, attract much foreign investment, or create much economic accumulation.

Meanwhile, elsewhere in Latin America a wave of civilian governments replaced military ones in the late 1980s. Economic conditions there have improved, not worsened, as a result. In states such as South Korea and Taiwan, which began industrializing under authoritarianism but have since shifted toward democracy, economic progress was not harmed. Relatively free elections and tolerance of dissent signaled greater stability and maturity, and did not discourage investment or slow economic growth (although the 1992 world recession did).

It has been suggested that authoritarian rule and the concentration of income in few hands represent a phase in the development process. First, capital must be concentrated to get accumulation started, and tight political control must be maintained during this painful phase. Later, more wealth is generated, income spreads to more people, the middle class expands, and political controls can be relaxed.

But again, the empirical reality does not support such a theory as a general rule. There is no guarantee that, even in early phases of accumulation, authoritarian control leads to economic development. In fact, flagrant human rights abuses seem to cause political instability at any stage of economic development. Some successful accumulators, such as China and Saudi Arabia, have maintained tight political control throughout the process. Others, such as South Korea and Turkey, have started with authoritarian rule and evolved into democracies. Still others, such as Costa Rica and Malaysia, have achieved good economic results while maintaining relative democracy and little repression. Similarly, among the countries that have done poorly in economic accumulation are both authoritarian regimes and democratic ones. Therefore, a state's form of political governance does not determine its success in economic development.

Web Link
Corruption

Corruption   Corruption is an important negative factor in economic development in many states; corruption also plays a role in some of the theories just discussed about various strategies for using trade, industry, and government to promote economic development.

Corruption centers on the government as the central actor in economic development, especially in its international aspects. Through foreign policy, the government mediates the national economy's relationship to the world economy. It regulates the conditions under which MNCs operate in the country. It enforces worker discipline—calling out the army if necessary to break strikes or suppress revolutions. It sets tax rates and wields other macroeconomic levers of control over the economy. And in most third world states it owns a sizable stake in major industries—a monopoly in some cases.

Corruption is a kind of privatization of politics in that it concerns the distribution of benefits from economic transactions (exchange and capital accumulation). For example, when a foreign MNC comes into a country to drill for oil, the surplus produced will be shared among the MNC (through profits), the state (through taxation and fees), the local capitalists who make money supplying the operation, the local workers who earn wages, and the foreign consumers who use the oil (which, due to the added supply, will be slightly cheaper on world markets).

State officials will decide whether to let the MNC into the country, which MNC to give the drilling rights to, and what terms to insist on (leasing fees, percentages of sales, etc.). These are complex deals struck after long negotiations. Corruption merely adds another player, the corrupt official, to share the benefits. For instance, a foreign oil company can pay off an official to award a favorable contract, and both can profit.

Corruption is by no means limited to the third world. But for several reasons corruption has a deeper effect in poor countries. First, there is simply less surplus to keep economic growth going; accumulation is fragile. Another difference is that in those third world countries dependent on exporting a few products, the revenue arrives in a very concentrated form—large payments in hard currency. This presents a greater opportunity for corruption than in a more diversified economy with more (smaller) deals.

Corruption Stinks Corruption is a major impediment to third world development. In South Korea in 1997, two former presidents were jailed for corruption and the ruling party lost power. Officials had taken bribes in exchange for granting government loans; these bad loans were a major factor in the 1997 financial crisis. Here, South Korean students, demanding the president's resignation for corruption, run from riot police early in 1997.

Furthermore, in third world countries incomes are often so low that corrupt officials are more tempted to accept payments.

Third world corruption presents a collective goods problem for states and MNCs in the global North: individually MNCs and their home states can profit by clinching a deal with a private payoff, but collectively the MNCs and states of the North lose money by having to make these payoffs. Therefore, there is an incentive to clamp down on corruption only if other industrialized states do likewise. The United States in recent decades has barred U.S. companies from making corrupt deals abroad, but other countries of the North had not done so until recently. Germany and Canada even allowed their companies to deduct foreign bribes on their taxes. U.S. officials estimated that in 1994 U.S. companies lost almost $50 billion in foreign deals because of this disparity in rules.

In the 1990s, high-level corruption cases became high-profile international news; governments fell in Brazil, Italy, Pakistan, and elsewhere. Two former presidents in South Korea went to jail. In this context, a Berlin-based NGO called Transparency International pushed successfully for action to stem corruption in international business deals. The group published annual surveys showing the countries that business executives considered most corrupt. In 1997, the IMF and World Bank announced plans to use their influence to curb corruption in the global South. These actions culminated in a 1997 agreement among the world's 29 leading industrialized states to forbid their companies from bribing foreign officials (payments to political parties were not forbidden, however). It was unclear how much effect this agreement would have in practice, but U.S. companies cheered the equalization of rules.

Occasionally, government officials serve not their own private interests but those of a foreign state. Such a government is called a *puppet government*. The officials of such a government are bought off to serve the interests of a more powerful state (which may have installed the government through military conquest). For example, during the Cold War, both superpowers justified installing friendly governments by reference to global power politics. Critics, however, believed the puppet governments served business interests of the controlling state, not security interests. This and other issues concern the role of international business in third world accumulation.

North-South Business

Given the importance of international trade and investment to third world economic development, not only governments but private banks and MNCs from the North are also major participants in the economies of the South. (Several large third world states have also created their own MNCs, though these play a fairly minor role.)

Foreign Investment Poor countries have little money available to invest in new factories, farms, mines, or oil wells. Foreign investment—investment in such capital goods by foreigners (most often MNCs)—is one way to get accumulation started (see pp. 263–265). Foreign investment has been crucial to the success of China and other Asian developing countries. The extent to which poor countries crave foreign investment was illustrated by a 1995 policy in Seychelles (population 75,000): anyone who invested $10 million or more was promised immunity from extradition or prosecution for crimes committed elsewhere. U.S. officials called it the "Welcome, Criminals" Act.

Overall, private capital flow to the global South reached nearly $300 billion in 1996 (far more than the $60 billion given in official development assistance). Three-quarters of this flow, however, went to just 12 countries in the South. More than one-third of the capital flow represented foreign direct investment, which was up fourfold since 1990.[1]

Foreigners who invest in a country then own the facilities; the investor by virtue of its ownership can control decisions about how many people to employ, whether to expand or shut down, what products to make, and how to market them. Also, the foreign investor can usually take the profits from the operation out of the country (repatriation of profits). However, the host government can share in the wealth by charging fees and taxes, or by leasing land or drilling rights (see pp. 265–268).

Because of past colonial experiences, many third world governments have feared the loss of control that comes with foreign investments by MNCs. Sometimes the presence

---

[1] Data from World Bank web site [http://www.worldbank.org].

of MNCs was associated with the painful process of concentrating capital and the sharpening of class disparities in the host state. Although such fears remain, they are counterbalanced by the ability of foreign investors to infuse capital and generate more surplus. By the 1980s and 1990s, as models based on autarky or state ownership were discredited and the NICs gained success, many poor states rushed to embrace foreign investment.

One way in which states have sought to soften the loss of control is through *joint ventures*, companies owned partly by a foreign MNC and partly by a local firm or the host government itself. Sometimes foreign ownership in joint ventures is limited to some percentage (often 49 percent), to ensure that ultimate control rests with the host country even though a large share of the profits go to the MNC. The percentage of ownership is usually proportional to the amount of capital invested; if a host government wants more control it must put up more money. Joint ventures work well for MNCs because they help ensure the host government's cooperation in reducing bureaucratic hassles and ensuring success (by giving the host government a direct stake in the outcome).

MNCs invest in a country because of some advantage of doing business there. In some cases, it is the presence of other natural resources. Sometimes it is cheap labor. Some states have better *absorptive capacity* than others—the ability to put investments to productive use—because of more highly developed infrastructure and a higher level of skills among workers. These are often middle-income states, so the funneling of investments to states with high absorptive capacity tends to sharpen disparities *within* the third world.

MNCs also look for a favorable *regulatory environment* in which a host state will facilitate, rather than impede, the MNC's business. For example, Motorola had decided to invest more than $1 billion in new facilities in India in the 1990s, but changed its mind after encountering India's bureaucracy and shifted its investments toward China instead.

MNC decisions about foreign investment also depend on prospects for *financial stability*, especially for low inflation and stable currency exchange rates. If a currency is not convertible into hard currency, an MNC will not be able to take profits back to its home state or reinvest them elsewhere.

Beyond these financial considerations, a foreign investor producing for local markets wants to know that the host country's *economic growth* will sustain demand for the goods being produced. For example, automobile producers who built factories in Thailand and other Southeast Asian countries in the 1990s to meet the demands of a growing middle class were burned by the 1997 financial crash; some pulled up stakes and left. Similarly, whether producing for local consumption or export, the MNC wants the local *labor* supply—whether semiskilled or just cheap—to be stable. Foreign investors often look to international financial institutions, such as the World Bank and the IMF, and to private analyses, to judge a state's economic stability before investing in it.

Of equal importance in attracting investment is *political stability* (see pp. 268–270). Banks and MNCs conduct *political risk analyses* to assess the risks of political disturbances in third world states in which they might invest.

Web Link
MNCs and Third
World Labor

Host countries for their part seek to assure potential foreign investors that they have stable political environments in which investments will not be at risk. For example, foreign states occasionally take out pages of advertising in U.S. newspapers to promote their country as a site for investment. Sometimes these appeals coincide with a summit meeting, as when Pakistan's Benazir Bhutto visited the United States in 1995. Or they may follow events in the host country.

Beyond their usual role in providing foreign investment, technology transfer, and loans (in the case of banks), MNCs also sometimes participate in more broadly conceived development projects in a host state. This is a way of investing in political goodwill as well as helping provide political stability by improving the condition of the population. The attitude of the government and the goodwill of the population affect the overall business prospects of the MNC. In the long run, blatant exploitation is not the most profitable way to do business.

Technology Transfer
Productive investment of capital depends on the knowledge and skills—business management, technical training, higher education, as well as basic literacy and education—of workers and managers. Of special importance are management and technical skills related to the key industries in a state's economy. In many former colonies, whites with such skills left after independence (see pp. 345–348). In other states, the skills needed to develop new industries have never existed. A few states in the Persian Gulf with large incomes and small populations have imported a whole work force from foreign countries. But this is rare.

Most third world states seek to build up their own educated elite with knowledge and skills to run the national economy. One way to do so is to send students to industrialized states for higher education. This entails some risks, however. Students may enjoy life in the North and fail to return home. In most third world countries, every student talented enough to study abroad represents a national resource and usually a long investment in primary and secondary education, which is lost if the student does not return. The same applies to professionals (for example, doctors) who emigrate later in their careers. The problem of losing skilled workers to richer countries is called the **brain drain**. It has impeded economic development in states such as India, Pakistan, the Philippines, and China.

Technology transfer refers to a third world state's acquisition of technology (knowledge, skills, methods, designs, and specialized equipment) from foreign sources, usually in conjunction with foreign direct investment or similar business operations. A third world state may allow an MNC to produce certain goods in the country under favorable conditions, provided the MNC shares knowledge of the technology and design behind the product. The state may try to get its own citizens into the management and professional work force of factories or facilities created by foreign investment. Not only can physical capital accumulate in the country, so can the related technological base for further development. But, MNCs are sometimes reluctant to share proprietary technology.

Technology transfer sometimes encounters difficulty when the technological style of the source country does not fit the needs of the recipient country. A good fit has been called *appropriate technology*. In particular, the Soviet Union was fond of creating the "world's largest" factory of some type, and it tended to apply the same overly centralized approach to its investments and development projects in the third world—such as the huge Nigerian steel plant mentioned earlier. Furthermore, technology that seemed useful to bureaucrats in Moscow might not be appropriate to a recipient country

The **green revolution**—a massive transfer of agricultural technology coordinated through international agencies—deserves special mention. This effort, which began in the 1960s, transplanted a range of agricultural technologies from rich countries to poor ones—new seed strains, fertilizers, tractors to replace oxen, and so forth. The green revolution increased crop yields in a number of states, especially in Asia, and helped food supplies keep up with growing populations.

However, it did have drawbacks. Critics said the green revolution made recipients dependent on imported technologies such as tractors and oil, that it damaged the environment with commercial pesticides and fertilizers, and that it disrupted traditional agriculture (driving more people off the land and into cities). Environmental reactions to the green revolution have led to recent declines in crop yields, forcing changes. For example, in Indonesia pesticides introduced in the green revolution created resistant strains of a rice parasite and killed off the parasite's natural predators. The pesticides also polluted water supplies. Recognizing the need to adapt imported technologies to local needs, the Indonesian government banned most pesticides in 1986 and adopted organic methods instead. In recent years, the Food and Agriculture Organization (FAO) has spread information about organic pest control through traditional village theater plays. Pesticide usage has declined sharply while rice production has increased.

In the 1990s, states in the North focused on technology transfer that promotes *environmentally sustainable development* (see pp. 410–411). Japan's MITI-funded International Center for Environmental Technology Transfer geared up to train 10,000 people from third world countries, over ten years, in energy conservation, pollution control, and other environmental technologies. Japan also hosts the International Environmental Technology Center, a project of the UN Environment Program (UNEP). Among other motives, Japan hopes these projects will encourage developing countries to choose Japanese technology and products.

Third World Debt

Borrowing money is an alternative to foreign investment as a way of obtaining funds to prime a cycle of economic accumulation. If accumulation succeeds, it produces enough surplus to repay the loan and still make a profit. Borrowing has several advantages. It keeps control in the hands of the state (or other local borrower) and does not impose painful sacrifices on local citizens, at least in the short term.

Debt has disadvantages too. The borrower must service the debt—making regular payments of interest and repaying the principal according to the terms of the loan. **Debt service** is a constant drain on whatever surplus is generated by investment of the money. With foreign direct investment, a money-losing venture is the problem of the foreign MNC; with debt, it is the problem of the borrowing state (which must find the money elsewhere). Often, a debtor must borrow new funds to service old loans, slipping further into debt. Debt service has created a net financial outflow from South to North in recent years, as the South has paid billions more in interest to banks and governments in the North than it has received in foreign investment or development aid.

The failure to make scheduled payments, called a **default,** is considered a drastic action because it destroys lender confidence and results in cutoff of future loans. Rather than defaulting, borrowers attempt **debt renegotiation**—a reworking of the terms on which a loan will be repaid. By renegotiating their debts with lenders, borrowers aim to come up with a mutually acceptable payment scheme to keep at least some money flowing to the lender. If interest rates have fallen since a loan was first taken out, the borrower can refinance. Borrowers and lenders can also negotiate to restructure a debt by changing the length of the loan (usually to a longer payback period) or the other terms.

Web Link
Debt Forgiveness

Occasionally state-to-state loans are written off altogether—forgiven—for political reasons, as happened with U.S. loans to Egypt after the Gulf War.

Third world debt encompasses several types of lending relationships, all of which are influenced by international politics. The *borrower* may be a private firm or bank in a third world country, or it may be the government itself. Loans to the government are somewhat more common because lenders consider the government less likely to default than a private borrower. The *lender* may be a private bank or company, or a state (both are important). Usually banks are more insistent on receiving timely payments and firmer in renegotiating debts than are states. Some state-to-state loans are made on artificially favorable *concessionary* terms, in effect subsidizing economic development in the borrowing state.

In the 1970s and 1980s, many third world states borrowed heavily from banks and states in the North, which encouraged the borrowing. The anticipated growth often did not materialize. In oil-exporting states such as Venezuela and Mexico, for instance, price declines reduced export earnings with which states planned to repay the loans. Other exporting states found that protectionist measures in the North, combined with a global economic slowdown, limited their ability to export. Sometimes borrowed funds were simply not spent wisely and produced too little surplus to service the debt.

As a result, by the 1980s a *third world debt crisis* had developed, particularly in Latin America. Many third world states could not generate enough export earnings to service their debts, much less to repay them—not to speak of retaining some surplus to generate sustained local accumulation. Major states of the global South such as Brazil, Mexico, and India found foreign debt a tremendous weight on economic development. Although the "crisis" is past, and many debts have been renegotiated to a longer-term basis, the weight of debt remains (see Table 7.4); in fact, third world debt increased by one-quarter between 1991 and 1996.

Many private banks in industrialized countries had overextended themselves with loans that third world states could not repay, and some economists worried that the banking system in the North could collapse. But the banking system rode out this

TABLE 7.4   Third World Debt, 1997

Region	Foreign Debt		Annual Debt Service	
	Billion $	% of GNP[a]	Billion $	% of Exports
Latin America	667	34%	130	36%
Asia	937	34	113	13
Africa	473	63	25	15
Total "South"	1,915	37	268	19

[a] GNP not calculated at purchasing-power parity.

Notes: Regions do not exactly match those used elsewhere in this book. Africa here includes North Africa. Asia includes China.

Source: United Nations, *World Economic and Social Survey 1999* (New York: United Nations, 1999), pp. 292–96. UN estimates based on IMF, OECD, and World Bank data.

crisis, writing off a portion of the uncollectible debts each year. Banks sold off the debts at a discount, and there is now a *secondary market* in third world debts. From 1986 to 1989, the average price for the bank debts of 15 heavily indebted countries in this secondary market dropped from 65 percent of face value to 30 percent (though values rebounded somewhat in later years). In the worst cases, holders of debts of some poor states could not unload them for more than 1 cent on the dollar.

Debt renegotiation has become a perennial occupation of third world states. Brazil had to do so three times in a decade, in the 1980s and early 1990s. Such renegotiations are complex international bargaining situations, like international trade or arms control negotiations but with more parties. The various lenders—private banks and states—try to extract as much as they can, and the borrower tries to hold out for more favorable terms. If a borrowing government accepts terms that are too burdensome, it may lose popularity at home; the local population and opposition politicians may accuse it of selling out to foreigners, neocolonialists, and so on. But if the borrowing state does not give enough to gain the agreement of the lenders, it might have to default and lose out on future loans and investments, which could greatly impede economic growth.

For the lenders, debt renegotiations involve a collective goods problem: all of them have to agree on the conditions of the renegotiation but each really cares only about getting its own money back. To solve this problem, state creditors meet together periodically as the **Paris Club**, and private creditors as the **London Club**, to work out their terms.

Through such renegotiations and the corresponding write-offs of debts by banks, third world states have largely avoided defaulting on their debts. Some large states have threatened to default—or even to lead a coalition of third world states all defaulting at once—but have backed off from such threats. Default is a risky course because of the integrated nature of the world economy, the need for foreign investment and foreign trade to accumulate wealth, and the risks of provoking international confrontations. Lenders too have always proven willing to absorb losses in the end rather than push a borrower over the edge and risk financial instability. Through various efforts, including the *Baker Plan* and *Brady Plan* in the 1980s (named after the U.S. treasury secretaries who proposed them) and the work of multilateral institutions such as the World Bank and the IMF, the third world debt situation had stabilized somewhat by the early 1990s.

Despite stabilization, third world states have not yet solved the debt problem. As shown in Table 7.4, the South owes almost $2 trillion in foreign debt, and pays about $250 billion a year to service that debt. The debt service (in hard currency) absorbs nearly a third of the entire hard-currency export earnings in Latin America—the region most affected. Africa's debt is equal to two-thirds of the annual GDP of the region. Asia has less serious debt problems, but many states in that region are vulnerable to debt problems as well (as some found out in the 1997 devaluations).

In the late 1990s, a group of NGOs called the Jubilee 2000 coalition worked to raise public consciousness about the need for debt relief. Partly as a result, the 1999 G8 summit agreed to forgive as much as $90 billion in debt service payments owed by some of the poorest states to governments in the North (and to the IMF). This relief was conditioned on the debtor states' using the savings for health and education. The IMF planned to sell up to several billion dollars worth of its gold reserves, invest the money, and put interest payments in a trust fund to help the poorest debtor countries.

IMF Conditionality   The International Monetary Fund (IMF) and the World Bank have a large supply of capital from their member states (see pp. 247–249). This capital plays an important role in funding the early stages of accumulation in third world states and in helping developing countries get through short periods of great difficulty. Also, as a political entity rather than a bank, the IMF can make funds available on favorable terms.

The IMF does not give away money indiscriminately. Rather, it scrutinizes third world states' economic plans and policies, withholding loans until it is satisfied that the right policies are in place. Then it makes loans to help states through the transitional process of implementing the IMF-approved policies. The IMF also sends important signals to private lenders and investors. Its approval of a state's economic plans is a "seal of approval" bankers and MNCs use to assess the wisdom of investing in that state. Thus, the IMF wields great power to influence the economic policies of third world states.

An agreement to loan IMF funds on the condition that certain government policies are adopted is called an **IMF conditionality** agreement; implementation of these conditions is referred to as a *structural adjustment program*. Dozens of third world states have entered into such agreements with the IMF in the past two decades. The terms insisted on by the IMF are usually painful for the citizens (and hence for national politicians). The IMF demands that inflation be brought under control, which requires reducing state spending and closing budget deficits. This often spurs unemployment and requires that

Miracle of Loaves   IMF conditionality agreements often called for reducing subsidies for food, transportation, and other basic needs. In Egypt, bread prices are heavily subsidized, forcing the government to use hard currency to import wheat. But public resistance to bread price increases is so strong that the government has not brought itself to cut the subsidy. Here, bread is delivered by bicycle in Cairo, 1996.

subsidies of food and basic goods be reduced or eliminated. Short-term consumption is curtailed in favor of longer-term investment. Surplus must be concentrated to service debt and invest in new capital accumulation. It wants to ensure that inflation does not eat away all progress and that the economy is stable enough to attract investment. In addition, the IMF demands steps to curtail corruption.

Because of the pain inflicted by a conditionality agreement—and to some extent by any debt renegotiation agreement—such agreements are often politically unpopular in the third world. On quite a few occasions, a conditionality agreement has brought rioters into the streets demanding the restoration of subsidies. Sometimes governments have backed out of the agreement or have broken their promises under such pressure. Occasionally, governments have been toppled. As a Peruvian economist noted in 1992, "You can reduce the debt, but is it worth it? [Terms are] too harsh, and it results in mass unemployment and the abandonment of any kind of social program." In a country such as Peru, facing a violent leftist guerrilla war that fed on mass poverty, such a choice was especially difficult.

The IMF formula for stability and success is remarkably universal from one country to the next. When the IMF negotiated terms for economic assistance to Russia and the former Soviet republics in the early 1990s, the terms were similar to those for any third world state: cut inflation, cut government spending, cut subsidies, crack down on corruption. Critics of the IMF argue that it does not adapt its program adequately to account for differences in the local cultural and economic conditions in different states. (The United States in the 1980s and early 1990s would not have qualified for IMF assistance because of government deficits!) A major question in the late 1990s was whether IMF conditions imposed on Asian economies such as Indonesia and South Korea, which sought IMF bailouts after the 1997 financial crash, unnecessarily choked off growth there, perhaps even accelerating crises in Russia and elsewhere in 1998.

The South in International Economic Regimes
Because of the need for capital and the wealth created by international trade, most third world states now see their future economic development as resting on a close interconnection with the world economy, not on national autarky or third world regional economic communities. This means that third world states must play by the rules embedded in international economic regimes, as discussed in Chapter 5.

The WTO trading regime tends to work against third world states relative to industrialized ones. A free-trade regime makes it harder for poor states to protect infant industries in order to build self-sufficient capital accumulation. It forces competition with more technologically advanced states. A poor state can be competitive only in low-wage, low-capital niches—especially those using natural resources that are scarce in the North, such as tropical agriculture, extractive (mining and drilling) industries, and textiles.

Yet just these economic sectors in which third world states have comparative advantages on world markets—agriculture and textiles in particular—were largely excluded from the free-trade rules of the GATT (see pp. 231–234). The GATT instead concentrated on free trade in manufactured goods, in which states in the North have comparative advantages. As a result, some third world states found that they were expected to open their home markets to foreign products, against which home industries are not competitive, yet see their own export products shut out of foreign markets.

To compensate for this inequity and help third world states use trade to boost economic growth, the GATT created the Generalized System of Preferences. These and other measures—such as the Lomé conventions in which EU states relaxed tariffs on third world goods—are exceptions to the overall rules of trade, intended to ensure that participation in world trade advances rather than impedes third world development. But critics claim that third world states are the losers in the overall world trading regime.

The World Bank came under criticism on its fiftieth anniversary in 1994. A coalition of activist groups including Greenpeace and Oxfam America accused the Bank of supporting authoritarian regimes and underwriting huge infrastructure projects that displaced poor people. Critics alleged that the Bank's portfolio of loans in the global South, totaling more than $100 billion, was more a hindrance than a help to true development. Bank officials responded that despite a few mistakes, the Bank and its mission were sound.

The tenuous position of the third world in international economic regimes reflects the role of power in IR. The global North, with two-thirds of the world's wealth, clearly has more power—more effective leverage—than the South. The global disparity of power is accentuated by the fact that the South is split up into more than a hundred actors whereas the North's power is concentrated in eight large states (the G8 members). Thus, when the rules of the world economy were created after World War II, and as they have been rewritten and adjusted over the years, the main actors shaping the outcome have been a handful of large industrialized states.

Third world states have responded in several ways to these problems with world economic regimes. In the 1970s, OPEC shifted the terms of trade for oil—bringing huge amounts of capital into the oil-exporting countries. Some third world states hoped such successes could be repeated for other commodities, resulting in broad gains for the third world, but this did not occur (see pp. 238–239 and 426–428).

Also in the 1970s, many third world states tried to form a broad political coalition to push for restructuring the world economy so as to make North-South economic transactions more favorable to the South. A summit meeting of the nonaligned movement (see pp. 80–82) in 1973 first called for a **New International Economic Order (NIEO)**. Central to the NIEO was a shift in the terms of trade to favor primary commodities relative to manufactured goods. The NIEO proposal also called for the promotion of industrialization in the third world, and for increased development assistance from the North.

The NIEO never became much more than a rallying cry for the global South, partly because of the South's lack of power and partly because disparities within the South created divergent interests among states there. In the 1980s, the terms of trade further deteriorated for raw material exporters, and economic development slowed down in much of the third world. But in China and some other Asian countries, development accelerated.

Web Link
UNCTAD

Third world states continue to pursue proposals to restructure world trade to benefit the South. These efforts now take place mainly through the *UN Conference on Trade and Development (UNCTAD)*, which meets periodically but lacks power to implement major changes in North-South economic relations. Attempts to promote South-South trade (reducing dependence on the North) have proven largely impractical. Efforts continue, however, to boost third world cooperation and solidarity through a variety of groups such as the nonaligned movement and the UN. Nonetheless, such efforts have done little to change the South's reliance on assistance from the North.

Foreign Assistance

Foreign assistance (or *overseas development assistance*) is money or other aid made available to third world states to help them speed up economic development or simply meet basic humanitarian needs. Along with the commercial economic activities just discussed, foreign assistance is a second major source of money for third world development. It covers a variety of programs—from individual volunteers lending a hand to massive government packages—in which money or some other form of value flows from North to South.

Different kinds of development assistance have different purposes. Some are humanitarian, some are political, and others are intended to create future economic advantages for the giver (these purposes often overlap). The state or organization that gives assistance is called a *donor*; the state or organization receiving the aid is the *recipient*. Foreign assistance creates, or extends, a relationship between donor and recipient that is simultaneously political and cultural as well as economic. Foreign assistance can be a form of power in which the donor seeks to influence the recipient, or a form of interdependence in which the donor and recipient create a mutually beneficial exchange.

Patterns of Foreign Assistance The majority of foreign assistance comes from governments in the North. Private donations provide a smaller amount, although sometimes a significant one. In 1997, for instance, George Soros, a speculator and Hungarian-American fund manager, contributed or pledged nearly $2 billion in aid to Russia and other countries.

Table 7.5 (p. 396) lists the major donors toward the $50.6 billion in governmental foreign assistance provided in 1997. More than 95 percent of government assistance comes from members of the **Development Assistance Committee (DAC)**, consisting of states from Western Europe, North America, and Japan/Pacific. Several oil-exporting Arab countries provide some foreign development assistance as well. Nearly 80 percent of the DAC countries' assistance goes directly to governments in the third world as state-to-state **bilateral aid**; the rest goes through the UN or other agencies as **multilateral aid.** The DAC countries have set themselves a goal to contribute 0.7 percent of their GNPs in foreign aid. But overall they give less than half this amount. Only Norway, Sweden, Denmark, and the Netherlands meet the target. France is close.

The United States gives the lowest percentage of GNP—about one-eighth of 1 percent—of any of the 29 states of the industrialized West that make up the OECD. In total economic aid given ($7 billion), the United States has slipped behind Japan ($14 billion), France ($8 billion), and Germany ($8 billion). In 1995, as the U.S. Congress was considering further cuts in foreign aid budgets, the OECD issued a report strongly criticizing the low level of U.S. foreign aid. The cuts were made anyway; U.S. foreign assistance dropped by nearly half from 1992 to 1995. This and other decreases brought the world total in foreign assistance down by more than 10 percent in those three years.

Types of Aid Bilateral aid takes a variety of forms. *Grants* are funds given free to a recipient state, usually for some stated purpose. *Technical cooperation* refers to grants given in the form of expert assistance in some project rather than just money or goods. *Credits* are

TABLE 7.5 Who's Helping?
Foreign Assistance, 1997

Donor	Assistance Given		Change from 1992
	Billion $	% of GNP[a]	
World total	50.6	0.2%	-31%
Total G7	36.4	0.2%	-37%
Japan	9.7	0.2%	-27%
United States	7.1	0.1%	-49%
France	6.5	0.5%	-34%
Germany	6.1	0.3%	-32%
Britain	3.5	0.3%	-8%
Canada	2.1	0.3%	-30%
Italy	1.3	0.1%	-72%
Netherlands	3.0	0.8%	
Sweden	1.8	0.8%	
Denmark	1.7	1.0%	
Norway	1.3	0.9%	
Other "North"	5.6		
Arab Countries	0.6		
Other "South"	0.3		

[a] GNP not calculated at purchasing-power parity.

Source: United Nations, *World Economic and Social Survey 1999* (New York: United Nations, 1999), p. 287. UN estimates based on OECD data; governmental aid only.

grants that can be used to buy certain products from the donor state. For instance, Japan might assist a state's agricultural development by giving credits that can be used to buy Japanese-built farm equipment. If people in a recipient country become accustomed to products from the donor state, they are likely to buy those same products in the future.

Loans are funds given to help in economic development, which must be repaid in the future out of the surplus generated by the development process (they too are often tied to the purchase of products from the donor state). Unlike commercial loans, government-to-government development loans are often on concessionary terms, with long repayment times and low interest rates. Although still an obligation for the recipient country, such loans are relatively easy to service.

Loan guarantees, which are used only occasionally, are promises by the donor state to back up commercial loans to the recipient. If the recipient state services such debts and ultimately repays them, there is no cost to the donor. But if the recipient cannot make the payments, the donor has to step in and cover the debts. A loan guarantee allows the recipient state to borrow money at lower interest rates from commercial banks (because the risk to the bank is much lower).

Military aid is not normally included in development assistance, but in a broad sense belongs there. It is money that flows from North to South, from government to government, and it does bring a certain amount of value into the third world economy. If a country is going to have a certain size army with certain weapons, getting them free from a donor state frees up money that can be used elsewhere in the economy. However, of all the forms of development assistance, military aid is certainly one of the least efficient and most prone to impede rather than help economic development. It is also geared almost exclusively to political alliances rather than actual development needs.

The main agency dispensing U.S. foreign economic assistance (but not military aid) is the State Department's *Agency for International Development (USAID)*, which works mainly through the U.S. embassy in each recipient country. Major recipients of U.S. foreign aid include Israel, Egypt, and Turkey—all important strategic allies in the volatile Middle East. Like other great powers, the United States uses the promise of foreign aid, or the threat of cutting it off, as a leverage in political bargaining with recipients. For example, when Pakistan proceeded in the late 1980s with a nuclear weapons program, despite U.S. warnings, a sizable flow of U.S. aid was terminated. In Indonesia and elsewhere, the United States has cut off foreign aid to protest human rights violations by the military. Thus foreign aid is used as a leverage to gain political influence in the third world.

The U.S. **Peace Corps** provides U.S. volunteers for technical development assistance in third world states. They work at the request and under the direction of the host state but are paid an allowance by the U.S. government. Started by President Kennedy in 1961, the Peace Corps now sends about 6,000 volunteers to 90 countries, where they participate in projects affecting about a million people. It is a small-scale program, but one that increases person-to-person contacts.

Web Link
Peace Corps

In foreign aid, the donor must have the permission of the recipient government to operate in the country. This goes back to the principle of national sovereignty and the history of colonialism. National governments have the right to control the distribution of aid and the presence of foreign workers on their soil. Only occasionally is this principle violated, as when the United States and its allies provided assistance to Iraqi Kurds against the wishes of the Iraqi government following the Gulf War. International norms may be starting to change in this regard, with short-term humanitarian assistance starting to be seen as a human right that should not be subject to government veto.

UN Programs Most of the multilateral development aid goes through *UN programs*. The place of these programs in the UN structure is described in Chapter 6. The overall flow of assistance through the UN is coordinated by the **UN Development Program (UNDP)**, which manages 5,000 projects at once around the world (focusing especially on technical development assistance). Other UN programs focus on concentrating capital, transferring technology, and developing work force skills for manufacturing. UNIDO works on industrialization, UNITAR on training and research. But most UN programs—such as UNICEF, UNFPA, and WFP—focus on meeting basic needs.

UN programs have three advantages in promoting economic development. One is that governments and citizens tend to perceive the UN as a friend of the third world, not an alien force, a threat to sovereignty, or a reminder of colonialism. The UN can sometimes mobilize technical experts and volunteers from other third world countries so that people who arrive to help do not look like white European colonialists. A team of Egyptian medical workers under a UN program may be more easily accepted in an African country than French or British workers, however well-intentioned.

Second, UN workers may be more likely to make appropriate decisions because of their backgrounds. UN workers who come from the third world or have worked in other poor countries in a region may be more sensitive to local conditions and to the pitfalls of development assistance than are aid workers from rich countries.

A third advantage is that the UN can organize its assistance on a global scale, giving priority to projects and avoiding duplication and the reinvention of the wheel in each state. For some issues—such as the fight against AIDS or the integration of development objectives with environmental preservation—there is no substitute for global organization.

A major disadvantage faced by UN development programs is that they are funded largely through voluntary contributions by rich states. Each program has to solicit contributions to carry on its activities. The contributions can be abruptly cut off if the program displeases a donor government (see p. 353). A second major disadvantage of UN programs is their reputation for operating in an inefficient, bureaucratic manner, without the cohesion and the resources that governments and MNCs in the North take for granted.

Forms of Development Assistance
The remainder of this chapter discusses three models of development assistance, which are distinguished by the type of assistance provided rather than the type of donor (all three models encompass both government and private aid).

The Disaster Relief Model First is the disaster relief model. It is the kind of foreign assistance given when poor people are afflicted by famine, drought, earthquakes, flooding, or other such natural disasters. (War is also a disaster and can compound naturally occurring disasters.) When disaster strikes a poor state, many people are left with no means of subsistence and often without their homes. **Disaster relief** is the provision of short-term relief to such people in the form of food, water, shelter, clothing, and other essentials.

Disaster relief is very important because disasters can wipe out years of progress in economic development in a single blow. Generally, the international community tries to respond with enough assistance to get people back on their feet. The costs of such assistance are relatively modest, the benefits visible and dramatic. Having a system of disaster relief in place provides the third world with a kind of insurance against sudden losses that could otherwise destabilize economic accumulation.

Disasters generally occur quickly and without much warning. Rapid response is difficult to coordinate. International disaster relief has become more organized and better coordinated in the past decade but is still a complex process that varies somewhat from one situation to the next. Contributions of governments, private charitable organizations, and other groups and agencies are coordinated through the *UN Office of the Disaster Relief Coordinator (UNDRO)* in Geneva. Typically, international contributions make up no more than about one-third of the total relief effort, the remainder coming from local communities and national governments in the affected states. The U.S. government's contributions are coordinated by the *Office of Foreign Disaster Assistance (OFDA)*, which is part of USAID.

Web Link
UN ReliefWeb

Disaster relief is something of a collective good because the states of the North do not benefit individually by contributing, yet they benefit in the long run from greater stability in the South. Despite this problem and the large number of actors, disaster relief is generally a positive example of international cooperation to get a job done. Food donated by the World Council of Churches may be carried to the scene in U.S. military aircraft and then distributed by the International Committee of the Red Cross (ICRC). Embarrassing failures in the past—of underresponse or overresponse, of duplication of efforts or agencies working at cross-purposes—became rarer in the 1990s.

The relationship of disasters with economic development is complex, and appropriate responses vary according to location, type and size of disaster, and phase of recovery. For instance, refugees displaced from their home communities have different needs from those of earthquake or hurricane victims whose entire communities have been damaged. Appropriate disaster relief can promote local economic development, whereas inappropriate responses can distort or impede such development.

When the disaster is *war*, the lead role often falls to the *International Committee of the Red Cross (ICRC)*, based in Switzerland. International norms and traditions treat the ICRC as an agency with special protected status (see p. 320). Red Cross societies in each country are autonomous agencies that also participate in disaster relief efforts (they are called Red Crescent societies in Islamic countries and the Red Star of David in Israel).

International norms regarding states' legal obligations to assist others in time of natural disaster and to accept such assistance if needed are changing. In the 1990s—designated by the UN as the International Decade for Natural Disaster Reduction—a new international regime in this area began solidifying.

THE MISSIONARY MODEL Beyond disaster relief, many governments and private organizations provide ongoing development assistance in the form of projects administered by agencies from the North in local communities in the South to help meet basic needs. Although such efforts vary, one could call the approach a *missionary* model because it resembles the charitable works performed by missionaries in poor countries in past centuries. In fact, many of these private programs are still funded by churches and carried out by missionaries. Often such assistance is considered "God's work."

Such charitable programs are helpful though not without problems. They are a useful means by which people in the North funnel resources to people in the South. Even during the colonial era, missionaries did much good despite sometimes perpetuating stereotypes of European superiority and native inferiority. Today's efforts to help poor people in third world states are helpful in giving local individuals and communities some resources with which they may better contribute to national economic development.

However, most handout programs provide only short-term assistance and do not create sustained local economic development. They do not address the causes of poverty, the position of poor countries in the world economy, or the local political conditions such as military rule or corruption.

One version of "missionary" assistance—advertised widely in the United States—lets citizens in rich countries "adopt" poor children in the third world. Photos of a hungry child stare at the reader from a magazine page while the accompanying text notes that a few cents a day can "save" the child. Although such programs raise awareness in the North of the extent of poverty in the South, at worst they tend to be exploitive and to reinforce racist and paternalistic stereotypes of the helplessness of third world people.

The U.S. military operation to restore food relief in war-torn Somalia in 1992–1993 contained elements of the missionary model. President Bush called the mission "God's work" and it was often referred to as one to "save" Somalia. U.S. leaders tried to focus the

Mouthwash for Mauritania   The missionary model of foreign assistance contributes goods to third world economies, but often with little understanding of local needs or long-term strategies. Here, free supplies including cartons of mouthwash are delivered by the U.S. ambassador and the captain of a U.S. Navy ship participating in Project Handclasp, 1989.

mission narrowly on delivering food to hungry people despite appeals from the UN secretary-general and others that only disarming the warring factions could solve the Somali crisis. Later, political negotiation and some forceful disarming of factions quieted the civil war at least temporarily, and without doubt the U.S. intervention helped the situation in Somalia greatly. But in the end, the United States and the UN pulled out without resolving the war and other political problems that had caused the famine and could do so again. The episode showed that helping starving people is often more complex than just sending in food shipments (even with military escorts to ensure their safe delivery). There is a danger in the missionary model that people from the North may provide assistance inappropriate for a third world state's local conditions and culture.

Web Link
Oxfam

THE OXFAM MODEL   A third model of development assistance can be found in the approach taken by the private charitable group **Oxfam America** (one of seven groups worldwide descended from the Oxford Committee for Famine Relief, founded in 1942 in Britain). Originally devoted to short-term aid to famine victims, and still active in that effort, Oxfam America realized that over the longer term people needed not just handouts of food but the means to feed themselves—land, water, seed, tools, and technical training.

The distinctive aspect of the Oxfam model is that it relies on local communities to determine the needs of their own people and to carry out development projects. Oxfam does not operate projects itself but provides funding to local organizations. Nor does Oxfam call itself a donor and these organizations recipients. Rather, it calls both sides "project partners"—working together to accomplish a task. In this model, a little outside money can go a long way toward building sustained local economic development. Furthermore, projects help participants empower themselves by organizing to meet their own needs.

For example, Oxfam America helped the Ethiopian women's cooperative mentioned on page 363. Oxfam did not design or organize the project; women in Addis Ababa did. But when their garment-making workshop became profitable and was ready to expand and employ twice as many women, Oxfam gave the group a $15,000 grant to build a new building. This small grant helped to consolidate a new center of accumulation in one of the world's poorest neighborhoods.

In this model, third world economic development is not charity; it is in the interests of people in the rich countries as well as the poor. A cooperative relationship between North and South is essential for a peaceful and prosperous world. Even in a narrow economic sense, development in the third world creates new markets and new products that will enrich the industrialized countries as well. In economics, the creation of wealth is a positive-sum game.

The Oxfam approach seeks to reconceptualize development assistance to focus on long-term development through a bottom-up basic needs strategy. "Genuine development," in Oxfam's view, "enables people to meet their essential needs; extends beyond food aid and emergency relief; reverses the process of impoverishment; enhances democracy; makes possible a balance between populations and resources; improves the well-being and status of women; respects local cultures; sustains the natural environment; measures progress in human, not just monetary terms; involves change, not just charity; requires the empowerment of the poor; and promotes the interests of the majority of people worldwide, in the global North as well as the South."

To promote its approach to North-South relations (and to raise funds for its project partners), Oxfam America carries on education and action programs in the United States. The most prominent is an annual Fast for a World Harvest, a week before Thanksgiving, that raises awareness among U.S. citizens about the extent and causes of third world hunger. Participants at "hunger banquets" are assigned randomly to one of three groups: 15 percent eat an elaborate gourmet meal, 25 percent get a modest meal of rice and beans, and 60 percent eat a small portion of rice and water. Thanks to the information revolution (see Chapter 8), information about third world poverty and economic development is now more widely available to people in industrialized countries.

Because of disappointment with the political uses of foreign aid in the past, Oxfam has tried to minimize the role in its projects of governments in both the North and South. For instance, Oxfam does not accept government funds nor does it make grants to governments.

The general goals of the Oxfam model of foreign aid are consistent with a broader movement in the global South toward grassroots **empowerment**. Efforts such as those of Oxfam partners are organized by poor people to gain some power over their situation and meet their basic needs—not by seizing control of the state in a revolution but by means that are more direct, more local, and less violent. The key to success is getting organized, finding information, gaining self-confidence, and obtaining needed resources to implement action plans.

Partner in Development
The Oxfam model of foreign assistance emphasizes support for local groups that can stimulate self-sustaining economic development at a local level. A mutually beneficial North-South partnership is the global goal of such projects. This woman manages a cooperative store in San Salvador, El Salvador.

For example, women in Bangladesh have a very low status in rural society (see pp. 362–363). Often they cannot own property, participate in politics, or even leave their houses without their husbands' permission. Now some women in rural Bangladesh have organized women's groups to raise women's self-esteem, promote their rights, and mobilize them to change conditions. In India, local women's groups using only the power of persuasion and logic have convinced some landowners to give them land for cooperative income-generating projects such as vegetable farming and raising silkworms. Elsewhere in India, women working as gatherers of wood and other forest products got organized to win the legal minimum wage for 250,000 female forest workers—three times what they had been paid before. In this case, government action was necessary, but the pressure for such action came from local organizing. The women took their case to the public and the press, staging protest marches and getting an art exhibit relating to their cause displayed in the provincial capital.

Atlas CD
Indian Women
Photo

Such examples do not mean that national and foreign governments are unimportant. On the contrary, government policies affect millions of people more quickly and more widely than do grassroots efforts. Indeed, grassroots organizing often has as an ultimate goal the restructuring of national political and social life so that policies reflect the needs of poor people. But the successes of grassroots empowerment show that poor communities can be more than victims of poverty waiting to be saved or passive bystanders in North-South relations. Nor do poor people need to place their hopes for change in violent revolutions aimed at toppling national governments—revolutions that lead to greater suffering more often than to stable economic development.

The Oxfam model has the advantage of promoting this trend toward grassroots empowerment, thereby overcoming the dangers of externally run programs under the disaster relief and missionary models. However, the Oxfam model to date has been tested only on a very small scale. Although the model may be effective in the local communities it reaches, it would have to be adopted widely and replicated on a much larger scale in order to influence the overall prospects for third world development. It is unclear whether the principles the model embodies, from a reliance on local community organizers to an avoidance of government involvement, would work on a massive scale.

CONFRONTING THE NORTH-SOUTH GAP All three models of development assistance have contributions to make. Given the extent of its poverty, the global South needs all the help from the North that it can get. Perhaps the most important point is for people in the North to be aware of the tremendous gap between North and South and to try to address the problem. Third world poverty can seem so overwhelming that citizens in rich countries can easily turn their backs and just try to live their own lives.

But in today's interdependent world this really is not possible. North-South relations have become a part of everyday life. The integrated global economy brings to the North products and people from the South. The information revolution puts images of third world poverty on TV sets in comfortable living rooms. The growing role of the UN brings North and South together in a worldwide community. This global integration is especially evident in the areas of environmental management and technological change, which occupy Chapter 8.

THINKING CRITICALLY

1. In North and South America, independence from colonialism was won by descendants of the colonists themselves. In Asia and Africa, it was won mainly by local populations with a long history of their own. How do you think this has affected the postcolonial history of one or more specific countries from each group?
2. Dozens of poor states appear to be stuck midway through the demographic transition; death rates have fallen, birthrates remain high, and per capita incomes are not increasing. How do you think these states, with or without foreign assistance, can best get unstuck and complete the demographic transition?
3. Some scholars criticize the IMF for imposing harsh terms in its conditionality agreements with poor states. Others applaud the IMF for demanding serious reforms before providing financial resources. If you were a third world leader negotiating with the IMF, what kinds of terms would you be willing to agree to and what terms would you resist? Why?

CHAPTER SUMMARY

◆ Most of the world's people live in poverty in the third world. About a billion live in extreme poverty, without access to adequate food, water, and other necessities.

◆ Moving from poverty to well-being requires the accumulation of capital. Capitalism and socialism take different views on this process. Capitalism emphasizes overall growth with considerable concentration of wealth, whereas socialism emphasizes a fair distribution of wealth.

◆ Most states have a mixed economy with some degree of private ownership of capital and some degree of state ownership. However, state ownership has not been very successful in accumulating wealth.

◆ Marxists view international relations, including global North-South relations, in terms of a struggle between economic classes (especially workers and owners) that have different roles in society and different access to power.

◆ Since Lenin's time, many Marxists have attributed poverty in the South to the concentration of wealth in the North. In this theory, capitalists in the North exploit the South economically and use the wealth thus generated to buy off workers in the North.

◆ IR scholars in the world-system school argue that the North is a core region specializing in producing manufactured goods and the South is a periphery specializing in extracting raw materials through agriculture and mining. Between these are semiperiphery states with light manufacturing.

◆ Today's North-South gap traces its roots to the colonization of the third world regions by Europe over the past several centuries. Because of the negative impact of colonialism on local populations, anticolonial movements arose throughout the third world at various times and using various methods. These culminated in a wave of successful independence movements primarily after World War II in Asia and Africa.

◆ Following independence, third world states were left with legacies of colonialism, including their basic economic infrastructures, that made wealth accumulation difficult in certain ways. These problems still remain in many countries.

◆ World population—now at 6 billion—will reach 8 or 9 billion in 30 years. Thereafter it is expected to level out over 150 years, ultimately reaching a stable level somewhere between about 10 and 20 billion.

◆ Future world population growth will be largely driven by the demographic transition. Death rates have fallen throughout the world, but birthrates will fall proportionally only as per capita incomes go up.

◆ The demographic transition sharpens disparities of wealth globally and locally. High per capita incomes and low population growth make rich states or groups richer, whereas low incomes and high population growth reinforce each other to keep poor states and groups poor.

◆ Within the overall shape of the demographic transition, government policies can reduce birthrates somewhat at a given level of per capita income. Effective policies are those that improve access to birth control and raise the status of women in society.

◆ Death rates are stable and little affected in the large picture by wars, famines, and other disasters. Raising the death rate is not a feasible way to limit population growth.

◆ Although the global AIDS epidemic may not greatly slow world population growth, it will impose huge costs on many poor states in the coming years. More than 30 million people are infected with HIV; most are in Africa and most new infections are now in Asia. Because states cannot wall themselves off from the outside world, international cooperation in addition to unilateral state actions will be necessary to contain AIDS.

◆ Population pressures do not cause, but do contribute to, a variety of international conflicts including ethnic conflicts, economic competition, and territorial disputes.

◆ Wealth accumulation depends on the meeting of basic human needs such as access to food, water, education, shelter, and health care. Third world states have had mixed success in meeting their populations' basic needs.

◆ War has been a major impediment to meeting basic needs, and to wealth accumulation generally, in poor countries. Almost all the wars of the past 50 years have been fought in the third world.

◆ Hunger and malnutrition are rampant in the third world. The most important cause is the displacement of subsistence farmers from their land because of war, population pressures, and the conversion of agricultural land into plantations growing export crops to earn hard currency.

◆ Urbanization is increasing throughout the third world as more people move from the countryside to cities. Huge slums have grown in the cities as poor people arrive and cannot find jobs.

◆ Women's central role in the process of accumulation has begun to be recognized. International agencies based in the North have started taking women's contributions into account in analyzing economic development in the South.

◆ Poverty in the South has led huge numbers of migrants to seek a better life in the North; this has created international political frictions. War and repression in the South have generated millions of refugees seeking safe haven.

◆ Many people throughout the third world have turned to political revolution as a strategy for changing economic inequality and poverty. Often, especially during the Cold War, states in the North were drawn into supporting one side or the other during such revolutions.

◆ Today the most potent third world revolutions are the Islamic revolutions in the Middle East directed against the North. Like communist ones, Islamic revolutions draw support and legitimacy from the plight of poor people.

◆ When revolutionaries succeed in taking power, they usually change their state's foreign policy. Over time, however, old national interests and strategies tend to reappear.

◆ North-South relations, although rooted in a basic economic reality—the huge gap in accumulated wealth—reflect the close connections of economics with international security.

◆ Economic development in the third world has been uneven; per capita GDP increased in the 1970s but, except in Asia, decreased in the 1980s. Growth in the 1990s was brisk in Asia but slow elsewhere.

◆ Evidence does not support a strong association of economic growth either with internal equality of wealth distribution or with internal inequality.

◆ The newly industrializing countries (NICs) in Asia—South Korea, Taiwan, Hong Kong, and Singapore—show that it is possible to rise out of poverty into sustained economic accumulation. Other third world states are trying to emulate these successes, but it is unclear whether these experiences can apply elsewhere.

◆ China has registered strong economic growth in the past 15 years of market-oriented economic reforms. Though still quite poor, China may be emerging as a leading success story in third world economic development.

◆ Economic development in other large third world countries such as India, Brazil, and Nigeria has been slowed by the inefficiency of state-owned enterprises, by corruption, and by debt.

◆ Import substitution has been largely rejected as a development strategy in favor of export-led growth. This reflects both the experiences of the NICs and the theory of comparative advantage.

◆ Most poor states want to develop a manufacturing base. But, even when focusing on low-capital industries, states have generally had to sharpen income disparities in the process of concentrating capital for manufacturing.

◆ The theory that democratization would strengthen economic development has not been supported by the experiences of third world countries. But the opposite theory—that authoritarian government is necessary to maintain control while concentrating capital for industrialization—has also not been supported.

◆ Government corruption is a major obstacle to development.

◆ Given the shortage of local capital in most poor states, foreign investment by MNCs is often courted as a means of stimulating economic growth. MNCs look for favorable local conditions, including political and economic stability, in deciding where to invest.

◆ States in the global South seek the transfer of technology to support their future economic development. Technology transfer can be appropriate or inappropriate to local needs depending on the circumstances of each case.

◆ The green revolution of the 1960s was a massive North-South transfer of agricultural technology, which had both good and bad effects. Today's "green" technologies being transferred to the third world are techniques for environmentally sustainable development.

◆ Third world debt, resulting largely from overborrowing in the 1970s and early 1980s, is a major problem. Despite renegotiations and other debt management efforts, the South remains almost $2 trillion in debt to the North, and annual debt service consumes about one-sixth of all hard-currency earnings from exports of the South.

◆ The IMF makes loans to states in the South conditional on economic and governmental reforms. These conditionality agreements often necessitate politically unpopular measures such as cutting food subsidies.

◆ The WTO trading regime works against the third world by allowing richer nations to protect sectors in which the third world has advantages—notably agriculture and textiles. The Generalized System of Preferences (GSP) tries to compensate by lowering barriers to third world exports.

◆ Efforts to improve the South's solidarity, cooperation, and bargaining position relative to the North—such as the New International Economic Order (NIEO)—have had little success.

◆ Foreign assistance, most of it from governments in the North, plays an important part in the economic development plans of the poorer states of the South. However, only a few states in the North meet the goal of contributing 0.7 percent of their GNPs as foreign assistance to the South. The United States, at 0.1 percent, contributes the smallest share of any industrialized state.

◆ Most foreign aid consists of bilateral grants and loans from governments in the North to specific governments in the South. Such aid is often used for political leverage, and promotes the export of products from the donor state.

◆ Disaster relief provides short-term aid to prevent a natural disaster from reversing a poor state's economic development efforts. Disaster relief generally involves cooperation by various donor governments, local governments, the UN, and private agencies.

◆ Handouts to poor communities to meet immediate needs for food and supplies outside times of disaster—here called the missionary model—can be helpful but also have drawbacks.

◆ Efforts to support local organizations working to empower poor people and generate community economic development—here called the Oxfam model—are promising but have been tried only on a small scale.

ONLINE PRACTICE TEST

Take an online practice test at
www.IRtext.com

Environment and Technology

Interdependence and the Environment

As we have seen, world industrialization and development have increased international interdependence through functional economic integration and North–South relationships. Industrialization and development have also intensified international interdependence in another, less direct way, through their impact on the world's natural environment. Actions taken by one state now routinely affect other states' access to natural resources and to the benefits of a healthy environment. The global threats to the natural environment are thus a major new source of interdependence. This chapter discusses this new source and then considers how information technologies are similarly strengthening interdependence.

Because environmental effects tend to be diffuse and long term, and because such effects easily spread, international environmental politics creates difficult collective goods problems (see pp. 88–89). Essentially, a sustainable natural environment is a collective good, and states bargain over how to distribute the costs of providing that good. The technical, scientific, and ethical aspects of managing the environment are complex, but the basic nature of states' interests is not. The collective goods problem arises in each issue area concerning the environment and natural resources.

For example, the world's major fisheries in international waters are not owned by any state; they are a collective good. The various fishing states must cooperate (partly by regulating nonstate actors such as MNCs) to avoid depleting stocks of fish. If too many states fail to cooperate, the fish populations are wiped out and everyone's catch is much reduced. In fact, this has already happened in many of the world's largest fisheries—fish catches worldwide dropped sharply in the early 1990s. The fishing industry worldwide started losing more than $50 billion a year, and relied increasingly on government subsidies.

Atlas CD
Oceans in
Distress
Video

But what is a state's fair quota of fish? There is no world government to decide such a question, so states must enter into multilateral negotiations, agreements, and regimes. Such efforts create new avenues for functionalism and international integration, but also new potentials for conflict and "prisoner's dilemmas." A UN-sponsored agreement among all the world's major fishing states in 1999 set goals to reduce fleet overcapacity. (There are 4 million fishing boats worldwide, of which 40,000 are ships larger than 100 tons.) Participating nations are supposed to cap the size of fishing fleets and then scale them back gradually, while reducing subsidies. The pain of unemployment and economic adjustment would thus be shared. However, the agreement is voluntary, its implementation delayed until at least 2003, and its effect probably too little, too late.

This type of collective goods dilemma has been called the **tragedy of the commons**. Centuries ago the commons was shared grazing land in Britain. As with fisheries, if too many people kept too many sheep, the commons would be overgrazed. Yet adding one more sheep was profitable to that sheep's owner. Britain solved this problem (although creating other problems) by **enclosure** of the commons—splitting it into privately owned pieces on each of which a single owner would have an incentive to manage resources responsibly. The world's states are gradually taking a similar approach to fisheries by extending territorial waters to put more fish under the control of single states (see pp. 428-430). The *global commons* refers to the shared parts of the earth, such as the oceans and outer space.

As in other areas of IPE, the solution of environmental collective goods problems is based on achieving shared benefits that depend on overcoming conflicting interests. *Regimes* are an important part of the solution, providing rules to govern bargaining over who gets the benefits and bears the costs of environmental protection. So are functional IOs that specialize in technical and management aspects of the environment.

Increasingly, these IOs overlap with broader communities of experts from various states that structure the way states manage environmental issues; these have been called **epistemic communities** (knowledge-based communities). For example, the transnational community of experts and policy makers concerned with pollution in the Mediterranean is an epistemic community.

In global environmental politics, it is hard to manage collective goods problems because of the large number of actors. Collective goods are easier to provide in small groups, where individual actions have more impact on the total picture and where cheating is more noticeable. The opposite is true with the environment. The actions of nearly 200 states (albeit some more than others) aggregate to cause indirect but serious

Too Many Cooks Management of environmental issues is complicated by the large numbers of actors involved, which make collective goods problems hard to resolve (individuals may be more tempted to free-ride). Here is the negotiating table at the 1992 "Earth Summit" (UN Conference on Environment and Development) in Rio de Janeiro, Brazil. It was the largest gathering of state leaders in history.

Web Link
Earth Summit

consequences throughout the world. This large number of actors was seen in the 1992 *UN Conference on Environment and Development* (the *"Earth Summit"*) in Rio de Janeiro, Brazil; it was the largest summit meeting of state leaders ever, more than a hundred in all.

With a few exceptions, only in the last two decades has the global environment become a major subject of international negotiation and of IR scholarship. Interest in the environment has grown rapidly since the first "Earth Day" was held by environmental activists in 1970. The energy crises of the 1970s seemed to underline the issue in industrialized regions. Oil spills, urban air pollution, pesticide residues, and difficulties at nuclear power plants elevated the environment on the international agenda.

Sustainable Economic Development At the 1992 Earth Summit, the major theme was *sustainable* economic development. This refers to economic growth that does not deplete resources and destroy ecosystems so quickly that the basis of that economic growth is itself undermined. The concept applies to both the industrialized regions and the global South.

In the past, the growth of population, industry, energy use, and the extraction of natural resources on the planet has been exponential—growing faster and faster over time. Such exponential growth cannot continue indefinitely. Several possibilities emerge. First, new technologies may allow *unabated economic growth* but may shift the basis of that growth away from the ever-increasing use of energy and other resources. This is what optimists with faith in technology expect. Goods and services would continue to multiply, raising the global standard of living, but would do so efficiently to reduce strains on the environment.

A second possibility is a *collapse* of population and living standards in the world, as excessive growth leads to ecological disaster. Pessimists worry that the present course will overshoot the **carrying capacity** of the planetary ecosystem and cause ecosystems to break down because of long-term environmental problems such as species depletion and global warming. By the time such problems produced severe short-term effects, it would be too late to correct them.

A third possibility is that the past curve of exponential growth will flatten out to form an *S-curve*. The curve rises from a fairly flat slope to an exponential growth curve and then levels off back to a flat slope (at a higher level). Instead of overshooting the planet's limits (triggering collapse), human beings would adapt to those limits in time to achieve a *steady-state* economy in which population, food production, energy use, and other key processes were stable from year to year. In this scenario, the key task of our generation would be to adapt our economics and our politics, including IR, to level out into a sustainable long-term relationship with the environment.

The Earth Summit produced an overall plan, called A*genda 21*, whereby large third world states promise to industrialize along cleaner lines (at a certain cost to economic growth) and industrialized states promise to funnel aid and technology to them to assist in that process. The Earth Summit also established the **Sustainable Development Commission**; it monitors states' compliance with the promises they made at the Earth Summit and hears evidence from environmental NGOs such as Greenpeace. But it lacks powers of enforcement over national governments—again reflecting the preeminence of state sovereignty over supranational authority (see pp. 277, 297–299). Of the 53 Commission members, 19 are from the industrialized regions, 12 from Africa, 12 from Asia, and 10 from Latin America. It was hoped that the Commission's ability to monitor and publicize state actions would discourage states from cheating on the Earth Summit plan. But the Commission's first meeting, two years after the meeting, found the states of the global North providing only half of the level of financial support pledged for sustainable development in the South. Funding for sustainable development in the global South—a collective good—continued to lag throughout the 1990s.

China and other developing countries in Asia stood at the center of the debate over sustainable development. In the drive for rapid economic growth, these countries have cut corners environmentally, resulting in the world's worst air pollution and other serious problems. China is building the Three Gorges Dam, which will be the world's largest hydroelectric station; it provides a clean source of energy in a coal-burning country, but environmentalists fear it will damage a large river ecosystem. Because of China's size, any success in developing its economy along Western industrialized lines (for example, with widespread ownership of automobiles) could create massive shocks to the global environment. Yet no practical alternative has been articulated.

Atlas CD
Three
Gorges Dam
Photo

Rethinking Interdependence
We have thus far treated international environmental issues as problems of interstate bargaining, an approach that reflects a neoliberal theoretical orientation. This approach has been challenged in recent years by an emerging theoretical framework that is more revolutionary in orientation, seeking

Not Sustainable   Pollution from Soviet industrialization caused great environmental damage, contributing to the stagnation and collapse of the Soviet economy—an unsustainable path. This steel plant in Novokuznetsk, Siberia, Russia, exemplifies the problem (1992 photo). Today's third world countries will have to industrialize along cleaner lines to realize sustainable development.

more fundamental change in the nature of the international community's approach to environmental problems. This approach is well reflected in the grassroots activism of Greenpeace and other environment-related NGOs. Environmentalists object to free trade provisions that weaken environmental standards by empowering international bureaucrats who care more about wealth generation than eco-preservation (see p. 417). Similarly, environmental groups have objected to management of economic development in the global South by international institutions, in particular the World Bank.

This more revolutionary theoretical perspective rejects the liberal goal of maximizing wealth (see pp. 210–212). Although liberal concepts of rationality are longer term than conservative ones (see p. 85), environmentalists take an even broader and longer term view. From this perspective, the collective goods problem among states is not the problem; it is the growth of industrial civilization out of balance with the planetary ecosystem that must ultimately support it. True rationality, for environmentalists, must include very long-term calculations about how the self-interest of humanity itself is undermined by a greedy drive to exploit nature—that is, interdependence and the collective goods problem are broadened to include humanity versus nature, not just state versus state.

Managing the Environment

The next two sections of the chapter will focus primarily on interstate bargaining processes concerning the environment, but will include the broader forces of concern to environmentalists. As these forces shape the contexts for interstate bargaining, they must be of concern even to liberals and conservatives. In discussing the issue areas in which states are bargaining over environmental problems, we begin with the most global problems—those that are collective goods for all states and people in the world.

The Atmosphere Preserving the health of the earth's atmosphere is a benefit that affects people throughout the world without regard for their own state's contribution to the problem or its solution. Two problems of the atmosphere have become major international issues—global warming and depletion of the ozone layer.

Atlas CD
Air Pollution, Global Warming
Article, Photos

GLOBAL WARMING Global climate change, or **global warming**, is a slow, long-term rise in the average world temperature. Scientists are not certain that such a rise is occurring, or how fast if so, but there is growing evidence that global warming is a real problem, that it is caused by the emission of carbon dioxide and other gases, and that it will get worse in the future. Many scientists believe it to be prudent to address the problem soon, because once the symptoms become obvious it will be too late to prevent disaster.

Web Link
Global Warming

It is not easy to guess who will be harmed and how soon. But over the next 50 years, according to most estimates, global temperatures may rise by between two and nine degrees Fahrenheit if nothing is done. The high end of this temperature range corresponds with the difference between today's climate and that of the last ice age; it is a major climate change. Possibly within a few decades the polar ice caps would begin to melt and cause the sea level to rise by as much as a few feet. Such a rise could flood many coastal cities and devastate low-lying areas such as the heavily populated coastal plains of Bangladesh. Among the most urgent voices calling for action to avert global warming are island states in the Pacific, which could be wiped off the map.

Atlas CD
Global Warming, Threat to Maldives
Photo

Global climate change could also change weather patterns in many regions, causing droughts, floods, and widespread disruption of natural ecosystems. It is also possible that climate changes (at least mild ones) could *benefit* some regions and make agriculture more productive. Nobody knows for sure, but sudden environmental changes are usually much more destructive than helpful.

It is very difficult to reduce the emissions of gases—mainly carbon dioxide—that cause global warming. These gases result from the broad spectrum of activities that drive an industrial economy. They are a by-product of burning **fossil fuels**—oil, coal, and natural gas—to run cars, tractors, furnaces, factories, and so forth. These activities create **greenhouse gases**—so named because when concentrated in the atmosphere these gases act like the glass in a greenhouse: they let energy in as short-wavelength solar radiation but reflect it back when it tries to exit again as longer-wavelength heat waves. The greenhouse gases are *carbon dioxide* (responsible for two-thirds of the effect), *methane gas, chlorofluorocarbons (CFCs),* and *nitrous oxide.* The concentration of these gases in the global atmosphere is slowly increasing, though the rates and processes involved are complicated.

Thus, the costs of reducing the greenhouse effect are high, because the solutions entail curbing economic growth or shifting it onto entirely new technological paths.

THE INFORMATION REVOLUTION   Silicon Versus Fossil Fuels?

The industrial revolution, which harnessed fossil fuels to power machinery, changed IR profoundly (see pp. 29–30). Now, perhaps, a comparable revolution in technology is driving world events in new directions. Some call information- and service-based economies "postindustrial." Is the information revolution the endpoint of industrialization and, if so, can the global South bypass industrialization and the global North decrease its energy use, thus reducing global warming?

To explore this question, go to www.IRtext.com

The political costs of such actions—which would likely increase unemployment, reduce corporate profits, and lower personal incomes—could be severe. For example, as the U.S. government headed to global warming negotiations in 1997, it faced lobbying against the proposed treaty by a powerful coalition of big business, labor unions, and agriculture. "The only thing this treaty will cool down is the U.S. economy," they argued. In the short term, they were right, since costs would take effect within years but benefits would materialize decades into the future (and are hard to quantify).

For individual states, the costs of reducing greenhouse emissions are almost unrelated to the benefits of a solution. If one state reduces its industrial production or makes expensive investments in new technologies, this will have little effect on the long-term outcome unless other states do likewise. And if most states took such steps, a free rider that did not go along would save money and still benefit from the solution.

Global warming thus presents states with a triple dilemma. First, there is the dilemma of short-term (and predictable) costs to gain long-term (and less predictable) benefits. Second, specific constituencies such as oil companies and industrial workers pay the costs, whereas the benefits are distributed more generally across domestic society. Third, there is the collective goods dilemma among states: benefits are shared globally but costs must be extracted from each state individually.

This third dilemma is complicated by the North-South divide, which creates divergent expectations about fair allocation of costs. Specifically, how can the industrialization of today's poor countries take place without pushing greenhouse emissions to unacceptable levels? Greenhouse gases are produced by each state roughly in proportion to its industrial activity. Eighty percent of greenhouse gases now come from the industrialized countries—25 percent from the United States alone. Yet the most severe impacts of global warming are likely to be felt in the global South. Naturally, serious international conflicts exist over who should pay the bills to avert global warming.

All of these elements make for a difficult multilateral bargaining situation, one not yet resolved. The *Framework Convention on Climate Change* adopted at the 1992 Earth Summit set a nonbinding goal, to limit greenhouse emissions to 1990 levels by the year 2000; that goal has not been met. The treaty did not commit the signatory states to meet target levels of greenhouse emissions by a particular date, owing to U.S. objections to such a commitment. Western Europe and Japan have been more willing to regulate greenhouse emissions than is the United States (which burns more fossil fuel per person). Europe and Japan later proposed a binding treaty requiring all states to stabilize their emissions at 1990 levels by the year 2000, and then reduce them 15 percent further by 2010. The United States modified its position in 1996, supporting a binding treaty, but with a target date of 2010 to reach 1990 levels and no subsequent targets.

The 1997 *Kyoto Protocol* adopted a complex formula for reducing greenhouse emissions to 1990 levels in the global North over about a decade. Countries in the global South received preferential treatment, however, since their levels (per capita) were much lower. Yet China in the 1990s was the world's second-largest producer of carbon dioxide (after the United States), and India the sixth largest (after Russia, Japan, and Germany). Objecting to this "free ride," the U.S. Congress promptly declared that it would not ratify the treaty. The dilemma of global warming thus remains fundamentally unsolved, and with no enforcement mechanism it is questionable whether states that signed the Kyoto Protocol will in fact meet their targets on schedule, if ever.

Technology may help to make the bargaining a bit easier in the future. Many technical experts now argue that dramatic gains can be made through energy efficiency measures and other solutions that do not reduce the amount of economic activity but do make it cleaner and more efficient. Although costly, such investments would ultimately pay for themselves through greater economic efficiency. If this approach succeeds, international conflicts over global warming will be reduced.

Japanese leaders think their country can profit by gaining a comparative advantage in environmental technologies. The government- and industry-funded *Research Institute of Innovative Technology for the Earth (RITE)* is developing methods to filter carbon dioxide out of industrial exhausts. RITE is part of a MITI campaign (called *New Earth 21*) to coordinate a movement of Japanese industry into environmental technologies.

The **UN Environment Program (UNEP)**, whose main function is to monitor environmental conditions, works with the World Meteorological Organization to measure changes in global climate from year to year. Since 1989 the UN-sponsored *Intergovernmental Panel on Climate Change* has served as a negotiating forum for this issue.

Web Link
Intergovernmental Panel on Climate Change

OZONE DEPLETION A second major atmospheric problem being negotiated by the world's governments is the depletion of the world's **ozone layer**. Ozone high in the atmosphere screens out harmful ultraviolet rays from the sun. Certain chemicals expelled by industrial economies float up to the top of the atmosphere and interact with ozone in a way that breaks it down. The chief culprits are CFCs, widely used in refrigeration and in aerosol sprays. (Unfortunately, ozone produced by burning fossil fuels does not replace the high-level ozone but only pollutes the lower atmosphere.)

As the ozone layer thins, more ultraviolet radiation is reaching the earth's surface. Over Antarctica, where the ozone is thinnest, a hole in the ozone appears to be growing larger and lasting longer year by year. Depleted ozone levels over North America were detected in the early 1990s, and people have been warned to limit exposure to the sun to lower the risk of skin cancer. Eventually, the increased radiation could begin to kill off vegetation, reduce agricultural yields, and disrupt entire ecosystems.

Clearly, this is another collective goods problem in that one state benefits from allowing the use of CFCs in its economy, provided that most other states prohibit their use. But the costs of replacing CFCs are much lower than the costs of addressing global

Melting Away International treaties have been much more successful at addressing ozone depletion than global warming, mostly because the costs of the latter are much higher and the results are further in the future. A 1997 conference in Kyoto, Japan, set goals for industrialized countries to reduce their output of carbon dioxide and related gases modestly over the next decade, but it is doubtful that the goals will be met. Here, U.S. Vice President Al Gore tries to dramatize the problem of global warming just before the Kyoto conference, by standing in front of a slowly melting glacier in Glacier National Park, Montana. If global warming similarly melts polar ice caps in the twenty-first century, sea levels could rise and devastate many cities.

warming: CFCs can be replaced with other chemicals at relatively modest costs. Furthermore, the consequences of ozone depletion are both better understood and more immediate than those of global warming.

Therefore, states have had more success in negotiating agreements and developing regimes to manage the ozone problem. In the 1987 **Montreal Protocol**, 22 states agreed to reduce CFCs by 50 percent by 1998. In 1990, the timetable was accelerated and the signatories were expanded: 81 states agreed to eliminate all CFCs by 2000. In 1992, as evidence of ozone depletion mounted, the schedule was again accelerated, with major industrial states phasing out CFCs by 1995. The signatories agreed in principle to establish a fund (of unspecified size and source) to help third world states pay for alternative refrigeration technologies not based on CFCs. Without such an effort, the third world states would be tempted to free-ride and could ultimately undermine the effort. These countries were also given until 2010 to phase out production. But with payments by rich countries lagging, and an emerging black market in CFCs, it was far from certain that countries in the global South would succeed in cutting out CFCs. By the mid-

1990s, China had the world's largest CFC emissions by far; the top ten included Mexico, Brazil, Thailand, India, and Argentina (but not the United States).

The Montreal Protocol on CFCs is the most important success yet achieved in international negotiations to preserve the global environment. It showed that states can agree to take action on urgent environmental threats, can agree on targets and measures to counter such threats, and can allocate the costs of such measures in a mutually acceptable way. Recent measurements of CFCs in the atmosphere show that the yearly rate of increase has slowed down—a promising start. But the international cooperation on the ozone problem has not been widely repeated on other environmental issues.

Biodiversity **Biodiversity** refers to the tremendous diversity of plant and animal species making up the earth's (global, regional, and local) ecosystems. Biologists believe that the 1.4 million species they have identified and named are only a small fraction of the total number of species in existence (most of which are microorganisms). Some species, such as humans, are distributed broadly around the world, whereas others live in just one locale.

Due to humans' destruction of ecosystems, large numbers of species are already *extinct* and others are in danger of becoming so. Extinct species can never return. The causes of their extinction include overhunting, overfishing, and introducing non-native species that crowd out previous inhabitants. But the most important cause is *loss of habitat*—the destruction of rain forests, pollution of lakes and streams, and loss of agricultural lands to urban sprawl. Because ecosystems are based on complex and often fragile interrelationships among species, the extinction of a few species can cause deeper changes in the environment. For example, the loss of native microorganisms can lead to chronic pollution of rivers, or to the transformation of arable land into deserts.

Atlas CD
Threatened
Species and
Habitats
Video

Because ecosystems are so complex, it is usually impossible to predict the consequences of a species' extinction or of the loss of a habitat or ecosystem. Generally the activities that lead to habitat loss are economically profitable, so there are real costs associated with limiting such activities. For example, logging in the U.S. Northwest has been restricted to save the northern spotted owl from extinction. Nobody can be sure what effect the owl's extinction would have, but the costs to loggers are clear and immediate.

Species preservation is thus a collective good resembling global warming; the costs are immediate and substantial but the benefits are long term and ill defined. As to biodiversity, the effects of policies tend to be more local than those of global warming, so the problem to some degree can be enclosed within the purview of states. But to a surprising extent the biodiversity in one state affects the quality of the environment in other states. Topsoil blown away in Africa is deposited in South America; monarch butterflies that failed to breed in Mexico in 1991 did not appear in New England in 1992.

Web Link
Species
Preservation

It has been difficult to reach international agreement on sharing the costs of preserving biodiversity. A UN convention on trade in endangered species has reduced but not eliminated such trade. At the 1992 Earth Summit, a treaty on biodiversity was adopted that committed signatories to preserving habitats, and got rich states to pay poor ones for the rights to use commercially profitable biological products extracted from rare species in protected habitats (such as medicines from rain forest trees). However, because of fears that it could limit U.S. patent rights in biotechnology, the United States did not sign the treaty. Later it agreed to sign, with stipulations, but by 1999 it was the only industrialized country that had not ratified the treaty.

Many environmentalists have a special concern for whales and dolphins, which like humans are large-brained mammals. In the past 20 years, environmental activists have gotten states to agree to international regimes to protect whales and dolphins. The **International Whaling Commission** (an IGO) sets quotas for hunting certain whale species; participation is voluntary, and Norway dropped out in 1992 when it decided unilaterally that it could increase its catch without endangering the species. The *Inter-American Tropical Tuna Commission* (another IGO) regulates methods used to fish for tuna, aiming to minimize dolphin losses.

The United States, which consumes half the world's tuna catch, has gone further and unilaterally requires—in the Marine Mammal Protection Act—that "dolphin-safe" methods be used for tuna sold in U.S. territory. Under this law, the United States in 1990 banned imports of tuna from Mexico and Venezuela. These countries, which could not comply with the U.S. law as easily as the U.S. tuna industry could, took their case to the GATT (see pp. 231–234) and won. But the United States did not comply with the GATT ruling, despite appeals from the EC and dozens of other states. Venezuela's tuna fleet was reduced to less than a third of its former size.

Such conflicts portend future battles between environmentalists and free-trade advocates. Free traders argue that states must not use domestic legislation to seek global environmental goals. Environmentalists do not want to give up national laws that they worked for decades to enact, over the opposition of industrial corporations. Environmentalists adopted the sea turtle as a symbol of their opposition to the WTO after the WTO overturned U.S. regulations that required shrimp to be caught in nets from which sea turtles (an endangered species) can escape. The WTO's actions in cases such as the shrimp dispute are based on unfair *application* of environmental rules to domestic versus foreign companies. In practical terms, however, the effect is negative from environmentalists' perspective.

In recent years, most spectacularly at the WTO's failed 1999 Seattle summit, a coalition of U.S. environmental groups campaigned against the "faceless bureaucrats" at the WTO who override national laws such as the tuna act; these bureaucrats are portrayed as agents of the MNCs, out to increase profits with no regard for the environment. (Note the similarity to earlier popular European resistance to "faceless Eurocrats.") Conflicts are developing over U.S. laws restricting imports of foods with pesticide residues, and over European laws on imports of genetically engineered agricultural and pharmaceutical products, which the United States wants to export worldwide. Environmentalists fear that the successful Montreal Protocol on ozone protection, which relies on trade sanctions for enforcement, could be threatened by new WTO agreements.

Thus, unilateral approaches to biodiversity issues are problematical because they disrupt free trade; multilateral approaches are problematical because of the collective goods problem. It is not surprising that the international response to species extinction has been fairly ineffective to date.

Forests and Oceans

Two types of habitat—tropical rain forests and oceans—are especially important to biodiversity *and* the atmosphere. Both are also reservoirs of commercially profitable resources such as fish and wood. They differ in that forests exist almost entirely within state territory, but oceans are largely beyond any state territory, in the global commons.

RAIN FORESTS As many as half the world's total species live in *rain forests*; they replenish oxygen and reduce carbon dioxide in the atmosphere—slowing down global warming. Rain forests thus benefit all the world's states; they are collective goods.

Atlas CD
Southeast Asia
Forests
Map

International bargaining on the preservation of rain forests has made considerable progress, probably because most rain forests belong to a few states. These few states have the power to speed up or slow down the destruction of forests—and international bargaining amounts to agreements to shift costs from those few states onto the broader group of states benefiting from the rain forests. This collective goods problem is simpler and has fewer actors than the global warming problem.

Although some rich states (including the United States) have large forests, most of the largest rain forests are in poor states such as Brazil, Indonesia and Malaysia, and Madagascar. Such states can benefit economically from exploiting the forests—freely cutting lumber, clearing land for agriculture, and mining. Until recently (and still to an extent), leaders of rich states have been most interested in encouraging maximum economic growth in poor states so that foreign debts could be paid—with little regard for environmental damage.

Atlas CD
Deforestation
Video

Now that rich states have an interest in protecting rain forests, they are using money and development assistance as leverage to induce poorer states to protect their forests rather than exploiting them maximally. Under international agreements of the early 1990s, rich countries are contributing hundreds of millions of dollars in foreign aid for this purpose. In some third world countries burdened by large foreign debts, environmentalists and bankers from rich countries have worked out "debt-for-nature swaps" in which a debt is canceled in exchange for the state's agreement to preserve forests.

Brazil in particular has responded to these agreements with significant steps. A major government-sponsored drive to settle and exploit the Amazon basin had begun in the 1960s. In the early 1990s, the government adopted sweeping new policies to balance economic exploitation of the Amazon basin with the needs of environmental preservation and the rights of indigenous peoples. Although the rain forest problem has not been solved, and thousands of square miles of forest continue to be destroyed each year, there is widespread awareness of the problem and creative efforts are being made to solve it.

For example, Cultural Survival, a U.S.-based activist group, has developed creative ways to preserve native cultures and their environments. One idea is to make the rain forest economically profitable in its native state so that people do not need to cut down the trees to make money. Cultural Survival has helped Brazilian nut gatherers form cooperatives and build a shelling factory. The nuts are shipped to Vermont and made into a brittle candy that goes into Ben and Jerry's "Rain Forest Crunch" ice cream. Such products satisfy the interests of U.S. consumers, Brazilian forest inhabitants, and the global environment.

OCEANS The oceans, covering 70 percent of the earth's surface, are (like the rain forest) a key to regulating climate and preserving biodiversity. Oceans, like forests, are attractive targets for short-term economic uses that cause long-term environmental damage. Such uses include overfishing, dumping toxic and nuclear waste (and other garbage), and long-distance oil shipments with their recurrent spills. Unlike rain forests, oceans belong to no state but are a global commons. This makes the collective goods problem more difficult because no authority exists to enforce regulations. Preserving the oceans depends on the cooperation of more than a hundred states and thousands of nonstate actors.

Free riders have great opportunities to profit. For example, *drift nets* are huge fishing nets, miles long, that scoop up everything in their path. They are very profitable but destructive of a sustainable ocean environment. Most states have now banned their use (under pressure from the environmental movement). However, no state has the authority to go onto the **high seas** (nonterritorial waters) and stop illegal use of these nets.

One solution that states have pursued involves "enclosing" more of the ocean. Territorial waters have expanded to hundreds of miles off the coast (and around islands), so that state sovereignty encloses substantial resources (fisheries and offshore oil and mineral deposits). This solution has been pursued in the context of larger multilateral negotiations on ocean management.

Those negotiations centered on the **UN Convention on the Law of the Sea (UNCLOS)** from 1973 to 1982. Building on two earlier rounds, this conference created a world treaty governing uses of the oceans. The UNCLOS treaty established rules on territorial waters—12 miles for shipping and 200 miles for economic activities, such as fishing and mining. The 200-mile limit placed a substantial share of the economically profitable ocean resources in the control of about a dozen states (see Figure 8.1).

A conflict developed over a small piece of the continental shelf off Newfoundland that was just beyond the 200-mile range controlled by Canada. The Canadian Navy harassed Spanish fishing ships there, which the Canadians claimed were overfishing and endangering fish populations that were mostly within the 200-mile limit. Although the European Union accused Canada of "piracy" on the high seas, the two sides in 1995 reached an agreement on fishing levels and practices. The agreement in turn stimulated progress in UN talks that had been trying to develop global rules and norms for ocean fishing. (These talks reached no quick breakthrough, however.) Similar conflicts may develop near Norway, West Africa, the South Pacific, and the Indian Ocean.

UNCLOS also developed the general principle that the oceans are a common heritage of humankind. A mechanism was created, through an International Sea-Bed Authority, for sharing some of the wealth that rich states might gain from extracting minerals on the ocean floor (beyond 200 miles).

The UNCLOS treaty faced uncertain prospects when the United States decided not to sign the treaty, believing that their country bore too great a share of the costs in the plan. The United States is the dominant naval power with de facto military control in much of the world's ocean space. It is also the state most likely to benefit from unilateral deep-sea mining. It was not willing to underwrite the costs of providing the collective good of ocean management. After more than a decade's delay and renegotiation of some of the deep-sea mining aspects, the United States signed UNCLOS in 1994.

Private environmental groups have been active players on oceans, as in rain forests—pressuring governments and MNCs to change policies and activities. Tactics include direct action (such as Greenpeace ships shadowing garbage barges), lobbying, lawsuits, and public education. These tactics have effectively used global communications—a dramatic event videotaped in a remote location on the high seas can be shown on millions of TV sets.

ANTARCTICA Like the oceans, Antarctica belongs to no state. The continent's strategic and commercial value are limited, however, and not many states care about it. Thus, states have been successful in reaching agreements on Antarctica because the costs were

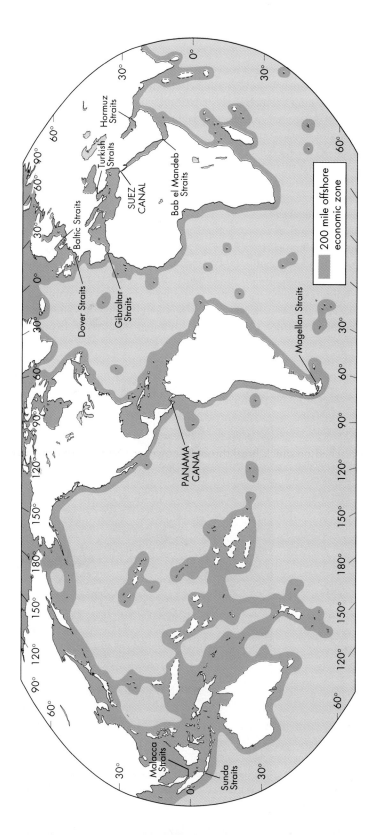

FIGURE 8.1 State-Controlled Waters Overfishing and similar problems of managing the "commons" of world oceans have been addressed by enclosing the most important
ocean areas under the exclusive control of states. Shaded areas are within the 200-mile
economic zones controlled by states under terms of the UNCLOS treaty.

Source: Adapted from Andrew Boyd, *An Atlas of World Affairs,* 9th ed. New York: Routledge, 1992.

low and the players few. The **Antarctic Treaty of 1959**—one of the first multilateral treaties concerning the environment—forbids military activity as well as the presence of nuclear weapons or the dumping of nuclear waste in Antarctica. It sets aside territorial claims on the continent for future resolution and establishes a regime under which various states conduct scientific research in Antarctica. The treaty was signed by all states with interests in the area, including both superpowers. By 1991, Greenpeace had convinced the treaty signatories to turn the continent into a "world park." Antarctica is largely a success story in international environmental politics.

Pollution   Pollution generally creates a collective goods problem, but one that is not often global in scale. Pollution is more often a regional or bilateral issue. With some exceptions—such as dumping at sea—the effects of pollution are limited to the state where it occurs and its close neighbors. For example, U.S. industrial smokestack emissions affect acid rain in Canada but do not directly affect distant states. Even when pollution crosses state borders, it often has its strongest effects closest to the source. This makes it a somewhat less intractable collective goods problem, because a polluting state can seldom get an entirely free ride, and there are a limited number of actors. The

Poisoned Waters   Pollution easily crosses national borders. For example, this spill of cyanide from a Romanian gold mine in 2000 killed off fish in Hungary and Serbia downstream. Pollution's effects are mainly regional rather than global in scope, however, reducing the collective goods problem somewhat.

effects of pollution also are not distant abstractions such as global warming.

In several regions—notably Western and Eastern Europe and the Middle East—states are closely packed in the same air, river, or sea basins. Here, pollution controls must often be negotiated multilaterally. In Europe during the Cold War, the international pollution problem was exacerbated by the inability of Western European states to impose any limits on Eastern ones, whose pollution was notorious. These problems are only now being addressed.

Atlas CD
Czech
Coal Mine
Photo

Several regional agreements seek to limit **acid rain**, caused by air pollution. Acid rain often crosses borders. European states—whose forests have been heavily damaged—have agreed to limit air pollution and acid rain for their mutual benefit. In 1988, 24 European states signed a treaty to limit nitrogen oxide emissions to 1988 levels by 1995. After long negotiations, the United States and Canada have signed bilateral agreements to limit such pollution as well. These regional agreements have worked fairly well.

Water pollution often crosses borders as well, especially because industrial pollution, human sewage, and agricultural fertilizers and pesticides all tend to run into rivers and seas. Long-standing international regional agencies that regulate shipping on heavily used European rivers now also deal with pollution. The Mediterranean basin is severely polluted, and difficult to manage because so many states border it. The Great Lakes on the U.S.-Canadian border had become heavily polluted by the 1970s. But because the issue affected only two countries, it was easier to address, and the situation has improved in recent years.

Toxic and *nuclear wastes* are a special problem because of their long-term dangers. States occasionally try to ship such wastes out of the country. International agreements now ban the dumping of toxic and nuclear wastes at sea (an obvious collective goods problem). But such wastes have been sent to third world countries for disposal, for a fee. For instance, toxic ash from Pennsylvania became material for bricks in Guinea, and Italian nuclear waste was shipped to Nigeria.

Atlas CD
Toxic Waste
Cleanup in
Newark
Photo

Norms have developed in recent years against exporting toxic wastes—a practice seen as exploitive of the receiving country. In 1989, 100 states signed a treaty under UN auspices to regulate shipments of toxic and nuclear wastes and prevent their secret movements under corrupt deals. Forty more countries, in Africa, did not sign the treaty but called for a complete halt to toxic waste shipments to Africa.

In 1986, a meltdown at the Soviet nuclear power plant at **Chernobyl**, in Ukraine, created airborne radioactivity that spread over much of Europe, from Italy to Sweden. The accident exemplified the new reality—that economic and technical decisions taken in one state can have grave environmental consequences for other countries. Soviet leaders made matters worse by failing to notify neighbors promptly of the accident.

Web Link
Chernobyl

On the various issues of water and air pollution, both unilateral state actions and international agreements have often been feasible and effective. In recent decades, river water quality has improved in most industrialized regions. Market economies have begun to deal with pollution as just another cost of production that should be charged to the polluter instead of to society at large. Some governments have begun to allocate "pollution rights" that companies can buy and sell on a free market.

In the former Soviet bloc, decades of centrally planned industrialization have created more severe environmental problems, which may prove more intractable. With staggering environmental damage and human health effects, the economically strapped former Soviet republics must bargain over limiting pollution and repairing the damage. For example, the severely polluted Aral Sea, formerly contained within one state, the Soviet Union, is now shared by two, Kazakhstan and Uzbekistan. Once the world's fourth largest inland sea, it has shrunk in half, its huge fisheries destroyed, after a Soviet-era mega-irrigation project diverted the Aral Sea's inlet rivers and polluted them with pesticides. Former fishing towns found themselves dozens of miles away from the shoreline. In the 1990s, environmentalists gave up efforts to save the Aral Sea, after local and international political leaders failed to implement plans to address the problem. Local populations suffered from widespread health effects of the disaster. Decisions by the former Soviet republics to keep operating old and unsafe nuclear power reactors, as well as the problems associated with dismantling nuclear weapons, also add to the region's long environmental agenda.

Atlas CD
Aral Sea
Shrinkage
Landsat Photos

Natural Resources

The natural environment is not only a delicate ecosystem requiring protection; it is also a repository of natural resources. The extraction of resources brings states wealth (and hence power), so these resources regularly become a source of international conflict. Because they are mostly located within individual states, they do not present a collective goods problem. Rather, states bargain (with leverage) as to these vital resources.

Three aspects of natural resources shape their role in international conflict. First, they are required for the operation of an industrial economy (sometimes even an agrarian one). Second, their sources—mineral deposits, rivers, and so forth—are associated with particular territories over which states may fight for control. Third, natural resources tend to be unevenly distributed, with plentiful supplies in some states and an absence in others. These aspects mean that trade in natural resources is extremely profitable; much additional wealth is created by such trade. They also mean that trade in resources is fairly politicized—creating market imperfections such as monopoly, oligopoly, price manipulation, and so on (see pp. 218–219).

World Energy Of the various natural resources required by states, energy resources (fuels) are central. The commercial fuels that power the world's industrial economies are oil (about 40 percent of world energy consumption), coal (30 percent), natural gas (25 percent), and hydroelectric and nuclear power (5 percent). The fossil fuels (coal, oil, gas) thus account for 95 percent of world energy consumption. (Some energy consumed as electricity comes from hydroelectric dams or nuclear power plants, but most of it comes from burning fossil fuels in electric-generating plants.)

Imagine a pile of coal weighing 24,000 pounds (11 metric tons, about the weight of ten automobiles). The energy released by burning that much coal is equivalent to the amount of energy North Americans use per person each year. Wealthier people, of course, consume more energy per person than do poorer people, but 11 tons is the average.

Table 8.1 shows energy consumption per person in the nine world regions. The four industrialized regions of the North use much more energy per person than those of the South. North America uses 30 times as much as Asia or Africa, because Asia and Africa have little industry. Among industrialized countries there are differences in the *efficiency* of energy use—GDP produced per unit of energy consumed. The least efficient

TABLE 8.1 Per Capita Energy Consumption and Net Energy Trade

1995, In Coal Equivalent

	Per Capita Consumption (metric tons)	Total Net Energy Exports[a] (million metric tons)
North America	11	–400
Western Europe	5	–630
Japan/Pacific	5	–550
Russia & Eastern Europe	5	+300
China	1.0	+50
Middle East	1.8	+1,400
Latin America	1.4	+260
South Asia	0.4	+60
Africa	0.3	+220
World as a whole	2.1	

[a] Net exports refers to production minus consumption. Net exports worldwide do not equal net imports for technical reasons.

Source: Calculated from data in United Nations, *1995 Energy Statistics Yearbook* (New York: United Nations, 1997).

are Russia and Eastern Europe (even before that region's current economic depression); North America is also rather inefficient; Europe and Japan are the most energy efficient.

International trade in energy plays a vital role in the world economy. As Table 8.1 shows, the regions of the industrialized West are all net importers of energy. Together they import from the rest of the world, each year, energy equivalent to 1.6 billion tons of coal. The other six world regions are net exporters of energy.

Although all forms of energy are traded internationally, the most important by far is oil, the cheapest to transport over long distances. Russia and Eastern Europe receive vital hard currency earnings from exporting oil. Venezuela and Mexico (in Latin America) and Nigeria and Angola (in Africa) are major oil exporters. But by far the largest source of oil exports is the Middle East—especially the countries around the Persian Gulf (Saudi Arabia, Kuwait, Iraq, Iran, and the small sheikdoms of United Arab Emirates, Qatar, Bahrain, and Oman). Saudi Arabia is the largest oil exporter and sits atop the largest oil reserves (see Table 5.1 on p. 238). The politics of world energy revolve around Middle East oil shipped to Western Europe, Japan/Pacific, and North America.

The importance of oil in the industrialized economies helps to explain the political importance of the Middle East in world politics. Iraq's 1990 invasion of Kuwait (and the mere possibility that Iraq's army could move into Saudi Arabia) threatened the West's access to stable, inexpensive supplies of oil. World oil prices immediately more than doubled. But Saudi Arabia could increase its own rate of oil exports massively enough to compensate for both Kuwaiti and Iraqi exports cut off during the invasion and the UN sanctions against Iraq. When it became clear that Saudi exports would not be disrupted, the price of oil dropped again on world markets. Thus, not only is energy a crucial economic sector (on which all industrial activity depends), but it is also one of the

Web Link
Oil and
International
Relations

most politically sensitive (because of the dependence of the West on energy imported from the Middle East and other third world regions).

To secure a supply of oil in the Middle East, Britain and other European countries colonized the area early this century, carving up territory into protectorates in which European power kept local monarchs on their thrones. (Iraq, for instance, argues that Kuwait is part of Iraq, that it was cut off and made into a separate state by the British.) The United States did not claim colonies or protectorates, but U.S. MNCs were heavily involved in the development of oil resources in the area from the 1920s through the 1960s—often wielding vast power. Local rulers depended on the expertise and capital investment of U.S. and European oil companies. The "seven sisters"—a cartel of Western oil companies—kept the price paid to local states low and their own profits high.

After World War II the British gave up colonial claims in the Middle East, but the Western oil companies kept producing cheap oil there for Western consumption. Then in 1973, during an Arab-Israeli war, the oil-producing Arab states of the region decided to punish the United States for supporting Israel. They cut off their oil exports to the United States and curtailed their overall exports. This sent world oil prices skyrocketing. OPEC realized its potential power and the high price the world was willing to pay for oil. After the war ended, OPEC agreed to limit production to keep oil prices high.

The 1973 **oil shock** had a profound effect on the world economy and on world politics. Huge amounts of hard currency accumulated in the treasuries of the Middle East oil-exporting countries, which in turn invested them around the world (these were called *petrodollars*). High inflation plagued the United States and Europe for years afterward. The economic instability and sense of U.S. helplessness—coming on top of the Vietnam debacle—seemed to mark a decline in American power and perhaps the rise of the third world.

In 1979, the revolution in Iran led to another major increase in oil prices. This second oil shock further weakened the industrialized economies. But these economies were already adjusting to the new realities of world energy. Higher oil prices led to the expansion of oil production in new locations outside of OPEC—in the North Sea (Britain and Norway), Alaska, Angola, Russia, and elsewhere. By the mid-1980s, the Middle East was rapidly losing its market share of world trade in oil. At the same time, industrialized economies learned to be more *energy efficient*. After drifting down toward $10 per barrel, however, oil prices shot up to around $30 by early 2000, because Asian economic recovery stimulated demand.

Because of market adjustments following high oil prices, the industrialized West is now somewhat less dependent on Middle East oil and the power of OPEC has been greatly reduced. Still, energy continues to be a crucial issue in which the Middle East plays a key role.

Atlas CD
Caspian Sea
Region
Map

In the late 1990s, the Caspian Sea region beckoned as a new and largely untapped oil source (see Figure 8.2). However, international politics and geography hampered the development of this zone. The oil must travel overland by pipeline to reach world markets (the Caspian is an inland sea). But the main pipeline from oil-producing Azerbaijan to the Black Sea (where tanker ships can load) travels through war-torn Chechnya in southern Russia, controlled by local armed forces that had defeated the Russian army. Negotiations to reopen the pipeline sputtered along in the late 1990s, but meanwhile Azerbaijan sought other pipeline routes that did not cross Russia. All such routes, however, would have to cross either Georgia (also war-torn), Armenia (still at war with Azerbaijan), or Iran (not acceptable to the United States). In 1999, oil companies and rel-

FIGURE 8.2 Dividing the Caspian Sea   The Caspian Sea is the world's largest inland body of water. It could be defined under international law as either a lake or a sea. The middle of a *lake* (beyond territorial waters) is a joint area (see left panel), which can be exploited only if the countries agree on terms. In a *sea* less than 400 miles wide, the bordering countries' Exclusive Economic Zones (EEZs) split up the whole sea (right panel).

After a 1921 treaty, the Soviet Union and Iran treated the Caspian as a lake and made agreements on fishing. Later, substantial oil deposits were found offshore. When the Soviet Union broke up a decade ago, the Caspian was suddenly bordered by five countries instead of two, with most of the oil and gas in or near Azerbaijan and Turkmenistan, not Russia. Under the "lake" interpretation, however, Russia could share in revenues from some of the offshore oil. In the past few years, more oil and gas has been discovered, including some potentially big fields near Russia. This makes Russia more inclined to accept a "sea" interpretation and begin drilling, without waiting to negotiate a complex deal with contentious neighbors.[a]

[a] Sciolino, Elaine. "It's a Sea! It's a Lake! No. It's a Pool of Oil!" *New York Times*, June 21, 1998.

evant states reached agreement on a pipeline route that goes just inside Georgia, then through Turkey to the Mediterranean, the route favored by the United States. The case of Caspian Sea oil thus illustrates that, although borders and geography may be less and less important in communications and business, they still matter greatly in many international economic transactions such as oil pipelines.

Low oil prices help the industrialized economies, but they have two major drawbacks. First, burning oil contributes to global warming, and low prices make it profitable to burn more oil and be less energy efficient. Second, low oil prices reduce the export earnings of oil-producing countries. Those like Saudi Arabia, with huge financial reserves and plenty of oil, feel only modest pain. But countries such as Venezuela and

Mexico had counted on oil revenues in their economic development plans and had borrowed foreign money to be repaid from future oil earnings. Some of these countries faced major debt problems as a result.

Minerals, Land, Water

To build the infrastructure and other manufactured goods that create wealth in a national economy, states need other raw materials in addition to energy. These include metals, other minerals, and related materials extracted through mining.

A combination of energy sources, other raw materials, and capital (machines, etc.) that all work together in an economy has been called a *technological style*. For instance, the combination of hay, farms, horse carts, and roads (etc.) makes up one technological style, and the combination of oil, steel, automobiles, and freeways (etc.) makes up a different style. The raw materials and fuels that a state requires depend on both its overall level of economic development (industrialization) and its technological style.

The political economy of minerals—iron, copper, platinum, and so forth—differs from that of world energy. The value of international trade in oil is many times greater than that of any mineral. Mineral production is distributed more evenly than is oil production—supply is not so concentrated in one region of the world. Industrialized countries have also reduced their vulnerability by stockpiling strategic minerals (easier to do with minerals than with energy because of the smaller quantities and values).

Nonetheless, industrialized countries do have certain vulnerabilities with regard to mineral supply, and these do affect international politics. Among the industrialized regions, Japan and Europe are most dependent on mineral imports; the United States is more self-sufficient. The former Soviet Union was a leading exporter of key minerals—a role that Russia may continue in the future. Despite its economic problems, one great strength of the Russian economy is being self-sufficient in both energy and mineral resources.

Another major exporter of key minerals is South Africa. For a few strategic minerals, notably manganese and chromium, South Africa controls three-quarters or more of the world's reserves. Western leaders worried that political instability in South Africa (where the black majority struggled for years under white minority rule) could disrupt the supply of these minerals. This is one reason why the industrialized countries were reluctant to impose trade sanctions on South Africa over human rights issues. South Africa's leading position in supplying diamonds, gold, and platinum to world markets gave South Africa a valuable source of income, but in the end the West did apply economic sanctions that hurt the South African economy and helped end apartheid.

Most important to industrialized economies are the minerals used to make industrial equipment. Traditionally most important is iron, from which steel is made. The leading producers of steel are the former Soviet Union, Japan, the United States, China, and Germany, followed by Brazil, Italy, South Korea, France, and Britain. Thus, major industrialized countries produce their own steel (Germany and Japan are the leading exporters worldwide). To preserve self-sufficiency in steel production, the United States and others have used trade policies to protect domestic steel industries.

Some industrialized countries, notably Japan, depend heavily on importing iron ore for their steel industry. Unlike oil, iron ore is not concentrated in a "Persian Gulf" but is exported from both third world and industrialized countries around the world. There is an *Association of Iron Ore Exporting Countries (AIOEC)*, but it is limited to consultation, and the United States, Canada, and the former Soviet Union are exporters not among the 12 members.

For other important industrial minerals such as copper and nickel, the pattern of supply and trade is much more diffuse than for oil, and the industrialized countries are largely self-sufficient. Even when third world states are the main suppliers, they have not gained the power held by OPEC. There is a producer cartel in some cases (copper), a producer–consumer cartel in some (tin), and separate producer and consumer cartels in others (bauxite).

Certain agricultural products have spawned producer cartels such as the Union of Banana Exporting Countries (UBEC) and the African Groundnut Council. Like minerals, some export crops come mainly from just a few countries. These include sugar (Cuba), cocoa (Ivory Coast, Ghana, Nigeria), tea (India, Sri Lanka, China), and coffee (Brazil, Colombia). Despite the concentrations, producer cartels have not been very successful in boosting prices of these products, which are less essential than energy.

WATER DISPUTES In addition to energy and minerals, states need water. Need of water increases as a society industrializes, as it intensifies agriculture, and as its population grows. World water use is 35 times higher than just a few centuries ago, and grew twice as fast as population in the twentieth century. Yet water supplies are relatively unchang-

Water, Water Everywhere   As population growth and economic development increase the demand for water, more international conflicts arise over water rights. Many important rivers pass through multiple states, and many states share access to seas and lakes. The Aral Sea, once part of the Soviet Union but now shared between Kazakhstan and Uzbekistan, was among the world's largest lakes until it was decimated by the diversion of its water sources to irrigate cotton. This scene shows the former seabed, now 70 miles from shore, in 1997.

ing, and are becoming depleted in many places. One-fifth of the world's population lacks safe drinking water, and 80 countries suffer water shortages. Water supplies—rivers and water tables—often cross international boundaries, so access to water is increasingly a source of international conflict. Sometimes—as when several states share access to a single water table—these conflicts are collective goods problems.

Water problems are especially important in the Middle East. For instance, the Euphrates River runs from Turkey through Syria to Iraq before reaching the Persian Gulf. Iraq objects to Syrian diversion of water from the river, and both Iraq and Syria object to Turkey's diversion.

Atlas CD
Jordan River
Map

The Jordan River originates in Syria and Lebanon and runs through Israel to Jordan. Soon after its independence in 1948 (never recognized by Syria, Lebanon, and Jordan), Israel began building a canal to take water from the Jordan River to "make the desert bloom." Jordan and its Arab neighbors complained to the UN Security Council, which tried (with the U.S. government) to mediate the dispute from 1953 to 1955. Israel's representative called the Jordan's water "the bloodstream and the life artery of our country" and "the very essence of national economic independence." The UN mediation efforts failed, and each state went ahead with its own water plans (although Israel and Jordan each agreed to stay within allocations suggested in a UN plan). In 1964, Israel's Arab neighbors decided to construct their own storage dams and diversion systems on three rivers in Syria and Lebanon to divert water before it reached Israel. This would have made Israel's water system, almost completely constructed, worthless. Turning to military leverage in this international bargaining situation, Israel launched air and artillery attacks on the Syrian construction site in 1964, forcing Syria to abandon its diversion project. Israel's capture of the Golan Heights in 1967 prevented Syria from renewing efforts to divert water from the Jordan River.

Water contains other resources such as fish and offshore oil deposits. The UNCLOS treaty enclosed more of these resources within states' territory; however, this enclosure creates new problems. Norms regarding territorial waters are not firmly entrenched; some states disagree on who owns what. Also, control of small islands now implies rights to surrounding oceans with their fish, offshore oil, and minerals. A potentially serious international dispute is brewing in the Spratly Islands, where China claims some tiny islands also claimed by Vietnam and other nearby countries (see p. 151). With the islands come nearby oil drilling rights and fisheries. China has invited a U.S. company to explore for oil there, promising protection by the Chinese Navy. This conflict could lead to military clashes.

A common theme runs through the conflicts over fuels, minerals, agricultural products, and territorial waters. They are produced in fixed locations but traded to distant places. Control of these locations gives a state both greater self-sufficiency (valued by mercantilists) and market commodities generating wealth (valued by liberals).

International Security and the Environment
In recent years, IR scholars have expanded their studies of environmental politics to systematically study the relationship of military and security affairs with the environment. One side of this relationship is the role of the environment as a source of international conflict. We have seen how environmental degradation can lead to collective goods problems among

War Is Not Green   Wars often bring environmental destruction sometimes deliberately and sometimes as a by-product. Military operations in peacetime also contribute to environmental problems. Hundreds of Kuwaiti oil wells, set on fire by retreating Iraqi troops in 1991, burned for months.

large numbers of states, and how competition for territory and resources can create conflicts among smaller groups of states.

The other side of the environment-security relationship concerns the effect of activities in the international security realm on the environment. Military activities—especially warfare—are important contributors to environmental degradation, above and beyond the degradation caused by economic activities such as mining and manufacturing.

These damaging effects were spotlighted during the Gulf War. Iraqi forces spilled large amounts of Kuwaiti oil into the Persian Gulf—either to try to stop an amphibious invasion, or simply to punish Saudi Arabia (in whose direction the currents pushed the oil). Then, before retreating from Kuwait, the Iraqis blew up hundreds of Kuwaiti oil wells, leaving them burning uncontrollably and covering the country with thick black smoke. Air pollution and weather effects lasted more than a year and were felt in other countries around the Gulf (such as Iran). Large lakes of oil remain in the Kuwaiti desert. Iraq's environment also suffered tremendous damage from the massive bombing campaign. (Since the war, Iraq has built a giant canal to drain marshes used for refuge by rebels; the draining is another potential environmental disaster.)

The deliberate environmental destruction seen in the Gulf War is not without precedent. Armies sometimes adopt a "scorched earth policy" to deny sustenance to their adversaries. Fields are burned and villages leveled. In World War II, the Soviets left a scorched earth behind as they retreated before the Nazi invasion. During World War II, Japan used incendiary devices carried in high-altitude balloons to start forest fires in the U.S. Northwest. The United States sprayed defoliants massively in Vietnam to destroy jungles in an attempt to expose guerrilla forces. The Vietnamese countryside still shows effects from these herbicides, as do U.S. veterans who suffer lingering health effects due to contact with chemicals such as *Agent Orange*.

Military activity short of war also tends to damage the environment. Military industries pollute. Military forces use energy less efficiently than civilians do. Military aircraft and missiles contribute to ozone depletion. Military bases contain many toxic-waste dumps.

The greatest *potential* environmental disaster imaginable would be a large nuclear war. Ecosystems would be severely damaged throughout the world by secondary effects of nuclear weapons—radioactive fallout and the breakdown of social order and technology. Some scientists also think that global climate changes, leading to famine and environmental collapse, could result—the "nuclear winter" mentioned on page 193.

In managing the daunting environmental threats discussed in this chapter, states and NGOs have begun to use new technologies productively. Information technologies, especially, allow scientists to confirm global warming, NGOs to mobilize public opinion against habitat destruction, and MNCs to produce more fuel-efficient cars. This information revolution also has far-reaching consequences for world politics far beyond issues of environmental management. The remainder of this chapter discusses those profound, yet still ambiguous, consequences.

The Power of Information

Global telecommunications are profoundly changing how information and culture function in international relations. Information is now a vital tool of national governments in their interactions with each other. Yet technology is at the same time undermining and disempowering those governments and shifting power to substate actors and individuals. Those newly empowered individuals and groups have begun to create new transnational networks worldwide, bypassing states.

Web Link
Wiring the World

Wiring the World Numerous international political possibilities are based on technological developments. Just a hundred years ago, the idea of instant global communication was incomprehensible. It would have seemed unthinkable that anyone could push a dozen buttons on a handheld instrument and be able to talk with any of billions of people anywhere in the economically developed areas of the world (and many of the poorer areas). Equally ridiculous was the idea that you could look at a box no bigger than a suitcase and see in it moving pictures of things happening at that moment in distant lands. For most of the history of the international system, until about 150 years ago, the fastest way to send information was to write it down and bring it to the recipient by horse or sailing ship.

The media over which information travels—telephones, television, films, magazines, and so forth—shape the way ideas take form and spread from one place to another. The media with the strongest political impact are radio and (especially) televi-

Wired   Global communication, a very new capability on the time scale of the international system, is changing the rules of IR and empowering nonstate transnational actors. Here, a villager in Iran brings home a color TV, 1995, perhaps fueling the vibrant Iranian democratization movement of the late 1990s.

sion. There are about one billion TV sets and more than two billion radio receivers in the world (roughly one-third are in North America, one-third in Western and Eastern Europe and Russia, and the rest in the global South and Japan/Pacific). The power of these media is to take a single source of information (a moving picture or a voice) and reproduce it in many copies in many locations.

Radio, and increasingly TV, reaches the poorest rural areas of the third world. Peasants who cannot read can understand radio. Shortwave radio—typically stations such as Voice of America (VOA), the British Broadcasting Corporation (BBC), and Radio Moscow—is very popular in remote locations.

TV is especially powerful. The combination of pictures and sounds affects viewers emotionally and intellectually. Viewers can experience distant events more fully. Traditionally this participation has been passive. But as technology has developed in recent decades, the passive nature of TV is changing. More and more channels of information on TV give viewers power over what they watch—from the local city council meeting, to simultaneous translation of the Russian evening news (in the United States), to MTV music videos (in Russia). Less and less are millions of TV viewers all forced to march to the beat of the same drummer; rather, the global TV audience is being fragmented into many small pieces, often not along national lines.

Ordinary over-the-air TV and radio signals are radio waves carried on specific frequencies. Frequencies are a limited resource in high demand, which governments regulate and allocate to users. Because radio waves do not respect national borders, the allocation of frequencies is a subject of interstate bargaining. International regimes have grown up around the regulation of international communications technologies.

Now the limitations of radio waves are yielding to new technologies. Cable TV does not use the airwaves of the radio spectrum and can carry hundreds of signals at once. Cable also has the potential to carry signals from viewers. Satellite transmissions also bypass the normal over-the-air radio spectrum and transmit signals over a huge area to dish-shaped antennas.

Images and sounds are being recorded, reproduced, and viewed in new ways through audiotapes and videotapes. Videocassette recorders (VCRs) have proliferated in many countries in recent years. Audio- and videotapes can be played repeatedly and passed from person to person, again giving the viewer more control. Video cameras are empowering ordinary citizens to create their own visual records, such as videos of political demonstrations in one country that end up on the TV news in another country.

Even more empowering of ordinary citizens is the telephone. Unlike TV and radio, phones are a two-way medium through which users interact without any centralized information source. Phones are becoming more powerful, with the advent of fiber-optic cables, communication satellites, cellular phones, fax machines, and modems. New satellite networks will soon allow a portable phone to use a single phone number worldwide. These forms of communication do not slow down for even a millisecond when they cross an international border. The increased flows of information from state to state reflect the growing functional interdependence of states in today's world.

Information technologies have security implications. Capabilities such as fiber-optic cables or satellite communications serve governments in conducting their foreign and military policies (see pp. 188–190). Because fiber-optic cables facilitate military command and control, the United States tried to prevent the sale of such cables to Russia even after the Cold War ended.

In a subtle but pervasive way, communication technologies may be diffusing power away from governments and toward ordinary people and other nonstate actors. Recall that new "smart weapons" technologies are empowering the foot soldier relative to large-weapons systems (see p. 189). New communications technologies may be doing the same for ordinary citizens relative to governments and political parties.

Information as a Tool of Governments

Not all aspects of the information revolution work against governments. With more information traveling around the world than ever before, information has become an important instrument of governments' power (domestic and interstate). Above all, governments want *access to information*. In 1992, U.S. Secretary of State James Baker made his first visit to the newly independent Asian republics of the former Soviet Union (the poorest and most remote CIS members). At each stop, one of the first questions Baker was asked by the state leader was, "How do I get CNN?" CNN, state leaders hoped, would tie them directly to the Western world and symbolize their independence from Russia. Access to CNN was also considered a status symbol.

Web Link
CNN

U.S. military leaders recognized the importance of playing to a global audience when, during the bombing of Bosnian Serb forces in 1995, they designated an ammunition dump close to Sarajevo the "CNN site" because they knew the explosion would make good footage for Sarajevo-based TV cameras. During the Gulf War, the U.S. military fed TV networks pictures of precision weapons striking their targets, to help "sanitize" the bombing campaign (which mostly used unguided bombs).

Governments spend large amounts of money and effort trying to gain information about what is happening both inside and outside their territories. They keep files on their citizens ranging from social security records to secret police files. They compile economic statistics to chart their own economic health and make estimates of the economic health of other states. Most operate intelligence-gathering agencies.

With today's information technologies, it is easier for governments to gather, organize, and store huge amounts of information. In this respect, the information revolution empowers governments more than ever. In the past, a wanted criminal, druglord, or terrorist could slip over the border and take refuge in a foreign country. Today, it is more likely that a routine traffic ticket in the foreign country could trigger an instant directive to arrest the person. Information technologies give repressive governments more power to keep tabs on citizens, spy on dissidents, and manipulate public opinion.

Just as domestic citizens find it harder to hide from their governments, so are state governments finding it harder to hide information from each other. The military importance of satellite reconnaissance has been cited (see p. 187). A powerful state such as the United States can increase its power through information technologies. It can and does monitor phone calls, faxes, data transmissions, and radio conversations in foreign countries.

As the cost of information technology decreases, it comes into reach of more states. The great powers have always been able to maintain a worldwide presence and gather information globally. Now small states can gain some of the same capabilities electronically—if only by monitoring world affairs on CNN. Even sophisticated information is becoming more available and cheaper—high-resolution satellite photos are now available commercially within the price range of most states. These images can be used for both military purposes and natural-resource management. The small but rich oil-producing state of Bahrain, for example, decided in the 1990s to buy a satellite that would help it keep track of the production and movement of oil worldwide.

The very nature of interstate interactions is affected by changes in information technology. The risks of surprise in IR are reduced by the information revolution. The security dilemma is less severe as a result (states do not need to arm against unknown potential threats since they know what the real threats are). Similarly, the ability to monitor performance of agreements makes collective goods problems easier to resolve. (Collective goods are more easily maintained when cheaters and free riders can be identified.)

The ability of governments to bargain effectively with each other and to reach mutually beneficial outcomes is enhanced by the availability of instant communications channels. During the Iraq-Kuwait crisis, the telephone was one of President George Bush's most potent instruments of power in assembling the international coalition against Iraq.

In addition to gaining access to information, governments use information as a power capability by disseminating it internationally and domestically. In today's information-intensive world, TV transmitters may be more powerful than tanks. Even in war itself, propaganda plays a key role. For instance, in the Gulf War pamphlets and loudspeakers appealed to Iraqi soldiers, ultimately contributing to their mass surrenders.

The information disseminated by a government often crosses international borders, intentionally and otherwise. The government of Jordan, for example, is well aware that its Arabic programs are received by Arab citizens of Israel and that its English programs are watched by Israeli Jews. When Jordanian TV broadcasts, say, a U.S. documentary about the U.S. civil rights movement (with Arabic subtitles), the message influences Israeli–Palestinian relations across the border.

Most governments create explicit channels of information dissemination to influence domestic and international audiences. Stations such as Radio Moscow broadcast radio programs in dozens of languages aimed at all the world's regions. The U.S. Information Agency (USIA) operates the U.S. government's VOA shortwave radio network, which is picked up in many third world regions where it may be one of the few outside information sources.

Governments spread false as well as true information as a means of international influence. This is called *disinformation*. In the 1930s, the Nazis discovered that the "big lie," if repeated enough times, would be accepted as truth by most people. It is harder to fool international audiences these days, but domestic ones can still respond to propagandistic misinformation, as the Serbian regime in the early 1990s showed. Anyone who follows international events should remember that even stories reported in the Western news as fact are sometimes disinformation.

Most governments (but not the U.S. government) own and operate at least one main TV station, and many hold a monopoly on TV stations. This suggests that TV signals often rank with military equipment and currency as capabilities so important to a government that it must control them itself. Indeed, in a military coup d'état, usually one of the first and most important targets seized is the television broadcasting facility. When power is up for grabs in a state, it is now as likely that fighting will occur in the government TV studios or at the transmitting antenna as at the legislature or presidential offices. As the Soviet Union broke up in the early 1990s, TV towers were the scene of confrontations in several republics. In Lithuania, a crowd of Lithuanian nationalists surrounded the TV tower, and Soviet troops killed a dozen people shooting their way in.

Information as a Tool Against Governments

Information can be used against governments as well, by foreign governments or by domestic political opponents. Governments, especially repressive ones, fear the free flow of information, for good reason. When they are allowed to circulate among a population, ideas become a powerful force that can sweep aside governments, as when the idea of democracy swept away the white-rule system of apartheid in South Africa in the early 1990s. New information technologies have become powerful tools of domestic opposition movements and their allies in foreign governments. Television coverage fed popular discontent regarding the U.S. war in Vietnam in the 1960s and 1970s, and the Russian war in Chechnya in 1995.

In Iran, the government was brought down in part by audiotapes containing speeches and sermons by Ayatollah Khomeini, who spoke against the inequalities and harsh repression of the pro-Western government of the Shah of Iran. Khomeini advocated a revolution to create an Islamic state. The power of his sermons could never have been captured in newspapers and pamphlets. The shah's secret police could spot a subversive pamphlet with one glance, but the content of audiotapes cannot be determined instantly. Khomeini made the tapes while in exile in France and had them smuggled into Iran, where they were passed around. When the Islamic revolution drove the shah from power in 1979, Khomeini arrived from France as a well-known and popular leader of a large movement.

Telling the World   Control of television news and other mass media has become an important instrument of political power, one that states often seek to control. Independent journalists are often directly or indirectly targeted in this effort. Here, 28-year-old American photographer Cynthia Elbaum works to show the world the effects of Russia's war in Chechnya (1994). She was killed an hour later in a Russian air raid on the site.

In Thailand in 1992, military leaders lost power in what some Thais called "the cellular phone revolution." Students protesting against the military government were joined by newly affluent Thais with access to cellular phones and fax machines. When the government shot the demonstrators in the streets, arrested them, and cut off their phone lines, the protesters stayed organized by using mobile phones and fax machines. Meanwhile, in next-door Burma, a harsh military government faced the power of shortwave radio broadcasts by the opposition movement, made using a transmitter owned by the government of Norway.

To counteract such uses of information, governments throughout the world try to limit the flow of unfavorable information—especially information from foreign sources. For example, China and several other developing countries have channeled all access to the Internet (and the World Wide Web) through a few state-controlled service providers. This lets the government monitor and control who can have access to the mass of information available through the Internet. During and after the 1989 Tiananmen protests, before the Internet was a factor, the Chinese government tried desperately to suppress the flow of information into and out of China. It stationed police at every fax machine in the country to screen incoming faxes after foreigners in Hong Kong, North America, and Europe began faxing in reports of the shooting of hundreds of protesters in Beijing.

Efforts by one government to project power through media broadcasts often bring counterefforts by other governments to block such broadcasts. The VOA, the BBC, and other foreign media were routinely jammed by the Soviet Union and other closed societies during the Cold War. But Soviet efforts to control information did not prevent collapse of that society. To the contrary, the effort to run a modern economy without photocopy machines, international phone lines, computers, and other information technologies clearly contributed to the economic stagnation of the country.

All in all, the tide of technology seems to be running against governments (though not all scholars would agree with this assessment). Information gets through, and no political power seems capable of holding it back for long. As more and more communication channels carry more information to more places, governments become just another player in a crowded field.

As the information revolution continues to unfold, it will further increase international interdependence, making actions in one state reverberate in other states more strongly than in the past. Information is thus slowly undermining the assumptions of state sovereignty and territorial integrity held dear by realists. At the same time, by empowering substate and transnational actors, information technology is undermining the centrality of states themselves in world affairs.

International Culture

Atlas CD
World
Languages
Map

As the information revolution increases the power and importance of transnational actors, it puts into motion two contradictory forces. One we have just discussed—the empowering of substate actors. This force was a factor in the disintegration of the Soviet Union and Yugoslavia, and the proliferation of civil wars since the end of the Cold War. As substate groups gain power, they demand their own national rights of sovereignty and autonomy. Nationalism reasserts itself in smaller but more numerous units.

The second force, however, is the forging of transnational communities and supranational identities—a process alluded to earlier with reference to the EU. Here regionalism or globalism asserts itself as an internationalized culture resting on communication links among people in different states. This second force, perhaps more than the first, challenges the realist emphasis on national borders and territorial integrity.

Web Link
Global Culture

Telecommunications and Global Culture Not only can people in one part of the world communicate with those elsewhere, they can also now find common interests to talk about. Riding the telecommunications revolution, a **global culture** is just beginning to develop, notwithstanding the great divisions remaining in culture and perspective (especially between the rich and poor regions of the world). In the global village, distance and borders matter less and less. Across dozens of countries, people are tuned in to the same news, the same music, the same sports events. Along with international politics, these activities now take place on a world stage with a world audience. The process might be seen as a form of cultural integration, similar to economic and technical integration.

Cultures, languages, and locations interact more quickly as the unfinished process of cultural integration proceeds. For example, in a rural town in Massachusetts, the local cable TV channel on weekends carries live news broadcasts from around the world (without translation), downloaded from a satellite consortium. One weekend, the Brazilian TV news on this broadcast included an ad for a U.S. film set in the Brazilian rain forest, dubbed in Portuguese. Information is bouncing around the world—Brazilian rain forest to Hollywood movie production to Brazilian movie theaters to Massachusetts cable TV. Such trends clearly undermine assumptions of state autonomy.

Ultimately, transnational cultural integration might lead to the emergence of supranational identities, including a global identity. If citizens in EU states can begin to think as Europeans, will citizens in UN member states someday begin to think as human beings and residents of Planet Earth? This is unclear. As we have seen, group identity is an important source of conflict between in-groups and out-groups (see "Ethnic Conflict" on pp. 158–162). Nationalism has tapped into the psychological dynamics of group identity in a powerful way that has legitimized the state as the ultimate embodiment of its people's aspirations and identity. Now the information revolution may aid the development of supranational identity. So far, nationalism continues to hold the upper hand. Global identity has not yet come to rival national identity in any state.

For a fleeting moment at the turn of the millennium, such a global identity seemed almost possible. The feared "Y2K" computer bug, which would cause old software to think time had jumped back 100 years, was fixed in a massive technology upgrade that

Triumph of Technology
Information, which easily crosses state borders, has become a major factor in both international and domestic politics, and may even be laying technological foundations for a global identity. The dawn of a new millennium was marked by global celebrations broadcast worldwide, as technology triumphed over the feared "Y2K" software flaw. Here, the Tokyo subway halts operations for a few minutes around midnight to check computer systems, January 1, 2000.

"leveraged the resources of the whole planet," in the words of an IBM executive. On December 31, as each time zone passed midnight, people around the world watched to see whether fears of computer failures, terrorist attacks, or riots would materialize. UN Secretary-General Annan said that "each city seemed to be rooting for cities in the next time zone to get through Y2K without any problems. It was like, 'O.K., Tokyo is through, now how about Beijing?' And then, 'Moscow is through, how about New York?' For one brief moment there was a pulling together all over the planet." As the feared problems did not materialize, the world was left with a 24-hour moment of good feeling broadcast live on CNN and the Internet.

CULTURAL IMPERIALISM Like international integration generally, global culture has its down side. The emerging global culture is primarily the culture of white Europeans and their descendants in rich areas of the world (mixed slightly with cultural elements of Japan and local third world elites). For many people, especially in the global South, the information revolution carrying global culture into their midst is, despite its empowering potential, an invasive force in practice.

Above all, the emerging global culture is dominated by the world's superpower, the United States; this dominance has been referred to as **cultural imperialism**. U.S. cul-

Mac Attack Some call it "global community," others "cultural imperialism." The power of information, opening up a wave of globalization in international business, is bringing together cultures in sometimes incongruous ways. Chinese leaders seemed unsure for years about whether McDonald's brought Western-style prosperity or spiritual pollution—maybe a bit of each.

tural influence is at least as strong as U.S. military influence. If there is a world language, it is English. If there is a "president of the world," it is more likely the U.S. president than the UN secretary-general.

U.S. films and TV shows dominate world markets, from Europe to Asia to Latin America (although top music titles, and most top TV shows, tend to be national, not American). Culture may be just another economic product, to be produced in the place of greatest comparative advantage, but culture also is central to national identity and politics. France held up the GATT agreement in 1994 until it could protect its film industry from U.S. competition. The prospect of cultural imperialism thus opens another front in the conflict of liberalism and mercantilism.

Industrialized countries have responded in various ways to U.S. cultural dominance. Canada has allowed U.S. cultural influence to become fairly pervasive, with some resentments but few severe frictions. France has been especially wary of U.S. influence; commissions periodically go through the French language trying to weed out expressions such as "le cash-and-carry" (not an easy task). However, Japan seemingly incorporated whole segments of U.S. culture after World War II, from baseball to hamburgers, yet remained Japanese.

Global culture and cultural imperialism shape the news that is reported by the TV, radio, and print media. In the United States alone, 50 million viewers watch network news nightly. To an increasing extent, everyone in the world follows the same story line of world news from day to day. To some extent, there is now a single drama unfolding at the global level, and the day's top international story on CNN very likely will also be reported by the other U.S. television networks, the national TV news in France, Japan, Russia, and most other states, and the world's radio and print media. The fact that everyone is following the same story reflects the globalizing influence of world communications. Cultural imperialism is reflected in the fact that the story often revolves around U.S. actions, reflects U.S. values, or is reported by U.S. reporters and news organizations. The attack on Iraq in 1991 illustrates in the extreme how the whole world watches one story—a story shaped by U.S. perspectives. When the bombing of Baghdad began, Saddam Hussein reportedly sat in his bunker watching the war unfold on CNN.

Transnational Communities
Although a global culture is still only nascent and the most powerful identity is still at the national level, people have begun to participate in specific communities that bridge national boundaries. International journalists, for example, are members of such a community. They work with colleagues from various countries and travel from state to state with each other. Though a journalist's identity *as* a journalist rarely takes precedence over his or her national identity, the existence of the transnational community of journalists creates a new form of international interdependence.

Like journalists, scientists and church members work in communities spanning national borders. So do members of transnational movements, such as those linking women from various countries, or environmentalists, or human rights activists. The effect once again is to undermine the state's role as the primary actor in international affairs. More important, the links forged in such transnational communities may create a new functionalism that could encourage international integration on a global scale.

International sports competition is one of the broadest-based transnational communities, especially strong at the regional level. Millions of fans watch their teams compete with teams from other countries. Of course, international sports competition can stir up animosities between neighbors, as when British soccer hooligans rampage through another European country after their team loses a game. But sports also create a sense of participation in a supranational community. This is especially true of world-level sports events in which a global athletic community participates. The Olympic Games (sponsored by the International Olympic Committee, an NGO) are a global event broadcast to a worldwide audience. Sponsors broadcast universalistic commercial messages such as Coca Cola's theme, "Shared Around the World."

Some people see sports as a force for peace. Sports events bring people from different countries together in shared activities. Citizens of different states share their admiration of sports stars, who become international celebrities. In Israel, one of the most successful programs for bridging the gap between Jewish and Arab children is a soccer camp in which Jewish and Arab star players (each admired in both communities) participate together as coaches. The U.S.-Chinese rapproachement of 1971 was so delicate that political cooperation was impossible until the way had first been paved by sports—the U.S. table tennis team that made the first official U.S. visit to China.

Most communication over the world's broadcasting networks is neither news nor sports, but drama—soap operas, films, situation comedies, documentaries, and so forth. Here U.S. cultural imperialism is strong, because so many films and TV shows watched around the world originate in Hollywood (home of the U.S. movie industry). The entertainment industry is a strong export sector of the U.S. economy. Large third world countries such as Brazil and India have concentrated their TV production efforts in an area where local contexts can gain viewers' interest and where production costs are modest—soap operas. They are immensely popular in these and other third world countries.

The popularity of Brazilian soap operas notwithstanding, many international viewers see less of their own experiences than of dramas set in the United States. These dramas, of course, give a distorted view of U.S. life, such as the impression that all Americans are rich. The power of such messages was demonstrated in 1991, when Albania's communist government was crumbling along with its economy. Desperately poor Albanians rode overloaded ferries to nearby Italy (where authorities eventually sent them back home). As it turned out, Albanians had an exaggerated view of Italian prosperity (though Italy was indeed more prosperous than Albania). Albanians had seen Italian TV commercials in which cats were fed their dinners on silver platters. Having been cut off from contact with the West for decades, many Albanians took such commercials literally!

Atlas CD
World Music
Video

Live performances and recordings of music have also become increasingly internationalized. In the world of classical music, a great conductor or violinist can roam the world in search of great orchestras and appreciative audiences, with almost complete disregard for national borders. International tours are a central element in rock music and jazz as well. Some genres of music are essentially more international than national, spanning several continents and explicitly global in outlook. Even highly specialized national music forms—such as Bulgarian chants or Mongolian throat singing—are gaining worldwide audiences. It is significant that people who cannot understand each other's language can understand each other's music.

Advertising is crucial to the emerging international culture. Advertising links the transnational products and services of MNCs with the transnational performances and works of actors, athletes, and artists. Most global broadcasts and performances—from the

THE INFORMATION

REVOLUTION World Wide Web

The Internet-based World Wide Web grew explosively in the late 1990s, becoming a ubiquitous element in corporate and cultural life, as well as increasingly a business venue. Will the Web create new transnational communities and interest groups that redraw international politics by empowering nonstate actors?

To explore this question, go to www.IRtext.com

Olympic Games to reruns of *Dallas*—are paid for by advertising. Advertising often carries subtle (or not so subtle) messages about culture, race, gender roles, and other themes. In Europe and Japan, international advertising may contain a subtext of U.S. superiority. In Eastern Europe and Russia, the advertising of products from Europe, Japan, and the United States may imply the superiority of the West over the East, whereas in the third world advertising may promote the values of the industrialized world over local and native cultures. For example, ads for cosmetics may portray stereotypical images of white Euro-American women as the ideal of beauty, even on billboards or TV shows in Asia or Latin America. Despite the cultural frictions that advertising can cause, it seems evident that without advertising the emerging global culture would lack the money needed to broadcast the Olympic Games or launch new communication satellites.

Finally, tourism also builds transnational communities. International tourists cross borders 500 million times a year. Tourism ranks among the top export industries worldwide. People who travel to another country often develop both a deeper understanding and a deeper appreciation for it. Person-to-person contacts and friendships maintained across borders make it harder for nationalism to succeed in promoting either war or protectionism. For example, a U.S. citizen who has visited Japan may be more likely to favor expanded U.S.-Japanese trade; a Greek who has visited Turkey and made friends there may be more likely to oppose a Greek-Turkish military confrontation.

Added to these contacts are exchange students and those who attend college in a foreign country. These students learn about their host countries, teach friends there about their home countries, and meet other foreign students from other countries. These kinds of person-to-person international contacts are amplified by the electronic media.

The Internet now allows transnational dialogues to take place at a global level. The World Wide Web allows people to move seamlessly from site to site around the world simply by clicking "links" on a computer screen. Significantly, the Web creates organizing structures and communities that can be almost totally divorced from physical location, bringing together people with common cultural or economic interest from anywhere in the world. In the 1990s, the Web quickly gained acceptance as a key infrastructure for business, and increasingly for governments.

The transnational connections forged by these various communities—sports, music, tourism, and so forth—deepen the international interdependence that links the well-being of one state to that of other states. This may promote peace, because a person who knows more about a foreign country and has developed empathy for it is likely to reject political conflict with that country and support positive cooperation with it. But sometimes cultural contact increases awareness of differences, creating distrust.

Furthermore, as the Internet wires parts of the world into a tight network centered on the United States, other regions are largely left out. Poor countries and poor people cannot afford computers—the equivalent of eight years' wages for a typical Bangladeshi, for example. Users of the World Wide Web in 1999 made up 26 percent of the population in the United States, 3 percent in Russia, 0.2 percent in Arab countries, and 0.04 percent in South Asia. English is the language of 80 percent of Web sites worldwide. Even the architecture of cyberspace assumes the United States as the default in such domain names as .gov (U.S. government) and .mil (U.S. military). Internet users are expected to increase from 150 million to 700 million worldwide just from 1999 to 2001 (with China going from 7 million to 20 million internet accounts). This explosive growth is mainly occurring among the richest strata of the world's people, however.

These supranational cultural influences are still in their infancy. Over the coming years and decades their shape will become clearer, and scholars will be able to determine more accurately how they are influencing world politics and state sovereignty.

Web Link
Poor Countries
and the Internet

Conclusion

Ultimately the conflicts and dramas of international relations are little different from those of other spheres of political and social life. The problems of IR are the problems of human society—struggles for power and wealth, efforts to cooperate despite differences, social dilemmas and collective goods problems, the balance between freedom and order, trade-offs of equity versus efficiency and of long-term versus short-term outcomes. These themes are inescapable in human society, from the smallest groups to the world community. The subject of international relations is in this sense an extension of everyday life and a reflection of the choices of individual human beings. IR belongs to all of us—North and South, women and men, citizens and leaders—who live together on this planet.

Technological development is just one aspect of the profound, yet incremental, changes taking place in international relations. New actors are gaining power, long-standing principles are becoming less effective, and new challenges are arising for states, groups, and individuals alike. The post-Cold War era, just a decade old, remains undefined. Will it, like past "postwar" eras, lapse slowly into the next "prewar" era, or will it lead to a robust and lasting "permanent peace"?

Consider a few aspects of these changes that this book has discussed. One major theme of the book was the nature of the international system as a well-developed set of rules based on state sovereignty, territoriality, and "anarchy"—a lack of central government. Yet, the international system is becoming more complex, more nuanced, and more interconnected with other aspects of planetary society. State sovereignty is now challenged by the principle of self-determination. International norms have begun to limit the right of a government to rule a population by force against its will and to violate human rights. Territorial integrity is also problematical, since national borders do not stop information, environmental changes, or missiles. Information allows actors—

state, substate, and supranational—to know what is going on everywhere in the world and to coordinate actions globally.

Technology is also profoundly changing the utility and role of military force. The power of defensive weaponry makes successful attacks more difficult, and the power of offensive weaponry makes retaliation an extremely potent threat to deter an attack. The twentieth-century superpowers could not attack each other without destroying themselves, and a large force cannot reliably defeat a small one (or, to be more accurate, the costs of doing so are too high), as demonstrated in the Vietnam and Afghanistan wars. Nonmilitary forms of leverage, particularly economic rewards, have become much more important power capabilities.

In IPE, we see simultaneous trends toward integration and disintegration among states. People continue to speak their own language, to fly their own flag, to use their own currency with its pictures and emblems. Nationalism continues to be an important force. At the same time, however, although people identify with their state, they also now hold competing identities based on ethnic ties, gender, and (in the case of Europe) region. In international trade, liberal economics prevails because it works so well. States have learned that in order to survive they must help, not impede, the creation of wealth by MNCs and other economic actors.

Environmental damage may become the single greatest obstacle to sustained economic growth in both the North and South (a trend presaged by Soviet-bloc environmental degradation, which contributed to that region's economic stagnation and collapse). Because of high costs, the large number of actors, and collective goods problems, international bargaining over the environment is difficult. However, the 1992 Earth Summit's call for sustainable economic growth that does not deplete resources and destroy ecosystems may be supported by new technology that moves information, instead of materials, to accomplish the same goals. The traditional technological style of industrialization cannot be sustained environmentally on the giant scale of countries like China and India.

North-South relations meanwhile are moving to the center of world politics. Demographic and economic trends are sharpening the global North-South gap, with the North continuing to accumulate wealth while much of the South lingers in great poverty. Ultimately, the North will bear a high cost for failing to address the economic development of the South. Perhaps, by using computerization and biotechnology innovations, poor states can develop their economies much more efficiently than did Europe or North America.

The future is unknowable now, but as it unfolds you can compare it—at mileposts along the way—to the worlds that you desire and expect. The comparison of alternative futures may be facilitated by examining a variety of possible branch points where alternative paths diverge. For example, you could ask questions such as the following (asking yourself, for each one, why you answer the way you do for your desired future and expected future):

1. Will state sovereignty be eroded by supranational authority?
2. Will norms of human rights and democracy become global?
3. Will the UN evolve into a quasi-government for the world?
4. Will the UN be restructured?

5. Will World Court judgments become enforceable?

6. Will the number of states increase?

7. Will China become democratic? Will it become rich?

8. What effects will information technologies have on IR?

9. Will military leverage become obsolete?

10. Will weapons of mass destruction proliferate?

11. Will disarmament occur?

12. Will women participate more fully in IR? With what effect?

13. Will there be a single world currency?

14. Will there be a global free-trade regime?

15. Will nationalism fade out or continue to be strong?

16. Will many people develop a global identity?

17. Will world culture become more homogeneous or more pluralistic?

18. Will the EU or other regional IOs achieve political union?

19. Will global environmental destruction be severe? How soon?

20. Will new technologies avert environmental constraints?

21. Will global problems create stronger or weaker world order?

22. Will population growth level out? If so, when and at what level?

23. Will the poorest countries accumulate wealth? How soon?

24. What role will the North play in the South's development?

The choices you make and actions you take will ultimately affect, in some way, the world you live in. You cannot opt out of involvement in international relations. You are involved, and year by year the information revolution and other aspects of interdependence are drawing you more closely into contact with the rest of the world. You can act in many ways, large and small, to bring the world you expect more into line with the world you desire. You can empower yourself by finding the actions and choices that define your place in international relations.

Now that you have completed the studies covered in this book, don't stop here. Keep learning about the world beyond your country's borders. Keep thinking about the world that might exist. Be a part of the changes that will carry this world through the coming decades. It's your world: study it, care for it, make it your own.

THINKING CRITICALLY

1. Does the record of the international community on environmental management reflect the views of mercantilists, of liberals, or of both? In what ways?

2. Some politicians call for the Western industrialized countries, including the United States, to be more self-sufficient in energy resources in order to reduce dependence on oil imports from the Middle East. In light of the overall world

energy picture and the economics of international trade, what are the pros and cons of such a proposal?

3. What are the good and bad effects, in your opinion, of the emergence of global communications and culture? Should we be cheering or lamenting the possibility of one world culture? Does the answer depend on where one lives in the world? Give concrete examples of the effects you discuss.

CHAPTER SUMMARY

◆ Environmental problems are an example of international interdependence and often create collective goods problems for the states involved. The large numbers of actors involved in global environmental problems make them more difficult to solve.

◆ To resolve such collective goods problems, states have used international regimes and IOs, and have in some cases extended state sovereignty (notably over territorial waters) to make management a national rather than an international matter.

◆ International efforts to solve environmental problems aim to bring about sustainable economic development. This was the theme of the 1992 UN Earth Summit.

◆ Global warming results from burning fossil fuels—the basis of industrial economies today. The industrialized states are much more responsible for the problem than are third world states. Solutions are difficult to reach because costs are substantial and dangers are somewhat distant and uncertain.

◆ Damage to the earth's ozone layer results from the use of specific chemicals, which are now being phased out under international agreements. Unlike global warming, the costs of solutions are much lower and the problem is better understood.

◆ Many species are threatened with extinction due to loss of habitats such as rain forests. An international treaty on biodiversity and an agreement on forests aim to reduce the destruction of local ecosystems, with costs spread among states.

◆ The UN Convention on the Law of the Sea (UNCLOS) establishes an ocean regime that puts most commercial fisheries and offshore oil under control of states as territorial waters. The United States signed the treaty after a decade's delay.

◆ Pollution—including acid rain, water and air pollution, and toxic and nuclear waste—tends to be more localized than global and has been addressed mainly through unilateral, bilateral, and regional measures rather than global ones.

◆ The economies of the industrialized West depend on fossil fuels. Overall, these economies import energy resources, mostly oil, whereas the other world regions export them. Oil prices rose dramatically in the 1970s but declined in the 1980s as the world economy adjusted by increasing supply and reducing demand.

◆ The most important source of oil traded worldwide is the Persian Gulf area of the Middle East. Consequently, this area has long been a focal point of international political conflict, including the 1991 Gulf War.

◆ States need other raw materials such as minerals, but no such materials have assumed the importance or political status of oil. Water resources are a growing source of local international conflicts, however.

◆ War and other military activities cause considerable environmental damage—sometimes deliberately inflicted as part of a war strategy.

◆ Supranational relationships and identities are being fostered by new information technologies, though such a process is still in an early stage.

◆ Greater access to information increases government power both domestically and internationally. Governments also use the dissemination of information across borders as a means of influencing other states. Thus information technologies can serve national and not just supranational purposes.

◆ Government access to information increases the stability of international relationships. The security dilemma and other collective goods problems are made less difficult in a transparent world where governments have information about each others' actions.

◆ The greater and freer flow of information around the world can undermine the authority and power of governments as well. It is now extremely difficult for authoritarian governments to limit the flow of information in and out of their states. Information technologies can empower ordinary citizens and contribute to transnational and supranational structures that bypass the state.

◆ Telecommunications are contributing to the development of global cultural integration. This process may hold the potential for the development of a single world culture. However, some politicians and citizens worry about cultural imperialism—that such a culture would be too strongly dominated by the United States.

◆ Transnational communities are developing in areas such as sports, music, and tourism. Such communities may foster supranational identities that could compete with the state for the loyalty of citizens someday.

ONLINE PRACTICE TEST

Take an online practice test at
www.IRtext.com

Glossary

acid rain   Caused by air pollution, it damages trees and often crosses borders. Limiting acid rain (via limiting nitrogen oxide emissions) has been the subject of several regional agreements. (p. 423)

airspace   The space above a state that is considered its territory, in contrast to outer space, which is considered international territory. (p. 152)

alliance cohesion   The ease with which the members hold together an alliance; it tends to be high when national interests converge and when cooperation among allies becomes institutionalized. (p. 76)

Amnesty International   An influential nongovernmental organization that operates globally to monitor and try to rectify glaring abuses of political (not economic or social) human rights. (p. 324)

anarchy   In IR theory, the term implies not complete chaos but the lack of a central government that can enforce rules. (p. 63)

Antarctic Treaty (1959)   One of the first multilateral treaties concerning the environment, it forbids military activity in Antarctica as well as the presence of nuclear weapons or the dumping of nuclear waste there, sets aside territorial claims on the continent for future resolution, and establishes a regime for the conduct of scientific research. (p. 422)

Antiballistic Missile (ABM) Treaty (1972)   It prohibited either the United States or the Soviet Union from using a ballistic missile defense as a shield, which would have undermined mutually assured destruction and the basis of deterrence. (p. 205) See also *mutually assured destruction (MAD)* and *Strategic Defense Initiative (SDI)*.

arms race   A reciprocal process in which two (or more) states build up military capabilities in response to each other. (p. 59)

autarky (self-reliance)   A policy of avoiding or minimizing trade and trying to produce everything one needs (or the most vital things) by oneself. (p. 223)

authoritarian (government)   A government that rules without the need to stand for free elections, respect civil and political rights, allow freedom of the press, and so forth. (p. 113)

balance of payments   A summary of all the flows of money in and out of a country. It includes three types of international transactions: the current account (including the merchandise trade balance), flows of capital, and changes in reserves. (p. 249)

balance of power   The general concept of one or more states' power being used to balance that of another state or group of states. The term can refer to (1) any ratio of power capabilities between states or alliances, (2) a relatively equal ratio, or (3) the process by which counterbalancing coalitions have repeatedly formed to prevent one state from conquering an entire region. (p. 66)

balance of trade   The value of a state's exports relative to its imports. (p. 219)

ballistic missiles   The major strategic delivery vehicles for nuclear weapons; they carry a warhead along a trajectory (typically rising at least 50 miles high) and let it drop on the target. (p. 193) See also *intercontinental ballistic missiles (ICBMs)*.

bargaining   Tacit or direct communication that is used in an attempt to reach agreement on an exchange of value. (p. 53)

basic human needs   The fundamental needs of people for adequate food, shelter, health care, sanitation, and education. Meeting such needs may be thought of as both a moral imperative and a form of investment in "human capital" essential for economic growth. (p. 357)

bilateral aid   Government assistance that goes directly to the third world governments as state-to-state aid. (p. 395)

biodiversity   The tremendous diversity of plant and animal species making up the earth's (global, regional, and local) ecosystems. (p. 417)

Biological Weapons Convention (1972)   It prohibits the development, production, and possession of biological weapons, but makes no provision for inspections. (p. 198)

brain drain   Poor countries' loss of skilled workers to rich countries. (p. 388)

Bretton Woods system   A post–World War II arrangement for managing the world economy, established at a meeting in Bretton Woods, New Hampshire, in 1944. Its main institutional components are the World Bank and the International Monetary Fund (IMF). (p. 247)

burden sharing   The distribution of the costs of an alliance among members; the term also refers to the conflicts that may arise over such distribution. (p. 76)

capital accumulation   The creation of standing wealth (capital) such as buildings, roads, factories, and so forth; such accumulation depends on investment and the creation of an economic surplus. (p. 335)

capitalism   An economic system based on private ownership of capital and the means of production (standing wealth and other forms of property). (p. 336) See also *socialism*.

carrying capacity   The limits of the planetary ecosystem's ability to absorb continual growth of population, industry, energy use, and extraction of natural resources. (p. 411)

cartel   An association of producers or consumers (or both) of a certain product, formed for the purpose of manipulating its price on the world market. (p. 238)

cash crops   Agricultural goods produced as commodities for export to world markets. (p. 361)

central bank   An institution common in industrialized countries whose major tasks are to maintain the value of the state's currency and to control inflation. (p. 246)

centrally planned (command) economy   An economy in which political authorities set prices and decide on quotas for production and consumption of each commodity according to a long-term plan. (p. 216)

chain of command   A hierarchy of officials (often civilian as well as military) through which states control military forces. (p. 179)

Chemical Weapons Convention (1992)   It bans the production and possession of chemical weapons, and includes strict verification provisions and the threat of sanctions against violators and against nonparticipants in the treaty. (p. 198)

Chernobyl   A city in Ukraine that was the site of a 1986 meltdown at a Soviet nuclear power plant. (p. 423)

civil war   A war between factions within a state trying to create, or prevent, a new government for the entire state or some territorial part of it. (p. 169)

Cold War   The hostile relations—punctuated by occasional periods of improvement, or détente—between the two superpowers, the U.S. and the U.S.S.R., from 1945 to 1990. (p. 35)

collective goods problem   A collective good is a tangible or intangible good, created by the members of a group, that is available to all group members regardless of their individual contributions; participants can gain by lowering their own contribution to the collective good, yet if too many participants do so, the good cannot be provided. (p. 88) See also *free riders*.

collective security   The formation of a broad alliance of most major actors in an international system for the purpose of jointly opposing aggression by any actor; sometimes seen as presupposing the existence of a universal organization (such as the United Nations) to which both the aggressor and its opponents belong. (p. 92) See also *League of Nations*.

Common Agricultural Policy (CAP)   An EU policy based on the principle that a subsidy extended to farmers in any member country should be extended to farmers in all member countries. (p. 301)

common market   A zone in which labor and capital (as well as goods) flow freely across borders. (p. 301)

Commonwealth of Independent States (CIS)   The loose coordinating structure linking the former republics of the Soviet Union (except the Baltic states) since 1991. (p. 38)

comparative advantage   The principle that says states should specialize in trading those goods which they produce with the greatest relative efficiency and at the lowest relative cost (relative, that is, to other goods produced by the same state). (p. 213)

compellence   The use of force to make another actor take some action (rather than, as in *deterrence*, refrain from taking an action). (p. 59)

Comprehensive Test Ban Treaty (1996)   It bans all nuclear weapons testing, thereby broadening the ban on atmospheric testing negotiated in 1963. (p. 205)

conditionality   See *IMF conditionality*.

conflict   A difference in preferred outcomes in a bargaining situation. (p. 143)

conflict and cooperation   The types of actions that states take toward each other through time. (p. 3)

conflict resolution   The development and implementation of peaceful strategies for settling conflicts. (p. 131)

constructivism   A movement in IR theory that examines how changing international norms help shape the content of state interests and the character of international institutions. (p. 130)

consumption goods   Goods whose consumption does not contribute directly to production of other goods and services, unlike some forms of investment. (p. 337)

containment   A policy adopted in the late 1940s by which the United States sought to halt the global expansion of Soviet influence on several levels—military, political, ideological, and economic. (p. 35)

Conventional Forces in Europe (CFE) Treaty (1990)   A U.S.-Soviet agreement that provided for asymmetrical reductions in Soviet forces in Europe and limited those of both sides. (p. 206)

convertible (currency)   The guarantee that the holder of a particular currency can exchange it for another currency. Some states' currencies are nonconvertible. (p. 242) See also *hard currency*.

core   The manufacturing regions of the world-system. (p. 341)

cost-benefit analysis   A calculation of the costs incurred by a possible action and the benefits it is likely to bring. (p. 60)

Council of Ministers   A European Union institution in which the relevant ministers (foreign, economic, agriculture, finance, etc.) of each member state meet to enact legislation and reconcile national interests. When the meeting takes place among the

state leaders it is called the "European Council." (p. 302) See also *European Commission*.

counterinsurgency   An effort to combat guerrilla armies, often including programs to "win the hearts and minds" of rural populations so that they stop sheltering guerrillas. (p. 170)

coup d'état   French for "blow against the state," it refers to the seizure of political power by domestic military forces—that is, a change of political power outside the state's constitutional order. (p. 181)

crimes against humanity   A category of legal offenses created at the Nuremberg trials after World War II to encompass genocide and other acts committed by the political and military leaders of the Third Reich (Nazi Germany). (p. 323) See also *dehumanization* and *genocide*.

cruise missile   A small winged missile that can navigate across thousands of miles of previously mapped terrain to reach a particular target; it can carry either a nuclear or a conventional warhead. (p. 196)

Cuban Missile Crisis (1962)   A superpower crisis, sparked by the Soviet Union's installation of medium-range nuclear missiles in Cuba, that marks the moment when the United States and the Soviet Union came closest to nuclear war. (p. 36)

cultural imperialism   A critical term for U.S. dominance of the emerging global culture. (p. 440)

customs union   A common external tariff adopted by members of a free-trade area; that is, participating states adopt a unified set of tariffs with regard to goods coming in from outside. (p. 301) See also *free-trade area*.

cycle theories   An effort to explain tendencies toward war in the international system as cyclical; for example, by linking wars with long waves in the world economy (Kondratieff cycles). (Ch. 4)

debt renegotiation   A reworking of the terms on which a loan will be repaid; frequently negotiated by third world debtor governments in order to avoid default. (p. 389)

debt service   An obligation to make regular interest payments and repay the principal of a loan according to its terms, which is a drain on many third world economies. (p. 389)

default   The failure to make scheduled debt payments. (p. 389)

dehumanization   Stigmatization of enemies as subhuman or nonhuman, leading frequently to widespread massacres or, in the worst cases, destruction of entire populations. (p. 161) See also *crimes against humanity* and *genocide*.

democracy   A government of "the people," usually through elected representatives, and usually with a respect for individual rights in society (especially rights to hold political ideas differing from those of the government). (p. 113)

democratic peace   The proposition, strongly supported by empirical evidence, that democracies almost never fight wars against each other (although they do fight against authoritarian states). (p. 113)

demographic transition   The pattern of falling death rates, followed by falling birthrates, that generally accompanies *industrialization* and *economic development*. (p. 349)

dependency theory   A Marxist-oriented theory that explains the lack of capital accumulation in the third world as a result of the interplay between domestic class relations and the forces of foreign capital. (p. 347) See also *enclave economy*.

deterrence   The threat to punish another actor if it takes a certain negative action (especially attacking one's own state or one's allies). The term has a somewhat more specific meaning in the context of the nuclear balance between the superpowers during the Cold War. (p. 58) See also *mutually assured destruction (MAD)*.

devaluation   A unilateral move to reduce the value of a currency by changing a fixed or official exchange rate. (p. 246) See also *exchange rate*.

developing countries   States in the global South, the poorest regions of the world—also called third world countries, less-developed countries, and undeveloped countries. (p. 332)

Development Assistance Committee (DAC)   A committee whose members—consisting of states from Western Europe, North America, and Japan/Pacific—provide 95 percent of official development assistance to countries of the global South. (p. 395) See also *foreign assistance*.

diplomatic immunity   Refers to diplomats' activity being outside the jurisdiction of the host country's national courts. (p. 316)

diplomatic recognition   The process by which the status of embassies and that of an ambassador as an official state representative are explicitly defined. (p. 316)

direct foreign investment   See *foreign direct investment*.

disaster relief   The provision of short-term relief in the form of food, water, shelter, clothing, and other essentials to people facing natural disasters. (p. 398)

discount rate   The interest rate charged by governments when they lend money to private banks. The discount rate is set by countries' central banks. (p. 246)

dumping   The sale of products in foreign markets at prices below the minimum level necessary to make a profit (or below cost). (p. 224)

economic conversion   The use of former military facilities and industries for new civilian production. (p. 175)

economic development   The combined processes of capital accumulation, rising per capita incomes (with consequent falling birthrates), the increasing of skills in the population, the adoption of new technological styles, and other related social and economic changes. (p. 370)

economic surplus   Made by investing money in productive capital rather than using it for consumption. (p. 335)

electronic warfare   The use of the electromagnetic spectrum (radio waves, radar, infrared, etc.) in war, such as employing electromagnetic signals for one's own benefit while denying their use to an enemy. (p. 188)

empowerment   In the development context, it refers to the grass-roots efforts of poor people to gain power over their situation and meet their basic needs. (p. 402)

enclave economy   An historically important form of dependency in which foreign capital is invested in a third world country to extract a particular raw material in a particular place—usually a mine, oil well, or plantation. (p. 347) See also *dependency theory*.

enclosure (of the commons)   The splitting of a common area or good into privately owned pieces, giving individual owners an incentive to manage resources responsibly. (p. 409)

epistemic communities   Transnational communities of experts who help structure the way states manage environmental and other issues. (p. 409)

ethnic cleansing   Forced displacement of an ethnic group or groups from a particular territory, accompanied by massacres and other human rights violations; it has occurred after the breakup of multinational states, notably in the former Yugoslavia. (p. 150)

ethnic groups Large groups of people who share ancestral, language, cultural, or religious ties and a common identity. (p. 158)

ethnocentrism (in-group bias) The tendency to see one's own group (in-group) in favorable terms and an out-group in unfavorable terms. (p. 160)

Euratom Created in the Treaty of Rome in 1957 to coordinate nuclear power development by pooling research, investment, and management. (p. 300)

euro Also called the *ECU (European currency unit)*, the euro is a single European currency being developed by the *European Union (EU)*. (p. 305)

European Commission A European Union body whose members, while appointed by states, are supposed to represent EU interests. Supported by a multinational civil service in Brussels, the Commission's role is to identify problems and propose solutions to the Council of Ministers. (p. 302) See also *Council of Ministers*.

European Court of Justice A judicial arm of the European Union, based in Luxembourg. The Court has actively established its jurisdiction and its right to overrule national law when it conflicts with EU law. (p. 303)

European Parliament A quasi-legislative body of the European Union that operates mainly as a watchdog over the *European Commission* and has little real legislative power. (p. 303)

European Union (EU) The official term for the European Community (formerly the European Economic Community) and associated treaty organizations. The EU has 15 member states and is negotiating with other states that have applied for membership. (p. 296) See also *Maastricht Treaty*.

exchange rate The rate at which one state's currency can be exchanged for the currency of another state. Since 1973, the international monetary system has depended mainly on flexible (or floating) rather than fixed exchange rates. (p. 241) See also *convertibility*; *fixed exchange rates*; *Exchange Rate Mechanism (ERM)*; and *managed float*.

Exchange Rate Mechanism (ERM) A system that establishes nearly fixed exchange rates among European currencies while letting them all float freely relative to the rest of the world. (p. 244)

export-led growth An economic development strategy that seeks to develop industries capable of competing in specific niches in the world economy. (p. 380)

fiscal policy A government's decisions about spending and taxation, and one of the two major tools of macroeconomic policy making (the other being *monetary policy*). (p. 252)

fissionable material The elements uranium-235 and plutonium, whose atoms split apart and release energy via a chain reaction when an atomic bomb explodes. (p. 191) See also *fusion weapons*.

fixed exchange rates The official rates of exchange for currencies set by governments; not a dominant mechanism in the international monetary system since 1973. (p. 243) See also *floating exchange rates*.

floating exchange rates The rates determined by global currency markets in which private investors and governments alike buy and sell currencies. (p. 243) See also *fixed exchange rates*.

foreign assistance Money or other aid made available to third world states to help them speed up economic development or meet humanitarian needs. Most foreign assistance is provided by governments and is called official development assistance (ODA). (p. 395) See also *Development Assistance Committee (DAC)*.

foreign direct investment The acquisition by residents of one country of control over a new or existing business in another country. Also called direct foreign investment. (p. 250)

foreign policy process The process by which foreign policies are arrived at and implemented. (p. 95)

fossil fuels Oil, coal, and natural gas, burnt to run factories, cars, tractors, furnaces, electrical generating plants, and other things that drive an industrial economy. (p. 413)

"four tigers"/"four dragons" The most successful newly industrialized areas of East Asia: South Korea, Taiwan, Hong Kong, and Singapore. (p. 373)

free economic zones The southern coastal provinces of China that were opened to foreign investment and run on capitalist principles with export-oriented industries, in the 1980s and 1990s. (p. 374)

free riders Those who benefit from someone else's provision of a collective good without paying their share of costs. (p. 88) See also *collective goods problem*.

free trade   The flow of goods and services across national boundaries unimpeded by tariffs or other restrictions; in principle (if not always in practice), free trade was a key aspect of Britain's policy after 1846 and of U.S. policy after 1945. (p. 29)

free-trade area   A zone in which there are no tariffs or other restrictions on the movement of goods and services across borders. (p. 300) See also *customs union.*

fusion weapons   Extremely destructive, expensive, and technologically sophisticated weapons in which two small atoms fuse together into a larger atom, releasing energy. Also referred to as "thermonuclear weapons" or "hydrogen bombs." (p. 191) See also *fissionable material.*

game theory   A branch of mathematics concerned with predicting bargaining outcomes. Games such as Prisoner's Dilemma have been used to analyze various sorts of international interactions. (p. 61)

gender gap   Refers to polls showing women lower than men on average in their support for military actions (as well as for various other issues and candidates). (p. 121)

General Agreement on Tariffs and Trade (GATT)   A world organization established in 1947 to work for freer trade on a multilateral basis; the GATT has been more of a negotiating framework than an administrative institution. It became the *World Trade Organization (WTO)* in 1995. (p. 231)

General Assembly   See *UN General Assembly.*

Generalized System of Preferences (GSP)   A mechanism by which some industrialized states began in the 1970s to give tariff concessions to third world states on certain imports; an exception to the most-favored nation (MFN) principle. (p. 232) See also *most-favored nation (MFN) concept.*

genocide   The intentional and systematic attempt to destroy a national, ethnic, racial, or religious group, in whole or part. It was confirmed as a crime under international law by the UN Genocide Convention (1948). (p. 220) See also *crimes against humanity* and *dehumanization.*

geopolitics   The use of geography as an element of power, and the ideas about it held by political leaders and scholars. (p. 52)

global culture   Worldwide cultural integration based on a massive increase in satellite television, radio, and Internet communication. (p. 438)

globalization   The increasing integration of the world in terms of communications, culture, and economics; may also refer to changing subjective experiences of space and time accompanying this process. (p. 438)

global warming   A slow, long-term rise in the average world temperature caused by the emission of greenhouse gases produced by burning fossil fuels—oil, coal, and natural gas. (p. 413) See also *greenhouse gases.*

gold standard   A system in international monetary relations, prominent for a century before the 1970s, in which the value of national currencies was pegged to the value of gold or other precious metals. (p. 240)

government bargaining model   It sees foreign policy decisions as flowing from a bargaining process among various government agencies that have somewhat divergent interests in the outcome ("where you stand depends on where you sit"). Also called the "bureaucratic politics model." (p. 98)

great powers   Generally, the half dozen or so most powerful states; the great-power club was exclusively European until the twentieth century. (p. 67) See also *middle powers.*

greenhouse gases   Carbon dioxide and other gases that, when concentrated in the atmosphere, act like the glass in a greenhouse, holding energy in and leading to *global warming.* (p. 413)

green revolution   The massive transfer of agricultural technology, such as high-yield seeds and tractors, to third world countries that began in the 1960s. (p. 388)

Gross Domestic Product (GDP)   The size of a state's total annual economic activity. (p. 9)

groupthink   The tendency of groups to validate wrong decisions by becoming overconfident and underestimating risks. (p. 102)

guerrilla war   Warfare without front lines and with irregular forces operating in the midst of, and often hidden or protected by, civilian populations. (p. 170)

hard currency   Money that can be readily converted to leading world currencies. (p. 243) See also *convertibility (of currency).*

hegemonic stability theory   The argument that regimes are most effective when power in the international system is most concentrated. (p. 91) See also *hegemony*.

hegemonic war　War for control of the entire world order—the rules of the international system as a whole. Also known as world war, global war, general war, or systemic war. (p. 169)

hegemony　The holding by one state of a preponderance of power in the international system, so that it can single-handedly dominate the rules and arrangements by which international political and economic relations are conducted. (p. 72) See also *hegemonic stability theory*.

high seas　That portion of the oceans considered common territory, not under any kind of exclusive state jurisdiction. (p. 420) See also *territorial waters*.

home country　The state where a *multinational corporation (MNC)* has its headquarters. (p. 265) See also *host country*.

host country　A state in which a foreign *multinational corporation (MNC)* operates. (p. 265) See also *home country*.

human rights　Rights of all persons to be free from abuses such as torture or imprisonment for their political beliefs (political and civil rights), and to enjoy certain minimum economic and social protections (economic and social rights). (p. 322)

humanitarian intervention　Armed intrusion into a state, without its consent, to prevent or alleviate widespread or severe human rights violations. (p. 282)

hyperinflation　An extremely rapid, uncontrolled rise in prices, such as occurred in Germany in the 1920s and some third world countries more recently. (p. 242)

idealism　An approach that emphasizes international law, morality, and international organization, rather than power alone, as key influences on international relations. (p. 45) See also *realism*.

IMF conditionality　An agreement to loan IMF funds on the condition that certain government policies are adopted. Dozens of third world states have entered into such agreements with the IMF in the past two decades. (p. 392) See also *International Monetary Fund (IMF)*.

immigration law　National laws that establish the conditions under which foreigners may travel and visit within a state's territory, work within the state,

and sometimes become citizens of the state (naturalization). (p. 315)

imperialism　The acquisition of colonies by conquest or otherwise. Lenin's theory of imperialism argued that European capitalists were investing in colonies where they could earn big profits, and then using part of those profits to buy off portions of the working class at home. (p. 339)

import substitution　A strategy of developing local industries, often conducted behind protectionist barriers, to produce items that a country had been importing. (p. 380)

industrialization　The use of fossil-fuel energy to drive machinery and the accumulation of such machinery along with the products created by it. (p. 29)

industrial policy　The strategies by which a government works actively with industries to promote their growth and tailor trade policy to their needs. (p. 227)

infant mortality rate　The proportion of babies who die within their first year of life. (p. 353)

infantry　Foot soldiers who use assault rifles and other light weapons (mines, machine guns, and the like). (p. 184)

informal sector　Those modes of business, such as black markets and street vendors, operating beyond state control; some scholars see this sector as the core of a new development strategy. (p. 382)

information screens　The subconscious or unconscious filters through which people put the information coming in about the world around them. (p. 99) See also *misperceptions and selective perceptions*.

intellectual property rights　The legal protection of the original works of inventors, authors, creators, and performers under patent, copyright, and trademark law. Such rights became a contentious area of trade negotiations in the 1990s. (p. 227)

intercontinental ballistic missiles (ICBMs)　The longest-range ballistic missiles, able to travel 5,000 miles. (p. 193) See also *ballistic missiles*.

interdependence　A political and economic situation in which two states are simultaneously dependent on each other for their well-being. The degree of interdependence is sometimes designated in terms of "sensitivity" or "vulnerability." (p. 220)

interest groups　Coalitions of people who share a common interest in the outcome of some political issue and who organize themselves to try to influence the outcome. (p. 107)

intergovernmental organizations (IGOs)
Organizations (such as the United Nations and its agencies) whose members are state governments. (p. 11)

Intermediate Nuclear Forces (INF) Treaty (1987)
It banned an entire class of missiles that both the Soviet Union and the United States had deployed in Europe. (p. 205)

International Committee of the Red Cross (ICRC) A *nongovernmental organization (NGO)* that provides practical support, such as medical care, food, and letters from home, to civilians caught in wars and to *prisoners of war (POWs)*. Exchanges of POWs are usually negotiated through the ICRC. (p. 320)

International Court of Justice See *World Court*.

international integration The process by which supranational institutions come to replace national ones; the gradual shifting upward of some sovereignty from the state to regional or global structures. (p. 297)

International Monetary Fund (IMF) An *intergovernmental organization (IGO)* that coordinates international currency exchange, the balance of international payments, and national accounts. Along with the *World Bank*, it is a pillar of the international financial system. (p. 247) See also *IMF conditionality*.

international norms The expectations held by participants about normal relations among states. (p. 326)

international organizations (IOs) They include *intergovernmental organizations (IGOs)* such as the UN, and *nongovernmental organizations (NGOs)* such as the *International Committee of the Red Cross (ICRC)*. (p. 276)

international political economy (IPE) The study of the politics of trade, monetary, and other economic relations among nations, and their connection to other transnational forces. (p. 3)

international regime A set of rules, norms, and procedures around which the expectations of actors converge in a certain international issue area (such as oceans or monetary policy). (p. 90)

international relations (IR) The relationships among the world's state governments and the connection of those relationships with other actors

(such as the United Nations, multinational corporations, and individuals), with other social relationships (including economics, culture, and domestic politics), and with geographic and historical influences. (p. 1)

international security A subfield of *international relations (IR)* that focuses on questions of war and peace. (p. 3)

international system The set of relationships among the world's states, structured by certain rules and patterns of interaction. (p. 8)

International Whaling Commission An *intergovernmental organization (IGO)* that sets quotas for hunting certain whale species; states' participation is voluntary. (p. 418)

investment Putting surplus wealth into capital-producing activities rather than consuming it, to produce long-term benefits. (p. 337)

Iran-Contra scandal An episode in which the Reagan administration secretly sold weapons to Iran in exchange for the freedom of U.S. hostages held in Lebanon, and then used the Iranian payments to illegally fund Nicaraguan Contra rebels. (p. 102)

irredentism A form of nationalism whose goal is the regaining of territory lost to another state; it can lead directly to violent interstate conflicts. (p. 147)

Islam, Muslims A broad and diverse world religion whose divergent populations include Sunni Muslims, Shiite Muslims, and many smaller branches and sects, practiced by Muslims, from Nigeria to Indonesia, centered in the Middle East. (p. 163)

issue areas Distinct spheres of international activity (such as global trade negotiations) within which policy makers of various states face conflicts and sometimes achieve cooperation. (p. 3)

just war doctrine A branch of international law and political theory that defines when wars can be justly started and how they can be justly fought. (p. 321) See also *war crimes*.

Keynesian economics The principles articulated by British economist John Maynard Keynes, used successfully in the Great Depression of the 1930s, including the view that governments should sometimes use deficit spending to stimulate economic growth. (p. 252)

land mines Concealed explosive devices, often left behind by irregular armies, which kill or maim civilians after wars end. Such mines number more than 100 million, primarily in Angola, Bosnia, Afghanistan, and Cambodia. A movement to ban land mines is underway; nearly 100 states have agreed to do so. (p. 184)

land reform Policies that aim to break up large land holdings and redistribute land to poor peasants for use in *subsistence farming*. (p. 362)

lateral pressure (theory of) It holds that the economic and population growth of states fuels geographic expansion as they seek natural resources beyond their borders, which in turn leads to conflicts and sometimes to war. (p. 155)

League of Nations Established after World War I and a forerunner of today's United Nations, the organization achieved certain humanitarian and other successes but was weakened by the absence of U.S. membership and by its own lack of effectiveness in ensuring collective security. (p. 31) See also *collective security*.

less-developed countries The world's poorest regions—the global South—where most people live; are also called underdeveloped countries, or *developing countries*. (p. 332)

liberal feminism A strand of feminism that emphasizes gender equality and views the "essential" differences in men's and women's abilities or perspectives as trivial or nonexistent. (p. 116)

liberalism (economic liberalism) In the context of IPE, an approach that generally shares the assumption of anarchy (the lack of a world government) but does not see this condition as precluding extensive cooperation to realize common gains from economic exchanges. It emphasizes absolute over relative gains and, in practice, a commitment to free trade, free capital flows, and an "open" world economy. (p. 210) See also *mercantilism* and *neoliberalism*.

limited war Military actions that seek objectives short of the surrender and occupation of the enemy. (p. 169)

London Club See *Paris Club*. (p. 391)

Maastricht Treaty Signed in the Dutch city of Maastricht and ratified in 1992, the treaty commits the European Union to monetary union (a single currency and European Central Bank) and to a common foreign policy. (p. 304) See also *European Union (EU)*.

malnutrition The lack of needed foods including protein and vitamins; about 10 million children die each year from malnutrition-related causes. (p. 360) See also *undernourishment*.

managed float A system of occasional multinational government interventions in currency markets to manage otherwise free-floating currency rates. (p. 243)

Maoism Official ideology of China under the rule of Mao Zedong (1949–1976) and after. In foreign affairs, it emphasized anti-imperialism and export of revolution, though China's actual foreign policy came to be guided by more pragmatic considerations. (p. 166)

Marxism A branch of socialism that emphasizes exploitation and class struggle and includes both communism and other approaches. (p. 338) See also *socialism*.

mediation The use of a third party (or parties) in *conflict resolution*. (p. 132)

mercantilism An economic theory and a political ideology opposed to free trade; it shares with *realism* the belief that each state must protect its own interests without seeking mutual gains through international organizations. (p. 210) See also *liberalism*.

microcredit The use of very small loans to small groups of individuals, often women, to stimulate economic development. (p. 382)

middle powers States that rank somewhat below the great powers in terms of their influence on world affairs (for example, Brazil and India). (p. 68) See also *great powers*.

migration Movement between states, usually emigration from the old state and immigration to the new state. (p. 363)

militarism The glorification of war, military force, and violence. (p. 134)

military governments States in which military forces control the government; most common in third world countries, where the military may be the only large modern institution. (p. 181)

military-industrial complex A huge interlocking network of governmental agencies, industrial corporations, and research institutes, all working together to promote and benefit from military spending. (p. 108)

misperceptions and selective perceptions The selective or mistaken processing of the available information about a decision; one of several ways—along with affective and cognitive bias—in which individual decision making diverges from the *rational model*. (p. 99) See also *information screens*.

Missile Technology Control Regime A set of agreements through which industrialized states try to limit the flow of missile-relevant technology to third world states. (p. 201)

mixed economies Economies such as those in the industrialized West that contain both some government control and some private ownership. (p. 218)

monetary policy A government's decisions about printing and circulating money, and one of the two major tools of macroeconomic policy making (the other being *fiscal policy*). (p. 252)

Montreal Protocol (1987) An agreement on protection of the ozone layer in which states pledged to reduce and then eliminate use of chlorofluorocarbons (CFCs). It is the most successful environmental treaty to date. (p. 416)

most-favored nation (MFN) concept The principle that one state, by granting another state MFN status, promises to give it the same treatment given to the first state's most-favored trading partner. (p. 232) See also *Generalized System of Preferences (GSP)*.

multilateral aid Government foreign aid from several states that goes through a third party, such as the UN or another agency. (p. 395)

multinational corporations (MNCs) Companies based in one state with affiliated branches or subsidiaries operating in other states. (p. 261) See also *home country* and *host country*.

multipolar system An international system with typically five or six centers of power that are not grouped into alliances. (p. 70)

Munich Agreement A symbol of the failed policy of appeasement, this agreement, signed in 1938, allowed Nazi Germany to occupy a part of Czechoslovakia. Rather than appease German aspirations, it was followed by further German expansions, which triggered World War II. (p. 31)

mutually assured destruction (MAD) The possession of second-strike nuclear capabilities, which ensures that neither of two adversaries could prevent the other from destroying it in an all-out war. (p. 202) See also *deterrence*.

national debt The amount a government owes in debt as a result of deficit spending. (p. 254)

national interest The interests of a state overall (as opposed to particular parties or factions within the state). (p. 60)

nationalism The identification with and devotion to the interests of one's nation. It usually involves a large group of people who share a national identity and often a language, culture, or ancestry. (p. 26)

nation-states States whose populations share a sense of national identity, usually including a language and culture. (p. 8)

negotiation The process of formal bargaining, usually with the parties talking back and forth across a table. (p. 54)

neocolonialism The continuation, in a former colony, of colonial exploitation without formal political control. (p. 346)

neofunctionalism The theory which holds that economic integration (functionalism) generates a "spillover" effect, resulting in increased political integration. (p. 298)

neoliberalism Shorthand for "neoliberal institutionalism," an approach that stresses the importance of international institutions in reducing the inherent conflict that realists assume in an international system; the reasoning is based on the core liberal idea that seeking long-term mutual gains is often more rational than maximizing individual short-term gains. (p. 86) See also *liberalism*.

neorealism A version of realist theory that emphasizes the influence on state behavior of the system's structure, especially the international distribution of power. (p. 70) See also *realism*.

New International Economic Order (NIEO) A third-world effort begun in the mid-1970s, mainly conducted in UN forums, to advocate restructuring of the world economy so as to make North-South economic transactions less unfavorable to the South. (p. 394)

newly industrializing countries (NICs) Third world states that have achieved self-sustaining capital accumulation, with impressive economic growth. The most successful are the "*four tigers*" or "*four dragons*" of East Asia—South Korea, Taiwan, Hong Kong, and Singapore. (p. 372)

"New World Order" Announced by U.S. President George Bush during the Iraq-Kuwait crisis, it included four principles: peaceful settlement of disputes, solidarity against aggression, reduced and controlled arsenals, and just treatment of all peoples. (p. 327)

nonaligned movement   Movement of third world states, led by India and Yugoslavia, that attempted to stand apart from the U.S.–Soviet rivalry during the Cold War. (p. 81)

nongovernmental organizations (NGOs) Transnational groups or entities (such as the Catholic Church and Greenpeace) that interact with states, multinational corporations (MNCs), other NGOs and intergovernmental organizations (IGOs). (p. 11)

Non-Proliferation Treaty (NPT) (1968)   It created a framework for controlling the spread of nuclear materials and expertise, including the International Atomic Energy Agency (IAEA), a UN agency based in Vienna that is charged with inspecting the nuclear power industry in NPT member states to prevent secret military diversions of nuclear materials. (p. 200)

nonstate actors   Actors other than state governments that operate either below the level of the state (that is, within states) or across state borders. (p. 10)

nontariff barriers   Forms of restricting imports other than tariffs, such as quotas (ceilings on how many goods of a certain kind can be imported). (p. 224)

nonviolence/pacifism   A philosophy based on a unilateral commitment to refrain from using any violent forms of leverage. More specifically, *pacifism* refers to a principled opposition to war in general rather than simply to particular wars. (p. 138)

normative bias   The personal norms and values that IR scholars bring to their studies, such as a preference for peace rather than war. (p. 131)

norms (of behavior)   The shared expectations about what behavior is considered proper. (p. 64)

North American Free Trade Agreement (NAFTA) A free-trade zone encompassing the United States, Canada, and Mexico since 1994. (p. 237)

North Atlantic Treaty Organization (NATO) A U.S.-led military alliance, formed in 1949 with mainly West European members, to oppose and deter Soviet power in Europe. It is currently expanding into the former Soviet bloc. (p. 76) See also *Warsaw Pact.*

North-South gap   The disparity in resources (income, wealth, and power) between the industrialized, relatively rich countries of the West (and the

former East) and the poorer countries of Africa, the Middle East, and much of Asia and Latin America. (p. 15)

oil shocks   The two sharp rises in the world price of oil that occurred in 1973–1974 and 1979. (p. 426)

optimizing   Picking the very best option; contrasts with satisficing, or finding a satisfactory but less than best solution to a problem. The model of "bounded rationality" postulates that decision makers generally "satisfice" rather than optimize. (p. 101)

organizational process model   A decision-making model in which policy makers or lower-level officials rely largely on standardized responses or standard operating procedures. (p. 97)

Organization of Petroleum Exporting Countries (OPEC)   The most prominent cartel in the international economy; its members control about half the world's total oil exports, enough to significantly affect the world price of oil. (p. 238)

Oxfam America   A private charitable group that works with local third world communities to determine the needs of their own people and to carry out development projects. Oxfam does not operate these projects but provides funding to local organizations to carry them out. (p. 400)

ozone layer   The part of the atmosphere that screens out harmful unltraviolet rays from the sun. Certain chemicals used in industrial economies break the ozone layer down. (p. 415)

Paris Club   A group of first world governments that have loaned money to third world governments; it meets periodically to work out terms of debt renegotiations. Private creditors meet as the London Club.

Peace Corps   Started by President John Kennedy in 1961, it provides U.S. volunteers for technical development assistance in third world states. (p. 397)

peace movements   Movements against specific wars or against war and militarism in general, usually involving large numbers of people and forms of direct action such as street protests. (p. 137)

periphery   The third world regions of the world-system that mostly extract raw materials from their area. (p. 341)

positive peace   A peace that resolves the underlying reasons for war; not just a cease-fire but a transformation of relationships, including elimination or reduction of economic exploitation and political oppression. (p.135) See also *structural violence.*

postmodern feminism An effort to combine feminist and postmodernist perspectives with the aim of uncovering the hidden influences of gender in IR and showing how arbitrary the construction of gender roles is. (p. 116)

postmodernism An approach that denies the existence of a single fixed reality, and pays special attention to texts and to discourses—that is, to how people talk and write about a subject. (p. 127)

power The ability or potential to influence others' behavior, as measured by the possession of certain tangible and intangible characteristics. (p. 47)

power projection The ability to use military force in areas far from a country's region or sphere of influence. (p. 185)

prisoners of war (POWs) Soldiers who have surrendered (and who thereby receive special status under the laws of war). (p. 320)

proliferation The spread of weapons of mass destruction (nuclear, chemical, or biological weapons) into the hands of more actors. (p. 199)

pronatalist policy A government policy that encourages or forces childbearing, and outlaws or limits access to contraception. (p. 351)

prospect theory A decision-making theory that holds that options are assessed by comparison to a reference point, which is often the status quo but might be some past or expected situation. The model also holds that decision makers fear losses more than they value gains. (p. 101)

protectionism The protection of domestic industries against international competition, by trade tariffs and other means. (p. 223)

proxy wars Wars in the third world—often civil wars—in which the United States and the Soviet Union jockeyed for position by supplying and advising opposing factions. (p. 36)

public opinion In IR, the range of views on foreign policy issues held by the citizens of a state. (p. 109)

rally 'round the flag syndrome The public's increased support for government leaders during wartime, at least in the short term. (p. 112)

rational actors Actors conceived as single entities that can "think" about their actions coherently, make choices, identify their interests, and rank the interests in terms of priority. (p. 59)

rational model (of decision making) A model in which decision makers calculate the costs and benefits of each possible course of action, then choose the one with the highest benefits and lowest costs. (p. 96)

realism (political realism) A broad intellectual tradition that explains international relations mainly in terms of power. (p. 45) See also *idealism* and *neorealism.*

reciprocity A response in kind to another's actions; a strategy of reciprocity uses positive forms of leverage to promise rewards and negative forms of leverage to threaten punishment. (p. 58)

refugees People fleeing their countries to find refuge from war, natural disaster, or political persecution. International law distinguishes them from migrants. (p. 364)

reserves Hard-currency stockpiles kept by states. (p. 243)

risk assessment The preinvestment efforts by corporations (especially banks) to determine how likely it is that future political conditions in the target country will change so radically as to disrupt the flow of income. (p. 269)

satisficing The act of finding a satisfactory or "good enough" solution to a problem. (p. 101)

Secretariat See *UN Secretariat.*

secular (state) A state created apart from religious establishments and in which there is a high degree of separation between religious and political organizations. (p. 163)

security community A situation in which low expectations of interstate violence permit a high degree of political cooperation—as, for example, among NATO members. (p. 298)

Security Council See *UN Security Council.*

security dilemma A situation in which states' actions taken to assure their own security (such as deploying more military forces) are perceived as threats to the security of other states. (p. 65)

semiperiphery The area in the world-system in which some manufacturing occurs and some capital concentrates, but not to the extent of the core areas. (p. 341)

service sector The part of an economy that concerns services (as opposed to the production of tangible goods); the key focus in international trade negotiations is on banking, insurance, and related financial services. (p. 228)

settlement The outcome of a bargaining process. (p. 143)

Single European Act (1985) It set a target date of the end of 1992 for the creation of a true *common market* (free cross-border movement of goods, capital, people, and services) in the European Community (EC). (p. 304)

Sino–Soviet split A rift in the 1960s between the communist powers of the Soviet Union and China, fueled by China's opposition to Soviet moves toward peaceful coexistence with the United States. (p. 35)

socialism A term encompassing many political movements, parties, economic theories, and ideologies, historical and present-day. With its idea that workers should have political power (or a larger share of power), socialism favors the redistribution of wealth toward the workers who produce it. In economic policy, socialists have favored different combinations of planning and reliance on market forces, as well as various patterns of ownership. (p. 337) See also *capitalism* and *Marxism*.

sovereignty A state's right, at least in principle, to do whatever it wants within its own territory; traditionally sovereignty is the most important international norm. (p. 64)

Special Drawing Right (SDR) A world currency created by the *International Monetary Fund (IMF)* to replace gold as a world standard. Valued by a "basket" of national currencies, the SDR has been called "paper gold." (p. 248)

standpoint feminism A strand of feminism that believes gender differences are not just socially constructed and that views women as inherently less warlike than men (on average). (p. 116)

state An inhabited territorial entity controlled by a government that exercises sovereignty on its territory. (p. 7)

state-owned industries Industries such as oil-production companies and airlines that are owned wholly or partly by the state because they are thought to be vital to the national economy. (p. 218)

state-sponsored terrorism The use of terrorist groups by states, usually under control of a state's intelligence agency, to achieve political aims. (p. 171)

stealth technology The use of special radar-absorbent materials and unusual shapes in the design of aircraft, missiles, and ships to scatter enemy radar. (p. 188)

Strategic Arms Limitation Treaties (SALT) SALT I (1972) and SALT II (1979) put formal ceilings on the growth of U.S. and Soviet strategic weapons. (p. 205)

Strategic Arms Reduction Treaties (START) START I (1991) called for reducing the superpowers' strategic arsenals by about 30 percent. START II (1992) proposes to cut the remaining weapons by more than half in the next decade. START III is under discussion. (p. 205)

Strategic Defense Initiative (SDI) A U.S. effort, also known as "star wars," to develop defenses that could shoot down incoming ballistic missiles, spurred by President Ronald Reagan in 1983. Critics call it an expensive failure that would violate the ABM Treaty. (p. 204) See also *Antiballistic Missile (ABM) Treaty*.

structural violence A term used by some scholars to refer to poverty, hunger, oppression, and other social and economic sources of conflict. (p. 136) See also *positive peace*.

subsistence farming Rural communities growing food mainly for their own consumption rather than for sale in local or world markets. (p. 361)

subtext Meanings that are implicit or hidden in a text rather than explicitly addressed. (p. 128) See also *postmodernism*.

summit meeting A meeting between heads of state, often referring to leaders of great powers, as in the Cold War superpower summits between the United States and the Soviet Union or today's meetings of the Group of Eight on economic coordination. (p. 36)

supranationalism The subordination of state authority or national identity to larger institutions and groupings such as the European Union. (p. 275)

Sustainable Development Commission An organization established at the 1992 UN Earth Summit that monitors states' compliance with their promises and hears evidence from environmental *nongovernmental organizations (NGOs)*. (p. 411)

tariff   A duty or tax levied on certain types of imports (usually as a percentage of their value) as they enter a country. (p. 224)

technology transfer   Third world states' acquisition of technology (knowledge, skills, methods, designs, specialized equipment, etc.) from foreign sources, usually in conjunction with foreign direct investment or similar business operations. (p. 388)

terms of trade   The overall relationship between prices of imported and exported goods. (p. 380)

territorial waters   The waters near states' shores generally treated as part of national territory. The UN Convention on the Law of the Sea provides for a 12-mile territorial sea (exclusive national jurisdiction over shipping and navigation) and a 200-mile exclusive economic zone (EEZ) covering exclusive fishing and mineral rights (but allowing for free navigation by all). (p. 152) See also *high seas* and *UN Convention on the Law of the Sea (UNCLOS)*.

third-world countries   See *less-developed countries*.

tit for tat   A strategy of strict reciprocity (matching the other player's response) after an initial cooperative move; it can bring about mutual cooperation in a repeated Prisoner's Dilemma game, since it ensures that defection will not pay. (p. 86)

total war   Warfare by one state waged to conquer and occupy another; modern total war originated in the Napoleonic Wars, which relied upon conscription on a mass scale. (p. 169)

tragedy of the commons   A collective goods dilemma that is created when common environmental assets (such as the world's fisheries) are depleted or degraded through the failure of states to cooperate effectively. One solution is to "enclose" the commons (split them into individually owned pieces); international regimes can also be a (partial) solution. (p. 409)

transitional economies   Countries in Russia and Eastern Europe that are trying to convert from communism to capitalism, with various degrees of success. (p. 216)

Treaty of Rome (1957)   The founding document of the European Economic Community (EEC) or Common Market, now subsumed by the European Union. (p. 300)

United Nations (UN)   An organization of nearly all world states, created after World War II to promote collective security. (p. 8)

UN Charter   The founding document of the United Nations; it is based on the principles that states are equal, have *sovereignty* over their own affairs, enjoy independence and territorial integrity, and must fulfill international obligations. The Charter also lays out the structure and methods of the UN. (p. 277)

UN Convention on the Law of the Sea (UNCLOS)   A world treaty (1982) governing use of the oceans. The UNCLOS treaty established rules on territorial waters and a 200-mile exclusive economic zone (EEZ). (p. 420) See also *territorial waters*.

UN Conference on Trade and Development (UNCTAD)   A structure established in 1964 to promote third world development through various trade proposals. (p. 295)

UN Development Program (UNDP)   It coordinates the flow of multilateral development assistance and manages 5,000 projects at once around the world (focusing especially on technical development assistance). (p. 397)

UN Environment Program (UNEP)   It monitors environmental conditions and, among other activities, works with the World Meteorological Organization to measure changes in global climate. (p. 415)

UN General Assembly   Comprised of representatives of all states, it allocates UN funds, passes nonbinding resolutions, and coordinates third world development programs and various autonomous agencies through the Economic and Social Council (ECOSOC). (p. 279)

UN Secretariat   The UN's executive branch, led by the secretary-general. (p. 279)

UN Security Council   A body of five great powers (which can veto resolutions) and ten rotating member states, which makes decisions about international peace and security including the dispatch of UN peacekeeping forces. (p. 279)

undernourishment   The lack of needed foods; a lack of calories. (p. 360) See also *malnutrition*.

urbanization   A shift of population from the countryside to the cities that typically accompanies economic development and is augmented by displacement of peasants from *subsistence farming*. (p. 361)

Uruguay Round   A series of negotiations under the *General Agreement on Tariffs and Trade (GATT)* that began in Uruguay in 1986, and concluded in 1994 with agreement to create the World Trade

Organization. The Uruguay Round followed earlier GATT negotiations such as the Kennedy Round and the Tokyo Round. (p. 233) See also *World Trade Organization (WTO)*.

U.S.–Japanese Security Treaty A bilateral alliance between the United States and Japan, created in 1951 against the potential Soviet threat to Japan. The United States maintains troops in Japan and is committed to defend Japan if attacked, and Japan pays the United States to offset about half the cost of maintaining the troops. (p. 78)

war crimes Violations of the law governing the conduct of warfare, such as by mistreating prisoners of war or unnecessarily targeting civilians. (p. 318) See also *just war doctrine*.

Warsaw Pact A Soviet-led Eastern European military alliance, founded in 1955 and disbanded in 1991. It opposed the NATO alliance. See also *North Atlantic Treaty Organization (NATO)*. (p. 77)

weapons of mass destruction Nuclear, chemical, and biological weapons, all distinguished from conventional weapons by their enormous potential lethality, and by their relative lack of discrimination in whom they kill. (p. 191)

World Bank Formally the International Bank for Reconstruction and Development (IBRD), it was established in 1944 as a source of loans to help reconstruct the European economies. Later, the main borrowers were third world countries and, in the 1990s, Eastern European ones. (p. 247)

World Court (International Court of Justice) The judicial arm of the UN; located in The Hague, it hears only cases between states. (p. 313)

world government A centralized world governing body with strong enforcement powers. (p. 136)

World Health Organization (WHO) Based in Geneva, it provides technical assistance to improve health conditions in the third world and conducts major immunization campaigns. (p. 296)

world-system theory A view of the world in terms of regional class divisions, with industrialized countries as the *core*, poorest third world countries as the *periphery*, and other areas (for example, some of the newly industrializing countries) as the *semiperiphery*. (p. 340)

World Trade Organization (WTO) An organization begun in 1995 that expanded the GATT's traditional focus on manufactured goods, and created monitoring and enforcement mechanisms. (p. 231) See also *General Agreement on Tariffs and Trade (GATT)* and *Uruguay Round*.

zero-sum games A situation in which one actor's gain is by definition equal to the other's loss, as opposed to a non-zero-sum game, in which it is possible for both actors to gain (or lose). (p. 62)

Photo Credits

Index

Note: **Boldface** entries and page numbers indicate key terms. Entries for tables and figures are followed by *"table"* and *"fig.,"* respectively.